# Introduction
# to
# Programming in Java

# Introduction
# to
# Programming in Java

*An Interdisciplinary Approach*

Robert Sedgewick
and
Kevin Wayne

Princeton University

**PEARSON**

Addison
Wesley

Boston  San Francisco  New York
London  Toronto  Sydney  Tokyo  Singapore  Madrid
Mexico City  Munich  Paris  Cape Town  Hong Kong  Montreal

| | |
|---|---|
| Publisher | Greg Tobin |
| Executive Editor | Michael Hirsch |
| Associate Editor | Lindsey Triebel |
| Associate Managing Editor | Jeffrey Holcomb |
| Senior Designer | Joyce Cosentino Wells |
| Digital Assets Manager | Marianne Groth |
| Senior Media Producer | Bethany Tidd |
| Senior Marketing Manager | Michelle Brown |
| Marketing Assistant | Sarah Milmore |
| Senior Author Support/<br>    Technology Specialist | Joe Vetere |
| Senior Manufacturing Buyer | Carol Melville |
| Copyeditor | Genevieve d'Entremont |
| Composition and Illustrations | Robert Sedgewick and Kevin Wayne |

Cover Image: © Robert Sedgewick and Kevin Wayne

Page 353 © 2006 C. Herscovici, Brussels / Artists Rights Society (ARS), New York Banque d' Images, ADAGP / Art Resource, NY

Many of the designations used by manufacturers and sellers to distinguish their products are claimed as trademarks. Where those designations appear in this book, and Addison-Wesley was aware of a trademark claim, the designations have been printed in initial caps or all caps.

The interior of this book was composed in Adobe InDesign.

**Library of Congress Cataloging-in-Publication Data**

Sedgewick, Robert, 1946-
  Introduction to programming in Java : an interdisciplinary approach / by Robert Sedgewick and Kevin Wayne.
     p. cm.
  Includes index.
  ISBN 978-0-321-49805-2 (alk. paper)
  1. Java (Computer program language) 2. Computer programming. I. Wayne, Kevin Daniel, 1971- II. Title.
  QA76.73.J38S413 2007
  005.13'3--dc22

                    2007020235

ISBN-13: 978-0-321-49805-2
ISBN-10: 0-321-49805-4

9 10—EBM—13 12

# Preface

THE BASIS FOR EDUCATION IN THE last millennium was "reading, writing, and arithmetic;" now it is reading, writing, and *computing*. Learning to program is an essential part of the education of every student in the sciences and engineering. Beyond direct applications, it is the first step in understanding the nature of computer science's undeniable impact on the modern world. This book aims to teach programming to those who need or want to learn it, in a scientific context.

Our primary goal is to *empower* students by supplying the experience and basic tools necessary to use computation effectively. Our approach is to teach students that writing a program is a natural, satisfying, and creative experience (not an onerous task reserved for experts). We progressively introduce essential concepts, embrace classic applications from applied mathematics and the sciences to illustrate the concepts, and provide opportunities for students to write programs to solve engaging problems.

We use the Java programming language for all of the programs in this book—we refer to Java after programming in the title to emphasize the idea that the book is about *fundamental concepts in programming*, not Java per se. This book teaches basic skills for computational problem-solving that are applicable in many modern computing environments, and is a self-contained treatment intended for people with no previous experience in programming.

This book is an *interdisciplinary* approach to the traditional CS1 curriculum, where we highlight the role of computing in other disciplines, from materials science to genomics to astrophysics to network systems. This approach emphasizes for students the essential idea that mathematics, science, engineering, and computing are intertwined in the modern world. While it is a CS1 textbook designed for any first-year college student interested in mathematics, science, or engineering (including computer science), the book also can be used for self-study or as a supplement in a course that integrates programming with another field.

**Coverage**    The book is organized around four stages of learning to program: basic elements, functions, object-oriented programming, and algorithms (with data structures). We provide the basic information readers need to build confidence in writing programs at each level before moving to the next level. An essential feature of our approach is to use example programs that solve intriguing problems, supported with exercises ranging from self-study drills to challenging problems that call for creative solutions.

*Basic elements* include variables, assignment statements, built-in types of data, flow of control (conditionals and loops), arrays, and input/output, including graphics and sound.

*Functions and modules* are the student's first exposure to modular programming. We build upon familiarity with mathematical functions to introduce Java static methods, and then consider the implications of programming with functions, including libraries of functions and recursion. We stress the fundamental idea of dividing a program into components that can be independently debugged, maintained, and reused.

*Object-oriented programming* is our introduction to data abstraction. We emphasize the concepts of a data type (a set of values and a set of operations on them) and an object (an entity that holds a data-type value) and their implementation using Java's class mechanism. We teach students how to *use*, *create*, and *design* data types. Modularity, encapsulation, and other modern programming paradigms are the central concepts of this stage.

*Algorithms and data structures* combine these modern programming paradigms with classic methods of organizing and processing data that remain effective for modern applications. We provide an introduction to classical algorithms for sorting and searching as well as fundamental data structures (including stacks, queues, and symbol tables) and their application, emphasizing the use of the scientific method to understand performance characteristics of implementations.

*Applications in science and engineering* are a key feature of the text. We motivate each programming concept that we address by examining its impact on specific applications. We draw examples from applied mathematics, the physical and biological sciences, and computer science itself, and include simulation of physical systems, numerical methods, data visualization, sound synthesis, image processing, financial simulation, and information technology. Specific examples include a treatment in the first chapter of Markov chains for web page ranks and case studies that address the percolation problem, $N$-body simulation, and the small-world phenomenon. These applications are an integral part of the text. They engage students in the material, illustrate the importance of the programming concepts, and provide persuasive evidence of the critical role played by computation in modern science and engineering.

Our primary goal is to teach the specific mechanisms and skills that are needed to develop effective solutions to any programming problem. We work with complete Java programs and encourage readers to use them. We focus on programming by individuals, not library programming or programming in the large (which we treat briefly in an appendix).

**Use in the Curriculum**   This book is intended for a first-year college course aimed at teaching novices to program in the context of scientific applications. Taught from this book, prospective majors in any area of science and engineering will learn to program in a familiar context. Students completing a course based on this book will be well-prepared to apply their skills in later courses in science and engineering and to recognize when further education in computer science might be beneficial.

Prospective computer science majors, in particular, can benefit from learning to program in the context of scientific applications. A computer scientist needs the same basic background in the scientific method and the same exposure to the role of computation in science as does a biologist, an engineer, or a physicist.

Indeed, our interdisciplinary approach enables colleges and universities to teach prospective computer science majors and prospective majors in other fields of science and engineering in the *same* course. We cover the material prescribed by CS1, but our focus on applications brings life to the concepts and motivates students to learn them. Our interdisciplinary approach exposes students to problems in many different disciplines, helping them to more wisely choose a major.

Whatever the specific mechanism, the use of this book is best positioned early in the curriculum. First, this positioning allows us to leverage familiar material in high school mathematics and science. Second, students who learn to program early in their college curriculum will then be able to use computers more effectively when moving on to courses in their specialty. Like reading and writing, programming is certain to be an essential skill for any scientist or engineer. Students who have grasped the concepts in this book will continually develop that skill through a lifetime, reaping the benefits of exploiting computation to solve or to better understand the problems and projects that arise in their chosen field.

**Prerequisites**  This book is meant to be suitable for typical science and engineering students in their first year of college. That is, we do not expect preparation beyond what is typically required for other entry-level science and mathematics courses.

*Mathematical maturity* is important. While we do not dwell on mathematical material, we do refer to the mathematics curriculum that students have taken in high school, including algebra, geometry, and trigonometry. Most students in our target audience (those intending to major in the sciences and engineering) automatically meet these requirements. Indeed, we take advantage of their familiarity with the basic curriculum to introduce basic programming concepts.

*Scientific curiosity* is also an essential ingredient. Science and engineering students bring with them a sense of fascination in the ability of scientific inquiry to help explain what goes on in nature. We leverage this predilection with examples of simple programs that speak volumes about the natural world. We do not assume any specific knowledge beyond that provided by typical high school courses in mathematics, physics, biology, or chemistry.

*Programming experience* is not necessary, but also is not harmful. Teaching programming is our primary goal, so we assume no prior programming experience. But writing a program to solve a new problem is a challenging intellectual task, so students who have written numerous programs in high school can benefit from taking an introductory programming course based on this book (just as students who have written numerous essays in high school can benefit from an introductory writing course in college). The book can support teaching students with varying backgrounds because the applications appeal to both novices and experts alike.

*Experience using a computer* is also not necessary, but also is not at all a problem. College students use computers regularly, to communicate with friends and relatives, listen to music, process photos, and many other activities. The realization that they can harness the power of their own computer in interesting and important ways is an exciting and lasting lesson.

In summary, virtually all students in science and engineering are prepared to take a course based on this book as a part of their first-semester curriculum.

**Goals**   What can *instructors* of upper-level courses in science and engineering expect of students who have completed a course based on this book?

We cover the CS1 curriculum, but anyone who has taught an introductory programming course knows that expectations of instructors in later courses are typically high: each instructor expects all students to be familiar with the computing environment and approach that he or she wants to use. A physics professor might expect some students to design a program over the weekend to run a simulation; an engineering professor might expect other students to be using a particular package to numerically solve differential equations; or a computer science professor might expect knowledge of the details of a particular programming environment. Is it realistic to meet such diverse expectations? Should there be a different introductory course for each set of students? Colleges and universities have been wrestling with such questions since computers came into widespread use in the latter part of the 20th century. Our answer to them is found in this common introductory treatment of programming, which is analogous to commonly accepted introductory courses in mathematics, physics, biology, and chemistry. *An Introduction to Programming* strives to provide the basic preparation needed by all students in science and engineering, while sending the clear message that there is much more to understand about computer science than programming. Instructors teaching students who have studied from this book can expect that they have the knowledge and experience necessary to enable them to adapt to new computational environments and to effectively exploit computers in diverse applications.

What can *students* who have completed a course based on this book expect to accomplish in later courses?

Our message is that programming is not difficult to learn and that harnessing the power of the computer is rewarding. Students who master the material in this book are prepared to address computational challenges wherever they might appear later in their careers. They learn that modern programming environments, such as the one provided by Java, help open the door to any computational problem they might encounter later, and they gain the confidence to learn, evaluate, and use other computational tools. Students interested in computer science will be well-prepared to pursue that interest; students in science and engineering will be ready to integrate computation into their studies.

**Booksite**    An extensive amount of information that supplements this text may be found on the web at

```
http://www.cs.princeton.edu/IntroProgramming
```

For economy, we refer to this site as the *booksite* throughout. It contains material for instructors, students, and casual readers of the book. We briefly describe this material here, though, as all web users know, it is best surveyed by browsing. With a few exceptions to support testing, the material is all publicly available.

One of the most important implications of the booksite is that it empowers instructors and students to use their own computers to teach and learn the material. Anyone with a computer and a browser can begin learning to program by following a few instructions on the booksite. The process is no more difficult than downloading a media player or a song. As with any website, our booksite is continually evolving. It is an essential resource for everyone who owns this book. In particular, the supplemental materials are critical to our goal of making computer science an integral component of the education of all scientists and engineers.

For *instructors*, the booksite contains information about teaching. This information is primarily organized around a teaching style that we have developed over the past decade, where we offer two lectures per week to a large audience, supplemented by two class sessions per week where students meet in small groups with instructors or teaching assistants. The booksite has presentation slides for the lectures, which set the tone.

For *teaching assistants*, the booksite contains detailed problem sets and programming projects, which are based on exercises from the book but contain much more detail. Each programming assignment is intended to teach a relevant concept in the context of an interesting application while presenting an inviting and engaging challenge to each student. The progression of assignments embodies our approach to teaching programming. The booksite fully specifies all the assignments and provides detailed, structured information to help students complete them in the allotted time, including descriptions of suggested approaches and outlines for what should be taught in class sessions.

For *students*, the booksite contains quick access to much of the material in the book, including source code, plus extra material to encourage self-learning. Solutions are provided for many of the book's exercises, including complete program code and test data. There is a wealth of information associated with programming assignments, including suggested approaches, checklists, FAQs, and test data.

For *casual readers* (including instructors, teaching assistants, and students!), the booksite is a resource for accessing all manner of extra information associated with the book's content. All of the booksite content provides web links and other routes to pursue more information about the topic under consideration. There is far more information accessible than any individual could fully digest, but our goal is to provide enough to whet any reader's appetite for more information about the book's content.

**Acknowledgements**   This project has been under development since 1992, so far too many people have contributed to its success for us to acknowledge them all here. Special thanks are due to Anne Rogers for helping to start the ball rolling; to Dave Hanson, Andrew Appel, and Chris van Wyk, for their patience in explaining data abstraction; and to Lisa Worthington, for being the first to truly relish the challenge of teaching this material to first-year students. We also gratefully acknowledge the efforts of /dev/126 (the summer students who have contributed so much of the content); the faculty, graduate students, and teaching staff who have dedicated themselves to teaching this material over the past 15 years here at Princeton; and the thousands of undergraduates who have dedicated themselves to learning it.

*Robert Sedgewick*
*Madeira, Portugal*

*Kevin Wayne*
*San Francisco, California*

*July, 2007*

# Contents

# Elements of Programming

OUR GOAL IN THIS CHAPTER IS to convince you that writing a program is easier than writing a piece of text, such as a paragraph or essay. Writing prose is difficult: we spend many years in school to learn how to do it. By contrast, just a few building blocks suffice to enable us to write programs that can help solve all sorts of fascinating, but otherwise unapproachable, problems. In this chapter, we take you through these building blocks, get you started on programming in Java, and study a variety of interesting programs. You will be able to express yourself (by writing programs) within just a few weeks. Like the ability to write prose, the ability to program is a lifetime skill that you can continually refine well into the future.

In this book, you will learn the Java programming language. This task will be much easier for you than, for example, learning a foreign language. Indeed, programming languages are characterized by no more than a few dozen vocabulary words and rules of grammar. Much of the material that we cover in this book could be expressed in the C or C++ languages, or any of several other modern programming languages. But we describe everything specifically in Java so that you can get started creating and running programs right away. On the one hand, we will focus on learning to program, as opposed to learning details about Java. On the other hand, part of the challenge of programming is knowing which details are relevant in a given situation. Java is widely used, so learning to program in this language will enable you to write programs on many computers (your own, for example). Also, learning to program in Java will make it easy for you learn other languages, including lower-level languages such as C and specialized languages such as MATLAB.

# 1.1 Your First Program

IN THIS SECTION, OUR PLAN IS to lead you into the world of Java programming by taking you through the basic steps required to get a simple program running. The Java system is a collection of applications, not unlike many of the other applications that you are accustomed to using (such as your word processor, email program, and internet browser). As with any application, you need to be sure that Java is properly installed on your computer. It comes preloaded on many computers, or you can download it easily. You also need a text editor and a terminal application. Your first task is to find the instructions for installing such a Java programming environment on *your* computer by visiting

```
http://www.cs.princeton.edu/IntroProgramming
```

We refer to this site as the *booksite*. It contains an extensive amount of supplementary information about the material in this book for your reference and use. You will find it useful to have your browser open to this site while programming.

**Programming in Java**   To introduce you to developing Java programs, we break the process down into three steps. To program in Java, you need to:

- *Create* a program by typing it into a file named, say, MyCode.java.
- *Compile* it by typing javac MyCode.java in a terminal window.
- *Run* (or *execute*) it by typing java MyCode in the terminal window.

In the first step, you start with a blank screen and end with a sequence of typed characters on the screen, just as when you write an email message or a paper. Programmers use the term *code* to refer to program text and the term *coding* to refer to the act of creating and editing the code. In the second step, you use a system application that *compiles* your program (translates it into a form more suitable for the computer) and puts the result in a file named MyCode.class. In the third step, you transfer control of the computer from the system to your program (which returns control back to the system when finished). Many systems have several different ways to create, compile, and execute programs. We choose the sequence described here because it is the simplest to describe and use for simple programs.

*Creating a program.* A Java program is nothing more than a sequence of characters, like a paragraph or a poem, stored in a file with a .java extension. To create one, therefore, you need only define that sequence of characters, in the same way as you do for email or any other computer application. You can use any *text editor* for this task, or you can use one of the more sophisticated program development environments described on the booksite. Such environments are overkill for the sorts of programs we consider in this book, but they are not difficult to use, have many useful features, and are widely used by professionals.

*Compiling a program.* At first, it might seem that Java is designed to be best understood by the computer. To the contrary, the language is designed to be best understood by the programmer (that's you). The computer's language is far more primitive than Java. A *compiler* is an application that translates a program from the Java language to a language more suitable for executing on the computer. The compiler takes a file with a .java extension as input (your program) and produces a file with the same name but with a .class extension (the computer-language version). To use your Java compiler, type in a terminal window the javac command followed by the file name of the program you want to compile.

*Executing a program.* Once you compile the program, you can run it. This is the exciting part, where your program takes control of your computer (within the constraints of what the Java system allows). It is perhaps more accurate to say that your computer follows your instructions. It is even more accurate to say that a part of the Java system known as the *Java Virtual Machine* (the *JVM*, for short) directs your computer to follow your instructions. To use the JVM to execute your program, type the java command followed by the program name in a terminal window.

*Developing a Java program*

*Program 1.1.1      Hello, World*
---

```
public class HelloWorld
{
   public static void main(String[] args)
   {
      System.out.print("Hello, World");
      System.out.println();
   }
}
```
---

*This code is a Java program that accomplishes a simple task. It is traditionally a beginner's first
program. The box below shows what happens when you compile and execute the program. The
terminal application gives a command prompt (% in this book) and executes the commands
that you type (javac and then java in the example below). The result in this case is that the
program prints a message in the terminal window (the third line).*

```
% javac HelloWorld.java
% java HelloWorld
Hello, World
```

PROGRAM 1.1.1 IS AN EXAMPLE OF a complete Java program. Its name is HelloWorld,
which means that its code resides in a file named HelloWorld.java (by convention
in Java). The program's sole action is to print a message back to the terminal window. For continuity, we will use some standard Java terms to describe the program,
but we will not define them until later in the book: PROGRAM 1.1.1 consists of a single
*class* named HelloWorld that has a single *method* named main(). This method uses
two other methods named System.out.print() and System.out.println() to
do the job. (When referring to a method in the text, we use () after the name to
distinguish it from other kinds of names.) Until SECTION 2.1, where we learn about
classes that define multiple methods, all of our classes will have this same structure.
For the time being, you can think of "class" as meaning "program."

The first line of a method specifies its name and other information; the rest is
a sequence of *statements* enclosed in braces and each followed by a semicolon. For
the time being, you can think of "programming" as meaning "specifying a class

name and a sequence of statements for its `main()` method." In the next two sections, you will learn many different kinds of statements that you can use to make programs. For the moment, we will just use statements for printing to the terminal like the ones in `HelloWorld`.

When you type `java` followed by a class name in your terminal application, the system calls the `main()` method that you defined in that class, and executes its statements in order, one by one. Thus, typing `java HelloWorld` causes the system to call on the `main()` method in PROGRAM 1.1.1 and execute its two statements. The first statement calls on `System.out.print()` to print in the terminal window the message between the quotation marks, and the second statement calls on `System.out.println()` to terminate the line.

*Anatomy of a program*

Since the 1970s, it has been a tradition that a beginning programmer's first program should print `"Hello, World"`. So, you should type the code in PROGRAM 1.1.1 into a file, compile it, and execute it. By doing so, you will be following in the footsteps of countless others who have learned how to program. Also, you will be checking that you have a usable editor and terminal application. At first, accomplishing the task of printing something out in a terminal window might not seem very interesting; upon reflection, however, you will see that one of the most basic functions that we need from a program is its ability to tell us what it is doing.

For the time being, all our program code will be just like PROGRAM 1.1.1, except with a different sequence of statements in `main()`. Thus, you do not need to start with a blank page to write a program. Instead, you can

- Copy `HelloWorld.java` into a new file having a new program name of your choice, followed by `.java`.
- Replace `HelloWorld` on the first line with the new program name.
- Replace the `System.out.print()` and `System.out.println()` statements with a different sequence of statements (each ending with a semicolon).

Your program is characterized by its sequence of statements and its name. Each Java program must reside in a file whose name matches the one after the word `class` on the first line, and it also must have a `.java` extension.

**Program 1.1.2   *Using a command-line argument***

```
public class UseArgument
{
   public static void main(String[] args)
   {
      System.out.print("Hi, ");
      System.out.print(args[0]);
      System.out.println(". How are you?");
   }
}
```

*This program shows the way in which we can control the actions of our programs: by providing an argument on the command line. Doing so allows us to tailor the behavior of our programs.*

```
% javac UseArgument.java
% java UseArgument Alice
Hi, Alice. How are you?
% java UseArgument Bob
Hi, Bob. How are you?
```

*Errors.* It is easy to blur the distinction among editing, compiling, and executing programs. You should keep them separate in your mind when you are learning to program, to better understand the effects of the errors that inevitably arise. You can find several examples of errors in the Q&A at the end of this section. You can fix or avoid most errors by carefully examining the program as you create it, the same way you fix spelling and grammatical errors when you compose an email message. Some errors, known as *compile-time* errors, are caught when you compile the program, because they prevent the compiler from doing the translation. Other errors, known as *run-time* errors, do not show up until you execute the program. In general, errors in programs, also commonly known as *bugs*, are the bane of a programmer's existence: the error messages can be confusing or misleading, and the source of the error can be very hard to find. One of the first skills that you will learn is to identify errors; you will also learn to be sufficiently careful when coding, to avoid making many of them in the first place.

**Input and Output**    Typically, we want to provide *input* to our programs: data that they can process to produce a result. The simplest way to provide input data is illustrated in UseArgument (PROGRAM 1.1.2). Whenever UseArgument is executed, it reads the *command-line argument* that you type after the program name and prints it back out to the terminal as part of the message. The result of executing this program depends on what we type after the program name. After compiling the program once, we can run it for different command-line arguments and get different printed results. We will discuss in more detail the mechanism that we use to pass arguments to our programs later, in SECTION 2.1. In the meantime, you can use args[0] within your program's body to represent the string that you type on the command line when it is executed, just as in UseArgu-

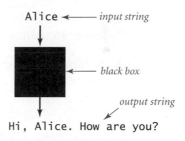

ment.

Again, accomplishing the task of getting a program to write back out what we type in to it may not seem interesting at first, but upon reflection you will realize that another basic function of a program is its ability to respond to basic information from the user to control what the program does. The simple model that UseArgument represents will suffice to allow us to consider Java's basic programming mechanism and to address all sorts of interesting computational problems.

*A bird's-eye view of a Java program*

Stepping back, we can see that UseArgument does neither more nor less than implement a function that maps a string of characters (the argument) into another string of characters (the message printed back to the terminal). When using it, we might think of our Java program as a black box that converts our input string to some output string. This model is attractive because it is not only simple but also sufficiently general to allow completion, in principle, of any computational task. For example, the Java compiler itself is nothing more than a program that takes one string of characters as input (a .java file) and produces another string of characters as output (the corresponding .class file). Later, we will be able to write programs that accomplish a variety of interesting tasks (though we stop short of programs as complicated as a compiler). For the moment, we live with various limitations on the size and type of the input and output to our programs; in SECTION 1.5, we will see how to incorporate more sophisticated mechanisms for program input and output. In particular, we can work with arbitrarily long input and output strings and other types of data such as sound and pictures.

## Q&A

**Q.** Why Java?

**A.** The programs that we are writing are very similar to their counterparts in several other languages, so our choice of language is not crucial. We use Java because it is widely available, embraces a full set of modern abstractions, and has a variety of automatic checks for mistakes in programs, so it is suitable for learning to program. There is no perfect language, and you certainly will be programming in other languages in the future.

**Q.** Do I really have to type in the programs in the book to try them out? I believe that you ran them and that they produce the indicated output.

**A.** Everyone should type in and run `HelloWorld`. Your understanding will be greatly magnified if you also run `UseArgument`, try it on various inputs, and modify it to test different ideas of your own. To save some typing, you can find all of the code in this book (and much more) on the booksite. This site also has information about installing and running Java on your computer, answers to selected exercises, web links, and other extra information that you may find useful or interesting.

**Q.** What is the meaning of the words `public`, `static` and `void`?

**A.** These keywords specify certain properties of `main()` that you will learn about later in the book. For the moment, we just include these keywords in the code (because they are required) but do not refer to them in the text.

**Q.** What is the meaning of the `//`, `/*`, and `*/` character sequences in the code?

**A.** They denote *comments*, which are ignored by the compiler. A comment is either text in between `/*` and `*/` or at the end of a line after `//`. As with most online code, the code on the booksite is liberally annotated with comments that explain what it does; we use fewer comments in code in this book because the accompanying text and figures provide the explanation.

**Q.** What are Java's rules regarding tabs, spaces, and newline characters?

**A.** Such characters are known as *whitespace* characters. Java compilers consider all whitespace in program text to be equivalent. For example, we could write `Hel`-

loWorld as follows:

```
public class HelloWorld { public static void main ( String []
args) { System.out.print("Hello, World")          ; System.out.
println() ;} }
```

But we do normally adhere to spacing and indenting conventions when we write Java programs, just as we always indent paragraphs and lines consistently when we write prose or poetry.

**Q.** What are the rules regarding quotation marks?

**A.** Material inside quotation marks is an exception to the rule defined in the previous question: things within quotes are taken literally so that you can precisely specify what gets printed. If you put any number of successive spaces within the quotes, you get that number of spaces in the output. If you accidentally omit a quotation mark, the compiler may get very confused, because it needs that mark to distinguish between characters in the string and other parts of the program.

**Q.** What happens when you omit a brace or misspell one of the words, like `public` or `static` or `void` or `main`?

**A.** It depends upon precisely what you do. Such errors are called *syntax errors* and are usually caught by the compiler. For example, if you make a program Bad that is exactly the same as `HelloWorld` except that you omit the line containing the first left brace (and change the program name from `HelloWorld` to Bad), you get the following helpful message:

```
% javac Bad.java
Bad.java:2: '{' expected
   public static void main(String[] args)
   ^
1 error
```

From this message, you might correctly surmise that you need to insert a left brace. But the compiler may not be able to tell you exactly what mistake you made, so the error message may be hard to understand. For example, if you omit the second left brace instead of the first one, you get the following messages:

```
% javac Bad.java
Bad.java:4: ';' expected
        System.out.print("Hello, World");
        ^
Bad.java:7: 'class' or 'interface' expected
}
^
Bad.java:8: 'class' or 'interface' expected
^
3 errors
```

One way to get used to such messages is to intentionally introduce mistakes into a simple program and then see what happens. Whatever the error message says, you should treat the compiler as a friend, for it is just trying to tell you that something is wrong with your program.

**Q.** Can a program use more than one command-line argument?

**A.** Yes, you can use many arguments, though we normally use just a few. Note that the count starts at 0, so you refer to the first argument as `args[0]`, the second one as `args[1]`, the third one as `args[2]`, and so forth.

**Q.** What Java methods are available for me to use?

**A.** There are literally thousands of them. We introduce them to you in a deliberate fashion (starting in the next section) to avoid overwhelming you with choices.

**Q.** When I ran `UseArgument`, I got a strange error message. What's the problem?

**A.** Most likely, you forgot to include a command-line argument:

```
% java UseArgument
Hi, Exception in thread "main"
java.lang.ArrayIndexOutOfBoundsException: 0
        at UseArgument.main(UseArgument.java:6)
```

The JVM is complaining that you ran the program but did not type an argument as promised. You will learn more details about array indices in SECTION 1.4. Remember this error message: you are likely to see it again. Even experienced programmers forget to type arguments on occasion.

# *Exercises*

**1.1.1**   Write a program that prints the `Hello, World` message 10 times.

**1.1.2**   Describe what happens if you omit the following in `HelloWorld.java`:
  *a.* `public`
  *b.* `static`
  *c.* `void`
  *d.* `args`

**1.1.3**   Describe what happens if you misspell (by, say, omitting the second letter) the following in `HelloWorld.java`:
  *a.* `public`
  *b.* `static`
  *c.* `void`
  *d.* `args`

**1.1.4**   Describe what happens if you try to execute `UseArgument` with each of the following command lines:
  *a.* `java UseArgument java`
  *b.* `java UseArgument @!&^%`
  *c.* `java UseArgument 1234`
  *d.* `java UseArgument.java Bob`
  *e.* `java UseArgument Alice Bob`

**1.1.5**   Modify `UseArgument.java` to make a program `UseThree.java` that takes three names and prints out a proper sentence with the names in the reverse of the order given, so that, for example, `java UseThree Alice Bob Carol` gives `Hi Carol, Bob, and Alice`.

# 1.2 Built-in Types of Data

WHEN PROGRAMMING IN JAVA, YOU MUST always be aware of the type of data that your program is processing. The programs in SECTION 1.1 process strings of characters, many of the programs in this section process numbers, and we consider numerous other types later in the book. Understanding the distinctions among them is so important that we formally define the idea: a *data type* is a *set of values* and a *set of operations* defined on those values. You are familiar with various types of numbers, such as integers and real numbers, and with operations defined on them,

such as addition and multiplication. In mathematics, we are accustomed to thinking of sets of numbers as being infinite; in computer programs we have to work with a finite number of possibilities. Each operation that we perform is well-defined *only* for the finite set of values in an associated data type.

There are eight *primitive* types of data in Java, mostly for different kinds of numbers. Of the eight primitive types, we most often use these: `int` for integers; `double` for real numbers; and `boolean` for true-false values. There are other types of data available in Java libraries: for example, the programs in SECTION 1.1 use the type `String` for strings of characters. Java treats the `String` type differently from other types because its usage for input and output is essential. Accordingly, it shares some characteristics of the primitive types: for example, some of its operations are built in to the Java language. For clarity, we refer to primitive types and `String` collectively as *built-in* types. For the time being, we concentrate on programs that arc based on computing with built-in types. Later, you will learn about Java library data types and building your own data types. Indeed, programming in Java is often centered on building data types, as you shall see in CHAPTER 3.

After defining basic terms, we consider several sample programs and code fragments that illustrate the use of different types of data. These code fragments do not do much real computing, but you will soon see similar code in longer programs. Understanding data types (values and operations on them) is an essential step in beginning to program. It sets the stage for us to begin working with more intricate programs in the next section. Every program that you write will use code like the tiny fragments shown in this section.

| type | set of values | common operators | sample literal values |
|------|---------------|------------------|-----------------------|
| int | integers | + - * / % | 99  -12  2147483647 |
| double | floating-point numbers | + - * / | 3.14  -2.5  6.022e23 |
| boolean | boolean values | && \|\| ! | true false |
| char | characters | | 'A'  '1'  '%'  '\n' |
| String | sequences of characters | + | "AB" Hello"  "2.5" |

*Basic built-in data types*

**Definitions**   To talk about data types, we need to introduce some terminology. To do so, we start with the following code fragment:

```
int a, b, c;
a = 1234;
b = 99;
c = a + b;
```

The first line is a *declaration* that declares the names of three *variables* to be the *identifiers* a, b, and c and their type to be int. The next three lines are *assignment statements* that change the values of the variables, using the *literals* 1234 and 99, and the *expression* a + b, with the end result that c has the value 1333.

*Identifiers.*  We use identifiers to name variables (and many other things) in Java. An identifier is a sequence of letters, digits, _, and $, the first of which is not a digit. The sequences of characters abc, Ab$, abc123, and a_b are all legal Java identifiers, but Ab*, 1abc, and a+b are not. Identifiers are case-sensitive, so Ab, ab, and AB are all different names. You cannot use certain *reserved words*—such as public, static, int, double, and so forth—to name variables.

*Literals.*  A literal is a source-code representation of a data-type value. We use strings of digits like 1234 or 99 to define int literal values, and add a decimal point as in 3.14159 or 2.71828 to define double literal values. To specify a boolean value, we use the keywords true or false, and to specify a String, we use a sequence of characters enclosed in quotes, such as "Hello, World". We will consider other kinds of literals as we consider each data type in more detail.

*Variables.*  A variable is a name that we use to refer to a data-type value. We use variables to keep track of changing values as a computation unfolds. For example, we use the variable n in many programs to count things. We create a variable in a *declaration* that specifies its type and gives it a name. We compute with it by using the name in an *expression* that uses operations defined for its type. Each variable always stores one of the permissible data-type values.

*Declaration statements.*  A declaration statement associates a variable name with a type at compile time. Java requires us to use declarations to specify the names and types of variables. By doing so, we are being explicit about any computation that we are specifying. Java is said to be a *strongly-typed* language, because the Java compiler can check for consistency at compile time (for example, it does not permit us to add a String to a double). This situation is precisely analogous to making sure that quantities have the proper units in a sci-

*Using a primitive data type*

entific application (for example, it does not make sense to add a quantity measured in inches to another measured in pounds). Declarations can appear anywhere before a variable is first used—most often, we put them *at* the point of first use.

*Assignment statements.*  An assignment statement associates a data-type value with a variable. When we write c = a + b in Java, we are not expressing mathematical equality, but are instead expressing an action: set the value of the variable c to be the value of a plus the value of b. It is true that c is mathematically equal to a + b immediately after the assignment statement has been executed, but the point of the statement is to change the value of c (if necessary). The left-hand side of an assignment statement must be a single variable; the right-hand side can be an arbitrary *expression* that produces values of the type. For example, we can say discriminant = b*b - 4*a*c in Java, but we cannot say a + b = b + a or 1 = a. In short, *the meaning of = is decidedly not the same as in mathematical equations*. For example, a  =  b is certainly not the same as b  =  a, and while the value of c is the value of a plus the value of b  after c =  a + b  has been executed, that may cease to be the case if subsequent statements change the values of any of the variables.

*Initialization.*  In a simple declaration, the initial value of the variable is undefined. For economy, we can combine a declaration with an assignment statement to provide an initial value for the variable.

*Tracing changes in variable values.* As a final check on your understanding of the purpose of assignment statements, convince yourself that the following code *exchanges* the values of a and b (assume that a and b are int variables):

```
int t = a;
a = b;
b = t;
```

To do so, use a time-honored method of examining program behavior: study a table of the variable values after each statement (such a table is known as a *trace*).

| | a | b | t |
|---|---|---|---|
| int a, b; | *undefined* | *undefined* | |
| a = 1234; | 1234 | *undefined* | |
| b = 99; | 1234 | 99 | |
| int t = a; | 1234 | 99 | **1234** |
| a = b; | 99 | 99 | 1234 |
| b = t; | 99 | **1234** | 1234 |

*Your first trace*

*Expressions.* An expression is a literal, a variable, or a sequence of operations on literals and/or variables that produces a value. For primitive types, expressions look just like mathematical formulas, which are based on familiar symbols or *operators* that specify data-type operations to be performed on one or more *operands*. Each operand can be any expression. Most of the operators that we use are *binary operators* that take exactly two operands, such as x + 1 or y / 2. An expression that is enclosed in parentheses is another expression with the same value. For example, we can write 4 * (x - 3) or 4*x - 12 on the right-hand side of an assignment statement and the compiler will understand what we mean.

*operands*
*(and expressions)*

*operator*

*Anatomy of an expression*

*Precedence.* Such expressions are shorthand for specifying a sequence of computations: in what order should they be performed? Java has natural and well-defined *precedence* rules (see the booksite) that fully specify this order. For arithmetic operations, multiplication and division are performed before addition and subtraction, so that a-b*c and a-(b*c) represent the same sequence of operations. When arithmetic operators have the same precedence, the order is determined by *left-associativity*, so that a-b-c and (a-b)-c represent the same sequence of operations. You can use parentheses to override the rules, so you should not need to worry about the details of precedence for most of the programs that you write. (Some of the programs that you *read* might depend subtly on precedence rules, but we avoid such programs in this book.)

*Converting strings to primitive values for command-line arguments.* Java provides the library methods that we need to convert the strings that we type as command-line arguments into numeric values for primitive types. We use the Java library methods `Integer.parseInt()` and `Double.parseDouble()` for this purpose. For example, typing `Integer.parseInt("123")` in program text yields the literal value 123 (typing 123 has the same effect) and the code `Integer.parseInt(args[0])` produces the same result as the literal value typed as a string on the command line. You will see several examples of this usage in the programs in this section.

*Converting primitive type values to strings for output.*  As mentioned at the beginning of this section, the Java built-in `String` type obeys special rules. One of these special rules is that you can easily convert any type of data to a `String`: whenever we use the + operator with a `String` as one of its operands, Java automatically converts the other to a `String`, producing as a result the `String` formed from the characters of the first operand followed by the characters of the second operand. For example, the result of these two code fragments

```
String a = "1234";          String a = "1234";
String b = "99";            int b = 99;
String c = a + b;           String c = a + b;
```

are both the same: they assign to `c` the value "123499". We use this automatic conversion liberally to form `String` values for `System.out.print()` and `System.out.println()` for output. For example, we can write statements like this one:

```
System.out.println(a + " + " + b + " = " + c);
```

If `a`, `b`, and `c` are `int` variables with the values 1234, 99, and 1333, respectively, then this statement prints out the string 1234 + 99 = 1333.

WITH THESE MECHANISMS, OUR VIEW OF each Java program as a black box that takes string arguments and produces string results is still valid, but we can now interpret those strings as numbers and use them as the basis for meaningful computation. Next, we consider these details for the basic built-in types that you will use most often (strings, integers, floating-point numbers, and true–false values), along with sample code illustrating their use. To understand how to use a data type, you need to know not just its defined set of values, but also which operations you can perform, the language mechanism for invoking the operations, and the conventions for specifying literal values.

**Characters and Strings**    A char is an alphanumeric character or symbol, like the ones that you type. There are $2^{16}$ different possible character values, but we usually restrict attention to the ones that represent letters, numbers, symbols, and whitespace characters such as tab and newline. Literals for char are characters enclosed in single quotes; for example, 'a' represents the letter a. For tab, newline, backslash, single quote and double quote, we use the special *escape sequences* '\t', '\n', '\\', '\'', and '\"', respectively. The characters are encoded as 16-bit integers using an encoding scheme known as Unicode, and there are escape sequences for specifying special characters not found on your keyboard (see the booksite). We usually do not perform any operations directly on characters other than assigning values to variables.

| values | sequences of characters |
|---|---|
| typical literals | "Hello," "1 " " * " |
| operation | concatenate |
| operator | + |

*Java's built-in* String *data type*

A String is a sequence of characters. A literal String is a sequence of characters within double quotes, such as "Hello, World". The String data type is *not* a primitive type, but Java sometimes treats it like one. For example, the *concatenation* operator (+) that we just considered is built in to the language as a binary operator in the same way as familiar operations on numbers.

The concatenation operation (along with the ability to declare String variables and to use them in expressions and assignment statements) is sufficiently powerful to allow us to attack some nontrivial computing tasks. As an example, Ruler (PROGRAM 1.2.1) computes a table of values of the *ruler function* that describes the relative lengths of the marks on a ruler. One noteworthy feature of this computation is that it illustrates how easy is is to craft short programs that produce huge amounts of output. If you extend this program in the obvious way to print five lines, six lines, seven lines, and so forth, you will see that each time you add just two statements to this program, you increase the size of its output by precisely one more than a factor of two. Specifically, if the program prints $n$ lines, the $n$th line contains $2^n - 1$ numbers. For example, if you were to add statements in this way so that the program prints 30 lines, it would attempt to print more than 1 *billion* numbers.

| expression | value |
|---|---|
| "Hi, " + "Bob" | "Hi, Bob" |
| "1" + " 2 " + "1" | "1 2 1" |
| "1234" + " + " + "99" | "1234 + 99" |
| "1234" + "99" | "123499" |

*Typical* String *expressions*

---

### Program 1.2.1   *String concatenation example*

```
public class Ruler
{
    public static void main(String[] args)
    {
        String ruler1 = "1";
        String ruler2 = ruler1 + " 2 " + ruler1;
        String ruler3 = ruler2 + " 3 " + ruler2;
        String ruler4 = ruler3 + " 4 " + ruler3;
        System.out.println(ruler1);
        System.out.println(ruler2);
        System.out.println(ruler3);
        System.out.println(ruler4);
    }
}
```

*This program prints the relative lengths of the subdivisions on a ruler. The nth line of output is the relative lengths of the marks on a ruler subdivided in intervals of $1/2^n$ of an inch. For example, the fourth line of output gives the relative lengths of the marks that indicate intervals of one-sixteenth of an inch on a ruler.*

```
% javac Ruler.java
% java Ruler
1
1 2 1
1 2 1 3 1 2 1
1 2 1 3 1 2 1 4 1 2 1 3 1 2 1
```

*The ruler function for n = 4*

As just discussed, our most frequent use (by far) of the concatenation operation is to put together results of computation for output with `System.out.print()` and `System.out.println()`. For example, we could simplify `UseArgument` (PROGRAM 1.1.2) by replacing its three statements with this single statement:

```
System.out.println("Hi, " + args[0] + ". How are you?");
```

We have considered the `String` type first precisely because we need it for output (and command-line input) in programs that process other types of data.

**Integers**    An int is an integer (natural number) between –2147483648 ($-2^{31}$) and 2147483647 ($2^{31}-1$). These bounds derive from the fact that integers are represented in binary with 32 binary digits: there are $2^{32}$ possible values. (The term *binary digit* is omnipresent in computer science, and we nearly always use the abbreviation *bit*: a bit is either 0 or 1.) The range of possible int values is asymmetric because zero is included with the positive values. See the booksite for more details about number representation, but in the present context it suffices to know that an int is one of the finite set of values in the range just given. Sequences of the characters 0 through 9, possibly with a plus or minus sign at the beginning (that, when interpreted as decimal numbers, fall within the defined range), are integer literal values. We use ints frequently because they naturally arise when implementing programs.

Standard arithmetic operators for addition/subtraction (+ and -), multiplication (*), division (/), and remainder (%) for the int data type are built in to Java. These operators take two int operands and produce an int result, with one significant exception—division or remainder by zero is not allowed. These operations are defined just as in grade school (keeping in mind that all results must be integers): given two int values a and b, the value of a / b is the number of times b goes into a *with the fractional part discarded*, and the value of a % b is the remainder that you get when you divide a by b. For example, the value of 17 / 3 is 5, and the value of 17 % 3 is 2. The int results that we get from arithmetic operations are just what we expect, except that if the result is too large to fit into int's 32-bit representation, then it will be truncated in a well-defined manner. This situation is known as *overflow*. In

| expression | value | comment |
|---|---|---|
| 5 + 3 | 8 | |
| 5 - 3 | 2 | |
| 5 * 3 | 15 | |
| 5 / 3 | 1 | no fractional part |
| 5 % 3 | 2 | remainder |
| 1 / 0 | | run-time error |
| 3 * 5 - 2 | 13 | * has precedence |
| 3 + 5 / 2 | 5 | / has precedence |
| 3 - 5 - 2 | -4 | left associative |
| ( 3 - 5 ) - 2 | -4 | better style |
| 3 - ( 5 - 2 ) | 0 | unambiguous |

*Typical* int *expressions*

| values | integers between $-2^{31}$ and $+2^{31}-1$ | | | | |
|---|---|---|---|---|---|
| typical literals | 1234  99  -99  0  1000000 | | | | |
| operations | add | subtract | multiply | divide | remainder |
| operators | + | – | * | / | % |

*Java's built-in* int *data type*

*Program 1.2.2    Integer multiplication and division*

```java
public class IntOps
{
   public static void main(String[] args)
   {
      int a = Integer.parseInt(args[0]);
      int b = Integer.parseInt(args[1]);
      int p = a * b;
      int q = a / b;
      int r = a % b;
      System.out.println(a + " * " + b + " = " + p);
      System.out.println(a + " / " + b + " = " + q);
      System.out.println(a + " % " + b + " = " + r);
      System.out.println(a + " = " + q + " * " + b + " + " + r);
   }
}
```

*Arithmetic for integers is built in to Java. Most of this code is devoted to the task of getting the values in and out; the actual arithmetic is in the simple statements in the middle of the program that assign values to* p, q, *and* r.

```
% javac IntOps.java
% java IntOps 1234 99
1234 * 99 = 122166
1234 / 99 = 12
1234 % 99 = 46
1234 = 12 * 99 + 46
```

general, we have to take care that such a result is not misinterpreted by our code. For the moment, we will be computing with small numbers, so you do not have to worry about these boundary conditions.

PROGRAM 1.2.2 illustrates basic operations for manipulating integers, such as the use of expressions involving arithmetic operators. It also demonstrates the use of `Integer.parseInt()` to convert `String` values on the command line to `int` values, as well as the use of automatic type conversion to convert `int` values to `String` values for output.

Three other built-in types are different representations of integers in Java. The `long`, `short`, and `byte` types are the same as `int` except that they use 64, 16, and 8 bits respectively, so the range of allowed values is accordingly different. Programmers use `long` when working with huge integers, and the other types to save space. You can find a table with the maximum and minimum values for each type on the booksite, or you can figure them out for yourself from the numbers of bits.

**Floating-point numbers**    The `double` type is for representing *floating-point* numbers, for use in scientific and commercial applications. The internal representation is like scientific notation, so that we can compute with numbers in a huge range. We use floating-point numbers to represent real numbers, but they are decidedly not the same as real numbers! There are infinitely many real numbers, but we can only represent a finite number of floating-points in any digital computer representation. Floating-point numbers do approximate real numbers sufficiently well that we can use them in applications, but we often need to cope with the fact that we cannot always do exact computations.

| expression | value |
| --- | --- |
| 3.141 + .03 | 3.171 |
| 3.141 - .03 | 3.111 |
| 6.02e23 / 2.0 | 3.01e23 |
| 5.0 / 3.0 | 1.6666666666666667 |
| 10.0 % 3.141 | 0.577 |
| 1.0 / 0.0 | Infinity |
| Math.sqrt(2.0) | 1.4142135623730951 |
| Math.sqrt(-1.0) | NaN |

*Typical* double *expressions*

We can use a sequence of digits with a decimal point to type floating-point numbers. For example, `3.14159` represents a six-digit approximation to $\pi$. Alternatively, we can use a notation like scientific notation: the literal `6.022e23` represents the number $6.022 \times 10^{23}$. As with integers, you can use these conventions to write floating-point literals in your programs or to provide floating-point numbers as string parameters on the command line.

The arithmetic operators +, -, *, and / are defined for `double`. Beyond the built-in operators, the Java `Math` library defines the square root, trigonometric

| | | | |
| --- | --- | --- | --- |
| *values* | real numbers (specified by IEEE 754 standard) | | |
| *typical literals* | 3.14159  6.022e23  -3.0  2.0  1.4142135623730951 | | |
| *operations* | add | subtract | multiply | divide |
| *operators* | + | - | * | / |

*Java's built-in* double *data type*

---

*Program 1.2.3    Quadratic formula*

```
public class Quadratic
{
   public static void main(String[] args)
   {
      double b = Double.parseDouble(args[0]);
      double c = Double.parseDouble(args[1]);
      double discriminant = b*b - 4.0*c;
      double d = Math.sqrt(discriminant);
      System.out.println((-b + d) / 2.0);
      System.out.println((-b - d) / 2.0);
   }
}
```

---

*This program prints out the roots of the polynomial $x^2 + bx + c$, using the quadratic formula. For example, the roots of $x^2 - 3x + 2$ are 1 and 2 since we can factor the equation as $(x - 1)(x - 2)$; the roots of $x^2 - x - 1$ are $\phi$ and $1 - \phi$, where $\phi$ is the golden ratio, and the roots of $x^2 + x + 1$ are not real numbers.*

```
% javac Quadratic.java
% java Quadratic -3.0 2.0
2.0
1.0
```

```
% java Quadratic -1.0 -1.0
1.618033988749895
-0.6180339887498949

% java Quadratic 1.0 1.0
NaN
NaN
```

functions, logarithm/exponential functions, and other common functions for floating-point numbers. To use one of these values in an expression, we write the name of the function followed by its argument in parentheses. For example, you can use the code `Math.sqrt(2.0)` when you want to use the square root of 2 in an expression. We discuss in more detail the mechanism behind this arrangement in SECTION 2.1 and more details about the `Math` library at the end of this section.

When working with floating point numbers, one of the first things that you will encounter is the issue of *precision*: 5.0/2.0 is 2.5 but 5.0/3.0 is 1.6666666666666667. In SECTION 1.5, you will learn Java's mechanism for controlling the number of significant digits that you see in output. Until then, we will work with the Java default output format.

The result of a calculation can be one of the special values `Infinity` (if the number is too large to be represented) or `NaN` (if the result of the calculation is undefined). Though there are myriad details to consider when calculations involve these values, you can use `double` in a natural way and begin to write Java programs instead of using a calculator for all kinds of calculations. For example, PROGRAM 1.2.3 shows the use of `double` values in computing the roots of a quadratic equation using the quadratic formula. Several of the exercises at the end of this section further illustrate this point.

As with `long`, `short`, and `byte` for integers, there is another representation for real numbers called `float`. Programmers sometimes use `float` to save space when precision is a secondary consideration. The `double` type is useful for about 15 significant digits; the `float` type is good for only about 7 digits. We do not use `float` in this book.

| | | | |
|---|---|---|---|
| *values* | true or false | | |
| *literals* | `true` `false` | | |
| *operations* | and | or | not |
| *operators* | `&&` | `\|\|` | `!` |

*Java's built-in* `boolean` *data type*

**Booleans** The `boolean` type has just two values: `true` and `false`. These are the two possible `boolean` literals. Every `boolean` variable has one of these two values, and every `boolean` operation has operands and a result that takes on just one of these two values. This simplicity is deceiving—`boolean` values lie at the foundation of computer science.

The most important operations defined for `boolean`s are *and* (`&&`), *or* (`||`), and *not* (`!`), which have familiar definitions:
- `a && b` is `true` if both operands are `true`, and `false` if either is `false`.
- `a || b` is `false` if both operands are `false`, and `true` if either is `true`.
- `!a` is `true` if `a` is `false`, and `false` if `a` is `true`.

Despite the intuitive nature of these definitions, it is worthwhile to fully specify each possibility for each operation in tables known as *truth tables*. The *not* function

| a | !a | | a | b | a && b | a \|\| b |
|---|---|---|---|---|---|---|
| true | false | | false | false | false | false |
| false | true | | false | true | false | true |
| | | | true | false | false | true |
| | | | true | true | true | true |

*Truth-table definitions of* `boolean` *operations*

| a     | b     | a && b | !a    | !b    | !a \|\| !b | !(!a \|\| !b) |
|-------|-------|--------|-------|-------|------------|---------------|
| false | false | false  | true  | true  | true       | false         |
| false | true  | false  | true  | false | true       | false         |
| true  | false | false  | false | true  | true       | false         |
| true  | true  | true   | false | false | false      | true          |

*Truth-table proof that* a && b *and* !(!a \|\| !b) *are identical*

has only one operand: its value for each of the two possible values of the operand is specified in the second column. The *and* and *or* functions each have two operands: there are four different possibilities for operand input values, and the values of the functions for each possibility are specified in the right two columns.

We can use these operators with parentheses to develop arbitrarily complex expressions, each of which specifies a well-defined boolean function. Often the same function appears in different guises. For example, the expressions (a && b) and !(!a || !b) are equivalent.

The study of manipulating expressions of this kind is known as *Boolean logic*. This field of mathematics is fundamental to computing: it plays an essential role in the design and operation of computer hardware itself, and it is also a starting point for the theoretical foundations of computation. In the present context, we are interested in boolean expressions because we use them to control the behavior of our programs. Typically, a particular condition of interest is specified as a boolean expression and a piece of program code is written to execute one set of statements if the expression is true and a different set of statements if the expression is false. The mechanics of doing so are the topic of SECTION 1.3.

**Comparisons**    Some *mixed-type* operators take operands of one type and produce a result of another type. The most important operators of this kind are the comparison operators ==, !=, <, <=, >, and >=, which all are defined for each primitive numeric type and produce a boolean result. Since operations are defined only

| | |
|---|---|
| *non-negative discriminant?* | (b*b - 4.0*a*c) >= 0.0 |
| *beginning of a century?* | (year % 100) == 0 |
| *legal month?* | (month >= 1) && (month <= 12) |

*Typical comparison expressions*

---

**Program 1.2.4    Leap year**

---

```
public class LeapYear
{
   public static void main(String[] args)
   {
      int year = Integer.parseInt(args[0]);
      boolean isLeapYear;
      isLeapYear = (year % 4 == 0);
      isLeapYear = isLeapYear && (year % 100 != 0);
      isLeapYear = isLeapYear || (year % 400 == 0);
      System.out.println(isLeapYear);
   }
}
```

---

*This program tests whether an integer corresponds to a leap year in the Gregorian calendar. A year is a leap year if it is divisible by 4 (2004), unless it is divisible by 100 in which case it is not (1900), unless it is divisible by 400 in which case it is (2000).*

```
% javac LeapYear.java
% java LeapYear 2004
true
% java LeapYear 1900
false
% java LeapYear 2000
true
```

with respect to data types, each of these symbols stands for many operations, one for each data type. It is required that both operands be of the same type. The result is always `boolean`.

Even without going into the details of number representation, it is clear that the operations for the various types are really quite different: for example, it is one thing to compare two `int`s to check that (2 <= 2) is `true` but quite another to compare two `double`s to check whether (2.0 <= 0.002e3) is `true` or `false`. Still, these operations are well-defined and useful to write code that tests for conditions such as (b*b - 4.0*a*c) >= 0.0, which is frequently needed, as you will see.

The comparison operations have lower precedence than arithmetic operators and higher precedence than boolean operators, so you do not need the parentheses in an expression like (b*b - 4.0*a*c) >= 0.0, and you could write an expression like month >= 1 && month <= 12 without parentheses to test whether the value of the int variable month is between 1 and 12. (It is better style to use the parentheses, however.)

Comparison operations, together with boolean logic, provide the basis for decision-making in Java programs. PROGRAM 1.2.4 is an example of their use, and you can find other examples in the exercises at the end of this section. More importantly, in SECTION 1.3 we will see the role that boolean expressions play in more sophisticated programs.

| op | meaning | true | false |
|----|---------|------|-------|
| == | equal | 2 == 2 | 2 == 3 |
| != | not equal | 3 != 2 | 2 != 2 |
| < | less than | 2 < 13 | 2 < 2 |
| <= | less than or equal | 2 <= 2 | 3 <= 2 |
| > | greater than | 13 > 2 | 2 > 13 |
| >= | greater than or equal | 3 >= 2 | 2 >= 3 |

*Comparisons with* int *operands and a* boolean *result*

**Library methods and APIs**   As we have seen, many programming tasks involve using Java library methods in addition to the built-in operations on data-type values. The number of available library methods is vast. As you learn to program, you will learn to use more and more library methods, but it is best at the beginning to restrict your attention to a relatively small set of methods. In this chapter, you have already used some of Java's methods for printing, for converting data from one type to another, and for computing mathematical functions (the Java Math library). In later chapters, you will learn not just how to use other methods, but how to create and use your own methods.

For convenience, we will consistently summarize the library methods that you need to know how to use in tables like this one:

```
public class System.out
```

| void  print(String s) | *print s* |
|---|---|
| void  println(String s) | *print s, followed by a newline* |
| void  println() | *print a newline* |

*Note: Any type of data can be used (and will be automatically converted to* String*).*

*Excerpts from Java's library for standard output*

Such a table is known as an *application programming interface (API)*. It provides the information that you need to write an *application program* that uses the methods. Here is an API for the most commonly used methods in Java's Math library:

---

`public class Math`

| | |
|---|---|
| `double abs(double a)` | *absolute value of a* |
| `double max(double a, double b)` | *maximum of a and b* |
| `double min(double a, double b)` | *minimum of a and b* |

*Note 1:* `abs()`, `max()`, *and* `min()` *are defined also for* `int`, `long`, *and* `float`.

| | |
|---|---|
| `double sin(double theta)` | *sine function* |
| `double cos(double theta)` | *cosine function* |
| `double tan(double theta)` | *tangent function* |

*Note 2: Angles are expressed in radians. Use* `toDegrees()` *and* `toRadians()` *to convert.*
*Note 3: Use* `asin()`, `acos()`, *and* `atan()` *for inverse functions.*

| | |
|---|---|
| `double exp(double a)` | *exponential ($e^a$)* |
| `double log(double a)` | *natural log ($\log_e a$, or ln a)* |
| `double pow(double a, double b)` | *raise a to the bth power ($a^b$)* |
| `long round(double a)` | *round to the nearest integer* |
| `double random()` | *random number in* $[0, 1)$ |
| `double sqrt(double a)` | *square root of a* |
| `double E` | *value of e (constant)* |
| `double PI` | *value of $\pi$ (constant)* |

*See booksite for other available functions.*

*Excerpts from Java's mathematics library*

With the exception of `random()`, these methods implement mathematical functions—they use their arguments to compute a value of a specified type. Each method is described by a line in the API that specifies the information you need to know in order to use the method. The code in the tables is *not* the code that you type to use the method; it is known as the method's *signature*. The signature specifies the type of the arguments, the method name, and the type of the value that the method computes (the *return value*). When your program is executed, we say that it *calls* the system library code for the method, which *returns* the value for use in your code.

*Anatomy of a method signature*

Note that `random()` does not implement a mathematical function because it does not take an argument. On the other hand, `System.out.print()` and `System.out.println()` do not implement mathematical functions because they do not return values and therefore do not have a return type. (This condition is specified in the signature by the keyword `void`.)

In your code, you can use a library method by typing its name followed by arguments of the specified type, enclosed in parentheses and separated by commas. You can use this code in the same way as you use variables and literals in expressions. When you do so, you can expect that method to compute a value of the appropriate type, as documented in the left column of the API. For example, you can write expressions like `Math.sin(x) * Math.cos(y)` and so on. Method arguments may also be expressions, as in `Math.sqrt(b*b - 4.0*a*c)`.

```
double d = Math.sqrt(b*b - 4.0*a*c);
```

*Using a library method*

The `Math` library also defines the precise constant values `PI` (for $\pi$) and `E` (for $e$), so that you can use those names to refer to those constants in your programs. For example, the value of `Math.sin(Math.PI/2)` is `1.0` and the value of `Math.log(Math.E)` is `1.0` (because `Math.sin()` takes its argument in radians and `Math.log()` implements the natural logarithm function).

To be complete, we also include here the following API for Java's conversion methods, which we use for command-line arguments:

|        |                                |                              |
|-------:|--------------------------------|------------------------------|
|    int | `Integer.parseInt(String s)`   | *convert* s *to an* int *value* |
| double | `Double.parseDouble(String s)` | *convert* s *to a* double *value* |
|   long | `Long.parseLong(String s)`     | *convert* s *to a* long *value* |

*Java library methods for converting strings to primitive types*

You *do not* need to use methods like these to convert from `int`, `double`, and `long` values to `String` values for *output*, because Java automatically converts any value used as an argument to `System.out.print()` or `System.out.println()` to `String` for output.

| expression | library | type | value |
|---|---|---|---|
| Integer.parseInt("123") | Integer | int | 123 |
| Math.sqrt(5.0*5.0 - 4.0*4.0) | Math | double | 3.0 |
| Math.random() | Math | double | *random in* $[0, 1)$ |
| Math.round(3.14159) | Math | long | 3 |

*Typical expressions that use Java library methods*

These APIs are typical of the online documentation that is the standard in modern programming. There is extensive online documentation of the Java APIs that is used by professional programmers, and it is available to you (if you are interested) directly from the Java website or through our booksite. You do not need to go to the online documentation to understand the code in this book or to write similar code, because we present and explain in the text all of the library methods that we use in APIs like these and summarize them in the endpapers. More important, in CHAPTERS 2 AND 3 you will learn in this book how to develop your own APIs and to implement functions for your own use.

**Type conversion**    One of the primary rules of modern programming is that you should always be aware of the type of data that your program is processing. Only by knowing the type can you know precisely which set of values each variable can have, which literals you can use, and which operations you can perform. Typical programming tasks involve processing multiple types of data, so we often need to convert data from one type to another. There are several ways to do so in Java.

*Explicit type conversion.*  You can use a method that takes an argument of one type (the value to be converted) and produces a result of another type. We have already used the Integer.parseInt() and Double.parseDouble() library methods to convert String values to int and double values, respectively. Many other methods are available for conversion among other types. For example, the library method Math.round() takes a double argument and returns a long result: the nearest integer to the argument. Thus, for example, Math.round(3.14159) and Math.round(2.71828) are both of type long and have the same value (3).

*Explicit cast.*  Java has some built-in type conversion conventions for primitive types that you can take advantage of when you are aware that you might lose information. You have to make your intention to do so explicit by using a device called a *cast*. You cast an expression from one primitive type to another by prepending the desired type name within parentheses. For example, the expression `(int) 2.71828` is a cast from `double` to `int` that produces an `int` with value 2. The conversion methods defined for casts throw away information in a reasonable way (for a full list, see the booksite). For example, casting a floating-point number to an integer discards the fractional part by rounding towards zero. If you want a different result, such as rounding to the nearest integer, you must use the explicit conversion method `Math.round()`, as just discussed (but you then need to use an explicit cast to `int`, since that method returns a `long`). RandomInt (PROGRAM 1.2.5) is an example that uses a cast for a practical computation.

*Automatic promotion for numbers.* You can use data of any primitive numeric type where a value whose type has a larger range of values is expected, because Java automatically converts to the type with the larger range. This kind of conversion is called *promotion*. For example, we used numbers all of type `double` in PROGRAM 1.2.3, so there is no conversion. If we had chosen to make b and c of type `int` (using `Integer.parseInt()` to convert the command-line arguments), automatic promotion would be used to evaluate the expression b*b - 4.0*c. First, c is promoted to `double` to multiply by the `double` literal 4.0, with a `double` result. Then, the `int` value b*b is promoted to `double` for the subtraction, leaving a `double` result.

| expression | expression type | expression value |
|---|---|---|
| "1234" + 99 | String | "123499" |
| Integer.parseInt("123") | int | 123 |
| (int) 2.71828 | int | 2 |
| Math.round(2.71828) | long | 3 |
| (int) Math.round(2.71828) | int | 3 |
| (int) Math.round(3.14159) | int | 3 |
| 11 * 0.3 | double | 3.3 |
| (int) 11 * 0.3 | double | 3.3 |
| 11 * (int) 0.3 | int | 0 |
| (int) (11 * 0.3) | int | 3 |

*Typical type conversions*

Or, we might have written b*b - 4*c. In that case, the expression b*b - 4*c would be evaluated as an `int` and then the result promoted to `double`, because that is what `Math.sqrt()` expects. Promotion is appropriate because your intent is clear and it can be done with no loss of information. On the other hand, a conversion that might involve loss of information (for example, assigning a `double` to an `int`) leads to a compile-time error.

---

**Program 1.2.5  *Casting to get a random integer***

```java
public class RandomInt
{
   public static void main(String[] args)
   {
      int N = Integer.parseInt(args[0]);
      double r = Math.random();   // uniform between 0 and 1
      int n = (int) (r * N);      // uniform between 0 and N-1
      System.out.println(n);
   }
}
```

*This program uses the Java method* Math.random() *to generate a random number* r *in the interval* [0, 1), *then multiplies* r *by the command-line argument* N *to get a random number greater than or equal to 0 and less than* N, *then uses a cast to truncate the result to be an integer* n *between 0 and* N-1.

---

```
% javac RandomInt.java

% java RandomInt 1000
548

% java RandomInt 1000
141

% java RandomInt 1000000
135032
```

Casting has higher precedence than arithmetic operations—any cast is applied to the value that immediately follows it. For example, if we write int n = (int) 11 * 0.3, the cast is no help: the literal 11 is already an integer, so the cast (int) has no effect. In this example, the compiler produces a possible loss of precision error message because there would be a loss of precision in converting the resulting value (3.3) to an int for assignment to n. The error is helpful because the intended computation for this code is likely (int) (11 * 0.3), which has the value 3, not 3.3.

BEGINNING PROGRAMMERS TEND TO FIND TYPE conversion to be an annoyance, but experienced programmers know that paying careful attention to data types is a key to success in programming. It is well worth your while to take the time to understand what type conversion is all about. After you have written just a few programs, you will understand that these rules help you to make your intentions explicit and to avoid subtle bugs in your programs.

**Summary**  *A data type is a set of values and a set of operations on those values.* Java has eight primitive data types: `boolean`, `char`, `byte`, `short`, `int`, `long`, `float`, and `double`. In Java code, we use operators and expressions like those in familiar mathematical expressions to invoke the operations associated with each type. The `boolean` type is for computing with the logical values `true` and `false`; the `char` type is the set of character values that we type; and the other six are numeric types, for computing with numbers. In this book, we most often use `boolean`, `int`, and `double`; we do not use `short` or `float`. Another data type that we use frequently, `String`, is not primitive, but Java has some built-in facilities for `String`s that are like those for primitive types.

When programming in Java, we have to be aware that every operation is defined only in the context of its data type (so we may need type conversions) and that all types can have only a finite number of values (so we may need to live with imprecise results).

The `boolean` type and its operations— `&&`, `||`, and `!` —are the basis for logical decision-making in Java programs, when used in conjunction with the mixed-type comparison operators `==`, `!=`, `<`, `>`, `<=`, and `>=`. Specifically, we use `boolean` expressions to control Java's conditional (`if`) and loop (`for` and `while`) constructs, which we will study in detail in the next section.

The numeric types and Java's libraries give us the ability to use Java as an extensive mathematical calculator. We write arithmetic expressions using the built-in operators `+`, `-`, `*`, `/`, and `%` along with Java methods from the `Math` library. Although the programs in this section are quite rudimentary by the standards of what we will be able to do after the next section, this class of programs is quite useful in its own right. You will use primitive types and basic mathematical functions extensively in Java programming, so the effort that you spend now understanding them will certainly be worthwhile.

## Q&A

**Q.** What happens if I forget to declare a variable?

**A.** The compiler complains, as shown below for a program `IntOpsBad`, which is the same as PROGRAM 1.2.2 except that the `int` variable p is omitted from the declaration statement.

```
% javac IntOpsBad.java
IntOpsBad.java:7: cannot resolve symbol
symbol : variable p
location: class IntOpsBad
p = a * b;
    ^
IntOpsBad.java:10: cannot resolve symbol
symbol : variable p
location: class IntOpsBad
System.out.println(a + " * " + b + " = " + p);
                                           ^
2 errors
```

The compiler says that there are two errors, but there is really just one: the declaration of p is missing. If you forget to declare a variable that you use often, you will get quite a few error messages. A good strategy is to correct the *first* error and check that correction before addressing later ones.

**Q.** What happens if I forget to initialize a variable?

**A.** The compiler checks for this condition and will give you a `variable might not have been initialized` error message if you try to use the variable in an expression.

**Q.** Is there a difference between = and == ?

**A.** Yes, they are quite different! The first is an assignment operator that changes the value of a variable, and the second is a comparison operator that produces a `boolean` result. Your ability to understand this answer is a sure test of whether you understood the material in this section. Think about how you might explain the difference to a friend.

**Q.** Why do `int` values sometime become negative when they get large?

**A.** If you have not experienced this phenomenon, see EXERCISE 1.2.10. The problem has to do with the way integers are represented in the computer. You can learn the details on the booksite. In the meantime, a safe strategy is using the `int` type when you know the values to be less than ten digits and the `long` type when you think the values might get to be ten digits or more.

**Q.** It seems wrong that Java should just let `int`s overflow and give bad values. Shouldn't Java automatically check for overflow?

**A.** Yes, this issue is a contentious one among programmers. The short answer for now is that the lack of such checking is one reason such types are called *primitive* data types. A little knowledge can go a long way in avoiding such problems. Again, it is fine to use the `int` type for small numbers, but when values run into the billions, you cannot.

**Q.** What is the value of `Math.abs(-2147483648)`?

**A.** `-2147483648`. This strange (but true) result is a typical example of the effects of integer overflow.

**Q.** It is annoying to see all those digits when printing a `float` or a `double`. Can we get `System.out.println()` to print out just two or three digits after the decimal point?

**A.** That sort of task involves a closer look at the method used to convert from `double` to `String`. The Java library function `System.out.printf()` is one way to do the job, and it is similar to the basic printing method in the C programming language and many modern languages, as discussed in SECTION 1.5. Until then, we will live with the extra digits (which is not all bad, since doing so helps us to get used to the different primitive types of numbers).

**Q.** How can I initialize a `double` variable to infinity?

**A.** Java has built-in constants available for this purpose: `Double.POSITIVE_IN-FINITY` and `Double.NEGATIVE_INFINITY`.

**Q.** What is the value of `Math.round(6.022e23)`?

**A.** You should get in the habit of typing in a tiny Java program to answer such questions yourself (and trying to understand why your program produces the result that it does).

**Q.** Can you compare a `double` to an `int`?

**A.** Not without doing a type conversion, but remember that Java usually does the requisite type conversion automatically. For example, if x is an `int` with the value 3, then the expression (x < 3.1) is `true`—Java converts x to `double` (because `3.1` is a `double` literal) before performing the comparison.

**Q.** Are expressions like `1/0` and `1.0/0.0` legal in Java?

**A.** No and yes. The first generates a run-time *exception* for division by zero (which stops your program because the value is undefined); the second is legal and has the value `Infinity`.

**Q.** Are there functions in Java's `Math` library for other trigonometric functions, like cosecant, secant, and cotangent?

**A.** No, because you could use `Math.sin()`, `Math.cos()`, and `Math.tan()` to compute them. Choosing which functions to include in an API is a tradeoff between the convenience of having every function that you need and the annoyance of having to find one of the few that you need in a long list. No choice will satisfy all users, and the Java designers have many users to satisfy. Note that there are plenty of redundancies even in the APIs that we have listed. For example, you could use `Math.sin(x)/Math.cos(x)` instead of `Math.tan(x)`.

**Q.** Can you use `<` and `>` to compare `String` variables?

**A.** No. Those operators are defined only for primitive types.

**Q.** How about `==` and `!=` ?

**A.** Yes, but the result may not be what you expect, because of the meanings these operators have for non-primitive types. For example, there is a distinction between a `String` and its value. The expression `"abc" == "ab" + x` is `false` when `x` is a `String` with value `"c"` because the two operands are stored in different places in memory (even though they have the same value). This distinction is essential, as you will learn when we discuss it in more detail in SECTION 3.1.

**Q.** What is the result of division and remainder for negative integers?

**A.** The quotient `a / b` rounds toward 0; the remainder `a % b` is defined such that `(a / b) * b + a % b` is always equal to `a`. For example, `-14/3` and `14/-3` are both `-4`, but `-14 % 3` is `-2` and `14 % -3` is `2`.

**Q.** Will `(a < b < c)` test whether three numbers are in order?

**A.** No, that will not compile. You need to say `(a < b && b < c)`.

**Q.** Fifteen digits for floating-point numbers certainly seems enough to me. Do I really need to worry much about precision?

**A.** Yes, because you are used to mathematics based on real numbers with infinite precision, whereas the computer always deals with approximations. For example, `(0.1 + 0.1 == 0.2)` is `true` but `(0.1 + 0.1 + 0.1 == 0.3)` is `false`! Pitfalls like this are not at all unusual in scientific computing. Novice programmers should avoid comparing two floating-point numbers for equality.

**Q.** Why do we say `(a && b)` and not `(a & b)`?

**A.** Java also has a `&` operator that we do not use in this book but which you may encounter if you pursue advanced programming courses.

**Q.** Why is the value of `10^6` not `1000000` but `12`?

**A.** The `^` operator is not an exponentiation operator, which you must have been thinking. Instead, it is an operator like `&` that we do not use in this book. You want the literal `1e6`. You could also use `Math.pow(10, 6)` but doing so is wasteful if you are raising 10 to a known power.

## *Exercises*

**1.2.1** Suppose that a and b are `int` values. What does the following sequence of statements do?

```
int t = a; b = t; a = b;
```

**1.2.2** Write a program that uses `Math.sin()` and `Math.cos()` to check that the value of $\cos^2\theta + \sin^2\theta$ is approximately 1 for any $\theta$ entered as a command-line argument. Just print the value. Why are the values not always exactly 1?

**1.2.3** Suppose that a and b are `int` values. Show that the expression

```
(!(a && b) && (a || b)) || ((a && b) || !(a || b))
```

is equivalent to `true`.

**1.2.4** Suppose that a and b are `int` values. Simplify the following expression: `(!(a < b) && !(a > b))`.

**1.2.5** The *exclusive or* operator ^ for `boolean` operands is defined to be `true` if they are different, `false` if they are the same. Give a truth table for this function.

**1.2.6** Why does 10/3 give 3 and not 3.333333333?

*Solution.* Since both 10 and 3 are integer literals, Java sees no need for type conversion and uses integer division. You should write 10.0/3.0 if you mean the numbers to be `double` literals. If you write 10/3.0 or 10.0/3, Java does implicit conversion to get the same result.

**1.2.7** What do each of the following print?
  *a.* `System.out.println(2 + "bc");`
  *b.* `System.out.println(2 + 3 + "bc");`
  *c.* `System.out.println((2+3) + "bc");`
  *d.* `System.out.println("bc" + (2+3));`
  *e.* `System.out.println("bc" + 2 + 3);`

Explain each outcome.

**1.2.8**  Explain how to use PROGRAM 1.2.3 to find the square root of a number.

**1.2.9**  What do each of the following print?
- *a.* `System.out.println('b');`
- *b.* `System.out.println('b' + 'c');`
- *c.* `System.out.println((char) ('a' + 4));`

Explain each outcome.

**1.2.10**  Suppose that a variable a is declared as `int a = 2147483647` (or equivalently, `Integer.MAX_VALUE`). What do each of the following print?
- *a.* `System.out.println(a);`
- *b.* `System.out.println(a+1);`
- *c.* `System.out.println(2-a);`
- *d.* `System.out.println(-2-a);`
- *e.* `System.out.println(2*a);`
- *f.* `System.out.println(4*a);`

Explain each outcome.

**1.2.11**  Suppose that a variable a is declared as `double a = 3.14159`. What do each of the following print?
- *a.* `System.out.println(a);`
- *b.* `System.out.println(a+1);`
- *c.* `System.out.println(8/(int) a);`
- *d.* `System.out.println(8/a);`
- *e.* `System.out.println((int) (8/a));`

Explain each outcome.

**1.2.12**  Describe what happens if you write `sqrt` instead of `Math.sqrt` in PROGRAM 1.2.3.

**1.2.13**  What is the value of `(Math.sqrt(2) * Math.sqrt(2) == 2)` ?

**1.2.14** Write a program that takes two positive integers as command-line arguments and prints `true` if either evenly divides the other.

**1.2.15** Write a program that takes three positive integers as command-line arguments and prints `true` if any one of them is greater than or equal to the sum of the other two and `false` otherwise. (*Note*: This computation tests whether the three numbers could be the lengths of the sides of some triangle.)

**1.2.16** A physics student gets unexpected results when using the code

```
F = G * mass1 * mass2 / r * r;
```

to compute values according to the formula $F = Gm_1m_2 / r^2$. Explain the problem and correct the code.

**1.2.17** Give the value of a after the execution of each of the following sequences:

```
int a = 1;          boolean a = true;      int a = 2;
a = a + a;          a = !a;                a = a * a;
a = a + a;          a = !a;                a = a * a;
a = a + a;          a = !a;                a = a * a;
```

**1.2.18** Suppose that x and y are `double` values that represent the Cartesian coordinates of a point $(x, y)$ in the plane. Give an expression whose value is the distance of the point from the origin.

**1.2.19** Write a program that takes two `int` values a and b from the command line and prints a random integer between a and b.

**1.2.20** Write a program that prints the sum of two random integers between 1 and 6 (such as you might get when rolling dice).

**1.2.21** Write a program that takes a `double` value t from the command line and prints the value of $\sin(2t) + \sin(3t)$.

**1.2.22** Write a program that takes three `double` values $x_0$, $v_0$, and $t$ from the command line and prints the value of $x_0 + v_0t + gt^2/2$, where g is the constant 9.78033. (*Note*: This value the displacement in meters after $t$ seconds when an object is thrown straight up from initial position $x_0$ at velocity $v_0$ meters per second.)

**1.2.23** Write a program that takes two `int` values m and d from the command line and prints `true` if day $d$ of month $m$ is between 3/20 and 6/20, `false` otherwise.

## Creative Exercises

**1.2.24** *Loan payments.* Write a program that calculates the monthly payments you would have to make over a given number of years to pay off a loan at a given interest rate compounded continuously, taking the number of years $t$, the principal $P$, and the annual interest rate $r$ as command-line arguments. The desired value is given by the formula $Pe^{rt}$. Use `Math.exp()`.

**1.2.25** *Wind chill.* Given the temperature $t$ (in Fahrenheit) and the wind speed $v$ (in miles per hour), the National Weather Service defines the effective temperature (the wind chill) to be:

$$w = 35.74 + 0.6215\,t + (0.4275\,t - 35.75)\,v^{0.16}$$

Write a program that takes two `double` command-line arguments t and v and prints out the wind chill. Use `Math.pow(a, b)` to compute $a^b$. *Note*: The formula is not valid if $t$ is larger than 50 in absolute value or if $v$ is larger than 120 or less than 3 (you may assume that the values you get are in that range).

**1.2.26** *Polar coordinates.* Write a program that converts from Cartesian to polar coordinates. Your program should take two real numbers x and y on the command line and print the polar coordinates $r$ and $\theta$. Use the Java method `Math.atan2(y, x)` which computes the arctangent value of y/x that is in the range from $-\pi$ to $\pi$.

*Polar coordinates*

**1.2.27** *Gaussian random numbers.* One way to generate a random number taken from the Gaussian distribution is to use the *Box-Muller* formula

$$w = \sin(2\,\pi\,v)\,(-2\ln u)^{1/2}$$

where $u$ and $v$ are real numbers between 0 and 1 generated by the `Math.random()` method. Write a program `StdGaussian` that prints out a standard Gaussian random variable.

**1.2.28** *Order check.* Write a program that takes three `double` values x, y, and z as command-line arguments and prints `true` if the values are strictly ascending or descending ( $x < y < z$ or $x > y > z$ ), and `false` otherwise.

**1.2.29** *Day of the week.* Write a program that takes a date as input and prints the day of the week that date falls on. Your program should take three command line parameters: m (month), d (day), and y (year). For m, use 1 for January, 2 for February, and so forth. For output, print 0 for Sunday, 1 for Monday, 2 for Tuesday, and so forth. Use the following formulas, for the Gregorian calendar:

$$y_0 = y - (14 - m) / 12$$
$$x = y_0 + y_0/4 - y_0/100 + y_0/400$$
$$m_0 = m + 12 \times ((14 - m) / 12) - 2$$
$$d_0 = (d + x + (31 \times m_0)/12) \% 7$$

*Example:* On what day of the week was February 14, 2000?

$$y_0 = 2000 - 1 = 1999$$
$$x = 1999 + 1999/4 - 1999/100 + 1999/400 = 2483$$
$$m_0 = 2 + 12 \times 1 - 2 = 12$$
$$d_0 = (14 + 2483 + (31 \times 12) / 12) \% 7 = 2500 \% 7 = 1$$

*Answer:* Monday.

**1.2.30** *Uniform random numbers.* Write a program that prints five uniform random values between 0 and 1, their average value, and their minimum and maximum value. Use Math.random(), Math.min(), and Math.max().

**1.2.31** *Mercator projection.* The *Mercator projection* is a conformal (angle preserving) projection that maps latitude $\varphi$ and longitude $\lambda$ to rectangular coordinates $(x, y)$. It is widely used—for example, in nautical charts and in the maps that you print from the web. The projection is defined by the equations $x = \lambda - \lambda_0$ and $y = 1/2 \ln((1 + \sin \varphi) / (1 - \sin \varphi))$, where $\lambda_0$ is the longitude of the point in the center of the map. Write a program that takes $\lambda_0$ and the latitude and longitude of a point from the command line and prints its projection.

**1.2.32** *Color conversion.* Several different formats are used to represent color. For example, the primary format for LCD displays, digital cameras, and web pages, known as the *RGB format,* specifies the level of red (R), green (G), and blue (B) on an integer scale from 0 to 255. The primary format for publishing books and magazines, known as the *CMYK format,* specifies the level of cyan (C), magenta (M), yellow (Y), and black (K) on a real scale from 0.0 to 1.0. Write a program RGBtoCMYK that converts RGB to CMYK. Take three integers—r, g, and b—from the command line and print the equivalent CMYK values. If the RGB values are all 0, then the CMY values are all 0 and the K value is 1; otherwise, use these formulas:

$$w = \max(r/255, g/255, b/255)$$
$$c = (w - (r/255))/w$$
$$m = (w - (g/255))/w$$
$$y = (w - (b/255))/w$$
$$k = 1 - w$$

**1.2.33** *Great circle.* Write a program GreatCircle that takes four command-line arguments—x1, y1, x2, and y2—(the latitude and longitude, in degrees, of two points on the earth) and prints out the great-circle distance between them. The great-circle distance (in nautical miles) is given by the equation:

$$d = 60 \arccos(\sin(x_1)\sin(x_2) + \cos(x_1)\cos(x_2)\cos(y_1 - y_2))$$

Note that this equation uses degrees, whereas Java's trigonometric functions use radians. Use Math.toRadians() and Math.toDegrees() to convert between the two. Use your program to compute the great-circle distance between Paris (48.87° N and −2.33° W) and San Francisco (37.8° N and 122.4° W).

**1.2.34** *Three-sort.* Write a program that takes three int values from the command line and prints them in ascending order. Use Math.min() and Math.max().

**1.2.35** *Dragon curves.* Write a program to print the instructions for drawing the dragon curves of order 0 through 5. The instructions are strings of F, L, and R characters, where F means "draw line while moving 1 unit forward," L means "turn left," and R means "turn right." A dragon curve of order N is formed when you fold a strip of paper in half N times, then unfold to right angles. The key to solving this problem is to note that a curve of order N is a curve of order N−1 followed by an L followed by a curve of order N−1 traversed in reverse order, and then to figure out a similar description for the reverse curve .

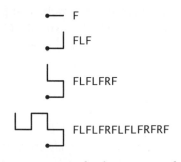

*Dragon curves of order 0, 1, 2, and 3*

# 1.3 Conditionals and Loops

IN THE PROGRAMS THAT WE HAVE examined to this point, each of the statements in the program is executed once, in the order given. Most programs are more complicated because the sequence of statements and the number of times each is executed can vary. We use the term *control flow* to refer to statement sequencing in a program. In this section, we introduce statements that allow us to change the control flow, using logic about the values of program variables. This feature is an essential component of programming.

Specifically, we consider Java statements that implement *conditionals*, where some other statements may or may not be executed depending on certain conditions, and *loops*, where some other statements may be executed multiple times, again depending on certain conditions. As you will see in numerous examples in this section, conditionals and loops truly harness the power of the computer and will equip you to write programs to accomplish a broad variety of tasks that you could not contemplate attempting without a computer.

**If statements**   Most computations require different actions for different inputs. One way to express these differences in Java is the `if` statement:

```
if (<boolean expression>) { <statements> }
```

This description introduces a formal notation known as a *template* that we will use to specify the format of Java constructs. We put within angle brackets (`< >`) a construct that we have already defined, to indicate that we can use any instance of that construct where specified. In this case, `<boolean expression>` represents an expression that has a boolean value, such as one involving a comparison operation, and `<statements>` represents a *statement block* (a sequence of Java statements, each terminated by a semicolon). This latter construct is familiar to you: the body of `main()` is such a sequence. If the sequence is a single statement, the curly braces are optional. It is possible to make formal definitions of `<boolean expression>` and `<statements>`, but we refrain from going into that level of detail. The meaning of an `if` statement is self-explanatory: the statement(s) in the sequence are to be executed if and only if the expression is `true`.

As a simple example, suppose that you want to compute the absolute value of an `int` value x. This statement does the job:

```
if (x < 0) x = -x;
```

As a second simple example, consider the following statement:

```
if (x > y)
{
    int t = x;
    x = y;
    y = t;
}
```

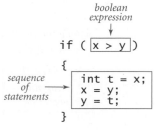

*Anatomy of an `if` statement*

This code puts x and y in ascending order by exchanging them if necessary.

You can also add an `else` clause to an `if` statement, to express the concept of executing either one statement (or sequence of statements) or another, depending on whether the boolean expression is `true` or `false`, as in the following template:

```
if (<boolean expression>) <statements T>
else                      <statements F>
```

As a simple example of the need for an `else` clause, consider the following code, which assigns the maximum of two `int` values to the variable max:

```
if (x > y) max = x;
else       max = y;
```

One way to understand control flow is to visualize it with a diagram called a *flow-chart*. Paths through the flowchart correspond to flow-of-control paths in the pro-

*Flowchart examples (`if` statements)*

| | |
|---|---|
| *absolute value* | ```if (x < 0) x = -x;``` |
| *put* x *and* y *into sorted order* | ```if (x > y)
{
    int t = x;
    y = x;
    x = t;
}``` |
| *maximum of* x *and* y | ```if (x > y) max = x;
else        max = y;``` |
| *error check for division operation* | ```if (den == 0) System.out.println("Division by zero");
else             System.out.println("Quotient = " + num/den);``` |
| *error check for quadratic formula* | ```double discriminant = b*b - 4.0*c;
if (discriminant < 0.0)
{
    System.out.println("No real roots");
}
else
{
    System.out.println((-b + Math.sqrt(discriminant))/2.0);
    System.out.println((-b - Math.sqrt(discriminant))/2.0);
}``` |

*Typical examples of using* if *statements*

gram. In the early days of computing, when programmers used low-level languages and difficult-to-understand flows of control, flowcharts were an essential part of programming. With modern languages, we use flowcharts just to understand basic building blocks like the if statement.

The accompanying table contains some examples of the use of if and if-else statements. These examples are typical of simple calculations you might need in programs that you write. Conditional statements are an essential part of programming. Since the *semantics* (meaning) of statements like these is similar to their meanings as natural-language phrases, you will quickly grow used to them.

PROGRAM 1.3.1 is another example of the use of the if-else statement, in this case for the task of simulating a coin flip. The body of the program is a single statement, like the ones in the table above, but it is worth special attention because it introduces an interesting philosophical issue that is worth contemplating: can a computer program produce *random* values? Certainly not, but a program *can* produce numbers that have many of the properties of random numbers.

*Program 1.3.1    Flipping a fair coin*

```
public class Flip
{
   public static void main(String[] args)
   {  // Simulate a coin flip.
      if (Math.random() < 0.5) System.out.println("Heads");
      else                     System.out.println("Tails");
   }
}
```

*This program uses* Math.random() *to simulate a coin flip. Each time you run it, it prints either heads or tails. A sequence of flips will have many of the same properties as a sequence that you would get by flipping a fair coin, but it is not a truly random sequence.*

```
% java Flip
Heads
% java Flip
Tails
% java Flip
Tails
```

**While loops**   Many computations are inherently repetitive. The basic Java construct for handling such computations has the following format:

```
while (<boolean expression>) { <statements> }
```

The while statement has the same form as the if statement (the only difference being the use of the keyword while instead of if), but the meaning is quite different. It is an instruction to the computer to behave as follows: if the expression is false, do nothing; if the expression is true, execute the sequence of statements (just as with if) but then check the expression again, execute the sequence of statements again if the expression is true, and *continue* as long as the expression is true. We often refer to the statement block in a loop as the *body* of the loop. As with the if statement, the braces are optional if a while loop body has just one statement. The while statement is equivalent to a sequence of identical if statements:

```
if (<boolean expression>) { <statements> }
if (<boolean expression>) { <statements> }
if (<boolean expression>) { <statements> }
...
```

*initialization is a separate statement*

*loop continuation condition*

```
int v = 1;
while ( v <= N/2 )
```

*braces are optional when body is a single statement*

```
{
    v = 2*v;
}
```

*body*

*Anatomy of a* while *loop*

At some point, the code in one of the statements must change something (such as the value of some variable in the boolean expression) to make the boolean expression false, and then the sequence is broken.

A common programming paradigm involves maintaining an integer value that keeps track of the number of times a loop iterates. We start at some initial value, and then increment the value by 1 each time through the loop, testing whether it exceeds a predetermined maximum before deciding to continue. TenHellos (PROGRAM 1.3.2) is a simple example of this paradigm that uses a while statement. The key to the computation is the statement

```
i = i + 1;
```

As a mathematical equation, this statement is nonsense, but as a Java assignment statement it makes perfect sense: it says to compute the value i + 1 and then assign the result to the variable i. If the value of i was 4 before the statement, it becomes 5 afterwards; if it was 5 it becomes 6; and so forth. With the initial condition in TenHellos that the value of i starts at 4, the statement block is executed five times until the sequence is broken, when the value of i becomes 11.

```
int i = 4;
while (i <= 10)
{
    System.out.println(i + "th Hello");
    i = i + 1;
}
```

```
          i = 4;

    ┌──→ i <= 10 ?  ──no──┐
    │       │ yes          │
    │  System.out.println(i + "th Hello");  │
    │       │              │
    │    i = i + 1;        │
    └─────────────────────┘
            │
```

*Flowchart example (while statement)*

Using the while loop is barely worthwhile for this simple task, but you will soon be addressing tasks where you will need to specify that statements be repeated far too many times to contemplate doing it without loops. There is a profound difference between programs with while statements and programs without them, because while statements allow us to specify a potentially unlimited number of statements to be executed in a program. In particular, the while statement allows us to specify lengthy computations in short programs. This ability opens the door to writing programs for tasks that we could not contemplate addressing without a

*Program 1.3.2   Your first while loop*

```
public class TenHellos
{
   public static void main(String[] args)
   {  // Print 10 Hellos.
      System.out.println("1st Hello");
      System.out.println("2nd Hello");
      System.out.println("3rd Hello");
      int i = 4;
      while (i <= 10)
      {  // Print the ith Hello.
         System.out.println(i + "th Hello");
         i = i + 1;
      }
   }
}
```

*This program uses a* while *loop for the simple, repetitive task of printing the output shown below. After the third line, the lines to be printed differ only in the value of the index counting the line printed, so we define a variable* i *to contain that index. After initializing the value of* i *to 4, we enter into a* while *loop where we use the value of* i *in the* System.out.println() *statement and increment it each time through the loop. After printing* 10th Hello, *the value of* i *becomes* 11 *and the loop terminates.*

```
% java TenHellos
1st Hello
2nd Hello
3rd Hello
4th Hello
5th Hello
6th Hello
7th Hello
8th Hello
9th Hello
10th Hello
```

| i | i <= 10 | *output* |
|----|---------|-----------|
| 4  | true    | 4th Hello |
| 5  | true    | 5th Hello |
| 6  | true    | 6th Hello |
| 7  | true    | 7th Hello |
| 8  | true    | 8th Hello |
| 9  | true    | 9th Hello |
| 10 | true    | 10th Hello |
| 11 | false   |           |

*Trace of* java TenHellos

computer. But there is also a price to pay: as your programs become more sophisticated, they become more difficult to understand.

PowersOfTwo (PROGRAM 1.3.3) uses a `while` loop to print out a table of the powers of 2. Beyond the loop control counter i, it maintains a variable v that holds the powers of two as it computes them. The loop body contains three statements: one to print the current power of 2, one to compute the next (multiply the current one by 2), and one to increment the loop control counter.

There are many situations in computer science where it is useful to be familiar with powers of 2. You should know at least the first 10 values in this table and you should note that $2^{10}$ is about 1 thousand, $2^{20}$ is about 1 million, and $2^{30}$ is about 1 billion.

PowersOfTwo is the prototype for many useful computations. By varying the computations that change the accumulated value and the way that the loop control variable is incremented, we can print out tables of a variety of functions (see EXERCISE 1.3.11).

It is worthwhile to carefully examine the behavior of programs that use loops by studying a *trace* of the program. For example, a trace of the operation of PowersOfTwo should show the value of each variable before each iteration of the loop and the value of the conditional expression that controls the loop. Tracing the operation of a loop can be very tedious, but it is nearly always worthwhile to run a trace because it clearly exposes what a program is doing.

PowersOfTwo is nearly a self-tracing program, because it prints the values of its variables each time through the loop. Clearly, you can make any program produce a trace of itself by adding appropriate `System.out.println()` statements. Modern programming environments provide sophisticated tools for tracing, but

| i | v | i <= N |
|---|---|---|
| 0 | 1 | true |
| 1 | 2 | true |
| 2 | 4 | true |
| 3 | 8 | true |
| 4 | 16 | true |
| 5 | 32 | true |
| 6 | 64 | true |
| 7 | 128 | true |
| 8 | 256 | true |
| 9 | 512 | true |
| 10 | 1024 | true |
| 11 | 2048 | true |
| 12 | 4096 | true |
| 13 | 8192 | true |
| 14 | 16384 | true |
| 15 | 32768 | true |
| 16 | 65536 | true |
| 17 | 131072 | true |
| 18 | 262144 | true |
| 19 | 524288 | true |
| 20 | 1048576 | true |
| 21 | 2097152 | true |
| 22 | 4194304 | true |
| 23 | 8388608 | true |
| 24 | 16777216 | true |
| 25 | 33554432 | true |
| 26 | 67108864 | true |
| 27 | 134217728 | true |
| 28 | 268435456 | true |
| 29 | 536870912 | true |
| 30 | 1073741824 | false |

*Trace of* `java PowersOfTwo 29`

### Program 1.3.3    Computing powers of two

```
public class PowersOfTwo
{
   public static void main(String[] args)
   {  // Print the first N powers of 2.
      int N = Integer.parseInt(args[0]);
      int v = 1;
      int i = 0;
      while (i <= N)
      {  // Print ith power of 2.
         System.out.println(i + " " + v);
         v = 2 * v;
         i = i + 1;
      }
   }
}
```

| N | loop termination value |
|---|---|
| i | loop control counter |
| v | current power of 2 |

This program takes a command-line argument N and prints a table of the powers of 2 that are less than or equal to $2^N$. Each time through the loop, we increment the value of i and double the value of v. We show only the first three and the last three lines of the table; the program prints N+1 lines.

```
% java PowersOfTwo 5
0 1
1 2
2 4
3 8
4 16
5 32
```

```
% java PowersOfTwo 29
0 1
1 2
2 4
...
27 134217728
28 268435456
29 536870912
```

this tried-and-true method is simple and effective. You certainly should add print statements to the first few loops that you write, to be sure that they are doing precisely what you expect.

There is a hidden trap in PowersOfTwo, because the largest integer in Java's int data type is $2^{31} - 1$ and the program does not test for that possibility. If you invoke it with java PowersOfTwo 31, you may be surprised by the last line of output:

```
...
1073741824
-2147483648
```

The variable v becomes too large and takes on a negative value because of the way Java represents integers. The maximum value of an int is available for us to use as Integer.MAX_VALUE. A better version of PROGRAM 1.3.3 would use this value to test for overflow and print an error message if the user types too large a value, though getting such a program to work properly for all inputs is trickier than you might think. (For a similar challenge, see EXERCISE 1.3.14.)

As a more complicated example, suppose that we want to compute the largest power of two that is less than or equal to a given positive integer N. If N is 13 we want the result 8; if N is 1000, we want the result 512; if N is 64, we want the result 64; and so forth. This computation is simple to perform with a while loop:

```
int v = 1;
while (v <= N/2)
    v = 2*v;
```

It takes some thought to convince yourself that this simple piece of code produces the desired result. You can do so by making these observations:

*Flowchart for the statements*
```
int v = 1;
while (v <= N/2)
    v = 2*v;
```

- v is always a power of 2.
- v is never greater than N.
- v increases each time through the loop, so the loop must terminate.
- After the loop terminates, 2*v is greater than N.

Reasoning of this sort is often important in understanding how while loops work. Even though many of the loops you will write are much simpler than this one, you should be sure to convince yourself that each loop you write is going to behave as you expect.

The logic behind such arguments is the same whether the loop iterates just a few times, as in TenHellos, dozens of times, as in PowersOfTwo, or millions of times, as in several examples that we will soon consider. That leap from a few tiny cases to a huge computation is profound. When writing loops, understanding how the values of the variables change each time through the loop (and checking that understanding by adding statements to trace their values and running for a small number of iterations) is essential. Having done so, you can confidently remove those training wheels and truly unleash the power of the computer.

**For loops**   As you will see, the `while` loop allows us to write programs for all manner of applications. Before considering more examples, we will look at an alternate Java construct that allows us even more flexibility when writing programs with loops. This alternate notation is not fundamentally different from the basic `while` loop, but it is widely used because it often allows us to write more compact and more readable programs than if we used only `while` statements.

*For notation.*   Many loops follow this scheme: initialize an index variable to some value and then use a `while` loop to test a loop continuation condition involving the index variable, where the last statement in the `while` loop increments the index variable. You can express such loops directly with Java's `for` notation:

```
for (<initialize>; <boolean expression>; <increment>)
{
    <statements>
}
```

This code is, with only a few exceptions, equivalent to

```
<initialize>;
while (<boolean expression>)
{
    <statements>
    <increment>;
}
```

Your Java compiler might even produce identical results for the two loops. In truth, *<initialize>* and *<increment>* can be any statements at all, but we nearly always use `for` loops to support this typical initialize-and-increment programming idiom. For example, the following two lines of code are equivalent to the corresponding lines of code in `TenHellos` (PROGRAM 1.3.2):

```
for (int i = 4; i <= 10; i = i + 1)
    System.out.println(i + "th Hello");
```

Typically, we work with a slightly more compact version of this code, using the shorthand notation discussed next.

*Compound assignment idioms.* Modifying the value of a variable is something that we do so often in programming that Java provides a variety of different short-hand notations for the purpose. For example, the following four statements all increment the value of i by 1 in Java:

```
i = i + 1;    i++;    ++i;    i += 1;
```

You can also say i-- or --i or i -= 1 or i = i-1 to decrement that value of i by 1. Most programmers use i++ or i-- in for loops, though any of the others would do. The ++ and -- constructs are normally used for integers, but the *compound assignment* constructs are useful operations for any arithmetic operator in any primitive numeric type. For example, you can say v *= 2 or v += v instead of v = 2*v. All of these idioms are for notational convenience, nothing more. This combination of shortcuts came into widespread use with the C programming language in the 1970s and have become standard. They have survived the test of time because they lead to compact, elegant, and easily understood programs. When you learn to write (and to read) programs that use them, you will be able to transfer that skill to programming in numerous modern languages, not just Java.

*Scope.* The scope of a variable is the part of the program where it is defined. Generally the scope of a variable is comprised of the statements that follow the declaration in the same block as the declaration. For this purpose, the code in the for loop header is considered to be in the same block as the for loop body. Therefore, the while and for formulations of loops are not quite equivalent: in a typical for loop, the incrementing variable is *not* available for use in later statements; in the corresponding while loop, it is. This distinction is often a reason to use a while instead of a for loop.

CHOOSING AMONG DIFFERENT FORMULATIONS OF THE same computation is a matter of each programmer's taste, as when a writer picks from among synonyms or chooses between using active and passive voice when composing a sentence. You will not find good hard-and-fast rules on how to compose a program any more than you will find such rules on how to compose a paragraph. Your goal should be to find a style that suits you, gets the computation done, and can be appreciated by others.

The accompanying table includes several code fragments with typical examples of loops used in Java code. Some of these relate to code that you have already seen; others are new code for straightforward computations. To cement your understanding of loops in Java, put these code snippets into a class's code that takes an integer N from the command line (like `PowersOfTwo`) and *compile and run them.* Then, write

*Anatomy of a* `for` *loop (that prints powers of 2)*

some loops of your own for similar computations of your own invention, or do some of the early exercises at the end of this section. There is no substitute for the experience gained by running code that you create yourself, and it is imperative that you develop an understanding of how to write Java code that uses loops.

| | |
|---|---|
| *print largest power of two less than or equal to N* | ```int v = 1;\nwhile (v <= N/2)\n    v = 2*v;\nSystem.out.println(v);``` |
| *compute a finite sum* $(1 + 2 + \ldots + N)$ | ```int sum = 0;\nfor (int i = 1; i <= N; i++)\n    sum += i;\nSystem.out.println(sum);``` |
| *compute a finite product* $(N! = 1 \times 2 \times \ldots \times N)$ | ```int product = 1;\nfor (int i = 1; i <= N; i++)\n    product *= i;\nSystem.out.println(product);``` |
| *print a table of function values* | ```for (int i = 0; i <= N; i++)\n    System.out.println(i + " " + 2*Math.PI*i/N);``` |
| *print the ruler function (see Program 1.2.1)* | ```String ruler = " ";\nfor (int i = 1; i <= N; i++)\n    ruler = ruler + i + ruler;\nSystem.out.println(ruler);``` |

*Typical examples of using* `for` *and* `while` *statements*

**Nesting** The `if`, `while`, and `for` statements have the same status as assignment statements or any other statements in Java. That is, we can use them whenever a statement is called for. In particular, we can use one or more of them in the *<body>* of another to make compound statements. As a first example, `DivisorPattern` (PROGRAM 1.3.4) has a `for` loop whose statements are a `for` loop (whose statement is an `if` statement) and a print statement. It prints a pattern of asterisks where the $i$th row has an asterisk in each position corresponding to divisors of $i$ (the same holds true for the columns).

To emphasize the nesting, we use indentation in the program code. We refer to the i loop as the *outer* loop and the j loop as the *inner* loop. The inner loop iterates all the way through for each iteration of the outer loop. As usual, the best way to understand a new programming construct like this is to study a trace.

`DivisorPattern` has a complicated control structure, as you can see from its flowchart. A diagram like this illustrates the importance of using a limited number of simple control structures in programming. With nesting, you can compose loops and conditionals to build programs that are easy to understand even though they may have a complicated control structure. A great many useful computations can be accomplished with just one or two levels of nesting. For example, many programs in this book have the same general structure as `DivisorPattern`.

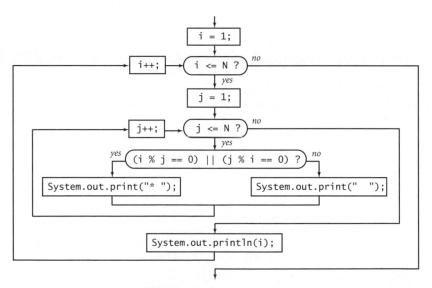

*Flowchart for* `DivisorPattern`

## Program 1.3.4  Your first nested loops

```
public class DivisorPattern
{
   public static void main(String[] args)
   { // Print a square that visualizes divisors.
      int N = Integer.parseInt(args[0]);
      for (int i = 1; i <= N; i++)
      { // Print the ith line.
         for (int j = 1; j <= N; j++)
         { // Print the jth entry in the ith line.
            if ((i % j == 0) || (j % i == 0))
               System.out.print("* ");
            else
               System.out.print("  ");
         }
         System.out.println(i);
      }
   }
}
```

| N | number of rows and columns |
| i | row index |
| j | column index |

*This program takes an integer N as the command-line argument and uses nested for loops to print an N-by-N table with an asterisk in row i and column j if either i divides j or j divides i. The loop control variables i and j control the computation.*

```
% java DivisorPattern 3
* * *  1
* *    2
*   *  3

% java DivisorPattern 16
* * * * * * * * * * * * * * * * 1
* *   *   *   *   *   *   *   * 2
*   *     *     *     *     *   3
* *   *       *       *       * 4
*       *         *         *   5
* * *     *           *         6
*         *           *         7
* *   *         *             * 8
*   *             *             9
* *     *             *         10
*               *               11
* * * *   *           *         12
*                 *             13
* *         *             *     14
*     *         *             * 15
* *     *             *         16
```

| i | j | i % j | j % i | output |
|---|---|---|---|---|
| 1 | 1 | 0 | 0 | * |
| 1 | 2 | 1 | 0 | * |
| 1 | 3 | 1 | 0 | * |
| | | | | 1 |
| 2 | 1 | 0 | 1 | * |
| 2 | 2 | 0 | 0 | * |
| 2 | 3 | 2 | 1 | |
| | | | | 2 |
| 3 | 1 | 0 | 1 | * |
| 3 | 2 | 1 | 2 | |
| 3 | 3 | 0 | 0 | * |
| | | | | 3 |

*Trace of java DivisorPattern 3*

As a second example of nesting, consider the following program fragment, which a tax preparation program might use to compute income tax rates:

```
if        (income <        0) rate = 0.0;
else if (income <   47450) rate = .22;
else if (income < 114650) rate = .25;
else if (income < 174700) rate = .28;
else if (income < 311950) rate = .33;
else                           rate = .35;
```

In this case, a number of `if` statements are nested to test from among a number of mutually exclusive possibilities. This construct is a special one that we use often. Otherwise, it is best to use braces to resolve ambiguities when nesting `if` statements. This issue and more examples are addressed in the Q&A and exercises.

**Applications**    The ability to program with loops immediately opens up the full world of computation. To emphasize this fact, we next consider a variety of examples. These examples all involve working with the types of data that we considered in SECTION 1.2, but rest assured that the same mechanisms serve us well for any computational application. The sample programs are carefully crafted, and by studying and appreciating them, you will be prepared to write your own programs containing loops, as requested in many of the exercises at the end of this section.

The examples that we consider here involve computing with numbers. Several of our examples are tied to problems faced by mathematicians and scientists throughout the past several centuries. While computers have existed for only 50 years or so, many of the computational methods that we use are based on a rich mathematical tradition tracing back to antiquity.

*Finite sum.*    The computational paradigm used by `PowersOfTwo` is one that you will use frequently. It uses two variables—one as an index that controls a loop and the other to accumulate a computational result. `Harmonic` (PROGRAM 1.3.5) uses the same paradigm to evaluate the finite sum $H_N = 1 + 1/2 + 1/3 + ... + 1/N$. These numbers, which are known as the *Harmonic numbers*, arise frequently in discrete mathematics. Harmonic numbers are the discrete analog of the logarithm. They also approximate the area under the curve $y = 1/x$. You can use PROGRAM 1.3.5 as a model for computing the values of other sums (see EXERCISE 1.3.16).

## Program 1.3.5    *Harmonic numbers*

```java
public class Harmonic
{
   public static void main(String[] args)
   {  // Compute the Nth Harmonic number.
      int N = Integer.parseInt(args[0]);
      double sum = 0.0;
      for (int i = 1; i <= N; i++)
      {  // Add the ith term to the sum
         sum += 1.0/i;
      }
      System.out.println(sum);
   }
}
```

| N | number of terms in sum |
|------|------------------------|
| i | loop index |
| sum | cumulated sum |

*This program computes the value of the Nth Harmonic number. The value is known from mathematical analysis to be about ln(N) + 0.57721 for large N. Note that ln(10000) ≈ 9.21034.*

```
% java Harmonic 2
1.5
% java Harmonic 10
2.9289682539682538
% java Harmonic 10000
9.787606036044348
```

*Computing the square root.*   How are functions in Java's Math library, such as Math.sqrt(), implemented? Sqrt (PROGRAM 1.3.6) illustrates one technique. To compute the square root function, it uses an iterative computation that was known to the Babylonians over 4,000 years ago. It is also a special case of a general computational technique that was developed in the 17th century by Isaac Newton and Joseph Raphson and is widely known as *Newton's method*. Under generous conditions on a given function $f(x)$, Newton's method is an effective way to find roots (values of $x$ for which the function is 0). Start with an initial estimate, $t_0$. Given the

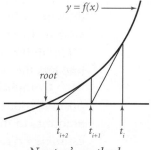

*Newton's method*

*Program 1.3.6    Newton's method*

```
public class Sqrt
{
   public static void main(String[] args)
   {
      double c = Double.parseDouble(args[0]);
      double epsilon = 1e-15;
      double t = c;
      while (Math.abs(t - c/t) > epsilon * t)
      {  // Replace t by the average of t and c/t.
         t = (c/t + t) / 2.0;
      }
      System.out.println(t);
   }
}
```

| | |
|---|---|
| c | *argument* |
| epsilon | *error tolerance* |
| t | *estimate of c* |

*This program computes the square root of its command-line argument to 15 decimal places of accuracy, using Newton's method (see text).*

```
% java Sqrt 2.0
1.414213562373095
% java Sqrt 2544545
1595.1630010754388
```

| *iteration* | t | c/t |
|---|---|---|
| | 2.0000000000000000 | 1.0 |
| 1 | 1.5000000000000000 | 1.3333333333333333 |
| 2 | 1.4166666666666665 | 1.4117647058823530 |
| 3 | 1.4142156862745097 | 1.4142114384748700 |
| 4 | 1.4142135623746899 | 1.4142135623715002 |
| 5 | 1.4142135623730950 | 1.4142135623730951 |

*Trace of* java Sqrt 2.0

estimate $t_i$, compute a new estimate by drawing a line tangent to the curve $y = f(x)$ at the point $(t_i, f(t_i))$ and set $t_{i+1}$ to the x-coordinate of the point where that line hits the x-axis. Iterating this process, we get closer to the root.

Computing the square root of a positive number $c$ is equivalent to finding the positive root of the function $f(x) = x^2 - c$. For this special case, Newton's method amounts to the process implemented in Sqrt (see EXERCISE 1.3.17). Start with the estimate $t = c$. If $t$ is equal to $c/t$, then $t$ is equal to the square root of $c$, so the computation is complete. If not, refine the estimate by replacing $t$ with the average of $t$

and *c/t*. With Newton's method, we get the value of the square root of 2 accurate to 15 places in just 5 iterations of the loop.

Newton's method is important in scientific computing because the same iterative approach is effective for finding the roots of a broad class of functions, including many for which analytic solutions are not known (so the Java `Math` library would be no help). Nowadays, we take for granted that we can find whatever values we need of mathematical functions; before computers, scientists and engineers had to use tables or computed values by hand. Computational techniques that were developed to enable calculations by hand needed to be very efficient, so it is not surprising that many of those same techniques are effective when we use computers. Newton's method is a classic example of this phenomenon. Another useful approach for evaluating mathematical functions is to use Taylor series expansions (see EXERCISES 1.3.35–36).

*Number conversion.* `Binary` (PROGRAM 1.3.7) prints the binary (base 2) representation of the decimal number typed as the command-line argument. It is based on decomposing a number into a sum of powers of two. For example, the binary representation of 19 is `10011`, which is the same as saying that $19 = 16 + 2 + 1$. To compute the binary representation of N, we consider the powers of 2 less than or equal to N in decreasing order to determine which belong in the binary decomposition (and therefore correspond to a 1 bit in the binary representation). The process corresponds precisely to using a balance scale to weigh an object, using weights whose values are powers of two. First, we find largest weight not heavier than the object. Then, considering the weights in decreasing order, we add each weight to test whether the object is lighter. If so, we remove the

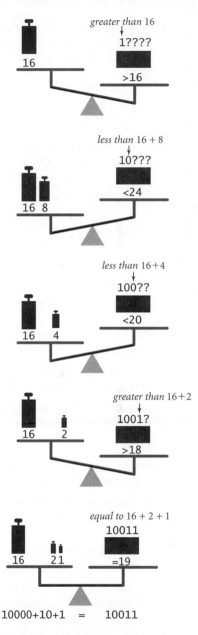

*Scale analog to binary conversion*

*Program 1.3.7    Converting to binary*

```
public class Binary
{
   public static void main(String[] args)
   {  // Print binary representation of N.
      int N = Integer.parseInt(args[0]);
      int v = 1;
      while (v <= N/2)
         v = 2*v;
      // Now v is the largest power of 2 <= N.

      int n = N;
      while (v > 0)
      {  // Cast out powers of 2 in decreasing order.
         if (n < v) { System.out.print(0);          }
         else       { System.out.print(1); n -= v; }
         v = v/2;
      }
      System.out.println();
   }
}
```

| N | integer to convert |
|---|--------------------|
| v | current power of 2 |
| n | current excess     |

*This program prints the binary representation of a positive integer given as the command-line argument, by casting out powers of 2 in decreasing order (see text).*

```
% java Binary 19
10011
% java Binary 100000000
101111101011110000100000000
```

weight; if not, we leave the weight and try the next one. Each weight corresponds to a bit in the binary representation of the weight of the object: leaving a weight corresponds to a 1 bit in the binary representation of the object's weight, and removing a weight corresponds to a 0 bit in the binary representation of the object's weight.

In Binary, the variable v corresponds to the current weight being tested, and the variable n accounts for the excess (unknown) part of the object's weight (to

| n | binary representation | v | v > 0 | binary representation | n < v | output |
|---|---|---|---|---|---|---|
| 19 | 10011 | 16 | true | 10000 | false | 1 |
| 3 | 0011 | 8 | true | 1000 | true | 0 |
| 3 | 011 | 4 | true | 100 | true | 0 |
| 3 | 01 | 2 | true | 10 | false | 1 |
| 1 | 1 | 1 | true | 1 | false | 1 |
| 0 | | 0 | false | | | |

*Trace of casting-out-powers-of-two loop for* java Binary 19

simulate leaving a weight on the balance, we just subtract that weight from n). The value of v decreases through the powers of two. When it is larger than n, Binary prints 0; otherwise, it prints 1 and subtracts v from n. As usual, a trace (of the values of n, v, n < v, and the output bit for each loop iteration) can be very useful in helping you to understand the program. Read from top to bottom in the rightmost column of the trace, the output is 10011, the binary representation of 19.

Converting data from one representation to another is a frequent theme in writing computer programs. Thinking about conversion emphasizes the distinction between an abstraction (an integer like the number of hours in a day) and a representation of that abstraction (24 or 11000). The irony here is that the computer's representation of an integer is actually based on its binary representation.

*Simulation.*  Our next example is different in character from the ones we have been considering, but it is representative of a common situation where we use computers to simulate what might happen in the real world so that we can make informed decisions. The specific example that we consider now is from a thoroughly studied class of problems known as *gambler's ruin*. Suppose that a gambler makes a series of fair $1 bets, starting with some given initial stake. The gambler always goes broke eventually, but when we set other limits on the game, various questions arise. For example, suppose that the gam-

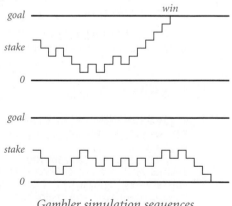

*Gambler simulation sequences*

**Program 1.3.8   *Gambler's ruin simulation***

```
public class Gambler
{
    public static void main(String[] args)
    {  // Run T experiments that start with $stake
       // and terminate on $0 or $goal.
       int stake = Integer.parseInt(args[0]);
       int goal  = Integer.parseInt(args[1]);
       int T     = Integer.parseInt(args[2]);
       int bets = 0;
       int wins = 0;
       for (int t = 0; t < T; t++)
       {  // Run one experiment.
          int cash = stake;
          while (cash > 0 && cash < goal)
          {  // Simulate one bet.
             bets++;
             if (Math.random() < 0.5) cash++;
             else                     cash--;
          }  // Cash is either 0 (ruin) or $goal (win).
          if (cash == goal) wins++;
       }
       System.out.println(100*wins/T + "% wins");
       System.out.println("Avg # bets: " + bets/T);
    }
}
```

| stake | initial stake |
|---|---|
| goal | walkaway goal |
| T | number of trials |
| bets | bet count |
| wins | win count |
| cash | cash on hand |

The inner while *loop in this program simulates a gambler with* $stake *who makes a series of* $1 *bets, continuing until going broke or reaching* $goal. *The running time of this program is proportional to T times the average number of bets. For example, the third command below causes nearly 100 million random numbers to be generated.*

```
% java Gambler 10 20 1000
50% wins
Avg # bets: 100
% java Gambler 50 250 100
19% wins
Avg # bets: 11050
% java Gambler 500 2500 100
21% wins
Avg # bets: 998071
```

bler decides ahead of time to walk away after reaching a certain goal. What are the chances that the gambler will win? How many bets might be needed to win or lose the game? What is the maximum amount of money that the gambler will have during the course of the game?

`Gambler` (PROGRAM 1.3.8) is a simulation that can help answer these questions. It does a sequence of trials, using `Math.random()` to simulate the sequence of bets, continuing until the gambler is broke or the goal is reached, and keeping track of the number of wins and the number of bets. After running the experiment for the specified number of trials, it averages and prints out the results. You might wish to run this program for various values of the command-line arguments, not necessarily just to plan your next trip to the casino, but to help you think about the following questions: Is the simulation an accurate reflection of what would happen in real life? How many trials are needed to get an accurate answer? What are the computational limits on performing such a simulation? Simulations are widely used in applications in economics, science, and engineering, and questions of this sort are important in any simulation.

In the case of `Gambler`, we are verifying classical results from probability theory, which say the *probability of success is the ratio of the stake to the goal* and that the *expected number of bets is the product of the stake and the desired gain* (the difference between the goal and the stake). For example, if you want to go to Monte Carlo to try to turn $500 into $2,500, you have a reasonable (20%) chance of success, but you should expect to make a million $1 bets! If you try to turn $1 into $1,000, you have a .1% chance and can expect to be done (ruin, most likely) in about 999 bets.

Simulation and analysis go hand-in-hand, each validating the other. In practice, the value of simulation is that it can suggest answers to questions that might be too difficult to resolve with analysis. For example, suppose that our gambler, recognizing that there will never be enough time to make a million bets, decides ahead of time to set an upper limit on the number of bets. How much money can the gambler expect to take home in that case? You can address this question with an easy change to PROGRAM 1.3.8 (see EXERCISE 1.3.24), but addressing it with mathematical analysis is not so easy.

*Factoring.* A *prime* is an integer greater than one whose only positive divisors are one and itself. The prime factorization of an integer is the multiset of primes whose product is the integer. For example, 3757208 = 2*2*2*7*13*13*397. Factors (PROGRAM 1.3.9) computes the prime factorization of any given positive integer. In contrast to many of the other programs that we have seen (which we could do in a few minutes with a calculator or even a pencil and paper), this computation would not be feasible without a computer. How would you go about trying to find the factors of a number like 287994837222311? You might find the factor 17 quickly, but even with a calculator it would take you quite a while to find 1739347.

Although Factors is compact and straightforward, it certainly will take some thought to for you to convince yourself that it produces the desired result for any given integer. As usual, following a trace that shows the values of the variables at the beginning of each iteration of the outer for loop is a good way to understand the computation. For the case where the initial value of N is 3757208, the inner while loop iterates three times when i is 2, to remove the three factors of 2; then zero times when i is 3, 4, 5, and 6, since none of those numbers divide 469651; and so forth. Tracing the program for a few example inputs clearly reveals its basic operation. To convince ourselves that the program will behave as expected for all inputs, we reason about what we expect each of the loops to do. The while loop clearly prints and removes from n all factors of i, but the key to understanding the program is to see that the following fact holds at the beginning of each iteration of the for loop: n has no factors between 2 and i-1. Thus, if i is not prime, it will not divide n; if i is prime, the while loop will do its job. Once we know that n has no factors less than or equal to i, we also know that it has no factors greater than n/i, so we need look no further when i is greater than n/i.

| i | N | output |
|---|---|---|
| 2 | 3757208 | 2  2  2 |
| 3 | 469651 | |
| 4 | 469651 | |
| 5 | 469651 | |
| 6 | 469651 | |
| 7 | 469651 | 7 |
| 8 | 67093 | |
| 9 | 67093 | |
| 10 | 67093 | |
| 11 | 67093 | |
| 12 | 67093 | |
| 13 | 67093 | 13  13 |
| 14 | 397 | |
| 15 | 397 | |
| 16 | 397 | |
| 17 | 397 | |
| 18 | 397 | |
| 19 | 397 | |
| 20 | 397 | |
| | | 397 |

*Trace of* java Factors 3757208

In a more naïve implementation, we might simply have used the condition (i < n) to terminate the for loop. Even given the blinding speed of modern computers, such a decision would have a dramatic effect on the size of the numbers that we could factor. EXERCISE 1.3.26 encourages you to experiment with the program to

---

### Program 1.3.9  *Factoring integers*

```java
public class Factors
{
   public static void main(String[] args)
   { // Print the prime factors of N.
      long N = Long.parseLong(args[0]);
      long n = N;
      for (long i = 2; i <= n/i; i++)
      { // Test whether i is a factor.
         while (n % i == 0)
         { // Cast out and print i factors.
            n /= i;
            System.out.print(i + " ");
         } // Any factors of n are greater than i.
      }
      if (n > 1) System.out.print(n);
      System.out.println();
   }
}
```

| N | integer to factor |
|---|---|
| n | unfactored part |
| i | potential factor |

*This program prints the prime factorization of any positive integer in Java's* long *data type. The code is simple, but it takes some thought to convince oneself that it is correct (see text).*

```
% java Factors 3757208
2 2 2 7 13 13 397
```

```
% java Factors 287994837222311
17 1739347 9739789
```

learn the effectiveness of this simple change. On a computer that can do billions of operations per second, we could factor numbers on the order of $10^9$ in a few seconds; with the (i <= n/i) test we can factor numbers on the order of $10^{18}$ in a comparable amount of time. Loops give us the ability to solve difficult problems, but they also give us the ability to construct simple programs that run slowly, so we must always be cognizant of performance.

In modern applications in cryptography, there are important situations where we wish to factor truly huge numbers (with, say, hundreds or thousands of digits). Such a computation is prohibitively difficult even *with* the use of a computer.

**Other conditional and loop constructs**   To more fully cover the Java language, we consider here four more control-flow constructs. You need not think about using these constructs for every program that you write, because you are likely to encounter them much less frequently than the `if`, `while`, and `for` statements. You certainly do not need to worry about using these constructs until you are comfortable using `if`, `while`, and `for`. You might encounter one of them in a program in a book or on the web, but many programmers do not use them at all and we do not use any of them outside this section.

*Break statement.*   In some situations, we want to immediately exit a loop without letting it run to completion. Java provides the `break` statement for this purpose. For example, the following code is an effective way to test whether a given integer $N>1$ is prime:

```
int i;
for (i = 2; i <= N/i; i++)
    if (N % i == 0) break;
if (i > N/i) System.out.println(N + " is prime");
```

There are two different ways to leave this loop: either the `break` statement is executed (because `i` divides `N`, so `N` is not prime) or the `for` loop condition is not satisfied (because no `i` with `i <= N/i` was found that divides `N`, which implies that `N` is prime). Note that we have to declare `i` outside the `for` loop instead of in the initialization statement so that its scope extends beyond the loop.

*Continue statement.*   Java also provides a way to skip to the next iteration of a loop: the `continue` statement. When a `continue` is executed within a loop body, the flow of control transfers directly to the increment statement for the next iteration of the loop.

*Switch statement.*   The `if` and `if-else` statements allow one or two alternatives in directing the flow of control. Sometimes, a computation naturally suggests more than two mutually exclusive alternatives. We could use a sequence or a chain of `if-else` statements, but the Java `switch` statement provides a direct solution. Let us move right to a typical example. Rather than printing an `int` variable day in a program that works with days of the weeks (such as a solution to EXERCISE 1.2.29), it is easier to use a `switch` statement, as follows:

```
switch (day)
{
    case 0: System.out.println("Sun"); break;
    case 1: System.out.println("Mon"); break;
    case 2: System.out.println("Tue"); break;
    case 3: System.out.println("Wed"); break;
    case 4: System.out.println("Thu"); break;
    case 5: System.out.println("Fri"); break;
    case 6: System.out.println("Sat"); break;
}
```

When you have a program that seems to have a long and regular sequence of if statements, you might consider consulting the booksite and using a switch statement, or using an alternate approach described in SECTION 1.4.

*Do-while loop.*  Another way to write a loop is to use the template

```
do { <statements> } while (<boolean expression>);
```

The meaning of this statement is the same as

```
while (<boolean expression>) { <statements> }
```

except that the first test of the condition is omitted. If the condition initially holds, there is no difference. For an example in which do-while is useful, consider the problem of generating points that are randomly distributed in the unit disk. We can use Math.random() to generate x and y coordinates independently to get points that are randomly distributed in the 2-by-2 square centered on the origin. Most points fall within the unit disk, so we just reject those that do not. We always want to generate at least one point, so a do-while loop is ideal for this computation. The following code sets x and y such that the point (x, y) is randomly distributed in the unit disk:

```
do
{  // Scale x and y to be random in (-1, 1).
    x = 2.0*Math.random() - 1.0;
    y = 2.0*Math.random() - 1.0;
} while (Math.sqrt(x*x + y*y) > 1.0);
```

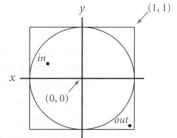

Since the area of the disk is $\pi$ and the area of the square is 4, the expected number of times the loop is iterated is $4/\pi$ (about 1.27).

**Infinite loops**   Before you write programs that use loops, you need to think about the following issue: what if the loop-continuation condition in a `while` loop is always satisfied? With the statements that you have learned so far, one of two bad things could happen, both of which you need to learn to cope with.

First, suppose that such a loop calls `System.out.println()`. For example, if the condition in `TenHellos` were (`i > 3`) instead of (`i <= 10`), it would always be `true`. What happens? Nowadays, we use *print* as an abstraction to mean *display in a terminal window* and the result of attempting to display an unlimited number of lines in a terminal window is dependent on operating-system conventions. If

```
public class BadHellos
...
int i = 4;
while (i > 3)
{
    System.out.println
      (i + "th Hello");
    i = i + 1;
}
...

% java BadHellos
1st Hello
2nd Hello
3rd Hello
5th Hello
6th Hello
7th Hello
...
```

*An infinite loop*

your system is set up to have *print* mean *print characters on a piece of paper*, you might run out of paper or have to unplug the printer. In a terminal window, you need a *stop printing* operation. Before running programs with loops on your own, you make sure that you know what to do to "pull the plug" on an infinite loop of `System.out.println()` calls and then test out the strategy by making the change to `TenHellos` indicated above and trying to stop it. On most systems, `<ctrl-c>` means *stop the current program*, and should do the job.

Second, *nothing* might happen. If your program has an infinite loop that does not produce any output, it will spin through the loop and you will see no results at all. When you find yourself in such a situation, you can inspect the loops to make sure that the loop exit condition always happens, but the problem may not be easy to identify. One way to locate such a bug is to insert calls to `System.out.println()` to produce a trace. If these calls fall within an infinite loop, this strategy reduces the problem to the case discussed in the previous paragraph, but the output might give you a clue about what to do.

You might not know (or it might not matter) whether a loop is infinite or just very long. Even `BadHellos` eventually would terminate after printing over a billion lines because of overflow. If you invoke PROGRAM 1.3.8 with arguments such as `java Gambler 100000 200000 100`, you may not want to wait for the answer. You will learn to be aware of and to estimate the running time of your programs.

Why not have Java detect infinite loops and warn us about them? You might be surprised to know that it is not possible to do so, in general. This counterintuitive fact is one of the fundamental results of theoretical computer science.

**Summary**   For reference, the accompanying table lists the programs that we have considered in this section. They are representative of the kinds of tasks we can address with short programs comprised of if, while, and for statements process-ing built-in types of data. These types of computations are an appropriate way to become familiar with the basic Java flow-of-control constructs. The time that you spend now working with as many such programs as you can will certainly pay off for you in the future.

| program | description |
|---------|-------------|
| Flip | simulate a coin flip |
| TenHellos | your first loop |
| PowersOfTwo | compute and print a table of values |
| DivisorPattern | your first nested loop |
| Harmonic | compute finite sum |
| Sqrt | classic iterative algorithm |
| Binary | basic number conversion |
| Gambler | simulation with nested loops |
| Factors | while loop within a for loop |

*Summary of programs in this section*

To learn how to use condition-als and loops, you must practice writ-ing and debugging programs with if, while, and for statements. The exer-cises at the end of this section provide many opportunities for you to begin this process. For each exercise, you will write a Java program, then run and test it. All programmers know that it is unusual to have a program work as planned the first time it is run, so you will want to have an understanding of your program and an expectation of what it should do, step by step. At first, use explicit traces to check your understanding and expectation. As you gain experience, you will find yourself thinking in terms of what a trace might produce as you compose your loops. Ask yourself the following kinds of questions: What will be the values of the variables after the loop iterates the first time? The second time? The final time? Is there any way this program could get stuck in an infinite loop?

Loops and conditionals are a giant step in our ability to compute: if, while, and for statements take us from simple straight-line programs to arbitrarily com-plicated flow of control. In the next several chapters, we will take more giant steps that will allow us to process large amounts of input data and allow us to define and process types of data other than simple numeric types. The if, while, and for statements of this section will play an essential role in the programs that we consider as we take these steps.

**Q.** What is the difference between = and ==?

**A.** We repeat this question here to remind you to be sure not to use = when you mean == in a conditional expression. The expression (x = y) assigns the value of y to x, whereas the expression (x == y) tests whether the two variables currently have the same values. In some programming languages, this difference can wreak havoc in a program and be difficult to detect, but Java's type safety usually will come to the rescue. For example, if we make the mistake of typing (t = goal) instead of (t == goal) in PROGRAM 1.3.8, the compiler finds the bug for us:

```
javac Gambler.java
Gambler.java:18: incompatible types
found   : int
required: boolean
if (t = goal) wins++;
      ^
1 error
```

Be careful about writing if (x = y) when x and y are boolean variables, since this will be treated as an assignment statement, which assigns the value of y to x and evaluates to the truth value of y. For example, instead of writing if (isPrime = false), you should write if (!isPrime).

**Q.** So I need to pay attention to using == instead of = when writing loops and conditionals. Is there something else in particular that I should watch out for?

**A.** Another common mistake is to forget the braces in a loop or conditional with a multi-statement body. For example, consider this version of the code in Gambler:

```
for (int t = 0; t < T; t++)
   for (cash = stake; cash > 0 && cash < goal; bets++)
      if (Math.random() < 0.5) cash++;
      else                          cash--;
   if (cash == goal) wins++;
```

The code appears correct, but it is dysfunctional because the second if is outside both for loops and gets executed just once. Our practice of using explicit braces for long statements is precisely to avoid such insidious bugs.

**Q.** Anything else?

**A.** The third classic pitfall is ambiguity in nested `if` statements:

```
if <expr1> if <expr2> <stmntA> else <stmntB>
```

In Java this is equivalent to

```
if <expr1> { if <expr2> <stmntA> else <stmntB> }
```

even if you might have been thinking

```
if <expr1> { if <expr2> <stmntA> } else <stmntB>
```

Again, using explicit braces is a good way to avoid this pitfall.

**Q.** Are there cases where I must use a `for` loop but not a `while`, or vice versa?

**A.** No. Generally, you should use a `for` loop when you have an initialization, an increment, and a loop continuation test (if you do not need the loop control variable outside the loop). But the equivalent `while` loop still might be fine.

**Q.** What are the rules on where we declare the loop-control variables?

**A.** Opinions differ. In older programming languages, it was required that all variables be declared at the beginning of a `<body>`, so many programmers are in this habit and there is a lot of code out there that follows this convention. But it makes a lot of sense to declare variables where they are first used, particularly in `for` loops, when it is normally the case that the variable is not needed outside the loop. However, it is not uncommon to need to test (and therefore declare) the loop-control variable outside the loop, as in the primality-testing code we considered as an example of the `break` statement.

**Q.** What is the difference between `++i` and `i++`?

**A.** As statements, there is no difference. In expressions, both increment `i`, but `++i` has the value after the increment and `i++` the value before the increment. In this book, we avoid statements like `x = ++i` that have the side effect of changing variable values. So, it is safe to not worry much about this distinction and just use `i++`

in for loops and as a statement. When we do use ++i in this book, we will call attention to it and say why we are using it.

**Q.** So, *<initialize>* and *<increment>* can be any statements whatsoever in a for loop. How can I take advantage of that?

**A.** Some experts take advantage of this ability to create compact code fragments, but, as a beginner, it is best for you to use a while loop in such situations. In fact, the situation is even more complicated because *<initialize>* and *<increment>* can be *sequences* of statements, separated by commas. This notation allows for code that initializes and modifies other variables besides the loop index. In some cases, this ability leads to compact code. For example, the following two lines of code could replace the last eight lines in the body of the main() method in PowersOfTwo (PROGRAM 1.3.3):

```
for (int i = 0, v = 1; i <= n; i++, v *= 2)
    System.out.println(i + " " + v);
```

Such code is rarely necessary and better avoided, particularly by beginners.

**Q** Can I use a double value as an index in a for loop?

**A** It is legal, but generally bad practice to do so. Consider the following loop:

```
for (double x = 0.0; x <= 1.0; x += 0.1)
    System.out.println(x + " " + Math.sin(x));
```

How many times does it iterate? The number of iterations depends on an equality test between double values, which may not always give the result that you expect.

**Q.** Anything else tricky about loops?

**A.** Not all parts of a for loop need to be filled in with code. The initialization statement, the boolean expression, the increment statement, and the loop body can each be omitted. It is generally better style to use a while statement than null statements in a for loop. In the code in this book, we avoid null statements.

```
int v = 1;
while (v <= N/2)              null increment
    v *= 2;                    statement
                                    ↓
for (int v = 1; v <= N/2; )
    v *= 2;

for (int v = 1; v <= N/2; v *= 2)
    ;   ← null loop body
```

*Three equivalent loops*

# Exercises

**1.3.1**    Write a program that takes three integer command-line arguments and prints `equal` if all three are equal, and `not equal` otherwise.

**1.3.2**    Write a more general and more robust version of `Quadratic` (Program 1.2.3) that prints the roots of the polynomial $ax^2 + bx + c$, prints an appropriate message if the discriminant is negative, and behaves appropriately (avoiding division by zero) if $a$ is zero.

**1.3.3**    What (if anything) is wrong with each of the following statements?

    *a.*  `if (a > b) then c = 0;`

    *b.*  `if a > b { c = 0; }`

    *c.*  `if (a > b) c = 0;`

    *d.*  `if (a > b) c = 0 else b = 0;`

**1.3.4**    Write a code fragment that prints `true` if the `double` variables x and y are both strictly between 0 and 1 and `false` otherwise.

**1.3.5**    Improve your solution to Exercise 1.2.25 by adding code to check that the values of the command-line arguments fall within the ranges of validity of the formula, and also adding code to print out an error message if that is not the case.

**1.3.6**    Suppose that i and j are both of type `int`. What is the value of j after each of the following statements is executed?

    *a.*  `for (i = 0, j = 0; i < 10; i++)  j += i;`

    *b.*  `for (i = 0, j = 1; i < 10; i++)  j += j;`

    *c.*  `for (j = 0; j < 10; j++) j += j;`

    *d.*  `for (i = 0, j = 0; i < 10; i++) j += j++;`

**1.3.7**    Rewrite `TenHellos` to make a program `Hellos` that takes the number of lines to print as a command-line argument. You may assume that the argument is less than 1000. Hint: Use i % 10 and i % 100 to determine when to use st, nd, rd, or th for printing the ith Hello.

**1.3.8**    Write a program that, using one `for` loop and one `if` statement, prints the integers from 1,000 to 2,000 with five integers per line. Hint: Use the % operation.

**1.3.9**   Write a program that takes an integer N as a command-line argument, uses Math.random() to print N uniform random values between 0 and 1, and then prints their average value (see EXERCISE 1.2.30).

**1.3.10**  Describe what happens when you try to print a ruler function (see the table on page 57) with a value of N that is too large, such as 100.

**1.3.11**  Write a program FunctionGrowth that prints a table of the values $\log N$, $N$, $N \log N$, $N^2$, $N^3$, and $2^N$ for $N = 16, 32, 64, \ldots, 2048$. Use tabs (\t characters) to line up columns.

**1.3.12**  What are the values of m and n after executing the following code?

```
int n = 123456789;
int m = 0;
while (n != 0)
{
   m = (10 * m) + (n % 10);
   n = n / 10;
}
```

**1.3.13**  What does the following program print ?

```
int f = 0, g = 1;
for (int i = 0; i <= 15; i++)
{
   System.out.println(f);
   f = f + g;
   g = f - g;
}
```

*Solution.*   Even an expert programmer will tell you that the only way to understand a program like this is to trace it. When you do, you will find that it prints the values 0, 1, 1, 2, 3, 5, 8, 13, 21, 34, 55, 89, 134, 233, 377, and 610. These numbers are the first sixteen of the famous *Fibonacci sequence*, which are defined by the following formulas: $F_0 = 0$, $F_1 = 1$, and $F_n = F_{n-1} + F_{n-2}$ for $n > 1$. The Fibonacci sequence arises in a surprising variety of contexts, they have been studied for centuries, and many of their properties are well-known. For example, the ratio of successive numbers approaches the *golden ratio* φ (about 1.618) as *n* approaches infinity.

**1.3.14** Write a program that takes a command-line argument *N* and prints all the positive powers of two less than or equal to *N*. Make sure that your program works properly for all values of *N*. (`Integer.parseInt()` will generate an error if *N* is too large, and your program should print nothing if *N* is negative.)

**1.3.15** Expand your solution to EXERCISE 1.2.24 to print a table giving the total amount paid and the remaining principal after each monthly payment.

**1.3.16** Unlike the harmonic numbers, the sum $1/1^2 + 1/2^2 + ... + 1/N^2$ *does* converge to a constant as *N* grows to infinity. (Indeed, the constant is $\pi^2/6$, so this formula can be used to estimate the value of π.) Which of the following `for` loops computes this sum? Assume that `N` is an `int` initialized to 1000000 and `sum` is a `double` initialized to 0.0.

   *a.* `for (int i = 1; i <= N; i++) sum += 1 / (i*i);`
   *b.* `for (int i = 1; i <= N; i++) sum += 1.0 / i*i;`
   *c.* `for (int i = 1; i <= N; i++) sum += 1.0 / (i*i);`
   *d.* `for (int i = 1; i <= N; i++) sum += 1 / (1.0*i*i);`

**1.3.17** Show that PROGRAM 1.3.6 implements Newton's method for finding the square root of *c*. *Hint*: Use the fact that the slope of the tangent to a (differentiable) function *f(x)* at *x = t* is *f′(t)* to find the equation of the tangent line and then use that equation to find the point where the tangent line intersects the *x*-axis to show that you can use Newton's method to find a root of any function as follows: at each iteration, replace the estimate *t* by *t − f(t) / f′(t)*.

**1.3.18** Using Newton's method, develop a program that takes integers N and k as command-line arguments and prints the kth root of N (*Hint*: see EXERCISE 1.3.17).

**1.3.19** Modify `Binary` to get a program `Kary` that takes i and k as command-line arguments and converts i to base k. Assume that i is an integer in Java's `long` data type and that k is an integer between 2 and 16. For bases greater than 10, use the letters A through F to represent the 11th through 16th digits, respectively.

**1.3.20** Write a code fragment that puts the binary representation of a positive integer `N` into a `String s`.

*Solution.*    Java has a built-in method `Integer.toBinaryString(N)` for this job, but the point of the exercise is to see how such a method might be implemented. Working from PROGRAM 1.3.7, we get the solution

```
String s = "";
int v = 1;
while (v <= n/2) v = 2*v;
while (v > 0)
{
    if (n < v) { s += 0;            }
    else       { s += 1; n -= v; }
    v = v/2;
}
```

A simpler option is to work from right to left:

```
String s = "";
for (int n = N; n > 0; n /= 2)
    s = (n % 2) + s;
```

Both of these methods are worthy of careful study.

**1.3.21** Write a version of `Gambler` that uses two nested `while` loops or two nested `for` loops instead of a `while` loop inside a `for` loop.

**1.3.22** Write a program `GamblerPlot` that traces a gambler's ruin simulation by printing a line after each bet in which one asterisk corresponds to each dollar held by the gambler.

**1.3.23** Modify `Gambler` to take an extra command-line argument that specifies the (fixed) probability that the gambler wins each bet. Use your program to try to learn how this probability affects the chance of winning and the expected number of bets. Try a value of *p* close to .5 (say, .48).

**1.3.24** Modify `Gambler` to take an extra command-line argument that specifies the number of bets the gambler is willing to make, so that there are three possible ways for the game to end: the gambler wins, loses, or runs out of time. Add to the output to give the expected amount of money the gambler will have when the game ends. *Extra credit*: Use your program to plan your next trip to Monte Carlo.

**1.3.25** Modify Factors to print just one copy each of the prime divisors.

**1.3.26** Run quick experiments to determine the impact of using the termination condition (i <= N/i) instead of (i < N) in Factors in PROGRAM 1.3.9. For each method, find the largest *n* such that when you type in an *n* digit number, the program is sure to finish within 10 seconds.

**1.3.27** Write a program Checkerboard that takes one command-line argument N and uses a loop within a loop to print out a two-dimensional N-by-N checkerboard pattern with alternating spaces and asterisks.

**1.3.28** Write a program GCD that finds the greatest common divisor (gcd) of two integers using *Euclid's algorithm*, which is an iterative computation based on the following observation: if x is greater than y, then if y divides x, the gcd of x and y is y; otherwise, the gcd of x and y is the same as the gcd of x % y and y.

**1.3.29** Write a program RelativelyPrime that takes one command-line argument N and prints out an N-by-N table such that there is an * in row i and column j if the gcd of i and j is 1 (i and j are relatively prime) and a space in that position otherwise.

**1.3.30** Write a program PowersOfK that takes an integer k as command-line argument and prints all the positive powers of k in the Java long data type. *Note*: The constant Long.MAX_VALUE is the value of the largest integer in long.

**1.3.31** Generate a random point $(x, y, z)$ on the surface of a sphere using Marsaglia's method: Pick a random point $(a, b)$ in the unit disk using the method described at the end of this section. Then, set $x = 2\, a\, \sqrt{1 - a^2 - b^2}$. $y = 2\, b\, \sqrt{1 - a^2 - b^2}$. and $z = 1 - 2\,(a^2 + b^2)$.

## *Creative Exercises*

**1.3.32** *Ramanujan's taxi.* Srinivasa Ramanujan was an Indian mathematician who became famous for his intuition for numbers. When the English mathematician G. H. Hardy came to visit him one day, Hardy remarked that the number of his taxi was 1729, a rather dull number. To which Ramanujan replied, "No, Hardy! No, Hardy! It is a very interesting number. It is the smallest number expressible as the sum of two cubes in two different ways." Verify this claim by writing a program that takes a command-line argument N and prints out all integers less than or equal to N that can be expressed as the sum of two cubes in two different ways. In other words, find distinct positive integers $a$, $b$, $c$, and $d$ such that $a^3 + b^3 = c^3 + d^3$. Use four nested for loops.

**1.3.33** *Checksum.* The International Standard Book Number (ISBN) is a 10-digit code that uniquely specifies a book. The rightmost digit is a checksum digit that can be uniquely determined from the other 9 digits, from the condition that $d_1 + 2d_2 + 3d_3 + ... + 10d_{10}$ must be a multiple of 11 (here $d_i$ denotes the $i$th digit from the right). The checksum digit $d_i$ can be any value from 0 to 10. The ISBN convention is to use the character 'X' to denote 10. Example: the checksum digit corresponding to 020131452 is 5 since 5 is the only value of $x$ between 0 and 10 for which

$$10 \cdot 0 + 9 \cdot 2 + 8 \cdot 0 + 7 \cdot 1 + 6 \cdot 3 + 5 \cdot 1 + 4 \cdot 4 + 3 \cdot 5 + 2 \cdot 2 + 1 \cdot x$$

is a multiple of 11. Write a program that takes a 9-digit integer as a command-line argument, computes the checksum, and prints out the the ISBN number.

**1.3.34** *Counting primes.* Write a program PrimeCounter that takes a command-line argument N and finds the number of primes less than or equal to N. Use it to print out the number of primes less than or equal to 10 million. *Note*: if you are not careful, your program may not finish in a reasonable amount of time!

**1.3.35** *2D random walk.* A two-dimensional random walk simulates the behavior of a particle moving in a grid of points. At each step, the random walker moves north, south, east, or west with probability equal to 1/4, independent of previous moves. Write a program RandomWalker that takes a command-line argument N and estimates how long it will take a random walker to hit the boundary of a 2N-by-2N square centered at the starting point.

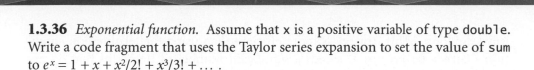

**1.3.36** *Exponential function.* Assume that x is a positive variable of type double. Write a code fragment that uses the Taylor series expansion to set the value of sum to $e^x = 1 + x + x^2/2! + x^3/3! + \ldots$ .

*Solution.*    The purpose of this exercise is to get you to think about how a library function like Math.exp() might be implemented in terms of elementary operators. Try solving it, then compare your solution with the one developed here.

We start by considering the problem of computing one term. Suppose that x and term are variables of type double and n is a variable of type int. The following code fragment sets term to $x^N / N!$ using the direct method of having one loop for the numerator and another loop for the denominator, then dividing the results:

```
double num = 1.0, dem = 1.0;
for (int i = 1; i <= n; i++) num *= x;
for (int i = 1; i <= n; i++) den *= i;
double term = num/den;
```

A better approach is to use just a single for loop:

```
double term = 1.0;
for (i = 1; i <= n; i++) term *= x/i;
```

Besides being more compact and elegant, the latter solution is preferable because it avoids inaccuracies caused by computing with huge numbers. For example, the two-loop approach breaks down for values like $x = 10$ and $N = 100$ because 100! is too large to represent as a double.

To compute $e^x$, we nest this for loop within another for loop:

```
double term = 1.0;
double sum = 0.0;
for (int n = 1; sum != sum + term; n++)
{
    sum += term;
    term = 1.0;
    for (int i = 1; i <= n; i++) term *= x/i;
}
```

The number of times the loop iterates depends on the relative values of the next term and the accumulated sum. Once the value of the sum stops changing, we leave the loop. (This strategy is more efficient than using the termination condition (`term > 0`) because it avoids a significant number of iterations that do not change the value of the sum.) This code is effective, but it is inefficient because the inner `for` loop recomputes all the values it computed on the previous iteration of the outer `for` loop. Instead, we can make use of the term that was added in on the previous loop iteration and solve the problem with a single `for` loop:

```
double term = 1.0;
double sum = 0.0;
for (int n = 1; sum != sum + term; n++)
{
    sum += term;
    term *= x/n;
}
```

**1.3.37** *Trigonometric functions.* Write two programs, `Sin` and `Cos`, that compute the sine and cosine functions using their Taylor series expansions $\sin x = x - x^3/3! + x^5/5! - ...$ and $\cos x = 1 - x^2/2! + x^4/4! - ...$ .

**1.3.38** *Experimental analysis.* Run experiments to determine the relative costs of `Math.exp()` and the methods from EXERCISE 1.3.36 for computing $e^x$: the direct method with nested `for` loops, the improvement with a single `for` loop, and the latter with the termination condition (`term > 0`). Use trial-and-error with a command-line argument to determine how many times your computer can perform each computation in 10 seconds.

**1.3.39** *Pepys problem.* In 1693 Samuel Pepys asked Isaac Newton which is more likely: getting 1 at least once when rolling a fair die six times or getting 1 at least twice when rolling it 12 times. Write a program that could have provided Newton with a quick answer.

**1.3.40** *Game simulation.* In the 1970s game show *Let's Make a Deal*, a contestant is presented with three doors. Behind one of them is a valuable prize. After the contestant chooses a door, the host opens one of the other two doors (never revealing the prize, of course). The contestant is then given the opportunity to switch to the other unopened door. Should the contestant do so? Intuitively, it might seem that the contestant's initial choice door and the other unopened door are equally likely to contain the prize, so there would be no incentive to switch. Write a program MonteHall to test this intuition by simulation. Your program should take a command-line argument N, play the game N times using each of the two strategies (switch or do not switch), and print the chance of success for each of the two strategies.

**1.3.41** *Median-of-5.* Write a program that takes five distinct integers from the command line and prints the median value (the value such that two of the others are smaller and two are larger). *Extra credit*: Solve the problem with a program that compares values fewer than seven times for any given input.

**1.3.42** *Sorting three numbers.* Suppose that the variables a, b, c, and t are all of the same numeric primitive type. Prove that the following code puts a, b, and c in ascending order:

```
if (a > b) { t = a; a = b; b = t; }
if (a > c) { t = a; a = c; c = t; }
if (b > c) { t = b; b = c; c = t; }
```

**1.3.43** *Chaos.* Write a program to study the following simple model for population growth, which might be applied to study fish in a pond, bacteria in a test tube, or any of a host of similar situations. We suppose that the population ranges from 0 (extinct) to 1 (maximum population that can be sustained). If the population at time $t$ is $x$, then we suppose the population at time $t + 1$ to be $rx(1-x)$, where the argument $r$, known as the *fecundity parameter*, controls the rate of growth. Start with a small population—say, $x = 0.01$—and study the result of iterating the model, for various values of $r$. For which values of $r$ does the population stabilize at $x = 1 - 1/r$? Can you say anything about the population when $r$ is 3.5? 3.8? 5?

**1.3.44** *Euler's sum-of-powers conjecture.* In 1769 Leonhard Euler formulated a generalized version of Fermat's Last Theorem, conjecturing that at least $n$ $n$th powers are needed to obtain a sum that is itself an $n$th power, for $n > 2$. Write a program to disprove Euler's conjecture (which stood until 1967), using a quintuply nested loop to find four positive integers whose 5th power sums to the 5th power of another positive integer. That is, find $a$, $b$, $c$, $d$, and $e$ such that $a^5 + b^5 + c^5 + d^5 = e^5$. Use the long data type.

# 1.4   Arrays

IN THIS SECTION, WE CONSIDER A fundamental programming construct known as the *array*. The primary purpose of an array is to facilitate storing and manipulating large quantities of data. Arrays play an essential role in many data processing tasks. They also correspond to vectors and matrices, which are widely used in science and in scientific programming. We will consider basic properties of array processing in Java, with many examples illustrating why they are useful.

An array stores a sequence of values that are all of the same type. Processing such a set of values is very common. We might have exam scores, stock prices, nucleotides in a DNA strand, or characters in a book. Each of these examples involve a large number of values that are all of the same type.

We want not only to store values but also directly access each individual value. The method that we use to refer to individual values in an array is numbering and then *indexing* them. If we have $N$ values, we think of them as being numbered from 0 to $N-1$. Then, we can unambiguously specify one of them by referring to the $i$th value for any value of $i$ from 0 to $N-1$. To refer to the $i$th value in an array a, we use the notation a[i], pronounced *a sub i*. This Java construct is known as a *one-dimensional* array.

The one-dimensional array is our first example in this book of a *data structure* (a method for organizing data). We also consider in this section a more complicated data structure known as *a two-dimensional array*. Data structures play an essential role in modern programming— CHAPTER 4 is largely devoted to the topic.

Typically, when we have a large amount of data to process, we first put all of the data into one or more arrays. Then we use array indexing to refer to individual values and to process the data. We consider such applications when we discuss data input in SECTION 1.5 and in the case study that is the subject of SECTION 1.6. In this section, we expose the basic properties of arrays by considering examples where our programs first populate arrays with computed values from experimental studies and then process them.

a

| |
|---|
| a[0] |
| a[1] |
| a[2] |
| a[3] |
| a[4] |
| a[5] |
| a[6] |
| a[7] |

*An array*

**Arrays in Java**    Making an array in a Java program involves three distinct steps:
- Declare the array name and type.
- Create the array.
- Initialize the array values.

To declare the array, you need to specify a name and the type of data it will contain. To create it, you need to specify its size (the number of values). For example, the following code makes an array of N numbers of type `double`, all initialized to `0.0`:

```java
double[] a;
a = new double[N];
for (int i = 0; i < N; i++)
    a[i] = 0.0;
```

The first statement is the array declaration. It is just like a declaration of a variable of the corresponding primitive type except for the square brackets following the type name, which specify that we are declaring an array. The second statement creates the array. This action is unnecessary for variables of a primitive type (so we have not seen a similar action before), but it is needed for all other types of data in Java (see SECTION 3.1). In the code in this book, we normally keep the array length in an integer variable N, but any integer-valued expression will do. The `for` statement initializes the N array values. We refer to each value by putting its index in brackets after the array name. This code sets all of the array entries to the value `0.0`.

When you begin to write code that uses an array, you must be sure that your code declares, creates, and initializes it. Omitting one of these steps is a common programming mistake. For economy in code, we often take advantage of Java's default array initialization convention and combine all three steps into a single statement. For example, the following statement is equivalent to the code above:

```java
double[] a = new double[N];
```

The code to the left of the equal sign constitutes the declaration; the code to the right constitutes the creation. The `for` loop is unnecessary in this case because the default initial value of variables of type `double` in a Java array is `0.0`, but it would be required if a nonzero value were desired. The default initial value is zero for all numbers and `false` for type `boolean`. For `String` and other non-primitive types, the default is the value `null`, which you will learn about in CHAPTER 3.

After declaring and creating an array, you can refer to any individual value anywhere you would use a variable name in a program by enclosing an integer index in braces after the array name. We refer to the ith item with the code a[i]. The explicit initialization code shown earlier is an example of such a use. The obvious advantage of using arrays is to avoid explicitly naming each variable individually. Using an array index is virtually the same as appending the index to the array name: for example, if we wanted to process eight variables of type double, we could declare each of them individually with the declaration

```
double a0, a1, a2, a3, a4, a5, a6, a7;
```

and then refer to them as a0, a1 and so forth instead of declaring them with double[] a = new double[8] and referring to them as a[0], a[1], and so forth. But naming dozens of individual variables in this way would be cumbersome and naming millions is untenable.

As an example of code that uses arrays, consider using arrays to represent *vectors*. We consider vectors in detail in SECTION 3.3; for the moment, think of a vector as a sequence of real numbers. The *dot product* of two vectors (of the same length) is the sum of the products of their corresponding components. The dot product of two vectors that are represented as one-dimensional arrays x[] and y[] that are each of length 3 is the expression x[0]*y[0] + x[1]*y[1] + x[2]*y[2]. If we represent the two vectors as one-dimensional arrays x[] and y[] that are each of length N and of type double, the dot product is easy to compute:

```
double sum = 0.0;
for (int i = 0; i < N; i++)
    sum += x[i]*y[i];
```

| i | x[i] | y[i] | x[i]*y[i] | sum |
|---|------|------|-----------|-----|
|   |      |      |           | 0   |
| 0 | .30  | .50  | .15       | .15 |
| 1 | .60  | .10  | .06       | .21 |
| 2 | .10  | .40  | .04       | .25 |
|   |      |      |           | .25 |

*Trace of dot product computation*

The simplicity of coding such computations makes the use of arrays the natural choice for all kinds of applications. (Note that when we use the notation x[], we are referring to the whole array, as opposed to x[i], which is a reference to the ith entry.)

The accompanying table has many examples of array-processing code, and we will consider even more examples later in the book, because arrays play a central role in processing data in many applications. Before considering more sophisticated examples, we describe a number of important characteristics of programming with arrays.

| | |
|---|---|
| *create an array with random values* | ```double[] a = new double[N];
for (int i = 0; i < N; i++)
   a[i] = Math.random();``` |
| *print the array values, one per line* | ```for (int i = 0; i < N; i++)
   System.out.println(a[i]);``` |
| *find the maximum of the array values* | ```double max = Double.NEGATIVE_INFINITY;
for (int i = 0; i < N; i++)
   if (a[i] > max) max = a[i];``` |
| *compute the average of the array values* | ```double sum = 0.0;
for (int i = 0; i < N; i++)
   sum += a[i];
double average = sum / N;``` |
| *copy to another array* | ```double[] b = new double[N];
for (int i = 0; i < N; i++)
   b[i] = a[i];``` |
| *reverse the elements within an array* | ```for (int i = 0; i < N/2; i++)
{
   double temp = b[i];
   b[i] = b[N-1-i];
   b[N-i-1] = temp;
}``` |

*Typical array-processing code (for arrays of N double values)*

*Zero-based indexing.* We always refer to the first element of an array as a[0], the second as a[1], and so forth. It might seem more natural to you to refer to the first element as a[1], the second value as a[2], and so forth, but starting the indexing with 0 has some advantages and has emerged as the convention used in most modern programming languages. Misunderstanding this convention often leads to *off-by one-errors* that are notoriously difficult to avoid and debug, so be careful!

*Array length.* Once we create an array, its size is fixed. The reason that we need to explicitly create arrays at runtime is that the Java compiler cannot know how much space to reserve for the array at compile time (as it can for primitive-type values). Our convention is to keep the size of the array in a variable N whose value can be set at runtime (usually it is the value of a command-line argument). Java's standard mechanism is to allow a program to refer to the length of an array a[] with the code a.length; we normally use N to create the array, or set the value of N to a.length. Note that the last element of an array is always a[a.length-1].

*Memory representation.* Arrays are fundamental data structures in that they have a direct correspondence with memory systems on virtually all computers. The elements of an array are stored consecutively in memory, so that it is easy to quickly access any array value. Indeed, we can view memory itself as a giant array. On modern computers, memory is implemented in hardware as a sequence of indexed memory locations that each can be quickly accessed with an appropriate index. When referring to computer memory, we normally refer to a location's index as its *address*. It is convenient to think of the name of the array—say, a—as storing the memory address of the first element of the array a[0]. For the purposes of illustration, suppose that the computer's memory is organized as 1,000 values, with addresses from 000 to 999. (This simplified model ignores the fact that array elements can occupy differing amounts of memory depending on their type, but you can ignore such details for the moment.) Now, suppose that an array of eight elements is stored in memory locations 523 through 530. In such a situation, Java would store the memory address (index) of the first array value somewhere else in memory, along with the array length. We refer to the address as a *pointer* and think of it as *pointing to* the referenced memory location. When we specify a[i], the compiler generates code that accesses the desired value by adding the index i to the memory address of the array a[]. For example, the Java code a[4] would generate machine code that finds the value at memory location 523 + 4 = 527. Accessing element i of an array is an efficient operation because it simply requires adding two integers and then referencing memory—just two elementary operations. Extending the model to handle different-sized array elements just involves multiplying the index by the element size before adding to the array address.

*Memory representation*

*Memory allocation.* When you use new to create an array, Java reserves space in memory for it. This process is called *memory allocation*. The same process is required for all variables that you use in a program. We call attention to it now because it is your responsibility to use new to allocate memory for an array before accessing any of its elements. If you fail to adhere to this rule, you will get a compile-time *uninitialized variable* error. Java automatically initializes all of the values in an array when it is created. You should remember that the time required to create an array is proportional to its length.

*Bounds checking.* As already indicated, you must be careful when programming with arrays. It is your responsibility to use legal indices when accessing an array element. If you have created an array of size N and use an index whose value is less than 0 or greater than N-1, your program will terminate with an `ArrayIndex-OutOfBounds` run-time exception. (In many programming languages, such *buffer overflow* conditions are not checked by the system. Such unchecked errors can and do lead to debugging nightmares, but it is also not uncommon for such an error to go unnoticed and remain in a finished program. You might be surprised to know that such a mistake can be exploited by a hacker to take control of a system, even your personal computer, to spread viruses, steal personal information, or wreak other malicious havoc.) The error messages provided by Java may seem annoying to you at first, but they are small price to pay to have a more secure program.

*Setting array values at compile time.* When we have a small number of literal values that we want to keep in array, we can declare and initialize it by listing the values between curly braces, separated by commas. For example, we might use the following code in a program that processes playing cards.

```
String[] suit = { "Clubs", "Diamonds", "Hearts", "Spades" };

String[] rank =
{
    "2", "3", "4", "5", "6", "7", "8", "9", "10",
    "Jack", "Queen", "King", "Ace"
};
```

After creating the two arrays, we can use them to print out a random card name, such as Queen of Clubs, as follows:

```
int i = (int) (Math.random() * rank.length);
int j = (int) (Math.random() * suit.length);
System.out.println(rank[i] + " of " + suit[j]);
```

This code uses the idiom introduced in SECTION 1.2 to generate random indices and then uses the indices to pick strings out of the arrays. Whenever the values of all array entries are known at compile time (and the size of the array is not too large) it makes sense to use this method of initializing the array—just put all the values in braces on the right hand side of an assignment in the array declaration. Doing so implies array creation, so the new keyword is not needed.

*Setting array values at runtime.* A more typical situation is when we wish to compute the values to be stored in an array. In this case, we can use array names with indices in the same way we use variable names on the left side of assignment statements. For example, we might use the following code to initialize an array of size 52 that represents a deck of playing cards, using the two arrays just defined:

```
String[] deck = new String[suit.length * rank.length];
for (int i = 0; i < suit.length; i++)
   for (int j = 0; j < rank.length; j++)
      deck[rank.length*i + j] = rank[i] + " of " + suit[j];
```

After this code has been executed, if you were to print out the contents of deck in order from deck[0] through deck[51] using System.out.println(), you would get the sequence

```
2 of Clubs
2 of Diamonds
2 of Hearts
2 of Spades
3 of Clubs
3 of Diamonds
...
Ace of Hearts
Ace of Spades
```

*Exchange.* Frequently, we wish to exchange two values in an array. Continuing our example with playing cards, the following code exchanges the cards at position i and j using the same idiom that we traced as our first example of the use of assignment statements in SECTION 1.2:

```
String t = deck[i];
deck[i] = deck[j];
deck[j] = t;
```

When we use this code, we are assured that we are perhaps changing the *order* of the values in the array but not the *set* of values in the array. When i and j are equal, the array is unchanged. When i and j are not equal, the values a[i] and a[j] are found in different places in the array. For example, if we were to use this code with i equal to 1 and j equal to 4 in the deck array of the previous example, it would leave 3 of Clubs in deck[1] and 2 of Diamonds in deck[4].

*Shuffle.* The following code shuffles our deck of cards:

```
int N = deck.length;
for (int i = 0; i < N; i++)
{
    int r = i + (int) (Math.random() * (N-i));
    String t = deck[i];
    deck[i] = deck[r];
    deck[r] = t;
}
```

Proceeding from left to right, we pick a random card from `deck[i]` through `deck[N-1]` (each card equally likely) and exchange it with `deck[i]`. This code is more sophisticated than it might seem: First, we ensure that the cards in the deck after the shuffle are the same as the cards in the deck before the shuffle by using the exchange idiom. Second, we ensure that the shuffle is random by choosing uniformly from the cards not yet chosen.

*Sampling without replacement.* In many situations, we want to draw a random sample from a set such that each member of the set appears at most once in the sample. Drawing numbered ping-pong balls from a basket for a lottery is an example of this kind of sample, as is dealing a hand from a deck of cards. `Sample` (PROGRAM 1.4.1) illustrates how to sample, using the basic operation underlying shuffling. It takes command-line arguments M and N and creates a *permutation* of size N (a rearrangement of the integers from 0 to N-1) whose first M entries com-

| i | r | perm |  |  |  |  |  |  |  |  |  |  |  |  |  |  |  |
|---|---|---|---|---|---|---|---|---|---|---|---|---|---|---|---|---|---|
|   |   | 0 | 1 | 2 | 3 | 4 | 5 | 6 | 7 | 8 | 9 | 10 | 11 | 12 | 13 | 14 | 15 |
|   |   | 0 | 1 | 2 | 3 | 4 | 5 | 6 | 7 | 8 | 9 | 10 | 11 | 12 | 13 | 14 | 15 |
| 0 | 9 | 9 | 1 | 2 | 3 | 4 | 5 | 6 | 7 | 8 | 0 | 10 | 11 | 12 | 13 | 14 | 15 |
| 1 | 5 | 9 | 5 | 2 | 3 | 4 | 1 | 6 | 7 | 8 | 0 | 10 | 11 | 12 | 13 | 14 | 15 |
| 2 | 13 | 9 | 5 | 13 | 3 | 4 | 1 | 6 | 7 | 8 | 0 | 10 | 11 | 12 | 2 | 14 | 15 |
| 3 | 5 | 9 | 5 | 13 | 1 | 4 | 3 | 6 | 7 | 8 | 0 | 10 | 11 | 12 | 2 | 14 | 15 |
| 4 | 11 | 9 | 5 | 13 | 1 | 11 | 3 | 6 | 7 | 8 | 0 | 10 | 4 | 12 | 2 | 14 | 15 |
| 5 | 8 | 9 | 5 | 13 | 1 | 11 | 8 | 6 | 7 | 3 | 0 | 10 | 4 | 12 | 2 | 14 | 15 |
|   |   | 9 | 5 | 13 | 1 | 11 | 8 | 6 | 7 | 3 | 0 | 10 | 4 | 12 | 2 | 14 | 15 |

*Trace of* `java Sample 6 16`

**Program 1.4.1  *Sampling without replacement***

```
public class Sample
{
   public static void main(String[] args)
   {  // Print a random sample of M integers
      // from 0 ... N-1 (no duplicates).
      int M = Integer.parseInt(args[0]);
      int N = Integer.parseInt(args[1]);
      int[] perm = new int[N];

      // Initialize perm[].
      for (int j = 0; j < N; j++)
         perm[j] = j;

      // Take sample.
      for (int i = 0; i < M; i++)
      {  // Exchange perm[i] with a random element to its right.
         int r = i + (int) (Math.random() * (N-i));
         int t = perm[r];
         perm[r] = perm[i];
         perm[i] = t;
      }

      // Print sample.
      for (int i = 0; i < M; i++)
         System.out.print(perm[i] + " ");
      System.out.println();
   }
}
```

| M | sample size |
|---|---|
| N | range |
| perm[] | permutation of 0 to N-1 |

*This program takes two command-line arguments M and N and produces a sample of M of the integers from 0 to N-1. This process is useful, not just in state and local lotteries, but in scientific applications of all sorts. If the first argument is equal to the second, the result is a random permutation of the integers from 0 to N-1. If the first argument is greater than the second, the program will terminate with an ArrayOutOfBounds exception.*

```
% java Sample 6 16
9 5 13 1 11 8

% java Sample 10 1000
656 488 298 534 811 97 813 156 424 109

% java Sample 20 20
6 12 9 8 13 19 0 2 4 5 18 1 14 16 17 3 7 11 10 15
```

prise a random sample. The accompanying trace of the contents of the perm[] array at the end of each iteration of the main loop (for a run where the values of *M* and *N* are 6 and 16, respectively) illustrates the process.

If the values of r are chosen such that each value in the given range is equally likely, then perm[0] through perm[M-1] are a random sample at the end of the process (even though some elements might move multiple times) because each element in the sample is chosen by taking each item not yet sampled, with equal probability for each choice. One important reason to explicitly compute the permutation is that we can use it to print out a random sample of *any* array by using the elements of the permutation as indices into the array. Doing so is often an attractive alternative to actually rearranging the array because it may need to be in order for some other reason (for instance, a company might wish to draw a random sample from a list of customers that is kept in alphabetical order). To see how this trick works, suppose that we wish to draw a random poker hand from our deck[] array, constructed as just described. We use the code in Sample with *N* = 52 and *M* = 5 and replace perm[i] with deck[perm[i]] in the System.out.print() statement (and change it to println()), resulting in output such as the following:

```
3 of Clubs
Jack of Hearts
6 of Spades
Ace of Clubs
10 of Diamonds
```

Sampling like this is widely used as the basis for statistical studies in polling, scientific research, and many other applications, whenever we want to draw conclusions about a large population by analyzing a small random sample.

*Precomputed values.* One simple application of arrays is to save values that you have computed, for later use. As an example, suppose that you are writing a program that performs calculations using small values of the harmonic numbers (see PROGRAM 1.3.5). An efficient approach is to save the values in an array, as follows:

```
double[] H = new double[N];
for (int i = 1; i < N; i++)
    H[i] = H[i-1] + 1.0/i;
```

Then you can just use the code H[i] to refer to any of the values. Precomputing values in this way is an example of a *space-time tradeoff:* by investing in space (to save the values) we save time (since we do not need to recompute them). This method is not effective if we need values for huge N, but it is very effective if we need values for small N many different times.

*Simplifying repetitive code.* As an example of another simple application of arrays, consider the following code fragment, which prints out the name of a month given its number (1 for January, 2 for February, and so forth):

```
if        (m ==  1) System.out.println("Jan");
else if (m ==  2) System.out.println("Feb");
else if (m ==  3) System.out.println("Mar");
else if (m ==  4) System.out.println("Apr");
else if (m ==  5) System.out.println("May");
else if (m ==  6) System.out.println("Jun");
else if (m ==  7) System.out.println("Jul");
else if (m ==  8) System.out.println("Aug");
else if (m ==  9) System.out.println("Sep");
else if (m == 10) System.out.println("Oct");
else if (m == 11) System.out.println("Nov");
else if (m == 12) System.out.println("Dec");
```

We could also use a `switch` statement, but a much more compact alternative is to use a `String` array consisting of the names of each month:

```
String[] months =
{
    "", "Jan", "Feb", "Mar", "Apr", "May", "Jun",
         "Jul", "Aug", "Sep", "Oct", "Nov", "Dec"
};
System.out.println(months[m]);
```

This technique would be especially useful if you needed to access the name of a month by its number in several different places in your program. Note that we intentionally waste one slot in the array (element 0) to make `months[1]` correspond to January, as required.

*Assignments and equality tests.* Suppose that you have created the two arrays `a[]` and `b[]`. What does it mean to assign one to the other with the code `a = b;`? Similarly, what does it mean to test whether the two arrays are equal with the code `(a == b)`? The answers to these questions may not be what you first assume, but if you think about the array memory representation, you will see that Java's interpretation of these operations makes sense: An assignment makes the names a and b refer to the same array. The alternative would be to have an implied loop that assigns each value in b to the corresponding value in a. Similarly, an equality test checks whether the two names refer to the same array. The alternative would be to have an implied loop that tests whether each value in one array is equal to the corresponding value in the other array. In both cases, the implementation in Java is very simple: it just performs the standard operation as if the array name were a variable whose value is the memory address of the array. Note that there are many other operations that you might want to perform on arrays: for example, it would be nice in some applications to say a = a + b and have it mean "add the corresponding element in b[] to each element in a[]," but that statement is not legal in Java. Instead, we write an explicit loop to perform all the additions. We will consider in detail Java's mechanism for satisfying such higher-level programming needs in SECTION 3.2. In typical applications, we use this mechanism, so we rarely need to use Java's assignments and equality tests with arrays.

WITH THESE BASIC DEFINITIONS AND EXAMPLES out of the way, we can now consider two applications that both address interesting classical problems and illustrate the fundamental importance of arrays in efficient computation. In both cases, the idea of using data to index into an array plays a central role and enables a computation that would not otherwise be feasible.

**Coupon collector**    Suppose that you have a shuffled deck of cards and you turn them face up, one by one. How many cards do you need to turn up before you have seen one of each suit? How many cards do you need to turn up before seeing one of each value? These are examples of the famous *coupon collector* problem. In general, suppose that a trading card company issues trading cards with $N$ different possible cards: how many do you have to collect before you have all $N$ possibilities, assuming that each possibility is equally likely for each card that you collect?

*Coupon collection*

Coupon collecting is no toy problem. For example, it is very often the case that scientists want to know whether a sequence that arises in nature has the same characteristics as a random sequence. If so, that fact might be of interest; if not, further investigation may be warranted to look for patterns that might be of importance. For example, such tests are used by scientists to decide which parts of genomes are worth studying. One effective test for whether a sequence is truly random is

**Program 1.4.2   *Coupon collector simulation***

```java
public class CouponCollector
{
    public static void main(String[] args)
    {   // Generate random values in (0..N] until finding each one.
        int N = Integer.parseInt(args[0]);
        boolean[] found = new boolean[N];
        int cardcnt = 0, valcnt = 0;
        while (valcnt < N)
        {   // Generate another value.
            int val = (int) (Math.random() * N);
            cardcnt++;
            if (!found[val])
            {
                valcnt++;
                found[val] = true;
            }
        }  // N different values found.
        System.out.println(cardcnt);
    }
}
```

| | |
|---|---|
| N | *range* |
| cardcnt | *values generated* |
| valcnt | *different values found* |
| found[] | *table of found values* |

*This program simulates coupon collection by taking a command-line argument N and generating random numbers between 0 and N-1 until getting every possible value.*

```
% java CouponCollector 1000
6583
% java CouponCollector 1000
6477
% java CouponCollector 1000000
12782673
```

the *coupon collector test*: compare the number of elements that need to be examined before all values are found against the corresponding number for a uniformly random sequence. CouponCollector (PROGRAM 1.4.2) is an example program that simulates this process and illustrates the utility of arrays. It takes the value of *N* from the command line and generates a sequence of random integer values between 0 and $N-1$ using the code (int) (Math.random() * N) (see PROGRAM 1.2.5). Each value represents a card: for each card, we want to know if we have seen that value before. To maintain that knowledge, we use an array found[], which uses the card value as an index: found[i] is true if we have seen a card with value i and false if we have not. When we get a new card that is represented by the integer val, we check whether we have seen its value before simply by accessing found[val]. The computation consists of keeping count of the number of distinct values seen and the number of cards generated and printing the latter when the former gets to N.

| val | found | | | | | | valcnt | cardcnt |
|-----|---|---|---|---|---|---|--------|---------|
|     | 0 | 1 | 2 | 3 | 4 | 5 |        |         |
|     | F | F | F | F | F | F | 0      | 0       |
| 2   | F | F | T | F | F | F | 1      | 1       |
| 0   | T | F | T | F | F | F | 2      | 2       |
| 4   | T | F | T | F | T | F | 3      | 3       |
| 0   | T | F | T | F | T | F | 3      | 4       |
| 1   | T | T | T | F | T | F | 4      | 5       |
| 2   | T | T | T | F | T | F | 4      | 6       |
| 5   | T | T | T | F | T | T | 5      | 7       |
| 0   | T | T | T | F | T | T | 5      | 8       |
| 1   | T | T | T | F | T | T | 5      | 9       |
| 3   | T | T | T | T | T | T | 6      | 10      |

*Trace for a typical run of* java CouponCollector 6

As usual, the best way to understand a program is to consider a trace of the values of its variables for a typical run. It is easy to add code to CouponCollector that produces a trace that gives the values of the variables at the end of the while loop for a typical run. In the accompanying figure, we use F for the value false and T for the value true to make the trace easier to follow. Tracing programs that use large arrays can be a challenge: when you have an array of size $N$ in your program, it represents $N$ variables, so you have to list them all. Tracing programs that use Math.random() also can be a challenge because you get a different trace every time you run the program. Accordingly, we check relationships among variables carefully. Here, note that valcnt always is equal to the number of true values in found[].

Without arrays, we could not contemplate simulating the coupon collector process for huge $N$; with arrays it is easy to do so. We will see many examples of such processes throughout the book.

**Sieve of Eratosthenes** Prime numbers play an important role in mathematics and computation, including cryptography. A *prime number* is an integer greater than one whose only positive divisors are one and itself. The prime counting function $\pi(N)$ is the number of primes less than or equal to $N$. For example, $\pi(25) = 9$ since the first nine primes are 2, 3, 5, 7, 11, 13, 17, 19, and 23. This function plays a central role in number theory.

*Program 1.4.3*  *Sieve of Eratosthenes*

```
public class PrimeSieve
{
   public static void main(String[] args)
   {  // Print the number of primes <= N.
      int N = Integer.parseInt(args[0]);
      boolean[] isPrime = new boolean[N+1];
      for (int i = 2; i <= N; i++)
         isPrime[i] = true;

      for (int i = 2; i <= N/i; i++)
      {  if (isPrime[i])
         {  // Mark multiples of i as nonprime.
            for (int j = i; j <= N/i; j++)
               isPrime[i * j] = false;
         }
      }

      // Count the primes.
      int primes = 0;
      for (int i = 2; i <= N; i++)
         if (isPrime[i]) primes++;
      System.out.println(primes);
   }
}
```

| N | argument |
|---|---|
| isPrime[i] | is i prime? |
| primes | prime counter |

*This program takes a command-line argument N and computes the number of primes less than or equal to N. To do so, it computes an array of boolean values with isPrime[i] set to true if i is prime, and to false otherwise. First, it sets to true all array elements in order to indicate that no numbers are initially known to be nonprime. Then it sets to false array elements corresponding to indices that are known to be nonprime (multiples of known primes). If a[i] is still true after all multiples of smaller primes have been set to false, then we know i to be prime. The termination test in the second for loop is i <= N/i instead of the naive i <= N because any number with no factor less than N/i has no factor greater than N/i, so we do not have to look for such factors. This improvement makes it possible to run the program for large N.*

```
% java PrimeSieve 25
9
% java PrimeSieve 100
25
% java PrimeSieve 1000000000
50847534
```

| i | 2 | 3 | 4 | 5 | 6 | 7 | 8 | 9 | 10 | 11 | 12 | 13 | 14 | 15 | 16 | 17 | 18 | 19 | 20 | 21 | 22 | 23 | 24 | 25 |
|---|---|---|---|---|---|---|---|---|----|----|----|----|----|----|----|----|----|----|----|----|----|----|----|----|
|   | T | T | T | T | T | T | T | T | T | T | T | T | T | T | T | T | T | T | T | T | T | T | T | T |
| 2 | T | T | F | T | F | T | F | T | F | T | F | T | F | T | F | T | F | T | F | T | F | T | F | T |
| 3 | T | T | F | T | F | T | F | F | F | F | T | F | T | F | F | F | T | F | T | F | F | T | F | T |
| 5 | T | T | F | T | F | T | F | F | F | F | T | F | T | F | F | F | T | F | T | F | F | T | F | F |
|   | T | T | F | T | F | T | F | F | F | F | T | F | T | F | F | F | T | F | T | F | F | T | F | F |

*Trace of* java PrimeSieve 25

One approach to counting primes is to use a program like Factors (PROGRAM 1.3.9). Specifically, we could modify the code in Factors to set a boolean value to be true if a given number is prime and false otherwise (instead of printing out factors), then enclose that code in a loop that increments a counter for each prime number. This approach is effective for small $N$, but becomes too slow as $N$ grows.

PrimeSieve (PROGRAM 1.4.3) takes a command-line integer N and computes the prime count using a technique known as the *Sieve of Eratosthenes*. The program uses a boolean array isPrime[] to record which integers are prime. The goal is to set isPrime[i] to true if i is prime, and to false otherwise. The sieve works as follows: Initially, set all array elements to true, indicating that no factors of any integer have yet been found. Then, repeat the following steps as long as i <= N/i:

- Find the next smallest i for which no factors have been found.
- Leave isPrime[i] as true since i has no smaller factors.
- Set the isPrime[] entries for all multiples of i to be false.

When the nested for loop ends, we have set the isPrime[] entries for all nonprimes to be false and have left the isPrime[] entries for all primes as true. With one more pass through the array, we can count the number of primes less than or equal to N. As usual, it is easy to add code to print a trace. For programs such as Prime-Sieve, you have to be a bit careful—it contains a nested for-if-for, so you have to pay attention to the braces in order to put the print code in the correct place. Note that we stop when i > N/i, just as we did for Factors.

With PrimeSieve, we can compute $\pi(N)$ for large $N$, limited primarily by the maximum array size allowed by Java. This is another example of a space-time tradeoff. Programs like PrimeSieve play an important role in helping mathematicians to develop the theory of numbers, which has many important applications.

**Two-dimensional arrays**   In many applications, a convenient way to store information is to use a table of numbers organized in a rectangular table and refer to *rows* and *columns* in the table. For example, a teacher might need to maintain a table with a row corresponding to each student and a column corresponding to each assignment, a scientist might need to maintain a table of experimental data with rows corresponding to experiments and columns corresponding to various outcomes, or a programmer might want to prepare an image for display by setting a table of pixels to various grayscale values or colors.

The mathematical abstraction corresponding to such tables is a *matrix*; the corresponding Java construct is a *two-dimensional array*. You are likely to have already encountered many applications of matrices and two-dimensional arrays, and you will certainly encounter many others in science, in engineering, and in computing applications, as we will demonstrate with examples throughout this book. As with vectors and one-dimensional arrays, many of the most important applications involve processing large amounts of data, and we defer considering those applications until we consider input and output, in SECTION 1.5.

*Anatomy of a two-dimensional array*

Extending Java array constructs to handle two-dimensional arrays is straightforward. To refer to the element in row i and column j of a two-dimensional array a[][], we use the notation a[i][j]; to declare a two-dimensional array, we add another pair of brackets; and to create the array, we specify the number of rows followed by the number of columns after the type name (both within brackets), as follows:

```
double[][] a = new double[M][N];
```

We refer to such an array as an *M*-by-*N* array. By convention, the first dimension is the number of rows and the second is the number of columns. As with one-dimensional arrays, Java initializes all entries in arrays of numbers to zero and in arrays of boolean values to `false`.

*Initialization.*   Default initialization of two-dimensional arrays is useful because it masks more code than for one-dimensional arrays. The following code is equivalent to the single-line create-and-initialize idiom that we just considered:

```
double[][] a;
a = new double[M][N];
for (int i = 0; i < M; i++)
{  // Initialize the ith row.
   for (int j = 0; j < N; j++)
      a[i][j] = 0.0;
}
```

This code is superfluous when initializing to zero, but the nested for loops are needed to initialize to some other value(s). As you will see, this code is a model for the code that we use to access or modify each element of a two-dimensional array.

*Output.* We use nested for loops for many array-processing operations. For example, to print an *M*-by-*N* array in the familiar tabular format, we would use the following code

```
for (int i = 0; i < M; i++)
{  // Print the ith row.
   for (int j = 0; j < N; j++)
      System.out.print(a[i][j] + " ");
   System.out.println();
}
```

regardless of the array elements' type. If desired, we could add code to embellish the output with row and column numbers (see EXERCISE 1.4.6), but Java programmers typically tabulate arrays with row numbers running top to bottom from 0 and column number running left to right from 0. Generally, we also do so and do not bother to use labels.

*Memory representation.* Java represents a two-dimensional array as an array of arrays. A matrix with *M* rows and *N* columns is actually an array of length *M*, each entry of which is an array of length *N*. In a two-dimensional Java array a[][], we can use the code a[i] to refer to the ith row (which is a one-dimensional array), but we have no corresponding way to refer to a column.

a[][]

| a[0][0] | a[0][1] | a[0][2] |
|---------|---------|---------|
| a[1][0] | a[1][1] | a[1][2] |
| a[2][0] | a[2][1] | a[2][2] |
| a[3][0] | a[3][1] | a[3][2] |
| a[4][0] | a[4][1] | a[4][2] |
| a[5][0] | a[5][1] | a[5][2] |
| a[6][0] | a[6][1] | a[6][2] |
| a[7][0] | a[7][1] | a[7][2] |
| a[8][0] | a[8][1] | a[8][2] |
| a[9][0] | a[9][1] | a[9][2] |

a[5]→

*A 10-by-3 array*

*Setting values at compile time.* The Java method for initializing an array of values at compile time follows immediately from the representation. A two-dimensional array is an array of rows, each row initialized as a one-dimensional array. To initialize a two-dimensional array, we enclose in braces a list of terms to initialize the rows, separated by commas. Each term in the list is itself a list: the values for the array elements in the row, enclosed in braces and separated by commas.

*Spreadsheets.* One familiar use of arrays is a *spreadsheet* for maintaining a table of numbers. For example, a teacher with $M$ students and $N$ test grades for each student might maintain an $(M+1)$-by-$(N+1)$ array, reserving the last column for each student's average grade and the last row for the average test grades. Even though we typically do such computations within specialized applications, it is worthwhile to study the underlying code as an introduction to array processing. To compute the average grade for each student (average values for each row), sum the entries for each row and divide by $N$. The row-by-row order in which this code processes the matrix

```
int[][] a =
{
    { 99, 85, 98,  0 },
    { 98, 57, 78,  0 },
    { 92, 77, 76,  0 },
    { 94, 32, 11,  0 },
    { 99, 34, 22,  0 },
    { 90, 46, 54,  0 },
    { 76, 59, 88,  0 },
    { 92, 66, 89,  0 },
    { 97, 71, 24,  0 },
    { 89, 29, 38,  0 },
    {  0,  0,  0,  0 }
};
```

*Compile-time initialization of a two-dimensional array*

*Compute row averages*

```
for (int i = 0; i < M; i++)
{   // Compute average for row i
    double sum = 0.0;
    for (int j = 0; j < N; j++)
        sum += a[i][j];
    a[i][N] = (int) Math.round(sum/N);
}
```

*Compute column averages*

```
for (int j = 0; j < N; j++)
{   // Compute average for column j
    double sum = 0.0;
    for (int i = 0; i < M; i++)
        sum += a[i][j];
    a[M][j] = (int) Math.round(sum/M);
}
```

*Typical spreadsheet calculations*

entries is known as *row-major* order. Similarly, to compute the average test grade (average values for each column), sum the entries for each column and divide by *M*. The column-by-column order in which this code processes the matrix entries is known as *column-major* order.

a[][]

```
.70 .20 .10
.30 .60 .10
.50 .10 .40
```
a[1][2]

b[][]
```
.80 .30 .50
.10 .40 .10
.10 .30 .40
```
b[1][2]

c[][]
```
1.5 .50 .60
.40 1.0 .20
.60 .40 .80
```
c[1][2]

*Matrix addition*

*Matrix operations.* Typical applications in science and engineering involve representing matrices as two-dimensional arrays and then implementing various mathematical operations with matrix operands. Again, even though such processing is often done within specialized applications, it is worthwhile for you to understand the underlying computation. For example, we can *add* two *N*-by-*N* matrices as follows:

```
double[][] c = new double[N][N];
for (int i = 0; i < N; i++)
    for (int j = 0; j < N; j++)
        c[i][j] = a[i][j] + b[i][j];
```

Similarly, we can *multiply* two matrices. You may have learned matrix multiplication, but if you do not recall or are not familiar with it, the Java code below for square matrices is essentially the same as the mathematical definition. Each entry c[i][j] in the product of a[] and b[] is computed by taking the dot product of row i of a[] with column j of b[].

```
double[][] c = new double[N][N];
for (int i = 0; i < N; i++)
{
    for (int j = 0; j < N; j++)
    {
        // Compute dot product of row i and column j.
        for (int k = 0; k < N; k++)
            c[i][j] += a[i][k]*b[k][j];
    }
}
```

The definition extends to matrices that are not necessarily square (see EXERCISE 1.4.17).

a[][]
```
.70 .20 .10
.30 .60 .10  ← row 1
.50 .10 .40
```

b[][]    column 2
            ↓
```
.80 .30 .50
.10 .40 .10
.10 .30 .40
```

c[1][2] = .3 *.5
        + .6 *.1
        + .1 *.4
        = .25

c[][]
```
.59 .32 .41
.31 .36 .25
.45 .31 .42
```

*Matrix multiplication*

*Special cases of matrix multiplication.* Two special cases of matrix multiplication are important. These special cases occur when one of the dimensions of one of the matrices is 1, so it may be viewed as a vector. We have *matrix-vector multiplication*, where we multiply an $M$-by-$N$ matrix by a *column vector* (an $N$-by-1 matrix) to get an $M$-by-1 column vector result (each entry in the result is the dot product of the corresponding row in the matrix with the operand vector). The second case is *vector-matrix multiplication*, where we multiply a *row vector* (a 1-by-$M$ matrix) by an $M$-by-$N$ matrix to get a 1-by-$N$ row vector result (each entry in the result is the dot product of the operand vector with the corresponding column in the matrix). These operations provide a succinct way to express numerous matrix calculations. For example, the row-average computation for such a spreadsheet with $M$ rows and $N$ columns is equivalent to a matrix-vector multiplication where the column vector has $M$ entries all equal to $1/M$. Similarly, the column-average computation in such a spreadsheet is equivalent to a vector-matrix multiplication where the row vector has $N$ entries all equal to $1/N$. We return to vector-matrix multiplication in the context of an important application at the end of this chapter.

*Matrix-vector multiplication* a[][]*x[] = b[]

```
for (int i = 0; i < M; i++)
{  // Dot product of row i and x[].
   for (int j = 0; j < N; j++)
      b[i] += a[i][j]*x[j];
}
```

*Vector-matrix multiplication* y[]*a[][] = c[]

```
for (int j = 0; j < N; j++)
{  // Dot product of y[] and column j.
   for (int i = 0; i < M; i++)
      c[j] += y[i]*a[i][j];
}
```

*Matrix-vector and vector-matrix multiplication*

*Ragged arrays.* There is actually no requirement that all rows in a two-dimensional array have the same length—an array with rows of nonuniform length is known as a *ragged array* (see EXERCISE 1.4.32 for an example application). The possibility of ragged arrays creates the need for more care in crafting array-processing code. For example, this code prints the contents of a ragged array:

```java
for (int i = 0; i < a.length; i++)
{
   for (int j = 0; j < a[i].length; j++)
      System.out.print(a[i][j] + " ");
   System.out.println();
}
```

This code tests your understanding of Java arrays, so you should take the time to study it. In this book, we normally use square or rectangular arrays, whose dimension is given by a variable M or N. Code that uses a[i].length in this way is a clear signal to you that an array is ragged.

*Multidimensional arrays.* The same notation extends to allow us to write code using arrays that have any number of dimensions. For instance, we can declare and initialize a three-dimensional array with the code

```java
double[][][] a = new double[N][N][N];
```

and then refer to an entry with code like a[i][j][k], and so forth.

TWO-DIMENSIONAL ARRAYS PROVIDE A NATURAL REPRESENTATION for matrices, which are omnipresent in science, mathematics, and engineering. They also provide a natural way to organize large amounts of data, a key factor in spreadsheets and many other computing applications. Through Cartesian coordinates, two- and three-dimensional arrays also provide the basis for a models of the physical world. We consider their use in all three arenas throughout this book.

**Example: self-avoiding random walks**  Suppose that you leave your dog in the middle of a large city whose streets form a familiar grid pattern. We assume that there are *N* north-south streets and *N* east-west streets all regularly spaced and fully intersecting in a pattern known as a *lattice.* Trying to escape the city, the dog makes a random choice of which way to go at each intersection, but knows by scent to avoid visiting any place previously visited. But it is possible for the dog to get stuck in a dead end where there is no choice but to revisit some intersection. What is the chance that this will happen? This amusing problem is a simple example of a famous model known as the *self-avoiding random walk,* which has important scientific applications in the study of polymers and in statistical mechanics, among many others. For example, you can see

*dead end*

*escape*

*Self-avoiding walks*

that this process models a chain of material growing a bit at a time, until no growth is possible. To better understand such processes, scientists seek to understand the properties of self-avoiding walks.

The dog's escape probability is certainly dependent on the size of the city. In a tiny 5-by-5 city, it is easy to convince yourself that the dog is certain to escape. But what are the chances of escape when the city is large? We are also interested in other parameters. For example, how long is the dog's path, on the average? How often does the dog come within one block of a previous position other than the one just left, on the average? How often does the dog come within one block of escaping? These sorts of properties are important in the various applications just mentioned.

`SelfAvoidingWalk` (PROGRAM 1.4.4) is a simulation of this situation that uses a two-dimensional `boolean` array, where each entry represents an intersection. The value `true` indicates that the dog has visited the intersection; `false` indicates that the dog has not visited the intersection. The path starts in the center and takes random steps to places not yet visited until getting stuck or escaping at a boundary. For simplicity, the code is written so that if a random choice is made to go to a spot that has already been visited, it takes no action, trusting that some subsequent random choice will find a new place (which is assured because the code explicitly tests for a dead end and leaves the loop in that case).

Note that the code depends on Java initializing all of the array entries to `false` for each experiment. It also exhibits an important programming technique where we code the loop exit test in the `while` statement as a *guard* against an illegal statement in the body of the loop. In this case, the `while` loop continuation test serves as a guard against an out-of-bounds array access within the loop. This corresponds to checking whether the dog has escaped. Within the loop, a successful dead-end test results in a `break` out of the loop.

As you can see from the sample runs, the unfortunate truth is that your dog is nearly certain to get trapped in a dead end in a large city. If you are interested in learning more about self-avoiding walks, you can find several suggestions in the exercises. For example, the dog is virtually certain to escape in the three-dimensional version of the problem. While this is an intuitive result that is confirmed by our tests, the development of a mathematical model that explains the behavior of self-avoiding walks is a famous open problem: despite extensive research, no one knows a succinct mathematical expression for the escape probability, the average length of the path, or any other important parameter.

**Program 1.4.4   Self-avoiding random walks**

```
public class SelfAvoidingWalk
{
   public static void main(String[] args)

   { // Do T random self-avoiding walks
     //    in an N-by-N lattice
     int N = Integer.parseInt(args[0]);
     int T = Integer.parseInt(args[1]);
     int deadEnds = 0;
     for (int t = 0; t < T; t++)
     {
        boolean[][] a = new boolean[N][N];
        int x = N/2, y = N/2;
        while (x > 0 && x < N-1 && y > 0 && y < N-1)
        { // Check for dead end and make a random move.
           a[x][y] = true;
           if (a[x-1][y] && a[x+1][y] && a[x][y-1] && a[x][y+1])
           { deadEnds++; break;  }
           double r = Math.random();
           if       (r < 0.25) { if (!a[x+1][y]) x++; }
           else if (r < 0.50) { if (!a[x-1][y]) x--; }
           else if (r < 0.75) { if (!a[x][y+1]) y++; }
           else if (r < 1.00) { if (!a[x][y-1]) y--; }
        }
     }
     System.out.println(100*deadEnds/T + "% dead ends");
   }
}
```

| N | lattice size |
|---|---|
| T | number of trials |
| deadEnds | trials resulting in a dead end |
| a[][] | intersections visited |
| x, y | current position |
| r | random number in (0, 1) |

This program takes command-line arguments N and T and computes T self-avoiding walks in an N-by-N lattice. For each walk, it creates a boolean array, starts the walk in the center, and continues until either a dead end or a boundary is reached. The result of the computation is the percentage of dead ends. As usual, increasing the number of experiments increases the precision of the results.

```
% java SelfAvoidingWalk 5 100
0% dead ends
% java SelfAvoidingWalk 20 100
36% dead ends
% java SelfAvoidingWalk 40 100
80% dead ends
% java SelfAvoidingWalk 80 100
98% dead ends
% java SelfAvoidingWalk 160 100
100% dead ends
```

```
% java SelfAvoidingWalk 5 1000
0% dead ends
% java SelfAvoidingWalk 20 1000
32% dead ends
% java SelfAvoidingWalk 40 1000
70% dead ends
% java SelfAvoidingWalk 80 1000
95% dead ends
% java SelfAvoidingWalk 160 1000
100% dead ends
```

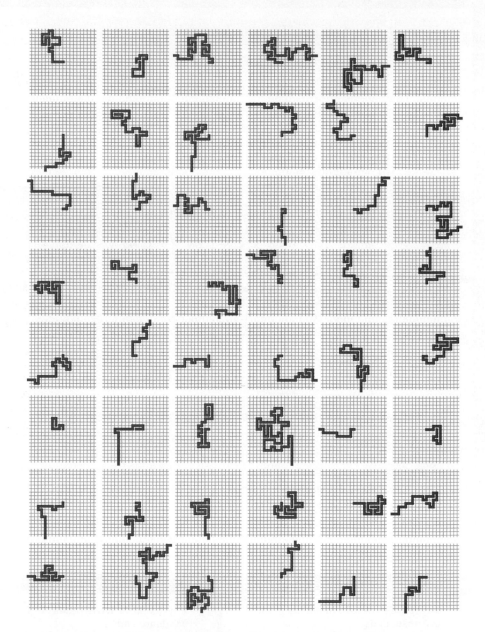

*Self-avoiding random walks in a 21-by-21 grid*

**Summary**   Arrays are the fourth basic element (after assignments, conditionals, and loops) found in virtually every programming language, completing our coverage of basic Java constructs. As you have seen with the sample programs that we have presented, you can write programs that can solve all sorts of problems using just these constructs.

Arrays are prominent in many of the programs that we consider, and the basic operations that we have discussed here will serve you well in addressing many programming tasks. When you are not using arrays explicitly (and you are sure to be doing so frequently), you will be using them implicitly, because all computers have a memory that is conceptually equivalent to an indexed array.

The fundamental ingredient that arrays add to our programs is a potentially huge increase in the size of a program's *state*. The state of a program can be defined as the information you need to know to understand what a program is doing. In a program without arrays, if you know the values of the variables and which statement is the next to be executed, you can normally determine what the program will do next. When we trace a program, we are essentially tracking its state. When a program uses arrays, however, there can be too huge a number of values (each of which might be changed in each statement) for us to effectively track them all. This difference makes writing programs with arrays more of a challenge than writing programs without them.

Arrays directly represent vectors and matrices, so they are of direct use in computations associated with many basic problems in science and engineering. Arrays also provide a succinct notation for manipulating a potentially huge amount of data in a uniform way, so they play a critical role in any application that involves processing large amounts of data, as you will see throughout this book.

## Q&A

**Q.** Some Java programmers use `int a[]` instead of `int[] a` to declare arrays. What's the difference?

**A.** In Java, both are legal and equivalent. The former is how arrays are declared in C. The latter is the preferred style in Java since the type of the variable `int[]` more clearly indicates that it is an *array* of integers.

**Q.** Why do array indices start at 0 instead of 1?

**A.** This convention originated with machine-language programming, where the address of an array element would be computed by adding the index to the address of the beginning of an array. Starting indices at 1 would entail either a waste of space at the beginning of the array or a waste of time to subtract the 1.

**Q.** What happens if I use a negative number to index an array?

**A.** The same thing as when you use an index that is too big. Whenever a program attempts to index an array with an index that is not between zero and the array length minus one, Java will issue an `ArrayIndexOutOfBoundsException` and terminate the program.

**Q.** What happens when I compare two arrays with `(a == b)`?

**A.** The expression evaluates to `true` only if `a[]` and `b[]` refer to the same array, not if they have the same sequence of elements. Unfortunately, this is rarely what you want.

**Q.** If `a[]` is an array, why does `System.out.println(a)` print out a hexadecimal integer, like `@f62373`, instead of the elements of the array?

**A.** Good question. It is printing out the memory address of the array, which, unfortunately, is rarely what you want.

**Q.** What other pitfalls should I watch out for when using arrays?

**A.** It is very important to remember that Java *always* initializes arrays when you create them, so that *creating an array takes time proportional to the size of the array*.

# *Exercises*

**1.4.1**   Write a program that declares and initializes an array a[] of size 1000 and accesses a[1000]. Does your program compile? What happens when you run it?

**1.4.2**   Describe and explain what happens when you try to compile a program with the following statement:

```
int N = 1000;
int[] a = new int[N*N*N*N];
```

**1.4.3**   Given two vectors of length N that are represented with one-dimensional arrays, write a code fragment that computes the *Euclidean distance* between them (the square root of the sums of the squares of the differences between corresponding entries).

**1.4.4**   Write a code fragment that reverses the order of a one-dimensional array a[] of String values. Do not create another array to hold the result. *Hint*: Use the code in the text for exchanging two elements.

**1.4.5**   What is wrong with the following code fragment?

```
int[] a;
for (int i = 0; i < 10; i++)
   a[i] = i * i;
```

*Solution.*   It does not allocate memory for a[] with new. This code results in a `variable a might not have been initialized` compile-time error.

**1.4.6**   Write a code fragment that prints the contents of a two-dimensional boolean array, using * to represent true and a space to represent false. Include row and column numbers.

**1.4.7**   What does the following code fragment print?

```
int[] a = new int[10];
for (int i = 0; i < 10; i++)
   a[i] = 9 - i;
for (int i = 0; i < 10; i++)
   a[i] = a[a[i]];
for (int i = 0; i < 10; i++)
   System.out.println(a[i]);
```

**1.4.8**    What values does the following code put in the array a[]?

```
int N = 10;
int[] a = new int[N];
a[0] = 1;
a[1] = 1;
for (int i = 2; i < N; i++)
   a[i] = a[i-1] + a[i-2];
```

**1.4.9**    What does the following code fragment print?

```
int[] a = { 1, 2, 3 };
int[] b = { 1, 2, 3 };
System.out.println(a == b);
```

**1.4.10**    Write a program Deal that takes an command-line argument N and prints N poker hands (five cards each) from a shuffled deck, separated by blank lines.

**1.4.11**    Write code fragments to create a two-dimensional array b[][] that is a copy of an existing two-dimensional array a[][], under each of the following assumptions:

    *a.*  a[][] is square

    *b.*  a[][] is rectangular

    *c.*  a[][] may be ragged

Your solution to *b* should work for *a*, and your solution to *c* should work for both *b* and *a*, but your code should get progressively more complicated.

**1.4.12**    Write a code fragment to print the *transposition* (rows and columns changed) of a square two-dimensional array. For the example spreadsheet array in the text, you code would print the following:

```
99  98  92  94  99  90  76  92  97  89
85  57  77  32  34  46  59  66  71  29
98  78  76  11  22  54  88  89  24  38
```

**1.4.13**    Write a code fragment to transpose a square two-dimensional array *in place* without creating a second array.

**1.4.14** Write a program that takes an integer *N* from the command line and creates an *N*-by-*N* boolean array a[][] such that a[i][j] is true if i and j are relatively prime (have no common factors), and false otherwise. Use your solution to EXERCISE 1.4.6 to print the array. *Hint*: Use sieving.

**1.4.15** Write a program that computes the product of two square matrices of boolean values, using the *or* operation instead of + and the *and* operation instead of *.

**1.4.16** Modify the spreadsheet code fragment in the text to compute a *weighted* average of the rows, where the weights of each test score are in a one-dimensional array weights[]. For example, to assign the last of the three tests in our example to be twice the weight of the others, you would use

```
double[] weights = { .25, .25, .50 };
```

Note that the weights should sum to 1.

**1.4.17** Write a code fragment to multiply two rectangular matrices that are not necessarily square. *Note*: For the dot product to be well-defined, the number of columns in the first matrix must be equal to the number of rows in the second matrix. Print an error message if the dimensions do not satisfy this condition.

**1.4.18** Modify SelfAvoidingWalk (PROGRAM 1.4.4) to calculate and print the average length of the paths as well as the dead-end probability. Keep separate the average lengths of escape paths and dead-end paths.

**1.4.19** Modify SelfAvoidingWalk to calculate and print the average area of the smallest axis-oriented rectangle that encloses the path. Keep separate statistics for escape paths and dead-end paths.

## Creative Exercises

**1.4.20** *Dice simulation.* The following code computes the exact probability distribution for the sum of two dice:

```
double[] dist = new double[13];
for (int i = 1; i <= 6; i++)
   for (int j = 1; j <= 6; j++)
      dist[i+j] += 1.0;

for (int k = 1; k <= 12; k++)
   dist[k] /= 36.0;
```

The value `dist[k]` is the probability that the dice sum to k. Run experiments to validate this calculation simulating $N$ dice throws, keeping track of the frequencies of occurrence of each value when you compute the sum of two random integers between 1 and 6. How large does $N$ have to be before your empirical results match the exact results to three decimal places?

**1.4.21** *Longest plateau.* Given an array of integers, find the length and location of the longest contiguous sequence of equal values where the values of the elements just before and just after this sequence are smaller.

**1.4.22** *Empirical shuffle check.* Run computational experiments to check that our shuffling code works as advertised. Write a program `ShuffleTest` that takes command-line arguments $M$ and $N$, does $N$ shuffles of an array of size $M$ that is initialized with `a[i]` = i before each shuffle, and prints an $M$-by-$M$ table such that row i gives the number of times i wound up in position j for all j. All entries in the array should be close to $N/M$.

**1.4.23** *Bad shuffling.* Suppose that you choose a random integer between 0 and N-1 in our shuffling code instead of one between i and N-1. Show that the resulting order is *not* equally likely to be one of the $N!$ possibilities. Run the test of the previous exercise for this version.

**1.4.24** *Music shuffling.* You set your music player to shuffle mode. It plays each of the $N$ songs before repeating any. Write a program to estimate the likelihood that you will not hear any sequential pair of songs (that is, song 3 does not follow song 2, song 10 does not follow song 9, and so on).

**1.4.24** *Minima in permutations.* Write a program that takes an integer N from the command line, generates a random permutation, prints the permutation, and prints the number of left-to-right minima in the permutation (the number of times an element is the smallest seen so far). Then write a program that takes integers M and N from the command line, generates M random permutations of size N, and prints the average number of left-to-right minima in the permutations generated. *Extra credit*: Formulate a hypothesis about the number of left-to-right minima in a permutation of size N, as a function of N.

**1.4.25** *Inverse permutation.* Write a program that reads in a permutation of the integers 0 to N-1 from N command-line arguments and prints the inverse permutation. (If the permutation is in an array a[], its inverse is the array b[] such that a[b[i]] = b[a[i]] = i.) Be sure to check that the input is a valid permutation.

**1.4.26** *Hadamard matrix.* The $N$-by-$N$ Hadamard matrix $H(N)$ is a boolean matrix with the remarkable property that any two rows differ in exactly $N/2$ entries. (This property makes it useful for designing error-correcting codes.) $H(1)$ is a 1-by-1 matrix with the single entry true, and for $N>1$, $H(2N)$ is obtained by aligning four copies of $H(N)$ in a large square, and then inverting all of the entries in the lower right $N$-by-$N$ copy, as shown in the following examples (with T representing true and F representing false, as usual).

| $H(1)$ | $H(2)$ | $H(4)$ |
|--------|--------|--------|
| T | T T | T T T T |
|   | T F | T F T F |
|   |     | T T F F |
|   |     | T F F T |

Write a program that takes one command-line argument $N$ and prints $H(N)$. Assume that $N$ is a power of 2.

**1.4.27** *Rumors.* Alice is throwing a party with $N$ other guests, including Bob. Bob starts a rumor about Alice by telling it to one of the other guests. A person hearing this rumor for the first time will immediately tell it to one other guest, chosen at random from all the people at the party except Alice and the person from whom they heard it. If a person (including Bob) hears the rumor for a second time, he or she will not propagate it further. Write a program to estimate the probability that everyone at the party (except Alice) will hear the rumor before it stops propagating. Also calculate an estimate of the expected number of people to hear the rumor.

**1.4.28** *Find a duplicate.* Given an array of N elements with each element between 1 and N, write an algorithm to determine whether there are any duplicates. You do not need to preserve the contents of the given array, but do not use an extra array.

**1.4.29** *Counting primes.* Compare PrimeSieve with the method that we used to demonstrate the break statement, at the end of SECTION 1.3. This is a classic example of a time-space tradeoff: PrimeSieve is fast, but requires a boolean array of size *N*; the other approach uses only two integer variables, but is substantially slower. Estimate the magnitude of this difference by finding the value of *N* for which this second approach can complete the computation in about the same time as java PrimeSeive 1000000.

**1.4.30** *Minesweeper.* Write a program that takes 3 command-line arguments *M*, *N*, and *p* and produces an *M*-by-*N* boolean array where each entry is occupied with probability *p*. In the minesweeper game, occupied cells represent bombs and empty cells represent safe cells. Print out the array using an asterisk for bombs and a period for safe cells. Then, replace each safe square with the number of neighboring bombs (above, below, left, right, or diagonal) and print out the solution.

```
* * . . .          * * 1 0 0
. . . . .          3 3 2 0 0
. * . . .          1 * 1 0 0
```

Try to write your code so that you have as few special cases as possible to deal with, by using an (*M*+2)-by-(*N*+2) boolean array.

**1.4.31** *Self-avoiding walk length.* Suppose that there is no limit on the size of the grid. Run experiments to estimate the average walk length.

**1.4.32** *Three-dimensional self-avoiding walks.* Run experiments to verify that the dead-end probability is 0 for a three-dimensional self-avoiding walk and to compute the average walk length for various values of *N*.

**1.4.33** *Random walkers.* Suppose that $N$ random walkers, starting in the center of an $N$-by-$N$ grid, move one step at a time, choosing to go left, right, up, or down with equal probability at each step. Write a program to help formulate and test a hypothesis about the number of steps taken before all cells are touched.

**1.4.34** *Bridge hands.* In the game of bridge, four players are dealt hands of 13 cards each. An important statistic is the distribution of the number of cards in each suit in a hand. Which is the most likely, 5-3-3-2, 4-4-3-2, or 4-3-3-3?

**1.4.35** *Birthday problem.* Suppose that people enter an empty room until a pair of people share a birthday. On average, how many people will have to enter before there is a match? Run experiments to estimate the value of this quantity. Assume birthdays to be uniform random integers between 0 and 364.

**1.4.36** *Coupon collector.* Run experiments to validate the classical mathematical result that the expected number of coupons needed to collect $N$ values is about $NH_N$. For example, if you are observing the cards carefully at the blackjack table (and the dealer has enough decks randomly shuffled together), you will wait until about 235 cards are dealt, on average, before seeing every card value.

**1.4.37** *Binomial coefficients.* Write a program that builds and prints a two-dimensional ragged array a such that a[N][k] contains the probability that you get exactly k heads when you toss a coin N times. Take a command-line argument to specify the maximum value of N. These numbers are known as the *binomial distribution*: if you multiply each entry in row $i$ by $2^N$, you get the *binomial coefficients* (the coefficients of $x^k$ in $(x+1)^N$) arranged in *Pascal's triangle*. To compute them, start with a[N][0] = 0 for all N and a[1][1] = 1, then compute values in successive rows, left to right, with a[N][k] = (a[N-1][k] + a[N-1][k-1])/2.

| *Pascal's triangle* | *binomial distribution* | | | | |
| --- | --- | --- | --- | --- | --- |
| 1 | 1 | | | | |
| 1 1 | 1/2 | 1/2 | | | |
| 1 2 1 | 1/4 | 1/2 | 1/4 | | |
| 1 3 3 1 | 1/8 | 3/8 | 3/8 | 1/8 | |
| 1 4 6 4 1 | 1/16 | 1/4 | 3/8 | 1/4 | 1/16 |

## 1.5    Input and Output

IN THIS SECTION WE EXTEND THE set of simple abstractions (command-line input and standard output) that we have been using as the interface between our Java programs and the outside world to include standard input, *standard drawing,* and *standard audio.* Standard input makes it convenient for us to write programs that process arbitrary amounts of input and to interact with our programs; standard drawing makes it possible for us to work with graphical representations of images, freeing us from having to encode everything as text; and standard audio adds

*Programs in this section*

sound. These extensions are easy to use, and you will find that they bring you to yet another new world of programming.

The abbreviation *I/O* is universally understood to mean *input/output,* a collective term that refers to the mechanisms by which programs communicate with the outside world. Your computer's operating system controls the physical devices that are connected to your computer. To implement the standard I/O abstractions, we use libraries of methods that interface to the operating system.

You have already been accepting argument values from the command line and printing strings in a terminal window; the purpose of this section is to provide you with a much richer set of tools for processing and presenting data. Like the `System.out.print()` and `System.out.println()` methods that you have been using, these methods do not implement mathematical functions—their purpose is to cause some side effect, either on an input device or an output device. Our prime concern is using such devices to get information into and out of our programs.

An essential feature of standard I/O mechanisms is that there is no limit on the amount of input or output data, from the point of view of the program. Your programs can consume input or produce output indefinitely.

One use of standard I/O mechanisms is to connect your programs to *files* on your computer's disk. It is easy to connect standard input, standard output, standard drawing, and standard audio to files. Such connections make it easy to have your Java programs save or load results to files for archival purposes or for later reference by other programs or other applications.

**Bird's-eye view**   The conventional model that we have been using for Java programming has served us since SECTION 1.1. To build context, we begin by briefly reviewing the model.

A Java program takes input values from the command line and prints a string of characters as output. By default, both *command-line input* and *standard output* are associated with the application that takes commands (the one in which you have been typing the java and javac commands). We use the generic term *terminal window* to refer to this application. This model has proven to be a convenient and direct way for us to interact with our programs and data.

*Command-line input.*   This mechanism, which we have been using to provide input values to our programs, is a standard part of Java programming. All classes have a main() method that takes a String array args[] as its argument. That array is the sequence of command-line arguments that we type, provided to Java by the operating system. By convention, both Java and the operating system process the arguments as strings, so if we intend for an argument to be a number, we use a method such as Integer.parseInt() or Double.parseDouble() to convert it from String to the appropriate type.

*Standard output.*   To print output values in our programs, we have been using the system methods System.out.println() and System.out.print(). Java puts the results of a program's sequence of calls on these methods into the form of an abstract stream of characters known as *standard output*. By default, the operating system connects standard output to the terminal window. All of the output in our programs so far has been appearing in the terminal window.

For reference, and as a starting point, RandomSeq (PROGRAM 1.5.1) is a program that uses this model. It takes a command-line argument *N* and produces an output sequence of *N* random numbers between 0 and 1.

NOW WE ARE GOING TO COMPLEMENT command-line input and standard output with three additional mechanisms that address their limitations and provide us with a far more useful programming model. These mechanisms give us a new bird's-eye view of a Java program in which the program converts a standard input stream and a sequence of command-line arguments into a standard output stream, a standard drawing, and a standard audio stream.

**Program 1.5.1    *Generating a random sequence***

```
public class RandomSeq
{
   public static void main(String[] args)
   {  // Print a random sequence of N real values in [0, 1)
      int N = Integer.parseInt(args[0]);
      for (int i = 0; i < N; i++)
         System.out.println(Math.random());
   }
}
```

*This program illustrates the conventional model that we have been using so far for Java programming. It takes a command-line argument N and prints N random numbers between 0 and 1. From the program's point of view, there is no limit on the length of the output sequence.*

```
% java RandomSeq 1000000
0.2498362534343327
0.5578468691774513
0.5702167639727175
0.32191774192688727
0.6865902823177537
...
```

*Standard input.* Our class StdIn is a library that implements a standard input abstraction to complement the standard output abstraction. Just as you can print a value to standard output at any time during the execution of your program, you can read a value from a standard input stream at any time.

*Standard drawing.* Our class StdDraw allows you to create drawings with your programs. It uses a simple graphics model that allows you to create drawings consisting of points and lines in a window on your computer. StdDraw also includes facilities for text, color, and animation.

*Standard audio.* Our class StdAudio allows you to create sound with your programs. It uses a standard format to convert arrays of numbers into sound.

To use both command-line input and standard output, you have been using built-in Java facilities. Java also has built-in facilities that support abstractions like standard input, standard draw, and standard audio, but they are somewhat more complicated to use, so we have developed a simpler interface to them in our StdIn, StdDraw, and StdAudio libraries. To logically complete our programming model, we also include a StdOut library. To use these libraries, download StdIn.java, StdOut.java, StdDraw.java, and StdAudio.java and place them in the same directory as your program (or use one of the other mechanisms for sharing libraries described on the booksite).

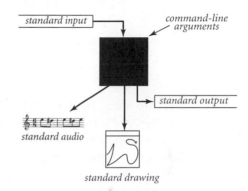

A bird's-eye view of a Java program (revisited)

The standard input and standard output abstractions date back to the development of the UNIX operating system in the 1970s and are found in some form on all modern systems. Although they are primitive by comparison to various mechanisms developed since, modern programmers still depend on them as a reliable way to connect data to programs. We have developed for this book standard draw and standard audio in the same spirit as these earlier abstractions to provide you with an easy way to produce visual and aural output.

**Standard output**   Java's System.out.print() and System.out.println() methods implement the basic standard output abstraction that we need. Nevertheless, to treat standard input and standard output in a uniform manner (and to provide a few technical improvements), starting in this section and continuing through the rest of the book, we use similar methods that are defined in our StdOut library. StdOut.print() and StdOut.println() are nearly the same as the Java methods that you have been using (see the booksite for a discussion of the differences, which need not concern you now). The StdOut.printf() method is a main topic of this section and will be of interest to you now because it gives you more control over the appearance of the output. It was a feature of the C language of the early 1970s that still survives in modern languages because it is so useful.

Since the first time that we printed double values, we have been distracted by excessive precision in the printed output. For example, when we use System.out.print(Math.PI) we get the output 3.141592653589793, even though we might

```
public class StdOut
```
---
|  |  |  |
| --- | --- | --- |
| void | print(String s) | *print* s |
| void | println(String s) | *print* s, *followed by newline* |
| void | println() | *print a new line* |
| void | printf(String f, ... ) | *formatted print* |

*API for our library of static methods for standard output*

prefer to see 3.14 or 3.14159. The print() and println() methods present each number to 15 decimal places even when we would be happy with just a few digits of precision. The printf() method is more flexible: it allows us to specify the number of digits and the precision when converting data type values to strings for output. With printf(), we can write StdOut.printf("%7.5f", Math.PI) to get 3.14159, and we can replace System.out.print(t) with

```
StdOut.printf("The square root of %.1f is %.6f", c, t);
```

in Newton (PROGRAM 1.3.6) to get output like

```
The square root of 2.0 is 1.414214
```

Next, we describe the meaning and operation of these statements, along with extensions to handle the other built-in types of data.

*Formatted printing basics.* In its simplest form, printf() takes two arguments. The first argument is a *format string* that describes how to convert the second argument into a string for output. The simplest type of format string begins with % and ends with a one-letter *conversion code*. The conversion codes that we use most frequently are d (for decimal values from Java's integer types), f (for floating-point values), and s (for String values). Between the % and the conversion code is an integer that specifies the *field width* of the converted value (the number of characters in the converted output string). By default, blanks are added on the left to make the length of the converted output equal to the field width; if we want the blanks on the right, we can insert a minus sign before the field width. (If the

*Anatomy of a formatted print statement*

converted output string is larger than the field width, the field width is ignored.) Following the width, we have the option of including a period followed by the number of digits to put after the decimal point (the precision) for a `double` value or the number of characters to take from the beginning of the string for a `String` value. The most important thing to remember about using `printf()` is that *the conversion code in the format and the type of the corresponding argument must match.* That is, Java must be able to convert from the type of the argument to the type required by the conversion code. Every type of data can be converted to `String`, but if you write `StdOut.printf("%12d", Math.PI)` or `StdOut.printf("%4.2f", 512)`, you will get an `IllegalFormatConversionException` run-time error.

*Format string.* The first argument of `printf()` is a `String` that may contain characters other than a format string. Any part of the argument that is not part of a format string passes through to the output, with the format string replaced by the argument value (converted to a string as specified). For example, the statement

```
StdOut.printf("PI is approximately %.2f\n", Math.PI);
```

prints the line

```
PI is approximately 3.14
```

Note that we need to explicitly include the newline character \n in the argument in order to print a new line with `printf()`.

| type | code | typical literal | sample format strings | converted string values for output |
|------|------|-----------------|-----------------------|-----------------------------------|
| int | d | 512 | `"%14d"`<br>`"%-14d"` | `"           512"`<br>`"512           "` |
| double | f<br>e | 1595.1680010754388 | `"%14.2f"`<br>`"%.7f"`<br>`"%14.4e"` | `"       1595.17"`<br>`"1595.1680011"`<br>`"    1.5952e+03"` |
| String | s | `"Hello, World"` | `"%14s"`<br>`"%-14s"`<br>`"%-14.5s"` | `"  Hello, World"`<br>`"Hello, World  "`<br>`"Hello         "` |

Format conventions for `printf()` *(see the booksite for many other options)*

*Multiple arguments.* The `printf()` function can take more than two arguments. In this case, the format string will have a format specifier for each additional argument, perhaps separated by other characters to pass through to the output. For example, if you were making payments on a loan, you might use code whose inner loop contains the statements

```
String formats = "%3s   $%6.2f   $%7.2f   $%5.2f\n";
StdOut.printf(formats, month[i], pay, balance, interest);
```

to print the second and subsequent lines in a table like this (see EXERCISE 1.5.14):

```
      payment    balance  interest
Jan   $299.00   $9742.67   $41.67
Feb   $299.00   $9484.26   $40.59
Mar   $299.00   $9224.78   $39.52
...
```

Formatted printing is convenient because this sort of code is much more compact than the string-concatenation code that we have been using.

**Standard input**   Our `StdIn` library takes data from a *standard input stream* that may be empty or may contain a sequence of values separated by whitespace (spaces, tabs, newline characters, and the like). Each value is a `String` or a value from one of Java's primitive types. One of the key features of the standard input stream is that your program *consumes* values when it reads them. Once your program has read a value, it cannot back up and read it again. This assumption is restrictive, but it reflects physical characteristics of some input devices and simplifies implementing the abstraction. The library consists of the nine methods: `isEmpty()`, `readInt()`, `readDouble()`, `readLong()`, `readBoolean()`, `readChar()`, `readString()`, `read-Line()`, and `readAll()`. Within the input stream model, these methods are largely self-documenting (the names describe their effect), but their precise operation is worthy of careful consideration, so we will consider several examples in detail.

*Typing input.* When you use the `java` command to invoke a Java program from the command line, you actually are doing three things: issuing a command to start executing your program, specifying the values of the command line arguments, and beginning to define the standard input stream. The string of characters that you type in the terminal window after the command line *is* the standard input stream. When you type characters, you are interacting with your program. The

```
public class StdIn
```

| | | |
|---:|:---|:---|
| boolean | isEmpty() | true *if no more values,* false *otherwise* |
| int | readInt() | *read a value of type* int |
| double | readDouble() | *read a value of type* double |
| long | readLong() | *read a value of type long* |
| boolean | readBoolean() | *read a value of type* boolean |
| char | readChar() | *read a value of type* char |
| String | readString() | *read a value of type* String |
| String | readLine() | *read the rest of the line* |
| String | readAll() | *read the rest of the text* |

*API for our library of static methods for standard input*

program *waits* for you to create the standard input stream. For example, consider the following program, which takes a command-line argument $N$, then reads $N$ numbers from standard input and adds them:

```java
public class AddInts
{
    public static void main(String[] args)
    {
        int N = Integer.parseInt(args[0]);
        int sum = 0;
        for (int i = 0; i < N; i++)
        {
            int value = StdIn.readInt();
            sum += value;
        }
        StdOut.println("Sum is " + sum);
    }
}
```

When you type java AddInts 4, after the program takes the command-line argument, it calls the method StdIn.readInt() and waits for you to type an integer. Suppose that you want 144 to be the first value. As you type 1, then 4, and then 4, nothing happens, because StdIn does not know that you are done typing the integer. But when you then type <return> to signify the end of your integer, StdIn.readInt() immediately returns the value 144, which your program adds to sum and then calls `StdIn.readInt()` again. Again, nothing happens until you type the second value: if you type 2, then 3, then 3, and then `<return>` to end the number, `StdIn.readInt()` returns the value 233, which your program again adds to `sum`. After you have typed four numbers in this way, `AddInts` expects no more input and prints out the sum, as desired.

*Input format.* If you type `abc` or `12.2` or `true` when `StdIn.readInt()` is expecting an `int`, it will respond with a `NumberFormatException`. The format for each type is the same as you have been using for literal values within Java programs. For convenience, `StdIn` treats strings of consecutive whitespace characters as identical to one space and allows you to delimit your numbers with such strings. It does not matter how many spaces you put between numbers, or whether you enter numbers on one line or separate them with tab characters or spread them out over several lines, (except that your

Anatomy of a command

terminal application processes standard input one line at a time, so it will wait until you type `<return>` before sending all of the numbers on that line to standard input). You can mix values of different types in an input stream, but whenever the program expects a value of a particular type, the input stream must have a value of that type.

*Interactive user input.* `TwentyQuestions` (PROGRAM 1.5.2) is a simple example of a program that interacts with its user. The program generates a random integer and then gives clues to a user trying to guess the number. (As a side note: by using *binary search*, you can always get to the answer in at most twenty questions. See SECTION 4.2.) The fundamental difference between this program and others that we have written is that the user has the ability to change the control flow *while* the program is executing. This capability was very important in early applications of computing, but we rarely write such programs nowadays because modern applications typically take such input through the graphical user interface, as discussed in CHAPTER 3. Even a simple program like `TwentyQuestions` illustrates that writing programs that support user interaction is potentially very difficult because you have to plan for all possible user inputs.

### Program 1.5.2   Interactive user input

```java
public class TwentyQuestions
{
    public static void main(String[] args)
    { // Generate a number and answer questions
      // while the user tries to guess the value.
        int N = 1 + (int) (Math.random() * 1000000);
        StdOut.print("I'm thinking of a number ");
        StdOut.println("between 1 and 1,000,000");
        int m = 0;
        while (m != N)
        { // Solicit one guess and provide one answer
            StdOut.print("What's your guess? ");
            m = StdIn.readInt();
            if (m == N) StdOut.println("You win!");
            if (m < N)  StdOut.println("Too low ");
            if (m > N)  StdOut.println("Too high");
        }
    }
}
```

| N | hidden value |
| m | user's guess |

This program plays a simple guessing game. You type numbers, each of which is an implicit
question ("Is this the number?") and the program tells you whether your guess is too high or
too low. You can always get it to print You win! with less than twenty questions. To use this
program, you need to first download StdIn.java and StdOut.java into the same directory
as this code (which is in a file named TwentyQuestions.java).

```
% java TwentyQuestions
I'm thinking of a number between 1 and 1,000,000
What's your guess? 500000
Too high
What's your guess? 250000
Too low
What's your guess? 375000
Too high
What's your guess? 312500
Too high
What's your guess? 300500
Too low
...
```

**Program 1.5.3   *Averaging a stream of numbers***

```
public class Average
{
   public static void main(String[] args)
   {  // Average the numbers on the input stream.
      double sum = 0.0;
      int cnt = 0;
      while (!StdIn.isEmpty())
      {  // Read a number and cumulate the sum.
         double value = StdIn.readDouble();
         sum += value;
         cnt++;
      }
      double average = sum / cnt;
      StdOut.println("Average is " + average);
   }
}
```

| cnt | count of numbers read |
|-----|----------------------|
| sum | cumulated sum |

*This program reads in a sequence of real numbers from standard input and prints their average on standard output (provided that the sum does not overflow). From its point of view, there is no limit on the size of the input stream. The commands on the right below use redirection and piping (discussed in the next subsection) to provide 100,000 numbers to average.*

```
% java Average
10.0 5.0 6.0
3.0
7.0 32.0
<ctrl-d>
Average is 10.5
```

```
% java RandomSeq 100000 > data.txt
% java Average < data.txt
Average is 0.5010473676174824

% java RandomSeq 100000 | java Average
Average is 0.5000499417963857
```

*Processing an arbitrary-size input stream.* Typically, input streams are finite: your program marches through the input stream, consuming values until the stream is empty. But there is no restriction of the size of the input stream, and some programs simply process all the input presented to them. Average (PROGRAM 1.5.3) is an example that reads in a sequence of real numbers from standard input and prints their average. It illustrates a key property of using an input stream: the length of the stream is not known to the program. We type all the numbers that we have, and then the program averages them. Before reading each number, the program uses the method `StdIn.isEmpty()` to check whether there are any more numbers in the input stream. How do we signal that we have no more data to type? By convention, we type a special sequence of characters known as the *end-of-file* sequence. Unfortunately, the terminal applications that we typically encounter on modern operating systems use different conventions for this critically important sequence. In this book, we use `<ctrl-d>` (many systems require `<ctrl-d>` to be on a line by itself); the other widely used convention is `<ctrl-z>` on a line by itself. `Average` is a simple program, but it represents a profound new capability in programming: with standard input, we can write programs that process an unlimited amount of data. As you will see, writing such programs is an effective approach for numerous data-processing applications.

STANDARD INPUT IS A SUBSTANTIAL STEP up from the command-line input model that we have been using, for two reasons, as illustrated by `TwentyQuestions` and `Average`. First, we can interact with our program—with command-line arguments, we can only provide data to the program *before* it begins execution. Second, we can read in large amounts of data—with command-line arguments, we can only enter values that fit on the command line. Indeed, as illustrated by `Average`, the amount of data can be potentially unlimited, and many programs are made simpler by that assumption. A third *raison d'être* for standard input is that your operating system makes it possible to change the source of standard input, so that you do not have to type all the input. Next, we consider the mechanisms that enable this possibility.

**Redirection and piping**   For many applications, typing input data as a standard input stream from the terminal window is untenable because our program's processing power is then limited by the amount of data that we can type (and our typing speed). Similarly, we often want to save the information printed on the standard output stream for later use. To address such limitations, we next focus on the idea that standard input is an *abstraction*—the program just expects its input and has no dependence on the source of the input stream. Standard output is a similar abstraction. The power of these abstractions derives from our ability (through the operating system) to specify various other sources for standard input and standard output, such as a file, the network, or another program. All modern operating systems implement these mechanisms.

*Redirecting standard output to a file.* By adding a simple directive to the command that invokes a program, we can *redirect* its standard output to a file, either for permanent storage or for input to another program at a later time. For example,

```
% java RandomSeq 1000 > data.txt
```

specifies that the standard output stream is not to be printed in the terminal window, but instead is to be written to a text file named `data.txt`. Each call to `System.out.print()` or `System.out.println()` appends text at the end of that file. In this example, the end result is a file that contains 1,000 random values. No output appears in the terminal window: it goes directly into the file named after the > symbol. Thus, we can save away information for later retrieval. Note that we do not have to change RandomSeq (PROGRAM 1.5.1) in any way for this mechanism to work—it is using the standard output abstraction and is unaffected by our use of a different implementation of that abstraction. You can use this mechanism to save output from any program that you write. Once we have expended a significant amount of effort to obtain a result, we often want to save the result for later reference. In a modern system,

*Redirecting standard output to a file*

you can save some information by using cut-and-paste or some similar mechanism that is provided by the operating system, but cut-and-paste is inconvenient for large amounts of data. By contrast, redirection is specifically designed to make it easy to handle large amounts of data.

*Redirecting from a file to standard input.* Similarly, we can redirect standard input so that `StdIn` reads data from a file instead of the terminal application:

```
% java Average < data.txt
```

This command reads a sequence of numbers from the file `data.txt` and computes their average value. Specifically, the < symbol is a directive that tells the operating system to implement the standard input stream by reading from the text file `data.txt` instead of waiting for the user to type something into the terminal window. When the program calls `StdIn.readDouble()`, the operating system reads the value from the file. The file `data.txt` could

*Redirecting from a file to standard input*

have been created by any application, not just a Java program—virtually every application on your computer can create text files. This facility to redirect from a file to standard input enables us to create *data-driven code* where we can change the data processed by a program without having to change the program at all. Instead, we keep data in files and write programs that read from standard input.

*Connecting two programs.* The most flexible way to implement the standard input and standard output abstractions is to specify that they are implemented by our own programs! This mechanism is called *piping*. For example, the command

```
% java RandomSeq 1000 | java Average
```

specifies that the standard output for RandomSeq and the standard input stream for Average are the *same* stream. The effect is as if RandomSeq were typing the numbers it generates into the terminal window while Average is running. This example also has the same effect as the following sequence of commands:

```
% java RandomSeq 1000 > data.txt
% java Average < data.txt
```

In this case, the file data.txt is not created. This difference is profound, because it removes another limitation on the size of the input and output streams that we can process. For example, we could replace 1000 in our example with 1000000000, even though we might not have the space to save a billion numbers on our computer (we do need the *time* to process them, however). When RandomSeq calls System.out.println(), a string is added to the end of the stream; when Average calls StdIn.readInt(), a string is removed from the beginning of the stream. The timing of precisely what happens is up to the operating

java RandomSeq 1000 | java Average

*Piping the output of one program to the input of another*

system: it might run RandomSeq until it produces some output, and then run Average to consume that output, or it might run Average until it needs some output, and then run RandomSeq until it produces the needed output. The end result is the same, but our programs are freed from worrying about such details because they work solely with the standard input and standard output abstractions.

**Program 1.5.4    A simple filter**

```
public class RangeFilter
{
    public static void main(String[] args)
    {  // Filter out numbers not between lo and hi.
        int lo = Integer.parseInt(args[0]);
        int hi = Integer.parseInt(args[1]);
        while (!StdIn.isEmpty())
        {  // Process one number.
            int t = StdIn.readInt();
            if (t >= lo && t <= hi) StdOut.print(t + " ");
        }
        StdOut.println();
    }
}
```

| lo | lower bound of range |
| hi | upper bound of range |
| t | current number |

*This filter copies to the output stream the numbers from the input stream that fall inside the range given by the command-line parameters. There is no limit on the length of the streams.*

```
% java RangeFilter 100 400
358 1330 55 165 689 1014 3066 387 575 843 203 48 292 877 65 998
<ctrl-d>
358 165 387 203 292
```

*Filters.*  Piping, a core feature of the original Unix system of the early 1970s, still survives in modern systems because it is a simple abstraction for communicating among disparate programs. Testimony to the power of this abstraction is that many Unix programs are still being used today to process files that are thousands or millions of times larger than imagined by the programs' authors. We can communicate with other Java programs via calls on methods, but standard input and standard output allow us to communicate with programs that were written at another time and, perhaps, in another language. With standard input and standard output, we are agreeing on a simple interface to the outside world. For many common tasks, it is convenient to think of each program as a *filter* that converts a standard input stream to a standard output stream in some way, with piping as the command mechanism to connect programs together. For example, `RangeFilter` (PROGRAM 1.5.4) takes two command-line arguments and prints on standard output those numbers from standard input that fall within the specified range. You might imagine standard input to be measurement data from some instrument, with the filter being used to throw away data outside the range of interest for the experiment at hand. Several standard filters that were designed for UNIX still survive (sometimes with different names) as commands in modern operating systems. For example, the `sort` filter puts the lines on standard input in sorted order:

```
% java RandomSeq 6 | sort
0.035813305516568916
0.14306638757584322
0.348292877655532103
0.5761644592016527
0.7234592733392126
0.9795908813988247
```

We discuss sorting in SECTION 4.2. A second useful filter is `grep`, which prints the lines from standard input that match a given pattern. For example, if you type

```
% grep lo < RangeFilter.java
```

you get the result

```
// Filter out numbers not between lo and hi.
int lo = Integer.parseInt(args[0]);
    if (t >= lo && t <= hi) StdOut.print(t + " ");
```

Programmers often use tools such as `grep` to get a quick reminder of variable names or language usage details. A third useful filter is `more`, which reads data from standard input and displays it in your terminal window one screenful at a time. For example, if you type

```
% java RandomSeq 1000 | more
```

you will see as many numbers as fit in your terminal window, but `more` will wait for you to hit the space bar before displaying each succeeding screenful. The term *filter* is perhaps misleading: it was meant to describe programs like `RangeFilter` that write some subsequence of standard input to standard output, but it is now often used to describe any program that reads from standard input and writes to standard output.

*Multiple streams.* For many common tasks, we want to write programs that take input from multiple sources and/or produce output intended for multiple destinations. In SECTION 3.1 we discuss our Out and In libraries, which generalize StdOut and StdIn to allow for multiple input and output streams. These libraries include provisions not just for redirecting these streams to and from files, but also from arbitrary web pages.

PROCESSING LARGE AMOUNTS OF INFORMATION PLAYS an essential role in many applications of computing. A scientist may need to analyze data collected from a series of experiments, a stock trader may wish to analyze information about recent financial transactions, or a student may wish to maintain collections of music and movies. In these and countless other applications, data-driven programs are the norm. Standard output, standard input, redirection, and piping provides us with the capability to address such applications with our Java programs. We can collect data into files on our computer through the web or any of the standard devices and use redirection and piping to connect data to our programs. Many (if not most) of the programming examples that we consider throughout this book have this ability.

**Standard drawing**   Up to this point, our input/output abstractions have focused exclusively on text strings. Now we introduce an abstraction for producing drawings as output. This library is easy to use and allows us to take advantage of a visual medium to cope with far more information than is possible with just text.

As with standard input, our standard drawing abstraction is implemented in a library that you need to download from the booksite, StdDraw.java. Standard drawing is very simple: we imagine an abstract drawing device capable of drawing lines and points on a two-dimensional canvas. The device is capable of responding to the commands that our programs issue in the form of calls to methods in Std-Draw such as the following:

public class StdDraw  *(basic drawing commands)*
```
    void  line(double x0, double y0, double x1, double y1)
    void  point(double x, double y)
```

Like the methods for standard input and standard output, these methods are nearly self-documenting: StdDraw.line() draws a straight line segment connecting the

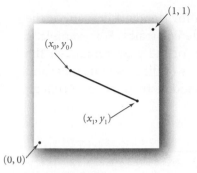

StdDraw.line(x0, y0, x1, y1);

point $(x_0, y_0)$ with the point $(x_1, y_1)$ whose coordinates are given as arguments. StdDraw.point() draws a spot centered on the point $(x, y)$ whose coordinates are given as arguments. The default scale is the unit square (all coordinates between 0 and 1). The standard implementation displays the canvas in a window on your computer's screen, with black lines and points on a white background. The window includes a menu option to save your drawing to a file, in a format suitable for publishing on paper or on the web.

*Your first drawing.* The HelloWorld equivalent for graphics programming with StdDraw is to draw a triangle with a point inside. To form the triangle, we draw three lines: one from the point (0, 0) at the lower left corner to the point (1, 0), one from that point to the third point at (1/2, $\sqrt{3}/2$), and one from that point back to (0, 0). As a final flourish, we draw a spot in the middle of the triangle. Once you have successfully downloaded StdDraw.java and then compiled and run Triangle, you are off and running to write your own programs that draw figures comprised of lines and points. This ability literally adds a new dimension to the output that you can produce.

```
public class Triangle
{
    public static void main(String[] args)
    {
        double t = Math.sqrt(3.0)/2.0;
        StdDraw.line(0.0, 0.0, 1.0, 0.0);
        StdDraw.line(1.0, 0.0, 0.5,   t);
        StdDraw.line(0.5,   t, 0.0, 0.0);
        StdDraw.point(0.5, t/3.0);
    }
}
```

When you use a computer to create drawings, you get immediate feedback (the drawing) so that you can refine and improve your program quickly. With a computer program, you can create drawings that you could not contemplate making by hand. In particular, instead of viewing our data as just numbers, we can use pictures, which are far more expressive. We will consider other graphics examples after we discuss a few other drawing commands.

*Your first drawing*

*Control commands.* The default coordinate system for standard drawing is the unit square, but we often want to draw plots at different scales. For example, a typical situation is to use coordinates in some range for the *x*-coordinate, or the *y*-coordinate, or both. Also, we often want to draw lines of different thickness and points of different size from the standard. To accommodate these needs, StdDraw has the following methods:

---

public class StdDraw *(basic control commands)*

---

   void setXscale(double x0, double x1)  *reset x range to $(x_0, x_1)$*

   void setYscale(double y0, double y1)  *reset y range to $(y_0, y_1)$*

   void setPenRadius(double r)        *set pen radius to r*

*Note: Methods with the same names but no arguments reset to default values.*

For example, when we issue the command StdDraw.setXscale(0, N), we are telling the drawing device that we will be using *x*-coordinates between 0 and N. Note that the two-call sequence

```
StdDraw.setXscale(x0, x1);
StdDraw.setYscale(y0, y1);
```

sets the drawing coordinates to be within a *bounding box* whose lower left corner is at $(x_0, y_0)$ and whose upper right corner is at $(x_1, y_1)$. If you use integer coordinates, Java casts them to double, as expected. Scaling is the simplest of the transformations commonly used in graphics. In the applications that we consider in this chapter, we use it in a straightforward way to match our drawings to our data.

    The pen is circular, so that lines have rounded ends, and when you set the pen radius to *r* and draw a point, you get a circle of radius *r*. The default pen radius is .002 and is not affected by coordinate scaling. This default is about 1/500 the width of the default window, so that if you draw 200 points equally spaced along a horizontal or vertical line, you will

```
int N = 50;
StdDraw.setXscale(0, N);
StdDraw.setYscale(0, N);
for (int i = 0; i <= N; i++)
    StdDraw.line(0, N-i, i, 0);
```

*Scaling to integer coordinates*

*Program 1.5.5    Input-to-drawing filter*

```
public class PlotFilter
{
   public static void main(String[] args)
   { // Plot points in standard input.

      // Scale as per first four values.
      double x0 = StdIn.readDouble();
      double y0 = StdIn.readDouble();
      double x1 = StdIn.readDouble();
      double y1 = StdIn.readDouble();
      StdDraw.setXscale(x0, x1);
      StdDraw.setYscale(y0, y1);

      // Read and plot the rest of the points.
      while (!StdIn.isEmpty())
      { // Read and plot a point.
         double x = StdIn.readDouble();
         double y = StdIn.readDouble();
         StdDraw.point(x, y);
      }
   }
}
```

| | |
|---|---|
| x0 | left bound |
| y0 | bottom bound |
| x1 | right bound |
| y1 | top bound |
| x, y | current point |

*Some data is inherently visual. The file* USA.txt *on the booksite has the coordinates of the US cities with populations over 500 (by convention, the first four numbers are the minimum and maximum x and y values).*

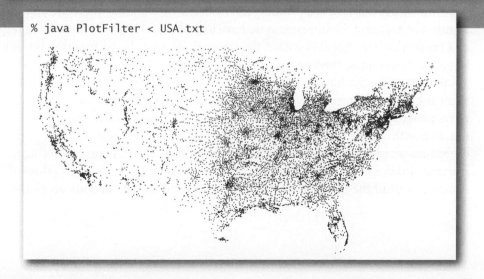

% java PlotFilter < USA.txt

be able to see individual circles, but if you draw 250 such points, the result will look like a line. When you issue the command `StdDraw.setPenRadius(.01)`, you are saying that you want the thickness of the lines and the size of the points to be five times the .002 standard.

*Filtering data to a standard drawing.* One of the simplest applications of standard draw is to plot data, by filtering it from standard input to the drawing. `Plot-Filter` (PROGRAM 1.5.5) is such a filter: it reads a sequence of points defined by ($x$, $y$) coordinates and draws a spot at each point. It adopts the convention that the first four numbers on standard input specify the bounding box, so that it can scale the plot without having to make an extra pass through all the points to determine the scale (this kind of convention is typical with such data files). The graphical representation of points plotted in this way is far more expressive (and far more compact) than the numbers themselves or anything that we could create with the standard output representation that our programs have been limited to until now. The plotted image that is produced by PROGRAM 1.5.5 makes it far easier for us to infer properties of the cities (such as, for example, clustering of population centers) than does a list of the coordinates. Whenever we are processing data that represents the physical world, a visual image is likely to be one of the most meaningful ways that we can use to display output. `PlotFilter` illustrates just how easily you can create such an image.

*Plotting a function graph.* Another important use of `StdDraw` is to plot experimental data or the values of a mathematical function. For example, suppose that we want to plot values of the function $y = \sin(4x) + \sin(20x)$ in the interval $[0, \pi]$. Accomplishing this task is a prototypical example of *sampling*: there are an infinite number of points in the interval, so we have to make do with evaluating the function at a finite number of points within the interval. We sample the function by choosing a set of $x$-values, then computing $y$-values by evaluating the function at each $x$-value. Plotting the function by connecting successive points with lines produces what is known as a *piecewise linear approximation*. The simplest way to proceed is to regularly space the $x$ values: we decide ahead of time on a sample size, then space the $x$-coordinates by the interval size divided by the sample size. To make sure that the values we plot fall in the visible canvas, we scale the $x$-axis corresponding to the interval and the $y$-axis corresponding to the maximum and minimum values of the function within the interval. The smoothness of the curve depends on properties of the function and the size of the sample. If the sample size is too small, the rendition of the function may not be at all accurate (it might not be very smooth, and it might miss major fluctuations); if the sample is too large, producing the plot may be time-consuming, since some functions are time-consuming to compute. (In SECTION 2.4, we will look at a method for plotting a smooth curve without using an excessive number of points.) You can use this same technique to plot the function graph of any function you choose: decide on an $x$-interval where you want to plot the function, compute function values evenly spaced through that interval and store them in an array, determine and set the $y$-scale, and draw the line segments.

```
double[] x = new double[N+1];
double[] y = new double[N+1];
for (int i = 0; i <= N; i++)
   x[i] = Math.PI * i / N;
for (int i = 0; i <= N; i++)
   y[i] = Math.sin(4*x[i]) + Math.sin(20*x[i]);
StdDraw.setXscale(0, Math.PI);
StdDraw.setYscale(-2.0, 2.0);
for (int i = 1; i <= N; i++)
   StdDraw.line(x[i-1], y[i-1], x[i], y[i]);
```

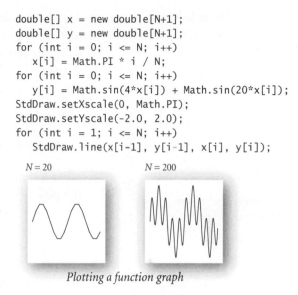

*Plotting a function graph*

*Outline and filled shapes.* StdDraw also includes methods to draw circles, rectangles, and arbitrary polygons. Each shape defines an outline. When the method name is just the shape name, that outline is traced by the drawing pen. When the name begins with filled, the named shape is instead filled solid, not traced. As usual, we summarize the available methods in an API:

| public class StdDraw (*shapes*) |
|---|
| void  circle(double x, double y, double r) |
| void  filledCircle(double x, double y, double r) |
| void  square(double x, double y, double r) |
| void  filledSquare(double x, double y, double r) |
| void  polygon(double[] x, double[] y) |
| void  filledPolygon(double[] x, double[] y) |

The arguments for circle() and filledCircle() define a circle of radius $r$ centered at $(x, y)$; the arguments for square() and filledSquare() define a square of side length 2*r* centered on (*x*, *y*); and the arguments for polygon() and filled-Polygon() define a sequence of points that we connect by lines, including one from the last point to the first point. If you want to define shapes other than squares or circles, use one of these methods. For example,

```
double[] xd = { x-r, x, x+r, x };
double[] yd = { y, y+r, y, y-r };
StdDraw.polygon(xd, yd);
```

plots a diamond (a rotated 2*r*-by-2*r* square) centered on the point (*x*,*y*).

StdDraw.circle(x, y, r);

*Text and color.* Occasionally, you may wish to annotate or highlight various elements in your drawings. StdDraw has a method for drawing text, another for setting parameters associated with text, and another for changing the color of the ink in the pen. We make scant use of these features in this book, but they can be very useful, particularly for drawings on your computer screen. You will find many examples of their use on the booksite.

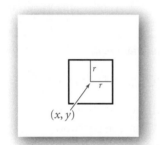

StdDraw.square(x, y, r);

public class StdDraw *(text and color commands)*

---

```
void text(double x, double y, String s)

void setFont(Font f)

void setPenColor(Color c)
```

```
double[] x = {x0, x1, x2, x3};
double[] y = {y0, y1, y2, y3};
StdDraw.polygon(x, y);
```

In this code, Font and Color are non-primitive types that you will learn about in SECTION 3.1. Until then, we leave the details to StdDraw. The available pen colors are BLACK, BLUE, CYAN, DARK_GRAY, GRAY, GREEN, LIGHT_GRAY, MAGENTA, ORANGE, PINK, RED, WHITE, and YELLOW, defined as constants within StdDraw. For example, the call StdDraw.setPenColor(StdDraw.GRAY) changes to gray ink. The default ink color is BLACK. The default font in StdDraw suffices for most of the drawings that you need (and you can find information on using other fonts on the booksite). For example, you might wish to use these methods to annotate function plots to highlight relevant values, and you might find it useful to develop similar methods to annotate other parts of your drawings.

Shapes, color, and text are basic tools that you can use to produce a dizzying variety of images, but you should use them sparingly. Use of such artifacts usually presents a design challenge, and our StdDraw commands are crude by the standards of modern graphics libraries, so that you are likely to need an extensive number of calls to them to produce the beautiful images that you may imagine. On the other hand, using color or labels to help focus on important information in drawings is often worthwhile, as is using color to represent data values.

*Animation.* The StdDraw library supplies additional methods that provide limitless opportunities for creating interesting effects.

```
StdDraw.square(.2, .8, .1);
StdDraw.filledSquare(.8, .8, .2);
StdDraw.circle(.8, .2, .2);
double[] xd = { .1, .2, .3, .2 };
double[] yd = { .2, .3, .2, .1 };
StdDraw.filledPolygon(xd, yd);
StdDraw.text(.2, .5, "black text");
StdDraw.setPenColor(StdDraw.WHITE);
StdDraw.text(.8, .8, "white text");
```

*Shape and text examples*

**public class StdDraw** *(advanced control commands)*

| | |
|---|---|
| void setCanvasSize(int w, int h) | *create canvas in screen window of width from w and height h (in pixels)* |
| void clear() | *clear the canvas to white (default)* |
| void clear(Color c) | *clear the canvas; color it c* |
| void show(int dt) | *draw, then pause dt milliseconds* |
| void show() | *draw, turn off pause mode* |

The default canvas size is 512-by-512 pixels; if you want to change it, call setCanvasSize() before any drawing commands. The clear() and show() methods support dynamic changes in the images on the computer screen. Such effects can provide compelling visualizations. We give an example next that also works for the printed page. There are more examples in the booksite that are likely to capture your imagination.

*Bouncing ball.* The `HelloWorld` of animation is to produce a black ball that appears to move around on the canvas. Suppose that the ball is at position $(r_x, r_y)$ and we want to create the impression of moving it to a new position nearby, such as, for example, $(r_x + .01, r_y + .02)$. We do so in two steps:

• Erase the drawing.

• Draw a black ball at the new position.

To create the illusion of movement, we iterate these steps for a whole sequence of positions (one that will form a straight line, in this case). But these two steps do not suffice, because the computer is so quick at drawing that the image of the ball will rapidly flicker between black and white instead of creating an animated image. Accordingly, `StdDraw` has a `show()` method that allows us to control when the results of drawing actions are actually shown on the display. You can think of it as collecting all of the lines, points, shapes, and text that we tell it to draw, and then immediately drawing them all when we issue the `show()` command. To control the apparent speed, `show()` takes an argument `dt` that tells `StdDraw` to wait `dt` milliseconds after doing the drawing. By default, `StdDraw` issues a `show()` after each `line()`, `point()`, or other drawing command; we turn that option off when we call `StdDraw.show(t)` and turn it back on when we call `StdDraw.show()` with no arguments. With these commands, we can create the illusion of motion with the following steps:

• Erase the drawing (but do not show the result).

• Draw a black ball at the new position.

• Show the result of both commands, and wait for a brief time.

`BouncingBall` (PROGRAM 1.5.6) implements these steps to create the illusion of a ball moving in the 2-by-2 box centered on the origin. The current position of the ball is $(r_x, r_y)$, and we compute the new position at each step by adding $v_x$ to $r_x$ and $v_y$ to $r_y$. Since $(v_x, v_y)$ is the fixed distance that the ball moves in each time unit, it represents the *velocity*. To keep the ball in the drawing, we simulate the effect of the ball bouncing off the walls according to the laws of elastic collision. This effect is easy to implement: when the ball hits a vertical wall, we just change the velocity in the $x$-direction from $v_x$ to $-v_x$, and when the ball hits a horizontal wall, we change the velocity in the $y$-direction from $v_y$ to $-v_y$. Of course, you have to download the code from the booksite and run it on your computer to see motion. To make the image clearer on the printed page, we modified `BouncingBall` to use a gray background that also shows the track of the ball as it moves (see EXERCISE 1.5.34).

**Program 1.5.6  Bouncing ball**

```
public class BouncingBall
{
   public static void main(String[] args)
   { // Simulate the movement of a bouncing ball.
      StdDraw.setXscale(-1.0, 1.0);
      StdDraw.setYscale(-1.0, 1.0);
      double rx = .480, ry = .860;
      double vx = .015, vy = .023;
      double radius = .05;
      while(true)
      { // Update ball position and draw it there.
         if (Math.abs(rx + vx) + radius > 1.0) vx = -vx;
         if (Math.abs(ry + vy) + radius > 1.0) vy = -vy;
         rx = rx + vx;
         ry = ry + vy;
         StdDraw.clear();
         StdDraw.filledCircle(rx, ry, radius);
         StdDraw.show(20);
      }
   }
}
```

| rx, ry | position |
|--------|----------|
| vx, vy | velocity |
| dt | wait time |
| radius | ball radius |

*This program simulates the movement of a bouncing ball in the box with coordinates between -1 and +1. The ball bounces off the boundary according to the laws of elastic collision. The 20-millisecond wait for* StdDraw.show() *keeps the black image of the ball persistent on the screen, even though most of the ball's pixels alternate between black and white. If you modify this code to take the wait time* dt *as a command-line argument, you can control the speed of the ball. The images below, which show the track of the ball, are produced by a modified version of this code (see Exercise 1.5.34).*

100 steps    200 steps    500 steps

STANDARD DRAWING COMPLETES OUR PROGRAMMING MODEL by adding a "picture is worth a thousand words" component. It is a natural abstraction that you can use to better open up your programs to the outside world. With it, you can easily produce the function plots and visual representations of data that are commonly used in science and engineering. We will put it to such uses frequently throughout this book. Any time that you spend now working with the sample programs on the last few pages will be well worth the investment. You can find many useful examples on the booksite and in the exercises, and you are certain to find some outlet for your creativity by using StdDraw to meet various challenges. Can you draw an *N*-pointed star? Can you make our bouncing ball actually bounce (add gravity)? You may be surprised at how easily you can accomplish these and other tasks.

```
public class StdDraw
```
---
```
   void  line(double x0, double y0, double x1, double y1)
   void  point(double x, double y)
   void  text(double x, double y, String s)
   void  circle(double x, double y, double r)
   void  filledCircle(double x, double y, double r)
   void  square(double x, double y, double r)
   void  filledSquare(double x, double y, double r)
   void  polygon(double[] x, double[] y)
   void  filledPolygon(double[] x, double[] y)

   void  setXscale(double x0, double x1)          reset x range to (x_0, x_1)
   void  setYscale(double y0, double y1)          reset y range to (y_0, y_1)
   void  setPenRadius(double r)                   set pen radius to r
   void  setPenColor(Color c)                     set pen color to c
   void  setFont(Font f)                          set text font to f
   void  setCanvasSize(int w, int h)              set canvas to w-by-h window
   void  clear(Color c)                           clear the canvas; color it c
   void  show(int dt)                             show all; pause dt milliseconds
   void  save(String filename)                    save to a .jpg or w.png file
```

*Note: Methods with the same names but no arguments reset to default values.*

*API for our library of static methods for standard drawing*

**Standard audio**   As a final example of a basic abstraction for output, we consider StdAudio, a library that you can use to play, manipulate, and synthesize sound files. You probably have used your computer to process music. Now you can write programs to do so. At the same time, you will learn some concepts behind a venerable and important area of computer science and scientific computing: *digital signal processing*. We will only scratch the surface of this fascinating subject, but you may be surprised at the simplicity of the underlying concepts.

*Concert A.*  Sound is the perception of the vibration of molecules, in particular, the vibration of our eardrums. Therefore, oscillation is the key to understanding sound. Perhaps the simplest place to start is to consider the musical note *A* above middle *C*, which is known as *concert A*. This note is nothing more than a sine wave, scaled to oscillate at a frequency of 440 times per second. The function $\sin(t)$ repeats itself once every $2\pi$ units on the *x*-axis, so if we measure *t* in seconds and plot the function $\sin(2\pi t \times 440)$, we get a curve that oscillates 440 times per second. When you play an *A* by plucking a guitar string, pushing air through a trumpet, or causing a small cone to vibrate in a speaker, this sine wave is the prominent part of the sound that you hear and recognize as concert *A*. We measure frequency in *hertz* (cycles per second). When you double or halve the frequency, you move up or down one octave on the scale. For example, 880 hertz is one octave above concert *A* and 110 hertz is two octaves below concert *A*. For reference, the frequency range of human hearing is about 20 to 20,000 hertz. The amplitude (*y*-value) of a sound corresponds to the volume. We plot our curves between $-1$ and $+1$ and assume that any devices that record and play sound will scale as appropriate, with further scaling controlled by you when you turn the volume knob.

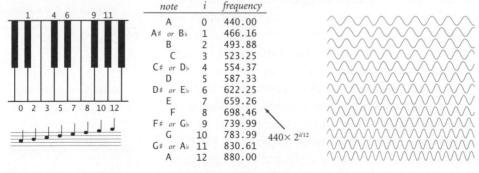

| note | i | frequency |
| --- | --- | --- |
| A | 0 | 440.00 |
| A♯ *or* B♭ | 1 | 466.16 |
| B | 2 | 493.88 |
| C | 3 | 523.25 |
| C♯ *or* D♭ | 4 | 554.37 |
| D | 5 | 587.33 |
| D♯ *or* E♭ | 6 | 622.25 |
| E | 7 | 659.26 |
| F | 8 | 698.46 |
| F♯ *or* G♭ | 9 | 739.99 |
| G | 10 | 783.99 |
| G♯ *or* A♭ | 11 | 830.61 |
| A | 12 | 880.00 |

$440 \times 2^{i/12}$

*Notes, numbers, and waves*

*Other notes.* A simple mathematical formula characterizes the other notes on the chromatic scale. There are twelve notes on the chromatic scale, divided equally on a logarithmic (base 2) scale. We get the *i*th note above a given note by multiplying its frequency by the $(i/12)$th power of 2. In other words, the frequency of each note in the chromatic scale is precisely the frequency of the previous note in the scale multiplied by the twelfth root of two (about 1.06). This information suffices to create music! For example, to play the tune *Frère Jacques*, we just need to play each of the notes *A B C# A* by producing sine waves of the appropriate frequency for about half a second and then repeat the pattern. The primary method in the StdAudio library, StdAudio.play(), allows you to do just that.

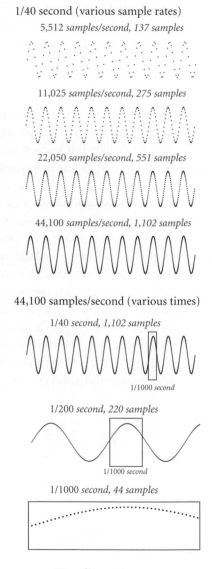

*Sampling.* For digital sound, we represent a curve by sampling it at regular intervals, in precisely the same manner as when we plot function graphs. We sample sufficiently often that we have an accurate representation of the curve—a widely used sampling rate for digital sound is 44,100 samples per second. For concert *A*, that rate corresponds to plotting each cycle of the sine wave by sampling it at about 100 points. Since we sample at regular intervals, we only need to compute the *y*-coordinates of the sample points. It is that simple: *we represent sound as an array of numbers* (double values that are between −1 and +1). Our standard sound library method StdAudio.play() takes an array as its argument and plays the sound represented by that array on your computer. For example, suppose that you want to play concert *A* for 10 seconds. At 44,100 samples per second, you need an array of 441,001 double values. To fill in the array, use a for loop that samples the function $\sin(2\pi t \times 440)$ at $t = 0/44100$,

*Sampling a sine wave*

1/44100, 2/44100, 3/44100, . . . 441000/44100. Once we fill the array with these values, we are ready for StdAudio.play(), as in the following code:

```
int sps = 44100;                    // samples per second
int hz = 440;                       // concert A
double duration = 10.0;             // ten seconds
int N = (int) (sps * duration);     // total number of samples
double[] a = new double[N+1];
for (int i = 0; i <= N; i++)
    a[i] = Math.sin(2*Math.PI * i * hz / sps);
StdAudio.play(a);
```

This code is the HelloWorld of digital audio. Once you use it to get your computer to play this note, you can write code to play other notes and make music! The difference between creating sound and plotting an oscillating curve is nothing more than the output device. Indeed, it is instructive and entertaining to send the same numbers to both standard draw and standard audio (see EXERCISE 1.5.27).

*Saving to a file.* Music can take up a lot of space on your computer. At 44,100 samples per second, a four-minute song corresponds to $4 \times 60 \times 44100 = 10,584,000$ numbers. Therefore, it is common to represent the numbers corresponding to a song in a binary format that uses less space than the string-of-digits representation that we use for standard input and output. Many such formats have been developed in recent years—StdAudio uses the .wav format. You can find some information about the .wav format on the booksite, but you do not need to know the details, because StdAudio takes care of the conversions for you. Our standard library for audio allows you to play .wav files, to write programs to create and manipulate arrays of double values, and to read and write them as .wav files.

| public class StdAudio | |
|---|---|
| void play(String file) | *play the given .wav file* |
| void play(double[] a) | *play the given sound wave* |
| void play(double x) | *play sample for 1/44100 second* |
| void save(String file, double[] a) | *save to a .wav file* |
| double[] read(String file) | *read from a .wav file* |

*API for our library of static methods for standard audio*

*Program 1.5.7    Digital signal processing*

```java
public class PlayThatTune
{
   public static void main(String[] args)
   {  // Read a tune from StdIn and play it.
      int sps = 44100;
      while (!StdIn.isEmpty())
      {  // Read and play one note.
         int pitch = StdIn.readInt();
         double duration = StdIn.readDouble();
         double hz = 440 * Math.pow(2, pitch / 12.0);
         int N = (int) (sps * duration);
         double[] a = new double[N+1];
         for (int i = 0; i <= N; i++)
            a[i] = Math.sin(2*Math.PI * i * hz / sps);
         StdAudio.play(a);
      }
   }
}
```

| pitch | distance from A |
|---|---|
| duration | note play time |
| hz | frequency |
| N | number of samples |
| a[] | sampled sine wave |

*This is a data-driven program that plays pure tones from the notes on the chromatic scale, specified on standard input as a pitch (distance from concert A) and a duration (in seconds). The test client reads the notes from standard input, creates an array by sampling a sine wave of the specified frequency and duration at 44100 samples per second, and then plays each note by calling* StdAudio.play()*.*

```
% more elise.txt
7 .25
6 .25
7 .25
6 .25
7 .25
2 .25
5 .25
3 .25
0 .50
```

```
% java PlayThatTune < elise.txt
```

PlayThatTune (PROGRAM 1.5.7) is an example that shows how easily we can create music with StdAudio. It takes notes from standard input, indexed on the chromatic scale from concert *A*, and plays them on standard audio. You can imagine all sorts of extensions on this basic scheme, some of which are addressed in the exercises. We include StdAudio in our basic arsenal of programming tools because sound processing is one important application of scientific computing that is certainly familiar to you. Not only has the commercial application of digital signal processing had a phenomenal impact on modern society, but the science and engineering behind it combines physics and computer science in interesting ways. We will study more components of digital signal processing in some detail later in the book. (For example, you will learn in SECTION 2.1 how to create sounds that are more musical than the pure sounds produced by PlayThatTune.)

I/O IS A PARTICULARLY CONVINCING EXAMPLE of the power of abstraction because standard input, standard output, standard draw, and standard audio can be tied to different physical devices at different times without making any changes to programs. Although devices may differ dramatically, we can write programs that can do I/O without depending on the properties of specific devices. From this point forward, we will use methods from StdOut, StdIn, StdDraw, and/or StdAudio in nearly every program in this book, and you will use them in nearly all of your programs, so make sure to download copies of these libraries. For economy, we collectively refer to these libraries as Std*. One important advantage of using such libraries is that you can switch to new devices that are faster, cheaper, or hold more data without changing your program at all. In such a situation, the details of the connection are a matter to be resolved between your operating system and the Std* implementations. On modern systems, new devices are typically supplied with software that resolves such details automatically for both the operating system and for Java.

Conceptually, one of the most significant features of the standard input, standard output, standard draw, and standard audio data streams is that they are *infinite*: from the point of view of your program, there is no limit on their length. This point of view not only leads to programs that have a long useful life (because they are less sensitive to changes in technology than programs with built-in limits). It also is related to the *Turing machine*, an abstract device used by theoretical computer scientists to help us understand fundamental limitations on the capabilities of real computers. One of the essential properties of the model is the idea of a finite discrete device that works with an unlimited amount of input and output.

**Q.** Why are we not using the standard Java libraries for input, graphics, and sound?

**A.** We *are* using them, but we prefer to work with simpler abstract models. The Java libraries behind StdIn, StdDraw, and StdAudio are built for production programming, and the libraries and their APIs are a bit unwieldy. To get an idea of what they are like, look at the code in StdIn.java, StdDraw.java, and StdAudio.java.

**Q.** So, let me get this straight. If I use the format %2.4f for a double value, I get two digits before the decimal point and four digits after, right?

**A.** No, that specifies just four digits after the decimal point. The first value is the width of the whole field. You want to use the format %7.2f to specify seven characters in total, four before the decimal point, the decimal point itself, and two digits after the decimal point.

**Q.** What other conversion codes are there for printf()?

**A.** For integer values, there is o for octal and x for hexadecimal. There are also numerous formats for dates and times. See the booksite for more information.

**Q.** Can my program re-read data from standard input?

**A.** No. You only get one shot at it, in the same way that you cannot undo a println() command.

**Q.** What happens if my program attempts to read data from standard input after it is exhausted?

**A.** You will get an error. StdIn.isEmpty() allows you to avoid such an error by checking whether there is more input available.

**Q.** What does the error message Exception in thread "main" java.lang. NoClassDefFoundError: StdIn mean?

**A.** You probably forgot to put StdIn.java in your working directory.

**Q.** I have a different working directory for each project that I am working on, so I have copies of StdOut.java, StdIn.java, StdDraw.java, and StdAudio.java in each of them. Is there some better way?

**A.** Yes. You can put them all in one directory and use the "classpath" mechanism to tell Java where to find them. This mechanism is operating-system dependent—you can find instructions on how to use it on the booksite.

**Q.** My terminal window hangs at the end of a program using StdAudio. How can I avoid having to use <ctrl-c> to get a command prompt?

**A.** Add a call to System.exit(0) as the last line in main(). Don't ask why.

**Q.** So I use negative integers to go below concert *A* when making input files for PlayThatTune?

**A.** Right. Actually, our choice to put concert *A* at 0 is arbitrary. A popular standard, known as the *MIDI Tuning Standard*, starts numbering at the *C* five octaves below concert *A*. By that convention, concert *A* is 69 and you do not need to use negative numbers.

**Q.** Why do I hear weird results on standard audio when I try to sonify a sine wave with a frequency of 30,000 Hertz (or more)?

**A.** The *Nyquist frequency*, defined as one-half the sampling frequency, represents the highest frequency that can be reproduced. For standard audio, the sampling frequency is 44,100, so the Nyquist frequency is 22,050.

## Exercises

**1.5.1**   Write a program that reads in integers (as many as the user enters) from standard input and prints out the maximum and minimum values.

**1.5.2**   Modify your program from the previous exercise to insist that the integers must be positive (by prompting the user to enter positive integers whenever the value entered is not positive).

**1.5.3**   Write a program that takes an integer $N$ from the command line, reads $N$ `double` values from standard input, and prints their mean (average value) and standard deviation (square root of the sum of the squares of their differences from the average, divided by $N-1$).

**1.5.4**   Extend your program from the previous exercise to create a filter that prints all the values that are further than 1.5 standard deviations from the mean. Use an array.

**1.5.5**   Write a program that reads in a sequence of integers and prints out both the integer that appears in a longest consecutive run and the length of the run. For example, if the input is 1 2 2 1 5 1 1 7 7 7 7 1 1, then your program should print `Longest run: 4 consecutive 7s`.

**1.5.6**   Write a filter that reads in a sequence of integers and prints out the integers, removing repeated values that appear consecutively. For example, if the input i 1 2 2 1 5 1 1 7 7 7 7 1 1 1 1 1 1 1 1, your program should print out 1 2 1 5 1 7 1.

**1.5.7**   Write a program that takes a command-line argument N, reads in N-1 distinct integers between 1 and N, and determines the missing value.

**1.5.8**   Write a program that reads in positive real numbers from standard input and prints out their geometric and harmonic means. The *geometric mean* of N positive numbers $x_1, x_2, ..., x_N$ is $(x_1 \times x_2 \times ... \times x_N)^{1/N}$. The *harmonic mean* is $(1/x_1 + 1/x_2 + ... + 1/x_N) / (1/N)$. *Hint*: For the geometric mean, consider taking logs to avoid overflow.

**1.5.9**   Suppose that the file `input.txt` contains the two strings F and F. What does the following command do (see EXERCISE 1.2.35)?

```
java Dragon < input.txt | java Dragon | java Dragon

public class Dragon
{
   public static void main(String[] args)
   {
      String dragon = StdIn.readString();
      String nogard = StdIn.readString();
      StdOut.print(dragon + "L" + nogard);
      StdOut.print(" ");
      StdOut.print(dragon + "R" + nogard);
      StdOut.println();
   }
}
```

**1.5.10** Write a filter TenPerLine that takes a sequence of integers between 0 and 99 and prints 10 integers per line, with columns aligned. Then write a program RandomIntSeq that takes two command-line arguments M and N and outputs N random integers between 0 and M-1. Test your programs with the command java RandomIntSeq 200 100 | java TenPerLine.

**1.5.11** Write a program that reads in text from standard input and prints out the number of words in the text. For the purpose of this exercise, a word is a sequence of non-whitespace characters that is surrounded by whitespace.

**1.5.12** Write a program that reads in lines from standard input with each line containing a name and two integers and then uses printf() to print a table with a column of the names, the integers, and the result of dividing the first by the second, accurate to three decimal places. You could use a program like this to tabulate batting averages for baseball players or grades for students.

**1.5.13** Which of the following *require* saving all the values from standard input (in an array, say), and which could be implemented as a filter using only a fixed number of variables? For each, the input comes from standard input and consists of $N$ real numbers between 0 and 1.

- Print the maximum and minimum numbers.
- Print the $k$th smallest value.
- Print the sum of the squares of the numbers.
- Print the average of the $N$ numbers.
- Print the percentage of numbers greater than the average.
- Print the $N$ numbers in increasing order.
- Print the $N$ numbers in random order.

**1.5.14** Write a program that prints a table of the monthly payments, remaining principal, and interest paid for a loan, taking three numbers as command-line arguments: the number of years, the principal, and the interest rate (see EXERCISE 1.2.24).

**1.5.15** Write a program that takes three command-line arguments $x$, $y$, and $z$, reads from standard input a sequence of point coordinates $(x_i, y_i, z_i)$, and prints the coordinates of the point closest to $(x, y, z)$. Recall that the square of the distance between $(x, y, z)$ and $(x_i, y_i, z_i)$ is $(x - x_i)^2 + (y - y_i)^2 + (z - z_i)^2$. For efficiency, do not use Math.sqrt() or Math.pow().

**1.5.16** Given the positions and masses of a sequence of objects, write a program to compute their center-of-mass, or *centroid*. The centroid is the average position of the $N$ objects, weighted by mass. If the positions and masses are given by $(x_i, y_i, m_i)$, then the centroid $(x, y, m)$ is given by:

$$m = m_1 + m_2 + \dots + m_N$$
$$x = (m_1 x_1 + \dots + m_n x_N) / m$$
$$y = (m_1 y_1 + \dots + m_n y_N) / m$$

**1.5.17** Write a program that reads in a sequence of real numbers between $-1$ and $+1$ and prints out their average magnitude, average power, and the number of zero crossings. The *average magnitude* is the average of the absolute values of the data values. The *average power* is the average of the squares of the data values. The number of *zero crossings* is the number of times a data value transitions from a strictly negative number to a strictly positive number, or vice versa. These three statistics are widely used to analyze digital signals.

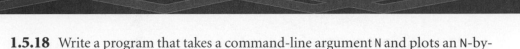

**1.5.18** Write a program that takes a command-line argument N and plots an N-by-N checkerboard with red and black squares. Color the lower left square red.

**1.5.19** Write a program that takes as command-line arguments an integer N and a double value p (between 0 and 1), plots N equally spaced points of size on the circumference of a circle, and then, with probability p for each pair of points, draws a gray line connecting them.

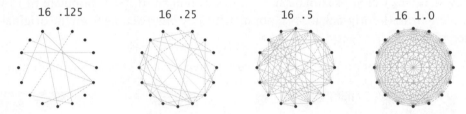

**1.5.20** Write code to draw hearts, spades, clubs, and diamonds. To draw a heart, draw a diamond, then attach two semicircles to the upper left and upper right sides.

**1.5.21** Write a program that takes a command-line argument $N$ and plots a rose with $N$ petals (if $N$ is odd) or $2N$ petals (if $N$ is even), by plotting the polar coordinates $(r, \theta)$ of the function $r = \sin(N\theta)$ for $\theta$ ranging from 0 to $2\pi$ radians.

**1.5.22** Write a program that takes a string s from the command line and displays it in banner style on the screen, moving from left to right and wrapping back to the beginning of the string as the end is reached. Add a second command-line argument to control the speed.

**1.5.23** Modify PlayThatTune to take additional command-line arguments that control the volume (multiply each sample value by the volume) and the tempo (multiply each note's duration by the tempo).

**1.5.24** Write a program that takes the name of a .wav file and a playback rate *r* as command-line arguments and plays the file at the given rate. First, use StdAudio.read() to read the file into an array a[]. If *r* = 1, just play a[]; otherwise create a new array b[] of approximate size *r* times a.length. If *r* < 1, populate b[] by *sampling* from the original; if *r* > 1, populate b[] by *interpolating* from the original. Then play b[].

**1.5.25** Write programs that uses StdDraw to create each of the following designs.

**1.5.26** Write a program Circles that draws filled circles of random size at random positions in the unit square, producing images like those below. Your program should take four command-line arguments: the number of circles, the probability that each circle is black, the minimum radius, and the maximum radius.

200 1 .01 .01        100 1 .01 .05        500 .5 .01 .05        50 .75 .1 .2

# Creative Exercises

**1.5.27** *Visualizing audio.* Modify PlayThatTune to send the values played to standard drawing, so that you can watch the sound waves as they are played. You will have to experiment with plotting multiple curves in the drawing canvas to synchronize the sound and the picture.

**1.5.28** *Statistical polling.* When collecting statistical data for certain political polls, it is very important to obtain an unbiased sample of registered voters. Assume that you have a file with N registered voters, one per line. Write a filter that prints out a random sample of size M (see PROGRAM 1.4.1).

**1.5.29** *Terrain analysis.* Suppose that a terrain is represented by a two-dimensional grid of elevation values (in meters). A *peak* is a grid point whose four neighboring cells (left, right, up, and down) have strictly lower elevation values. Write a program Peaks that reads a terrain from standard input and then computes and prints the number of peaks in the terrain.

**1.5.30** *Histogram.* Suppose that the standard input stream is a sequence of double values. Write a program that takes an integer N and two double values $l$ and $r$ from the command line and uses StdDraw to plot a histogram of the count of the numbers in the standard input stream that fall in each of the N intervals defined by dividing $(l, r)$ into N equal-sized intervals.

**1.5.31** *Spirographs.* Write a program that takes three parameters $R$, $r$, and $a$ from the command line and draws the resulting *spirograph*. A spirograph (technically, an epicycloid) is a curve formed by rolling a circle of radius $r$ around a larger fixed circle of radius $R$. If the pen offset from the center of the rolling circle is $(r+a)$, then the equation of the resulting curve at time $t$ is given by

$$x(t) = (R + r) \cos (t) - (r + a) \cos ((R + r)t/r)$$
$$y(t) = (R + r) \sin (t) - (r + a) \sin ((R + r)t/r)$$

Such curves were popularized by a best-selling toy that contains discs with gear teeth on the edges and small holes that you could put a pen in to trace spirographs.

**1.5.32** *Clock.* Write a program that displays an animation of the second, minute, and hour hands of an analog clock. Use the method `StdDraw.show(1000)` to update the display roughly once per second.

**1.5.33** *Oscilloscope.* Write a program to simulate the output of an oscilloscope and produce Lissajous patterns. These patterns are named after the French physicist, Jules A. Lissajous, who studied the patterns that arise when two mutually perpendicular periodic disturbances occur simultaneously. Assume that the inputs are sinusoidal, so that the following parametric equations describe the curve:

$$x(t) = A_x \sin(w_x t + \theta_x)$$
$$y(t) = A_y \sin(w_y t + \theta_y)$$

Take the six parameters $A_x$, $w_x$, $\theta_x$, $A_y$, $w_y$, and $\theta_y$ from the command line.

**1.5.34** *Bouncing ball with tracks.* Modify `BouncingBall` to produce images like the ones shown in the text, which show the track of the ball on a gray background.

**1.5.35** *Bouncing ball with gravity.* Modify `BouncingBall` to incorporate gravity in the vertical direction. Add calls to `StdAudio.play()` to add one sound effect when the ball hits a wall and a different one when it hits the floor.

**1.5.36** *Random tunes.* Write a program that uses `StdAudio` to play random tunes. Experiment with keeping in key, assigning high probabilities to whole steps, repetition, and other rules to produce reasonable melodies.

**1.5.37** *Tile patterns.* Using your solution to EXERCISE 1.5.25, write a program `TilePattern` that takes a command-line argument N and draws an N-by-N pattern, using the tile of your choice. Add a second command-line argument that adds a checkerboard option. Add a third command-line argument for color selection. Using the patterns on the facing page as a starting point, design a tile floor. Be creative! *Note*: These are all designs from antiquity that you can find in many ancient (and modern) buildings.

# 1.6   Case Study: Random Web Surfer

COMMUNICATING ACROSS THE WEB HAS BECOME an integral part of everyday life. This communication is enabled in part by scientific studies of the structure of the web, a subject of active research since its inception. We next consider a simple model of the web that has proven to be a particularly successful approach to understanding some of its properties. Variants of this model are widely used and have been a key factor in the explosive growth of search applications on the web.

The model is known as the *random surfer* model, and is simple to describe. We consider the web to be a fixed set of *pages*, with each page containing a fixed set of *hyperlinks* (for brevity, we use the term *links*), and each link a reference to some other page. We study what happens to a person (the random surfer) who randomly moves from page to page, either by typing a page name into the address bar or by clicking a link on the current page.

The underlying mathematical model behind the web model is known as the *graph*, which we will consider in detail at the end of the book (in SECTION 4.5). We defer discussion of details about processing graphs until then. Instead, we concentrate on calculations associated with a natural and well-studied probabilistic model that accurately describes the behavior of the random surfer.

The first step in studying the random surfer model is to formulate it more precisely. The crux of the matter is to specify what it means to randomly move from page to page. The following intuitive *90-10 rule* captures both methods of moving to a new page: *Assume that 90 per cent of the time the random surfer clicks a random link on the current page (each link chosen with equal probability) and that 10 percent of the time the random surfer goes directly to a random page (all pages on the web chosen with equal probability).*

*Pages and links*

You can immediately see that this model has flaws, because you know from your own experience that the behavior of a real web surfer is not quite so simple:

• No one chooses links or pages with equal probability.
• There is no real potential to surf directly to each page on the web.
• The 90-10 (or any fixed) breakdown is just a guess.
• It does not take the back button or bookmarks into account.
• We can only afford to work with a small sample of the web.

Despite these flaws, the model is sufficiently rich that computer scientists have learned a great deal about properties of the web by studying it. To appreciate the model, consider the small example on the previous page. Which page do you think the random surfer is most likely to visit?

Each person using the web behaves a bit like the random surfer, so understanding the fate of the random surfer is of intense interest to people building web infrastructure and web applications. The model is a tool for understanding the experience of each of the hundreds of millions of web users. In this section, you will use the basic programming tools from this chapter to study the model and its implications.

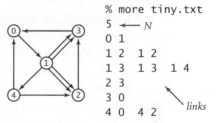

**Input format**  We want to be able to study the behavior of the random surfer on various web models, not just one example. Consequently, we want to write *data-driven code*, where we keep data in files and write programs that read the data from standard input. The first step in this approach is to define an *input format* that we can use to structure the information in the input files. We are free to define any convenient input format.

*Random surfer input format*

Later in the book, you will learn how to read web pages in Java programs (SECTION 3.1) and to convert from names to numbers (SECTION 4.4) as well as other techniques for efficient graph processing. For now, we assume that there are *N* web pages, numbered from 0 to N-1, and we represent links with ordered pairs of such numbers, the first specifying the page containing the link and the second specifying the page to which it refers. Given these conventions, a straightforward input format for the random surfer problem is an input stream consisting of an integer (the value of *N*) followed by a sequence of pairs of integers (the representations of all the links). StdIn treats all sequences of whitespace characters as a single delimiter, so we are free to either put one link per line or arrange them several to a line.

**Transition matrix**   We use a two-dimensional matrix, that we refer to as the *transition matrix*, to completely specify the behavior of the random surfer. With $N$ web pages, we define an $N$-by-$N$ matrix such that the entry in row i and column j is the probability that the random surfer moves to page j when on page i. Our first task is to write code that can create such a matrix for any given input. By the 90-10 rule, this computation is not difficult. We do so in three steps:

- Read $N$, and then create arrays counts[][] and outDegree[].
- Read the links and accumulate counts so that counts[i][j] counts the links from i to j and outDegree[i] counts the links from i to anywhere.
- Use the 90-10 rule to compute the probabilities.

The first two steps are elementary, and the third is not much more difficult: multiply counts[i][j] by .90/degree[i] if there is a link from i to j (take a random link with probability .9), and then add .10/N to each entry (go to a random page with probability .1). Transition (PROGRAM 1.6.1) performs this calculation: It is a filter that converts the list-of-links representation of a web model into a transition-matrix representation.

The transition matrix is significant because each row represents a *discrete probability distribution*—the entries fully specify the behavior of the random surfer's next move, giving the probability of surfing to each page. Note in particular that the entries sum to 1 (the surfer always goes somewhere).

The output of Transition defines another file format, one for matrices of double values: the numbers of rows and columns followed by the values for matrix entries. Now, we can write programs that read and process transition matrices.

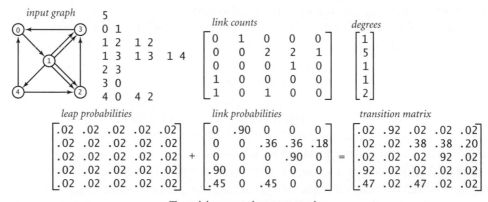

*Transition matrix computation*

**Program 1.6.1   *Computing the transition matrix***

```
public class Transition
{
   public static void main(String[] args)
   {  // Print random-surfer probabilites.
      int N = StdIn.readInt();
      int[][] counts = new int[N][N];
      int[] outDegree = new int[N];
      while (!StdIn.isEmpty())
      {  // Accumulate link counts.
         int i = StdIn.readInt();
         int j = StdIn.readInt();
         outDegree[i]++;
         counts[i][j]++;
      }

      StdOut.println(N + " " + N);
      for (int i = 0; i < N; i++)
      {  // Print probability distribution for row i.
         for (int j = 0; j < N; j++)
         {  // Print probability for column j.
            double p = .90*counts[i][j]/outDegree[i] + .10/N;
            StdOut.printf("%8.5f", p);
         }
         StdOut.println();
      }
   }
}
```

| | |
|---|---|
| N | *number of pages* |
| counts[i][j] | *count of links from page i to page j* |
| outDegree[i] | *count of links from page i to anywhere* |
| p | *transition probability* |

*This program is a filter that reads links from standard input and produces the corresponding transition matrix on standard output. First, it processes the input to count the outlinks from each page. Then it applies the 90-10 rule to compute the transition matrix (see text). It assumes that there are no pages that have no outlinks in the input (see Exercise 1.6.3).*

```
% more tiny.txt
5
0 1
1 2   1 2
1 3   1 3   1 4
2 3
3 0
4 0   4 2
```

```
% java Transition < tiny.txt
5 5
 0.02000 0.92000 0.02000 0.02000 0.02000
 0.02000 0.02000 0.38000 0.38000 0.20000
 0.02000 0.02000 0.02000 0.92000 0.02000
 0.92000 0.02000 0.02000 0.02000 0.02000
 0.47000 0.02000 0.47000 0.02000 0.02000
```

**Simulation**   Given the transition matrix, simulating the behavior of the random surfer involves surprisingly little code, as you can see in RandomSurfer (PROGRAM 1.6.2). This program reads a transition matrix and surfs according to the rules, starting at page 0 and taking the number of moves as a command-line argument. It counts the number of times that the surfer visits each page. Dividing that count by the number of moves yields an estimate of the probability that a random surfer winds up on the page. This probability is known as the page's *rank*. In other words, RandomSurfer computes an estimate of all page ranks.

*One random move.*   The key to the computation is the random move, which is specified by the transition matrix. We maintain a variable page whose value is the current location of the surfer. Row page of the matrix gives, for each j, the probability that the surfer next goes to j. In other words, when the surfer is at page, our task is to generate a random integer between 0 and N−1 according to the distribution given by row page in the transition matrix (the one-dimensional array p[page]). How can we accomplish this task? We can use Math.random() to generate a random number r between 0 and 1, but how does that help us get to a random page? One-way to answer this question is to think of the probabilities in row page as defining a set of N intervals in (0, 1) with each probability corresponding to an interval length. Then our random variable r falls into one of the intervals, with probability precisely specified by the interval length. This reasoning leads to the following code:

*Generating a random integer from a discrete distribution*

```
double sum = 0.0;
for (int j = 0; j < N; j++)
{  // Find interval containing r.
    sum += p[page][j];
    if (r < sum) { page = j; break; }
}
```

The variable sum tracks the endpoints of the intervals defined in row p[page], and the for loop finds the interval containing the random value r. For example, suppose that the surfer is at page 4 in our example. The transition probabilities are .47,

**Program 1.6.2   *Simulating a random surfer***

```
public class RandomSurfer
{
   public static void main(String[] args)
   { // Simulate random-surfer leaps and links.
      int T = Integer.parseInt(args[0]);
      int N = StdIn.readInt();
      StdIn.readInt();

      // Read transition matrix.
      double[][] p = new double[N][N];
      for (int i = 0; i < N; i++)
         for (int j = 0; j < N; j++)
            p[i][j] = StdIn.readDouble();

      int page = 0; // Start at page 0.
      int[] freq = new int[N];
      for (int t = 0; t < T; t++)
      {  // Make one random move.
         double r = Math.random();
         double sum = 0.0;
         for (int j = 0; j < N; j++)
         {  // Find interval containing r.
            sum += p[page][j];
            if (r < sum) { page = j; break; }
         }
         freq[page]++;
      }

      for (int i = 0; i < N; i++)      // Print page ranks.
         StdOut.printf("%8.5f", (double) freq[i] / T);
      StdOut.println();
   }
}
```

| | |
|---|---|
| T | *number of moves* |
| N | *number of pages* |
| page | *current page* |
| p[i][j] | *probability that the surfer moves from page i to page j* |
| freq[i] | *number of times the surfer hits page i* |

*This program uses a transition matrix to simulate the behavior of a random surfer. It takes the number of moves as a command-line argument, reads the transition matrix, performs the indicated number of moves as prescribed by the matrix, and prints the relative frequency of hitting each page. The key to the computation is the random move to the next page (see text).*

```
% java Transition < tiny.txt | java RandomSurfer 100
 0.24000 0.23000 0.16000 0.25000 0.12000
% java Transition < tiny.txt | java RandomSurfer 10000
 0.27280 0.26530 0.14820 0.24830 0.06540
% java Transition < tiny.txt | java RandomSurfer 1000000
0.27324 0.26568 0.14581 0.24737 0.06790
```

.02, .47, .02, and .02, and sum takes on the values 0.0, 0.47, 0.49, 0.96, 0.98, and 1.0. These values indicate that the probabilities define the five intervals (0, .47), (.47, .49), (.49, .96), (.96, .98), and (.98, 1), one for each page. Now, suppose that Math.random() returns the value .71. We increment j from 0 to 1 to 2 and stop there, which indicates that .71 is in the interval (.49, .96), so we send the surfer to the third page (page 2). Then, we perform the same computation for p[2], and the random surfer is off and surfing. For large $N$, we can use *binary search* to substantially speed up this computation (see EXERCISE 4.2.36). Typically, we are interested in speeding up the search in this situation because we are likely to need a huge number of random moves, as you will see.

*Markov chains.* The random process that describes the surfer's behavior is known as a *Markov chain*, named after the Russian mathematician Andrey Markov, who developed the concept in the early 20th century. Markov chains are widely applicable, well-studied, and have many remarkable and useful properties. For example, you may have wondered why RandomSurfer starts the random surfer at page 0 whereas you might have expected a random choice. A basic limit theorem for Markov chains says that the surfer could start *anywhere*, because the probability that a random surfer eventually winds up on any particular page is the same for all starting pages! No matter where the surfer starts, the process eventually stabilizes to a point where further surfing provides no further information. This phenomenon is known as *mixing*. Though this phenomenon is perhaps counterintuitive at first, it explains coherent behavior in a situation that might seem chaotic. In the present context, it captures the idea that the web looks pretty much the same to everyone after surfing for a sufficiently long time. However, not all Markov chains have this mixing property. For example, if we eliminate the random leap from our model, certain configurations of web pages can present problems for the surfer. Indeed, there exist on the web sets of pages known as *spider traps,* which are designed to attract incoming links but have no outgoing links. Without the random leap, the surfer could get stuck in a spider trap. The primary purpose of the 90-10 rule is to guarantee mixing and eliminate such anomalies.

*Page ranks.* The RandomSurfer simulation is straightforward: it loops for the indicated number of moves, randomly surfing through the graph. Because of the mixing phenomenon, increasing the number of iterations gives increasingly accurate estimates of the probability that the surfer lands on each page (the page ranks). How do the results compare with your intuition when you first thought about the question? You might have guessed that page 4 was the lowest-ranked page, but did you think that pages 0 and 1 would rank higher than page 3? If we want to know which page is the highest rank, we need more precision and more accuracy. RandomSurfer needs $10^n$ moves to get answers precise to $n$ decimal places and many more moves for those answers to stabilize to an accurate value. For our example, it takes tens of thousands of iterations to get answers accurate to two decimal places and millions of iterations to get answers accurate to three places (see Exercise 1.6.5). The end result is that page 0 beats page 1 by 27.3% to 26.6%. That such a tiny difference would appear in such a small problem is quite surprising: if you guessed that page 0 is the most likely spot for the surfer to end up, you were lucky! Accurate page rank estimates for the web are valuable in practice for many reasons. First, using them to put in order the pages that match the search criteria for web searches proved to be vastly more in line with people's expectations than previous methods. Next, this measure of confidence and reliability led to the investment of huge amounts of money in web advertising based on page ranks. Even in our tiny example, page ranks might be used to convince advertisers to pay up to four times as much to place an ad on page 0 as on page 4. Comput-

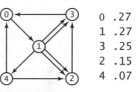

ing page ranks is mathematically sound, an interesting computer science problem, and big business, all rolled into one.

| | |
|---|---|
| 0 | .27 |
| 1 | .27 |
| 3 | .25 |
| 2 | .15 |
| 4 | .07 |

*Visualizing the histogram.* With StdDraw, it is also easy to create a visual representation that can give you a feeling for how the random surfer visit frequencies converge to the page ranks. Simply add

```
StdDraw.clear();
StdDraw.setXscale(-1, N);
StdDraw.setYscale(0, t);
StdDraw.setPenRadius(.5/N);
for (int i = 0; i < N; i++)
    StdDraw.line(i, 0, i, freq[i]);
StdDraw.show(20);
```

*Page ranks with histogram*

to the random move loop, run RandomSurfer for large values of T, and you will see a drawing of the frequency histogram that eventually stabilizes to the page ranks. After you have used this tool once, you are likely to find yourself using it *every* time you want to study a new model (perhaps with some minor adjustments to handle larger models).

*Studying other models.* RandomSurfer and Transition are excellent examples of data-driven programs. You can easily create a data model just by creating a file like tiny.txt that starts with an integer N and then specifies pairs of integers between 0 and N-1 that represent links connecting pages. You are encouraged to run it for various data models as suggested in the exercises, or to make up some models of your own to study. If you have ever wondered how web page ranking works, this calculation is your chance to develop better intuition about what causes one page to be ranked more highly than another. What kind of page is likely to be rated highly? One that has many links to other pages, or one that has just a few links to other pages? The exercises in this section present many opportunities to study the behavior of the random surfer. Since RandomSurfer uses standard input, you can write simple programs that generate large input models, pipe their output to RandomSurfer, and therefore study the random surfer on large models. Such flexibility is an important reason to use standard input and standard output.

DIRECTLY SIMULATING THE BEHAVIOR OF A random surfer to understand the structure of the web is appealing, but it has limitations. Think about the following question: Could you use it to compute page ranks for a web model with millions (or billions!) of web pages and links? The quick answer to this question is *no*, because you cannot even afford to store the transition matrix for such a large number of pages. A matrix for millions of pages would have *trillions* of entries. Do you have that much space on your computer? Could you use RandomSurfer to find page ranks for a smaller model with, say, thousands of pages? To answer this question, you might run multiple simulations, record the results for a large number of trials, and then interpret those experimental results. We do use this approach for many scientific problems (the gambler's ruin problem is one example; SECTION 2.4 is devoted to another), but it can be very time-consuming, as a huge number of trials may be necessary to get the desired accuracy. Even for our tiny example, we saw that it takes millions of iterations to get the page ranks accurate to three or four decimal places. For larger models, the required number of iterations to obtain accurate estimates becomes truly huge.

**Mixing a Markov chain**    It is important to remember that the page ranks are a property of the web model, not any particular approach for computing it. That is, RandomSurfer is just *one* way to compute page ranks. Fortunately, a simple computational model based on a well-studied area of mathematics provides a far more efficient approach than simulation to the problem of computing page ranks. That model makes use of the basic arithmetic operations on two-dimensional matrices that we considered in SECTION 1.4.

*Squaring a Markov chain.*  What is the probability that the random surfer will move from page i to page j in *two* moves? The first move goes to an intermediate page k, so we calculate the probability of moving from i to k and then from k to j for all possible k and add up the results. For our example, the probability of moving from 1 to 2 in two moves is the probability of moving from 1 to 0 to 2 (.02×.02), plus the probability of moving from 1 to 1 to 2 (.02×.38), plus the probability of moving from 1 to 2 to 2 (.38×.02), plus the probability of moving from 1 to 3 to 2 (.38×.02), plus the probability of moving from 1 to 4 to 2 (.20×.47), which adds up to a grand total of .1172. The same process works for each pair of pages. *This calculation is one that we have seen before*, in the definition of matrix multiplication: the entry in row i and column j in the result is the dot product of row i and column j in the original. In other words, the result of multiplying p[][] by itself is a matrix where the entry in row i and column j is the probability that the random surfer moves from page i to page j in two moves. Studying the entries of the two-move transition matrix for our example is well worth your time and will help you better understand the movement of the random surfer. For instance, the largest entry in the square is the one in row 2 and column 0, reflecting the fact that a surfer starting on page 2 has only one link out, to page 3, where there is also only one link out, to page 0. Therefore, by far the most likely outcome for a surfer start-

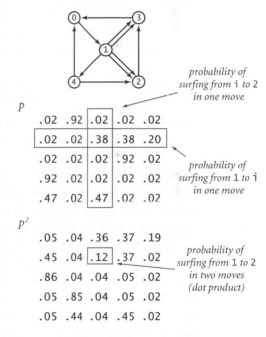

*probability of surfing from i to 2 in one move*

*p*

| | | | | |
|---|---|---|---|---|
| .02 | .92 | .02 | .02 | .02 |
| .02 | .02 | .38 | .38 | .20 |
| .02 | .02 | .02 | .92 | .02 |
| .92 | .02 | .02 | .02 | .02 |
| .47 | .02 | .47 | .02 | .02 |

*probability of surfing from 1 to i in one move*

*p²*

| | | | | |
|---|---|---|---|---|
| .05 | .04 | .36 | .37 | .19 |
| .45 | .04 | .12 | .37 | .02 |
| .86 | .04 | .04 | .05 | .02 |
| .05 | .85 | .04 | .05 | .02 |
| .05 | .44 | .04 | .45 | .02 |

*probability of surfing from 1 to 2 in two moves (dot product)*

*Squaring a Markov chain*

ing on page 2 is to end up in page 0 after two moves. All of the other two-move routes involve more choices and are less probable. It is important to note that this is an exact computation (up to the limitations of Java's floating-point precision), in contrast to `RandomSurfer`, which produces an estimate and needs more iterations to get a more accurate estimate.

*The power method.* We might then calculate the probabilities for three moves by multiplying by `p[][]` again, and for four moves by multiplying by `p[][]` yet again, and so forth. However, matrix-matrix multiplication is expensive, and we are actually interested in a *vector*-matrix calculation. For our example, we start with the vector

```
[1.0 0.0 0.0 0.0 0.0 ]
```

which specifies that the random surfer starts on page 0. Multiplying this vector by the transition matrix gives the vector

```
[.02 .92 .02 .02 .02 ]
```

which is the probabilities that the surfer winds up on each of the pages after one step. Now, multiplying *this* vector by the transition matrix gives the vector

```
[.05 .04 .36 .37 .19 ]
```

which contains the probabilities that the surfer winds up on each of the pages after *two* steps. For example, the probability of moving from 0 to 2 in two moves is the probability of moving from 0 to 0 to 2 ($.02 \times .02$), plus the probability of moving from 0 to 1 to 2 ($.92 \times .38$), plus the probability of moving from 0 to 2 to 2 ($.02 \times .02$), plus the probability of moving from 0 to 3 to 2 ($.02 \times .02$), plus the probability of moving from 0 to 4 to 2 ($.02 \times .47$), which adds up to a grand total of .36 . From these initial calculations, the pattern is clear: *The vector giving the probabilities that the random surfer is at each page after t steps is precisely the product of the corresponding vector for t − 1 steps and the transition matrix.* By the basic limit theorem for Markov chains, this process converges to the same vector no matter where we start; in other words, after a sufficient number of moves, the probability that the surfer ends up on any given page is independent of the starting point. `Markov` (PROGRAM 1.6.3) is an implementation that you can use to check convergence for our example. For instance, it gets the same results (the page ranks accurate to two decimal places) as `RandomSurfer`, but with just 20 matrix-vector multiplications

```
            rank[]                      p[][]                      newRank[]
first move              ⎡.02 .92 .02 .02 .02⎤
                        ⎢.02 .02 .38 .38 .20⎥
      [ 1.0 0.0 0.0 0.0 0.0 ] *  ⎢.02 .02 .02 .92 .02⎥ = [ .02 .92 .02 .02 .02 ]
                        ⎢.92 .02 .02 .02 .02⎥
                        ⎣.47 .02 .47 .02 .02⎦
```

*probabilities of surfing
from 0 to i in one move*

*second move*

*probabilities of surfing
from i to 2 in one move*

*probabilities of surfing
from 0 to i in one move*

```
      [ .02 .92 .02 .02 .02 ] *  ⎢.02 .02 .38 .38 .20⎥
                        ⎡.02 .92 .02 .02 .02⎤
                        ⎢.02 .02 .02 .92 .02⎥
                        ⎢.92 .02 .02 .02 .02⎥
                        ⎣.47 .02 .47 .02 .02⎦
```

*probability of surfing from 0 to 2
in two moves (dot product)*

= [ .05 .04 .36 .37 .19 ]

*probabilities of surfing
from 0 to i in two moves*

*third move*

*probabilities of surfing
from 0 to i in two moves*

```
      [ .05 .04 .36 .37 .19 ] *  ⎡.02 .92 .02 .02 .02⎤
                        ⎢.02 .02 .38 .38 .20⎥
                        ⎢.02 .02 .02 .92 .02⎥ = [ .44 .06 .12 .36 .03 ]
                        ⎢.92 .02 .02 .02 .02⎥
                        ⎣.47 .02 .47 .02 .02⎦
```

*probabilities of surfing
from 0 to i in three moves*

.
.
.

*20th move*

*probabilities of surfing
from 0 to i in 19 moves*

```
      [ .27 .26 .15 .25 .07 ] *  ⎡.02 .92 .02 .02 .02⎤
                        ⎢.02 .02 .38 .38 .20⎥
                        ⎢.02 .02 .02 .92 .02⎥ = [ .27 .26 .15 .25 .07 ]
                        ⎢.92 .02 .02 .02 .02⎥
                        ⎣.47 .02 .47 .02 .02⎦
```

*probabilities of surfing
from 0 to i in 20 moves
(steady state)*

*The power method for computing page ranks (limit values of transition probabilities)*

*Program 1.6.3    Mixing a Markov chain*

```
public class Markov
{  //  Compute page ranks after T moves.
   public static void main(String[] args)
   {
      int T = Integer.parseInt(args[0]);
      int N = StdIn.readInt();
      StdIn.readInt();

      // Read p[][] from StdIn.
      double[][] p = new double[N][N];
      for (int i = 0; i < N; i++)
         for (int j = 0; j < N; j++)
            p[i][j] = StdIn.readDouble();

      // Use the power method to compute page ranks.
      double[] rank = new double[N];
      rank[0] = 1.0;
      for (int t = 0; t < T; t++)
      {  // Compute effect of next move on page ranks.
         double[] newRank = new double[N];
         for (int j = 0; j < N; j++)
         {  //  New rank of page j is dot product
            //  of old ranks and column j of p[][].
            for (int k = 0; k < N; k++)
               newRank[j] += rank[k]*p[k][j];
         }

         for (int j = 0; j < N; j++)
            rank[j] = newRank[j];
      }

      for (int i = 0; i < N; i++)    // Print page ranks.
         StdOut.printf("%8.5f", rank[i]);
      StdOut.println();
   }
}
```

| | |
|---|---|
| T | *number of iterations* |
| N | *number of pages* |
| p[][] | *transition matrix* |
| rank[] | *page ranks* |
| newRank[] | *new page ranks* |

*This program reads a transition matrix from standard input and computes the probabilities that a random surfer lands on each page (page ranks) after the number of steps specified as command-line argument.*

```
% java Transition < tiny.txt | java Markov 20
 0.27245 0.26515 0.14669 0.24764 0.06806

% java Transition < tiny.txt | java Markov 40
 0.27303 0.26573 0.14618 0.24723 0.06783
```

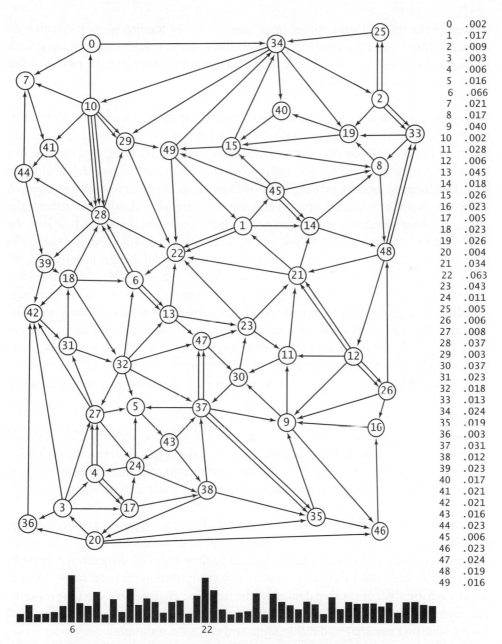

| | |
|---|---|
| 0 | .002 |
| 1 | .017 |
| 2 | .009 |
| 3 | .003 |
| 4 | .006 |
| 5 | .016 |
| 6 | .066 |
| 7 | .021 |
| 8 | .017 |
| 9 | .040 |
| 10 | .002 |
| 11 | .028 |
| 12 | .006 |
| 13 | .045 |
| 14 | .018 |
| 15 | .026 |
| 16 | .023 |
| 17 | .005 |
| 18 | .023 |
| 19 | .026 |
| 20 | .004 |
| 21 | .034 |
| 22 | .063 |
| 23 | .043 |
| 24 | .011 |
| 25 | .005 |
| 26 | .006 |
| 27 | .008 |
| 28 | .037 |
| 29 | .003 |
| 30 | .037 |
| 31 | .023 |
| 32 | .018 |
| 33 | .013 |
| 34 | .024 |
| 35 | .019 |
| 36 | .003 |
| 37 | .031 |
| 38 | .012 |
| 39 | .023 |
| 40 | .017 |
| 41 | .021 |
| 42 | .021 |
| 43 | .016 |
| 44 | .023 |
| 45 | .006 |
| 46 | .023 |
| 47 | .024 |
| 48 | .019 |
| 49 | .016 |

*Page ranks with histogram for a larger example*

instead of the tens of thousands of iterations needed by RandomSurfer. Another 20 multiplications gives the results accurate to three decimal places, as compared with millions of iterations for RandomSurfer, and just a few more give the results to full precision (see EXERCISE 1.6.6).

MARKOV CHAINS ARE WELL-STUDIED, BUT THEIR impact on the web was not truly felt until 1998, when two graduate students, Sergey Brin and Lawrence Page, had the audacity to build a Markov chain and compute the probabilities that a random surfer hits each page for *the whole web*. Their work revolutionized web search and is the basis for the page ranking method used by GOOGLE, the highly successful web search company that they founded. Specifically, the company periodically recomputes the random surfer's probability for each page. Then, when you do a search, it lists the pages related to your search keywords in order of these ranks. Such page ranks now predominate because they somehow correspond to the expectations of typical web users, reliably providing them with *relevant* web pages for typical searches. The computation that is involved is enormously time-consuming, due to the huge number of pages on the web, but the result has turned out to be enormously profitable and well worth the expense. The method used in Markov is far more efficient than simulating the behavior of a random surfer, but it is still too slow to actually compute the probabilities for a huge matrix corresponding to all the pages on the web. That computation is enabled by better data structures for graphs (see CHAPTER 4).

**Lessons**   Developing a full understanding of the random surfer model is beyond the scope of this book. Instead, our purpose is to show you an application that involves writing a bit more code than the short programs that we have been using to teach specific concepts. What specific lessons can we learn from this case study?

*We already have a full computational model.*   Primitive types of data and strings, conditionals and loops, arrays, and standard input/output enable you to address interesting problems of all sorts. Indeed, it is a basic precept of theoretical computer science that this model suffices to specify any computation that can be performed on any reasonable computing device. In the next two chapters, we discuss two critical ways in which the model has been extended to drastically reduce the amount of time and effort required to develop large and complex programs.

*Data-driven code is prevalent.* The concept of using standard input and output streams and saving data in files is a powerful one. We write filters to convert from one kind of input to another, generators that can produce huge input files for study, and programs that can handle a wide variety of different models. We can save data for archiving or later use. We can also process data derived from some other source and then save it in a file, whether it is from a scientific instrument or a distant website. The concept of data-driven code is an easy and flexible way to support this suite of activities.

*Accuracy can be elusive.* It is a mistake to assume that a program produces accurate answers simply because it can print numbers to many decimal places of precision. Often, the most difficult challenge that we face is ensuring that we have accurate answers.

*Uniform random numbers are only a start.* When we speak informally about random behavior, we often are thinking of something more complicated than the "every value equally likely" model that `Math.random()` gives us. Many of the problems that we consider involve working with random numbers from other distributions, such as `RandomSurfer`.

*Efficiency matters.* It is also a mistake to assume that your computer is so fast that it can do *any* computation. Some problems require much more computational effort than others. CHAPTER 4 is devoted to a thorough discussion of evaluating the performance of the programs that you write. We defer detailed consideration of such issues until then, but remember that you always need to have some general idea of the performance requirements of your programs.

PERHAPS THE MOST IMPORTANT LESSON TO learn from writing programs for complicated problems like the example in this section is that *debugging is difficult.* The polished programs in the book mask that lesson, but you can rest assured that each one is the product of a long bout of testing, fixing bugs, and running the programs on numerous inputs. Generally we avoid describing bugs and the process of fixing them in the text because that makes for a boring account and overly focuses attention on bad code, but you can find some examples and descriptions in the exercises and on the booksite.

## *Exercises*

**1.6.1**   Modify Transition to take the leap probability from the command line and use your modified version to examine the effect on page ranks of switching to an 80-20 rule or a 95-5 rule.

**1.6.2**   Modify Transition to ignore the effect of multiple links. That is, if there are multiple links from one page to another, count them as one link. Create a small example that shows how this modification can change the order of page ranks.

**1.6.3**   Modify Transition to handle pages with no outgoing links, by filling rows corresponding to such pages with the value $1/N$.

**1.6.4**   The code fragment in RandomSurfer that generates the random move fails if the probabilities in the row p[page] do not add up to 1. Explain what happens in that case, and suggest a way to fix the problem.

**1.6.5**   Determine, to within a factor of 10, the number of iterations required by RandomSurfer to compute page ranks to four decimal places and to five decimal places for tiny.txt.

**1.6.6.**   Determine the number of iterations required by Markov to compute page ranks to three decimal places, to four decimal places, and to ten decimal places for tiny.txt.

**1.6.7**   Download the file medium.txt from the booksite (which reflects the 50-page example depicted in this section) and add to it links *from* page 23 *to* every other page. Observe the effect on the page ranks, and discuss the result.

**1.6.8**   Add to medium.txt (see the previous exercise) links *to* page 23 *from* every other page, observe the effect on the page ranks, and discuss the result.

**1.6.9**   Suppose that your page is page 23 in medium.txt. Is there a link that you could add from your page to some other page that would *raise* the rank of *your* page?

**1.6.10**   Suppose that your page is page 23 in medium.txt. Is there a link that you could add from your page to some other page that would *lower* the rank of *that* page?

**1.6.11** Use `Transition` and `RandomSurfer` to determine the transition probabilities for the eight-page example shown below.

**1.6.12** Use `Transition` and `Markov` to determine the transition probabilities for the eight-page example shown below.

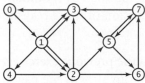

*Eight-page example*

## Creative Exercises

**1.6.13** *Matrix squaring.* Write a program like Markov that computes page ranks by repeatedly squaring the matrix, thus computing the sequence $p$, $p^2$, $p^4$, $p^8$, $p^{16}$, and so forth. Verify that all of the rows in the matrix converge to the same values.

**1.6.14** *Random web.* Write a generator for Transition that takes as input a page count N and a link count M and prints to standard output N followed by M random pairs of integers from 0 to N-1. (See SECTION 4.5 for a discussion of more realistic web models.)

**1.6.15** *Hubs and authorities.* Add to your generator from the previous exercise a fixed number of *hubs*, which have links pointing to them from 10% of the pages, chosen at random, and *authorities*, which have links pointing from them to 10% of the pages. Compute page ranks. Which rank higher, hubs or authorities?

**1.6.16** *Page ranks.* Design an array of pages and links where the highest-ranking page has fewer links pointing to it than some other page.

**1.6.17** *Hitting time.* The hitting time for a page is the expected number of moves between times the random surfer visits the page. Run experiments to estimate page hitting times for tiny.txt, compare with page ranks, formulate a hypothesis about the relationship, and test your hypothesis on medium.txt.

**1.6.18** *Cover time.* Write a program that estimates the time required for the random surfer to visit every page at least once, starting from a random page.

**1.6.19** *Graphical simulation.* Create a graphical simulation where the size of the dot representing each page is proportional to its rank. To make your program data-driven, design a file format that includes coordinates specifying where each page should be drawn. Test your program on medium.txt.

# Chapter Two

# *Functions and Modules*

THIS CHAPTER IS CENTERED ON A construct that has as profound an impact on control flow as do conditionals and loops: the *function*, which allows us to transfer control back and forth between different pieces of code. Functions (which are known as *static methods* in Java) are important because they allow us to clearly separate tasks within a program and because they provide a general mechanism that enables us to reuse code.

We group functions together in *modules*, which we can compile independently. We use modules to break a computational task into subtasks of a reasonable size. You will learn in this chapter how to build modules of your own and to use them, in a style of programming known as *modular programming*.

Some modules are developed with the primary intent of providing code that can be reused later by many other programs. We refer to such modules as *libraries*. In particular, we consider in this chapter libraries for generating random numbers, analyzing data, and input/output for arrays. Libraries vastly extend the set of operations that we use in our programs.

We pay special attention to functions that transfer control to themselves. This process is known as *recursion*. At first, recursion may seem counterintuitive, but it allows us to develop simple programs that can address complex tasks that would otherwise be much more difficult to handle.

*Whenever you can clearly separate tasks within programs, you should do so*. We repeat this mantra throughout this chapter, and end the chapter with an example showing how a complex programming task can be handled by breaking it into smaller subtasks, then independently developing modules that interact with one another to address the subtasks.

## 2.1 Static Methods

THE JAVA CONSTRUCT FOR IMPLEMENTING FUNCTIONS is known as the *static method*. The modifier `static` distinguishes this kind of method from the kind discussed later in CHAPTER 3—we will apply it consistently for now and discuss the difference then.

You have actually been using static methods since the beginning of this book, from printing with `System.out.print-ln()` to mathematical functions such as `Math.abs()` and `Math.sqrt()` to all of the methods in `StdIn`, `StdOut`, `StdDraw`, and `StdAudio`. Indeed, every Java program that you have written has a static

*Programs in this section*

method named `main()`. In this section, you will learn how to define and use static methods.

In mathematics, a *function* maps a value of a specified type (the *domain*) to another value of another specified type (the *range*). For example, the function $f(x) = x^2$ maps 2 to 4, 3 to 9, 4 to 16, and so forth. At first, we work with static methods that implement mathematical functions, because they are so familiar. Many standard functions are implemented in Java's `Math` library, but scientists and engineers work with a broad variety of mathematical functions, which cannot all be included in the library. At the beginning of this section, you will learn how to implement and use such functions on your own.

Later, you will learn that we can do more with static methods than implement mathematical functions: static methods can have strings and other types as their range or domain, and they can have side effects such as producing output. We also consider in this section how to use static methods to organize programs and thus to simplify complicated programming tasks.

Static methods support a key concept that will pervade your approach to programming from this point forward: *Whenever you can clearly separate tasks within programs, you should do so.* We will be overemphasizing this point throughout this section and reinforcing it throughout this book. When you write an essay, you break it up into paragraphs; when you write a program, you will break it up into methods. Separating a larger task into smaller ones is much more important in programming than in writing, because it greatly facilitates *debugging*, *maintenance*, and *reuse*, which are all critical in developing good software.

**Using and defining static methods**   As you know from using Java's `Math` library, the use of static methods is easy to understand. For example, when you write `Math.abs(a-b)` in a program, the effect is as if you were to replace that code by the value that is computed by Java's `Math.abs()` method when presented with the value `a-b`. This usage is so intuitive that we have hardly needed to comment on it. If you think about what the system has to do to create this effect, you will see that it involves changing a program's *control flow*. The implications of being able to change the control flow in this way is as profound as doing so for conditionals and loops.

You can define static methods other than `main()` in a `.java` file, as illustrated in `Newton` (PROGRAM 2.1.1). This implementation is better than our original implementation of Newton's algorithm (PROGRAM 1.3.6) because it clearly separates the two primary tasks performed by the program: calculating the square root and interacting with the user. *Whenever you can clearly separate tasks within programs, you should do so.* The code here differs from PROGRAM 1.3.6 in two additional respects. First, `sqrt()` returns `Double.NaN` when its argument is negative; second, `main()` tests `sqrt()` not just for one value, but for all the values given on the command line. A static method must return a well-defined value for each possible argument, and taking multiple command-line arguments facilitates testing that `Newton` operates as expected for various input values.

While `Newton` appeals to our familiarity with mathematical functions, we will examine it in detail so that you can think carefully about what a static method is and how it operates.

```
public class Newton
{
    public static double sqrt(double c)
    {
        if (c < 0) return Double.NaN;
        double err = 1e-15;
        double t = c;
        while (Math.abs(t - c/t) > err * t)
            t = (c/t + t) / 2.0;
        return t;
    }

    public static void main(String[] args)
    {
        int N = args.length;
        double[] a = new double[N];
        for (int i = 0; i < N; i++)
            a[i] = Double.parseDouble(args[i]);
        for (int i = 0; i < N; i++)
        {
            double x = sqrt(a[i]);
            StdOut.println(x);
        }
    }
}
```

*Flow of control for a call on a static method*

*Control flow.*  `Newton` comprises two static methods: `sqrt()` and `main()`. Even though `sqrt()` appears first in the code, the first statement executed when the program is executed is, as always, the first statement in `main()`. The next few statements operate as usual, except that the code `sqrt(a[i])`, which is known as a *function call* on the static method `sqrt()`, causes a *transfer of control* (to the first line of code in `sqrt()`) , each time that it is encountered. Moreover, the value of `c` within

*Program 2.1.1    Newton's method (revisited)*

```java
public class Newton
{
   public static double sqrt(double c)
   {  // Compute the square root of c.
      if (c < 0) return Double.NaN;
      double err = 1e-15;
      double t = c;
      while (Math.abs(t - c/t) > err * t)
         t = (c/t + t) / 2.0;
      return t;
   }

   public static void main(String[] args)
   {  // Print square roots of arguments.
      int N = args.length;
      double[] a = new double[N];
      for (int i = 0; i < N; i++)
         a[i] = Double.parseDouble(args[i]);
      for (int i = 0; i < N; i++)
      {  // Print square root of ith argument.
         double x = sqrt(a[i]);
         StdOut.println(x);
      }
   }
}
```

| err | desired precision |
| t | current estimate |

| N | argument count |
| a[] | argument values |

*This program defines two static methods, one named* sqrt() *that computes the square root of its argument using Newton's algorithm (see Program 1.3.6) and one named* main(), *which tests* sqrt() *on command-line argument values. The constant values* NaN *and* Infinity *stand for "not a number" and infinity, respectively.*

```
% java Newton 1.0 2.0 3.0 1000000.1
1.0
1.414213562373095
1.7320508075688772
1000.000499999875

% java Newton NaN Infinity 0 -0 -2
NaN
Infinity
0.0
-0.0
NaN
```

sqrt() is initialized to the value of a[i] within main() at the time of the call. Then the statements in sqrt() are executed in sequence, as usual, until reaching a return statement, which transfers control back to the statement in main() containing the call on sqrt(). Moreover, the effect of the call is the same as if sqrt(a[0]) were a variable whose value is the value of t in sqrt() when the return t statement is executed. The end result exactly matches our intuition: the first value assigned to x and printed is precisely the value computed by code in sqrt() (with the value of c initialized to a[0]). Next, the same process transfers control to sqrt again (with the value of c initialized to a[1]), and so forth.

*Function call trace.* One simple approach to following the control flow through function calls is to imagine that each function prints its name and argument when it is called and its return value just before returning, with indentation added on calls and subtracted on returns. The result is a special case of the process of tracing a program by printing the values of its variables, which we have been using since SECTION 1.2. However, the added indentation exposes the flow of the control, and helps us check that each function has the effect that we expect. Adding calls on StdOut.printf() to trace

```
main({1, 2})
    sqrt(1)
        Math.abs(0)
        return 0.0
    return 1.0
    sqrt(2)
        Math.abs(1.0)
        return 1.0
        Math.abs(1.416666666666667)
        return 1.416666666666667
        ...
    return 1.414213562373095
return
```

*Function call trace for* java Newton 1 2

a program's control flow in this way is a fine way to begin to understand what it is doing (see EXERCISE 2.1.7). If the return values match our expectations, we need not trace the function code in detail, saving us a substantial amount of work.

*Anatomy of a static method.* The square root function maps a nonnegative real number to a nonnegative real number; the sqrt() static method in Newton maps a double to a double. The first line of a static method, known as its *signature*, describes this information. The type of the domain is indicated in parentheses after the function name, along with a name called an *argument variable* that we will use to refer to the argument. The type of the range is indicated before the function name—we can put code that calls this function anywhere we could put an expression of that type. We will discuss the meaning of the public keyword in the next section and the meaning of the static keyword in CHAPTER 3. (Technically, the signature in Java does not include these keyword modifiers or the return type, but we leave that distinction for experts.) Following the signature is the *body* of the method, enclosed in braces. For `sqrt()` this code is the same as we discussed in SECTION 1.3, except that the last statement is a `return` statement, which causes a transfer of control back to the point where the static method was called. For any given initial value of the argument variable, the method must compute a return value. The variables that

*Anatomy of a static method*

are declared and used in the body of the method are known as *local variables*. There are two local variables in `sqrt()`: `err` and `t`. These variables are local to the code in the body of the method and cannot be used outside of the method.

**Properties of static methods**    For the rest of this chapter, your programming will be centered on creating and using static methods, so it is worthwhile to consider in more detail their basic properties.

*Terminology.*  As we have been doing throughout, it is useful to draw a distinction between abstract concepts and Java mechanisms to implement them (the Java `if` statement implements the conditional, the `while` statement implements the loop, and so forth). There are several concepts rolled up in the idea of a function, and Java constructs corresponding to each, as summarized in the following table:

| concept | Java construct | description |
|---|---|---|
| function | static method | mapping |
| domain | argument type | set of values where function is defined |
| range | return type | set of values a function can return |
| formula | method body | function definition |

When we use a symbolic name in a formula that defines a mathematical function (such as $f(x) = 1 + x + x^2$), the symbol is a placeholder for some value in the domain that will be substituted into the formula when computing the function value. In Java, the symbol that we use is the name of an argument variable. It represents the particular value of interest where the function is to be evaluated.

*Scope.* The *scope* of a variable name is the set of statements that can refer to that name. The general rule in Java is that the scope of the variables in a block of statements is limited to the statements in that block. In particular, the scope of a variable in a static method is limited to that method's body. Therefore, you cannot refer to a variable in one static method that is declared in another. If the method includes smaller blocks—for example, the body of an `if` or a `for` statement—the scope of any variables declared in one of those blocks is limited to just the statements within the block. Indeed, it is common practice to use the same variable names in independent blocks of code. When we do so, we are declaring different independent variables. For example, we have been following this practice when we use an index i in two different `for` loops in the same program. A guiding principle when designing software is that each variable should be defined so that its scope is as small as possible. One of the important reasons that we use static methods is that they ease debugging by limiting variable scope.

```
public class Newton
{                                                   this code cannot refer to
   public static double sqrt(double c)                args[], N, or a[]
   {
      if (c < 0) return Double.NaN;
      double err = 1e-15;
      double t = c;                 scope of
      while (Math.abs(t - c/t) > err * t)    c, err, and t
         t = (c/t + t) / 2.0;
      return t;
   }


   public static void main(String[] args)          this code cannot refer to
   {                                                  c[], err, or t
      int N = args.length;
      double[] a = new double[N];
      for (int i = 0; i < N; i++)
         a[i] = Double.parseDouble(args[i]);
                                          scope of i
      for (int i = 0; i < N; i++)      scope of
      {                                 args[], N, and a[]          two different
         double x = sqrt(a[i]);                                       variables
         StdOut.println(x);
      }                              scope of i and x
   }
}
```

*Scope of local and argument variables*

*Argument variables.*  You can use argument variables anywhere in the code in the body of the function in the same way you use local variables. The only difference between an argument variable and a local variable is that the argument variable is initialized with the argument value provided by the calling code. This approach is known as *pass by value*. The method works with the *value* of its arguments, not the arguments themselves. One consequence of this approach is that changing the value of an argument variable within a static method has no effect on the calling code. An alternative known as *pass by reference,* where the method actually works with the calling code's variable, is favored in some programming environments (and actually is akin to the way Java works for nonprimitive arguments, as we will see). For clarity, we do not change argument variables in the code in this book: our static methods take the values of argument variables and produce a result.

*Multiple methods.*  You can define as many static methods as you want in a `.java` file. Each has a body that consists of a sequence of statements enclosed in braces. These methods are independent, except that they may refer to each other through calls. They can appear in any order in the file.

*Calling other static methods.*  As evidenced by `main()` calling `sqrt()` and `sqrt()` calling `Math.abs()` in `Newton`, any static method defined in a `.java` file can call any other static method in the same file or any static method in a Java library such as `Math`. Also, as we see in the next section, a static method can call a static method in any `.java` file in the same directory. In SECTION 2.3, we consider the ramifications of the idea that a static method can even call *itself*.

*Multiple arguments.*  Like a mathematical function, a Java static method can take on more than one argument, and therefore can have more than one argument variable. For example, the following method computes the length of the hypotenuse of a right triangle with sides of length a and b:

```
public static double hypotenuse(double a, double b)
{   return Math.sqrt(a*a + b*b);   }
```

Although the argument variables are of the same type in this case, in general they can be of different types. The type and the name of each argument variable is declared in the function signature, separated by commas.

| | |
|---|---|
| *absolute value of an* int *value* | ```java
public static int abs(int x)
{
    if (x < 0) return -x;
    else        return  x;
}
``` |
| *absolute value of a* double *value* | ```java
public static double abs(double x)
{
    if (x < 0.0) return -x;
    else          return  x;
}
``` |
| *primality test* | ```java
public static boolean isPrime(int N)
{
    if (N < 2) return false;
    for (int i = 2; i <= N/i; i++)
        if (N % i == 0) return false;
    return true;
}
``` |
| *hypotenuse of a right triangle* | ```java
public static double hypotenuse(double a, double b)
{   return Math.sqrt(a*a + b*b);   }
``` |
| *Harmonic number* | ```java
public static double H(int N)
{
    double sum = 0.0;
    for (int i = 1; i <= N; i++)
        sum += 1.0 / i;
    return sum;
}
``` |
| *uniform random integer in* $[0, N)$ | ```java
public static int uniform(int N)
{   return (int) (Math.random() * N);   }
``` |
| *draw a triangle* | ```java
public static void drawTriangle(double x0, double y0,
                                double x1, double y1,
                                double x2, double y2 )
{
    StdDraw.line(x0, y0, x1, y1);
    StdDraw.line(x1, y1, x2, y2);
    StdDraw.line(x2, y2, x0, y0);
}
``` |

*Typical code for implementing functions*
```

*Overloading.* Static methods whose signatures differ are different static methods. For example, we often want to define the same operation for values of different numeric types, as in the following static methods for computing absolute values:

```
public static int abs(int x)
{
   if (x < 0) return -x;
   else       return  x;
}

public static double abs(double x)
{
   if (x < 0.0) return -x;
   else         return  x;
}
```

These are two different methods, but sufficiently similar so as to justify using the same name (abs). Using one name for two static methods whose signatures differ is known as *overloading*, and is common in Java programming. For example, the Java Math library uses this approach to provide implementations of Math.abs(), Math.min(), and Math.max() for all primitive numeric types. Another common use of overloading is to define two different versions of a function, one that takes an argument and another that uses a default value of that argument.

*Single return value.* Like a mathematical function, a Java static method can provide only one return value, of the type declared in the method signature. This policy is not as restrictive as it might seem. First, you will see in CHAPTER 3 that many types of data in Java can contain more information than a value of a single primitive type. Second, you will see later in this section that we can use arrays as arguments and return values for static methods.

*Multiple return statements.* Control goes back to the calling program as soon as the first return statement in a static method is reached. You can put return statements wherever you need them, as in sqrt(). Even though there may be multiple return statements, any static method returns a single value each time it is invoked: the value following the first return statement encountered. Some programmers insist on having only one return per function, but we are not so strict in this book.

*Side effects.*  A static method may use the keyword `void` as its return type, to indicate that it has no return value. An explicit `return` is not necessary in a `void` static method: control returns to the caller after the last statement. In this book, we use `void` static methods for two primary purposes:

- For I/O, using `StdIn`, `StdOut`, `StdDraw`, and `StdAudio`
- To manipulate the contents of arrays

You have been using `void` static methods for output since `main()` in `HelloWorld`, and we will discuss their use with arrays later in this section. A `void` static method is said to produce *side effects* (consume input, produce output, or otherwise change the state of the system). For example, the `main()` static method in our programs has a `void` return type because its purpose is to produce output. It is possible in Java to write methods that have other side effects, but we will avoid doing so until CHAPTER 3, where we do so in a specific manner supported by Java. Technically, `void` static methods do not implement mathematical functions (and neither does `Math.random()` or the methods in `StdIn`, which take no arguments but do produce return values).

**Implementing mathematical functions**   Why not just use the static methods that are defined within Java, such as `Math.sqrt()`? The answer to this question is that we *do* use such implementations when they are present. Unfortunately, there are an unlimited number of mathematical functions that we may wish to use and only a small set of basic functions in the library. When you encounter a function that is not in the library, you need to implement a corresponding static method.

As an example, we consider the kind of code required for a familiar and important application that is of interest to many high school and college students in the United States. In a recent year, over 1 million students took a standard college entrance examination. Scores range from 400 (lowest) to 1600 (highest) on the multiple-choice parts of the test. These scores play a role in making important decisions: for example, student athletes are required to have a score of at least 820, and the minimum eligibility requirement for certain academic scholarships is 1500. What percentage of test takers are ineligible for athletics? What percentage are eligible for the scholarships?

Two functions from statistics enable us to compute accurate answers to these questions. The *Gaussian (normal) distribution function* is characterized by the familiar bell-shaped curve and defined by the formula $\phi(x) = e^{-x^2/2}/\sqrt{2\pi}$ . The *cumulative Gaussian distribution function* $\Phi(z)$ is defined to be the area under the curve defined by $\phi(x)$ above the $x$-axis and to the left of the vertical line $x = z$. These functions play an important role in science, engineering, and finance because they arise as accurate models throughout the natural world and because they are essential in understanding experimental error.

    In particular, these functions are known to accurately describe the distribution of test scores in our example, as a function of the mean (average value of the scores) and the standard deviation (square root of the sum of the squares of the differences between each score and the mean), which are published each year. Given the mean $\mu$ and the standard deviation $\sigma$ of the test scores, the percentage of students with scores less than a given value $z$ is closely approximated by the function $\Phi((z-\mu)/\sigma)$. Static methods to calculate $\phi$ and $\Phi$ are not available in Java's Math library, so we need to develop our own implementations.

*Closed form.* In the simplest situation, we have a closed-form mathematical formula defining our function in terms of functions that are implemented in the library. This situation is the case for $\phi$—the Java Math library includes methods to compute the exponential and the square root functions (and a constant value for $\pi$), so a static method phi() corresponding to the mathematical definition is easy to implement (see PROGRAM 2.1.2).

*No closed form.* Otherwise, we may need a more complicated algorithm to compute function values. This situation is the case for $\Phi$—no closed-form expression exists for this function. Such algorithms sometimes follow immediately from Taylor series approximations, but developing reliably accurate implementations of mathematical functions is an art that needs to be addressed carefully, taking advantage of the knowledge built up in mathematics over the past several centuries. Many different approaches have been studied for evaluating $\Phi$. For example, a Taylor series approximation to the ratio of $\Phi$ and $\phi$ turns out to be an effective basis for evaluating the function:

$$\Phi(z) = 1/2 + \phi(z)\,(z + z^3/3 + z^5/(3{\cdot}5) + z^7/(3{\cdot}5{\cdot}7) + \dots).$$

*distribution* $\phi$

*area is* $\Phi(z_0)$

$\phi(x)$

$z_0$

*cumulative* $\Phi$

$\Phi(z_0)$

$z_0$

*Gaussian probability functions*

*Program 2.1.2   Gaussian functions*

```
public class Gaussian
{ // Implement Gaussian (normal) distribution functions.
   public static double phi(double x)
   {
      return Math.exp(-x*x/2) / Math.sqrt(2*Math.PI);
   }

   public static double Phi(double z)
   {
      if (z < -8.0) return 0.0;
      if (z >  8.0) return 1.0;
      double sum = 0.0, term = z;
      for (int i = 3; sum != sum + term; i += 2)
      {
         sum  = sum + term;
         term = term * z * z / i;
      }
      return 0.5 + phi(z) * sum;
   }

   public static void main(String[] args)
   {
      double z     = Double.parseDouble(args[0]);
      double mu    = Double.parseDouble(args[1]);
      double sigma = Double.parseDouble(args[2]);
      StdOut.printf("%.3f\n", Phi((z - mu) / sigma));
   }
}
```

| sum  | cumulated sum |
| term | current term  |

*This code implements the Gaussian (normal) density (phi) and cumulative distribution (Phi) functions, which are not implemented in Java's Math library. The phi() implementation follows directly from its definition, and the Phi() implementation uses a Taylor series and also calls phi() (see accompanying text at left and Exercise 1.3.36).*

```
% java Gaussian 820 1019 209
0.171

% java Gaussian 1500 1019 209
0.989

% java Gaussian 1500 1025 231
0.980
```

This formula readily translates to the Java code for the static method Phi () in Pro-GRAM 2.1.2. For small (respectively large) $z$, the value is extremely close to 0 (respectively 1), so the code directly returns 0 (respectively 1); otherwise, it uses the Taylor series to add terms until the sum converges.

Running Gaussian with the appropriate arguments on the command line tells us that about 17% of the test takers were ineligible for athletics and that only about 1% qualified for the scholarship. In a year when the mean was 1025 and the standard deviation 231, about 2% qualified for the scholarship.

COMPUTING WITH MATHEMATICAL FUNCTIONS OF ALL sorts has always played a central role in science and engineering. In a great many applications, the functions that you need are expressed in terms of the functions in Java's Math library as we have just seen with phi (), or in terms of Taylor series approximations that are easy to compute, as we have just seen with Phi (). Indeed, support for such computations has played a central role throughout the evolution of computing systems and programming languages. You will find many examples on the booksite and throughout this book.

### Using static methods to organize code

Beyond evaluating mathematical functions, the process of calculating a result value on the basis of an input value is important as a general technique for organizing control flow in *any* computation. Doing so is a simple example of an extremely important principle that is a prime guiding force for any good programmer: *Whenever you can clearly separate tasks within programs, you should do so.*

Functions are natural and universal for expressing computational tasks. Indeed, the "bird's-eye view" of a Java program that we began with in SECTION 1.1 was equivalent to a function: we began by thinking of a Java program as a function that transforms command-line arguments into an output string. This view expresses itself at many different levels of computation. In particular, it is generally the case that a long program is more naturally expressed in terms of functions instead of as a sequence of Java assignment, conditional, and loop statements. With the ability to define functions, we can better organize our programs by defining functions within them when appropriate.

For example, Coupon (PROGRAM 2.1.3) is a version of CouponCollector (PRO-GRAM 1.4.2) that better separates the individual components of the computation. If you study PROGRAM 1.4.2, you will identify three separate tasks:

**Program 2.1.3   Coupon collector (revisited)**

```
public class Coupon
{
   public static int uniform(int N)
   {  // Generate a random integer between 0 and N-1.
      return (int) (Math.random() * N);
   }

   public static int collect(int N)
   {  // Collect coupons until getting one of each value.
      boolean[] found = new boolean[N];
      int cardcnt = 0, valcnt = 0;
      while (valcnt < N)
      {
         int val = uniform(N);
         cardcnt++;
         if (!found[val]) valcnt++;
         found[val] = true;
      }
      return cardcnt;
   }

   public static void main(String[] args)
   {  // Print the number of coupons collected
      // to get N different coupons.
      int N = Integer.parseInt(args[0]);
      int count = collect(N);
      StdOut.println(count);
   }
}
```

| found[] | cumulated sum |
|---------|---------------|
| cardcnt | number collected |
| valcnt | number that differ |
| val | current value |

This version of Program 1.4.2 illustrates the style of encapsulating computations in static methods. This code has the same effect as CouponCollector, but better separates the code into its three constituent pieces: generating a random integer between 0 and N-1, running a collection experiment, and managing the I/O.

```
% java Coupon 1000
6522

% java Coupon 1000
6481

% java Coupon 1000000
12783771
```

- Given *N*, compute a random coupon value.
- Given *N*, do the coupon collection experiment.
- Get *N* from the command line, then compute and print the result.

Coupon rearranges the code in CouponCollect to reflect the reality that these three functions underlie the computation.

With this organization, we could change uniform() (for example, we might want to draw the random numbers from a different distribution) or main() (for example, we might want to take multiple inputs or run multiple experiments) without worrying about the effect of any changes on collect().

Using static methods isolates the implementation of each component of the collection experiment from others, or *encapsulates* them. Typically, programs have many independent components, which magnifies the benefits of separating them into different static methods. We will discuss these benefits in further detail after we have seen several other examples, but you certainly can appreciate that it is better to express a computation in a program by breaking it up into functions, just as it is better to express an idea in an essay by breaking it up into paragraphs. *Whenever you can clearly separate tasks within programs, you should do so.*

**Implementing static methods for arrays**   A static method can take an array as an argument or as a return value. This capability is a special case of Java's object orientation, which is the subject of CHAPTER 3. We consider it in the present context because the basic mechanisms are easy to understand and to use, leading us to compact solutions to a number of problems that naturally arise when we use arrays to help us process large amounts of data.

*Arrays as arguments.* When a static method takes an array as an argument, it implements a function that operates on an arbitrary number of values of the same type. For example, the following static method computes the mean (average) value of an array of double values.

```
public static double mean(double[] a)
{
    double sum = 0.0;
    for (int i = 0; i < a.length; i++)
        sum = sum + a[i];
    return sum / a.length;
}
```

We have been using arrays as arguments from the beginning. The code

```
public static void main(String[] args)
```

defines `main()` as a static method that takes an array of strings as an argument and returns nothing. By convention, the Java system collects the strings that you type after the program name in the `java` command into an array `args[]` and calls `main()` with that array as argument. (Most programmers use the name `args` for the argument variable, even though any name at all would do.) Within `main()`, we can manipulate that array just like any other array. The `main()` method in `Newton` (PROGRAM 2.1.1) is an example of such code.

*Side effects with arrays.*  It is often the case that the purpose of a static method that takes an array as argument is to produce a side effect (change values of array elements). A prototypical example of such a method is one that exchanges the values at two given indices in a given array. We can adapt the code that we examined at the beginning of SECTION 1.4:

```
public static void exch(String[] a, int i, int j)
{
   String t = a[i];
   a[i] = a[j];
   a[j] = t;
}
```

This implementation stems naturally from the Java array representation. The argument variable in `exch()` is a reference to the array, not to all of the array's values: when you pass an array as argument to a static method, you are giving it the opportunity to operate on that array (not a copy of it). A second prototypical example of a static method that takes an array argument and produces side effects is one that randomly shuffles the values in the array, using this version of the algorithm that we examined in SECTION 1.4 (and the `exch()` and `uniform()` methods just defined):

```
public static void shuffle(String[] a)
{
   int N = a.length;
   for (int i = 0; i < N; i++)
      exch(a, i, i + uniform(N-i));
}
```

| | |
|---|---|
| *find the maximum of the array values* | ```java
public static double max(double[] a)
{
    double max = Double.NEGATIVE_INFINITY;
    for (int i = 0; i < a.length; i++)
        if (a[i] > max) max = a[i];
    return max;
}
``` |
| *dot product* | ```java
public static double dot(double[] a, double[] b)
{
    double sum = 0.0;
    for (int i = 0; i < a.length; i++)
        sum += a[i] * b[i];
    return sum;
}
``` |
| *exchange two elements in an array* | ```java
public static void exch(String[] a, int i, int j)
{
    String t = a[i];
    a[i] = a[j];
    a[j] = t;
}
``` |
| *print a 1D array (and its length)* | ```java
public static void print(double[] a)
{
    StdOut.println(a.length);
    for (int i = 0; i < a.length; i++)
        StdOut.println(a[i]);
}
``` |
| *read a 2D array of* double *values (with dimensions) in row-major order* | ```java
public static double[][] readDouble2D()
{
    int M = StdIn.readInt();
    int N = StdIn.readInt();
    double[][] a = new double[M][N];
    for (int i = 0; i < M; i++)
        for (int j = 0; j < N; j++)
            a[i][j] = StdIn.readDouble();
    return a;
}
``` |

*Typical code for implementing functions with arrays*
```

Similarly, we will consider in SECTION 4.2 methods that *sort* an array (rearrange its values so that they are in order). All of these examples highlight the basic fact that the mechanism for passing arrays in Java is a *call-by-reference* mechanism with respect to the contents of the array. Unlike primitive-type arguments, the changes that a method makes in the contents of an array *are* reflected in the client program. A method that takes an array as argument cannot change the array itself—the reference is the same memory location assigned when the array was created, and the length is the value set when the array was created—but it can change the contents of the array to any values whatsoever.

*Arrays as return values.* A method that sorts, shuffles, or otherwise modifies an array taken as argument does not have to return a reference to that array, because it is changing the contents of a client array, not a copy. But there are many situations where it is useful for a static method to provide an array as a return value. Chief among these are static methods that create arrays for the purpose of returning multiple values of the same type to a client. For example, the following static method produces an array of the kind used by StdAudio (see PROGRAM 1.5.7) that contains values sampled from a sine wave of a given frequency (in hertz) and duration (in seconds), sampled at the standard 44,100 samples per second.

```java
public static double[] tone(double hz, double t)
{
   int sps = 44100;
   int N = (int) (sps * t);
   double[] a = new double[N+1];
   for (int i = 0; i <= N; i++)
      a[i] = Math.sin(2 * Math.PI * i * hz / sps);
   return a;
}
```

In this code, the size of the array returned depends on the duration: if the given duration is t, the size of the array is about 44100*t. With static methods like this one, we can write code that treats a sound wave as a single entity (an array containing sampled values), as we will see next in PROGRAM 2.1.4.

**Example: superposition of sound waves**  As discussed in SECTION 1.5, the simple audio model that we studied there needs to be embellished in order to create sound that resembles the sound produced by a musical instrument. Many different embellishments are possible; with static methods we can systematically apply them to produce sound waves that are far more complicated than the simple sine waves that we produced in SECTION 1.5. As an illustration of the effective use of static methods to solve an interesting computational problem, we consider a program that has essentially the same functionality as PlayThatTune (PROGRAM 1.5.7), but adds harmonic tones one octave above and one octave below each note in order to produce a more realistic sound.

*Chords and harmonics.*  Notes like concert *A* have a pure sound that is not very musical, because the sounds that you are accustomed to hearing have many other components. The sound from the guitar string echoes off the wooden part of the instrument, the walls of the room that you are in, and so forth. You may think of such effects as modifying the basic sine wave. For example, most musical instruments produce harmonics (the same note in different octaves and not as loud), or you might play chords (multiple notes at the same time). To combine multiple sounds, we use *superposition*: simply add their waves together and rescale to make sure that all values stay between $-1$ and $+1$. As it turns out, when

*A major chord*

*concert A with harmonics*

*Superposing waves to make composite sounds*

we superpose sine waves of different frequencies in this way, we can get arbitrarily complicated waves. Indeed, one of the triumphs of 19th century mathematics was the development of the idea that any smooth periodic function can be expressed as a sum of sine and cosine waves, known as a *Fourier series*. This mathematical idea corresponds to the notion that we can create a large range of sounds with musical instruments or our vocal chords and that all sound consists of a composition of various oscillating curves. Any sound corresponds to a curve and any curve corresponds to a sound, and we can create arbitrarily complex curves with superposition.

*Superposition.* Since we represent sound waves by arrays of numbers that represent their values at the same sample points, superposition is simple to implement: we add together their sample values at each sample point to produce the combined result and then rescale. For greater control, we specify a relative weight for each of the two waves to be added, with the property that the weights are positive and sum to 1. For example, if we want the first sound to have three times the effect of the second, we would assign the first a weight of .75 and the second a weight of .25. Now, if one wave is in an array a[] with relative weight awt and the other is in an array b[] with relative weight bwt, we compute their weighted sum with the following code:

```
double[] c = new double[a.length];
for (int i = 0; i < a.length; i++)
   c[i] = a[i]*awt + b[i]*bwt;
```

The conditions that the weights are positive and sum to 1 ensure that this operation preserves our convention of keeping the values of all of our waves between $-1$ and $+1$.

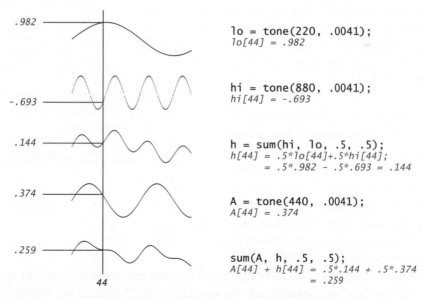

*Adding harmonics to concert A (180 samples at 44,100 samples/sec)*

PROGRAM 2.1.4 IS AN IMPLEMENTATION THAT applies these concepts to produce a more realistic sound than that produced by PROGRAM 1.5.7. In order to do so, it makes use of functions to divide the computation into four parts:

- Given a frequency and duration, create a pure tone.
- Given two sound waves and relative weight, superpose them.
- Given a pitch and duration, create a note with harmonics.
- Read and play a sequence of pitch/duration pairs from standard input.

These tasks are each amenable to implementation as functions, which depend on one another. Each function is well-defined and straightforward to implement. All of them (and `StdAudio`) represent sound as a series of discrete values kept in an array, corresponding to sampling a sound wave at 44,100 samples per second.

Up to this point, the use of functions has been somewhat of a notational convenience. For example, the control flow in PROGRAMS 2.1.1–2.1.3 is simple—each function is called in just one place in the code. By contrast, `PlayThatTuneDeluxe` (PROGRAM 2.1.4) is a convincing example of the effectiveness of defining functions to or-

```java
public class PlayThatTune
{
    public static double[] sum(double[] a, double[] b,
                               double awt, double bwt)
    {
        double[] c = new double[a.length];
        for (int i = 0; i < a.length; i++)
            c[i] = a[i]*awt + b[i]*bwt;
        return c;
    }

    public static double[] tone(double hz, double t)
    {
        int sps = 44100;
        int N = (int) (sps * t);
        double[] a = new double[N+1];
        for (int i = 0; i <= N; i++)
            a[i] = Math.sin(2 * Math.PI * i * hz / sps);
        return a;
    }

    public static double[] note(int pitch, double t)
    {
        double hz = 440.0 * Math.pow(2, pitch / 12.0);
        double[] a  = tone(hz, t);
        double[] hi = tone(2*hz, t);
        double[] lo = tone(hz/2, t);
        double[] h  = sum(hi, lo, .5, .5);
        return sum(a, h, .5, .5);
    }

    public static void main(String[] args)
    {
        while (!StdIn.isEmpty())
        {
            int pitch = StdIn.readInt();
            double duration = StdIn.readDouble();
            double[] a = note(pitch, duration);
            StdAudio.play(a);
        }
    }
}
```

*Flow of control among several static methods*

ganize a computation because the functions are each called multiple times. For example, the function `note()` calls the function `tone()` three times and the function `sum()` twice. Without static methods, we would need multiple copies of the code in

**Program 2.1.4   Play that Tune (revisited)**

```
public class PlayThatTuneDeluxe
{
   public static double[] sum(double[] a, double[] b,
                              double awt, double bwt)
   {  // Superpose a and b, weighted.
      double[] c = new double[a.length];
      for (int i = 0; i < a.length; i++)
         c[i] = a[i]*awt + b[i]*bwt;
      return c;
   }
   public static double[] tone(double hz, double t)
      // see text

   public static double[] note(int pitch, double t)
   {  // Play note of given pitch, with harmonics.
      double hz = 440.0 * Math.pow(2, pitch / 12.0);
      double[] a  = tone(hz, t);
      double[] hi = tone(2*hz, t);
      double[] lo = tone(hz/2, t);
      double[] h  = sum(hi, lo, .5, .5);
      return sum(a, h, .5, .5);
   }
   public static void main(String[] args)
   {  // Read and play a tune, with harmonics.
      while (!StdIn.isEmpty())
      {  // Read and play a note, with harmonics.
         int pitch = StdIn.readInt();
         double duration = StdIn.readDouble();
         double[] a = note(pitch, duration);
         StdAudio.play(a);
      }
   }
}
```

| hz | frequency |
|---|---|
| a[] | pure tone |
| hi[] | upper harmonic |
| lo[] | lower harmonic |
| h[] | tone with harmonics |

*This code embellishes the sounds produced by Program 1.5.7 by using static methods to create harmonics, which results in a more realistic sound than the pure tone.*

```
% more elise.txt
7 .25
6 .25
7 .25
6 .25
7 .25
...
```

```
% java PlayThatTuneDeluxe < elise.txt
```

tone() and sum(); with static methods, we can deal directly with concepts close to the application. As with loops, methods have a simple but profound effect: we have one sequence of statements (those in the method definition) executed multiple times during the execution of our program—once for each time the method is called in the control flow in main().

STATIC METHODS ARE IMPORTANT BECAUSE THEY give us the ability to *extend* the Java language within a program. Having implemented and debugged static methods such as sqrt(), phi(), Phi(), mean(), abs(), exch(), shuffle(), isPrime(), H(), uniform(), sum(), note(), and tone(), we can use them almost as if they were built into Java. The flexibility to do so opens up a whole new world of programming. Before, you were safe in thinking about a Java program as a sequence of statements. Now you need to think of a Java program as a *set of static methods* that can call one another. The statement-to-statement control flow to which you have been accustomed is still present within static methods, but programs have a higher-level control flow defined by static method calls and returns. This ability enables you to think in terms of operations called for by the application, not just the simple arithmetic operations on primitive types that are built in to Java.

*Whenever you can clearly separate tasks within programs, you should do so.* The examples in this section (and the programs throughout the rest of the book) clearly illustrate the benefits of adhering to this maxim. With static methods, we can
  • Divide a long sequence of statements into independent parts.
  • Reuse code without having to copy it.
  • Work with higher-level concepts (such as sound waves).
This produces code that is easier to understand, maintain, and debug than a long program composed solely of Java assignment, conditional, and loop statements. In the next section, we discuss the idea of using static methods defined in *other* programs, which again takes us to another level of programming.

## Q&A

**Q.** Why do I need to use the return type void? Why not just omit the return type?

**A.** Java requires it; we have to include it. Second-guessing a decision made by a programming-language designer is the first step on the road to becoming one.

**Q.** Can I return from a void function by using return? If so, what return value should I use?

**A.** Yes. Use the statement return; with no return value.

**Q.** What happens if I leave out the keyword static?

**A.** As usual, the best way to answer a question like this is to try it yourself and see what happens. Here is the result of omitting static for sqrt() in Newton:

```
Newton.java:13: non-static method sqrt(double)
cannot be referenced from a static context
        double x = sqrt(i);
                   ^
1 error
```

Non-static methods are different from static methods. You will learn about the former in CHAPTER 3.

**Q.** What happens if I write code after a return statement?

**A.** Once a return statement is reached, control immediately returns to the caller, so any code after a return statement is useless. The Java compiler identifies this situation as an error, reporting unreachable code .

**Q.** What happens if I do not include a return statement?

**A.** No problem, if the return type is void. In this case, control will return to the caller after the last statement. When the return type is not void, the compiler will report a missing return statement error if there is *any* path through the code that does not end in a return.

**Q.** This issue with side effects and arrays passed as arguments is confusing. Is it really all that important?

**A.** Yes. Properly controlling side effects is one of a programmer's most important tasks in large systems. Taking the time to be sure that you understand the difference between passing a value (when arguments are of a primitive type) and passing a reference (when arguments are arrays) will certainly be worthwhile. The very same mechanism is used for all other types of data, as you will learn in Chapter 3.

**Q.** So why not just eliminate the possibility of side effects by making all arguments pass-by-value, including arrays?

**A.** Think of a huge array with, say, millions of elements. Does it make sense to copy all of those values for a static method that is just going to exchange two of them? For this reason, most programming languages support passing an array to a function without creating a copy of the array elements—Matlab is a notable exception.

*Exercises*

**2.1.1**  Write a static method max3() that takes three int values as arguments and returns the value of the largest one. Add an overloaded function that does the same thing with three double values.

**2.1.2**  Write a static method odd() that takes three boolean inputs and returns true if an odd number of inputs are true, and false otherwise.

**2.1.3**  Write a static method majority() that takes three boolean arguments and returns true if at least two of the arguments have the value true, and false otherwise. Do not use an if statement.

**2.1.4**  Write a static method eq() that takes two arrays of integers as arguments and returns true if they contain the same number of elements and all corresponding pairs of elements are equal.

**2.1.5**  Write a static method areTriangular() that takes three double values as arguments and returns true if they could be the sides of a triangle (none of them is greater than or equal to the sum of the other two). See EXERCISE 1.2.15.

**2.1.6**  Write a static method sigmoid() that takes a double argument $x$ and returns the double value obtained from the formula $1/(1-e^{-x})$.

**2.1.7**  If the argument of sqrt() in Newton (PROGRAM 2.1.1) has the value Infinity, then Newton.sqrt() returns the value Infinity, as desired. Explain why.

**2.1.8**  Add a method abs() to Newton (PROGRAM 2.1.1), change sqrt() to use abs() instead of Math.abs(), and add print statements to produce a function call trace, as described in the text. *Hint*: You need to add an argument to each function to give the level of indentation.

**2.1.9**  Give the function call trace for java Newton 4.0 9.0.

**2.1.10**  Write a static method lg() that takes a double value N as argument and returns the base 2 logarithm of N. You may use Java's Math library.

**2.1.11**  Write a static method lg() that takes an int value N as argument and returns the largest int not larger than the base-2 logarithm of N. Do *not* use Math.

**2.1.12** Write a static method `signum()` that takes an `int` value N as argument and returns -1 if N is less than 0, 0 if N is equal to 0, and +1 if N is greater than 0.

**2.1.13** Consider the static method `duplicate()` below.

```
public static String duplicate(String s)
{
    String t = s + s;
    return t;
}
```

What does the following code fragment do?

```
String s = "Hello";
s = duplicate(s);
String t = "Bye";
t = duplicate(duplicate(duplicate(t)));
StdOut.println(s + t);
```

**2.1.14** Consider the static method `cube()` below.

```
public static void cube(int i)
{
    i = i * i * i;
}
```

How many times is the following `for` loop iterated?

```
for (int i = 0; i < 1000; i++)
    cube(i);
```

*Answer:* Just 1,000 times. A call to `cube()` has no effect on client code. It changes the value of its local argument variable i, but that change has no effect on the i in the `for` loop, which is a different variable. If you replace the call to `cube(i)` with the statement `i = i * i * i;` (maybe that was what you were thinking), then the loop is iterated five times, with i taking on the values 0, 1, 2, 9, and 730 at the beginning of the five iterations.

**2.1.15** The following *checksum* formula is widely used by banks and credit card

companies to validate legal account numbers:
$$d_0 + f(d_1) + d_2 + f(d_3) + d_4 + f(d_5) + \ldots = 0 \pmod{10}$$
The $d_i$ are the decimal digits of the account number and $f(d)$ is the sum of the decimal digits of $2d$ (for example, $f(7) = 5$ because $2{\times}7 = 14$ and $1+ 4 = 5$). For example 17327 is valid because $1+5+3+4+7=20$, which is a multiple of 10. Implement the function $f$ and write a program to take a 10-digit integer as a command-line argument and print a valid 11-digit number with the given integer as its first 10 digits and the checksum as the last digit.

**2.1.16** Given two stars with angles of declination and right ascension $(d_1, a_1)$ and $(d_2, a_2)$, the angle they subtend is given by the formula

$$2 \arcsin((\sin^2(d/2) + \cos(d_1)\cos(d_2)\sin^2(a/2))^{1/2}),$$

where $a_1$ and $a_2$ are angles between $-180$ and $180$ degrees, $d_1$ and $d_2$ are angles between $-90$ and $90$ degrees, $a = a_2 - a_1$, and $d = d_2 - d_1$. Write a program to take the declination and right ascension of two stars as command-line arguments and print the angle they subtend. *Hint*: Be careful about converting from degrees to radians.

**2.1.17** Write a `readBoolean2D()` method that reads a two-dimensional boolean matrix (with dimensions) into an array.

*Solution*: The body of the method is virtually the same as for the corresponding method given in the table in the text for 2D arrays of `double` values:

```
public static boolean[][] readBoolean2D()
{
    int M = StdIn.readInt();
    int N = StdIn.readInt();
    boolean[][] a = new boolean[M][N];
    for (int i = 0; i < M; i++)
        for (int j = 0; j < N; j++)
            a[i][j] = StdIn.readBoolean();
    return a;
}
```

Note that `StdIn` accepts 0 and 1 as `boolean` values in the input stream.

**2.1.18** Write a method that takes an array of `double` values as argument and re-scales the array so that each element is between 0 and 1 (by subtracting the minimum value from each element and then dividing each element by the difference between the minimum and maximum values). Use the max() method defined in the table in the text, and write and use a matching min() method.

**2.1.19**  Write a method histogram() that takes an array a[] of int values and an integer M as argument and returns an array of length M whose ith entry is the number of times the integer i appeared in the argument array. If the values in a[] are all between 0 and M-1, the sum of the values in the returned array should be equal to a.length.

**2.1.20**  Assemble code fragments in this section and in SECTION 1.4 to develop a program that takes *N* from the command line and prints *N* five-card hands, separated by blank lines, drawn from a randomly shuffled card deck, one card per line using card names like Ace of Clubs.

**2.1.21**  Write a method multiply() that takes two square matrices of the same dimension as arguments and produces their product (another square matrix of that same dimension). *Extra credit*: Make your program work whenever the number of rows in the first matrix is equal to the number of columns in the second matrix.

**2.1.22**  Write a method any() that takes an array of boolean values as argument and returns true if any of the entries in the array is true, and false otherwise. Write a method all() that takes an array of boolean values as argument and returns true if all of the entries in the array are true, and false otherwise.

**2.1.23**  Develop a version of getCoupon() that better models the situation when one of the coupons is rare: choose one value at random, return that value with probability *N*/1000, and return all other values with equal probability. *Extra credit*: How does this change affect the average value of the coupon collector function?

**2.1.24**  Modify PlayThatTune to add harmonics two octaves away from each note, with half the weight of the one-octave harmonics.

## Creative Exercises

**2.1.25** *Birthday problem.* Develop a class with appropriate static methods for studying the birthday problem (see EXERCISE 1.4.35).

**2.1.26** *Euler's totient function.* Euler's totient function is an important function in number theory: $\varphi(n)$ is defined as the number of positive integers less than or equal to $n$ that are relatively prime with $n$ (no factors in common with $n$ other than 1). Write a class with a function that takes an integer argument $n$ and returns $\varphi(n)$, and a `main()` that takes an integer from the command line, calls the function, and prints the result.

**2.1.27** *Harmonic numbers.* Write a program `Harmonic` that contains three static methods `H()`, `Hsmall()`, and `Hlarge()` for computing the Harmonic numbers. The `Hsmall()` method should just compute the sum (as in PROGRAM 1.3.5), the `Hlarge()` method should use the approximation $H_N = \log_e(N) + \gamma + 1/(2N) - 1/(12N^2) + 1/(120N^4)$ (the number $\gamma = .577215664901532...$ is known as *Euler's constant*), and the `H()` method should call `Hsmall()` for $N < 100$ and `Hlarge()` otherwise.

**2.1.28** *Gaussian random values.* Experiment with the following method for generating random variables from the Gaussian distribution, which is based on generating a random point in the unit circle and using a form of the Box-Muller formula (see EXERCISE 1.2.27 and the discussion of `do-while` at the end of SECTION 1.3).

```
public static double gaussian()
{
   double r, x, y;
   do
   {
      x = uniform(-1.0, 1.0);
      y = uniform(-1.0, 1.0);
      r = x*x + y*y;
   } while (r >= 1 || r == 0);
   return x * Math.sqrt(-2 * Math.log(r) / r);
}
```

Take a command-line argument N and generate N random numbers, using an array a[20] to count the numbers generated that fall between i*.05 and (i+1)*.05 for i from 0 to 19. Then use StdDraw to plot the values and to compare your result with the normal bell curve.

**2.1.29** *Binary search.* A general method that we study in detail in SECTION 4.2 is effective for computing the inverse of a cumulative probability density function like Phi(). Such functions are continuous and nondecreasing from $(0,0)$ to $(1,1)$. To find the value $x_0$ for which $f(x_0) = y_0$, check the value of $f(.5)$. If it is greater than $y_0$, then $x_0$ must be between 0 and .5; otherwise, it must be between .5 and 1. Either way, we halve the length of the interval known to contain $x_0$. Iterating, we can compute $x_0$ to within a given tolerance. Add a method PhiInverse() to Gaussian that uses binary search to compute the inverse. Change main() to take a number $p$ between 0 and 100 as a third command-line argument and print the minimum score that a student would need to be in the top $p$ percent of students taking the SAT in a year when the mean and standard deviation were the first two command-line arguments.

**2.1.30** *Black-Scholes option valuation.* The Black-Scholes formula supplies the theoretical value of a European call option on a stock that pays no dividends, given the current stock price $s$, the exercise price $x$, the continuously compounded risk-free interest rate $r$, the standard deviation $\sigma$ of the stock's return (volatility), and the time (in years) to maturity $t$. The value is given by the formula $s\,\Phi(a) - xe^{-rt}\Phi(b)$, where $\Phi(z)$ is the Gaussian cumulative distribution function, $a = (\ln(s/x) + (r + \sigma^2/2)\,t)\,/\,(\sigma\sqrt{t})$, and $b = a - \sigma\sqrt{t}$. Write a program that takes s, x, r, sigma, and t from the command line and prints the Black-Scholes value.

**2.1.31** *Implied volatility.* Typically the volatility is the unknown value in the Black-Scholes formula. Write a program that reads s, x, r, t, and the current price of the European call option from the command line and uses binary search (see EXERCISE 2.1.29) to compute $\sigma$.

**2.1.32** *Horner's method.* Write a class Horner with a method double eval(double x, double[] p) that evaluates the polynomial $p(x)$ whose coefficients are the entries in p[]:

$$p_0 + p_1x^1 + p_2x^2 + \ldots + p_{N-2}x^{N-2} + p_{N-1}x^{N-1}$$

Use *Horner's method*, an efficient way to perform the computations that is suggested by the following parenthesization:

$$p_0 + x\,(p_1 + x\,(p_2 + \ldots + x\,(p_{N-2} + xp_{N-1}))\ldots)$$

Write a test client with a static method `exp()` that uses `Horner.eval()` to compute an approximation to $e^x$, using the first $N$ terms of the Taylor series expansion $e^x = 1 + x + x^2/2! + x^3/3! + \ldots$. Take an argument x from the command-line, and compare your result against that computed by `Math.exp(x)`.

**2.1.33** *Benford's law.* The American astronomer Simon Newcomb observed a quirk in a book that compiled logarithm tables: the beginning pages were much grubbier than the ending pages. He suspected that scientists performed more computations with numbers starting with 1 than with 8 or 9, and postulated the first digit law, which says that under general circumstances, the leading digit is much more likely to be 1 (roughly 30%) than the digit 9 (less than 4%). This phenomenon is known as *Benford's law* and is now often used as a statistical test. For example, IRS forensic accountants rely on it to discover tax fraud. Write a program that reads in a sequence of integers from standard input and tabulates the number of times each of the digits 1–9 is the leading digit, breaking the computation into a set of appropriate static methods. Use your program to test the law on some tables of information from your computer or from the web. Then, write a program to foil the IRS by generating random amounts from $1.00 to $1,000.00 with the same distribution that you observed.

**2.1.34** *Binomial distribution.* Write a function

```
public static double binomial(int N, int k, double p)
```

to compute the probability of obtaining exactly $k$ heads in $N$ biased coin flips (heads with probability $p$) using the formula

$$f(N, k, p) = p^k(1-p)^{N-k}N!/(k!(N-k)!).$$

*Hint*: To stave off overflow, compute $x = \ln f(N, k, p)$ and then return $e^x$. In `main()`, take $N$ and $p$ from the command line and check that the sum over all values of $k$ between 0 and $N$ is (approximately) 1. Also, compare every value computed with the normal approximation

$$f(N, k, p) \approx \phi(Np, Np(1-p))$$

(see EXERCISE 2.2.1).

**2.1.35** *Coupon collecting from a binomial distribution.* Develop a version of get-Coupon() that uses binomial() from the previous exercise to return coupon values according to the binomial distribution with $p = 1/2$. *Hint*: Generate a uniformly distributed random number $x$ between 0 and 1, then return the smallest value of $k$ for which the sum of $f(N, j, p)$ for all $j < k$ exceeds $x$. *Extra credit*: Develop a hypothesis for describing the behavior of the coupon collector function under this assumption.

**2.1.36** *Chords.* Develop a version of PlayThatTune that can handle songs with chords (including harmonics). Develop an input format that allows you to specify different durations for each chord and different amplitude weights for each note within a chord. Create test files that exercise your program with various chords and harmonics, and create a version of *Für Elise* that uses them.

0 ‖ıııı
1 ııı‖
2 ıılıl
3 ııllı
4 ılııl
5 ılılı
6 ıllıı
7 lıııl
8 lıılı
9 lılıı

**2.1.37** *Postal bar codes.* The barcode used by the U.S. Postal System to route mail is defined as follows: Each decimal digit in the zip code is encoded using a sequence of three half-height and two full-height bars. The barcode starts and ends with a full-height bar (the guard rail) and includes a checksum digit (after the five-digit zip code or ZIP+4), computed by summing up the original digits modulo 10. Implement the following functions

08540 ‖llııılıılıılıılıılııllııılııll

       /  0  8  5  4  0  7  \
   *guard*                         *guard*
   *rail*                          *rail*
               *checksum*
                 *digit*

- Draw a half-height or full-height bar on StdDraw.
- Given a digit, draw its sequence of bars.
- Compute the checksum digit.

and a test client that reads in a five- (or nine-) digit zip code as the command-line argument and draws the corresponding postal bar code.

**2.1.38** *Calendar.* Write a program Calendar that takes two command-line arguments M and Y and prints out the monthly calendar for the Mth month of year Y, as in this example:

```
% java Calendar 2 2009
February 2009
 S  M Tu  W Th  F  S
 1  2  3  4  5  6  7
 8  9 10 11 12 13 14
15 16 17 18 19 20 21
22 23 24 25 26 27 28
```

*Hint*: See `LeapYear` (PROGRAM 1.2.4) and EXERCISE 1.2.29.

**2.1.39** *Fourier spikes.* Write a program that takes a command-line argument $N$ and plots the function

$$(\cos(t) + \cos(2\,t) + \cos(3\,t) + \ldots + \cos(N\,t))\,/\,N$$

for 500 equally spaced samples of $t$ from $-10$ to $10$ (in radians). Run your program for $N = 5$ and $N = 500$. *Note*: You will observe that the sum converges to a spike (0 everywhere except a single value). This property is the basis for a proof that *any* smooth function can be expressed as a sum of sinusoids.

# 2.2 Libraries and Clients

EACH PROGRAM THAT YOU HAVE WRITTEN consists of Java code that resides in a single
.java file. For large programs, keeping all the code in a single file in this way is
restrictive and unnecessary. Fortunately,
it is very easy in Java to refer to a method
in one file that is defined in another. This
ability has two important consequences
on our style of programming.

First, it enables *code reuse*. One program can make use of code that is already
written and debugged, not by copying the
code, but just by referring to it. This abil-
ity to define code that can be reused is an essential part of modern programming. It
amounts to extending Java—you can define and use your own operations on data.

Second, it enables *modular programming*. You can not only divide a program
up into static methods, as just described in SECTION 2.1, but also keep them in different files, grouped together according to the needs of the application. Modular
programming is important because it allows us to *independently* develop, compile,
and debug parts of big programs one piece at a time, leaving each finished piece in
its own file for later use without having to worry about its details again. We develop
libraries of static methods for use by any other program, keeping each library in
its own file and using its methods in any other program. Java's Math library and
our Std* libraries for input/output are examples that you have already used. More
important, you will soon see that it is very easy to define libraries of your own. The
ability to define libraries and then to use them in multiple programs is a critical
ingredient in our ability to build programs to address complex tasks.

Having just moved in SECTION 2.1 from thinking of a Java program as a sequence of statements to thinking of a Java program as a class comprising a set of
methods (one of which is main()), you will be ready after this section to think of
a Java program as a set of *classes*, each of which is an independent module consisting of a set of methods. Since each method can call a method in another class, all
of your code can interact as a network of methods that call one another, grouped
together in classes. With this capability, you can start to think about managing
complexity when programming by breaking up programming tasks into classes
that can be implemented and tested independently.

**Using static methods in other programs**   To refer to a static method in one class that is defined in another, we use the same mechanism that we have been using to invoke methods such as `StdOut.printf()` and `StdAudio.play()`:

• Keep both classes in the same directory in your computer.

• To call a method, prepend its class name and a period separator.

For example, consider `Gaussian` (PROGRAM 2.1.2). The definition of one of its methods requires the square root function. For purposes of illustration, suppose that we wish to use the `sqrt()` implementation from `Newton` (PROGRAM 2.1.1). All that we need to do is to keep `Gaussian.java` in the same directory as `Newton.java` and prepend the class name when calling `sqrt()`. If we want to use the standard

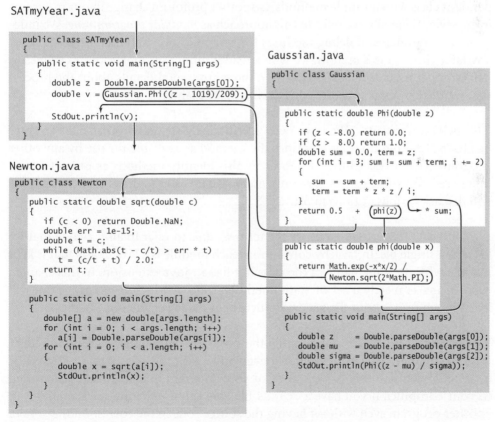

*A modular program*

Java implementation, we call `Math.sqrt()`; if we want to use our own implementation, we call `Newton.sqrt()`. Moreover, any other class in that directory can make use of the methods defined in `Gaussian`, by calling `Gaussian.phi()` or `Gaussian.Phi()`. For example, we might wish to have a simple client `SATmyYear.java` that takes a value z from the command line and prints $\Phi((z-1019)/209)$, so that we do not need to type in the mean and standard deviation each time we want to know the percentage scoring less than a given value for a certain year. The files `Gaussian.java`, `Newton.java`, and `SATmyYear.java` implement Java classes that interact with one another: `SATmyYear` calls a method in `Gaussian`, which calls a method that calls a method in `Newton`.

The potential effect of programming by defining multiple files, each an independent class with multiple methods, is another profound change in our programming style. Generally, we refer to this approach as *modular programming*. We independently develop and debug methods for an application and then utilize them at any later time. In this section, we will consider numerous illustrative examples to help you get used to the idea. However, there are several details about the process that we need to discuss before considering more examples.

*The* `public` *keyword.* We have been identifying every method as `public` since `HelloWorld`. This modifier identifies the method as available for use by any other program with access to the file. You can also identify methods as `private` (and there are a few other categories), but you have no reason to do so at this point. We will discuss various options in SECTION 3.3.

*Each module is a* `class`. We use the term *module* to refer to all the code that we keep in a single file. In Java, by convention, each module is a Java `class` that is kept in a file with the same name of the class but has a `.java` extension. In this chapter, each `class` is merely a set of static methods (one of which is `main()`). You will learn much more about the general structure of the Java `class` in CHAPTER 3.

*The* `.class` *file.* When you compile the program (by typing `javac` followed by the class name), the Java compiler makes a file with the class name followed by a `.class` extension that has the code of your program in a language more suited to your computer. If you have a `.class` file, you can use the module's methods in another program even without having the source code in the corresponding `.java` file (but you are on your own if you discover a bug!).

*Compile when necessary.* When you compile a program, the Java compiler will compile everything that needs to be compiled in order to run that program. If you call `Newton.sqrt()` in `Gaussian`, then, when you type `javac Gaussian.java`, the compiler will also check whether you modified `Newton.java` since the last time it was compiled (by checking the time it was last changed against the time `Newton.class` was created). If so, it will also compile `Newton`! If you think about this policy, you will agree that it is actually quite helpful. If you find a bug in `Newton` (and fix it), you want all the classes that call `Newton.sqrt()` to use the new version.

*Multiple main methods.* Another subtle point is to note that more than one class might have a `main()` method. In our example, `SATmyYear`, `Newton` and `Gaussian` each have `main()` methods. If you recall the rule for executing a program, you will see that there is no confusion: when you type `java` followed by a class name, Java transfers control to the machine code corresponding to the `main()` static method defined in that class. Typically, we put a `main()` static method in every class, to test and debug its methods. When we want to run `SATmyYear`, we type `java SATmyYear`; when we want to debug `Newton` or `Gaussian`, we type `java Newton` or `java Gaussian` (with appropriate command-line arguments).

IF YOU THINK OF EACH PROGRAM that you write as something that you might want to make use of later, you will soon find yourself with all sorts of useful tools. Modular programming allows us to view every solution to a computational problem that we may develop as adding value to our computational environment.

For example, suppose that you need to evaluate Φ for some future application. Why not just cut and paste the code that implements `Phi()` from `Gaussian`? That would work, but would leave you with two copies of the code, making it more difficult to maintain. If you later want to fix or improve it, you would need to do so in both copies. Instead, you can just call `Gaussian.Phi()`. Our implementations and uses of them are soon going to proliferate, so having just one copy of each is a worthy goal.

From this point forward, you should write *every* program by identifying a reasonable way to divide the computation into separate parts of a manageable size and implementing each part as if someone will want to use it later. Most frequently, that someone will be you, and you will have yourself to thank for saving the effort of rewriting and re-debugging code.

**Libraries**   We refer to a module whose methods are primarily intended for use by many other programs as a *library*. One of the most important characteristics of programming in Java is that many, many methods have been predefined for you, in literally thousands of Java libraries that are available for your use. We reveal information about those that might be of interest to you throughout the book, but we will postpone a detailed discussion of the scope of Java libraries until the end of the book, because many of them are designed for use by experienced programmers. Instead, we focus in this chapter on the even more important idea that we can build *user-defined libraries*, which are nothing more than classes that each contain a set of related methods for use by other programs. No Java library can contain all the methods that we might need for a given computation, so this ability is a crucial step in addressing complex programming applications.

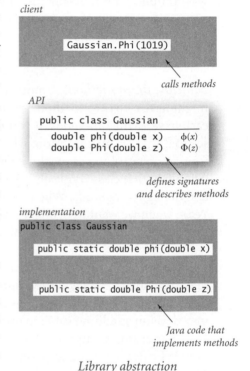

*Library abstraction*

*Clients.* We use the term *client* to refer to the program that calls a given method. When a class contains a method that is a client of a method in another class, we say that the first class is a client of the second class. In our example, `Gaussian` is a client of `Newton`. A given class might have multiple clients. For example, all of the programs that you have written that call `Math.sqrt()` or `Math.random()` are `Math` clients. When you implement a new static method or a new class, you need to have a very clear of idea of what it is going to do for its clients.

*APIs.* Programmers normally think in terms of a *contract* between the client and the implementation that is a clear specification of what the method is to do. When you are writing both clients and implementations, you are making contracts with yourself, which by itself is helpful because it provides extra help in debugging. More important, this approach enables code reuse. You have been able to write programs that are clients of Std* and Math and other built-in Java classes because of an informal contract (an English-language description of what they are supposed to do) along with a precise specification of the signatures of the methods that are available for use. Collectively, this information is known as an *application programming interface* (API). This same mechanism is effective for user-defined libraries. The API allows any client to use the library without having to examine the code in the implementation, just as you have been doing for Math and Std*. The guiding principle in API design is to *provide to clients the methods they need and no others*. An API with a huge number of methods may be a burden to implement; an API that is lacking important methods may be unnecessarily inconvenient for clients.

*Implementations.* We use the term *implementation* to describe the Java code that implements the methods in an API, kept by convention in a file with the library name and a .java extension. Every Java program is an implementation of some API, and no API is of any use without some implementation. Our goal when developing an implementation is to honor the terms of the contract. Often, there are many ways to do so, and separating client code from implementation code gives us the freedom to substitute new and improved implementations.

FOR EXAMPLE, CONSIDER THE GAUSSIAN DISTRIBUTION functions. These do not appear in Java's Math library but are important in applications, so it is worthwhile for us to put them in a library for use by future client programs and to articulate this API:

```
public class Gaussian
```

| | |
|---|---|
| double  phi(double x) | $\phi(x)$ |
| double  phi(double x, double m, double s) | $\phi(x, \mu, \sigma)$ |
| double  Phi(double z) | $\Phi(z)$ |
| double  Phi(double z, double m, double s) | $\Phi(z, \mu, \sigma)$ |

*API for our library of static methods for $\phi$ and $\Phi$*

Implementing these four static methods is straightforward from the code in Gaussian (PROGRAM 2.1.2)—see EXERCISE 2.2.1. Adding the three-argument versions of phi() and Phi() to the Gaussian library saves us from having to worry about those cases later on.

How much information should an API contain? This is a gray area and a hotly debated issue among programmers and computer-science educators. We might try to put as much information as possible in the API, but (as with any contract!) there are limits to the amount of information that we can productively include. In this book, we stick to a principle that parallels our guiding design principle: *provide to client programmers the information they need and no more.* Doing so gives us vastly more flexibility than the alternative of providing detailed information about implementations. Indeed, any extra information amounts to implicitly extending the contract, which is undesirable. Many programmers fall into the bad habit of checking implementation code to try to understand what it does. Doing so might lead to client code that depends on behavior not specified in the API, which would not work with a new implementation. Implementations change more often than you might think. For example, each new release of Java contains many new implementations of library functions.

Often, the implementation comes first. You might have a working module that you later decide might be useful for some task, and you can just start using its methods in other programs. In such a situation, it is wise to carefully articulate the API at some point. The methods may not have been designed for reuse, so it is worthwhile to use an API to do such a design (as we did for Gaussian).

The remainder of this section is devoted to several examples of libraries and clients. Our purpose in considering these libraries is twofold. First, they provide a richer programming environment for your use as you develop increasingly sophisticated client programs of your own. Second, they serve as examples for you to study as you begin to develop libraries for your own use.

**Random numbers**    We have written several programs that use Math.random(), but our code often uses particular idioms that convert the random double values between 0 and 1 that Math.random() provides to the type of random numbers that we want to use (random boolean values or random int values in a specified range, for example). To effectively reuse our code that implements these idioms, we will, from now on, use the StdRandom library in PROGRAM 2.2.1. StdRandom uses overloading to generate random numbers from various distributions. You can use any of them in the same way that you use our standard I/O libraries (download StdRandom.java and keep it in a directory with your client programs, or use your operating system's classpath mechanism). As usual, we summarize the methods in our StdRandom library with an API:

```
public class StdRandom
```
| | | |
|---:|:---|:---|
| int | uniform(int N) | *integer between* 0 *and* N-1 |
| double | uniform(double lo, double hi) | *real between* lo *and* hi |
| boolean | bernoulli(double p) | true *with probability* p |
| double | gaussian() | *normal, mean* 0, *standard deviation* 1 |
| double | gaussian(double m, double s) | *normal, mean* m, *standard deviation* s |
| int | discrete(double[] a) | i *with probability* a[i] |
| void | shuffle(double[] a) | *randomly shuffle the array* a[] |

*API for our library of static methods for random numbers*

These methods are sufficiently familiar that the short descriptions in the API suffice to specify what they do. By collecting all of these methods that use Math.random() to generate random numbers of various types in one file (StdRandom.java), we concentrate our attention on generating random numbers to this one file (and reuse the code in that file) instead of spreading them through every program that uses these methods. Moreover, each program that uses one of these methods is more clear than code that calls Math.random() directly, because its purpose for using Math.random() is clearly articulated by the choice of method from Std-Random.

*API design.* We make certain assumptions about the values passed to each method in StdRandom. For example, we assume that clients will call uniform(N) only for positive integers N, bernoulli(p) only for p between 0 and 1, and discrete() only for an array whose entries are between 0 and 1 and sum to 1. All of these assumptions are part of the contract between the client and the implementation. We strive to design libraries such that the contract is clear and unambiguous and to avoid getting bogged down with details. As with many tasks in programming, a good API design is often the result of several iterations of trying and living with various possibilities. We always take special care in designing APIs, because when we change an API we might have to change all clients and all implementations. Our goal is to articulate what clients are to expect *separate from the code* in the API. This practice frees us to change the code, and perhaps to use an implementation that achieves the desired effect more efficiently or with more accuracy.

*Program 2.2.1    Random number library*

```java
public class StdRandom
{
   public static int uniform(int N)
   {  return (int) (Math.random() * N);   }

   public static double uniform(double lo, double hi)
   {  return lo + Math.random() * (hi - lo);   }

   public static boolean bernoulli(double p)
   {  return Math.random() < p;   }

   public static double gaussian()
   {  /* See Exercise 2.1.28. */   }

   public static double gaussian(double m, double s)
   {  return m + s * gaussian();   }

   public static int discrete(double[] a)
   {  // See Program 1.6.2.
      double r = uniform(0.0, 1.0);
      double sum = 0.0;
      for (int i = 0; i < a.length; i++)
      {
         sum += a[i];
         if (sum > r) return i;
      }
      return a.length - 1;
   }

   public static void shuffle(double[] a)
   {  /* See Exercise 2.2.4. */   }

   public static void main(String[] args)
   {  /* See text. */   }
}
```

*This is a library of methods to compute various types of random numbers: random non-negative integer less than a given value, uniformly distributed in a given range, random bit (Bernoulli), Gaussian, Gaussian with given mean and standard deviation, and distributed according to a given discrete distribution.*

```
% java StdRandom 5
90 26.36076 false 8.79269 0
13 18.02210 false 9.03992 1
58 56.41176 true  8.80501 0
29 16.68454 false 8.90827 0
85 86.24712 true  8.95228 0
```

*Unit testing.* Even though we implement StdRandom without reference to any particular client, it is good programming practice to include a *test client* main() that, although not used when a client class uses the library, is helpful for use when debugging and testing the methods in the library. *Whenever you create a library, you should include a* main() *method for unit testing and debugging.* Proper unit testing can be a significant programming challenge in itself (for example, the best way of testing whether the methods in StdRandom produce numbers that have the same characteristics as truly random numbers is still debated by experts). At a minimum, you should always include a main() method that

 • Exercises all the code
 • Provides some assurance that the code is working
 • Takes an argument from the command line to allow more testing

Then, you should refine that main() method to do more exhaustive testing as you use the library more extensively. For example, we might start with the following code for StdRandom (leaving the testing of shuffle() for an exercise):

```
public static void main(String[] args)
{
   int N = Integer.parseInt(args[0]);
   double[] t = { .5, .3, .1, .1 };
   for (int i = 0; i < N; i++)
   {
      StdOut.printf(" %2d " , uniform(100));
      StdOut.printf("%8.5f ", uniform(10.0, 99.0));
      StdOut.printf("%5b "  , bernoulli(.5));
      StdOut.printf("%7.5f ", gaussian(9.0, .2));
      StdOut.printf("%2d "  , discrete(t));
      StdOut.println();
   }
}
```

When we include this code in StdRandom.java and invoke this method as illustrated in PROGRAM 2.2.1, the output carries no surprises: the integers in the first column might be equally likely to be any value from 0 to 99; the numbers in the second column might be uniformly spread between 10.0 and 99.0; about half of the values in the third column are true; the numbers in the fourth column seem to average about 9.0, and seem unlikely to be too far from 9.0; and the last column seems to be not far from 50% 0s, 30% 1s, 10% 2s, and 10% 3s. If something seems amiss in one of the columns, we can type java StdRandom 10 or 100 to see many more results. In this particular case, we can (and should) do far more extensive testing in a separate client to check that the numbers have many of the same properties as truly random numbers drawn from the cited distributions (see EXERCISE 2.2.3). One effective approach is to write test clients that use StdDraw, as data visualization can be a quick indication that a program is behaving as intended. For example, a plot of a large number of points whose *x* and *y* coordinates are both drawn from various distributions often produces a pattern that gives direct insight into the important properties of the distribution. More important, a bug in the random number generation code is likely to show up immediately in such a plot.

```
public class RandomPoints
{
   public static void main(String[] args)
   {
      int N = Integer.parseInt(args[0]);
      for (int i = 0; i < N; i++)
      {
         double x = StdRandom.gaussian(.5, .2);
         double y = StdRandom.gaussian(.5, .2);
         StdDraw.point(x, y);
      }
   }
}
```

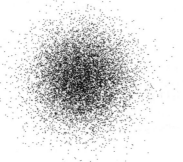

*A StdRandom test client*

*Stress testing.* An extensively used library such as StdRandom should also be subject to *stress testing*, where we make sure that it does not crash when the client does not follow the contract or makes some assumption that is not explicitly covered. You can be sure that Java libraries have been subject to such testing, which requires carefully examining each line of code and questioning whether some condition might cause a problem. What should discrete() do if array entries do not sum to exactly 1? What if the argument is an array of size 0? What should the two-argument uniform()

do if one or both of its arguments is NaN? Infinity? Any question that you can think of is fair game. Such cases are sometimes referred to as *corner cases*. You are certain to encounter a teacher or a supervisor who is a stickler about corner cases. With experience, most programmers learn to address them early, to avoid an unpleasant bout of debugging later. Again, a reasonable approach is to implement a stress test as a separate client.

**Input and output for arrays**    We have seen and will see many examples where we wish to keep data in arrays for processing. Accordingly, it is useful to build a library of static methods that complements `StdIn` and `StdOut` by providing static methods for reading arrays of primitive types from standard input and printing them to standard output, as expressed in this API:

| public class StdArrayIO | | |
|---|---|---|
| double[]   | readDouble1D() | *read a one-dimensional array of* double *values* |
| double[][] | readDouble2D() | *read a two-dimensional array of* double *values* |
| void | print(double[] a) | *print a one-dimensional array of* double *values* |
| void | print(double[][] a) | *print a two-dimensional array of* double *values* |

*Notes:*

   *1.* 1D *format is an integer N followed by N values.*

   *2.* 2D *format is two integers M and N followed by M×N values in row-major order.*

   *3. Methods for* int *and* boolean *are also included.*

*API for our library of static methods for array input and output*

The first two notes at the bottom of the table reflect the idea that we need to settle on a *file format*. For simplicity and harmony, we adopt the convention that all values appearing in standard input include the dimension(s) and appear in the order indicated. The `read*()` methods expect this format, the `print()` methods produce output in this format, and we can easily create files in this format for data from some other source. The third note at the bottom of the table indicates that `StdArrayIO` actually contains twelve methods—four each for `int`, `double`, and `boolean`. The `print()` methods are overloaded (they all have the same name `print()` but different types of arguments), but the `read*()` methods need different names, formed by adding the type name (capitalized, as in `StdIn`) followed by `1D` or `2D`.

Implementing these methods is straightforward from the array-processing code that we have considered in Section 1.4 and in Section 2.1, as shown in `StdArrayIO` (Program 2.2.2). Packaging up all of these static methods into one file—`StdArrayIO.java`—allows us to easily reuse the code and saves us from having to worry about the details of reading and printing arrays when writing client programs later on.

*Program 2.2.2    Array I/O library*

```
public class StdArrayIO
{
   public static double[] readDouble1D()
   {  /* See Exercise 2.2.6  */  }

   public static double[][] readDouble2D()
   {
      int M = StdIn.readInt();
      int N = StdIn.readInt();
      double[][] a = new double[M][N];
      for (int i = 0; i < M; i++)
         for (int j = 0; j < N; j++)
            a[i][j] = StdIn.readDouble();
      return a;
   }

   public static void print(double[] a)
   {  /* See Exercise 2.2.6  */  }

   public static void print(double[][] a)
   {
      int M = a.length;
      int N = a[0].length;
      System.out.println(M + " " + N);
      for (int i = 0; i < M; i++)
      {
         for (int j = 0; j < N; j++)
            StdOut.print(a[i][j] + " ");
         StdOut.println();
      }
      StdOut.println();
   }

   // Methods for other types are similar (see booksite).

   public static void main(String[] args)
   {  print(readDouble2D());  }

}
```

```
% more tiny.txt
4 3
  .000   .270   .000
  .246   .224  -.036
  .222   .176   .0893
 -.032   .739   .270

% java StdArrayIO < tiny.txt
4 3
  0.00000  0.27000  0.00000
  0.24600  0.22400 -0.03600
  0.22200  0.17600  0.08930
 -0.03200  0.73900  0.27000
```

*This library of static methods facilitates reading one-dimensional and two-dimensional arrays from standard input and printing them to standard output. The file format includes the dimensions (see accompanying text). Numbers in the output in the example are truncated.*

**Iterated function systems**   Scientists have discovered that complex visual images can arise unexpectedly from simple computational processes. With `StdRandom`, `StdDraw`, and `StdArrayIO`, we can easily study the behavior of such systems.

*Sierpinksi triangle.* As a first example, consider the following simple process: Start by plotting a point at one of the vertices of a given equilateral triangle. Then pick one of the three vertices at random and plot a new point halfway between the point just plotted and that vertex. Continue performing this same operation. Each time, we are picking a random vertex from the triangle to establish the line whose midpoint will be the next point plotted. Since we are making a random choice, the set of points should have some of the characteristics of random points, and that does seem to be the case after the first few iterations:

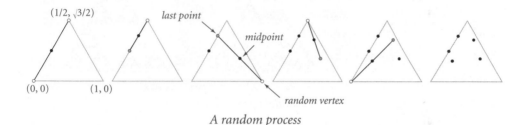

*A random process*

But we can study the process for a large number of iterations by writing a program to plot T points according to the rules:

```
double[] cx = { 0.000, 1.000, 0.500 };
double[] cy = { 0.000, 0.000, 0.866 };
double x = 0.0, y = 0.0;
for (int t = 0; t < T; t++)
{
    int r = StdRandom.uniform(3);
    x = (x + cx[r]) / 2.0;
    y = (y + cy[r]) / 2.0;
    StdDraw.point(x, y);
}
```

We keep the $x$ and $y$ coordinates of the triangle vertices in the arrays `cx[]` and `cy[]`, respectively. We use `StdRandom.uniform()` to choose a random index `r` into these arrays—the coordinates of the chosen vertex are (cx[r], cy[r]). The *x*-coordinate of the midpoint of the line from (*x*, *y*) to that vertex is given by the expression (x + cx[r])/2.0, and a similar calculation gives the *y* coordinate. Adding a call to StdDraw.point() and putting this code in a loop completes the implementation. Remarkably, despite the randomness, the same figure always emerges after a large number of iterations! This figure is known as the *Sierpinski triangle* (see EXERCISE 2.3.27). Understanding why such a regular figure should arise from such a random process is a fascinating question.

*A random process?*

*Barnsley fern.* To add to the mystery, we can produce pictures of remarkable diversity by playing the same game with different rules. One striking example is known as the *Barnsley fern*. To generate it, we use the same process, but this time driven by the following table of formulas. At each step, we choose the formulas to use to update *x* and *y* with the indicated probability (1% of the time we use the first pair of formulas, 85% of the time we use the second pair of formulas, and so forth).

| *probability* | *x-update* | | *y-update* | |
|:---:|:---|---:|:---|---:|
| 1%  | $x =$ | $.500$                  | $x =$ | $.160y$                |
| 85% | $x =$ | $.85x + .04y + .075$    | $y =$ | $.04x + .85y + .180$   |
| 7%  | $x =$ | $.20x - .26y + .400$    | $y =$ | $.23x + .22y + .045$   |
| 7%  | $x =$ | $.15x + .28y + .575$    | $y =$ | $.26x + .24y - .086$   |

We could write code just like the code we just wrote for the Sierpinski triangle to iterate these rules, but matrix processing provides a uniform way to generalize that

## Program 2.2.3    Iterated function systems

```java
public class IFS
{
   public static void main(String args[])
   {  // Plot T iterations of IFS on StdIn.
      int T = Integer.parseInt(args[0]);
      double[] dist    = StdArrayIO.readDouble1D();
      double[][] cx    = StdArrayIO.readDouble2D();
      double[][] cy    = StdArrayIO.readDouble2D();
      double x = 0.0, y = 0.0;
      for (int t = 0; t < T; t++)
      {  // Plot 1 iteration.
         int r = StdRandom.discrete(dist);
         double x0 = cx[r][0]*x + cx[r][1]*y + cx[r][2];
         double y0 = cy[r][0]*x + cy[r][1]*y + cy[r][2];
         x = x0;
         y = y0;
         StdDraw.point(x, y);
      }
   }
}
```

| T | iterations |
|---|---|
| dist[] | probabilities |
| cx[][] | x coefficients |
| cy[][] | y coefficients |
| x, y | current point |

*This data-driven client of* StdArrayIO, StdRandom, *and* StdDraw *iterates the function system defined by a 1-by-M vector (probabilities) and two M-by-3 matrices (coefficients for updating x and y, respectively) on standard input, plotting the result as a set of points on standard draw. Curiously, this code does not need to know the value of M, as it uses separate methods to create and process the matrices.*

```
% more sierpinski.txt

3
  .33 .33 .34
3 3
  .50 .00 .00
  .50 .00 .50
  .50 .00 .25
3 3
  .00 .50 .00
  .00 .50 .00
  .00 .50 .433
```

```
% java IFS 10000 < sierpinski.txt
```

```
% more barnsley.txt
4
   .01 .85 .07 .07
4 3
    .00   .00   .500
    .85   .04   .075
    .20  -.26   .400
   -.15   .28   .575
4 3
    .00   .16   .000
   -.04   .85   .180
    .23   .22   .045
    .26   .24  -.086
```

% java IFS 20000 < barnsley.txt

```
% more tree.txt
6
   .1 .1 .2 .2 .2 .2
6 3
    .00   .00   .550
   -.05   .00   .525
    .46  -.15   .270
    .47  -.15   .265
    .43   .26   .290
    .42   .26   .290
6 3
    .00   .60   .000
   -.50   .00   .750
    .39   .38   .105
    .17   .42   .465
   -.25   .45   .625
   -.35   .31   .525
```

% java IFS 20000 < tree.txt

% java IFS 20000 < coral.txt

```
% more coral.txt
3
   .40 .15 .45
3 3
    .3077  -.5315   .8863
    .3077  -.0769   .2166
    .0000   .5455   .0106
3 3
   -.4615  -.2937  1.0962
    .1538  -.4476   .3384
    .6923  -.1958   .3808
```

*Examples of iterated function systems*

code to handle any set of rules. We have $M$ different transformations, chosen from a 1-by-$M$ vector with `StdRandom.discrete()`. For each transformation, we have an equation for updating $x$ and an equation for updating $y$, so we use two $M$-by-3 matrices for the equation coefficients, one for $x$ and one for $y$. IFS (PROGRAM 2.2.3) implements this data-driven version of the computation. This program enables limitless exploration: it performs the iteration for any input containing a vector that defines the probability distribution and the two matrices that define the coefficients, one for updating $x$ and the other for updating $y$. For the coefficients just given, again, even though we choose a random equation at each step, the same figure emerges every time that we do this computation: an image that looks remarkably similar to a fern that you might see in the woods, not something generated by a random process on a computer.

*Generating a Barnsley fern*

That the same short program that takes a few numbers from standard input and plots points on standard draw can (given different data) produce both the Sierpinski triangle and the Barnsley fern (and many, many other images) is truly remarkable. Because of its simplicity and the appeal of the results, this sort of calculation is useful in making synthetic images that have a realistic appearance in computer-generated movies and games. Perhaps more significantly, the ability to produce such realistic diagrams so easily suggests intriguing scientific questions: What does computation tell us about nature? What does nature tell us about computation?

**Standard statistics**   Next, we consider a library for a set of mathematical calculations and basic visualization tools that arise in all sorts of applications in science and engineering and are not all implemented in standard Java libraries. These calculations relate to the task of understanding the statistical properties of a set of numbers. Such a library is useful, for example, when we perform a series of scientific experiments that yield measurements of a quantity. One of the most important challenges facing modern scientists is proper analysis of such data, and computation is playing an increasingly important role in such analysis. These basic data analysis methods that we will consider are summarized in the following API:

public class StdStats

| | |
|---|---|
| double max(double[] a) | *largest value* |
| double min(double[] a) | *smallest value* |
| double mean(double[] a) | *average* |
| double var(double[] a) | *sample variance* |
| double stddev(double[] a) | *sample standard deviation* |
| double median(double[] a) | *median* |
| void plotPoints(double[] a) | *plot points at (i, a[i])* |
| void plotLines(double[] a) | *plot lines connecting points at (i, a[i])* |
| void plotBars(double[] a) | *plot bars to points at (i, a[i])* |

*Note: overloaded implementations are included for all numeric types*

*API for our library of static methods for data analysis*

*Basic statistics.*  Suppose that we have $N$ measurements $x_0, x_1, .., x_{N-1}$. The average value of those measurements, otherwise known as the *mean*, is given by the formula $\mu = (x_0 + x_1 + \ldots + x_{N-1})/N$ and is an estimate of the value of the quantity. The minimum and maximum values are also of interest, as is the median (the value which is smaller than and larger than half the values). Also of interest is the *sample variance*, which is given by the formula

$$\sigma^2 = ((x_0 - \mu)^2 + (x_1 - \mu)^2 + \ldots + (x_{N-1} - \mu)^2)) / (N-1)$$

*Program 2.2.4    Data analysis library*

```
public class StdStats
{
   public static double max(double[] a)
   {  // Compute maximum value in a[].
      double max = Double.NEGATIVE_INFINITY;
      for (int i = 0; i < a.length; i++)
         if (a[i] > max) max = a[i];
      return max;
   }

   public static double mean(double[] a)
   {  // Compute the average of the values in a[].
      double sum = 0.0;
      for (int i = 0; i < a.length; i++)
         sum = sum + a[i];
      return sum / a.length;
   }

   public static double var(double[] a)
   {  // Compute the sample variance of the values in a[].
      double avg = mean(a);
      double sum = 0.0;
      for (int i = 0; i < a.length; i++)
         sum += (a[i] - avg) * (a[i] - avg);
      return sum / (a.length - 1);
   }

   public static double stddev(double[] a)
   {  return Math.sqrt(var(a));  }

   // See Program 2.2.5 for plotting methods.

   public static void main(String[] args)
   {  /* See text. */  }

}
```

*This code implements methods to compute the maximum, mean, variance, and standard deviation of numbers in a client array. The method for computing the minimum is omitted, and plotting methods are in Program 2.2.5 (see Section 4.2 for a discussion of the median).*

```
% more tiny.txt
5
3.0 1.0 2.0 5.0 4.0
```

```
% java StdStats < tiny.txt
     min    1.000
    mean    3.000
     max    5.000
 std dev    1.581
```

and the *sample standard deviation,* the square root of the sample variance. Std-
Stats (PROGRAM 2.2.3) shows implementations of static methods for computing
these basic statistics (the median is more difficult to compute than the others—we
will consider the implementation of median() in SECTION 4.2). The main() test client for StdStats reads numbers from standard input into an array and calls each
of the methods to print out the minimum, mean, maximum, and standard deviation, as follows:

```
public static void main(String[] args)
{
    double[] a = StdArrayIO.readDouble1D();
    StdOut.printf("        min %7.3f\n", min(a));
    StdOut.printf("       mean %7.3f\n", mean(a));
    StdOut.printf("        max %7.3f\n", max(a));
    StdOut.printf("    std dev %7.3f\n", stddev(a));
}
```

As with StdRandom, a more extensive test of the calculations is called for (see EX-
ERCISE 2.2.3). Typically, as we debug or test new methods in the library, we adjust
the unit testing code accordingly, testing the methods one at a time. A mature and
widely used library like StdStats also deserves a stress-testing client for extensively
testing everything after any change. If you are interested in seeing what such a client
might look like, you can find one for StdStats on the booksite. Most experienced
programmers will advise you that any time spent doing unit testing and stress testing will more than pay for itself later.

*Plotting.* One important use of StdDraw is to help us visualize data rather than
relying on tables of numbers. In a typical situation, we perform experiments, save
the experimental data in an array, and then compare the results against a model,
perhaps a mathematical function that describes the data. To expedite this process
for the typical case where values of one variable are equally spaced, our StdStats
library contains static methods that you can use for plotting data in an array. PRO-
GRAM 2.2.5 is an implementation of the plotPoints(), plotLines(), and plot-
Bars() methods for StdStats. These methods display the values in the argument
array at regularly spaced intervals in the drawing window, either connected together by line segments (lines), filled circles at each value (points), or bars from
the x-axis to the value (bars). They all plot the points with x coordinate i and y
coordinate a[i] using filled circles, lines through the points, and bars, respectively.

---

*Program 2.2.5  Plotting data values in an array*

---

```
public static void plotPoints(double[] a)
{  // Plot points at (i, a[i]).
   int N = a.length;
   StdDraw.setXscale(0, N-1);
   StdDraw.setPenRadius(1/(3.0*N));
   for (int i = 0; i < N; i++)
      StdDraw.point(i, a[i]);
}

public static void plotLines(double[] a)
{  // Plot lines through points at (i, a[i]).
   int N = a.length;
   StdDraw.setXscale(0, N-1);
   StdDraw.setPenRadius();
   for (int i = 1; i < N; i++)
      StdDraw.line(i-1, a[i-1], i, a[i]);
}

public static void plotBars(double[] a)
{  // Plot bars from (0, a[i]) to (i, a[i]).
   int N = a.length;
   StdDraw.setXscale(0, N-1);
   StdDraw.setPenRadius(0.5 / N);
   for (int i = 0; i < N; i++)
      StdDraw.line(i, 0, i, a[i]);
}
```

---

*This code implements three methods in* StdStats *(Program 2.2.4) for plotting data. They plot the points* (i, a[i]) *with filled circles, connecting line segments, and bars, respectively.*

```
int N = 20;
double[] a = new double[N];
for (int i = 0; i < N; i++)
   a[i] = 1.0/(i+1);
```

plotPoints(a);   plotLines(a);   plotBars(a);

(0.0, 1.0)

(9.0, 0.1)

They all rescale *x* to fill the drawing window (so that the points are evenly spaced along the *x*-coordinate) and leave to the client scaling the *y*-coordinates.

These methods are not intended to be a general-purpose plotting package, you can certainly think of all sorts of things that you might want to add: different types of spots, labeled axes, color, and many other artifacts are commonly found in modern systems that can plot data. Some situations might call for more complicated methods than these.

Our intent with StdStats is to introduce you to data analysis while showing you how easy it is to define a library to take care of useful tasks. Indeed, this library has already proven useful—we use these plotting methods to produce the figures in this book that depict function graphs, sound waves, and experimental results. Next, we consider several examples of their use.

*Plotting function graphs.* You can use the StdStats.plot*() methods to draw a plot of the function graph for any function at all: choose an *x*-interval where you want to plot the function, compute function values evenly spaced through that interval and store them in an array, determine and set the *y* scale, and then call StdStats. plotLines() or another plot*() method. For example, to plot a sine function, rescale the *y*-axis to cover values between $-1$ and $+1$. Scaling the *x*-axis is automatically handled by the StdStats methods. If you do not know the range, you can handle the situation by calling:

```
int N = 50;
double[] a = new double[N+1];
for (int i = 0; i <= N; i++)
    a[i] = Gaussian.phi(-4.0 + 8.0*i/N);
StdStats.plotPoints(a);
StdStats.plotLines(a);
```

*Plotting a function graph*

```
StdDraw.setYscale(StdStats.min(a), StdStats.max(a));
```

The smoothness of the curve is determined by properties of the function and by the number of points plotted. As we discussed when first considering StdDraw, you have to be careful to sample enough points to catch fluctuations in the function. We will consider another approach to plotting functions based on sampling values that are not equally spaced in Section 2.4.

*Plotting sound waves.* Both the StdAudio library and the StdStats plot methods work with arrays that contain sampled values at regular intervals. The diagrams of sound waves in SECTION 1.5 and at the beginning of this section were each produced by first scaling the *y*-axis with StdDraw.setYscale(-1, 1), then plotting the points with StdStats.plotPoints(). As you have seen, such plots give direct insight into processing audio. You can also produce interesting effects by plotting sound waves as you play them with StdAudio, although this task is a bit challenging because of the huge amount of data involved (see EXERCISE 1.5.23).

```
StdDraw.setYscale(-1.0, 1.0);
double[] hi;
hi = PlayThatTune.tone(880, .01);
StdStats.plotPoints(hi);
```

*Plotting a sound wave*

*Plotting experimental results* You can put multiple plots on the same drawing. One typical reason to do so is to compare experimental results with a theoretical model. For example, Bernoulli (PROGRAM 2.2.6) counts the number of heads found when a fair coin is flipped *N* times and compares the result with the predicted normal (Gaussian) distribution function. A famous result from probability theory is that the distribution of this quantity is the binomial distribution, which is extremely well-approximated by the normal distribution function $\phi$ with mean *N/2* and standard deviation $\sqrt{N}/2$. The more often we run the experiment, the more accurate the approximation. The drawing produced by Bernoulli is a succinct summary of the results of the experiment and a convincing validation of the theory. This example is prototypical of a scientific approach to applications programming that we use often throughout this book and that you should use whenever you run an experiment. If a theoretical model that can explain your results is available, a visual plot comparing the experiment to the theory can validate both.

THESE FEW EXAMPLES ARE INTENDED TO indicate to you what is possible with a well-designed library of static methods for data analysis. Several extensions and other ideas are explored in the exercises. You will find StdStats to be useful for basic plots, and you are encouraged to experiment with these implementations and to modify them or to add methods to make your own library that can draw plots of your own design. As you continue to address an ever-widening circle of programming tasks, you will naturally be drawn to the idea of developing tools like these for your own use.

*Program 2.2.6    Bernoulli trials*

```java
public class Bernoulli
{
   public static int binomial(int N)
   {  // Simulate flipping a coin N times.
      int heads = 0;
      for (int i = 0; i < N; i++)
         if (StdRandom.bernoulli(0.5)) heads++;
      return heads;
   }
   public static void main(String[] args)
   {  // Perform experiments, plot results and model.
      int N = Integer.parseInt(args[0]);
      int T = Integer.parseInt(args[1]);

      int[] freq = new int[N+1];
      for (int t = 0; t < T; t++)
         freq[binomial(N)]++;

      double[] norm = new double[N+1];
      for (int i = 0; i <= N; i++)
         norm[i] = (double) freq[i] / T;
      StdStats.plotBars(norm);

      double stddev = Math.sqrt(N)/2.0;
      double stddev = Math.sqrt(N)/2.0;
      double[] phi  = new double[N+1];
      for (int i = 0; i <= N; i++)
         phi[i] = Gaussian.phi(i, mean, stddev);
      StdStats.plotLines(phi);
   }
}
```

| N | *number of flips per trial* |
|---|---|
| T | *number of trials* |
| freq[] | *experimental results* |
| norm[] | *normalized results* |
| phi[] | *Gaussian model* |

This `StdStats`, `StdRandom`, *and* `Gaussian` *client provides convincing visual evidence that the number of heads observed when a fair coin is flipped N times obeys a Gaussian distribution. It uses the overloaded* `Gaussian.phi()` *that takes as arguments the mean and standard deviation (see Exercise 2.2.1).*

```
% java Bernoulli 20 100000
```

**Modular programming**    The library implementations that we have developed illustrate a programming style known as *modular programming*. Instead of writing a new program that is self-contained in its own file to address a new problem, we break up each task into smaller, more manageable subtasks, then implement and independently debug code that addresses each subtask. Good libraries facilitate modular programming by allowing us to define and to provide solutions of important subtasks for future clients. *Whenever you can clearly separate tasks within a program, you should do so.* Java supports such separation by allowing us to independently debug and later use classes in separate files. Traditionally, programmers use the term *module* to refer to code that can be compiled and run independently; in Java each *class* is a module.

IFS (PROGRAM 2.2.3) exemplifies modular programming because it is a relatively sophisticated computation that is implemented with several relatively small modules, developed independently. It uses StdRandom and StdArrayIO), as well as the methods from Integer and StdDraw that we are accustomed to using. If we were to put all of the code required for IFS in a single file, we would have a large amount of code on our hands to maintain and debug; with modular programming, we can study iterated function systems with some confidence that the arrays are read properly and that the random number generator will produce properly distributed values, because we already implemented and tested the code for these tasks in separate modules.

| API | description |
|---|---|
| Gaussian | Gaussian distribution functions |
| StdRandom | random numbers |
| StdArrayIO | input and output for arrays |
| IFS | client for iterated function systems |
| StdStats | functions for data analysis |
| Bernoulli | client for Bernoulli trials experiments |

*Summary of classes in this section*

Similarly, Bernoulli (PROGRAM 2.2.6) also exemplifies modular programming. It is a client of Gaussian, Integer, Math, StdRandom, and StdStats. Again, we can have some confidence that the methods in these modules produce the expected results because they are system libraries or libraries that we have tested, debugged, and used before.

To describe the relationships among modules in a modular program, we often draw a *dependency graph*, where we connect two class names with an arrow labeled with the name of a method if the first class contains a call on the method and the second class contains the definition of the method. Such diagrams play an impor-

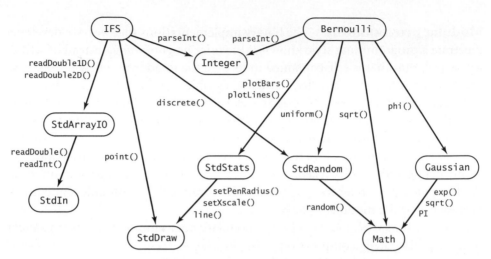

*Dependency graph for the modules in this section*

tant role because understanding the relationships among modules is necessary for proper development and maintenance.

We emphasize modular programming throughout this book because it has many important advantages that have come to be accepted as essential in modern programming, including the following:

   • We can have programs of a reasonable size, even in large systems.
   • Debugging is restricted to small pieces of code.
   • We can reuse code without having to reimplement it.
   • Maintaining (and improving) code is much simpler.

The importance of these advantages is difficult to overstate, so we will expand upon each of them.

*Programs of a reasonable size.* No large task is so complex that it cannot be divided into smaller subtasks. If you find yourself with a program that stretches to more than a few pages of code, you must ask yourself the following questions: Are there subtasks that could be implemented separately? Do some of these subtasks logically group together in a separate library? Could other clients use this code in the future? At the other end of the range, if you find yourself with a huge number of tiny modules, you must ask yourself questions such as: Is there some group of subtasks that logically belong in the same module? Is each module likely to be used by multiple clients? There is no hard-and-fast rule on module size: one implementation of a critically important abstraction might properly be a few lines of code, whereas another library with a large number of overloaded methods might properly stretch to hundreds of lines of code.

*Debugging.* Tracing a program rapidly becomes more difficult as the number of statements and interacting variables increases. Tracing a program with hundreds of variables requires keeping track of hundreds of values, as any statement might affect or be affected by any variable. To do so for hundreds or thousands of statements or more is untenable. With modular programming and our guiding principle of keeping the scope of variables local to the extent possible, we severely restrict the number of possibilities that we have to consider when debugging. Equally important is the idea of a contract between client and implementation. Once we are satisfied that an implementation is meeting its end of the bargain, we can debug all its clients under that assumption.

*Code reuse.* Once we have implemented libraries such as `StdStats` and `StdRandom`, we do not have to worry about writing code to compute averages or standard deviations or to generate random numbers again—we can simply reuse the code that we have written. Moreover, we do not need to make copies of the code: any module can just refer to any public method in any other module.

*Maintenance.* Like a good piece of writing, a good program can always be improved, and modular programming facilitates the process of continually improving your Java programs because improving a module improves all of its clients. For example, it is normally the case that there are several different approaches to solving a particular problem. With modular programming, you can implement more than one and try them independently. More importantly, suppose that while developing a new client, you find a bug in some module. With modular programming, fixing that bug amounts to fixing bugs in all of the module's clients.

IF YOU ENCOUNTER AN OLD PROGRAM (or a new program written by an old programmer!), you are likely to find one huge module—a long sequence of statements, stretching to several pages or more, where any statement can refer to any variable in the program. Variables whose scope extends to a whole program are known as *global variables*. We avoid global variables in modular programs, but their use is common in lower-level and older programming languages. Huge modules that use global variables are extremely difficult to understand, maintain, and debug. Old programs of this kind are found in critical parts of our computational infrastructure (for example, some nuclear power plants and some banks) precisely because the programmers charged with maintaining them cannot even understand them well enough to rewrite them in a modern language! With support for modular programming, modern languages like Java help us avoid such situations by separately developing libraries of methods in independent classes.

The ability to share static methods among different files fundamentally extends our programming model in two different ways. First, it allows us to reuse code without having to maintain multiple copies of it. Second, by allowing us to organize a program into files of manageable size that can be independently debugged and compiled, it strongly supports our basic message: *Whenever you can clearly separate tasks within a program, you should do so.* We use the term *library* to capture the idea of developing methods for later reuse and *modular programming* to capture the idea of independently developing pieces connected by well-defined interfaces instead of a big, monolithic piece of code.

In this section, we have supplemented the Std* libraries of SECTION 1.5 with several other libraries that you can use: Gaussian, StdArrayIO, StdRandom, and StdStats. Furthermore, we have illustrated their use with several client programs. These tools are centered on basic mathematical concepts that arise in any scientific project or engineering task. Our intent is not just to provide tools, but also to illustrate to you that it is easy for you to create your own tools. The first question that most modern programmers ask when addressing a complex task is "What tools do I need?" When the needed tools are not conveniently available, the second question is "How difficult would it be to implement them?" To be a good programmer, you need to have the confidence to build a software tool when you need it and the wisdom to know when it might be better to seek a solution in a library.

After libraries and modular programming, you have one more step to learn a complete modern programming model: *object-oriented programming*, the topic of CHAPTER 3. With object-oriented programming, you can build libraries of functions that use side effects (in a tightly controlled manner) to vastly extend the Java programming model. Before moving to object-oriented programming, we consider in this chapter the profound ramifications of the idea that any method can call itself (in SECTION 2.3) and a more extensive case study (in SECTION 2.4) of modular programming than the small clients in this section.

## Q&A

**Q.** I tried to use `StdRandom`, but got the error message `Exception in thread "main" java.lang.NoClassDefFoundError: StdRandom`. What's wrong?

**A.** You need to download `StdRandom.java` into the directory containing your client, or use your operating system's classpath mechanism, as described on the booksite.

**Q.** Is there a keyword that identifies a class as a library?

**A.** No, any set of public methods will do. There is a bit of a conceptual leap in this viewpoint because it is one thing to sit down to create a `.java` file that you will compile and run, quite another thing to create a `.java` file that you will rely on much later in the future, and still another thing to create a `.java` file for *someone else* to use in the future. You need to develop some libraries for your own use before engaging in this sort of activity, which is the province of experienced systems programmers.

**Q.** How do I develop a new version of a library that I have been using for a while?

**A.** With care. Any change to the API might break any client program, so it is best to work in a separate directory. But then you are working with a copy of the code. If you are changing a library that has a lot of clients, you can appreciate the problems faced by companies putting out new versions of their software. If you just want to add a few methods to a library, go ahead: that is usually not too dangerous, though you should realize that you might find yourself in a situation where you have to support that library for years!

**Q.** How do I know that an implementation behaves properly? Why not automatically check that it satisfies the API?

**A.** We use informal specifications because writing a detailed specification is not much different than writing a program. Moreover, a fundamental tenet of theoretical computer science says that doing so does not even solve the basic problem, because generally there is no way to check that two different programs perform the same computation.

## Exercises

**2.2.1**   Add to Gaussian (PROGRAM 2.1.2) the method implementation phi(x, mu, sigma) specified in the API that computes the Gaussian distribution with a given mean $\mu$ and standard deviation $\sigma$, based on the formula $\phi(x, \mu, \sigma) = \phi((x-\mu)/\sigma)/\sigma$. Also include the implementation of the associated cumulative distribution function Phi(z, mu, sigma), based on the formula $\Phi(z, \mu, \sigma) = \Phi((z-\mu)/\sigma)$.

**2.2.2**   Write a static method library that implements the *hyperbolic* trigonometric functions based on the definitions $\sinh(x) = (e^x - e^{-x})/2$ and $\cosh(x) = (e^x + e^{-x})/2$, with $\tanh(x)$, $\coth(x)$, $\operatorname{sech}(x)$, and $\operatorname{csch}(x)$ defined in a manner analogous to standard trigonometric functions.

**2.2.3**   Write a test client for both StdStats and StdRandom that checks that the methods in both libraries operate as expected. Take a command-line argument $N$, generate $N$ random numbers using each of the methods in StdRandom, and print out their statistics. *Extra credit*: Defend the results that you get by comparing them to those that are to be expected from analysis.

**2.2.4**   Add to StdRandom a method shuffle() that takes an array of double values as argument and rearranges them in random order. Implement a test client that checks that each permutation of the array is produced about the same number of times.

**2.2.5**   Develop a client that does stress testing for StdRandom. Pay particular attention to discrete(). For example, do the probabilities sum to 1?

**2.2.6**   Develop a full implementation of StdArrayIO (implement all 12 methods indicated in the API).

**2.2.7**   Write a method that takes double values ymin and ymax (with ymin strictly less than ymax), and a double array a[] as arguments and uses the StdStats library to linearly scale the values in a[] so that they are all between ymin and ymax.

**2.2.8**   Write a Gaussian and StdStats client that explores the effects of changing the mean and standard deviation on the Gaussian distribution curve. Create one plot with curves having a fixed mean and various standard deviations and another with curves having a fixed standard deviation and various means.

**2.2.9** Add to `StdRandom` a static method `maxwellBoltzmann()` that returns a random value drawn from a *Maxwell-Boltzmann* distribution with parameter $\sigma$. To produce such a value, return the square root of the sum of the squares of three Gaussian random variables with mean 0 and standard deviation $\sigma$. The speeds of molecules in an ideal gas have a Maxwell-Boltzmann distribution.

**2.2.10** Modify `Bernoulli` (PROGRAM 2.2.6) to animate the bar graph, replotting it after each experiment, so that you can watch it converge to the normal distribution. Then add a command-line argument and an overloaded `binomial()` implementation to allow you to specify the probability $p$ that a biased coin comes up heads, and run experiments to get a feeling for the distribution corresponding to a biased coin. Be sure to try values of $p$ that are close to 0 and close to 1.

**2.2.11** Write a library `Matrix` that implements the following API:

| public class Matrix | | |
|---|---|---|
| `double` | `dot(double[] a, double[] b)` | *vector dot product* |
| `double[][]` | `multiply(double[][] a, double[][] b)` | *matrix-matrix product* |
| `double[][]` | `transpose(double[][] a)` | *transpose* |
| `double[]` | `multiply(double[][] a, double[] x)` | *matrix-vector product* |
| `double[]` | `multiply(double[] x, double[][] a)` | *vector-matrix product* |

(See SECTION 1.4.) As a test client, use the following code, which performs the same calculation as `Markov` (PROGRAM 1.6.3).

```
public static void main(String[] args)
{
   int T = Integer.parseInt(args[0]);
   double[][] p = StdArrayIO.readDouble2D();
   double[] rank = new double[p.length];
   rank[0] = 1.0;
   for (int t = 0; t < T; t++)
       rank = Matrix.multiply(rank, p);
   StdArrayIO.print(rank);
}
```

Mathematicians and scientists use mature libraries or special-purpose matrix-processing languages for such tasks (see the CONTEXT section at the end of this book for some details). See the booksite for information on using such libraries.

**2.2.12** Write a Matrix client that implements the version of Markov described in SECTION 1.6 but is based on squaring the matrix, instead of iterating the vector-matrix multiplication.

**2.2.13** Rewrite RandomSurfer (PROGRAM 1.6.2) using the StdArrayIO and Std-Random libraries.

*Partial solution.*

```
...
double[][] p = StdArrayIO.readDouble2D();
int page = 0; // Start at page 0.
int[] freq = new int[N];
for (int t = 0; t < T; t++)
{
    page = StdRandom.discrete(p[page]);
    freq[page]++;
}
...
```

**2.2.14** Add a method exp() to StdRandom that takes an argument $\lambda$ and returns a random number from the *exponential distribution* with rate $\lambda$. *Hint*: If $x$ is a random number uniformly distributed between 0 and 1, then $-\ln x / \lambda$ is a random number from the exponential distribution with rate $\lambda$.

# Creative Exercises

**2.2.15** *Sicherman dice.* Suppose that you have two six-sided dice, one with faces labeled 1, 3, 4, 5, 6, and 8 and the other with faces labeled 1, 2, 2, 3, 3, and 4. Compare the probabilities of occurrence of each of the values of the sum of the dice with those for a standard pair of dice. Use `StdRandom` and `StdStats`.

**2.2.16** *Craps.* The following are the rules for a *pass bet* in the game of *craps*. Roll two six-sided dice, and let $x$ be their sum.
   • If $x$ is 7 or 11, you win.
   • If $x$ is 2, 3, or 12, you lose.
Otherwise, repeatedly roll the two dice until their sum is either $x$ or 7.
   • If their sum is $x$, you win.
   • If their sum is 7, you lose.
Write a modular program to estimate the probability of winning a pass bet. Modify your program to handle loaded dice, where the probability of a die landing on 1 is taken from the command line, the probability of landing on 6 is 1/6 minus that probability, and 2–5 are assumed equally likely. *Hint*: Use `StdRandom.discrete()`.

**2.2.17** *Dynamic histogram.* Suppose that the standard input stream is a sequence of `double` values. Write a program that takes an integer `N` and two `double` values `l` and `r` from the command line and uses `StdStats` to plot a histogram of the count of the numbers in the standard input stream that fall in each of the $N$ intervals defined by dividing $(l, r)$ into $N$ equal-sized intervals. Use your program to add code to your solution to EXERCISE 2.2.3 to plot a histogram of the distribution of the numbers produced by each method, taking `N` from the command line.

**2.2.18** *Tukey plot.* A Tukey plot is a data visualization that generalizes a histogram, and is appropriate for use when each integer in a given range is associated with a set of $y$ values. For each integer in the range, we compute the mean, standard deviation, 10th percentile, and 90th percentile of all the associated $y$ values; draw a vertical line with $x$-coordinate i running from the 10th percentile $y$ value to the 90th percentile $y$ value; and then draw a thin rectangle centered on the line that runs from one standard deviation below the mean to one standard deviation above the mean. Suppose that the standard input stream is a sequence of pairs of numbers where the first number in each pair is an `int` and the second a `double` value. Write a `StdStats` and `StdDraw` client that takes an integer *N* from the command line and, assuming that all the `int` values on the input stream are between 0 and N-1, uses `StdDraw` to make a Tukey plot of the data.

**2.2.19** *IFS.* Experiment with various inputs to `IFS` to create patterns of your own design like the Sierpinski triangle, the Barnsley fern, or the other examples in the table in the text. You might begin by experimenting with minor modifications to the given inputs.

**2.2.20** *IFS matrix implementation.* Write a version of `IFS` that uses `Matrix.multiply()` (see EXERCISE 2.2.11) instead of the equations that compute the new values of x0 and y0.

**2.2.21** *Stress test.* Develop a client that does stress testing for `StdStats`. Work with a classmate, with one person writing code and the other testing it.

**2.2.22** *Gambler's ruin.* Develop a `StdRandom` client to study the gambler's ruin problem (see PROGRAM 1.3.8 and EXERCISES 1.3.21–24. *Note*: Defining a static method for the experiment is more difficult than for `Bernoulli` because you cannot return two values.

**2.2.23** *Library for properties of integers.* Develop a library based on the functions that we have considered in this book for computing properties of integers. Include functions for determining whether a given integer is prime; whether two integers are relatively prime; computing all the factors of a given integer; the greatest common divisor and least common multiple of two integers; Euler's totient function (EXERCISE 2.1.26); and any other functions that you think might be useful. Include overloaded implementations for `long` values. Create an API, a client that performs stress testing, and clients that solve several of the exercises earlier in this book.

**2.2.24** *Voting machines.* Develop a `StdRandom` client (with appropriate static methods of its own) to study the following problem: Suppose that in a population of 100 million voters, 51% vote for candidate *A* and 49% vote for candidate *B*. However, the voting machines are prone to make mistakes, and 5% of the time they produce the wrong answer. Assuming the errors are made independently and at random, is a 5% error rate enough to invalidate the results of a close election? What error rate can be tolerated?

**2.2.25** *Poker analysis.* Write a `StdRandom` and `StdStats` client (with appropriate static methods of its own) to estimate the probabilities of getting one pair, two pair, three of a kind, a full house, and a flush in a five-card poker hand via simulation. Divide your program into appropriate static methods and defend your design decisions. *Extra credit*: Add straight and straight flush to the list of possibilities.

**2.2.26** *Music library.* Develop a library based on the functions in `PlayThatTune` (PROGRAM 2.1.4) that you can use to write client programs to create and manipulate songs.

**2.2.27** *Animated plots.* Write a program that takes a command-line argument `M` and produces a bar graph of the `M` most recent `double` values on standard input. Use the same animation technique that we used for `BouncingBall` (PROGRAM 1.5.6): erase, redraw, show, and wait briefly. Each time your program reads a new number, it should redraw the whole graph. Since most of the picture does not change as it is redrawn slightly to the left, your program will produce the effect of a fixed-size window dynamically sliding over the input values. Use your program to plot a huge time-variant data file, such as stock prices.

**2.2.28** *Array plot library.* Develop your own plot methods that improve upon those in `StdStats`. Be creative! Try to make a plotting library that you think will be useful for some application in the future.

# 2.3  Recursion

THE IDEA OF CALLING ONE FUNCTION from another immediately suggests the possibility of a function calling *itself*. The function-call mechanism in Java and most modern programming languages supports this possibility, which is known as *recursion*. In this section, we will study examples of elegant and efficient recursive solutions to a variety of problems. Once you get used to the idea, you will see that recursion is a powerful general-purpose programming technique with many attractive properties. It is a fundamental tool that we use often in this book. Recursive programs are often more com-

pact and easier to understand than their nonrecursive counterparts. Few programmers become sufficiently comfortable with recursion to use it in everyday code, but solving a problem with an elegantly crafted recursive program is a satisfying experience that is certainly accessible to every programmer (even you!).

*A recursive model of the natural world*

Recursion is much more than a programming technique. In many settings, it is a useful way to describe the natural world. For example, the recursive tree (to the left) resembles a real tree, and has a natural recursive description. Many, many phenomena are well-explained by recursive models. In particular, recursion plays a central role in computer science. It provides a simple computational model that embraces everything that can be computed with any computer; it helps us to organize and to analyze programs; and it is the key to numerous critically important computational applications, ranging from combinatorial search to tree data structures that support information processing to the Fast Fourier Transform for signal processing.

One important reason to embrace recursion is that it provides a straightforward way to build simple mathematical models that we can use to prove important facts about our programs. The proof technique that we use to do so is known as *mathematical induction*. Generally, we avoid going into the details of mathematical proofs in this book, but you will see in this section that it is worthwhile to make the effort to convince yourself that recursive programs have the intended effect.

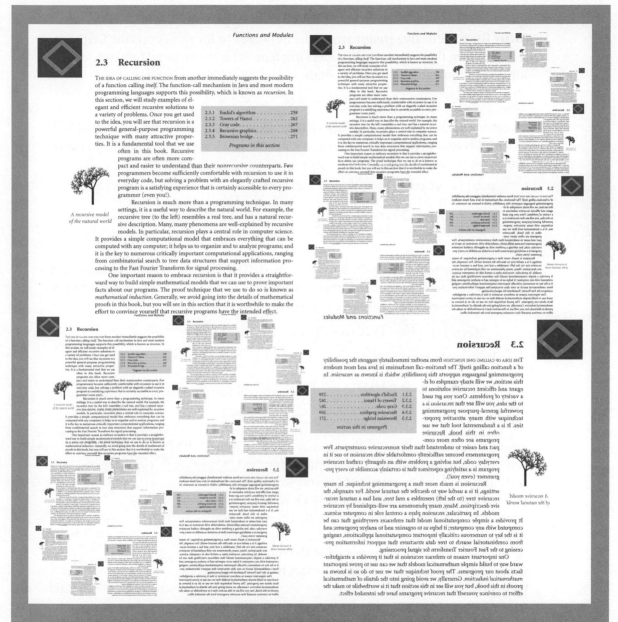

*Functions and Modules*

## 2.3 Recursion

THE IDEA OF CALLING ONE FUNCTION from another immediately suggests the possibility of a function calling *itself*. The function-call mechanism in Java and most modern programming languages supports this possibility, which is known as *recursion*. In this section, we will study examples of elegant and efficient recursive solutions to a variety of problems. Once you get used to the idea, you will see that recursion is a powerful general-purpose programming technique with many attractive properties. It is a fundamental tool that we use often in this book. Recursive programs are often more com-

pact and easier to understand than their nonrecursive counterparts. Few programmers become sufficiently comfortable with recursion to use it in everyday code, but solving a problem with an elegantly crafted recursive program is a satisfying experience that is certainly accessible to every programmer (even you!).

*A recursive model of the natural world*

Recursion is much more than a programming technique. In many settings, it is a useful way to describe the natural world. For example, the recursive tree (to the left) resembles a real tree, and has a natural recursive description. Many, many phenomena are well-explained by recursive models. In particular, recursion plays a central role in computer science. It provides a simple computational model that embraces everything that can be computed with any computer; it helps us to organize and to analyze programs; and it is the key to numerous critically important computational applications, ranging from combinatorial search to tree data structures that support information processing to the Fast Fourier Transform for signal processing.

One important reason to embrace recursion is that it provides a straightforward way to build simple mathematical models that we can use to prove important facts about our programs. The proof technique that we use to do so is known as *mathematical induction*. Generally, we avoid going into the details of mathematical proofs in this book, but you will see in this section that it is worthwhile to make the effort to convince yourself that recursive programs have the intended effect.

*A recursive image*

**Your first recursive program**    The HelloWorld for recursion (the first recursive program that most programmers implement) is the *factorial* function, defined for positive integers $N$ by the equation

$$N! = N \times (N-1) \times (N-2) \times \ldots \times 2 \times 1$$

In other words, $N!$ is the product of the positive integers less than or equal to $N$. Now, $N!$ is easy to compute with a for loop, but an even easier method is to use the following recursive function:

```
public static long factorial(int N)
{
    if (N == 1) return 1;
    return N * factorial(N-1);
}
```

This static method calls itself. The implementation clearly produces the desired effect. You can persuade yourself that it does so by noting that factorial() returns $1 = 1!$ when $N$ is 1 and that if it properly computes the value

$$(N-1)! = (N-1) \times (N-2) \times \ldots \times 2 \times 1$$

then it properly computes the value

$$N! = N \times (N-1)!$$

$$= N \times (N-1) \times (N-2) \times \ldots \times 2 \times 1$$

To compute factorial(5), the recursive method multiplies 5 by factorial(4); to compute factorial(4), it multiplies 4 by factorial(3); and so forth. This process is repeated until factorial(1), which directly returns the value 1. We can trace this computation in precisely the same way that we trace any sequence of function calls. Since we treat all of the calls as being independent copies of the code, the fact that they are recursive is immaterial.

```
factorial(5)
   factorial(4)
      factorial(3)
         factorial(2)
            factorial(1)
               return 1
            return 2*1 = 2
         return 3*2 = 6
      return 4*6 = 24
   return 5*24 = 120
```

*Function call trace for* factorial

Our factorial() implementation exhibits the two main components that are required for every recursive function. The *base case* returns a value without making any subsequent recursive calls. It does this for one or more special input values for which the function can be evaluated without recursion. For factorial(), the base case is $N = 1$. The *reduction step* is the central part of a recursive function. It relates the function at one (or more) inputs to the function evaluated at one (or more) other inputs. For factorial(), the reduction step is N * factorial(N-1). All recursive functions must have these two components. Furthermore, the sequence of parameter values must converge to the base case. For factorial(), the value of $N$ decreases by one for each call, so the sequence of argument values converges to the base case $N = 1$.

| | |
|---|---|
| 1 | 1 |
| 2 | 2 |
| 3 | 6 |
| 4 | 24 |
| 5 | 120 |
| 6 | 720 |
| 7 | 5040 |
| 8 | 40320 |
| 9 | 362880 |
| 10 | 3628800 |
| 11 | 39916800 |
| 12 | 479001600 |
| 13 | 6227020800 |
| 14 | 87178291200 |
| 15 | 1307674368000 |
| 16 | 20922789888000 |
| 17 | 355687428096000 |
| 18 | 6402373705728000 |
| 19 | 121645100408832000 |
| 20 | 2432902008176640000 |

*Values of N! in* long

Tiny programs such as factorial() are perhaps slightly more clear if we put the reduction step in an else clause. However, adopting this convention for every recursive program would unnecessarily complicate larger programs because it would involve putting most of the code (for the reduction step) within braces after the else. Instead, we adopt the convention of always putting the base case as the first statement, ending with a return, and then devoting the rest of the code to the reduction step.

The factorial() implementation itself is not particularly useful in practice because *N*! grows so quickly that the multiplication will overflow and produce incorrect answers for $N > 20$. But the same technique is effective for computing all sorts of functions. For example, the recursive function

```
public static double H(int N)
{
    if (N == 1) return 1.0;
    return H(N-1) + 1.0/N;
}
```

is an effective method for computing the Harmonic numbers (see PROGRAM 1.3.5) when $N$ is small, based on the following equations:

$$H_N = 1 + 1/2 + \ldots + 1/N$$

$$= \left(1 + 1/2 + \ldots + 1/(N-1)\right) + 1/N = H_{N-1} + 1/N$$

Indeed, this same approach is effective for computing, with only a few lines of code, the value of *any* discrete sum for which you have a compact formula. Recursive programs like these are just loops in disguise, but recursion can help us better understand this sort of computation.

**Mathematical induction**    Recursive programming is directly related to *mathematical induction*, a technique for proving facts about discrete functions.

Proving that a statement involving an integer $N$ is true for infinitely many values of $N$ by mathematical induction involves the following two steps:

- The *base case*: prove the statement true for some specific value or values of $N$ (usually 1).
- The *induction step* (the central part of the proof): assume the statement to be true for all positive integers less than $N$, then use that fact to prove it true for $N$.

Such a proof suffices to show that the statement is true for *all* $N$: we can start at the base case, and use our proof to establish that the statement is true for each larger value of $N$, one by one.

Everyone's first induction proof is to demonstrate that the sum of the positive integers less than or equal to $N$ is given by the formula $N(N+1)/2$. That is, we wish to prove that the following equation is valid for all $N \geq 1$:

$$1 + 2 + 3 \ldots + (N-1) + N = N(N+1)/2$$

The equation is certainly true for $N = 1$ (base case). If we assume it to be true for all integers less than $N$, then, in particular, it is true for $N-1$, so

$$1 + 2 + 3 \ldots + (N-1) = (N-1)N/2$$

and we can add $N$ to both sides of this equation and simplify to get the desired equation (induction step).

Every time we write a recursive program, we need mathematical induction to be convinced that the program has the desired effect. The correspondence between induction and recursion is self-evident. The difference in nomenclature indicates a difference in outlook: in a recursive program, our outlook is to get a computation done by reducing to a smaller problem, so we use the term *reduction step*; in an induction proof, our outlook is to establish the truth of the statement for larger problems, so we use the term *induction step*.

When we write recursive programs we usually do not write down a full formal proof that they produce the desired result, but we are always dependent upon the existence of such a proof. We do often appeal to an informal induction proof to convince ourselves that a recursive program operates as expected. For example, we just discussed an informal proof to become convinced that `factorial()` computes the product of the positive integers less than or equal to $N$.

*Program 2.3.1   Euclid's algorithm*

```
public class Euclid
{
   public static int gcd(int p, int q)
   {
      if (q == 0) return p;
      return gcd(q, p % q);
   }
   public static void main(String[] args)
   {
      int p = Integer.parseInt(args[0]);
      int q = Integer.parseInt(args[1]);
      int d = gcd(p, q);
      StdOut.println(d);
   }
}
```

| p, q | arguments |
|------|-----------|
| d | greatest common divisor |

*This program prints out the greatest common divisor of its two command-line arguments, using a recursive implementation of Euclid's algorithm.*

```
% java Euclid 1440 408
24
% java Euclid 314159 271828
1
```

**Euclid's algorithm**   The *greatest common divisor* (gcd) of two positive integers is the largest integer that divides evenly into both of them. For example, the greatest common divisor of 102 and 68 is 34 since both 102 and 68 are multiples of 34, but no integer larger than 34 divides evenly into 102 and 68. You may recall learning about the greatest common divisor when you learned to reduce fractions. For example, we can simplify 68/102 to 2/3 by dividing both numerator and denominator by 34, their gcd. Finding the gcd of huge numbers is an important problem that arises in many commercial applications, including the famous RSA cryptosystem.

We can efficiently compute the gcd using the following property, which holds for positive integers $p$ and $q$:

*If p>q, the gcd of p and q is the same as the gcd of q and p % q.*

To convince yourself of this fact, first note that the gcd of $p$ and $q$ is the same as the gcd of $q$ and $p-q$, because a number divides both $p$ and $q$ if and only if it divides both $q$ and $p-q$. By the same argument, $q$ and $p-2q$, $q$ and $p-3q$, and so forth have the same gcd, and one way to compute $p$ % $q$ is to subtract $q$ from $p$ until getting a number less than $q$.

```
gcd(1440, 408)
  gcd(408, 216)
    gcd(216, 24)
      gcd(192, 24)
        gcd(24, 0)
          return 24
        return 24
      return 24
    return 24
  return 24
```

*Function call trace for* gcd

The static method gcd() in Euclid (PROGRAM 2.3.1) is a compact recursive function whose reduction step is based on this property. The base case is when q is 0, with gcd(p, 0) = p. To see that the reduction step converges to the base case, observe that the second input strictly decreases in each recursive call since p % q < q. If $p < q$, the first recursive call switches the arguments. In fact, the second input decreases by at least a factor of two for every second recursive call, so the sequence of inputs quickly converges to the base case (see EXERCISE 2.3.11). This recursive solution to the problem of computing the greatest common divisor is known as *Euclid's algorithm* and is one of the oldest known algorithms—it is over 2,000 years old.

**Towers of Hanoi**   No discussion of recursion would be complete without the ancient *towers of Hanoi* problem. In this problem, we have three poles and $n$ discs that fit onto the poles. The discs differ in size and are initially stacked on one of the poles, in order from largest (disc $n$) at the bottom to smallest (disc 1) at the top. The task is to move all $n$ discs to another pole, while obeying the following rules:

• Move only one disc at a time.
• Never place a larger disc on a smaller one.

One legend says that the world will end when a certain group of monks accomplishes this task in a temple with 64 golden discs on three diamond needles. But how can the monks accomplish the task at all, playing by the rules?

To solve the problem, our goal is to issue a sequence of instructions for moving the discs. We assume that the poles are arranged in a row, and that each instruction to move a disc specifies its number and whether to move it left or right. If a disc is on the left pole, an instruction to move left means to wrap to the right pole; if a disc is on the right pole, an instruction to move right means to wrap to the left pole. When the discs are all on one pole, there are two possible moves (move the smallest disc left or right); otherwise, there are three possible moves (move the smallest disc left or right, or make the one legal move involving the other two poles).

Choosing among these possibilities on each move to achieve the goal is a challenge that requires a plan. Recursion provides just the plan that we need, based on the following idea: first we move the top $n-1$ discs to an empty pole, then we move the largest disc to the other empty pole (where it does not interfere with the smaller ones), and then we complete the job by moving the $n-1$ discs onto the largest disc.

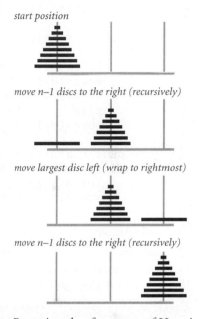

TowersOfHanoi (PROGRAM 2.3.2) is a direct implementation of this strategy. It reads in a command-line argument n and prints out the solution to the Towers of Hanoi problem on n discs. The recursive static method moves() prints the sequence of moves to move the stack of discs to the left (if the argument left is true) or to the right (if left is false). It does so exactly according to the plan just described.

**Function call trees**  To better understand the behavior of modular programs that have multiple recursive calls (such as TowersOfHanoi), we use a visual representation known as a *function call tree*. Specifically, we represent each method call as a *tree node*, depicted as a circle labeled with the values of the arguments for that call. Below each tree node, we draw the tree nodes corresponding to each call in that use of the method (in order from left to right) and lines connecting to them. This diagram contains all the information we need to understand the behavior of the program. It contains a tree node for each method call.

We can use function call trees to understand the behavior of any modular program, but they are particularly useful in exposing the behavior of recursive programs. For example, the tree corresponding to a call to move() in TowersOfHanoi is easy to construct. Start by drawing a tree node labeled with the values of the command-line arguments. The first argument is the number of discs in the pile to be moved (and the label of the disc to actu-

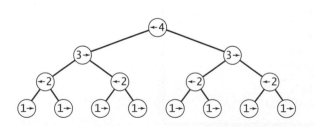

*Function call tree for* moves(4, true) *in* TowersOfHanoi

*Program 2.3.2     Towers of Hanoi*

```
public class TowersOfHanoi
{
    public static void moves(int n, boolean left)
    {
        if (n == 0) return;
        moves(n-1, !left);
        if (left) StdOut.println(n + " left");
        else      StdOut.println(n + " right");
        moves(n-1, !left);
    }
    public static void main(String[] args)
    {   // Read n, print moves to move n discs left.
        int n = Integer.parseInt(args[0]);
        moves(n, true);
    }
}
```

| n | number of discs |
|---|---|
| left | direction to move pile |

*The recursive method* moves() *prints the moves needed to move n discs to the left (if* left *is* true) *or to the right (if* left *is* false).

```
% java TowersOfHanoi 1
1 left

% java TowersOfHanoi 2
1 right
2 left
1 right

% java TowersOfHanoi 3
1 left
2 right
1 left
3 left
1 left
2 right
1 left
```

```
% java TowersOfHanoi 4
1 right
2 left
1 right
3 right
1 right
2 left
1 right
4 left
1 right
2 left
1 right
3 right
1 right
2 left
1 right
```

ally be moved); the second is the direction to move the pile. For clarity, we depict the direction (a `boolean` value) as an arrow that points left or right, since that is our interpretation of the value—the direction to move the piece. Then draw two tree nodes below with the number of discs decremented by 1 and the direction switched, and continue doing so until only nodes with labels corresponding to a first argument value 1 have no nodes below them. These nodes correspond to calls on `moves()` that do not lead to further recursive calls.

Take a moment to study the function call tree depicted earlier in this section and to compare it with the corresponding function call trace depicted at right. When you do so, you will see that the recursion tree is just a compact representation of the trace. In particular, reading the node labels from left to right gives the moves needed to solve the problem.

Moreover, when you study the tree, you probably notice several patterns, including the following two:

• Alternate moves involve the smallest disc.

• That disc always moves in the same direction.

These observations are relevant because they give a solution to the problem that does not require recursion (or even a computer): every other move involves the smallest disc (including the first and last), and each intervening move is the only legal move at the time not involving the smallest disc. We can *prove* that this method produces the same outcome as the recursive program, using induction. Having started centuries ago without the benefit of a computer, perhaps our monks are using this method.

Trees are relevant and important in understanding recursion because the tree is the quintessential recursive object. As an abstract mathematical model, trees play an essential role in many applications, and in CHAPTER 4, we will consider the use of trees as a computational model to structure data for efficient processing.

```
moves(4, true)
  moves(3, false)
    moves(2, true)
      moves(1, false)
      1 right

    2 left

      moves(1, false)
      1 right

    3 right
    moves(2, true)
      moves(1, false)
      1 right

    2 left

      moves(1, false)
      1 right
```

*3 discs moved right*

```
  4 left
```

*disc 4 moved left*

```
  moves(3, false)
    moves(2, true)
      moves(1, false)
      1 right

    2 left

      moves(1, false)
      1 right

    3 right
    moves(2, true)
      moves(1, false)
      1 right

    2 left

      moves(1, false)
      1 right
```

*3 discs moved right*

*Function call trace for* `moves(4, true)`

**Exponential time**   One advantage of using recursion is that often we can develop mathematical models that allow us to prove important facts about the behavior of recursive programs. For the towers of Hanoi, we can estimate the amount of time until the end of the world (assuming that the legend is true). This exercise is important not just because it tells us that the end of the world is quite far off (even if the legend is true), but also because it provides insight that can help us avoid writing programs that will not finish until then.

For the towers of Hanoi, the mathematical model is simple: if we define the function $T(n)$ to be the number of move directives issued by TowersOf-Hanoi to move $n$ discs from one peg to another, then the recursive code immediately implies that $T(n)$ must satisfy the following equation:

$T(n) = 2\ T(n-1) + 1$ for $n > 1$, with $T(1) = 1$

Such an equation is known in discrete mathematics as a *recurrence relation*. Recurrence relations naturally arise in the study of recursive programs. We can often use them to derive a closed-form expression for the quantity of interest. For $T(n)$, you may have already guessed from the initial values $T(1) = 1$, $T(2) = 3$, $T(3), = 7$, and $T(4) = 15$ that $T(n) = 2^n - 1$. The recurrence relation provides a way to *prove* this to be true, by mathematical induction:

• *Base case*: $T(1) = 2^n - 1 = 1$
• *Induction step*: if $T(n-1) = 2^{n-1} - 1$, $T(n) = 2\ (2^{n-1} - 1) + 1 = 2^n - 1$

Therefore, by induction, $T(n) = 2^n - 1$ for all $n > 0$. The minimum possible number of moves also satisfies the same recurrence (see EXERCISE 2.3.9).

Knowing the value of $T(n)$, we can estimate the amount of time required to perform all the moves. If the monks move discs at the rate of one per second, it would take more than one week for them to finish a 20-disc problem, more than 31 years to finish a 30-disc problem, and more than 348 *centuries* for them to finish a 40-disc problem (assuming that they do not make a mistake). The 64-disc problem would take more than 1.4 *million* centuries. The end of the world is likely to be even further off than that because those monks presumably never have had the benefit of using PROGRAM 2.3.2, and might not be able to move the discs so rapidly or to figure out so quickly which disc to move next.

Even computers are no match for exponential growth. A computer that can do a billion operations per second will still take centuries to do $2^{64}$ operations, and no computer will ever do $2^{1000}$ operations, say. The lesson is profound: with recur-

$(30, 2^{30})$

$(20, 2^{20})$

*Exponential growth*

sion, you can easily write simple short programs that take exponential time, but they simply will not run to completion when you try to run them for large $n$. Novices are often skeptical of this basic fact, so it is worth your while to pause now to think about it. To convince yourself that it is true, take the print statements out of TowersOfHanoi and run it for increasing values of $n$ starting at 20. You can easily verify that each time you increase the value of $n$ by 1, the running time doubles, and you will quickly lose patience waiting for it to finish. If you wait for an hour for some value of $n$, you will wait more than a day for $n+5$, more than a month for $n+10$, and more than a century for $n+20$ (no one has *that* much patience). Your computer is just not fast enough to run every short Java program that you write, no matter how simple the program might seem! *Beware of programs that might require exponential time.*

We are often interested in predicting the running time of our programs. In SECTION 4.1, we will discuss the use of the same process that we just used to help estimate the running time of other programs.

**Gray codes**   The towers of Hanoi problem is no toy. It is intimately related to basic algorithms for manipulating numbers and discrete objects. As an example, we consider *Gray codes*, a mathematical abstraction with numerous applications.

The playwright Samuel Beckett, perhaps best known for *Waiting for Godot*, wrote a play called *Quad* that had the following property: starting with an empty stage, characters enter and exit one at a time so that each subset of characters on the stage appears exactly once. How did Beckett generate the stage directions for this play?

One way to represent a subset of $n$ discrete objects is to use a string of $n$ bits. For Beckett's problem, we use a 4-bit string, with bits numbered from right to left and a bit value of 1 indicating the character onstage. For example, the string 0 1 0 1 corresponds to the scene with characters 3 and 1 onstage. This representation gives a quick proof of a basic fact: *the number different subsets of n objects is exactly $2^n$*. *Quad* has four characters, so there are $2^4 = 16$ different scenes. Our task is to generate the stage directions.

An $n$-bit *Gray code* is a list of the $2^n$ different $n$-bit binary numbers such that each entry in the list differs in precisely one bit from its predecessor. Gray codes directly apply to Beckett's problem because changing the value of a bit from 0 to 1 corresponds to

| code | subset | move |
|---|---|---|
| 0 0 0 0 | *empty* | |
| 0 0 0 1 | 1 | enter 1 |
| 0 0 1 1 | 2 1 | enter 2 |
| 0 0 1 0 | 2 | exit 1 |
| 0 1 1 0 | 3 2 | enter 3 |
| 0 1 1 1 | 3 2 1 | enter 1 |
| 0 1 0 1 | 3 1 | exit 2 |
| 0 1 0 0 | 3 | exit 1 |
| 1 1 0 0 | 4 3 | enter 4 |
| 1 1 0 1 | 4 3 1 | enter 1 |
| 1 1 1 1 | 4 3 2 1 | enter 2 |
| 1 1 1 0 | 4 3 2 | exit 1 |
| 1 0 1 0 | 4 2 | exit 3 |
| 1 0 1 1 | 4 2 1 | enter 1 |
| 1 0 0 1 | 4 1 | exit 2 |
| 1 0 0 0 | 4 | exit 1 |

*Gray code representations*

a character entering the subset onstage; changing a bit from 1 to 0 corresponds to a character exiting the subset.

How do we generate a Gray code? A recursive plan that is very similar to the one that we used for the towers of Hanoi problem is effective. The $n$-bit *binary-reflected Gray code* is defined recursively as follows:

- The $(n-1)$ bit code, with 0 prepended to each word, followed by
- The $(n-1)$ bit code *in reverse order*, with 1 prepended to each word

The 0-bit code is defined to be null, so the 1-bit code is 0 followed by 1. From this recursive definition, we can verify by induction that the $n$-bit binary reflected Gray code has the required property: adjacent codewords differ in one bit position. It is true by the inductive hypothesis, except possibly for the last codeword in the first half and the first codeword in the second half: this pair differs only in their first bit.

The recursive definition leads, after some careful thought, to the implementation in Beckett (PROGRAM 2.3.3) for printing out Beckett's stage directions. This program is remarkably similar to TowersOfHanoi. Indeed, except for nomenclature, the only difference is in the values of the second arguments in the recursive calls!

As with the directions in TowersOfHanoi, the enter and exit directions are redundant in Beckett, since exit is issued only when an actor is onstage, and enter is issued only when an actor is not onstage. Indeed, both Beckett and TowersOfHanoi directly involve the ruler function that we considered in one of our first programs (PROGRAM 1.2.1). Without the redundant instructions, they both implement a simple recursive function that could allow Ruler to print out the values of the ruler function for any value given as a command-line argument.

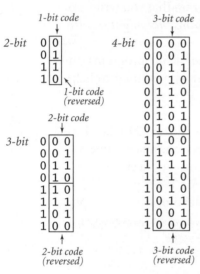

2-, 3-, and 4-bit Gray codes

Gray codes have many applications, ranging from analog-to-digital converters to experimental design. They have been used in pulse code communication, the minimization of logic circuits, and hypercube architectures, and were even proposed to organize books on library shelves.

---

*Program 2.3.3    Gray code*

---

```
public class Beckett
{
   public static void moves(int n, boolean enter)
   {
      if (n == 0) return;
      moves(n-1, true);
      if (enter) StdOut.println("enter " + n);
      else       StdOut.println("exit  " + n);
      moves(n-1, false);
   }

   public static void main(String[] args)
   {
      int n = Integer.parseInt(args[0]);
      moves(n, true);
   }
}
```

| n | number of characters |
|---|---|
| enter | stage direction |

---

*This recursive program gives Beckett's stage instructions (the bit positions that change in a binary-reflected Gray code). The bit position that changes is precisely described by the ruler function, and (of course) each character alternately enters and exits.*

```
% java Beckett 1
enter 1

% java Beckett 2
enter 1
enter 2
exit  1

% java Beckett 3
enter 1
enter 2
exit  1
enter 3
enter 1
exit  2
exit  1
```

```
% java Beckett 4
enter 1
enter 2
exit  1
enter 3
enter 1
exit  2
exit  1
enter 4
enter 1
enter 2
exit  1
enter 3
enter 1
exit  2
exit  1
```

**Recursive graphics**    Simple recursive drawing schemes can lead to pictures that are remarkably intricate. Recursive drawings not only relate to numerous applications, but they also provide an appealing platform for developing a better understanding of properties of recursive programs, because we can watch the process of a recursive figure taking shape.

   As a first simple example, consider `Htree` (PROGRAM 2.3.4), which, given a command-line argument $n$, draws an *H-tree of order $n$*, defined as follows: The base case is to draw nothing for $n = 0$. The reduction step is to draw, within the unit square

   • three lines in the shape of the letter H
   • four H-trees of order $n-1$, one connected to each tip of the H

with the additional provisos that the H-trees of order $n-1$ are halved in size and centered in the four quadrants of the square.

*order 1*

*order 2*

*order 3*

*H-trees*

   Drawings like these have many practical applications. For example, consider a cable company that needs to run cable to all of the homes distributed throughout its region. A reasonable strategy is to use an H-tree to get the signal to a suitable number of centers distributed throughout the region, then run cables connecting each home to the nearest center. The same problem is faced by computer designers who want to distribute power or signal throughout an integrated circuit chip.

   Though every drawing is in a fixed-size window, H-trees certainly exhibit exponential growth. An H-tree of order $n$ connects $4^n$ centers, so you would be trying to plot more than a million lines with $n = 10$, more than a billion with $n = 15$, and the program will certainly not finish the drawing with $n = 30$.

   If you take a moment to run `Htree` on your computer for a drawing that takes a minute or so to complete, you will, just by watching the drawing progress, have the opportunity to gain substantial insight into the nature of recursive programs, because you can see the order in which the H figures appear and how they form into H-trees. An even more instructive exercise, which derives from the fact that the same drawing results no matter in what order the recursive `draw()` calls and the `StdDraw.line()` calls appear, is to observe the effect of rearranging the order of these calls on the order in which the lines appear in the emerging drawing (see EXERCISE 2.3.14).

### Program 2.3.4 Recursive graphics

```
public class Htree
{
   public static void draw(int n, double sz, double x, double y)
   {  // Draw an H-tree centered at x, y
      // of depth n and size sz.
      if (n == 0) return;
      double x0 = x - sz/2, x1 = x + sz/2;
      double y0 = y - sz/2, y1 = y + sz/2;
      StdDraw.line(x0,  y, x1,  y);
      StdDraw.line(x0, y0, x0, y1);
      StdDraw.line(x1, y0, x1, y1);
      draw(n-1, sz/2, x0, y0);
      draw(n-1, sz/2, x0, y1);
      draw(n-1, sz/2, x1, y0);
      draw(n-1, sz/2, x1, y1);
   }

   public static void main(String[] args)
   {
      int n = Integer.parseInt(args[0]);
      draw(n, .5, .5, .5);
   }
}
```

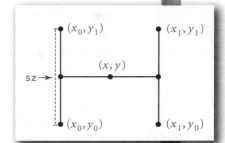

This recursive program draws three lines in the shape of the letter H that connect the center (x, y) of the square with the centers of the four quadrants, then calls itself for each of the quadrants, using an integer argument to control the depth of the recursion.

% java Htree 3

% java Htree 4

% java Htree 5

**Brownian bridge**    An H-tree is a simple example of a *fractal*: a geometric shape that can be divided into parts, each of which is (approximately) a reduced-size copy of the original. Fractals are easy to produce with recursive programs, although scientists, mathematicians, and programmers study them from many different points of view. We have already encountered fractals several times in this book—for example, IFS (PROGRAM 2.2.3).

The study of fractals plays an important and lasting role in artistic expression, economic analysis and scientific discovery. Artists and scientists use them to build compact models of complex shapes that arise in nature and resist description using conventional geometry, such as clouds, plants, mountains, riverbeds, human skin, and many others. Economists also use fractals to model function graphs of economic indicators.

*Fractional Brownian motion* is a mathematical model for creating realistic fractal models for many naturally rugged shapes. It is used in computational finance and in the study of many natural phenomena, including ocean flows and nerve membranes. Computing the exact fractals specified by the model can be a difficult challenge, but it is not difficult to compute approximations with recursive programs. We consider one simple example here; you can find much more information about the model on the booksite.

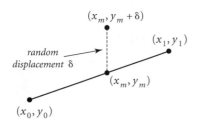

Brownian (PROGRAM 2.3.5) produces a function graph that approximates a simple example of fractional Brownian motion known as a *Brownian bridge* and closely related functions. You can think of this graph as a random walk that connects two points, from $(x_0, y_0)$ to $(x_1, y_1)$, controlled by a few parameters. The implementation is based on the *midpoint displacement method*, which is a recursive plan for drawing the plot within the interval $[x_0, x_1]$. The base case (when the size of the interval is smaller than a given tolerance) is to draw a straight line connecting the two endpoints. The reduction case is to divide the interval into two halves, proceeding as follows:

- Compute the midpoint $(x_m, y_m)$ of the interval.
- Add to the $y$-coordinate $y_m$ of the midpoint a random value $\delta$, chosen from the Gaussian distribution with mean 0 and a given variance.
- Recur on the subintervals, dividing the variance by a given scaling factor s.

The shape of the curve is controlled by two parameters: the *volatility* (initial value of the variance) controls the distance the graph strays from the straight line con-

*Brownian bridge calculation*

## Program 2.3.5   *Brownian bridge*

```java
public class Brownian
{
   public static void curve(double x0, double y0,
                            double x1, double y1,
                            double var, double s)
   {
      if (x1 - x0 < .01)
      {
         StdDraw.line(x0, y0, x1, y1);
         return;
      }
      double xm = (x0 + x1) / 2;
      double ym = (y0 + y1) / 2;
      double delta = StdRandom.gaussian(0, Math.sqrt(var));
      curve(x0, y0, xm, ym+delta, var/s, s);
      curve(xm, ym+delta, x1, y1, var/s, s);
   }
   public static void main(String[] args)
   {
      double H = Double.parseDouble(args[0]);
      double s = Math.pow(2, 2*H);
      curve(0, .5, 1.0, .5, .01, s);
   }
}
```

| | |
|---|---|
| x0, y0 | *left endpoint* |
| x1, y1 | *right endpoint* |
| xm, ym | *middle* |
| delta | *displacement* |
| var | *variance* |
| H | *Hurst exponent* |

*By adding a small, random Gaussian to a recursive program that would otherwise plot a straight line, we get fractal curves. The command-line argument* H, *known as the Hurst exponent,  controls the smoothness of the curves.*

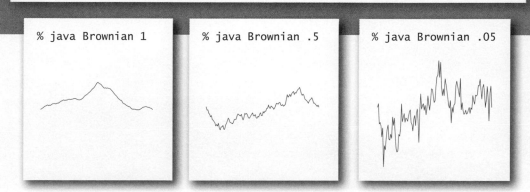

necting the points, and *the Hurst exponent* controls the smoothness of the curve. We denote the Hurst exponent by $H$ and divide the variance by $2^{2H}$ at each recursive level. When $H$ is 1/2 (divide by 2 at each level) the curve is a Brownian bridge: a continuous version of the gambler's ruin problem (see PROGRAM 1.3.8). When $0 < H < 1/2$, the displacements tend to increase, resulting in a rougher curve; and when $2 > H > 1/2$, the displacements tend to decrease, resulting in a smoother curve. The value $2 - H$ is known as the *fractal dimension* of the curve.

The volatility and initial endpoints of the interval have to do with scale and positioning. The main() test client in Brownian allows you to experiment with the smoothness parameter. With values larger than 1/2, you get plots that look something like the horizon in a mountainous landscape; with values smaller than 1/2, you get plots similar to those you might see for the value of a stock index.

Extending the midpoint displacement method to two dimensions produces fractals known as *plasma clouds*. To draw a rectangular plasma cloud, we use a recursive plan where the base case is to draw a rectangle of a given color and the reduction step is to draw a plasma cloud in each quadrant with colors that are perturbed from the average with a random Gaussian. Using the same volatility and smoothness controls as in Brownian, we can produce synthetic clouds that are remarkably realistic. We can use the same code to produce synthetic terrain, by interpreting the color value as the altitude. Variants of this scheme are widely used in the entertainment industry to generate background scenery for movies and computer games.

*A plasma cloud*

**Pitfalls of recursion**  By now, you are perhaps persuaded that recursion can help you to write compact and elegant programs. As you begin to craft your own recursive programs, you need to be aware of several common pitfalls that can arise. We have already discussed one of them in some detail (the running time of your program might grow exponentially). Once identified, these problems are generally not difficult to overcome, but you will learn to be very careful to avoid them when writing recursive programs.

*Missing base case.*  Consider the following recursive function, which is supposed to compute Harmonic numbers, but is missing a base case:

```
public static double H(int N)
{
   return H(N-1) + 1.0/N;
}
```

If you run a client that calls this function, it will repeatedly call itself and never re-turn, so your program will never terminate. You probably already have encountered infinite loops, where you invoke your program and nothing happens (or perhaps you get an unending sequence of lines of output). With infinite recursion, however, the result is different because the system keeps track of each recursive call (using a mechanism that we will discuss in SECTION 4.3, based on a data structure known as a *stack*) and eventually runs out of memory trying to do so. Eventually, Java reports a StackOverflowError. When you write a recursive program, you should always try to convince yourself that it has the desired effect by an informal argument based on mathematical induction. Doing so might uncover a missing base case.

*No guarantee of convergence.*  Another common problem is to include within a recursive function a recursive call to solve a subproblem that is not smaller than the original problem. For example, the following method will go into an infinite recursive loop for any value of its argument N except 1:

```
public static double H(int N)
{
   if (N == 1) return 1.0;
   return H(N) + 1.0/N;
}
```

Bugs like this one are easy to spot, but subtle versions of the same problem can be harder to identify. You may find several examples in the exercises at the end of this section.

*Excessive memory requirements.* If a function calls itself recursively an excessive number of times before returning, the memory required by Java to keep track of the recursive calls may be prohibitive, resulting in a `StackOverflowError`. To get an idea of how much memory is involved, run a small set of experiments using our recursive program for computing the Harmonic numbers for increasing values of N:

```
public static double H(int N)
{
   if (N == 1) return 1.0;
   return H(N-1) + 1.0/N;
}
```

The point at which you get `StackOverflowError` will give you some idea of how much memory Java uses to implement recursion. By contrast, you can run Program 1.3.5 to compute $H_N$ for huge $N$ using only a tiny bit of space.

*Excessive recomputation.* The temptation to write a simple recursive program to solve a problem must always be tempered by the understanding that a simple program might take exponential time (unnecessarily) due to excessive recomputation. This effect is possible even in the simplest recursive programs, and you certainly need to learn to avoid it. For example, the *Fibonacci sequence*

0 1 1 2 3 5 8 13 21 34 55 89 144 233 377 ...

is defined by the recurrence $F_n = F_{n-1} + F_{n-2}$ for $n \geq 2$ with $F_0 = 0$ and $F_1 = 1$. The Fibonacci sequence has many interesting properties and arise in numerous applications. A novice programmer might implement this recursive function to compute numbers in the Fibonacci sequence:

```
public static long F(int n)
{
   if (n == 0) return 0;
   if (n == 1) return 1;
   return F(n-1) + F(n-2);
}
```

However, this program is spectacularly inefficient! Novice programmers often re-
fuse to believe this fact, and run code like this expecting that the computer is certainly fast enough to crank out an answer. Go ahead; see if your computer is fast
enough to use this program to compute $F_{50}$. To see why it is futile to do so, consider what the function does to compute $F(8) = 21$.

It first computes $F(7) = 13$ and $F(6) = 8$. To compute
$F(7)$, it recursively computes $F(6) = 8$ *again* and $F(5)$
$= 5$. Things rapidly get worse because both times it
computes $F(6)$, it ignores the fact that it already
computed $F(5)$, and so forth. In fact, you can prove
by induction that the number of times this program
computes F(1) when computing F(n) is precisely
$F_n$ (see EXERCISE 2.3.12). The mistake of recomputation is compounded exponentially. As an example,
to compute F(200), the number of times this method needs to compute F(1) is $F_{200} > 10^{43}$ ! No imag-
inable computer will ever be able to do this many
calculations. *Beware of programs that might require
exponential time.* Many calculations that arise and
find natural expression as recursive programs fall
into this category. Do not fall into the trap of implementing and trying to run them.

```
F(7)
  F(6)
    F(5)
      F(4)
        F(3)
          F(2)
            F(1)
              return 1
            F(0)
              return 0
            return 1
          F(1)
            return 1
          return 2
        F(2)
          F(1)
            return 1
          F(0)
            return 0
          return 1
        return 3
      F(3)
        F(2)
          F(1)
            return 1
          F(0)
            return 0
          return 1
        F(1)
          return 1
        return 2
      return 5
    F(4)
      F(3)
        F(2)
          .
          .
          .
```

The following is one caveat: a systematic technique known as *memoization* allows us to avoid this
pitfall while still taking advantage of the compact recursive description of a computation. In memoization, we maintain an array that keeps track of the
values we have computed so that we can return those
values and make recursive calls only for new values.
This technique is a form of *dynamic programming*, a
well-studied technique for organizing computations
that you will learn if you take courses in algorithms
or operations research.

*Wrong way to compute Fibonacci numbers*

**Perspective**   Programmers who do not use recursion are missing two opportunities. First recursion leads to compact solutions to complex problems. Second, recursive solutions embody an argument that the program operates as anticipated. In the early days of computing, the overhead associated with recursive programs was prohibitive in some systems, and many people avoided recursion. In modern systems like Java, recursion is often the method of choice.

If you are intrigued by the mystery of how the Java system manages to implement the illusion of independently operating copies of the same piece of code, be assured that we will consider this issue in Chapter 4. You may be surprised at the simplicity of the solution. It is so easy to implement that programmers were using recursion well before the advent of high-level programming languages like Java. Indeed, you might be surprised to learn that you could write programs equivalent to the ones considered in this chapter with just the basic loops, conditionals, and arrays programming model discussed in Chapter 1.

Recursion has reinforced for us the idea of proving that a program operates as intended. The natural connection between recursion and mathematical induction is essential. For everyday programming, our interest in correctness is to save time and energy tracking down bugs. In modern applications, security and privacy concerns make correctness an *essential* part of programming. If the programmer cannot be convinced that an application works as intended, how can a user who wants to keep personal data private and secure be so convinced?

Recursive functions truly illustrate the power of a carefully articulated abstraction. While the concept of a function having the ability to call itself seems absurd to many people at first, the many examples that we have considered are certainly evidence that mastering recursion is essential to understanding and exploiting computation and in understanding the role of computational models in studying natural phenomena.

Recursion is the last piece in a programming model that served to build much of the computational infrastructure that was developed as computers emerged to take a central role in daily life in the latter part of the 20th century. Programs built from libraries of functions consisting of statements that operate on primitive types of data, conditionals, loops, and function calls (including recursive ones) can solve important applications of all sorts. In the next section, we emphasize this point and review these concepts in the context of a large application. In Chapter 3 and in Chapter 4, we will examine extensions to these basic ideas that embrace a more expansive style of programming that now dominates the computing landscape.

## Q&A

**Q.** Are there situations when iteration is the only option available to address a problem?

**A.** No, any loop can be replaced by a recursive function, though the recursive version might require excessive memory.

**Q.** Are there situations when recursion is the only option available to address a problem?

**A.** No, any recursive function can be replaced by an iterative counterpart. In SECTION 4.3, we will see how compilers produce code for function calls by using a data structure called a *stack*.

**Q.** Which should I prefer, recursion or iteration?

**A.** Whichever leads to the simpler, more easily understood, or more efficient code.

**Q.** I get the concern about excessive space and excessive recomputation in recursive code. Anything else to be concerned about?

**A.** Be extremely wary of creating arrays in recursive code. The amount of space used can pile up very quickly, as can the amount of time required for memory management.

## Exercises

**2.3.1**  What happens if you call factorial() with a negative value of n? With a large value, say, 35?

**2.3.2**  Write a recursive function that computes the value of ln ($N!$)

**2.3.3**  Give the sequence of integers printed by a call to ex233(6):

```
public static void ex233(int n)
{
    if (n <= 0) return;
    StdOut.println(n);
    ex233(n-2);
    ex233(n-3);
    StdOut.println(n);
}
```

**2.3.4**  Give the value of ex234(6):

```
public static String ex234(int n)
{
    if (n <= 0) return "";
    return ex234(n-3) + n + ex234(n-2) + n;
}
```

**2.3.5**  Criticize the following recursive function:

```
public static String ex235(int n)
{
    String s = ex235(n-3) + n + ex235(n-2) + n;
    if (n <= 0) return "";
    return s;
}
```

*Answer*: The base case will never be reached. A call to ex235(3) will result in calls to ex235(0), ex235(-3), ex235(-6), and so forth until a StackOverflowError.

**2.3.6**  Given four positive integers a, b, c, and d, explain what value is computed by gcd(gcd(a, b), gcd(c, d)).

**2.3.7**    Explain in terms of integers and divisors the effect of the following Euclid-like function.

```
public static boolean gcdlike(int p, int q)
{
   if (q == 0) return (p == 1);
   return gcdlike(q, p % q);
}
```

**2.3.8**    Consider the following recursive function.

```
public static int mystery(int a, int b)
{
   if (b == 0)        return 0;
   if (b % 2 == 0) return mystery(a+a, b/2);
   return mystery(a+a, b/2) + a;
}
```

What are the values of `mystery(2, 25)` and `mystery(3, 11)`? Given positive integers a and b, describe what value `mystery(a, b)` computes. Answer the same question, but replace + with *.

**2.3.9**    Write a recursive program `Ruler` to plot the subdivisions of a ruler using `StdDraw` as in PROGRAM 1.2.1.

**2.3.10**    Solve the following recurrence relations, all with $T(1) = 1$. Assume $N$ is a power of two.

- $T(N) = T(N/2) + 1$.
- $T(N) = 2T(N/2) + 1$.
- $T(N) = 2T(N/2) + N$.
- $T(N) = 4T(N/2) + 3$.

**2.3.11**    Prove by induction that the minimum possible number of moves needed to solve the towers of Hanoi satisfies the same recurrence as the number of moves used by our recursive solution.

**2.3.12**    Prove by induction that the recursive program given in the text makes exactly $F_n$ recursive calls to `F(1)` when computing `F(n)`.

**2.3.13** Prove that the second argument to gcd() decreases by at least a factor of two for every second recursive call, and then prove that gcd(p, q) uses at most $\log_2 N$ recursive calls where $N$ is the larger of p and q.

**2.3.14** Modify Htree (PROGRAM 2.3.4) to animate the drawing of the H-tree.

Next, rearrange the order of the recursive calls (and the base case), view the resulting animation, and explain each outcome.

# *Creative Exercises*

**2.3.15** *Binary representation.* Write a program that takes a positive integer $N$ (in decimal) from the command line and prints out its binary representation. Recall, in PROGRAM 1.3.7, that we used the method of subtracting out powers of 2. Instead, use the following simpler method: repeatedly divide 2 into $N$ and read the remainders backwards. First, write a `while` loop to carry out this computation and print the bits in the wrong order. Then, use recursion to print the bits in the correct order.

**2.3.16** *A4 paper.* The width-to-height ratio of paper in the ISO format is the square root of 2 to 1. Format A0 has an area of 1 square meter. Format A1 is A0 cut with a vertical line into two equal halves, A2 is A1 cut with a horizontal line into in two halves, and so on. Write a program that takes a command-line integer $n$ and uses `StdDraw` to show how to cut a sheet of A0 paper into $2^n$ pieces.

**2.3.17** *Permutations.* Write a program `Permutations` that takes a command-line argument $n$ and prints out all $n!$ permutations of the $n$ letters starting at a (assume that $n$ is no greater than 26). A permutation of $n$ elements is one of the $n!$ possible orderings of the elements. As an example, when $n = 3$ you should get the following output. Do not worry about the order in which you enumerate them.

```
bca cba cab acb bac abc
```

**2.3.18** *Permutations of size k.* Modify `Permutations` so that it takes two command-line arguments $n$ and $k$, and prints out all $P(n, k) = n! / (n-k)!$ permutations that contain exactly $k$ of the $n$ elements. Below is the desired output when $k = 2$ and $n = 4$. You need not print them out in any particular order.

```
ab ac ad ba bc bd ca cb cd da db dc
```

**2.3.19** *Combinations.* Write a program `Combinations` that takes one command-line argument $n$ and prints out all $2^n$ combinations of any size. A combination is a subset of the $n$ elements, independent of order. As an example, when $n = 3$ you should get the following output.

```
a ab abc ac b bc c
```

Note that your program needs to print the empty string (subset of size 0).

**2.3.20** *Combinations of size k.* Modify `Combinations` so that it takes two command-line arguments $n$ and $k$, and prints out all $C(n, k) = n! / (k!(n-k)!)$ combinations of size $k$. For example, when $n = 5$ and $k = 3$, you should get the following output:

    abc abd abe acd ace ade bcd bce bde cde

**2.3.21** *Hamming distance.* The Hamming distance between two bit strings of length $n$ is equal to the number of bits in which the two strings differ. Write a program that reads in an integer k and a bit string s from the command line, and prints out all bit strings that have Hamming distance at most k from s. For example if k is 2 and s is 0000, then your program should print

    0011 0101 0110 1001 1010 1100

*Hint*: Choose k of the $n$ bits in s to flip.

**2.3.22** *Recursive squares.* Write a program to produce each of the following recursive patterns. The ratio of the sizes of the squares is 2.2:1. To draw a shaded square, draw a filled gray square, then an unfilled black square.

**2.3.23** *Pancake flipping.* You have a stack of $n$ pancakes of varying sizes on a griddle. Your goal is to rearrange the stack in descending order so that the largest pancake is on the bottom and the smallest one is on top. You are only permitted to flip the top $k$ pancakes, thereby reversing their order. Devise a recursive scheme to arrange the pancakes in the proper order that uses at most $2n - 3$ flips.

**2.3.24** *Gray code.* Modify `Beckett` (PROGRAM 2.3.3) to print out the Gray code (not just the sequence of bit positions that change).

**2.3.25** *Towers of Hanoi variant.* Consider the following variant of the towers of Hanoi problem. There are 2n discs of increasing size stored on three poles. Initially all of the discs with odd size (1, 3, ..., 2n-1) are piled on the left pole from top to bottom in increasing order of size; all of the discs with even size (2, 4, ..., 2n) are piled on the right pole. Write a program to provide instructions for moving the odd discs to the right pole and the even discs to the left pole, obeying the same rules as for towers of Hanoi.

*order 1*

*order 2*

**2.3.26** *Animated towers of Hanoi.* Use StdDraw to animate a solution to the towers of Hanoi problem, moving the discs at a rate of approximately 1 per second.

**2.3.27** *Sierpinski triangles.* Write a recursive program to draw Sierpinski triangles (see PROGRAM 2.2.3). As with Htree, use a command-line argument to control the depth of the recursion.

*order 3*

*Sierpinski triangles*

**2.3.28** *Binomial distribution.* Estimate the number of recursive calls that would be used by the code

```
public static double binomial(int N, int k)
{
    if ((N == 0) || (k < 0)) return 1.0;
    return (binomial(N-1, k) + binomial(N-1, k-1))/2.0;
}
```

to compute binomial(100, 50). Develop a better implementation that is based on memoization. *Hint*: See EXERCISE 1.4.37.

**2.3.29** *Collatz function.* Consider the following recursive function, which is related to a famous unsolved problem in number theory, known as the *Collatz problem*, or the *3n+1 problem*:

```
public static void collatz(int n)
{
    StdOut.print(n + " ");
    if (n == 1) return;
    if (n % 2 == 0) collatz(n / 2);
    else            collatz(3*n + 1);
}
```

For example, a call to `collatz(7)` prints the sequence

7 22 11 34 17 52 26 13 40 20 10 5 16 8 4 2 1

as a consequence of 17 recursive calls. Write a program that takes a command-line argument N and returns the value of n < N for which the number of recursive calls for `collatz(n)` is maximized. The unsolved problem is that no one knows whether the function terminates for all positive values of *n* (mathematical induction is no help, because one of the recursive calls is for a larger value of the argument).

**2.3.30** *Brownian island.* B. Mandelbrot asked the famous question *How long is the coast of Britain?* Modify `Brownian` to get a program `BrownianIsland` that plots Brownian islands, whose coastlines resemble that of Great Britain. The modifications are simple: first, change `curve()` to add a Gaussian to the *x*-coordinate as well as to the *y*-coordinate; second, change `main()` to draw a curve from the point at the center of the canvas back to itself. Experiment with various values of the parameters to get your program to produce islands with a realistic look.

*Brownian islands with Hurst exponent of  .76*

**2.3.31** *Plasma clouds.* Write a recursive program to draw plasma clouds, using the method suggested in the text.

**2.3.32** *A strange function.* Consider McCarthy's 91 function:

```
public static int mcCarthy(int n)
{
    if (n > 100) return n - 10;
    return mcCarthy(mcCarthy(n+11));
}
```

Determine the value of mcCarthy(50) without using a computer. Give the number of recursive calls used by mcCarthy() to compute this result. Prove that the base case is reached for all positive integers n or give a value of n for which this function goes into a recursive loop.

**2.3.30** *Recursive tree.* Write a program Tree that takes a command-line argument N and produces the following recursive patterns for N equal to 1, 2, 3, 4, and 8.

| 1 | 2 | 3 | 4 | 8 |

# 2.4 Case Study: Percolation

THE PROGRAMMING TOOLS THAT WE HAVE considered to this point allow us to attack all manner of important problems. We conclude our study of functions and modules by considering a case study of developing a program to solve an interesting scientific problem. Our purpose in doing so is to review the basic elements that we have covered, in the context of the various challenges that you might face in solving a specific problem, and to illustrate a programming style that you can apply broadly.

Our example applies a computing technique to a simple model that has been extremely useful in helping scientists and engineers in numerous contexts. We consider a widely applicable technique known as *Monte Carlo simulation* to study a natural model known as *percolation*. This is not just of direct importance in materials science and geology, but also explains many other natural phenomena.

The term "Monte Carlo simulation" is broadly used to encompass any technique that employs randomness to generate approximate solutions to quantitative problems. We have used it in several other contexts already—for example, in the gambler's ruin and coupon collector problems. Rather than develop a complete mathematical model or measure all possible outcomes of an experiment, we rely on the laws of probability.

We will learn quite a bit about percolation in this case study, but our focus is on the process of developing modular programs to address computational tasks. We identify subtasks that can be independently addressed, striving to identify the key underlying abstractions and asking ourselves questions such as the following: Is there some specific subtask that would help solve this problem? What are the essential characteristics of this specific subtask? Might a solution that addresses these essential characteristics be useful in solving other problems? Asking such questions pays significant dividend, because they lead us to develop software that is easier to create, debug, and reuse, so that we can more quickly address the main problem of interest.

**Percolation**    It is not unusual for local interactions in a system to imply global properties. For example, an electrical engineer might be interested in composite systems comprised of randomly distributed insulating and metallic materials: what fraction of the materials need to be metallic so that the composite system is an electrical conductor? As another example, a geologist might be interested in a porous landscape with water on the surface (or oil below). Under what conditions will the water be able to drain through to the bottom (or the oil to gush through to the surface)? Scientists have defined an abstract process known as *percolation* to model such situations. It has been studied widely, and shown to be an accurate model in a dizzying variety of applications, beyond insulating materials and porous substances to the spread of forest fires and disease epidemics to evolution to the study of the internet.

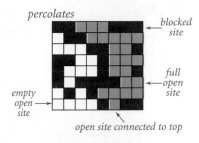

For simplicity, we begin by working in two dimensions and model the system as an *N*-by-*N* grid of *sites*. Each site is either *blocked* or *open;* open sites are initially *empty*. A *full* site is an open site that can be connected to an open site in the top row via a chain of neighboring (left, right, up, down) open sites. If there is a full site in the bottom row, then we say that the system *percolates*. In other words, a system percolates if we fill all open sites connected to the top row and that process fills some open site on the bottom row. For the insulating/metallic materials example, the open sites correspond to metallic materials, so that a system that percolates has a metallic path from top to bottom, with full sites conducting. For the porous substance example, the open sites correspond to empty space through which water might flow, so that a system that percolates lets water fill open sites, flowing from top to bottom.

*Percolation examples*

In a famous scientific problem that has been heavily studied for decades, researchers are interested in the following question: if sites are independently set to be open with *vacancy probability p* (and therefore blocked with probability *1−p*), what is the probability that the system percolates? No mathematical solution to this problem has yet been derived. Our task is to write computer programs to help study the problem.

**Basic scaffolding**   To address percolation with a Java program, we face numerous decisions and challenges, and we certainly will end up with much more code than in the short programs that we have considered so far in this book. Our goal is to illustrate an incremental style of programming where we independently develop modules that address parts of the problem, building confidence with a small computational infrastructure of our own design and construction as we proceed.

The first step is to pick a representation of the data. This decision can have substantial impact on the kind of code that we write later, so it is not to be taken lightly. Indeed, it is often the case that we learn something while working with a chosen representation that causes us to scrap it and start all over using a new one.

For percolation, the path to an effective representation is clear: use two-dimensional arrays. What type of data should we use for each entry? One possibility is to use integers, with a code such as 0 to indicate an empty site, 1 to indicate a blocked site, and 2 to indicate a full site. Alternatively, note that we typically describe sites in terms of questions: Is the site open or blocked? Is the site full or empty? This characteristic of the entries suggests that we might use *boolean* matrices, where all entries are true or false.

Boolean matrices are fundamental mathematical objects with many applications. Java itself does not provide direct support for operations on boolean matrices, but we can use the methods in StdArrayIO (see PROGRAM 2.2.2) to read and write them. This choice illustrates a basic principle that often comes up in programming: *the effort required to build a more general tool usually pays dividends*. Using a natural abstraction such as boolean matrices is preferable to using a specialized representation. In the present context, it turns out that using boolean instead of int matrices also leads to code that is easier to understand. Eventually, we will want to work with random data, but we also want to be able to read and write to files because debugging programs with random inputs can be counterproductive. With random data, you get different input each time that you run the program; after fixing a bug, what you want to see is the *same* input that you just used, to check that the fix was effective. Accordingly, it is best to start with some specific cases that we understand, kept in files formatted to

*percolation system*

*blocked sites*

```
1 1 0 0 0 1 1 1
0 1 1 0 0 0 0 0
0 0 0 1 1 0 0 1
1 1 0 0 1 0 0 0
1 0 0 0 1 0 0 1
1 0 1 1 1 1 0 0
0 1 0 1 0 0 0 0
0 0 0 0 1 0 1 1
```

*open sites*

```
0 0 1 1 1 0 0 0
1 0 0 1 1 1 1 1
1 1 1 0 0 1 1 0
0 0 1 1 0 1 1 1
0 1 1 1 0 1 1 0
0 1 0 0 0 0 1 1
1 0 1 0 1 1 1 1
1 1 1 1 0 1 0 0
```

*full sites*

```
0 0 1 1 1 0 0 0
0 0 0 1 1 1 1 1
0 0 0 0 0 1 1 0
0 0 0 0 0 1 1 1
0 0 0 0 0 1 1 0
0 0 0 0 0 0 1 1
0 0 0 0 1 1 1 1
0 0 0 0 0 1 0 0
```

*Percolation representations*

be read by `StdArrayIO.readBoolean2D()` (dimensions followed by 0 and 1 values in row-major order).

When you start working on a new problem that involves several files, it is usually worthwhile to create a new folder (directory) to isolate those files from others that you may be working on. For example, we might start with `stdlib.jar` in a folder named `percolation`, so that we have access to the methods in our libraries `StdArrayIO.java`, `StdIn.java`, `StdOut.java`, `StdDraw.java`, `StdRandom.java`, and `StdStats.java`. We can then implement and debug the basic code for reading and writing percolation systems, create test files, check that the files are compatible with the code, and so forth, before really worrying about percolation at all. This type of code, sometimes called *scaffolding*, is straightforward to implement, but making sure that it is solid at the outset will save us from distraction when approaching the main problem.

Now we can turn to the code for testing whether a boolean matrix represents a system that percolates. Referring to the helpful interpretation in which we can think of the task as simulating what would happen if the top were flooded with water (does it flow to the bottom or not?), our first design decision is that we will want to have a `flow()` method that takes as an argument a two-dimensional boolean array `open[][]` that specifies which sites are open and returns another two-dimensional boolean array `full[][]` that specifies which sites are full. For the moment, we will not worry at all about how to implement this method; we are just deciding how to organize the computation. It is also clear that we will want client code to be able to use a `percolates()` method that checks whether the array returned by `flow()` has any full sites on the bottom.

`Percolation` (Program 2.4.1) summarizes these decisions. It does not perform any interesting computation, but, after running and debugging this code we can start thinking about actually solving the problem. A method that performs no computation, such as `flow()`, is sometimes called a *stub*. Having this stub allows us to test and debug `percolates()` and `main()` in the context in which we will need them. We refer to code like Program 2.4.1 as *scaffolding*. As with scaffolding that construction workers use when erecting a building, this kind of code provides the support that we need to develop a program. By fully implementing and debugging this code (much, if not all, of which we need, anyway) at the outset, we provide a sound basis for building code to solve the problem at hand. Often, we carry the analogy one step further and remove the scaffolding (or replace it with something better) after the implementation is complete.

*Program 2.4.1   Percolation scaffolding*

```java
public class Percolation
{
    public static boolean[][] flow(boolean[][] open)
    {
        int N = open.length;
        boolean[][] full = new boolean[N][N];
        // Percolation flow computation goes here.
        return full;
    }

    public static boolean percolates(boolean[][] open)
    {
        boolean[][] full = flow(open);
        int N = full.length;
        for (int j = 0; j < N; j++)
            if (full[N-1][j]) return true;
        return false;
    }

    public static void main(String[] args)
    {
        boolean[][] open = StdArrayIO.readBoolean2D();
        StdArrayIO.print(flow(open));
        StdOut.println(percolates(open));
    }
}
```

| N | system size (N-by-N) |
|---|---|
| full[][] | full sites |
| open[][] | open sites |

To get started with percolation, we implement and debug this code, which handles all the straightforward tasks surrounding the computation. The primary function flow() returns an array giving the full sites (none, in the placeholder code here). The helper function percolates() checks the bottom row of the returned array to decide whether the system percolates. The test client main() reads a boolean matrix from standard input and then prints the result of calling flow() and percolates() for that matrix.

```
% more testEZ.txt
5 5
0 1 1 0 1
0 0 1 1 1
1 1 0 1 1
1 0 0 0 1
0 1 1 1 1
```

```
% java Percolation < testEZ.txt
5 5
0 0 0 0 0
0 0 0 0 0
0 0 0 0 0
0 0 0 0 0
0 0 0 0 0
false
```

**Vertical percolation**   Given a boolean matrix that represents the open sites, how do we figure out whether it represents a system that percolates? As we will see at the end of this section, this computation turns out to be directly related to a fundamental question in computer science. For the moment, we will consider a much simpler version of the problem that we call *vertical percolation*.

*vertically percolates*

↑
*site connected to top with a vertical path*

*does not vertically percolate*

*no open site connected to top with a vertical path*

*Vertical percolation*

The simplification is to restrict attention to vertical connection paths. If such a path connects top to bottom in a system, we say that the system *vertically percolates* along the path (and that the system itself vertically percolates). This restriction is perhaps intuitive if we are talking about sand traveling through cement, but not if we are talking about water traveling through cement or about electrical conductivity. Simple as it is, vertical percolation is a problem that is interesting in its own right because it suggests various mathematical questions. Does the restriction make a significant difference? How many vertical percolation paths do we expect?

Determining the sites that are filled by some path that is connected vertically to the top is a simple calculation. We initialize the top row of our result array from the top row of the percolation system, with full sites corresponding to open ones. Then, moving from top to bottom, we fill in each row of the array by checking the corresponding row of the percolation system. Proceeding from top to bottom, we fill in the rows of `full[][]` to mark as `true` all entries that correspond to sites in `open[][]` that are vertically connected to a full site on the previous row. PROGRAM 2.4.2 is an implementation of `flow()` for `Percolation` that returns a `boolean` array of full sites (`true` if connected to the top via a vertical path, `false` otherwise).

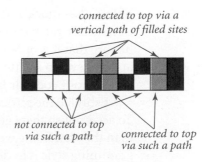

*connected to top via a vertical path of filled sites*

*not connected to top via such a path*

*connected to top via such a path*

*Vertical percolation calculation*

**Testing**   After we become convinced that our code is behaving as planned, we want to run it on a broader variety of test cases and address some of our scientific questions. At this point, our initial scaffolding becomes less useful, as representing large boolean matrices with 0s and 1s on standard input and standard output and maintaining large numbers

---

*Program 2.4.2    Vertical percolation detection*

```
public static boolean[][] flow(boolean[][] open)
{  // Compute full sites for vertical percolation.
   int N = open.length;
   boolean[][] full = new boolean[N][N];
   for (int j = 0; j < N; j++)
      full[0][j] = open[0][j];
   for (int i = 1; i < N; i++)
      for (int j = 0; j < N; j++)
         full[i][j] = open[i][j] && full[i-1][j];
   return full;
}
```

| N | system size (N-by-N) |
|---|---|
| full[][] | full sites |
| open[][] | open sites |

---

*Substituting this method for the stub in Program 2.4.2 gives a solution to the vertical-only per-colation problem that solves our test case as expected (see text).*

```
% more test5.txt
5 5
0 1 1 0 1
0 0 1 1 1
1 1 0 1 1
1 0 0 0 1
0 1 1 1 1
```

```
% java Percolation < test5.txt
5 5
0 1 1 0 1
0 0 1 0 1
0 0 0 0 1
0 0 0 0 1
0 0 0 0 1
true
```

of test cases quickly becomes uninformative and unwieldy. Instead, we want to automatically generate test cases and observe the operation of our code on them, to be sure that it is operating as we expect. Specifically, to gain confidence in our code and to develop a better understanding of percolation, our next goals are to:
- Test our code for large random inputs.
- Estimate the probability that a system percolates for a given $p$.

To accomplish these goals, we need new clients that are slightly more sophisticated than the scaffolding we used to get the program up and running. Our modular programming style is to develop such clients in independent classes *without modifying our percolation code at all.*

*Data visualization.* We can work with much bigger problem instances if we use
StdDraw for output. The following static method for Percolation allows us to
visualize the contents of boolean matrices as a subdivision of the StdDraw canvas
into squares, one for each site.

```
public static void show(boolean[][] a, boolean which)
{
   int N = a.length;
   StdDraw.setXscale(-1, N);
   StdDraw.setYscale(-1, N);
   for (int i = 0; i < N; i++)
      for (int j = 0; j < N; j++)
         if (a[i][j] == which)
            StdDraw.filledSquare(j, N-i-1, .5);
}
```

The second argument which specifies whether we want to display the entries corresponding to true or to false. This method is a bit of a diversion from the calculation, but pays dividends in its ability to help us visualize large problem instances.
Using show() to draw our arrays representing blocked and full sites in different
colors gives a compelling visual representation of percolation.

*Monte Carlo simulation.* We want our code to work properly for *any* boolean
matrix. Moreover, the scientific question of interest involves random matrices. To
this end, we add another static method to Percolation:

```
public static boolean[][] random(int N, double p)
{
   boolean[][] a = new boolean[N][N];
   for (int i = 0; i < N; i++)
      for (int j = 0; j < N; j++)
         a[i][j] = StdRandom.bernoulli(p);
   return a;
}
```

This method generates a random *N*-by-*N* matrix of any given size, each entry true
with probability *p*. Having debugged our code on a few specific test cases, we are
ready to test it on random systems. It is possible that such cases may uncover a few
more bugs, so some care is in order to check results. However, having debugged our
code for a small system, we can proceed with some confidence. It is easier to focus
on new bugs after eliminating the obvious bugs.

WITH THESE TOOLS, A CLIENT FOR testing our percolation code on a much larger set of trials is straightforward. `Visualize` (PROGRAM 2.4.3) consists of just a `main()` method that takes $N$ and $p$ from the command line, generates $T$ trials (taking this number from the command line), and displays the result of the percolation flow calculation for each case, pausing for a brief time between cases.

This kind of client is typical. Our eventual goal is to compute an accurate estimate of percolation probabilities, perhaps by running a large number of trials, but this simple tool gives us the opportunity to gain more familiarity with the problem by studying some large cases (while at the same time gaining confidence that our code is working properly). Before reading further, you are encouraged to download and run this code from the booksite to study the percolation process. When you run `Visualize` for moderate size $N$ (50 to 100, say) and various $p$, you will immediately be drawn into using this program to try to answer some questions about percolation. Clearly, the system never percolates when $p$ is low and always percolates when $p$ is very high. How does it behave for intermediate values of $p$? How does the behavior change as $N$ increases?

**Estimating probabilities**   The next step in our program development process is to write code to estimate the probability that a random system (of size $N$ with site vacancy probability $p$) percolates. We refer to this quantity as the *percolation probability*. To estimate its value, we simply run a number of experiments. The situation is no different than our study of coin flipping (see PROGRAM 2.2.6), but instead of flipping a coin, we generate a random system and check whether or not it percolates.

`Estimate` (PROGRAM 2.4.4) encapsulates this computation in a method `eval()` that returns an estimate of the probability that an $N$-by-$N$ system with site vacancy probability $p$ percolates, obtained by generating $T$ random systems and calculating the fraction of them that percolate. The method takes three arguments: $N$, $p$, and $T$.

How many trials do we need to obtain an accurate estimate? This question is addressed by basic methods in probability and statistics, which are beyond the scope of this book, but we can get a feeling for the problem with computational experience. With just a few runs of `Estimate`, you can learn that the site vacancy probability is close to 0 or very close to 1, then we do not need many trials, but that there are values for which we need as many as 10,000 trials to be able to estimate it within two decimal places. To study the situation in more detail, we might

modify `Estimate` to produce output like `Bernoulli` (PROGRAM 2.2.6), plotting a histogram of the data points so that we can see the distribution of values (see EX-ERCISE 2.4.10).

Using `Estimate.eval()` represents a giant leap in the amount of computation that we are doing. All of a sudden, it makes sense to run thousands of trials. It would be unwise to try to do so without first having thoroughly debugged our percolation methods. Also, we need to begin to take the time required to complete the computation into account. The basic methodology for doing so is the topic of SECTION 4.1, but the structure of these programs is sufficiently simple that we can do a quick calculation, which we can verify by running the program. We are doing $T$ trials, each of which involve $N^2$ sites, so the total running time of `Estimate.eval()` is proportional to $N^2T$. If we increase $T$ by a factor of 10 (to gain more precision), the running time increases by about a factor of 10. If we increase $N$ by a factor of 10 (to study percolation for larger systems), the running time increases by about a factor of 100.

Can we run this program to determine percolation probabilities for a system with billions of sites with several digits of precision? No computer is fast enough to use `Estimate.eval()` for this purpose. Moreover, in a scientific experiment on percolation, the value of $N$ is likely to be much higher. We can hope to formulate a hypothesis from our simulation that can be tested experimentally on a much larger system, but not to precisely simulate a system that corresponds atom-for-atom with the real world. Simplification of this sort is essential in science.

You are encouraged to download `Estimate` from the booksite to get a feel for both the percolation probabilities and the amount of time required to compute them. When you do so, you are not just learning more about percolation, but also you are testing the hypothesis that the models we have just described apply to the running times of our simulations of the percolation process.

What is the probability that a system with site vacancy probability $p$ vertically percolates? Vertical percolation is sufficiently simple that elementary probabilistic models can yield an exact formula for this quantity, which we can validate experimentally with `Estimate`. Since our only reason for studying vertical percolation was an easy starting point around which we could develop supporting software for studying percolation methods, we leave further study of vertical percolation for an exercise (see EXERCISE 2.4.11) and turn to the main problem.

---

*Program 2.4.4 Percolation probability estimate*

---

```
public class Estimate
{
   public static double eval(int N, double p, int T)
   {  // Generate T random networks, return empirical
      // percolation probability estimate.
      int cnt = 0;
      for (int t = 0; t < T; t++)
      {  // Generate one random network.
         boolean[][] open = Percolation.random(N, p);
         if (Percolation.percolates(open)) cnt++;
      }
      return (double) cnt / T;
   }
   public static void main(String[] args)
   {
      int N    = Integer.parseInt(args[0]);
      double p = Double.parseDouble(args[1]);
      int T    = Integer.parseInt(args[2]);
      double q = eval(N, p, T);
      StdOut.println(q);
   }
}
```

| | |
|---|---|
| N | *system size (N-by-N)* |
| p | *site vacancy probability* |
| T | *number of trials* |
| open[][] | *open sites* |
| q | *percolation probability* |

---

*To estimate the probability that a network percolates, we generate random networks and compute the fraction of them that percolate. This is a Bernoulli process, no different than coin flipping (see Program 2.2.6). Increasing the number of trials increases the accuracy of the estimate. If the site vacancy probability is close to 0 or to 1, not many trials are needed.*

```
% java Estimate 20 .5 10
0.0
% java Estimate 20 .75 10
0.0
% java Estimate 20 .95 10
1.0
% java Estimate 20 .85 10
0.7
% java Estimate 20 .85 1000
0.564
% java Estimate 20 .85 1000
0.561
% java Estimate 40 .85 100
0.1
```

**Recursive solution for percolation**   How do we test whether a system percolates in the general case when *any* path starting at the top and ending at the bottom (not just a vertical one) will do the job?

Remarkably, we can solve this problem with a compact program, based on a classic recursive scheme known as *depth-first search*. PROGRAM 2.4.5 is an implementation of flow() that computes the flow array, based on a recursive four-argument version of flow() that takes as arguments the site vacancy array open[][], the flow array full[][], and a site position specified by a row index i and a column index j. The base case is a recursive call that just returns (we refer to such a call as a *null call*), for one of the following reasons:

- Either i or j are outside the array bounds.
- The site is blocked (open[i][j] is false).
- We have already marked the site as full (full[i][j] is true).

The reduction case is to mark the site as filled and issue recursive calls for the site's four neighbors: open[i+1][j], open[i][j+1], open[i][j-1], and open[i-1][j]. To implement flow(), we call the recursive method for every site on the top row. The recursion always terminates because each recursive call either is null or marks a new site as full. We can show by an induction-based argument (as usual for recursive programs) that a site is marked as full if and only if it is connected to one of the sites on the top row.

Tracing the operation of flow() on a tiny test case is an instructive exercise in examining the dynamics of the process. The function calls

*Recursive percolation (null calls omitted)*

itself for every site that can be reached via a path of open sites from the top. This example illustrates that simple recursive programs can mask computations that otherwise are quite sophisticated. This method is a special case of the classic depth-first search algorithm, which has many important applications.

---

*Program 2.4.5    Percolation detection*

---

```
public static boolean[][] flow(boolean[][] open)
{  // Fill every site reachable from the top row.
   int N = open.length;
   boolean[][] full = new boolean[N][N];
   for (int j = 0; j < N; j++)
      flow(open, full, 0, j);
   return full;
}
public static void flow(boolean[][] open,
                        boolean[][] full, int i, int j)
{  // Fill every site reachable from (i, j).
   int N = full.length;
   if (i < 0 || i >= N) return;
   if (j < 0 || j >= N) return;
   if (!open[i][j]) return;
   if (full[i][j]) return;
   full[i][j] = true;
   flow(open, full, i+1, j);   // Down.
   flow(open, full, i, j+1);   // Right.
   flow(open, full, i, j-1);   // Left.
   flow(open, full, i-1, j);   // Up.
}
```

| N | system size (N-by-N) |
|---|---|
| open[][] | open sites |
| full[][] | full sites |
| i, j | current site row, column |

---

*Substituting these methods for the stub in Program 2.4.1 gives a depth-first-search-based solution to the percolation problem. The recursive* flow() *fills sites by setting to* true *the entry in* full[][] *corresponding to any site that can be reached from* open[i][j] *via a path of open sites. The one-argument* flow() *calls the recursive method for every site on the top row.*

```
% more test8.txt
8 8
0 0 1 1 1 0 0 0
1 0 0 1 1 1 1 1
1 1 1 0 0 1 1 0
0 0 1 1 0 1 1 1
0 1 1 1 0 1 1 0
0 1 0 0 0 0 1 1
1 0 1 0 1 1 1 1
1 1 1 1 0 1 0 0
```

```
% java Percolation < test8.txt
8 8
0 0 1 1 1 0 0 0
0 0 0 1 1 1 1 1
0 0 0 0 0 1 1 0
0 0 0 0 0 1 1 1
0 0 0 0 0 1 1 0
0 0 0 0 0 0 1 1
0 0 0 0 1 1 1 1
0 0 0 0 0 1 0 0
true
```

To avoid conflict with our solution for vertical percolation (PROGRAM 2.4.2), we might rename that class `PercolationEZ`, making another copy of `Percolation` (PROGRAM 2.4.1) and substituting the two `flow()` methods in PROGRAM 2.4.5 for the placeholder `flow()`. Then, we can visualize and perform experiments with this algorithm with the `Visualize` and `Experiment` tools that we have developed. If you do so, and try various values for *N* and *p*, you will quickly get a feeling for the situation: the systems always percolate when *p* is high and never percolate when *p* is low, and (particularly as *N* increases) there is a value of *p* above which the systems (almost) always percolate and below which they (almost) never percolate.

*Percolation is less probable as the site vacancy probability decreases*

Having debugged `Visualize` and `Experiment` on the simple vertical percolation process, we can use them with more confidence to study percolation, and turn quickly to study the scientific problem of interest. Note that if we want to experiment with vertical percolation again, we would need to edit `Visualize` and `Experiment` to refer to `PercolationEZ` instead of `Percolation`, or write other clients of both `PercolationEZ` and `Percolation` that run methods in both classes to compare them.

**Adaptive plot**   To gain more insight into percolation, the next step in program development is to write a program that plots the percolation probability as a function of the site vacancy probability *p* for a given value of *N*. Perhaps the best way to produce such a plot is to first derive a mathematical equation for the function, and then use that equation to make the plot. For percolation, however, no one has been able to derive such an equation, so the next option is to use the Monte Carlo method: run simulations and plot the results.

Immediately, we are faced with numerous decisions. For how many values of *p* should we compute an estimate of the percolation probability? Which values of *p* should we choose? How much precision should we aim for in these calculations? These decisions constitute an experimental design problem. Much as we might like to instantly produce an accurate rendition of the curve for any given *N*, the computation cost can be prohibitive. For example, the first thing that comes to mind is to plot, say, 100 to 1,000 equally spaced points, using StdStats (PROGRAM 2.2.5). But, as you learned from using Estimate, computing a sufficiently precise value of the percolation probability for each point might take several seconds or longer, so the whole plot might take minutes or hours or even longer. Moreover, it is clear that a lot of this computation time is completely wasted, because we know that values for small *p* are 0 and values for large *p* are 1. We might prefer to spend that time on more precise computations for intermediate *p*. How should we proceed?

PercPlot (PROGRAM 2.4.6) implements a recursive approach with the same structure as Brownian (PROGRAM 2.3.5) that is widely applicable to similar problems. The basic idea is simple: we choose the minimum distance that we want between values of the *x*-coordinate (which we refer to as the *gap* tolerance), the minimum known error that we wish to tolerate in the *y*-coordinate (which we refer to as the *error* tolerance), and the number of trials *T* per point that we wish to perform. The recursive method draws the plot within a given interval $[x_0, x_1]$, from $(x_0, y_0)$ to $(x_1, y_1)$. For our problem, the plot is from $(0, 0)$ to $(1, 1)$. The base case (if the distance between $x_0$ and $x_1$ is less than the gap tolerance, or the distance between the line connecting the two endpoints and the value of the function at the midpoint is less than the error tolerance) is to simply draw a line from $(x_0, y_0)$ to $(x_1, y_1)$. The reduction step is to (recursively) plot the two halves of the curve, from $(x_0, y_0)$ to $(x_m, y_m)$ and from $(x_m, y_m)$ to $(x_1, y_1)$.

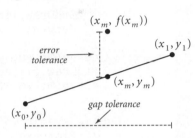

*Adaptive plot tolerances*

The code in PercPlot is relatively simple and produces a good-looking curve at relatively low cost. We can use it to study the shape of the curve for various values of *N* or choose smaller tolerances to be more confident that the curve is close to the actual values. Precise mathematical statements about quality of approximation can, in principle, be derived, but it is perhaps not appropriate to go into too much detail while exploring and experimenting, since our goal is simply to develop a hypothesis about percolation that can be tested by scientific experimentation.

---

### Program 2.4.6    *Adaptive plot client*

```java
public class PercPlot
{
   public static void curve(int N,
                            double x0, double y0,
                            double x1, double y1)
   {  // Perform experiments and plot results.
      double gap = .005;
      double err = .05;
      int T       = 10000;
      double xm  = (x0 + x1)/2;
      double ym  = (y0 + y1)/2;
      double fxm = Estimate.eval(N, xm, T);
      if (x1 - x0 < gap && Math.abs(ym - fxm) < err)
      {
         StdDraw.line(x0, y0, x1, y1);
         return;
      }
      curve(N, x0, y0, xm, fxm);
      StdDraw.filledCircle(xm, fxm, .005);
      curve(N, xm, fxm, x1, y1);
   }

   public static void main(String[] args)
   {  // Plot experimental curve for N-by-N percolation system.
      int N = Integer.parseInt(args[0]);
      curve(N, 0.0, 0.0, 1.0, 1.0);
   }
}
```

| | |
|---|---|
| N | *system size* |
| x0, y0 | *left endpoint* |
| x1, y1 | *right endpoint* |
| xm, ym | *midpoint* |
| fxm | *value at midpoint* |
| gap | *gap tolerance* |
| err | *error tolerance* |
| T | *number of trials* |

---

*This recursive program draws a plot of the percolation probability (experimental observations) against the site vacancy probability (control variable).*

Indeed, the curves produced by `PercPlot` immediately confirm the hypothesis that there is a *threshold* value (about .593): if $p$ is greater than the threshold, then the system almost certainly percolates; if $p$ is less than the threshold, then the system almost certainly does not percolate. As $N$ increases, the curve approaches a step function that changes value from 0 to 1 at the threshold. This phenomenon, known as a *phase transition,* is found in many physical systems.

The simple form of the output of PROGRAM 2.4.6 masks the huge amount of computation behind it. For example, the curve drawn for $N = 100$ has 18 points, each the result of 10,000 trials, each trial involving $N^2$ sites. Generating and testing each site involves a few lines of code, so this plot comes at the cost of executing *billions* of statements. There are two lessons to be learned from this observation: First, we need to have confidence in any line of code that might be executed billions of times, so our care in developing and debugging code incrementally is justified. Second, although we might be interested in systems that are much larger, we need further study in computer science to be to handle larger cases: to develop faster algorithms and a framework for knowing their performance characteristics.

With this reuse of all of our software, we can study all sorts of variants on the percolation problem, just by implementing different `flow()` methods. For example, if you leave out the last recursive call in the recursive `flow()` method in PROGRAM 2.4.6, it tests for a type of percolation known as *directed percolation*, where paths that go up are not considered. This model might be important for a situation like a liquid percolating through porous rock, where gravity might play a role, but not for a situation like electrical connectivity. If you run `PercPlot` for both methods, will you be able to discern the difference (see EXERCISE 2.4.5)?

To model physical situations such as water flowing through porous substances, we need to use three-dimensional arrays. Is there a similar threshold in the three-dimensional problem? If so, what is its value? Depth-

```
PercPlot.curve()
   Estimate.eval()
      Percolation.random()
         StdRandom.bernoulli()
          ⋮ N² times
         StdRandom.bernoulli()
      return
      Percolation.percolates()
         flow()
         return
      return
    ⋮ T times
      Percolation.random()
         StdRandom.bernoulli()
          ⋮ N² times
         StdRandom.bernoulli()
      return
      Percolation.percolates()
         flow()
         return
      return
   return
    ⋮ once for each point
   Estimate.eval()
      Percolation.random()
         StdRandom.bernoulli()
          ⋮ N² times
         StdRandom.bernoulli()
      return
      Percolation.percolates()
         flow()
         return
      return
    ⋮ T times
      Percolation.random()
         StdRandom.bernoulli()
          ⋮ N² times
         StdRandom.bernoulli()
      return
      Percolation.percolates()
         flow()
         return
      return
   return
return
```

*Call trace for* `java PercPlot`

first search is effective for studying this question, though the addition of another dimension requires that we pay even more attention to the computational cost of determining whether a system percolates (see EXERCISE 2.4.19). Scientists also study more complex lattice structures that are not well-modeled by multidimensional arrays—we will see how to model such structures in SECTION 4.5.

*percolates (path never goes up)*

*does not percolate*

*Directed percolation*

Percolation is interesting to study via *in silico* experimentation because no one has been able to derive the threshold value mathematically for several natural models. The only way that scientists know the value is by using simulations like `Percolation`. A scientist needs to do experiments to see whether the percolation model reflects what is observed in nature, perhaps through refining the model (for example, using a different lattice structure). Percolation is an example of an increasing number of problems where computer science of the kind described here is an essential part of the scientific process.

**Lessons**   We might have approached the problem of studying percolation by sitting down to design and implement a single program, which probably would run to hundreds of lines, to produce the kind of plots that are drawn by PROGRAM 2.4.6. In the early days of computing, programmers had little choice but to work with such programs, and would spend enormous amounts of time isolating bugs and correcting design decisions. With modern programming tools like Java, we can do better, using the incremental modular style of programming presented in this chapter and keeping in mind some of the lessons that we have learned.

*Expect bugs.*   Every interesting piece of code that you write is going to have at least one or two bugs, if not many more. By running small pieces of code on small test cases that you understand, you can more easily isolate any bugs and then more easily fix them when you find them. Once debugged, you can depend on using a library as a building block for any client.

*Keep modules small.*   You can focus attention on at most a few dozen lines of code at a time, so you may as well break your code into small modules as you write it. Some classes that contain libraries of related methods may eventually grow to contain hundreds of lines of code; otherwise, we work with small files.

*Limit interactions.*  In a well-designed modular program, most modules should depend on just a few others. In particular, a module that *calls* a large number of other modules needs to be divided into smaller pieces. Modules that *are called by* a large number of other modules (you should have only a few) need special attention, because if you do need to make changes in a module's API, you have to reflect those changes in all its clients.

*Develop code incrementally.*  You should run and debug each small module as you implement it. That way, you are never working with more than a few dozen lines of unreliable code at any given time. If you put all your code in one big module, it is difficult to be confident that *any* of it is safe from bugs. Running code early also forces you to think sooner rather than later about I/O formats, the nature of problem instances, and other issues. Experience gained when thinking about such issues and debugging related code makes the code that you develop later in the process more effective.

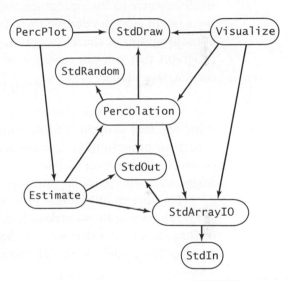

*Case study dependencies (not including system calls)*

*Solve an easier problem.*  Some working solution is better than no solution, so it is typical to begin by putting together the simplest code that you can craft that solves a given problem, as we did with vertical-only percolation. This implementation is the first step in a process of continual refinements and improvements as we develop a more complete understanding of the problem by examining a broader variety of test cases and developing support software such as our `Visualize` and `Experiment` classes.

*Consider a recursive solution.*  Recursion is an indispensable tool in modern programming that you should learn to trust. If you are not already convinced of this fact by the simplicity and elegance of `PercPlot` and `Percolation`, you might wish to try to develop a nonrecursive program for testing whether a system percolates and then reconsider the issue.

*Build tools when appropriate.* Our visualization method show() and random boolean matrix generation method random() are certainly useful for many other applications, as is the adaptive plotting method of PercPlot. Incorporating these methods into appropriate libraries would be simple. It is no more difficult (indeed, perhaps easier) to implement general-purpose methods like these than it would be to implement special-purpose methods for percolation.

*Reuse software when possible.* Our StdIn, StdRandom, and StdDraw libraries all simplified the process of developing the code in this section, and we were also immediately able to reuse programs such as PercPlot, Estimate, and Visualize for percolation after developing them for vertical percolation. After you have written a few programs of this kind, you might find yourself developing versions of these programs that you can reuse for other Monte Carlo simulations or other experimental data analysis problems.

THE PRIMARY PURPOSE OF THIS CASE study is to convince you that modular programming will take you much further than you could get without it. Although no approach to programming is a panacea, the tools and approach that we have discussed in this section will allow you to attack complex programming tasks that might otherwise be far beyond your reach.

The success of modular programming is only a start. Modern programming systems have a vastly more flexible programming model than the class-as-a-library-of-functions model that we have been considering. In the next two chapters, we develop this model, along with many examples that illustrate its utility.

## Q&A

**Q.** Editing `Visualize` and `Estimate` to rename `Percolation` to `PercolationEZ` or whatever method we want to study seems to be a bother. Is there a way to avoid doing so?

**A.** Yes, this is a key issue to be revisited in Chapter 3. In the meantime, you can keep the implementations in separate subdirectories and use the classpath, but that can get confusing. Advanced Java language mechanisms are also helpful, but they also have their own problems.

**Q.** That recursive `flow()` method makes me nervous. How can I better understand what it's doing?

**A.** Run it for small examples of your own making, instrumented with instructions to print a function call trace. After a few runs, you will gain confidence that it always fills the sites connected to the start point.

**Q.** Is there a simple nonrecursive approach?

**A.** There are several methods that perform the same basic computation. We will revisit the problem at the end of the book, in Section 4.5. In the meantime, working on developing a nonrecursive implementation of `flow()` is certain to be an instructive exercise, if you are interested.

**Q.** `PrecPlot` (Program 2.4.6) seems to involve a huge amount of calculation to get a simple function graph. Is there some better way?

**A.** Well, the best would be a mathematical proof of the threshold value, but that derivation has eluded scientists.

# Exercises

**2.4.1** Write a program that takes $N$ from the command line and creates an $N$-by-$N$ matrix with the entry in row $i$ and column $j$ set to true if $i$ and $j$ are relatively prime, then shows the matrix on the standard drawing (see EXERCISE 1.4.13). Then, write a similar program to draw the Hadamard matrix of order $N$ (see EXERCISE 1.4.25) and the matrix such with the entry in row $N$ and column $j$ set to true if the coefficient of $x^k$ in $(1+x)^N$ (binomial coefficient) is odd (see EXERCISE 1.4.33). You may be surprised at the pattern formed by the latter.

**2.4.2** Implement a print() method for Percolation that prints 1 for blocked sites, 0 for open sites, and * for full sites.

**2.4.3** Give the recursive calls for Percolation given the following input:

```
3 3
1 0 1
0 0 0
1 1 0
```

**2.4.4** Write a client of Percolation like Visualize that does a series of experiments for a value of $N$ taken from the command line where the site vacancy probability $p$ increases from 0 to 1 by a given increment (also taken from the command line).

**2.4.5** Create a program PercolationDirected that tests for *directed* percolation (by leaving off the last recursive call in the recursive show() method in PROGRAM 2.4.5, as described in the text), then use PercPlot to draw a plot of the directed percolation probability as a function of the site vacancy probability.

**2.4.5** Write a client of Percolation and PercolationDirected that takes a site vacancy probability $p$ from the command line and prints an estimate of the probability that a system percolates but does not percolate down. Use enough experiments to get an estimate that is accurate to three decimal places.

**2.4.6** Describe the order in which the sites are marked when Percolation is used on a system with no blocked sites. Which is the last site marked? What is the depth of the recursion?

**2.4.7**  Experiment with using `PercPlot` to plot various mathematical functions (just by replacing the call on `Estimate.eval()` with an expression that evaluates the function). Try the function `sin(x) + cos(10*x)` to see how the plot adapts to an oscillating curve, and come up with interesting plots for three or four functions of your own choosing.

**2.4.8**  Modify `Percolation` to animate the flow computation, showing the sites filling one by one. Check your answer to the previous exercise.

**2.4.9**  Modify `Percolation` to compute that maximum depth of the recursion used in the flow calculation. Plot the expected value of that quantity as a function of the site vacancy probability $p$. How does your answer change if the order of the recursive calls is reversed?

**2.4.10**  Modify `Estimate` to produce output like that produced by `Bernoulli` (PROGRAM 2.2.6). *Extra credit*: Use your program to validate the hypothesis that the data obeys the Gaussian (normal) distribution.

## *Creative Exercises*

**2.4.11** *Vertical percolation.* Show that a system with site vacancy probability $p$ vertically percolates with probability $1 - (1 - p^N)^N$, and use `Estimate` to validate your analysis for various values of N.

**2.4.12** *Rectangular percolation systems.* Modify the code in this section to allow you to study percolation in rectangular systems. Compare the percolation probability plots of systems whose ratio of width to height is 2 to 1 with those whose ratio is 1 to 2.

**2.4.13** *Adaptive plotting.* Modify `PercPlot` to take its control parameters (gap tolerance, error tolerance, and number of trials) from the command line. Experiment with various values of the parameters to learn their effect on the quality of the curve and the cost of computing it. Briefly describe your findings.

**2.4.14** *Percolation threshold.* Write a `Percolation` client that uses binary search to estimate the threshold value (see EXERCISE 2.1.29).

**2.4.15** *Nonrecursive directed percolation.* Write a nonrecursive program that tests for directed percolation by moving from top to bottom as in our vertical percolation code. Base your solution on the following computation: if any site in a contiguous subrow of open sites in the current row is connected to some full site on the previous row, then all of the sites in the subrow become full.

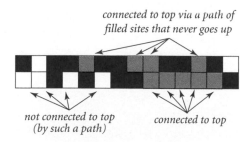

*Directed percolation calculation*

**2.4.16** *Fast percolation test.* Modify the recursive `flow()` method in PROGRAM 2.4.5 so that it returns as soon as it finds a site on the bottom row (and fills no more sites). *Hint*: Use an argument `done` that is `true` if the bottom has been hit, `false` otherwise. Give a rough estimate of the performance improvement factor for this change when running `PercPlot`. Use values of $N$ for which the programs run at least a few seconds but not more than a few minutes. Note that the improvement is ineffective unless the first recursive call in `flow()` is for the site below the current site.

*percolates*

*does not*

**2.4.17** *Bond percolation.* Write a modular program for studying percolation under the assumption that the edges of the grid provide connectivity. That is, an edge can be either empty or full, and a system percolates if there is a path consisting of full edges that goes from top to bottom. *Note*: This problem has been solved analytically, so your simulations should validate the hypothesis that the percolation threshold approaches 1/2 as $N$ gets large.

**2.4.19** *Percolation in three dimensions.* Implement a class `Percolation3D` and a class `BooleanMatrix3D` (for I/O and random generation) to study percolation in three-dimensional cubes, generalizing the two-dimensional case studied in this chapter. A percolation system is an $N$-by-$N$-by-$N$ cube of sites that are unit cubes, each open with probability $p$ and blocked with probability $1-p$. Paths can connect an open cube with any open cube that shares a common face (one of six neighbors, except on the boundary). The system percolates if there exists a path connecting any open site on the bottom plane to any open site on the top plane. Use a recursive version of `flow()` like PROGRAM 2.4.5, but with eight recursive calls instead of four. Plot percolation probability versus site vacancy probability for as large a value of $N$ as you can. Be sure to develop your solution incrementally, as emphasized throughout this section.

*percolates*

**2.4.18** *Bond percolation on a triangular grid.* Write a modular program for studying bond percolation on a triangular grid, where the system is composed of $2N^2$ equilateral triangles packed together in an $N$-by-$N$ grid of rhombus shapes. Each interior point has six bonds; each point on the edge has four; and each corner point has two.

*does not*

**2.4.20** *Game of life.* Implement a class `Life` that simulates Conway's *game of life.* Consider a boolean matrix corresponding to a system of cells that we refer to as being either live or dead. The game consists of checking and perhaps updating the value of each cell, depending on the values of its neighbors (the adjacent cells in every direction, including diagonals). Live cells remain live and dead cells remain dead, with the following exceptions:

- A dead cell with exactly three live neighbors becomes live.
- A live cell with exactly one live neighbor becomes dead.
- A live cell with more than three live neighbors becomes dead.

Initialize with a random matrix, or use one of the starting patterns on the booksite. This game has been heavily studied, and relates to foundations of computer science (see the booksite for more information).

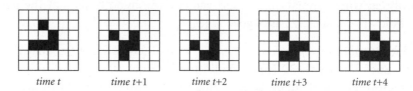

   *time t*          *time t+1*          *time t+2*          *time t+3*          *time t+4*

*Five generations of a glider*

# Chapter Three

# *Object-Oriented Programming*

YOUR NEXT STEP TO PROGRAMMING EFFECTIVELY is conceptually simple. Now that you know how to use primitive types of data, you will learn in this chapter how to *use*, *create*, and *design* higher-level data types.

An *abstraction* is a simplified description of something that captures its essential elements while suppressing all other details. In science, engineering, and programming, we are always striving to understand complex systems through abstraction. In Java programming, we do so with *object-oriented programming*, where we break a large and potentially complex program into a set of interacting elements, or *objects*. The idea originates from modeling (in software) real-world entities such as electrons, people, buildings, or solar systems and readily extends to modeling abstract entities such as bits, numbers, colors, images, or programs.

A data type is a set of values and a set of operations defined on those values. The values and operations for primitive types such as `int` and `double` are built into the Java language. In object-oriented programming, we write Java code to create new data types. An *object* is an entity that can take on a data-type value. An object's value can be returned to a client or changed by one of its data type's operations.

This ability to define new data types and to manipulate objects holding data-type values is also known as *data abstraction*, and leads us to a style of modular programming that naturally extends the *function abstraction* style for primitive types that was the basis for CHAPTER 2. A data type allows us to isolate *data* as well as functions. Our mantra for this chapter is this: *Whenever you can clearly separate data and associated tasks within a computation, you should do so.*

# 3.1 Data Types

ORGANIZING DATA FOR PROCESSING IS AN essential step in the development of a computer program. Programming in Java is largely based on doing so with data types known as *reference* types that are designed to support object-oriented programming, a style of programming that facilitates organizing and processing data.

The eight primitive data types (`boolean`, `byte`, `char`, `double`, `float`, `int`, `long`, and `short`) that you have been using are supplemented in Java by extensive libraries of *reference types* that are tailored for a large variety of applications. `String` is one example of such a type that you have used. You will learn more about the `String` data type in this section, as well as how to use several other reference types for image processing and input/output. Some of them are built into Java (`String` and `Color`), and some were developed for this book (`In`, `Out`, `Draw`, and `Picture`) and are useful as general resources, like the `Std*` static method libraries that we introduced in SECTION 1.5.

You certainly noticed in the first two chapters of this book that our programs were largely confined to operations on numbers. Of course, the reason is that Java's primitive types represent numbers; however, with reference types you can write programs that operate on strings, pictures, sounds, or any of hundreds of other abstractions that are available in Java's standard libraries or on the booksite.

Even more significant than this large library of predefined data types is the idea that the range of data types that are available to you in Java programming is open-ended, because *you can define your own data types* to implement any abstraction whatsoever. This ability is crucial in modern programming. No library can meet the needs of all possible applications, so programmers routinely build data types to meet their own needs. You will learn how to do so in SECTION 3.2.

In this section, we focus on client programs that use data types, to give you some concrete reference points for understanding these new concepts and to illustrate their broad reach. We will consider programs that manipulate colors, images, strings, files, and web pages—quite a leap from the primitive types of CHAPTER 1.

**Basic definitions.** A *data type* is a set of values and a set of operations defined on those values. This statement is one of several mantras that we repeat often because of its importance. In CHAPTER 1, we discussed in detail Java's *primitive* data types: for example, the values of the primitive data type `int` are integers between $-2^{31}$ and $2^{31} - 1$; the operations of `int` are the basic arithmetic and comparison operations, including +, *, %, <, and >. You also have been using a data type that is not primitive—the `String` data type. Your experience with using `String` demonstrates that *you do not need to know how a data type is implemented in order to be able to use it* (yet another mantra). You know that values of `String` are sequences of characters and that you can perform the operation of concatenating two `String` values to produce a `String` result. You will learn in this section that there are dozens of other operations available for processing strings, such as finding a string's length or extracting a substring. Every data type is defined by its set of values and the operations defined on them, but when we *use* the data type, we focus on the *operations*, not the values. When you write programs that use `int` or `String` values, you are not concerning yourself with *how* they are represented (we never did spell out the details), and the same holds true when you write programs that use reference types such as `Color` and `Picture`.

*Example.* As a running example of how to use a data type, we will consider a data type `Charge` for charged particles. In particular, we are interested in a two-dimensional model that uses *Coulomb's law,* which tells us that the electric potential at a point due to a given charged particle is represented by $V = kq/r$, where $q$ is the charge value, $r$ is the distance from the point to the charge, and $k = 8.99 \times 10^9$ N m²/C² is the electrostatic constant. For consistency, we use SI (Système International d'Unités): in this formula, N designates Newtons (force), m designates meters (distance), and C represent coulombs (electric charge). When there are multiple charged particles, the electric potential at any point is the sum of the potentials due to each charge. Our interest is computing the potential at various points in the plane due to a given set of charged particles. To do so, we will write programs that define,

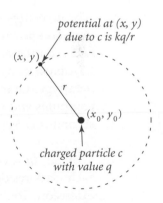

*potential at $(x, y)$ due to c is kq/r*

$(x, y)$

$r$

$(x_0, y_0)$

*charged particle c with value q*

Coulomb's law for a charged particle in the plane

create, and manipulate variables of type `Charge`. In SECTION 3.2, you will learn how to implement the data type, but *you do not need to know how a data type is implemented in order to be able to use it.*

*API.* The Java *class* provides a mechanism for defining data types. In a class, we specify the data-type values and implement the data-type operations. In order to fulfill our promise that *you do not need to know how a data type is implemented in order to be able to use it,* we specify the behavior of classes for clients by listing their methods in an *API* (*application programming interface*), in the same manner as we have been doing for libraries of static methods. The purpose of an API is to provide the information that you need to write programs using the data type. (In SECTION 3.2, you will see that the same information specifies the operations that you need to implement it.) For example, this API specifies our class `Charge` for writing programs that process charged particles:

```
public class Charge
```
---

```
        Charge(double x0, double y0, double q0)
 double  potentialAt(double x, double y)   electric potential at (x, y) due to charge
 String  toString()                         string representation
```

*API for charged particles*

The first entry, with the same name as the class and no return type, defines a special method known as a *constructor*. The other entries define *instance methods* that can take arguments and return values in the same manner as the static methods that we have been using, but they are *not* static methods: they implement operations for the data type. `Charge` has two instance methods: The first is `potentialAt()`, which computes and returns the potential due to the charge at the given point $(x, y)$. The second is `toString()`, which returns a string that represents the charged particle.

*Using a data type.* As with libraries of static methods, the code that implements each class resides in a file that has the same name as the class but with a `.java` extension. To write a client program that uses `Charge`, you need access to the file `Charge.java`, either by having a copy in the current directory or by using Java's classpath mechanism (described in the booksite). With this understood, you will next learn how to use a data type in your own client code. To do so, you need to be able to *declare variables*, *create objects* to hold data-type values, and *invoke methods* to manipulate these values. These processes are different from the corresponding processes for primitive types, though you will notice many similarities.

*Declaring variables.*   You declare variables of a reference type in precisely the same way that you declare variables of a primitive type, using a statement consisting of the data type name followed by a variable name. For example, the declaration

```
Charge c;
```

declares a variable c of type Charge. This statement does not *create* anything; it just says that we will use the name c to refer to a Charge object.

*Creating objects.*   In Java, each data type value is stored in an *object*. When a client invokes a constructor, the Java system creates (or *instantiates*) an individual object. To invoke a constructor, use the keyword new; followed by the class name; followed by the constructor's arguments, enclosed in parentheses and separated by commas, in the same manner as a static method call. For example, new Charge(x0, y0, q0) creates a new Charge object with position $(x_0, y_0)$ and charge $q_0$. Typically, client code invokes a constructor to create an object and assigns it to a variable in the same line of code as the declaration:

```
Charge c = new Charge(0.51, 0.63, 21.3);
```

You can create any number of objects from the same class; each object has its own identity and may or may not store the same value as another object of the same type. For example, the code

```
Charge c1 = new Charge(0.51, 0.63, 21.3);
Charge c2 = new Charge(0.13, 0.94, 85.9);
Charge c3 = new Charge(0.51, 0.63, 21.3);
```

creates three different Charge objects. In particular, c1 and c3 refer to different objects, even though the objects store the same value.

*Invoking methods.*   The most important difference between a variable of a reference type and a variable of a primitive type is that you can use reference type variables to invoke the methods that implement data type operations (in contrast to the built-in syntax involving operators such as + and * that we used for primitive types). Such methods are known as *instance methods*. Invoking an instance method is similar to invoking a static method in another class, except that an instance method is associated not just with a class, but also with an individual object. Accordingly, we use an *object* name (variable of the given type) instead of the *class* name to identify the method. For example, if c is a variable of type Charge, then

**Program 3.1.1    Charged particles**

```
public class ChargeClient
{
    public static void main(String[] args)
    {  // Print total potential at (x, y).
        double x = Double.parseDouble(args[0]);
        double y = Double.parseDouble(args[1]);
        Charge c1 = new Charge(.51, .63, 21.3);
        Charge c2 = new Charge(.13, .94, 81.9);
        double v1 = c1.potentialAt(x, y);
        double v2 = c2.potentialAt(x, y);
        StdOut.printf("%.1e\n", v1+v2);
    }
}
```

| x, y | query point |
|------|-------------|
| c1 | first charge |
| v1 | potential due to c1 |
| c2 | second charge |
| v2 | potential due to c2 |

*This object-oriented client takes a query point (x, y) as command-line argument, creates two charges c1 and c2 with fixed position and electric charge, and uses the potentialAt() instance method in Charge to compute the potential at (x, y) due to the two charges.*

```
% java ChargeClient .2 .5
2.2e+12
% java ChargeClient .51 .94
2.5e+12
```

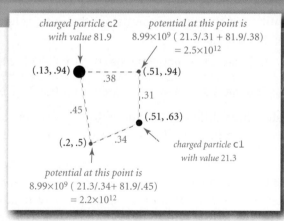

`c.potentialAt(x, y)` returns a double value that represents the potential at $(x, y)$ due to the charge $q_0$ at $(x_0, y_0)$. The values $x$ and $y$ belong to the *client*; the values $x_0$, $y_0$, and $q_0$ belong to the object. For example, `ChargeClient` (PROGRAM 3.1.1) creates two `Charge` objects and computes the total potential at a query point taken from the command line due to the two charges. This code clearly exhibits the idea of developing an abstract model and separating the code that implements the abstraction from the code that uses it. This ability characterizes object-oriented programming and is a turning point in this book: we have not yet seen any code of this nature, but virtually all of the code that we write from this point forward will be based on defining and invoking methods that implement data types operations.

one object

*References.* A constructor creates an object and returns to the client a *reference* to the object, not the object itself (hence the name *reference type*). What is a reference? Nothing more than a mechanism for accessing an object. There are several different ways for Java to implement references, but we do not need to know the details in order to use them. Still, it is worthwhile to have a mental model of one common implementation. One approach is for new to assign memory space to hold the object's current data type value and return a *pointer* (machine address) to that space. We refer to the memory space associated with the object as the object's *identity*. Why not just process the object itself? For small objects, it might make sense to do so, but for large objects, cost becomes an issue: data-type values can be complicated and consume large amounts of memory. It does not make sense to copy or move all of its data every time that we pass an object as an argument to a method. If this reasoning seems familiar to you, it is because we have used precisely the same reasoning before, when talking about passing arrays as arguments to static methods in SECTION 2.1. Indeed, arrays *are* objects, as we will see later in this section. By contrast, primitive types have values that are natural to represent directly in memory and operations that translate directly to machine operations, so that it does not make sense to use a reference to access each value. We will discuss references in more detail after you have seen several examples of client code that uses reference types. Your Java system might use something more complicated than machine addresses to implement references, but this model captures the essential difference between primitive and reference types.

*declare a variable (object name)*

*invoke a constructor to create an object*

```
Charge c1;
c1 = new Charge(.51, .63, 21.3) ;
double v = c1.potentialAt(x, y) ;
```

*object name*

*invoke an instance method that operates on the object's value*

Using a reference data type

two objects

Object representation

*Using objects.* A declaration give us a variable name for an object that we can use in code in much the same way as we use a variable name for an integer or floating-point number:

- As an argument or return value for a method
- In an assignment statement
- In an array

We have been using `String` objects in this way ever since `HelloWorld`: most of our programs call `StdOut.println()` with a `String` argument, and all of our programs have a `main()` method that takes an argument that is an array of `String` objects. As we have already seen, there is one critically important addition to this list for variables that refer to objects:

- To invoke an instance method defined on it

This usage is not available for variables of a primitive type, where all operations are built into the language and invoked using operators such as +, -, *, and /.

*Type conversion.* If you want to convert an object from one type to another, you have to write code to do it. Often, there is no issue, because values for different data types are so different that no conversion is contemplated. For instance, what would it mean to convert a `Charge` to a `Color`? But you have already seen one case where conversion is worthwhile: all Java reference types have a method `toString()` that returns a `String`. Moreover, Java automatically calls this method for any object when a `String` is expected. One consequence of this convention is that it enables you to write `StdOut.println(x)` for any variable x. For example, adding the call `StdOut.println(c1);` to ChargeClient would add `charge 21.3 at (0.51, 0.63)` to the output. The nature of the conversion is completely up to the implementation, but usually the string encodes the object's value.

*Uninitialized variables.* When you declare a variable of a reference type but do not assign a value to it, the variable is *uninitialized*, which leads to the same behavior as for primitive types when you try to use the variable. For example, the code

```
Charge bad;
double v = bad.potentialAt(.5, .5);
```

will not compile, because it is trying to use an uninitialized variable, which leads to the error `variable bad might not have been initialized`.

*Distinction between instance methods and static methods.* Finally, you are ready to appreciate the meaning of the keyword `static` that we have been using since PROGRAM 1.1, one of the last mysterious details in the Java programs that you have been writing. The primary purpose of static methods is to implement functions; the primary purpose of non-static (instance) methods is to implement data-type operations. You can distinguish between the uses of the two types of methods in our client code, because a static method call always starts with a *class* name (uppercase, by convention) and a non-static method call always starts with an *object* name (lowercase, by convention). These differences are summarized in the following table, but after you have written some client code yourself, you will be able to quickly recognize the difference.

| | instance method | static method |
|---|---|---|
| sample call | `c1.potentialAt(x, y)` | `Math.sqrt(2.0)` |
| invoked with | object name | class name |
| parameters | reference to object and argument(s) | argument(s) |
| primary purpose | manipulate object value | compute return value |

*Instance methods vs. static methods*

THE BASIC CONCEPTS THAT WE HAVE just covered are the starting point for object-oriented programming, so it is worthwhile to briefly summarize them: A *data type* is a set of values and a set of operations defined on those values. We implement data types in independent modules and write client programs that use them. An *object* is an *instance* of a data type. Objects are characterized by three essential properties: *state*, *behavior*, and *identity*. The *state* of an object is a value from its data type. The *behavior* of an object is defined by the data type's operations. The *identity* of an object is the place where it is stored in memory. In object-oriented programming, we invoke constructors to create objects and then modify their state by invoking their instance methods.

To demonstrate the power of object orientation, we next consider several more examples. First, we consider the familiar world of image processing, where we process `Color` and `Picture` objects. Then, we consider the operations associated with `String` objects and their importance in a scientific application.

**Color.**    *Color* is a sensation in the eye from electromagnetic radiation. Since we want to view and manipulate color images on our computers, color is a widely used abstraction in computer graphics, and Java provides a `Color` data type. In professional publishing in print and on the web, working with color is a complex task. For example, the appearance of a color image depends in a significant way on the medium used to present it. The `Color` data type separates the creative designer's problem of specifying a desired color from the system's problem of faithfully reproducing it.

Java has hundreds of data types in its libraries, so we need to explicitly list which Java libraries we are using in our program to avoid naming conflicts. Specifically, we include the statement

    import java.awt.Color;

at the beginning of any program that uses `Color`. (Until now, we have been using standard Java libraries or our own, so there has been no need to import them.)

To represent color values, `Color` uses the *RGB system* where a color is defined by three integers (each between 0 and 255) that represent the intensity of the red, green, and blue (respectively) components of the color. Other color values are obtained by mixing the red, green, and blue components. That is, the data type values of `Color` are three 8-bit integers. We do not need to know whether the implementation uses `int`, `short`, or `char` values to represent these integers. With this convention, Java is using 24 bits to represent each color

| red | green | blue | |
|---|---|---|---|
| 255 | 0 | 0 | red |
| 0 | 255 | 0 | green |
| 0 | 0 | 255 | blue |
| 0 | 0 | 0 | black |
| 100 | 100 | 100 | dark gray |
| 255 | 255 | 255 | white |
| 255 | 255 | 0 | yellow |
| 255 | 0 | 255 | magenta |
| 9 | 90 | 166 | this color |

*Some color values*

and can represent $256^3 = 2^{24} \approx 16.7$ million possible colors. Scientists estimate that the human eye can distinguish only about 10 million distinct colors.

`Color` has a constructor that takes three integer arguments, so that you can write, for example

```
Color red      = new Color(255,   0,   0);
Color bookBlue = new Color(  9,  90, 166);
```

to create objects whose values represent red and the blue used to print this book, respectively. We have been using colors in `StdDraw` since SECTION 1.5, but have been limited to a set of predefined colors, such as `StdDraw.BLACK`, `StdDraw.RED`, and `StdDraw.PINK`. Now you have millions of available colors. `AlbersSquares` (PROGRAM 3.1.2) is a `StdDraw` client that allows you to experiment with them.

*Program 3.1.2    Albers squares*

```java
import java.awt.Color;

public class AlbersSquares
{
    public static void main(String[] args)
    { // Display Albers squares for the two RGB
      // colors entered on the command line.
        int r1 = Integer.parseInt(args[0]);
        int g1 = Integer.parseInt(args[1]);
        int b1 = Integer.parseInt(args[2]);
        Color c1 = new Color(r1, g1, b1);

        int r2 = Integer.parseInt(args[3]);
        int g2 = Integer.parseInt(args[4]);
        int b2 = Integer.parseInt(args[5]);
        Color c2 = new Color(r2, g2, b2);

        StdDraw.setPenColor(c1);
        StdDraw.filledSquare(.25, .5, .2);
        StdDraw.setPenColor(c2);
        StdDraw.filledSquare(.25, .5, .1);
        StdDraw.setPenColor(c2);
        StdDraw.filledSquare(.75, .5, .2);
        StdDraw.setPenColor(c1);
        StdDraw.filledSquare(.75, .5, .1);
    }

}
```

| | |
|---|---|
| r1, g1, b1 | *RGB values* |
| c1 | *first color* |
| r2, g2, b2 | *RGB values* |
| c2 | *second color* |

*This program displays the two colors entered in RGB representation on the command line in the familiar format developed in the 1960s by the color theorist Josef Albers that revolutionized the way that people think about color.*

% java AlbersSquares 9 90 166   100 100 100

As usual, when we address a new abstraction, we are introducing you to `Color` by describing the essential elements of Java's color model, not all of the details. The API for `Color` contains several constructors and over 20 methods; the ones that we will use are briefly summarized next.

```
public class java.awt.Color
```
---

|              | `Color(int r, int g, int b)` |                                          |
|-------------:|------------------------------|------------------------------------------|
|        `int` | `getRed()`                   | *red intensity*                          |
|        `int` | `getGreen()`                 | *green intensity*                        |
|        `int` | `getBlue()`                  | *blue intensity*                         |
|      `Color` | `brighter()`                 | *brighter version of this color*         |
|      `Color` | `darker()`                   | *darker version of this color*           |
|     `String` | `toString()`                 | *string representation of this color*    |
|    `boolean` | `equals(Color c)`            | *is this color's value the same as* `c`*'s?* |

*See online documentation and booksite for other available methods.*

*Excerpts from the API for Java's Color data type*

Our primary purpose is to use `Color` as an example to illustrate object-oriented programming, while at the same time developing a few useful tools that we can use to write programs that process colors. Accordingly, we choose one color property as an example to convince you that writing object-oriented code to process abstract concepts like color is a convenient and useful approach

*Luminance.* The quality of the images on modern displays such as LCD monitors, plasma TVs, and cellphone screens depends on an understanding of a color property known as *monochrome luminance*, or effective brightness. A standard formula for luminance is derived from the eye's sensitivity to red, green, and blue. It is a linear combination of the three intensities: if a color's red, green, and blue values are *r*, *g*, and *b*, respectively, then its luminance is defined by this equation:

$$Y = 0.299\,r + 0.587g + 0.114b$$

Since the coefficients are positive and sum to 1 and the intensities are all integers between 0 and 255, the luminance is a real number between 0 and 255.

*Grayscale.* The RGB system has the property that when all three color intensities are the same, the resulting color is on a grayscale that ranges from black (all 0s) to white (all 255s). To print a color photograph in a black-and-white newspaper (or a book), we need a static method to convert from color to grayscale. A simple way to convert a color to grayscale is to replace the color with a new one whose red, green, and blue values equal its monochrome luminance.

*Color compatibility.* The luminance value is also crucial in determining whether two colors are compatible, in the sense that printing text in one of the colors on a background in the other color will be readable. A widely used rule of thumb is that the difference between the luminance of the foreground and background colors should be at least 128. For example, black text on a white background has a luminance difference of 255, but black text on a (book) blue background has a luminance difference of only 74. This rule is important in the design of advertising, road signs, websites, and many other applications. Luminance (PROGRAM 3.1.3) is a static method library that we can use to convert a color to grayscale and to test whether two colors are compatible, for example, when we use colors in StdDraw

| red | green | blue | |
|-----|-------|------|------------------|
| 9 | 90 | 166 | *this color* |
| 74 | 74 | 74 | *grayscale version* |
| 0 | 0 | 0 | *black* |

0.299 * 9 + 0.587 * 90 + 0.114 * 166 = 74.445

*Grayscale example*

applications. The methods in Luminance illustrate the utility of using data types to organize information. Using the Color reference type and passing objects as arguments makes these implementations substantially simpler than the alternative of having to pass around the three intensity values. Returning multiple values from a function also would be problematic without reference types.

| luminance | | difference |
|-----------|--------------|-----------|
| 0 | compatible | 232 |
| 74 | compatible | 158 |
| 232 | not compatible | 74 |

*Compatibility example*

HAVING AN ABSTRACTION FOR COLOR IS important not just for direct use, but also in building higher-level data types that have Color values. Next, we illustrate this point by building on the color abstraction to develop a data type that allows us to write programs to process digital images.

***Program 3.1.3    Luminance library***

```java
import java.awt.Color;

public class Luminance
{
   public static double lum(Color color)
   {  // Compute luminance of color.
      int r = color.getRed();
      int g = color.getGreen();
      int b = color.getBlue();
      return .299*r + .587*g + .114*b;
   }

   public static Color toGray(Color color)
   {  // Use luminance to convert to grayscale.
      int y = (int) Math.round(lum(color));
      Color gray = new Color(y, y, y);
      return gray;
   }

   public static boolean compatible(Color a, Color b)
   {  // Print true if colors are compatible, false otherwise.
      return Math.abs(lum(a) - lum(b)) >= 128;

   }

   public static void main(String[] args)
   {  // Are the two given RGB colors compatible?
      int[] a = new int[6];
      for (int i = 0; i < 6; i++)
         a[i] = Integer.parseInt(args[i]);
      Color c1 = new Color(a[0], a[1], a[2]);
      Color c2 = new Color(a[3], a[4], a[5]);
      StdOut.println(compatible(c1, c2));
   }
}
```

| | |
|---|---|
| r, g, b | *RGB values* |

| | |
|---|---|
| y | *luminance of arg color* |

| | |
|---|---|
| a[] | int *values of args* |
| c1 | *first color* |
| c2 | *second color* |

*This library comprises three important functions for manipulating color: luminance, conversion to gray, and background/foreground compatibility.*

```
% java Luminance 232 232 232    0   0   0
true
% java Luminance   9  90 166  232 232 232
true
% java Luminance   9  90 166    0   0   0
false
```

**Digital image processing**   You are familiar with the concept of a *photograph*. Technically, we might define a photograph as a two-dimensional image created by collecting and focusing visible wavelengths of electromagnetic radiation that constitutes a representation of a scene at a point in time. That technical definition is beyond our scope, except to note that the history of photography is a history of technological development. During the last century, photography was based on chemical processes, but its future is now based in computation. Your camera and your cellphone are computers with lenses and light-sensitive devices capable of capturing images in digital form, and your computer has photo-editing software that allows you to process those images. You can crop them, enlarge and reduce them, adjust the contrast, brighten or darken them, remove red-eye, or perform scores of other operations. Many such operations are remarkably easy to implement, given a simple basic data type that captures the idea of a digital image, as you will now see.

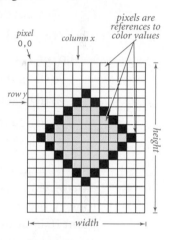

*Digital images.*  We have been using `StdDraw` to plot geometric objects (points, lines, circles, squares) in a window on the computer screen. Which set of values do we need to process digital images, and which operations do we need to perform on those values? The basic abstraction for computer displays is the same one that is used for digital photographs and is very simple: A *digital image* is a rectangular grid of *pixels* (picture elements), where the color of each pixel is individually defined. Digital images are sometimes referred to as *raster* or *bitmapped* images, in contrast to the types of images we produce with `StdDraw`, which are referred to as *vector* images.

*Anatomy of a digital image*

Our class `Picture` is a data type for digital images whose definition follows immediately from the digital image abstraction. The set of values is nothing more than a two-dimensional matrix of `Color` values, and the operations are what you might expect: create an image (either a blank one with a given width and height or one initialized from a picture file), set the value of a pixel to a given color, return the color of a given pixel, return the width or the height, show the image in a window on your computer screen, and save the image to a file. In this description, we intentionally use the word *matrix* instead of *array* to emphasize that we are referring to an abstraction (a matrix of pixels), not a specific implementation (a Java two-dimensional array of `Color` objects). *You do not need to know how a class is implemented in order to be able to use it.* Indeed, typical images have so many pixels that implementations are likely to use a more efficient representation than an array of `Color` values (see EXERCISE 3.1.29). Such considerations are interesting, but can be dealt with independent of client code. To write client programs that manipulate images, you just need to know this API:

`public class Picture`

| | | |
|---|---|---|
| | `Picture(String filename)` | *create a picture from a file* |
| | `Picture(int w, int h)` | *create a blank w-by-h picture* |
| `int` | `width()` | *return the width of the picture* |
| `int` | `height()` | *return the height of the picture* |
| `Color` | `get(int x, int y)` | *return the color of pixel (x, y)* |
| `void` | `set(int x, int y, Color c)` | *set the color of pixel (x, y) to* c |
| `void` | `show()` | *display the image in a window* |
| `void` | `save(String filename)` | *save the image to a file* |

*API for our data type for image processing*

By convention, (0, 0) is the upper leftmost pixel, so the image is laid as in the customary order for arrays (by contrast, the convention for `StdDraw` is to have the point (0,0) at the lower left corner, so that drawings are oriented as in the customary manner for Cartesian coordinates). Most image processing programs are filters that scan through the pixels in a source image as they would a two-dimensional array and then perform some computation to determine the color of each pixel in a target image. The supported file formats for the first constructor and the `save()` method are the widely used `.png` and `.jpg` formats, so that you can write programs to process your own photographs and add the results to an album or a website. The `show()` window also has an interactive option for saving to a file. These methods, together with Java's `Color` data type, open the door to image processing.

*Grayscale.* You will find many examples of color images on the booksite, and all of the methods that we describe are effective for full-color images, but all our example images in the text will be grayscale. Accordingly, our first task is to write a program that can convert images from color to grayscale. This task is a prototypical image-

*Program 3.1.4    Converting color to grayscale*

```java
import java.awt.Color;

public class Grayscale
{
    public static void main(String[] args)
    { // Show image in grayscale.
        Picture pic = new Picture(args[0]);
        for (int x = 0; x < pic.width(); x++)
        {
            for (int y = 0; y < pic.height(); y++)
            {
                Color color = pic.get(x, y);
                Color gray  = Luminance.toGray(color);
                pic.set(x, y, gray);
            }
        }
        pic.show();
    }
}
```

| | |
|---|---|
| pic | *image from file* |
| x, y | *pixel coordinates* |
| color | *pixel color* |
| gray | *pixel grayscale* |

*This program illustrates a simple image processing client. First, it creates a* Picture *object initialized with an image file named by the command-line argument. Then it converts each pixel in the image to grayscale by creating a grayscale version of each pixel's color and resetting the pixel to that color. Finally, it shows the image. You can perceive individual pixels in the image on the right, which was upscaled from a low-resolution image (see "Scaling" on the next page).*

% java Grayscale mandrill.jpg

% java Grayscale darwin.jpg

processing task: for each pixel in the source, we have a pixel in the target with a different color. Grayscale (PROGRAM 3.1.4) is a filter that takes a file name from the command line and produces a grayscale version of that image. It creates a new Picture object initialized with the color image, then sets the color of each pixel to a new Color having a grayscale value computed by applying the toGray() method in Luminance (PROGRAM 3.1.3) to the color of the corresponding pixel in the source.

*downscaling*

*source*

*target*

*upscaling*

*source*

*target*

*Scaling a digital image*

*Scaling.* One of the most common image-processing tasks is to make an image smaller or larger. Examples of this basic operation, known as *scaling*, include making small thumbnail photos for use in a chat room or a cellphone, changing the size of a high-resolution photo to make it fit into a specific space in a printed publication or on a web page, or zooming in on a satellite photograph or an image produced by a microscope. In optical systems, we can just move a lens to achieve a desired scale, but in digital imagery, we have to do more work.

In some cases, the strategy is clear. For example, if the target image is to be half the size (in each dimension) of the source image, we simply choose half the pixels, say, by deleting half the rows and half the columns. This technique is known as *sampling*. If the target image is to be double the size (in each dimension) of the source image, we can replace each source pixel by four target pixels of the same color. Note that we can lose information when we downscale, so halving an image and then doubling it generally does not give back the same image.

A single strategy is effective for both downscaling and upscaling. Our goal is to produce the target image, so we proceed through the pixels in the target, one by one, scaling each pixel's coordinates to identify a pixel in the source whose color can be assigned to the target. If the width and height of the source are $w_s$ and $h_s$ (respectively) and the width and height of the target are $w_t$ and $h_t$ (respectively), then we scale the column index by $w_s/w_t$ and the row index by $h_s/h_t$. That is, we get the color of the pixel in row $y$ and column $x$ of the target from row $y \times h_s/h_t$ and column $x \times w_s/w_t$ in the source. For example, if we are halving the size of a picture, the scale factors are 2, so the pixel in row 2 and column 3 of the target

*Program 3.1.5  Image scaling*

```
public class Scale
{
   public static void main(String[] args)
   {
      int w = Integer.parseInt(args[1]);
      int h = Integer.parseInt(args[2]);
      Picture source = new Picture(args[0]);
      Picture target = new Picture(w, h);
      for (int tx = 0; tx < w; tx++)
      {
         for (int ty = 0; ty < h; ty++)
         {
            int sx = tx * source.width()  / w;
            int sy = ty * source.height() / h;
            target.set(tx, ty, source.get(sx, sy));
         }
      }
      source.show();
      target.show();
   }
}
```

| w, h | *target dimensions* |
|---|---|
| source | *source image* |
| target | *target image* |
| tx, ty | *target pixel coords* |
| sx, sy | *source pixel coords* |

*This program takes the name of a picture file and two integers (width* w *and height* h*) as command-line arguments and scales the image to* w-*by-*h.

java Scale mandrill.jpg 800 800

600 300

200 400

200 200

gets the color of the pixel in row 4 and column 6 of the source; if we are doubling the size of the picture, the scale factors are 1/2, so the pixel in row 6 and column 4 of the target gets the color of the pixel in row 3 and column 2 of the source. Scale (PROGRAM 3.1.5) is an implementation of this strategy. More sophisticated strate-

```
java Fade mandrill.jpg Darwin.jpg 9
```

gies can be effective for low-resolution images of the sort that you might find on old web pages or from old cameras. For example, we might downscale to half size by averaging the values of four pixels in the source to make one pixel in the target. For the high-resolution images that are common in most applications today, the simple approach used in Scale is effective.

The same basic idea of computing the color value of each target pixel as a function of the color values of specific source pixels is effective for all sorts of image-processing tasks. Next, we consider two more examples, and you will find numerous other examples in the exercises and on the booksite.

*Fade effect.* Our next image-processing example is an entertaining computation where we transform one image to another in a series of discrete steps. Such a transformation is sometimes known as a *fade effect*. Fade (PROGRAM 3.1.6) is a Picture and Color client that uses a *linear interpolation* strategy to implement this effect. It computes $M-1$ intermediate images, with each pixel in the $t$th image a weighted average of the corresponding pixels in the source and target. The static method blend() implements the interpolation: the source color is weighted by a factor of $1 - t / M$ and the target color by a factor of $t / M$ (when $t$ is 0, we have the source color, and when $t$ is $M$, we have the target color). This simple computation can produce striking results. When you run Fade on your computer, the change appears to happen dynamically. Try running it on some images from your photo library. Note that Fade assumes that the images have the same width and height; if you have images for which this is not the case, you can use Scale to created a scaled version of one or both of them for Fade.

*Program 3.1.6    Fade effect*

```
import java.awt.Color;

public class Fade
{
   public static Color blend(Color c, Color d, double alpha)
   {  // Compute blend of c and d, weighted by x.
      double r = (1-alpha)*c.getRed()   + alpha*d.getRed();
      double g = (1-alpha)*c.getGreen() + alpha*d.getGreen();
      double b = (1-alpha)*c.getBlue()  + alpha*d.getBlue();
      return new Color((int) r, (int) g, (int) b);
   }
   public static void main(String[] args)
   {  // Show M-image fade sequence from source to target.
      Picture source = new Picture(args[0]);
      Picture target = new Picture(args[1]);
      int M = Integer.parseInt(args[2]);
      int width  = source.width();
      int height = source.height();
      Picture pic = new Picture(width, height);
      for (int t = 0; t <= M; t++)
      {
         for (int x = 0; x < width; x++)
         {
            for (int y = 0; y < height; y++)
            {
               Color c0 = source.get(x, y);
               Color cM = target.get(x, y);
               Color c = blend(c0, cM, (double) t / M);
               pic.set(x, y, c);
            }
         }
         pic.show();
      }
   }
}
```

| M | number of images |
|---|---|
| pic | current image |
| t | image counter |
| c0 | source color |
| c1 | target color |
| c | blended color |

*To fade from one image into another in M steps, we set each pixel in the tth image to a weighted average of the corresponding pixel in the source and the destination, with the source getting weight 1-t/M and the destination getting weight t/M. An example transformation is shown on the facing page.*

*Potential value visualization.*  Image processing is also helpful in scientific visualization. As an example, we consider a Picture client for visualizing properties of the Charge data type that we introduced at the beginning of this chapter. Potential (PROGRAM 3.1.7) visualizes the potential values created by a set of charged particles. First, Potential creates an array of particles, with values taken from standard input. Next, it creates a Picture object and sets each pixel in the picture to a shade of gray that is proportional to the potential value at the corresponding point. The calculation at the heart of the method is very simple: for each pixel, we compute corresponding $(x, y)$ values in the unit square, then call potentialAt() to find the potential at that point due to all of the charges, summing the values returned. With appropriate assignment of potential values to grayscale values (scaling them to fall between 0 and 255), we get a striking visual representation of the electric potential that is an excellent aid to understanding interactions among such particles. We could produce a similar image using filledSquare() in StdDraw, but Picture provides us with more accurate control over the color of each pixel on the screen. The same basic method is useful in many other settings—you can find several examples on the booksite.

```
% more charges.txt
9
.51  .63  -100
.50  .50    40
.50  .72    10
.33  .33     5
.20  .20   -10
.70  .70    10
.82  .72    20
.85  .23    30
.90  .12   -50
% java Potential < charges.txt
```

*Potential value visualization for a set of charges*

IT IS WORTHWHILE TO REFLECT BRIEFLY on the code in Potential, because it exemplifies data abstraction and object-oriented programming. We want to produce an image that shows interactions among charged particles, and our code reflects precisely the process of creating that image, using a Picture object for the image (which is manipulated via Color objects) and Charge objects for the particles. When we want information about a Charge, we invoke the appropriate method directly for that Charge; when we want to create a Color, we use a Color constructor; when we want to set a pixel, we directly involve the appropriate method for the Picture. These data types are independently developed, but their use together in a single client is easy and natural. We next consider several more examples, to illustrate the broad reach of data abstraction while at the same time adding a number of useful data types to our basic programming model.

---

**Program 3.1.7    Visualizing electric potential**

---

```
import java.awt.Color;

public class Potential
{
   public static void main(String[] args)
   {  // Read charges from StdIn into a[].
      int N = StdIn.readInt();
      Charge[] a = new Charge[N];
      for (int k = 0; k < N; k++)
      {
         double x0 = StdIn.readDouble();
         double y0 = StdIn.readDouble();
         double q0 = StdIn.readDouble();
         a[k] = new Charge(x0, y0, q0);
      }

      // Create and show image depicting potential values.
      int size = 512;
      Picture pic = new Picture(size, size);
      for (int i = 0; i < size; i++)
      {
         for (int j = 0; j < size; j++)
         {  // Compute pixel color.
            double x = (double) i / size;
            double y = (double) j / size;
            double V = 0.0;
            for (int k = 0; k < N; k++)
               V += a[k].potentialAt(x, y);
            int g = 128 + (int) (V / 2.0e10);
            if (g < 0)   g = 0;
            if (g > 255) g = 255;
            Color c = new Color(g, g, g);
            pic.set(i, size-1-j, c);
         }
      }
      pic.show();
   }
}
```

| | |
|---|---|
| N | number of charges |
| a[] | array of charges |
| x0, y0 | charge position |
| q0 | charge value |

| | |
|---|---|
| i, j | pixel position |
| x, y | point in unit square |
| g | scaled potential value |
| c | pixel color |

---

*This program reads values from standard input to create an array of charged particles, sets each pixel color in an image to a grayscale value proportional to the total of the potentials due to the particles at corresponding points, and shows the resulting image.*

**String processing**   You have been using strings since your first Java program. Java's `String` data type includes a long list of other operations on strings. It is one of Java's most important data types because string processing is critical to many computational applications. Strings lie at the heart of our ability to compile and run Java programs and to perform many other core computations; they are the basis of the information-processing systems that are critical to most business systems; people use them every day when typing into email, blog, or chat applications or preparing documents for publication; and they have proven to be critical ingredients in scientific progress in several fields, particularly molecular biology.

A `String` value is an indexed sequence of `char` values. We summarize here the methods from the Java API that we use most often. Several of the methods use integers to refer to a character's index within a string; as with arrays, these indices start at 0. As indicated in the note at the bottom, this list is a small subset of the `String` API; the full API has over 60 methods!

`public class String` (Java string data type)

| | | |
|---:|---|---|
| | `String(String s)` | *create a string with the same value as* s |
| `int` | `length()` | *string length* |
| `char` | `charAt(int i)` | i*th character* |
| `String` | `substring(int i, int j)` | i*th through (*j*-1)st characters* |
| `boolean` | `contains(String sub)` | *does string contain* sub *as a substring?* |
| `boolean` | `startsWith(String pre)` | *does string start with* pre*?* |
| `boolean` | `endsWith(String post)` | *does string end with* post*?* |
| `int` | `indexOf(String p)` | *index of first occurrence of* p |
| `int` | `indexOf(String p, int i)` | *index of first occurrence of* p *after* i |
| `String` | `concat(String t)` | *this string with* t *appended* |
| `int` | `compareTo(String t)` | *string comparison* |
| `String` | `replaceAll(String a, String b)` | *result of changing* as *to* bs |
| `String[]` | `split(String delim)` | *strings between occurrences of* delim |
| `boolean` | `equals(String t)` | *is this string's value the same as* t*'s?* |

*See online documentation and booksite for many other available methods.*

*Excerpts from the API for Java's* `String` *data type*

Java provides special language support for manipulating strings. Instead of initializing a string with a constructor, we can use a string literal, and instead of invoking the method concat(), we can use the + operator:

| | | |
|---|---|---|
| *shorthand* | `String s = "abc";` | `String t = r + s;` |
| *longhand* | `String s = new String("abc");` | `String t = r.concat(s);` |

These notations arc shorthand for standard data-type mechanisms.

String values are not the same as arrays of characters, but the two are similar, and novice Java programmers sometimes confuse them. For example, the differences are evident in one of the most common code idioms for both strings and arrays: for loops to process each element (for arrays) or character (for strings):

```
for (int i = 0; i < a.length; i++)     for (int i = 0; i < s.length(); i++)
{ ... a[i] ... }                       { ... s.charAt(i) ... }
```
array        string

For arrays, we have direct language support: brackets for indexed access and .length (with no parentheses) for length. For strings, both indexed access and length are just String methods.

The split() method in the String API is powerful because many options, known as *regular expressions*, are available for delim. For example, "\\s+" means "one or more whitespace characters." Using this delimiter with split() transforms a string of words delimited by whitespace into an array of words.

Why not just use arrays of characters instead of String values? When we process strings, we want to write client code that operates on strings, not arrays. The methods in Java's String data type implement natural operations on String values and also simplify client code, as you will see. We have been working with programs that use a few short strings for output, but it is not unusual for *strings*, not numbers, to be the primary data type of interest in an application, and to have programs that process huge strings or huge numbers of strings. Next, we consider in detail such an application.

```
String a = "now is ";
String b = "the time ";
String c = "to"
```

| call | value |
|---:|:---|
| a.length() | 7 |
| a.charAt(4) | i |
| a.substring(2, 5) | "w i" |
| b.startsWith("the") | true |
| a.indexOf("is") | 4 |
| a.concat(c) | "now is to" |
| b.replace('t','T') | "The Time " |
| a.split(" ")[0] | "now" |
| a.split(" ")[1] | "is" |
| b.equals(c) | false |

*Examples of string operations*

| | |
|---|---|
| *is the string a palindrome?* | ```java
public static boolean isPalindrome(String s)
{
    int N = s.length();
    for (int i = 0; i < N/2; i++)
        if (s.charAt(i) != s.charAt(N-1-i))
            return false;
    return true;
}
``` |
| *extract file name and extension from a command-line argument* | ```java
String s = args[0];
int dot = s.indexOf(".");
String base      = s.substring(0, dot);
String extension = s.substring(dot + 1, s.length());
``` |
| *print all lines on standard input that contain a string specified from a command line argument* | ```java
String query = args[0];
while (!StdIn.isEmpty())
{
    String s = StdIn.readLine();
    if (s.contains(query)) StdOut.println(s);
}
``` |
| *create an array of the strings on standard input delimited by whitespace* | ```java
String input = StdIn.readAll();
String[] words = input.split("\\s+");
``` |
| *check whether an array of strings is in alphabetical order* | ```java
public boolean isSorted(String[] a)
{
    for (int i = 1; i < a.length; i++)
    {
        if (a[i-1].compareTo(a[i]) > 0)
            return false;
    }
    return true;
}
``` |
| *print all the hyperlinks (to educational institutions) of the strings on standard input* | ```java
while (!StdIn.isEmpty())
{
    String s = StdIn.readString();
    if (s.startsWith("http://") && s.endsWith(".edu"))
        StdOut.println(s);
}
``` |

*Typical string-processing code*

**String-processing application: genomics**   To give you more experience with string processing, we will give a very brief overview of the field of *genomics* and consider a Java program that solves a basic problem known as *gene finding*. Genomics is a quintessential string-processing application.

Biologists use a simple model to represent the building blocks of life: The letters A, C, T, and G represent the four nucleotides in the DNA of living organisms. In each living organism, these basic building blocks appear in a set of long sequences (one for each chromosome) known as a *genome*. Scientists know that understanding properties of the genome is a key to understanding the processes that manifest themselves in living organisms. The genomic sequences for many living things are known, including a human genome, which is a sequence of about three billion characters. You can find these sequences in many places on the web. (We have collected several on the booksite: for instance, the file genomeVirus.txt, which is the 6252-character genome of a simple virus.) Knowing the sequences, scientists are now writing computer programs to study the structure of these sequences. String processing is now one of the most important methodologies—experimental or computational—in molecular biology for elucidating biological function.

*Gene finding.*   A *gene* is a substring of a genome that represents a functional unit of critical importance in understanding life processes. Genes are substrings of the genome of varying length, and there are varying numbers of them within a genome. A gene is a sequence of *codons*, each of which is a nucleotide triplet that represents one amino acid. The *start codon* ATG marks the beginning of a gene, and any of the *stop codons* TAG, TAA, or TGA mark the end of a gene (and there are no occurrences of any of the codons ATG, TAA, TAG, or TGA within the gene). One of the first steps in analyzing a genome is to identify its genes, which, as you certainly now realize, is a string-processing problem that Java's String data type equips us to solve. GeneFind (Program 3.1.8) is a Java program that can do the job. To understand how it works, we will consider a tiny example that does not represent a real genome. Take a moment to identify the genes marked by the start codon ATG and the end codon TAG in the following string:

ATAGATGCATAGCGCATAGCTAGATGTGCTAGC

There are several occurrences of both ATG and TAG, and they overlap in various ways, so you have to do a bit of work to identify the genes. GeneFind accomplishes the task in one left-to-right scan through the genome, as shown next.

**Program 3.1.8   Finding genes in a genome**

```
public class GeneFind
{
   public static void main(String[] args)
   { // Use start and stop to find genes in genome.
      String start  = args[0];
      String stop   = args[1];
      String genome = StdIn.readAll();
      int beg = -1;
      for (int i = 0; i < genome.length() - 2; i++)
      { // Check next codon for start or stop.
         String codon = genome.substring(i, i+3);
         if (codon.equals(start)) beg = i;
         if ((codon.equals(stop)) && beg != -1)
         { // Check putative gene alignment.
            String gene = genome.substring(beg+3, i);
            if (gene.length() % 3 == 0)
            { // Print and restart.
               StdOut.println(gene);
               beg = -1;
            }
         }
      }
   }
}
```

| start | start *codon* |
|---|---|
| stop | stop *codon* |
| genome | *full genome* |
| beg | *putative gene start position* |
| i | *character index* |
| codon | *next codon* |
| gene | *discovered gene* |

*This program prints all the genes in the genome on standard input defined by the start and stop codes on the command line. To find a gene in a genome, we scan for the start codon, remember its index, and then scan to the next stop codon. If the length of the intervening sequence is a multiple of 3, we have found a gene.*

```
% more genomeTiny.txt
ATAGATGCATAGCGCATAGCTAGATGTGCTAGC

% java GeneFind ATG TAG < genomeTiny.txt
CATAGCGCA
TGC

% java GeneFind ATG TAG < genomeVirus.txt
CGCCTGCGTCTGTAC
TCGAGCGGATCGCTCACAACCAGTCGG
...
AGATTATCAAAAAGGATCTTCACC
```

| i | codon | | beg | gene | *remaining portion of input string* |
|---|-------|------|-----|------|-------------------------------------|
|   | *start* | *stop* | | | |
| 0 | | | -1 | | ATAGATGCATAGCGCATAGCTAGATGTGCTAGC |
| 1 | | TAG | -1 | | ATAGATGCATAGCGCATAGCTAGATGTGCTAGC |
| 4 | ATG | | 4 | | ATAGATGCATAGCGCATAGCTAGATGTGCTAGC |
| 9 | | TAG | 4 | | ATAGATGCATAGCGCATAGCTAGATGTGCTAGC |
| 16 | | TAG | 4 | CATAGCGCA | ATAGATGCATAGCGCATAGCTAGATGTGCTAGC |
| 20 | | TAG | -1 | | ATAGATGCATAGCGCATAGCTAGATGTGCTAGC |
| 23 | ATG | | 23 | | ATAGATGCATAGCGCATAGCTAGATGTGCTAGC |
| 29 | | TAG | 23 | TGC | ATAGATGCATAGCGCATAGCTAGATGTGCTAGC |

The variable `beg` holds the index of the most recently encountered ATG start codon: the value -1 indicates that the current portion of the genome could not be a gene, either because no ATG has been seen (at the beginning) or because no ATG has been seen since the last gene was found. If we encounter a TAG stop codon when `beg` is -1, we ignore it; otherwise, we have found a gene. This trace illustrates the cases of interest: we ignore the TAG codons at 1 and 20 because `beg` is -1, indicating that we have not seen an ATG; we set `beg` to the current index each time that we encounter an ATG; we ignore the TAG at 9 because it marks the putative gene CA whose length is not a multiple of 3, so it could not be a sequence of codons; and we output genes at 16 and 29 because we have valid start and stop codons with no intervening stop codons and a gene length that is a multiple of 3.

GeneFind is simple but subtle, typical of string processing programs. In practice, the rules that define genes are more complicated than those we have sketched: other codons may be prohibited, there may be bounds on the length, some genes have to be spliced from multiple pieces, and genes satisfying various other criteria may be of interest. GeneFind is intended to exemplify how a basic knowledge of Java programming can enable a scientist to make appropriate tools to study these sequences. Actual genomes are similar to our test case, just much longer. You can experiment with GeneFind to look for genes in genomeVirus.txt and several other genomes on the booksite. The quick leap from examining a toy programming example that illustrates the basic Java String data type to studying scientific questions on actual data is a remarkable characteristic of modern genomics. As we will see, some of the very same algorithms that were developed by computer scientists that underly basic computational mechanisms and have proven important in commercial applications are also now playing a critical role in genomic research.

**Input and output revisited**   In SECTION 1.5 you learned how to read and write numbers and text using StdIn and StdOut and to make drawings with StdDraw. You have certainly come to appreciate the utility of these mechanism in getting information into and out of your programs. One reason that they are convenient is that the "standard" conventions make them accessible from anywhere within a program. One disadvantage of these conventions is that they leave us dependent upon the operating system's piping and redirection mechanism for access to files, and they restrict us to working with just one input file, one output file, and one drawing for any given program. With object-oriented programming, we can define mechanisms that are similar to StdIn, StdOut, and StdDraw but allow us to work with *multiple* input streams, output streams, and drawings within one program.

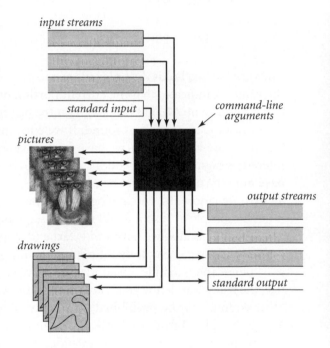

Specifically, we define in this section the data types In, Out, and Draw for input streams, output streams, and drawings (respectively). As usual, you can download the files In.java, Out. java, and Draw.java from the booksite to use these data types.

These data types give us the flexibility that we need to address many common data-processing

*A bird's-eye view of a Java program (revisited again)*

tasks within our Java programs. Rather than being restricted to just one input stream, one output stream, and one drawing, we can easily define multiple objects of each type, connecting the streams to various sources and destinations. We also get the flexibility to assign such objects to variables, pass them as arguments or return values from methods, and to create arrays of them, manipulating them just as we manipulate objects of any type. We will consider several examples of their use after we have presented the APIs.

*Input stream data type.* The data type `In` is a more general version of `StdIn` that supports reading numbers and text from files and websites as well as the standard input stream. It implements the *input stream* data type, with the following API:

`public class In`

| | | |
|---|---|---|
| | `In()` | *create an input stream from standard input* |
| | `In(String name)` | *create an input stream from a file or website* |
| boolean | `isEmpty()` | `true` *if no more input,* `false` *otherwise* |
| int | `readInt()` | *read a value of type* `int` |
| double | `readDouble()` | *read a value of type* `double` |
| | `...` | |

*Note: All operations supported by* `StdIn` *are also supported for* `In` *objects.*

API for our data type for input streams

Instead of being restricted to one abstract input stream (standard input), you now also have the ability to directly specify the source of an input stream. Moreover, that source can be either a *file* or a *website*. When invoked with a constructor having a `String` argument, `In` will first try to find a file in the current directory of your local computer that has that name. If it cannot do so, it will assume the argument to be a website name and will try to connect to that website. (If no such website exists, it will issue a runtime exception.) In either case, the specified file or website becomes the source of the input for the input stream object thus created, and the `read*()` methods will provide values from that stream. This arrangement makes it possible to process multiple files within the same program. Moreover, the ability to directly access the web opens up the whole web as potential input for your programs. For example, it allows you to process data that is provided and maintained by someone else. You can find such files all over the web. Scientists now regularly post data files with measurements or results of experiments, ranging from genome and protein sequences to satellite photographs to astronomical observations; financial services companies, such as stock exchanges, regularly publish on the web detailed information about the performance of stock and other financial instruments; governments publish election results; and so forth. Now you can write Java programs that read these kinds of files directly. `In` gives you a great deal of flexibility to take advantage of the multitude of data sources that are now available.

*Output stream data type.* Similarly, our data type Out is a more general version of StdOut that supports writing text to a variety of output streams, including standard output and files. Again, the API specifies the same methods as its StdOut counterpart. You specify the file that you want to use for output by using the one-argument constructor with the file's name as argument. Out interprets this string as the name of a new file on your local computer, and sends its output there. If you use the no-argument constructor, then you obtain standard output.

```
public class Out
```
| | | |
|---|---|---|
| | Out() | *create an output stream to standard output* |
| | Out(String name) | *create an output stream to a file* |
| void | print(String s) | *print s to the output stream* |
| void | println(String s) | *print s and a newline to the output stream* |
| void | println() | *print a newline to the output stream* |
| void | printf(String f, ...) | *formatted print to the output steam* |

*API for our data type for output streams*

*File concatenation and filtering.* PROGRAM 3.1.9 is a sample client of In and Out that uses multiple input streams to concatenate several input files into a single output file. Some operating systems have a command known as cat that implements this function. However, a Java program that does the same thing is perhaps more useful, because we can tailor it to *filter* the input files in various ways: we might wish to ignore irrelevant information, change the format, or select only some of the data, to name just a few examples. We now consider one example of such processing, and you can find several others in the exercises.

*Screen scraping.* The combination of In (which allows us to create an input stream from any page on the web) and String (which provides powerful tools for processing text strings) opens up the entire web to direct access by our Java programs, without any direct dependence on the operating system or the browser. One paradigm is known as *screen scraping*: the goal is to extract some information from a web page with a program rather than having to browse to find it. To do so, we take

---

### Program 3.1.9   Concatenating files

```
public class Cat
{
   public static void main(String[] args)
   { // Copy input files to out (last argument).
      Out out = new Out(args[args.length-1]);
      for (int i = 0; i < args.length - 1; i++)
      { // Copy input file named on ith arg to out.
         In in = new In(args[i]);
         String s = in.readAll();
         out.println(s);
      }
   }
}
```

| out | output stream |
|-----|---------------|
| i   | argument index |
| in  | current input stream |
| s   | contents of in |

*This program creates an output file whose name is given by the last argument and whose contents are copies of the input files whose names are given as the other arguments.*

```
% more in1.txt
This is

% more in2.txt
a tiny
test.
```

```
% java Cat in1.txt in2.txt out.txt

% more out.txt
This is
a tiny
test.
```

advantage of the fact that many web pages are defined with text files in a highly structured format (because they are created by computer programs!). Your browser has a mechanism that allows you to examine the source code that produces the web page that you are viewing, and by examining that source you can often figure out what to do. For example, suppose that we want to take a stock trading symbol as a command-line argument and print out its current trading price. Such information is published on the web by financial service companies and internet service providers. For example, you can find the stock price of a company whose symbol is goog by browsing to http://finance.yahoo.com/q?s=goog. Like many web pages, the name encodes an argument (goog), and we could substitute any other ticker symbol to get a web page with financial information for any other company. Also, like many other files on the web, the referenced file is a text file, written in a formatting language known as HTML. (See the CONTEXT section at the end of this book for some details about this language.) From the point of view of a Java program, it is just a `String` value accessible through an `In` input stream. You can use your browser to download the source of that file, or you could use

```
java Cat "http://finance.yahoo.com/q?s=goog" mycopy.txt
```

to put the source into a local file `mycopy.txt` on your computer (though there is no real need to do so). Now, suppose that `goog` is trading at $475.11 at the moment. If you search for the string `"475.11"` in the source of that page, you will find the stock price buried within some HTML code. Without having to know details of HTML, you can figure out something about the context in which the price appears. In this case, you can see that the stock price is enclosed between the tags `"<b>"` and `"</b>"`, a bit after the string `"Last Trade:"`. With the `String` data type methods `indexOf()` and `substring()` you can easily grab this information, as illustrated in `StockQuote` (PROGRAM 3.1.10). This program depends on the web page format of `http://finance.yahoo.com`; if this format changes, `StockQuote` not work. Still, making appropriate changes is not likely to be difficult. You can entertain yourself by embellishing `StockQuote` in all kinds of interesting ways. For example, you could grab the stock price on a periodic basis and plot it, compute a moving average, or save the results to a file for later analysis. Of course, the same technique works for sources of data found all over the web. You can find many examples in the exercises at the end of this section and on the booksite.

```
...
<tr>
<td class="yfnc_tablehead1"
width="48%">
Last Trade:
</td>
<td class="yfnc_tabledata1">
<big><b>475.11</b></big>
</td></tr>
<tr>
<td class="yfnc_tablehead1"
width="48%">
Trade Time:
</td>
<td class="yfnc_tabledata1">
11:13AM ET
...
```

*HTML code from the web*

*Extracting data.* The ability to maintain multiple input and output streams gives us a great deal of flexibility in meeting the challenges of processing large amounts of data coming from a variety of sources. We consider one more example: Suppose that a scientist or a financial analyst has a large amount of data within a spreadsheet program. Typically such spreadsheets are tables with a relatively large number of rows and a relatively small number of columns. You are not likely to be interested

---

**Program 3.1.10   Screen scraping for stock quotes**

---

```
public class StockQuote
{
   public static double price(String symbol)
   {  // Return current stock price for symbol.
      In page = new In("http://finance.yahoo.com/q?s=" + symbol);
      String in = page.readAll();
      int trade = in.indexOf("Last Trade:", 0);
      int from =  in.indexOf("<b>", trade);
      int to =    in.indexOf("</b>", from);
      String price = in.substring(from + 3, to);
      return Double.parseDouble(price);
   }

   public static void main(String[] args)
   {  StdOut.println(price(args[0]));   }
}
```

| page | input stream |
|------|--------------|
| in | contents of page |
| trade | Last... index |
| from | <b> index |
| to | </b> index |
| price | current price |

---

*This program takes the ticker symbol of a stock as a command-line argument, reads a web page containing the stock price, finds the stock price using the String method indexOf(), extracts it using the method substring(), and prints the price out to standard output.*

```
% java StockQuote goog
475.11
% java StockQuote adbe
41.125
```

in all the data in the spreadsheet, but you may be interested in a few of the columns. You can do some calculations within the spreadsheet program (this is its purpose, after all), but you certainly do not have the flexibility that you have with Java programming. One way to address this situation is to have the spreadsheet *export* the data to a text file, using some special character to delimit the columns, and then write a Java program that reads that file from an input stream. One standard practice is to use commas as delimiters: print one line per column, with commas separating row entries. Such files are known as *comma-separated-value* or .csv files. With the split() method in Java's String data type, we can read the file line-by-

*Program 3.1.11  Splitting a file*

```
public class Split
{
   public static void main(String[] args)
   {  // Split file by column into N files.
      String name = args[0];
      int N = Integer.parseInt(args[1]);
      String delim = ",";

      // Create output streams.
      Out[] out = new Out[N];
      for (int i = 0; i < N; i++)
         out[i] = new Out(name + i + ".txt");

      In in = new In(name + ".csv");
      while (!in.isEmpty())
      {  // Read a line and write fields to output streams.
         String line = in.readLine();
         String[] fields = line.split(delim);
         for (int i = 0; i < N; i++)
            out[i].println(fields[i]);
      }
   }
}
```

| | |
|---|---|
| name | *base file name* |
| N | *argument index* |
| delim | *delimiter (comma)* |
| in | *input stream* |
| out[] | *output streams* |
| line | *current line* |
| fields[] | *values in current line* |

*This program uses multiple output streams to split a* `.csv` *file into separate files, one for each comma-delimited field. The name of the output file corresponding to the* i*th field is formed by concatenating* i *and then* `.txt` *to the end of the original file name.*

```
% more DJIA.csv
...
31-Oct-29,264.97,7150000,273.51
30-Oct-29,230.98,10730000,258.47
29-Oct-29,252.38,16410000,230.07
28-Oct-29,295.18,9210000,260.64
25-Oct-29,299.47,5920000,301.22
24-Oct-29,305.85,12900000,299.47
23-Oct-29,326.51,6370000,305.85
22-Oct-29,322.03,4130000,326.51
21-Oct-29,323.87,6090000,320.91
...
```

```
% java Split DJIA 3

% more DJIA2.txt
...
7150000
10730000
16410000
9210000
5920000
12900000
6370000
4130000
6090000
...
```

line and isolate the data that we want. We will see several examples of this approach later in the book. Split (PROGRAM 3.1.11) is an In and Out client that goes one step further: it creates multiple output streams and makes one file for each column.

THESE EXAMPLES ARE CONVINCING ILLUSTRATIONS OF the utility of working with text files, with multiple input and output streams, and with direct access to web pages. Web pages are written in HTML precisely so that they are accessible to any program that can read strings. People use text formats such as .csv files rather than data formats that are beholden to particular applications precisely in order to allow as many people as possible to access the data with simple programs like Split.

*Drawing data type.* When using the Picture data type that we considered earlier in this section, we could write programs that manipulated multiple pictures, arrays of pictures, and so forth, precisely because the data type provides us with the capability for computing with Picture objects. Naturally, we would like the same capability for computing with the kinds of objects that we create with StdDraw. Accordingly, we have a Draw data type with the following API:

```
public class Draw
```
---
```
          Draw()
    void  line(double x0, double y0, double x1, double y1)
    void  point(double x, double y)

          . . .
```

*Note: All operations supported by* StdDraw *are also supported for* Draw *objects.*

As for any data type, you can create a new drawing by using new to create a Draw object, assign it to a variable, and use that variable name to call the methods that create the graphics. For example, the code

```
    Draw d = new Draw();
    d.circle(.5, .5, .2);
```

draws a circle in the center of a window on your screen. As with Picture, each drawing has its own window, so that you can address applications that call for multiple different drawings.

**Properties of reference types**   Now that you have seen several examples of reference types (Charge, Color, Picture, String, In, Out, and Draw) and client programs that use them, we discuss in more detail some of their essential properties. To a large extent, Java protects novice programmers from having to know these details. Experienced programmers know that a firm understanding of these properties is helpful in writing correct, effective, and efficient object-oriented programs.

A reference captures the distinction between a thing and its name. This distinction is a familiar one, as illustrated in these examples:

| type | typical object | typical name |
|---|---|---|
| website | our booksite | www.cs.princeton.edu/IntroProgramming |
| person | father of computer science | Alan Turing |
| planet | third rock from the sun | Earth |
| building | our office | 35 Olden Street |
| ship | superliner that sank in 1912 | RMS Titanic |
| number | circumference/diameter in a circle | $\pi$ |
| Picture | new Picture("mandrill.jpg") | pic |

A given object may have multiple names, but each object has its own identity. We can create a new name for an object without changing the object's value (via an assignment statement), but when we change an object's value (by invoking an instance method), all of the object's names refer to the changed object.

The following analogy may help you keep this crucial distinction clear in your mind. Suppose that you want to have your house painted, so you write the street address of your house in pencil on a piece of paper and give it to a few house painters. Now, if you hire one of the painters to paint the house, it becomes a different color. No changes have been made to any of the pieces of paper, but the house that they all refer to has changed. One of the painters might erase what you've written and write the address of another house, but changing what is written on one piece of paper does not change what is written on another piece of paper. Java references are like the pieces of paper: they hold names of objects. Changing a reference does not change the object, but changing an object makes the change apparent to everyone having a reference to it.

The famous Belgian artist René Magritte captured this same concept in a painting where he created an image of a pipe along with the caption *ceci n'est pas une pipe* (*this is not a pipe*) below it. We might interpret the caption as saying that the image is not actually a pipe, just an image of a pipe. Or perhaps Magritte meant that the caption is neither a pipe nor an image of a pipe, just a caption! In the present context, this image reinforces the idea that a reference to an object is nothing more than a reference; it is not the object itself.

*Ceci n'est pas une pipe.*

*This is a picture of a pipe*

*Aliasing.* An assignment statement with a reference type creates a second copy of the reference. The assignment statement *does not create a new object*, just another reference to an existing object. This situation is known as *aliasing*: both variables refer to the same object. The effect of aliasing is a bit unexpected, because it is different than for variables holding values of a primitive type. *Be sure that you understand the difference.* If x and y are variables of a primitive type, then the assignment statement x = y copies the value of y to x. For reference types, the reference is copied (not the value). Aliasing is a common source of bugs in Java programs, as illustrated by the following example:

```java
Picture a = new Picture("mandrill.jpg");
Picture b = a;
a.set(i, j, color1);  // a is updated
b.set(i, j, color2);  // a is updated again
```

After the assignment statement, the variables a and b both refer to the same Picture. Changing the state of an object impacts *all* code involving aliased variables referencing that object. We are used to thinking of two different variables of primitive types as being independent, but that intuition does not carry over to reference objects. For example, if the code above is assuming that a and b refer to different Picture objects, then it will produce the wrong result. Such *aliasing bugs* are common in programs written by people without much experience in using reference objects (that's you, so pay attention here!).

```java
Color a =
  new Color(160, 82, 45);
Color b = a;
```

| a | 811 | } references to same object |
| b | 811 | |

| 811 | 160 | |
| 812 | 82 | ← sienna |
| 813 | 45 | |

*Aliasing*

*Immutable types.* For this very reason, it is common to define data types whose values cannot change. A data type that has no methods that can change an object's value is said to be *immutable* (as are objects of that type). For example, Java's `Color` and `String` objects are immutable (there are no operations available to clients that change a color's value), but `Picture` objects are mutable (we can change pixel colors). We will consider immutability in detail in SECTION 3.3.

*Comparing objects.* When applied to references, the `==` operator checks whether the two *references* have the same identity (that is, whether they point to the same object). That is not the same as checking whether the *objects* have the same value. For example, consider the following code:

```
Color a = new Color(142, 213, 87);
Color b = new Color(142, 213, 87);
Color c = b;
```

Now (a `==` b) is `false` and (b `==` c) is `true`, but when you are thinking about equality testing for `Color`, you probably are thinking that you want to test whether their *values* are the same—you might want all three of these to test as equal. Java does not have an automatic mechanism for testing equality of object values, which leaves programmers with the opportunity (and responsibility) to define it for themselves by defining for any class a customized method named `equals()`, as described in SECTION 3.3. For example, `Color` has such a method, and `a.equals(c)` is `true` in our example. `String` also contains an implementation of `equals()` because we often want to test that two `String` objects have the same value.

*Pass by value.* When we call a method with arguments, the effect in Java is as if each argument value were to appear on the right-hand side of an assignment statement with the corresponding argument name on the left. That is, Java passes a *copy* of the argument value from the calling program to the method. This arrangement is known as *pass by value*. One important consequence is that the method cannot change the value of a caller's variable. For primitive types, this policy is what we expect (the two variables are independent), but each time that we use a reference type as a method argument, we create an alias, so we must be cautious. In other words, the convention is to pass the *reference* by value (make a copy of it) but to pass the *object* by reference. For example, if we pass a reference to an object of type `Picture`, the method cannot change the original reference (make it point to a different `Picture`), but it *can* change the value of the object, for example by invoking the method `set()` to change a pixel's color.

*Arrays are objects.* In Java, every value of any nonprimitive type is an object. In particular, arrays are objects. As with strings, there is special language support for certain operations on arrays: declarations, initialization, and indexing. As with any other object, when we pass an array to a method or use an array variable on the right hand side of an assignment statement, we are making a copy of the array reference, not a copy of the array. Arrays are mutable objects: This convention is appropriate for the typical case where we expect the method to be able to modify the array by rearranging its entries, as in, for example, the `exch()` and `shuffle()` methods that we considered in SECTION 2.1.

*Arrays of objects.* Array entries can be of any type, as we have already seen on several occasions, from `args[]` (an array of strings) in our `main()` implementations, to the array of `Charge` objects in PROGRAM 3.1.7. When we create an array of objects, we do so in two steps:
• Create the array, using the bracket syntax for array constructors
• Create each object in the array, using a standard constructor
For example, we would use the following code to create an array of two `Charge` objects:

```
Charge[] a = new Charge[2];
a[0] = new Charge(.51, .63, 21.3);
a[1] = new Charge(.13, .94, 85.9);
```

Naturally, an array of objects in Java is an array of *references*, not the objects themselves. If the objects are large, then we gain efficiency by not having to move them around, just their references. If they are small, we lose efficiency by having to follow a reference each time we need to get to some information.

*An array of objects*

*Safe pointers.* To provide the capability to manipulate memory addresses that refer to data, many programming languages include the *pointer* (which is like the Java reference) as a primitive data type. Programming with pointers is notoriously error prone, so operations provided for pointers need to be carefully designed to help programmers avoid errors. Java takes this point of view to an extreme (that is favored by many modern programming-language designers). In Java, there is only *one* way to create a reference (new) and only *one* way to change a reference (with an assignment statement). That is, the only things that a programmer can do with references is to create them and copy them. In programming-language jargon, Java references are known as *safe pointers*, because Java can guarantee that each reference points to an object of the specified type. Programmers used to writing code that directly manipulates pointers think of Java as having no pointers at all, but people still debate whether it is really desirable to have unsafe pointers. In short, when you program in Java, you will not be directly accessing pointer values, but if you find yourself doing so in some other language in the future, be careful!

```
Color a =
   new Color(160, 82, 45);
Color b =
   new Color(255, 255, 0);
Color b = a;
```

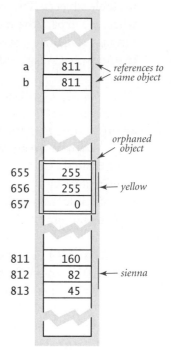

*An orphaned object*

*Orphaned objects.* The ability to assign a new value to a reference variable creates the possibility that a program may have created an object that it can no longer reference. For example, consider the three assignment statements in the figure at right. After the third assignment statement, not only do a and b refer to the same Color object (the one whose RGB values are 160, 82, and 45), but also there is no longer a reference to the Color object that was created and used to initialize b. The only reference to that object was in the variable b, and this reference was overwritten by the assignment, so there is no way to refer to the object again. Such an object is said to be *orphaned*. Objects are also orphaned when they go out of scope. Java programmers pay little attention to orphaned objects because the system automatically reuses the memory that they occupy, as we discuss next.

*Memory management.* Programs tend to create huge numbers of objects (and primitive-type variables) but only have a need for a small number of them at any given point in time. Accordingly, programming languages and systems need mechanisms to *allocate* memory for data type values during the time they are needed and to *free* the memory when they are no longer needed (for an object, sometime after it is orphaned). Memory management is easier for primitive types because all of the information needed for memory allocation is known at compile time. Java (and most other systems) take care of reserving space for variables when they are declared and freeing that space when they go out of scope. Memory management for objects is more complicated: the compiler knows to allocate memory for an object when it is created, but cannot know precisely when to free the memory associated with an object, because the dynamics of a program in execution determine when an object is orphaned.

*Memory leaks.* In many languages (such as C and C++) the programmer is responsible for both allocating and freeing memory. Doing so is tedious and notoriously error-prone. For example, suppose that a program deallocates the memory for an object, but then continues to refer to it (perhaps much later in the program). In the meantime, the system may have allocated the same memory for another use, so all kinds of havoc can result. Another insidious problem occurs when a programmer neglects to ensure that the memory for an orphaned object is deallocated. This bug is known as a *memory leak* because it can result in a steadily increasing amount of memory devoted to orphaned objects (and therefore not available for use). The effect is that performance degrades, just as if memory were leaking out of your computer. Have you ever had to reboot your computer because it was gradually getting less and less responsive? A common cause of such behavior is a memory leak in one of your applications.

*Garbage collection.* One of Java's most significant features is its ability to automatically manage memory. The idea is to free the programmers from the responsibility of managing memory by keeping track of orphaned objects and returning the memory they use to a pool of free memory. Reclaiming memory in this way is known as *garbage collection*, and Java's safe pointer policy enables it to do this efficiently and automatically. Garbage collection is an old idea, but people still debate whether the overhead of automatic garbage collection justifies the convenience of not having to worry about memory management. The same conclusion that we drew for pointers holds: when you program in Java, you will not be writing code to allocate and free memory, but if you find yourself doing so in some other language in the future, be careful!

For reference, we summarize the examples that we have considered in this section in the table below. These examples are chosen to help you understand the essential properties of data types and object-oriented programming.

*A data type is a set of values and a set of operations defined on those values.* With primitive data types, we worked with a small and simple set of values. Colors, pictures, strings, and input-output streams are high-level data types that indicate the breadth of applicability of data abstraction. *You do not need to know how a data type is implemented in order to be able to use it.* Each data type (there are hundreds in the Java libraries, and you will soon learn to create your own) is characterized by an API (application programming interface) that provides the information that you need in order to use it. A client program creates objects that hold data type values and invokes instance methods to manipulate those values. We write client programs with the basic statements and control constructs that you learned in Chapters 1 and 2, but now have the capability to work with a vast variety of data types, not just the primitive ones to which you have grown accustomed.

| API | description |
|---|---|
| Charge | electrical charges |
| Color | colors |
| Picture | digital images |
| String | character strings |
| In | input streams |
| Out | output streams |
| Draw | drawings |

*Summary of data types in this section*

which you have grown accustomed. With experience, you will find that this ability opens up for you new horizons in programming.

Our Charge example indicates that you can tailor one or more data types to the needs of your application. The ability to do so is profound, and also is the subject of the next section. When properly designed and implemented, data types lead to client programs that are clearer, easier to develop, and easier to maintain than equivalent programs that do not take advantage of data abstraction. The client programs in this section are testimony to this claim. Moreover, as you will see in the next section, implementing a data type is a straightforward application of the basic programming skills that you have already learned. In particular, addressing a large and complex application becomes a process of understanding its data and the operations to be performed on it, then writing programs that directly reflect this understanding. Once you have learned to do so, you might wonder how programmers *ever* developed large programs without using data abstraction.

## Q&A

**Q.** Why the distinction between primitive and reference types?

**A.** Performance. Java provides the *wrapper* reference types `Integer`, `Double`, and so forth that correspond to primitive types and can be used by programmers who prefer to ignore the distinction. Primitive types are closer to the types of data that are supported by computer hardware, so programs that use them usually run faster than programs that use corresponding reference types.

**Q.** What happens if I forget to use `new` when creating an object?

**A.** To Java, it looks as though you want to call a static method with a return value of the object type. Since you have not defined such a method, the error message is the same as when you refer to an undefined symbol. If you compile the code

```
Charge c = Charge(.51, .63, 21.3);
```

you get this error message:

```
cannot find symbol
symbol  : method Charge(double,double,double)
```

Constructors do not provide return values (their signature has no return value type)—they can only follow `new`. You get the same kind of error message if you provide the wrong number of arguments to a constructor or method.

**Q.** Why don't we write `StdOut.println(x.toString())` to print objects that are not strings?

**A.** Good question. That code works fine, but Java saves us the trouble of writing it by automatically invoking `toString()` for us anytime a `String` type is needed. This policy implies that every data type must have a `toString()` method. We will discuss in SECTION 3.3. Java's mechanism for ensuring that this is the case.

**Q.** What is the difference between =, ==, and `equals()`?

**A.** The single equals sign (=) is the basis of the assignment statement—you certainly are familiar with that. The double equals sign (==) is a binary operator for checking whether its two operands are identical. If the operands are of a primitive type, the result is true if they have the same value, and false otherwise. If the operands are references, the result is true if they refer to the same object, and false otherwise. That is, we use == to test object identity equality. The data-type method equals() is included in every Java type so that the implementation can provide the capability for clients to test whether two objects have the same *value*. Note that (a == b) implies a.equals(b), but not the other way around.

**Q.** How can I arrange to pass an array to a function in such a way that the function cannot change the array?

**A.** There is no direct way to do so—arrays are mutable. In Section 3.3, you will see how to achieve the same effect by building a wrapper data type and passing a value of that type instead (Vector, in Program 3.3.3).

**Q.** What happens if I forget to use new when creating an array of objects?

**A.** You need to use new for each object that you create, so when you create an array of N objects, you need to use new N+1 times: once for the array and once for each of the N objects. If you forget to create the array:

```
Charge[] a;
a[0] = new Charge(0.51, 0.63, 21.3);
```

you get the same error message that you would get when trying to assign a value to any uninitialized variable:

```
variable a might not have been initialized
        a[0] = new Charge(0.51, 0.63, 21.3);
        ^
```

but if you forget to use new when creating an object within the array and then try to use it to invoke a method:

```
Charge[] a = new Charge[2];
double x = a[0].potentialAt(.5, .5);
```

you get a NullPointerException. As usual, the best way to answer such questions is to write and compile such code yourself, then try to interpret Java's error message. Doing so might help you more quickly recognize mistakes later.

**Q.** Where can I find more details on how Java implements references and garbage collection?

**A.** One Java system might differ completely from another. For example, one natural scheme is to use a pointer (machine address); another is to use a handle (a pointer to a pointer). The former gives faster access to data; the latter provides for better garbage collection.

**Q.** Why red, green, and blue instead of red, *yellow*, and blue?

**A.** In theory, any three colors that contain some amount of each primary would work, but two different schemes have evolved: one (RGB) that has proven to produce good colors on television screens, computer monitors, and digital cameras, and the other (CMYK) that is typically used for the printed page (see EXERCISE 1.2.21). CMYK does include yellow (cyan, magenta, yellow, and black). Two different schemes are appropriate because printed inks *absorb* color, so where there are two different inks there are more colors absorbed and *fewer* reflected; but video displays *emit* color, so where there are two different colored pixels there are *more* colors emitted.

**Q.** What exactly does it mean to `import` a name?

**A.** Not much: it just saves some typing. You could type `java.awt.Color` everywhere in your code instead of using the `import` statement.

**Q.** Is there anything wrong with allocating and deallocating thousands of `Color` objects, as in `Grayscale` (PROGRAM 3.1.4)?

**A.** All programming-language constructs come at some cost. In this case the cost is reasonable, since the time for these allocations is tiny compared to the time to actually draw the picture.

**Q.** Why does the `String` method call `s.substring(i, j)` return the substring of `s` starting at index `i` and ending at `j-1` (and not `j`)?

**A.** Why do the indices of an array `a[]` go from `0` to `a.length-1` instead of from `1` to `length`? Programming-language designers make choices; we live with them.

**3.1.1**   Write a program that takes a `double` value w from the command line, creates four `Charge` objects with charge value 1.0 that are each distance w in each of the four cardinal directions from (.5, .5), and prints the potential at (.25, .5).

**3.1.2**   Write a program that takes from the command line three integers between 0 and 255 that represent red, green, and blue values of a color and then creates and shows a 256-by-256 `Picture` of that color.

**3.1.3**   Modify `AlbersSquares` (PROGRAM 3.1.2) to take *nine* command-line arguments that specify *three* colors and then draws the six squares showing all the Albers squares with the large square in each color and the small square in each different color.

**3.1.4**   Write a program that takes the name of a grayscale picture file as a command-line argument and uses `StdDraw` to plot a histogram of the frequency of occurrence of each of the 256 grayscale intensities.

**3.1.5**   Write a program that takes the name of a picture file as a command-line argument and flips the image horizontally.

**3.1.6**   Write a program that takes the name of an picture file as a command-line input, and creates three images, one that contains only the red components, one for green, and one for blue.

**3.1.7**   Write a program that takes the name of an picture file as a command-line argument and prints the pixel coordinates of the lower left corner and the upper right corner of the smallest bounding box (rectangle parallel to the *x*- and *y*-axes) that contains all of the non-white pixels.

**3.1.8**   Write a program that takes as command line arguments the name of an image file and the pixel coordinates of a rectangle within the image; reads from standard input a list of `Color` values (represented as triples of `int` values); and serves as a filter, printing out those color values for which all pixels in the rectangle are background/foreground compatible. (Such a filter can be used to pick a color for text to label an image.)

**3.1.9** Write a function `isValidDNA()` that takes a string as input and returns `true` if and only if it is comprised entirely of the characters A, C, T, and G.

**3.1.10** Write a function `complementWC()` that takes a DNA string as its inputs and returns its *Watson-Crick complement*: replace A with T, C with G, and vice versa.

**3.1.11** Write a function `palindromeWC()` that takes a DNA string as its input and returns `true` if the string is a Watson-Crick complemented palindrome, and `false` otherwise. A *Watson-Crick complemented palindrome* is a DNA string that is equal to the reverse of its Watson-Crick complement.

**3.1.12** Write a program to check whether an ISBN number is valid (see EXERCISE 1.3.33), taking into account that an ISBN number can have hyphens inserted at arbitrary places.

**3.1.13** What does the following code fragment print?

```
String string1 = "hello";
String string2 = string1;
string1 = "world";
StdOut.println(string1);
StdOut.println(string2);
```

**3.1.14** What does the following code fragment print?

```
String s = "Hello World";
s.toUpperCase();
s.substring(6, 11);
StdOut.println(s);
```

*Answer:* "Hello World". `String` objects are immutable—string methods each return a new `String` object with the appropriate value (but they do not change the value of the object that was used to invoke them). This code ignores the objects returned and just prints the original string. To print "WORLD", use `s = s.toUpperCase()` and `s = s.substring(6, 11)`.

**3.1.15** A string s is a *circular shift* of a string t if it matches when the characters are circularly shifted by any number of positions. For example, ACTGACG is a circular shift of TGACGAC, and vice versa. Detecting this condition is important in the study of genomic sequences. Write a program that checks whether two given strings s and t are circular shifts of one another. *Hint*: The solution is a one-liner with indexOf() and string concatenation.

**3.1.16** Given a string site that represents a website, write a code fragment to determine its domain type. For example, the domain type for the string http://www.cs.princeton.edu/IntroProgramming is edu.

**3.1.17** Write a static method that takes a domain name as argument and returns the reverse domain (reverse the order of the strings between periods). For example, the reverse domain of cs.princeton.edu is edu.princeton.cs. This computation is useful for web log analysis. (See EXERCISE 4.2.35.)

**3.1.18** What does the following recursive function return?

```
public static String mystery(String s)
{
    int N = s.length();
    if (N <= 1) return s;
    String a = s.substring(0, N/2);
    String b = s.substring(N/2, N);
    return mystery(b) + mystery(a);
}
```

**3.1.19** Modify GeneFind to handle all three stop codes (instead of handling them one at a time through the command line). Also add command-line arguments to allow the user to specify lower and upper bounds on the length of the gene sought.

**3.1.20** Write a version of GeneFind based on using the indexOf() method in String to find patterns.

**3.1.21** Write a program that takes a start string and a stop string as command-line arguments and prints all substrings of a given string that start with the first, end with the second, and otherwise contain neither. *Note*: Be especially careful of overlaps!

**3.1.22** Write a filter that reads text from an input stream and prints it to an output stream, removing any lines that consist only of whitespace.

**3.1.23** Modify `Potential` (PROGRAM 3.1.7) to take an integer *N* from the command line and generate *N* random `Charge` objects in the unit square, with potential values drawn randomly from a Gaussian distribution with mean 50 and standard deviation 10.

**3.1.24** Modify `StockQuote` (PROGRAM 3.1.10) to take multiple symbols on the command line.

**3.1.25** The example file `data` used for `Split` (PROGRAM 3.1.11) lists the date, high price, volume, and low price of the Dow Jones stock market average for every day since records have been kept. Download this file from the booksite and write a program that creates two `Draw` objects, one for the prices and one for the volumes, and plots them at a rate taken from the command line.

**3.1.26** Write a program `Merge` that takes a delimiter string followed by an arbitrary number of file names as command line arguments, concatenates the corresponding lines of each file, separated by the delimiter, and then writes the result to standard output, thus performing the opposite operation from `Split` (PROGRAM 3.1.11).

**3.1.27** Find a website that publishes the current temperature in your area, and write a screen-scraper program `Weather` so that typing `java Weather` followed by your zip code will give you a weather forecast.

**3.1.28** Suppose that a[] and b[] are each integer arrays consisting of millions of integers. What does the following code do, and how long does it take?

```
int[] t = a; a = b; b = t;
```

*Answer.* It swaps them, but it does so by copying references, so that it is not necessary to copy millions of elements.

# Creative Exercises

**3.1.29** *Picture filtering.* Write a library RawPicture with read() and write() methods for use with standard input and standard output. The write() method takes a Picture as argument and writes the picture to standard output, using the following format: if the picture is *w*-by-*h*, write *w*, then *h*, then *wh* triples of integers representing the pixel color values, in row major order. The read() method takes no arguments and returns a Picture, which it creates by reading a picture from standard input, in the format just described. *Note*: Be aware that this will use up much more disk space than the picture—the standard formats *compress* this information so that it will not take up so much space.

**3.1.30** *Sound visualization.* Write a program that uses StdAudio and Picture to create an interesting two-dimensional color visualization of a sound file while it is playing. Be creative!

**3.1.31** *Kama Sutra cipher.* Write a filter KamaSutra that takes two strings as command-line argument (the *key* strings), then reads standard input, substitutes for each letter as specified by the key strings, and writes the result to standard output. This operation is the basis for one of the earliest known cryptographic systems. The condition on the key strings is that they must be of equal length and that any letter in standard input must be in one of them. For example, if input is all capital letters and the keys are THEQUICKBROWN and FXJMPSVRLZYDG, then we make the table.

```
T H E Q U I C K B R O W N
F X J M P S V L A Z Y D G
```

which tells us that we should substitute F for T, T for F, H for X, X for H, and so forth when copying the input to the output. The message is encoded by replacing each letter with its pair. For example, the message MEET AT ELEVEN is encoded as QJJF BF JKJCJG. Someone receiving the message can use the same keys to get the message back.

**3.1.32** *Safe password verification.* Write a static method that takes a string as argument and returns true if it meets the following conditions, false otherwise:
  • At least eight characters long
  • Contains at least one digit (0-9)
  • Contains at least one upper-case letter

• Contains at least one lower-case letter
• Contains at least one character that is neither a letter nor a number
Such checks are commonly used for passwords on the web.

**3.1.33** *Color study.* Write a program that displays the color study shown at right, which gives Albers squares corresponding to each of the 256 levels of blue and gray that were used to print this book.

**3.1.34** *Entropy.* The *Shannon entropy* measures the information content of an input string and plays a cornerstone role in information theory and data compression. Given a string of $N$ characters, let $f_c$ be the frequency of occurrence of character $c$ The quantity $p_c = f_c / N$ is an estimate of the probability that $c$ would be in the string if it were a random string, and the entropy is defined to be the sum of the quantity $-p_c \log_2 p_c$, over all characters that appear in the string. The entropy is said to measure the *information content* of a string: if each character appears the same number times, the entropy is at its minimum value. Write a program that computes

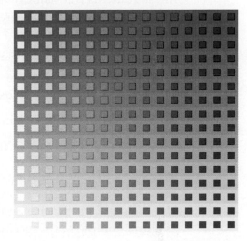

*A color study*

and prints the entropy of the string on standard input. Run your program on a web page that you read regularly, a recent paper that you wrote, and on the fruit fly genome found on the website.

**3.1.35** *Minimize potential.* Write a function that takes an array of `Charge` objects with positive potential as its argument and finds a point such that the potential at that point is within 1% of the minimum potential anywhere in the unit square. Use a `Charge` object to return this information. Add a call to this function and print out the point coordinates and charge value for the data given in the text and for the random charges described in EXERCISE 3.1.23.

**3.1.36** *Slide show.* Write a program that takes the names of several image files as command-line arguments and displays them in a slide show (one every two seconds), using a fade effect to black and a fade from black between pictures

**3.1.37** *Tile.* Write a program that takes the name of an image file and two integers $M$ and $N$ as command-line arguments and creates an $M$-by-$N$ tiling of the picture.

**3.1.38** *Rotation filter.* Write a program that takes two command-line arguments (the name of an image file and a real number theta) and rotates the image $\theta$ degrees counterclockwise. To rotate, copy the color of each pixel $(s_i, s_j)$ in the source image to a target pixel $(t_i, t_j)$ whose coordinates are given by the following formulas:

*rotate 30 degrees*

$$t_i = (s_i - c_i)\cos\theta - (s_j - c_j)\sin\theta + c_i$$

$$t_j = (s_i - c_i)\sin\theta + (s_j - c_j)\cos\theta + c_j$$

where $(c_i, c_j)$ is the center of the image.

**3.1.39** *Swirl filter.* Creating a swirl effect is similar to rotation, except that the angle changes as a function of distance to the center. Use the same formulas as in the previous exercise, but compute $\theta$ as a function of $(s_i, s_j)$, specifically $\pi/256$ times the distance to the center.

*swirl filter*

**3.1.40** *Wave filter.* Write a filter like those in the previous two exercises that creates a wave effect, by copying the color of each pixel $(s_i, s_j)$ in the source image to a target pixel $(t_i, t_j)$, where $t_i = s_i$ and $t_j = s_j + 20\sin(2\pi s_j/128)$. Add code to take the amplitude (20 in the accompanying figure) and the frequency (128 in the accompanying figure) as command-line arguments. Experiment with various values of these parameters.

*wave filter*

*glass filter*

**3.1.41** *Glass filter.* Write a program that takes the name of an image file as a command-line argument and applies a *glass filter*: set each pixel $p$ to the color of a random neighboring pixel (whose pixel coordinates both differ from $p$'s coordinates by at most 5).

*Exercises in filtering*

**3.1.42** *Morph.* The example images in the text for Fade do not quite line up in the vertical direction (the mandrill's mouth is much lower than Darwin's). Modify Fade to add a transformation in the vertical dimension that makes a smoother transition.

**3.1.43** *Digital zoom.* Write a program Zoom that takes the name of an image file and three numbers $s$, $x$, and $y$ as command-line arguments and shows an output image that zooms in on a portion of the input image. The numbers are all between 0 and 1, with $s$ to be interpreted as a scale factor and $(x, y)$ as the relative coordinates of the point that is to be at the center of the output image. Use this program to zoom in on your dog or a friend in some digital image on your computer. (If your image came from a cell phone or an old camera, you may not be able to zoom in too close without having visible artifacts from scaling.)

java Zoom pup.jpg 1 .5 .5

java Zoom pup.jpg .3 .40 .45

java Zoom pup.jpg .1 .39 .47

*Digital zoom*

**3.1.44** *Edge detection.* An edge is an area of a picture with a strong contrast or discontinuity in intensity from one pixel to the next. Finding the edges of an image is a fundamental problem in image processing and computer vision because edges characterize the object boundaries. Write a program EdgeDetect that takes the name of an image file and produces an image with the edges highlighted.

java Picture kitten.jpg

java EdgeDetect kitten.jpg

*Edge detection*

# 3.2 Creating Data Types

IN PRINCIPLE, WE COULD WRITE ALL of our programs using only the eight built-in primitive types, but, as we saw in the last section, it is much more convenient to write programs at a higher level of abstraction. Thus, a variety of data types are built into the Java language and libraries. Still, we certainly cannot expect Java to contain every conceivable data type that we might ever wish to use, so we need to be able to *define* our own. The purpose of this section is to explain how to build data types with the familiar Java `class`.

Implementing a data type as a Java class is not very different from implementing a function library as a set of static methods. The primary difference is that we associate *data* with the method implementations. The API specifies the methods that we need to implement, but we are free to choose any convenient representation. To cement the basic concepts, we begin by considering the implementation of the data type for charged particles that we introduced at the beginning of SECTION 3.1. Next, we illustrate the process of creating data types by considering a range of examples, from complex numbers to stock accounts, including a number of software tools that we will use later in the book. Useful client code is testimony to the value of any data type, so we also consider a number of clients, including one that depicts the famous and fascinating *Mandelbrot set*.

The process of defining a data type is known as *data abstraction* (as opposed to the *function abstraction* style that is the basis of CHAPTER 2). We focus on the data and implement operations on that data. *Whenever you can clearly separate data and associated operations within a program, you should do so.* Modeling physical objects or familiar mathematical abstractions is straightforward and extremely useful, but the true power of data abstraction is that it allows us to model *anything* that we can precisely specify. Once you gain experience with this style of programming, you will see that it naturally helps us address programming challenges of arbitrary complexity.

**Basic elements of a data type**    To illustrate the process of implementing a data type in a Java `class`, we discuss in detail an implementation of the `Charge` data type of SECTION 3.1. We have already considered client programs that demonstrate the utility of having such a data type (in PROGRAMS 3.1.1 and 3.1.7)—now we focus on the *implementation* details. Every data-type implementation that you will develop has the same basic ingredients as this simple example.

*API.*  The application programming interface is the contract with all clients and, therefore, the starting point for any implementation. To emphasize that APIs are critical for implementations, we repeat here our example `Charge` API:

```
public class Charge

        Charge(double x0, double y0, double q0)

  double  potentialAt(double x, double y)    electric potential at (x, y) due to charge

  String  toString()                         string representation
```

*API for charged particles* (*see* PROGRAM 3.2.1)

To implement `Charge`, we need to define the data type values, implement the constructor that creates objects having specified values, and implement two methods that manipulate those values. When faced with the problem of creating a completely new class for some application, the first step is to develop an API. This step is a design activity that we will address in SECTION 3.3. We need to design APIs with care because after we implement classes and write client programs that use them, we *do not change the API*, because that would imply changing all clients.

*Class.*  The data-type implementation is a Java `class`. As with the libraries of static methods that we have been using, we put the code for a data type in a file with the same name as the class, followed by the `.java` extension. We have been implementing Java classes, but the classes that we have been implementing do not have the key features of data types: *instance variables*, *constructors*, and *instance methods*. Instance variables are similar to the variables that we have been using in our program, and constructors and methods are similar to functions, but their effect is quite different. Each of these building blocks is also qualified by an *access* (or *visibility*) *modifier*. We next consider these four concepts, with examples.

*Access modifiers.* The keywords `public`, `private`, and `final` that sometimes precede class and variable names are known as *access modifiers*. The `public` and `private` modifiers control access from client code: we designate every instance variable and method within a class as either `public` (this entity is accessible by clients) or `private` (this entity is not accessible by clients). The `final` modifier indicates that the value of the variable will not change once it is initialized—its access is read-only. Our convention is to use `public` for the constructors and methods in the API (since we are promising to provide them to clients) and `private` for everything else. Typically, our private methods are helper methods used to simplify code in other methods in the class. Java is not so restrictive on its usage of modifiers—we defer to SECTION 3.3 a discussion of our reasons for these conventions.

*Instance variables.* To write code for the methods that manipulate data type values, the first thing that we need is to declare variables that we can use to refer to these values in code. These variables can be any type of data. We declare the types and names of these *instance variables* in the same way as we declare local variables: for `Charge`, we use three `double` values, two to describe the charge's position in the plane and one to describe the amount of charge. These declarations appear as the first statements in the class, not inside `main()` or any other method. There is a critical distinction between instance variables and the local variables within a static method or a block that you are accustomed to: there is just *one* value corresponding to each local variable at a given time, but there are *numerous* values corresponding to each instance variable (one for each object that is an instance of the data type). There is no ambiguity with this arrangement, because each time that we invoke an instance method, we do so with an object name—that object is the one whose value we are manipulating.

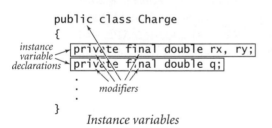

*Constructors.* A constructor creates an object and provides a reference to that object. Java automatically invokes a constructor when a client program uses the keyword `new`. Java does most of the work: our code only needs to initialize the instance variables to meaningful values. Constructors always share the same name as the class, but we can overload the name and have multiple constructors with different signatures, just as with static methods. To the client, the combination of

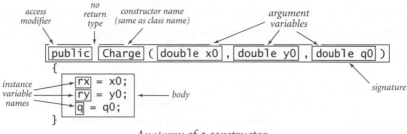

*Anatomy of a constructor*

new followed by a constructor name (with argument values enclosed within parentheses) is the same as a function call that returns a value of the corresponding type.
A constructor signature has no return type, because constructors always return
a reference to an object of its data type (the name of the type, the class, and the
constructor are all the same). Each time that a client invokes a constructor, Java
automatically:

• Allocates memory space for the object
• Invokes the constructor code to initialize the instance variables
• Returns a reference to the object

The constructor in Charge is typical: it initializes the instance variables with the
values provided by the client as arguments.

*Instance methods.* To implement instance methods, we write code that is precisely like the code that we learned in CHAPTER 2 to implement static methods (functions). Each method has a signature (which specifies its return type and the types
and names of its argument variables) and a body (which consists of a sequence of

*Anatomy of an instance method*

statements, including a return statement that provides a value of the return type back to the client). When a client invokes a method, the system initializes the argument variables with client values; executes statements until reaching a `return` statement; and returns the computed value to the client, with the same effect as if the method invocation in the client were replaced with that return value. All of this action is the same as for static methods, but there is one critical distinction for instance methods: *they can perform operations on instance variables.*

*Variables within methods.* Accordingly, the Java code that we write to implement instance methods uses *three* kinds of variables:
- Argument variables
- Local variables
- *Instance variables*

The first two are the same as for static methods: argument variables are specified in the method signature and initialized with client values when the method is called, and local variables are declared and initialized within the method body. The scope of argument variables is the entire method; the scope of local variables is the following statements in the block where they are defined. Instance variables are completely different: they hold data-type values for objects in a class, and their scope is the entire class. How do we specify which object's value we want to use? If you think for a moment about this question, you will recall the answer. Each object in the class has a value: the code in a class method refers to the value *for the object that was used to invoke the method.* When we say `c1.potentialAt(x, y)`, the code in `potentialAt()` is referring to the instance variables for `c1`. The code in `potentialAt()` uses all three kinds of variable names, as summarized in this table:

| variable | purpose | example | scope |
|----------|---------|---------|-------|
| instance | specify data-type value | `rx, ry` | class |
| argument | pass value from client to method | `x, y` | method |
| local | temporary use within method | `dx, dy` | block |

*Variables within instance methods*

*Be sure that you understand the distinctions among these three kinds of variables. These differences are a key to object-oriented programming.*

## Program 3.2.1  Charged-particle implementation

```
public class Charge
{
    private final double rx, ry;
    private final double q;

    public Charge(double x0, double y0, double q0)
    {  rx = x0; ry = y0; q = q0;  }

    public double potentialAt(double x, double y)
    {
        double k = 8.99e09;
        double dx = x - rx;
        double dy = y - ry;
        return k * q / Math.sqrt(dx*dx + dy*dy);
    }

    public String toString()
    {
        return q + " at " + "(" + rx + ", " + ry + ")";
    }

    public static void main(String[] args)
    {
        double x = Double.parseDouble(args[0]);
        double y = Double.parseDouble(args[1]);
        Charge c1 = new Charge(.51, .63, 21.3);
        Charge c2 = new Charge(.13, .94, 81.9);
        double v1 = c1.potentialAt(x, y);
        double v2 = c2.potentialAt(x, y);
        StdOut.printf("%.1e\n", (v1 + v2));
    }
}
```

| | |
|---|---|
| rx, ry | *query point* |
| q | *charge* |

| | |
|---|---|
| k | *electrostatic constant* |
| dx, dy | *delta distances to query point* |

| | |
|---|---|
| x, y | *query point* |
| c1 | *first charge* |
| v1 | *potential due to c1* |
| c2 | *second charge* |
| v2 | *potential due to c2* |

*This implementation of our data type for charged particles contains the basic elements found in every data type: instance variables* rx, ry, *and* q; *a constructor* Charge(); *instance methods* potentialAt() *and* toString(); *and a test client* main() *(see also Program 3.1.1).*

```
% java Charge .2 .5
2.2e+12
% java Charge .51 .94
2.5e+12
```

THESE ARE THE BASIC COMPONENTS THAT you need to understand to be able to build data types in Java. Every data-type implementation (Java class) that we will consider has instance variables, constructors, instance methods, and a test client. In each data type that we develop, we go through the same steps. Rather than thinking about what action we need to take next to accomplish a computational goal (as we did when first learning to program), we think about the needs of a client, then accommodate them in a data type.

The first step in creating a data type is to specify an API. The purpose of the API is to *separate clients from implementations*, to enable modular programming. We have two goals when specifying an API. First, we want to enable clear and correct client code. Indeed, it is a good idea to write some client code before finalizing the API to gain confidence that the specified data-type operations are the ones that clients need. Second, we want to be able to implement the operations. There is no point specifying operations that we have no idea how to implement.

The second step in creating a data type is to implement a Java class that meets the API specifications. First, we choose the instance variables, then we write the code that manipulates the instance variables to implement the specified methods.

The third step in creating a data type is to write test clients, to validate the design decisions made in the first two steps.

In this section, we start each example with an API, and then consider implementations, then clients. You will find many exercises at the end of this section intended to give you experience with data-type creation. SECTION 3.3 is an overview of the design process and related language mechanisms.

What are the values that define the type, and what operations do clients need to perform on those values? With these basic decisions made, you can create new data types and write clients that use the data types that you have defined in the same way as you have been using built-in types.

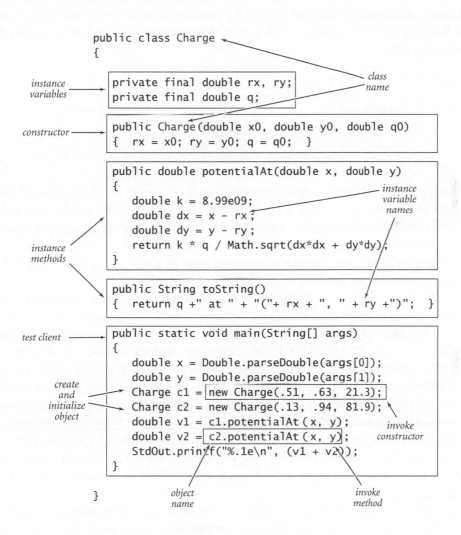

```
                     public class Charge
                     {
                                                                              class
instance                 private final double rx, ry;                        name
variables                private final double q;

constructor              public Charge(double x0, double y0, double q0)
                         {  rx = x0; ry = y0; q = q0;   }

                         public double potentialAt(double x, double y)
                         {
                                                                          instance
                             double k = 8.99e09;                          variable
                             double dx = x - rx;                          names
                             double dy = y - ry;
                             return k * q / Math.sqrt(dx*dx + dy*dy);
instance                 }
methods
                         public String toString()
                         {  return q +" at " + "("+ rx + ", " + ry +")";   }

test client              public static void main(String[] args)
                         {
                             double x = Double.parseDouble(args[0]);
                             double y = Double.parseDouble(args[1]);
create                       Charge c1 = new Charge(.51, .63, 21.3);
and                          Charge c2 = new Charge(.13, .94, 81.9);
initialize                   double v1 = c1.potentialAt(x, y);
object                       double v2 = c2.potentialAt(x, y);         invoke
                             StdOut.printf("%.1e\n", (v1 + v2));        constructor
                         }
                     }
                           object                          invoke
                           name                            method
```

*Anatomy of a class*

**Stopwatch**    One of the hallmarks of object-oriented programming is the idea
of easily modeling real-world objects by creating abstract programming objects.
As a simple example, consider `Stopwatch` (PROGRAM 3.3.2), which implements the
following API:

```
public class Stopwatch
```
---

|                    `Stopwatch()` | *create a new stopwatch and start it running* |
|---|---|
| `double  elapsedTime()` | *return the elapsed time since creation, in seconds* |

*API for stopwatches (see* PROGRAM 3.2.2*)*

In other words, a `Stopwatch` is a stripped-down version of an old-fashioned stopwatch. When you create one, it starts running, and you can ask it how long it has
been running by invoking the method `elapsedTime()`. You might imagine adding
all sorts of bells and whistles to `Stopwatch`, limited only by your imagination. Do
you want to be able to reset the stopwatch? Start and stop it? Include a lap timer?
These sorts of things are easy to add (see EXERCISE 3.2.11).

   The implementation in PROGRAM 3.2.2 uses the Java system method `System.`
`currentTimeMillis()`, which (as well-described by its name) returns a `long` value
giving the current time in milliseconds (the number of milliseconds since midnight on January 1, 1970 UTC). The data-type implementation could hardly be
simpler. A `Stopwatch` saves its creation time in an instance variable, then returns
the difference between that time and the current time whenever a client invokes
its `elapsedTime()` method. A `Stopwatch` itself does not actually tick (an internal
system clock on your computer does all the ticking for all `Stopwatch` objects and
many other data types); it just creates the illusion that it does for clients. Why not
just use `System.currentTimeMillis()` in clients? We could do so, but using the
higher-level `Stopwatch` abstraction leads to client code that is easier to understand
and maintain.

   The test client is typical. It creates two `Stopwatch` objects, uses them to measure the running time of two different computations, then prints the ratio of the
running times. The question of whether one approach to solving a problem is better than another has been lurking since the first few programs that you have run,
and plays an essential role in program development. In SECTION 4.1, we will develop
a scientific approach to understanding the cost of computation. `Stopwatch` is a
useful tool in that approach.

---

*Program 3.2.2   Stopwatch*

---

```
public class Stopwatch
{
   private final long start;
   public Stopwatch()
   {  start = System.currentTimeMillis();  }
   public double elapsedTime()
   {
       long now = System.currentTimeMillis();
       return (now - start) / 1000.0;
   }
   public static void main(String[] args)
   {
      int N = Integer.parseInt(args[0]);

      double totalMath = 0.0;
      Stopwatch swMath = new Stopwatch();
      for (int i = 0; i < N; i++)
         totalMath += Math.sqrt(i);
      double timeMath = swMath.elapsedTime();

      double totalNewton = 0.0;
      Stopwatch swNewton = new Stopwatch();
      for (int i = 0; i < N; i++)
         totalNewton += Newton.sqrt(i);
      double timeNewton = swNewton.elapsedTime();

      StdOut.println(totalNewton/totalMath);
      StdOut.println(timeNewton/timeMath);
   }
}
```

| start | creation time |
|-------|---------------|

---

*This class implements a simple data type that we can use to compare running times of performance-critical methods (see Section 4.1). The test client compares the method for computing square roots in Java's* Math *library with our implementation from Program 2.1.1 that uses Newton's method for the task of computing the sum of the square roots of the numbers from 0 to N-1. For this quick test, the Java implementation* Math.sqrt() *is about 20 times faster than our* Newton.sqrt() *(as it should be!).*

```
% java Stopwatch 1000000
1.0
19.961538461538463
```

**Histogram**   Data-type instance variables can be arrays. As an illustration, consider `Histogram` (PROGRAM 3.2.3), which maintains an array of the frequency of occurrence of integer values in a given interval $[0, N)$ and uses `StdStats.plotBars()` to display a histogram of the values, controlled by this API:

```
public class Histogram
```
---
|  | `Histogram(int N)` | *create a dynamic histogram for the N int values in [0, N)* |
|---|---|---|
| `double` | `addDataPoint(int i)` | *add an occurrence of the value i* |
| `void` | `draw()` | *draw the histogram using standard draw* |

*API for histograms (see* PROGRAM 3.2.3)

By creating a simple class such as `Histogram`, we reap the benefits of modular programming (reusable code, independent development of small programs, and so forth) that we discussed in CHAPTER 2, with the additional benefit that we also separate the *data*. A histogram client need not maintain the data (or know anything about its representation); it just creates a histogram and calls `addDataPoint()`.

When studying this code and the next several examples, it is best to carefully consider the client code. Each class that we implement essentially extends the Java language, allowing us to declare variables of the new data type, instantiate them with values, and perform operations on them. All client programs are conceptually the same as the first programs that you learned that use primitive types and built-in operations. Now you have the ability to define whatever types and operations you need in your client code! In this case, using `Histogram` actually *enhances* readability of the client code, as the `addDataPoint()` call focuses attention on the data being studied. Without `Histogram`, we would have to mix the code for creating the histogram with the code for the computation of interest, resulting in a program much more difficult to understand and maintain than the two separate programs. *Whenever you can clearly separate data and associated operations within a program, you should do so.*

Once you understand how a data type will be used in client code, you can consider the implementation. An implementation is characterized by its instance variables (data type values). `Histogram` maintains an array with the frequency of each point and a `double` value `max` that stores the height of the tallest bar (for scaling). Its private `draw()` method scales the drawing and then plots the frequencies.

**Program 3.2.3   Histogram**

```java
public class Histogram
{
    private final double[] freq;
    private double max;

    public Histogram(int N)
    {  // Create a new histogram.
       freq = new double[N];
    }

    public void addDataPoint(int i)
    {  // Add one occurrence of the value i.
       freq[i]++;
       if (freq[i] > max) max = freq[i];
    }

    public void draw()
    {  // Draw (and scale) the histogram.
       StdDraw.setYscale(0, max);
       StdStats.plotBars(freq);
    }

    public static void main(String[] args)
    {  // See Program 2.2.6.
       int N = Integer.parseInt(args[0]);
       int T = Integer.parseInt(args[1]);
       Histogram histogram = new Histogram(N+1);
       for (int t = 0; t < T; t++)
           histogram.addDataPoint(Bernoulli.binomial(N));
       StdDraw.setCanvasSize(500, 100);
       histogram.draw();
    }
}
```

| freq[] | *frequency counts* |
|---|---|
| max | *maximum frequency* |

% java Histogram 50 1000000

*This data type supports simple client code to create dynamic histograms of the frequency of occurrence of values in [0, N). The frequencies are kept in an instance-variable array, and an instance variable max tracks the maximum frequency (for scaling). To make a dynamically changing histogram, add a call to StdDraw.clear() before and a call to StdDraw.show(20) after the call to histogram.draw() in the client code..*

**Turtle graphics**   *Whenever you can clearly separate tasks within a program, you should do so.* In object-oriented programming, we extend that mantra to include *state* with the tasks. A small amount of state can be immensely valuable in simplifying a computation. Next, we consider *turtle graphics*, which is based on the data type defined by this API:

```
public class Turtle
```
---

| | |
|---|---|
| Turtle(double x0, double y0, double a0) | *create a new turtle at $(x_0, y_0)$ facing $a_0$ degrees counterclockwise from the x-axis* |
| void turnLeft(double delta) | *rotate* delta *degrees counterclockwise* |
| void goForward(double step) | *move distance* step, *drawing a line* |

*API for turtle graphics (see* PROGRAM 3.2.4)

Imagine a turtle that lives in the unit square and draws lines as it moves. It can move a specified distance in a straight line, or it can rotate left (counterclockwise) a specified number of degrees. According to the API, when we create a turtle, we place it at a specified point, facing a specified direction. Then, we create drawings by giving the turtle a sequence of goForward() and turnLeft() commands.

```
double x0   = 0.5;
double y0   = 0.0;
double a0   = 60.0;
double step = Math.sqrt(3)/2;
Turtle t    = new Turtle(x0, y0, a0);
t.goForward(step);
```

For example, to draw a triangle we create a Turtle at (0, .5) facing at an angle of 60 degrees counterclockwise from the origin, then direct it to take a step forward, then rotate 120 degrees counterclockwise, then take another step forward, then rotate another 120 degrees counterclockwise, and then take a third step forward to complete the triangle. Indeed, all of the turtle clients that we will examine simply create a turtle, then give it an alternating series of step and rotate commands, varying the step size and the amount of rotation. As you will see in the next several pages, this simple model

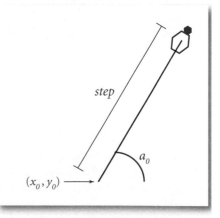

*A turtle's first step*

allows us to create arbitrarily complex drawings, with many important applications.

Turtle (PROGRAM 3.2.4) is an implementation of this API that uses StdDraw. It maintains three instance variables: the coordinates of the turtle's position and the current direction it is facing, measured in degrees counterclockwise from the *x*-axis. Implementing the two methods requires *updating* the values of these variables, so they are not final. The necessary updates are straightforward: turnLeft(delta) adds delta to the current angle, and goForward(step) adds the step size times the cosine of its argument to the current *x*-coordinate and the step size times the sine of its argument to the current *y*-coordinate.

The test client in Turtle takes an integer N as command-line argument and draws a regular polygon with N sides. If you are interested in elementary analytic geometry, you might enjoy verifying that fact. Whether or not you choose to do so, think about what you would need to do to compute the coordinates of all the points in the polygon. The simplicity of the turtle's approach is very appealing. In short, turtle graphics serves as a useful abstraction for describing geometric shapes of all sorts. For example, we obtain a good approximation to a circle by taking *N* to a sufficiently large value.

You can use a Turtle as you use any other object. Programs can create arrays of Turtle objects, pass them as arguments to functions, and so forth. Our examples will illustrate these capabilities and convince you that creating a data type like Turtle is both very easy and very useful. For each of them, as with regular polygons, it is *possible* to compute the coordinates of all the points and draw straight lines to get the drawings, but it is *easier* to do so with a Turtle. Turtle graphics exemplifies the value of data abstraction.

`t.goForward(step);`

`t.turnLeft(120.0);`

`t.goForward(step);`

`t.turnLeft(120.0);`

`t.goForward(step);`

*Your first turtle graphics drawing*

$(x_0 + d \cos \alpha, y_0 + d \sin \alpha)$

$d$

$d \sin \alpha$

$\alpha$

$(x_0, y_0)$

$d \cos \alpha$

*Turtle trigonometry*

*Program 3.2.4*    *Turtle graphics*

| x, y | position (in unit square) |
|------|---------------------------|
| angle | direction of motion (degrees, counterclockwise from x axis) |

```
public class Turtle
{
    private double x, y;
    private double angle;

    public Turtle(double x0, double y0, double a0)
    {  x = x0; y = y0; angle = a0;  }

    public void turnLeft(double delta)
    {  angle += delta;  }

    public void goForward(double step)
    {  // Compute new position, move and draw line to it.
       double oldx = x, oldy = y;
       x += step * Math.cos(Math.toRadians(angle));
       y += step * Math.sin(Math.toRadians(angle));
       StdDraw.line(oldx, oldy, x, y);
    }

    public static void main(String[] args)
    {  // Draw an N-gon.
       int N = Integer.parseInt(args[0]);
       double angle = 360.0 / N;
       double step = Math.sin(Math.toRadians(angle/2));
       Turtle turtle = new Turtle(.5, .0, angle/2);
       for (int i = 0; i < N; i++)
       {
          turtle.goForward(step);
          turtle.turnLeft(angle);
       }
    }
}
```

*This data type supports turtle graphics, which often simplifies the creation of drawings.*

% java Turtle 3                   % java Turtle 7                   % java Turtle 1000

*Recursive graphics.* A *Koch curve* of order 0 is a straight line. To form a Koch curve of order $n$, draw a Koch curve of order $n-1$, turn left 60 degrees, draw a second Koch curve of order $n-1$, turn right 120 degrees (left -120 degrees), draw a third Koch curve of order $n-1$, turn left 60 degrees, and draw a fourth Koch curve of order $n-1$. These recursive instructions lead immediately to turtle client code. With appropriate modifications, recursive schemes like this have proven useful in modeling self-similar patterns found in nature, such as snowflakes.

The client code below is straightforward, except for the value of the step size sz. If you carefully examine the first few examples, you will see (and be able to prove by induction) that the width of the curve of order $n$ is $3^n$ times the step size, so setting the step size to $1/3^n$ produces a curve of width 1. Similarly, the number of steps in a curve of order $n$ is $4^n$, so Koch will not finish if you invoke it for large $n$.

You can find many examples of recursive patterns of this sort that have been studied and developed by mathematicians, scientists, and artists from many cultures in many contexts. Here, our interest in them is that the turtle graphics abstraction greatly simplifies client code that draws them.

```
public class Koch                                              0
{
    public static void koch(int n, double step, Turtle turtle)
    {
        if (n == 0)
        {                                                      1
            turtle.goForward(step);
            return;
        }
        koch(n-1, step, turtle);
        turtle.turnLeft(60.0);                                 2
        koch(n-1, step, turtle);
        turtle.turnLeft(-120.0);
        koch(n-1, step, turtle);
        turtle.turnLeft(60.0);
        koch(n-1, step, turtle);                               3
    }

    public static void main(String[] args)
    {                                                          4
        int n = Integer.parseInt(args[0]);
        double step = 1.0 / Math.pow(3.0, n);
        Turtle turtle = new Turtle(0.0, 0.0, 0.0);
        koch(n, step, turtle);
    }
}
```

*Drawing Koch curves with turtle graphics*

*Spira mirabilis.* Perhaps the turtle is a bit tired after taking $4^n$ steps to draw a Koch curve. Accordingly, imagine that the turtle's step size decays by a tiny constant factor each time that it takes a step. What happens to our drawings? Remarkably, modifying the polygon-drawing test client in PROGRAM 3.2.4 to answer this question leads to an image known as a *logarithmic spiral*, a curve that is found in many contexts in nature.

Spiral (PROGRAM 3.2.5) is an implementation of this curve. It takes N and the decay factor as command-line arguments and instructs the turtle to alternately step and turn until it has wound around itself 10 times. As you can see from the four examples given with the program, the path spirals into the center of the drawing. The argument N controls the shape of the spiral. You are encouraged to experiment with Spiral yourself in order to develop an understanding of the way in which the parameters control the behavior of the spiral.

The logarithmic spiral was first described by René Descartes in 1638. Jacob Bernoulli was so amazed by its mathematical properties that he named it the *spira mirabilis* (miraculous spiral) and even asked to have it engraved on his tombstone. Many people also consider it to be "miraculous" that this precise curve is clearly present in a broad variety of natural phenomena. Three examples are depicted below: the chambers of a nautilus shell, the arms of a spiral galaxy, and the cloud formation in a tropical storm. Scientists have also observed it as the path followed by a hawk approaching its prey and the path followed by a charged particle moving perpendicular to a uniform magnetic field.

One of the goals of scientific enquiry is to provide simple but accurate models of complex natural phenomena. Our tired turtle certainly passes that test!

*nautilus shell*　　*galaxy*　　*storm*

*Examples of the spira mirabilis in nature*

*Program 3.2.5* *Spira mirabilis*

```
public class Spiral
{
   public static void main(String[] args)
   {
      int N        = Integer.parseInt(args[0]);
      double decay = Double.parseDouble(args[1]);
      double angle = 360.0 / N;
      double step  = Math.sin(Math.toRadians(angle/2));
      Turtle turtle = new Turtle(0.5, 0, angle/2);

      for (int i = 0; i < 10 * 360 / angle; i++)
      {
         step /= decay;
         turtle.goForward(step);
         turtle.turnLeft(angle);
      }
   }
}
```

| step | *step size* |
| decay | *decay factor* |
| angle | *rotation amount* |
| turtle | *tired turtle* |

*This code is a modification of the test client in Program 3.2.4 that decreases the step size at each step and cycles around 10 times. The angle controls the shape; the decay controls the nature of the spiral.*

% java Spiral 3 1.0

% java Spiral 3 1.2

% java Spiral 1440 1.00004

% java Spiral 1440 1.0004

*Brownian motion.* Or, perhaps the turtle has had one too many. Accordingly, imagine that the disoriented turtle (again following its standard alternating turn and step regimen) turns in a *random* direction before each step. Again, it is easy to plot the path followed by such a turtle for millions of steps, and again, such paths are found in nature in many contexts. In 1827, the botanist Robert Brown observed through a microscope that pollen grains immersed in water seemed to move about in just such a random fashion, which later became known as *Brownian motion* and led to Albert Einstein's insights into the atomic nature of matter.

Or perhaps our turtle has friends, all of whom have had one too many. After they have wandered around for a sufficiently long time, their paths merge together and become indistinguishable from a single path. Astrophysicists today are using this model to understand observed properties of distant galaxies.

TURTLE GRAPHICS WAS ORIGINALLY DEVELOPED BY Seymour Papert at MIT in the 1960s as part of an educational programming language, LOGO, that is still used today in toys. But turtle graphics is no toy, as we have just seen in numerous scientific examples. Turtle graphics also has numerous commercial applications. For example, it is the basis for POSTSCRIPT, a programming language for creating printed pages that is used for most newspapers, magazines, and books. In the present context, `Turtle` is a quintessential object-oriented programming example, showing that a small amount of saved state (data abstraction using objects, not just functions) can vastly simplify a computation.

10000 .01

```
public class DrunkenTurtle
{
    public static void main(String[] args)
    {
        int T = Integer.parseInt(args[0]);
        double step = Double.parseDouble(args[1]);
        Turtle turtle = new Turtle(0.5, 0.5, 0.0);
        for (int t = 0; t < T; t++)
        {
            turtle.turnLeft(360.0 * Math.random());
            turtle.goForward(step);
        }
    }
}
```

*Brownian motion of a drunken turtle (moving a fixed distance in a random direction)*

```
public class DrunkenTurtles
{
   public static void main(String[] args)
   {
      int N = Integer.parseInt(args[0]);        // number of turtles
      int T = Integer.parseInt(args[1]);        // number of steps
      double step = Double.parseDouble(args[2]);  // step size
      Turtle[] turtles = new Turtle[N];
      for (int i = 0; i < N; i++)
         turtles[i] = new Turtle(Math.random(), Math.random(), 0.0);
      for (int t = 0; t < T; t++)
      {  // All turtles take one step.
         for (int i = 0; i < N; i++)
         {  // Turtle i takes one step in a random direction.
            turtles[i].turnLeft(360.0 * Math.random());
            turtles[i].goForward(step);
         }
      }
   }
}
```

20 500 .005

20 5000 .005

20 1000 .005

*Brownian motion of a bale of drunken turtles*

**Complex numbers**    A *complex number* is a number of the form $x + iy$, where $x$ and $y$ are real numbers and $i$ is the square root of $-1$. The number $x$ is known as the *real* part of the complex number, and the number $y$ is known as the *imaginary* part. This terminology stems from the idea that the square root of $-1$ has to be an imaginary number, because no real number can have this value. Complex numbers are a quintessential mathematical abstraction: whether or not one believes that it makes sense physically to take the square root of $-1$, complex numbers help us understand the natural world. They are used extensively in applied mathematics and play an essential role in many branches of science and engineering. They are used to model physical systems of all sorts, from circuits to sound waves to electromagnetic fields. These models typically require extensive computations involving manipulating complex numbers according to well-defined arithmetic operations, so we want to write computer programs to do the computations. In short, we need a new data type.

Developing a data type for complex numbers is a prototypical example of object-oriented programming. No programming language can provide implementations of every mathematical abstraction that we might need, but the ability to implement data types give us not just the ability to write programs to easily manipulate abstractions such as complex numbers, polynomials, vectors, matrices, but also the freedom to think in terms of new abstractions.

The operations on complex numbers that are needed for basic computations are to add and multiply them by applying the commutative, associative, and distributive laws of algebra (along with the identity $i^2 = -1$); to compute the magnitude; and to extract the real and imaginary parts, according to the following equations:

- *Addition*: $(x+iy) + (v+iw) = (x+v) + i(y+w)$
- *Multiplication*: $(x + iy) * (v + iw) = (xv - yw) + i(yv + xw)$
- *Magnitude*: $|x + iy| = \sqrt{x^2 + y^2}$
- *Real part*: $\mathrm{Re}(x + iy) = x$
- *Imaginary part*: $\mathrm{Im}(x + iy) = y$

For example, if $a = 3 + 4i$ and $b = -2 + 3i$, then $a + b = 1 + 7i$, $a * b = -18 + i$, $\mathrm{Re}(a) = 3$, $\mathrm{Im}(a) = 4$, and $|a| = 5$.

With these basic definitions, the path to implementing a data type for complex numbers is clear. As usual, we start with an API that specifies the data-type operations:

```
public class Complex
```

|  | Complex(double real, double imag) |  |
|---|---|---|
| Complex | plus(Complex b) | *sum of this number and* b |
| Complex | times(Complex b) | *product of this number and* b |
| double | abs() | *magnitude* |
| double | re() | *real part* |
| double | im() | *imaginary part* |
| String | toString() | *string representation* |

*API for complex numbers (see Program 3.2.6)*

For simplicity, we concentrate in the text on just the basic operations in this API, but EXERCISE 3.2.19 asks you to consider several other useful operations that might be included in such an API.

Complex (PROGRAM 3.2.2) is a class that implements this API. It has all of the same components as did Charge (and every Java data type implementation): instance variables (re and im), a constructor, instance methods (plus(), times(), abs(), re(), im(), and toString()), and a test client. The test client first sets $z_0$ to $1 + i$, then sets $z$ to $z_0$, and then evaluates:

$$z = z^2 + z_0 = (1 + i)^2 + (1 + i) = (1 + 2i - 1) + (1 + i) = 1 + 3i$$
$$z = z^2 + z_0 = (1 + 3i)^2 + (1 + i) = (1 + 6i - 9) + (1 + i) = -7 + 7i$$

This code is straightforward and similar to code that you have seen earlier in this chapter, with one exception: the code that implements the arithmetic methods makes use of a new mechanism for accessing object values.

*Accessing instance variables in objects of this type.* Both plus() and times() need to access values in two objects: the object passed as an argument and the object used to invoke the method. If we call the method with a.plus(b), we can access the instance variables of a using the names re and im, as usual, but to access the instance variables of of b we use the code b.re and b.im. Keeping the instance variables private means that *client code cannot access directly instance variables in another class* (but code in the same class can access any object's instance variables directly).

*Chaining.* Observe the manner in which `main()` *chains* two method calls into one compact expression: the expression `z.times(z).plus(z0)` evaluates to $z^2 + z_0$. This usage is convenient because we do not have to invent a variable name for the intermediate value. If you study the expression, you can see that there is no ambiguity: moving from left to right, each method returns a reference to a `Complex` object, which is used to invoke the next method. If desired, we can use parentheses to override the default precedence order (for example, `z.times(z.plus(z0))` evaluates to $z(z + z_0)$).

*Creating and returning new objects.* Observe the manner in which `plus()` and `times()` provide return values to clients: they need to return a `Complex` value, so they each compute the requisite real and imaginary parts, use them to create a new object, and then return a reference to that object. This arrangement allow clients to manipulate complex numbers by manipulating local variables of type `Complex`.

*Final values.* The two instance variables in `Complex` are `final`, meaning that their values are set for each `Complex` object when it is created and do not change during the lifetime of an object. Again, we discuss the reasons behind this design decision in SECTION 3.3.

COMPLEX NUMBERS ARE THE BASIS FOR sophisticated calculations from applied mathematics that have many applications. Some programming languages have complex numbers built in as a primitive type, and provide special language support for use of operators such as * and + to perform addition, multiplication, and other operations, in the same way as for integers or floating-point numbers. *Java does not support overloading for built-in operators.* Java's support for data types is much more general, allowing us to compute with abstractions of all description. `Complex` is but one example.

To give you a feeling for the nature of calculations involving complex numbers and the utility of the complex number abstraction, we next consider a famous example of a `Complex` client.

### Program 3.2.6 Complex numbers

```
public class Complex
{
    private final double re;
    private final double im;

    public Complex(double real, double imag)
    {   re = real;  im = imag;   }

    public Complex plus(Complex b)
    {   // Return the sum of this number and b.
        double real = re + b.re;
        double imag = im + b.im;
        return new Complex(real, imag);
    }

    public Complex times(Complex b)
    {   // Return the product of this number and b.
        double real = re * b.re - im * b.im;
        double imag = re * b.im + im * b.re;
        return new Complex(real, imag);
    }

    public double abs()
    {   return Math.sqrt(re*re + im*im);   }

    public double re()  { return re; }
    public double im()  { return im; }

    public String toString()
    {   return re + " + " + im + "i";   }

    public static void main(String[] args)
    {
        Complex z0 = new Complex(1.0, 1.0);
        Complex z = z0;
        z = z.times(z).plus(z0);
        z = z.times(z).plus(z0);
        StdOut.println(z);
    }
}
```

| re | real part |
| im | imaginary part |

*This data type is the basis for writing Java programs that manipulate complex numbers.*

```
% java Complex
-7.0 + 7.0i
```

**Mandelbrot set**   The *Mandelbrot set* is a specific set of complex numbers discovered by Benoît Mandelbrot. It has many fascinating properties. It is a fractal pattern that is related to the Barnsley fern, the Sierpinski triangle, the Brownian bridge, the Koch curve, the drunken turtle, and other recursive (self-similar) patterns and programs that we have seen in this book. Patterns of this kind are found in natural phenomena of all sorts, and these models and programs are very important in modern science.

The set of points in the Mandelbrot set cannot be described by a single mathematical equation. Instead, it is defined by an *algorithm*, and therefore a perfect candidate for a `Complex` client: we study the set by writing programs to plot it.

The rule for determining whether a complex number $z_0$ is in the Mandelbrot set is simple: Consider the sequence of complex numbers $z_0, z_1, z_2, \ldots, z_t, \ldots$, where $z_{t+1} = (z_t)^2 + z_0$. For example, this table shows the first few entries in the sequence corresponding to $z_0 = 1 + i$:

| $t$ | $z_t$ | | | $(z_t)^2$ | | | $(z_t)^2 + z_0$ | | |
|---|---|---|---|---|---|---|---|---|---|
| 0 | $1 + i$ | $1 +\ 2i +$ | $i^2 =$ | | $2i$ | $2i + (1 + i) =$ | | $1\ + 3i$ |
| 1 | $1 + 3i$ | $1 +\ 6i +$ | $9i^2 =$ | $-8 + 6i$ | | $-8 + 6i + (1 + i) = -7 + 7i$ | | |
| 2 | $-7 + 7i$ | $49 - 98i +$ | $49i^2 =$ | | $-98i$ | $-98i + (1 + i) =$ | | $1- 97i$ |

*Mandelbrot sequence computation*

Now, if the sequence $|z_t|$ diverges to infinity, then $z_0$ is *not* in the Mandelbrot set; if the sequence is bounded, then $z_0$ *is* in the Mandelbrot set. For many points, the test is simple; for many other points, the test requires more computation, as indicated by the examples in this table:

| $t$ | $0 + 0i$ | $2 + 0i$ | $1 + i$ | $-.5 + 0i$ | $.10 - .64i$ |
|---|---|---|---|---|---|
| 0 | $0 + 0i$ | $2 + 0i$ | $1 + i$ | $-.5 + 0i$ | $.10 - .64i$ |
| 1 | $0 + 0i$ | $6 + 0i$ | $1 + 3i$ | $-.25 + 0i$ | $-.30 - .77i$ |
| 2 | $0 + 0i$ | $36 + 0i$ | $-7 + 7i$ | $-.44 + 0i$ | $-.40 - .18i$ |
| 3 | $0 + 0i$ | $1446 + 0i$ | $1 - 97i$ | $-.31 + 0i$ | $.23 - .50i$ |
| 4 | $0 + 0i$ | $2090918 + 0i$ | $-9407 - 193i$ | $-.40 + 0i$ | $-.09 - .87i$ |
| *in the set?* | *yes* | *no* | *no* | *yes* | *yes* |

*Mandelbrot sequence for several starting points*

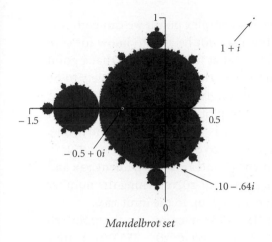

*Mandelbrot set*

For brevity, the numbers in the rightmost two columns of this table are given to just two decimal places. In some cases, we can prove whether numbers are in the set: for example, $0 + 0i$ is certainly in the set (since the magnitude of all the numbers in its sequence is 0), and $2 + 0i$ is certainly not in the set (since its sequence dominates the powers of 2, which diverges). In some other cases, the growth is readily apparent: for exam-

.1015 -.633 1.0

ple, $1 + i$ does not seem to be in the set. Other sequences exhibit a periodic behavior: for example, $i$ maps to $-1 + i$ to $-i$ to $-1 + i$ to $-i \ldots$. And some sequences go on for a very long time before the magnitude of the numbers begins to get large.

.1015 -.633 .10

To visualize the Mandelbrot set, we sample *complex* points, just as we sample real-valued points to plot a real-valued function. Each complex number $x + iy$ corresponds to a point $(x, y)$ in the plane, so we can plot the results as follows: for a specified resolution $N$, we define a regularly spaced $N$-by-$N$ pixel grid within a specified square and draw a black pixel if the corresponding point is in the Mandelbrot set and a white pixel if it is not. This plot is a strange and wondrous pattern, with all the black dots connected and falling roughly within the 2-by-2 square centered on the point $-1/2 + 0i$. Large values of $N$ will produce higher-resolution images, at the cost of more computation. Looking closer reveals self-similarities throughout the plot. For example, the same bulbous pattern with self-similar appendages appears all around the contour of the main black cardioid region, of sizes that resemble the simple ruler function of PROGRAM 1.2.1. When we zoom in near the edge of the cardioid, tiny self-similar cardioids appear!

.1015 -.633 .01

.1015 -.633 .001

But how, precisely, do we produce such plots? Actually, no one knows for sure, because there is no simple test that would enable us to

*Zooming in on the set*

conclude that a point is surely in the set. Given a complex point, we can compute the terms at the beginning of its sequence, but may not be able to know for sure that the sequence remains bounded. There *is* a test that tells us for sure that a point is *not* in the set: if the magnitude of any number in the sequence ever gets to be greater than 2 (such as $2 + 0i$), then the sequence surely will diverge.

Mandelbrot (PROGRAM 3.2.7) uses this test to plot a visual representation of the Mandelbrot set. Since our knowledge of the set is not quite black-and-white, we use grayscale in our visual representation. It is based on the function mand() (a Complex client), which takes a Complex argument z0 and an int argument max and computes the Mandelbrot iteration sequence starting at z0, returning the number of iterations for which the magnitude stays less than 2, up to the limit max.

For each pixel, the method main() in Mandelbrot computes the point z0 corresponding to the pixel and then computes 255 - mand(z0, 255) to create a grayscale color for the pixel. Any pixel that is not black corresponds to a point that we know to be not in the Mandelbrot set because the magnitude of the numbers in its sequence grew past 2 (and therefore will go to infinity). The black pixels (grayscale value 0) correspond to points that we assume to be in the set because the magnitude stayed less than 2 for 255 iterations, but we do not necessarily know for sure.

The complexity of the images that this simple program produces is remarkable, even when we zoom in on a tiny portion of the plane. For even more dramatic pictures, we can use use color (see EXERCISE 3.2.34). And the Mandelbrot set is derived from iterating just one function ($z^2 + z_0$): we have a great deal to learn from studying the properties of other functions, as well.

The simplicity of the code masks a substantial amount of computation. There are about one-quarter million pixels in a 512-by-512 image, and all of the black ones require 255 iterations, so producing an image with Mandelbrot requires hundreds of millions of operations on Complex values.

Fascinating as it is to study, our primary interest in Mandelbrot is as an example client of Complex, to illustrate that computing with a type of data that is not built into Java (complex numbers) is a natural and useful programming activity. Mandelbrot is a simple and natural expression of the computation, made so by the design and implementation of Complex. You could implement Mandelbrot without using Complex, but the code would essentially have to merge together the code in PROGRAMS 3.2.6 and 3.2.7 and therefore would be much more difficult to understand. *Whenever you can clearly separate tasks within a program, you should do so.*

Program 3.2.7    Mandelbrot set

```java
import java.awt.Color;

public class Mandelbrot
{
   private static int mand(Complex z0, int max)
   {
      Complex z = z0;
      for (int t = 0; t < max; t++)
      {
         if (z.abs() > 2.0) return t;
         z = z.times(z).plus(z0);
      }
      return max;
   }

   public static void main(String[] args)
   {
      double xc   = Double.parseDouble(args[0]);
      double yc   = Double.parseDouble(args[1]);
      double size = Double.parseDouble(args[2]);
      int N = 512;
      Picture pic = new Picture(N, N);
      for (int i = 0; i < N; i++)
         for (int j = 0; j < N; j++)
         {
            double x0 = xc - size/2 + size*i/N;
            double y0 = yc - size/2 + size*j/N;
            Complex z0 = new Complex(x0, y0);
            int t = 512 - mand(z0, 512);
            Color c = new Color(t, t, t);
            pic.set(i, N-1-j, c);
         }
      pic.show();
   }
}
```

| | |
|---|---|
| x0, y0 | point in square |
| z0 | $x_0 + i\,y_0$ |
| max | iteration limit |
| xc, yc | center of square |
| size | square is size-by-size |
| N | grid is N-by-N pixels |
| pic | image for output |
| c | pixel color for output |

-.5 0 2

-.1015 -.633 .01

This program takes three command-line arguments that specify the center and size of a square region of interest, and makes a digital image showing the result of sampling the Mandelbrot set in that region at a 512*512 grid of equally spaced pixels. It colors each pixel with a grayscale value that is determined by counting the number of iterations before the Mandelbrot sequence for the corresponding complex number grows past 2.0, up to 255.

**Commercial data processing**   One of the driving forces behind the development of object-oriented programming has been the need for an extensive amount of reliable software for commercial data processing. As an illustration, we consider next an example of a data type that might be used by a financial institution to keep track of customer information.

Suppose that a stock broker needs to maintain customer accounts containing shares of various stocks. That is, the set of values the broker needs to process includes the customer's name, numbers of different stocks held, amount of shares and ticker symbols for each, and perhaps the total value of the stocks in the account. To process an account, the broker needs at least the operations defined in this API:

```
public class StockAccount
```

| | |
|---|---|
| `StockAccount(In in)` | *create a new account from information in input stream* |
| `double value()` | *total value in dollars* |
| `void buy(int amount, String symbol)` | *add shares of stock to account* |
| `double sell(int amount, String symbol)` | *subtract shares of stock from account* |
| `void write(Out out)` | *save account to an output stream* |
| `void printReport()` | *print a detailed report of stocks and values* |

*API for processing stock accounts (see* PROGRAM 3.2.8)

The broker certainly needs to buy, sell, and provide reports to the customer, but the first key to understanding this kind of data processing is to consider the `StockAccount()` constructor and the `write()` method in this API. The customer information has a long lifetime and needs to be saved in a *file* or *database*. To process an account, a client program needs to read information from the corresponding file; process the information as appropriate; and, if the information changes, write it back to the file, saving it for later. To enable this kind of processing, we need a *file format* and an *internal representation*, or a *data structure*, for the account information. The situation is analogous to what we saw for matrix processing in CHAPTER 1, where we defined a file format (numbers of rows and columns followed by entries in row-major order) and an internal representation (Java two-dimensional arrays) to enable us to write programs for the random surfer and other applications.

As a (whimsical) running example, we imagine that a broker is maintaining a small portfolio of stock in leading software companies for Alan Turing, the father of computing. *As an aside*: Turing's life story is a fascinating one that is worth pursuing. Among many other things, he worked on computational cryptography that helped to bring about the end of the Second World War, he developed the basis for modern theoretical computer science, he designed and built one of the first computers, and he was a pioneer in artificial intelligence research. It is perhaps safe to assume that Turing, whatever his financial situation as an academic researcher in the middle of the last century, would be sufficiently optimistic about the potential impact of computing software in today's world that he would make some small investments.

*File format.* Modern systems normally use text files, even for data, to minimize dependence on formats defined by any one program. For simplicity, we use a direct representation where we list the account holder's name (a string), cash balance (a floating-point number), and number of stocks held (an integer), followed by a line for each stock giving the number of shares and the ticker symbol. It is also wise to use *tags* such as <Name> and <Number of shares> and so forth to label all the information, to further minimize dependencies on any one program, but we omit tags here for brevity.

```
% more Turing.txt
Turing, Alan
10.24
5
100 ADBE
 25 GOOG
 97 IBM
250 MSFT
200 YHOO
```

*File format*

*Data structure.* To represent information for processing by Java programs, we use *object instance variables.* They specify the type of information and provide the structure that we need in order to clearly refer to it in code. For our example, we clearly need the following:

- A `String` value for the account name
- A `double` value for the cash balance
- An `int` value for the number of stocks
- An array of `String` values for stock symbols
- An array of `int` values for numbers of shares

```
public class StockAccount
{
    private final String name;
    private double cash;
    private int N;
    private int[] shares;
    private String[] stocks;
    ...
}
```

*Data structure blueprint*

We directly reflect these choices in the instance variable declarations in `StockAccount` (PROGRAM 3.2.8). The arrays `stocks[]` and `shares[]` are known as *parallel arrays*. Given an index i, `stocks[i]` gives a stock symbol and `shares[i]` give the number of shares of that stock in the account. An alternative design would be to define a separate data type for stocks to manipulate this information for each stock and maintain an array of objects of that type in StockAccount.

StockAccount includes a constructor, which reads a file and builds an account with this internal representation, and the method implementation for value(), which uses StockQuote (PROGRAM 3.1.10) to get each stock's price from the web. For example, our broker needs to provide a periodic detailed report to customers, perhaps using the following code for printReport() in StockAccount:

```
public void printReport()
{
    StdOut.printf("%s\n", name);
    StdOut.printf("                      Cash: $%9.2f\n", cash);
    double total = cash;
    for (int i = 0; i < N; i++)
    {
        int amount = shares[i];
        double p = StockQuote.price(stocks[i]);
        StdOut.printf("%4d  %4s ", amount, stocks[i]);
        StdOut.printf("  $%6.2f    $%9.2f\n", p, amount * p);
        total += amount * p;
    }
    StdOut.printf("                      Total: $%9.2f\n", total);
}
```

On the one hand, this client illustrates the kind of computing that was one of the primary drivers in the evolution of computing in the 1950s. Banks and other companies bought early computers precisely because of the need to do such financial reporting. For example, formatted printing was developed precisely for such applications. On the other hand, this client exemplifies modern web-centric computing, as it gets information directly from the web, without using a browser.

The implementations of buy() and sell() require the use of basic mechanisms introduced in SECTION 4.4, so we defer them to that section. Beyond these basic methods, an actual application of these ideas would likely use a number of other clients. For example, a broker might want to build an array of all accounts, then process a list of transactions that both modify the information in those accounts and actually carry out the transactions through the web. Of course, such code needs to be developed with great care!

## Program 3.2.8   Stock account

```java
public class StockAccount
{
   private final String name;
   private double cash;
   private int N;
   private int[] shares;
   private String[] stocks;

   public StockAccount(In in)
   {  // Build data structure from input stream.
      name = in.readLine();
      cash = in.readDouble();
      N = in.readInt();
      shares = new int[N];
      stocks = new String[N];
      for (int i = 0; i < N; i++)
      {  // Process one stock.
         shares[i] = in.readInt();
         stocks[i] = in.readString();
      }
   }

   public void printReport()
   {  /* See text. */  }

   public static void main(String[] args)
   {
      In in = new In(args[0]);
      StockAccount acct = new StockAccount(in);
      acct.printReport();
   }
}
```

| name | customer name |
|------|------|
| cash | cash balance |
| N | number of stocks |
| shares[] | share counts |
| stocks[] | stock symbols |

| in | input stream |
|----|----|

*This class for processing stock accounts illustrates typical usage of object-oriented programming for commercial data processing.*

```
% more Turing.txt
Turing, Alan
10.24
5
100 ADBE
 25 GOOG
 97 IBM
250 MSFT
200 YHOO
```

```
% java StockAccount Turing.txt
Turing, Alan
                  Cash: $      10.24
100   ADBE   $ 42.23   $  4222.91
 25   GOOG   $473.25   $ 11831.25
 97   IBM    $104.40   $ 10126.80
250   MSFT   $ 30.25   $  7562.50
200   YHOO   $ 28.39   $  5678.00
                 Total: $ 39431.70
```

WHEN YOU LEARNED HOW TO DEFINE functions that can be used in multiple places in a program (or in other programs) in CHAPTER 2, you moved from a world where programs are simply lists of statements in a single file to the world of modular programming, summarized in our mantra: *whenever you can clearly separate subtasks within a program, you should do so.* The analogous capability for data, introduced in this chapter, moves you from a world where data has to be one of a few elementary types of data to a world where you can define your own types of data. This profound new capability vastly extends the scope of your programming. As with the concept of a function, once you have learned to implement and use data types, you will marvel at the primitive nature of programs that do not use them.

But object-oriented programming is much more than structuring data. It enables us to associate the data relevant to a subtask with the operations that manipulate that data and to keep both separate in an independent module. With object-oriented programming, our mantra is this: *whenever you can clearly separate data and associated operations for subtasks within a computation, you should do so.*

The examples that we have considered are persuasive evidence that object-oriented programming can play a useful role in a broad range of activities. Whether we are trying to design and build a physical artifact, develop a software system, understand the natural world, or process information, a key first step is to define an appropriate abstraction, such as a geometric description of the physical artifact, a modular design of the software system, a mathematical model of the natural world, or a data structure for the information. When we want to write programs to manipulate instances of a well-defined abstraction, we can just implement it as a data type in a Java class and write Java programs to create and manipulate objects of that type.

Each time that we develop a class that makes use of other classes by creating and manipulating objects of the type defined by the class, we are programming at a higher layer of abstraction. In the next section, we discuss some of the design challenges inherent in this kind of programming.

# Q & A

**Q.** Do instance variables have initial values that we can depend upon?

**A** Yes. They are automatically set to 0 for numeric types, `false` for the `boolean` type, and the special value `null` for all reference types. These values are consistent with the way array entries are initialized. This automatic initialization ensures that every instance variable always stores a legal (but not necessarily meaningful) value. Writing code that depends on these values is controversial: some experienced programmers embrace the idea because the resulting code can be very compact; others avoid it because the code is opaque to someone who does not know the rules.

**Q.** What is `null`?

**A** It is a literal value that refers to no object. Invoking a method using the `null` reference is meaningless and results in a `NullPointerException`. If you get this error message, check to make sure that your constructor properly initializes all of its instance variables.

**Q.** Can we initialize instance variables to other values when declaring them?

**A.** Yes, you can initialize instance variables using the same conventions as you have been using for initializing local variables. Each time a client creates an object with new, Java initializes its instance variables with those values, and then calls the constructor.

**Q.** Must every class have a constructor?

**A.** Yes, but if you do not specify a constructor, Java provides a default (no-argument) constructor automatically. When the client invokes that constructor with new, the instance variables are auto-initialized as usual. If you *do* specify a constructor, the default no-argument constructor disappears.

**Q.** Suppose I do not include a `toString()` method. What happens if I try to print an object of that type with `StdOut.println()`?

**A.** The printed output is an integer that is unlikely to be of much use to you.

**Q.** Can I have a static method in a class that implements a data type?

**A.** Of course. For example, all of our classes have `main()`. But it is easy to get confused when static methods and instance methods are mixed up in the same code. For example, it is natural to consider using static methods for operations that involve multiple objects where none of them naturally suggests itself as the one that should invoke the method. For example, we say `z.abs()` to get $|z|$, but saying `a.plus(b)` to get the sum is perhaps not so natural. Why not `b.plus(a)`? An alternative is to define a static method like the following within `Complex`:

```
public static Complex plus(Complex a, Complex b)
{
    return new Complex(a.re + b.re, a.im + b.im);
}
```

We generally avoid such usage and live with expressions that do not mix static and instance methods to avoid having to write code like this:

```
z = Complex.plus(Complex.times(z, z), z0)
```

Instead, we would write:

```
z = z.times(z).plus(z0)
```

**Q.** These computations with `plus()` and `times()` seem rather clumsy. Is there some way to use symbols like + and * in expressions involving objects where they make sense, like `Complex` and `Vector`, so that we could write expressions like `z = z * z + z0` instead?

**A.** Some languages (notably C++) support this feature, which is known as *operator overloading*, but Java does not do so (except that there is language support for overloading + with string concatenation). As usual, this is a decision of the language designers that we just live with, but many Java programmers do not consider this to be much of a loss. Operator overloading makes sense only for types that represent numeric or algebraic abstractions, a small fraction of the total, and many programs are easier to understand when operations have descriptive names such as `plus` and `times`. The APL programming language of the 1970s took this issue to the opposite extreme by insisting that *every* operation be represented by a single symbol (including Greek letters).

**Q.** Are there other kinds of variables besides argument, local, and instance variables in a class?

**A** If you include the keyword `static` in a variable declaration (outside of any method), it creates a completely different type of variable, known as a *static variable* or *class variable*. Like instance variables, static variables are accessible to every method in the class; however, they are not associated with any object—there is one variable per class. In older programming languages, such variables are known as *global variables* because of their global scope. In modern programming, we focus on limiting scope and therefore rarely use such variables.

**Q.** `Mandelbrot` creates hundreds of millions of `Complex` objects. Doesn't all that object-creation overhead slow things down?

**A.** Yes, but not so much that we cannot generate our plots. Our goal is to make our programs readable and easy to maintain—limiting scope via the complex number abstraction helps us achieve that goal. You certainly could speed up `Mandelbrot` by bypassing the complex number abstraction or by using a different implementation of `Complex`. We will revisit this issue in the next section.

**3.2.1** Consider the following data-type implementation for (axis-aligned) rectangles, which represents each rectangle with the coordinates of its center point and its width and height:

```
public class Rectangle
{
    private final double x
    private final double y;

    private final double width
    private final double height;

    public Rectangle(double x0, double y0, double w, double h)
    {
        x = x0;
        y = y0;
        width = w;
        height = h;
    }
    public double area()
    {   return width * height;   }

    public double perimeter()
    {   /* Compute perimeter. */   }

    public boolean intersects(Rectangle b)
    {   /* Does this rectangle intersect b? */   }

    public boolean contains(Rectangle b)
    {   /* Is b inside this rectangle? */   }

    public void show(Rectangle b)
    {   /* Draw rectangle on StdDraw. */   }

}
```

*representation*

*height* — (x, y) •

*width*

*intersects*

a

b

*contains*

a

b

Write an API for this class, and fill in the code for `perimeter()`, `intersects()`, and `contains()`. *Note*: Treat coincident lines as intersecting, so that, for example, `a.intersects(a)` is `true` and `a.contains(a)` is `false`.

**3.2.2** Write a test client for `Rectangle` that takes three command-line arguments N, min, and max; generates N random rectangles whose width and height are uni-

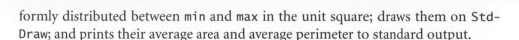

formly distributed between min and max in the unit square; draws them on Std-Draw; and prints their average area and average perimeter to standard output.

**3.2.3** Add code to your test client from the previous exercise code to compute the average number of pairs of rectangles that intersect and are contained in one another.

**3.2.4** Develop an implementation of your Rectangle API from EXERCISE 3.2.1 that represents rectangles with the coordinates of their lower left and upper right corners. Do *not* change the API.

**3.2.5** What is wrong with the following code?

```
public class Charge
{
    private double rx, ry;    // position
    private double q;         // charge
    public Charge(double x0, double y0, double q0)
    {
        double rx = x0;
        double ry = y0;
        double q = q0;
    }
    ...
}
```

*Answer.* The assignment statements in the constructor are also *declarations* that create new local variables rx, ry, and q, which are assigned values from the arguments but are never used. The instance variables rx, ry, and q remain at their default value of 0. *Note*: A local variable with the same name as an instance variable is said to *shadow* the instance variable—we discuss in the next section a way to refer to shadowed instance variables, which are best avoided by beginners.

**3.2.6** Create a data type Location that represents a location on Earth using latitudes and longitudes. Include a method distanceTo() that computes distances using the great-circle distance (see EXERCISE 1.2.33).

**3.2.7**   Implement a data type `Rational` for rational numbers that supports addition, subtraction, multiplication, and division.

```
public class Rational
```
|   |   |   |
|---|---|---|
|   | Rational(int numerator, int denominator) |   |
| Rational | plus(Rational b) | *sum of this number and b* |
| Rational | minus(Rational b) | *difference of this number and b* |
| Rational | times(Rational b) | *product of this number and b* |
| Rational | over(Rational b) | *quotient of this number and b* |
| String | toString() | *string representation* |

Use `Euclid.gcd()` (PROGRAM 2.3.1) to ensure that the numerator and denominator never have any common factors. Include a test client that exercises all of your methods. Do not worry about testing for overflow (see EXERCISE 3.3.24).

**3.2.8**   Write a data type `Interval` that implements the following API:

```
public class Interval
```
|   |   |   |
|---|---|---|
|   | Interval(double left, double right) |   |
| boolean | contains(double x) | *is x in this interval?* |
| boolean | intersects(Interval b) | *does this interval and b intersect?* |
| String | toString() | *string representation* |

An interval is defined to be the set of all points on the line greater than or equal to `left` and less than or equal to `right`. In particular, an interval with `right` less than `left` is empty. Write a client that is a filter that takes a `double` value x from the command line and prints all of the intervals on standard input (each defined by a pair of `double` values) that contain x.

**3.2.9**   Write a client for your `Interval` class from the previous exercise that takes an `int` value $N$ as command-line argument, reads $N$ intervals (each defined by a pair of `double` values) from standard input, and prints all pairs that intersect.

**3.2.10** Develop an implementation of your `Rectangle` API from EXERCISE 3.2.1 that takes advantage of `Interval` to simplify and clarify the code.

**3.2.11** Write a data type `Point` that implements the following API:

```
public class Point
```
---
|  | `Point(double x, double y)` |  |
| `double` | `distanceTo(Point q)` | *Euclidean distance between this point and* `q` |
| `String` | `toString()` | *string representation* |

**3.2.12** Add methods to `Stopwatch` that allow clients to stop and restart the stopwatch.

**3.2.13** Use a `Stopwatch` to compare the cost of computing Harmonic numbers with a `for` loop (see PROGRAM 1.3.5) as opposed to using the recursive method given in SECTION 2.3.

**3.2.14** Develop a version of `Histogram` that uses `Draw`, so that a client can create multiple histograms. Add to the display a red vertical line showing the sample mean and blue vertical lines at a distance of two standard deviations from the mean. Use a test client that creates histograms for flipping coins (Bernoulli trials) with a biased coin that is heads with probability $p$, for $p = .2, .4, .6.$ and $.8$, taking the number of flips and the number of trials from the command line, as in PROGRAM 3.2.3.

**3.2.15** Modify the test client in `Turtle` to produce stars with N points for odd N.

**3.2.16** Modify the `toString()` method in `Complex` (PROGRAM 3.2.2) so that it prints complex numbers in the traditional format. For example, it should print the value $3 - i$ as 3 - i instead of 3.0 + -1.0i, the value 3 as 3 instead of 3.0 + 0.0i, and the value $3i$ as 3i instead of 0.0 + 3.0i.

**3.2.17** Write a `Complex` client that takes three `double` values $a$, $b$, and $c$ as command-line arguments and prints out the complex roots of $ax^2 + bx + c$.

**3.2.18** Write a `Complex` client `Roots` that takes two `double` values $a$ and $b$ and an integer $N$ from the command line and prints the $N$th roots of $a + bi$. *Note*: skip this exercise if you are not familiar with the operation of taking roots of complex numbers.

**3.2.19** Implement the following additions to the `Complex` API:

| | |
|---|---|
| `double  theta()` | *phase (angle) of this number* |
| `Complex minus(Complex b)` | *difference of this number and* b |
| `Complex conjugate()` | *conjugate of this number* |
| `Complex divides(Complex b)` | *result of dividing this number by* b |
| `Complex power(int b)` | *result of raising this number to the* b*th power* |

Write a test client that exercises all of your methods.

**3.2.20** Suppose you want to add a constructor to `Complex` that takes a `double` value as argument and creates a `Complex` number with that value as the real part (and no imaginary part). You write the following code:

```
public void Complex(double real)
{
    re = real;
    im = 0.0;
}
```

But then `Complex c = new Complex(1.0)` does not compile. Why?

*Answer*:   Constructors do not have return types, not even `void`. The code above defines a method named `Complex`, not a constructor. Remove the keyword `void`.

**3.2.21** Find a `Complex` value for which `mand()` returns a number greater than 100, and then zoom in on that value, as in the example in the text.

**3.2.22** Implement the `write()` method for `StockAccount` (PROGRAM 3.2.8).

**3.2.23** *Mutable charges.* Modify `Charge` so that the charge q is not `final`, and add a method `increaseCharge()` that takes a `double` argument and adds the given value to the charge. Then, write a client that initializes an array with:

```
Charge[] a = new Charge[3];
a[0] = new Charge(.4, .6, 50);
a[1] = new Charge(.5, .5, -5);
a[2] = new Charge(.6, .6, 50);
```

and then displays the result of slowly decreasing the charge value of a[i] by wrapping the code that computes the picture in a loop like the following:

```
for (int t = 0; t < 100; t++)
{
    // compute the picture
    pic.show();
    a[1].change(-2);
}
```

-5

-55

**3.2.24** *Complex timing.* Write a `Stopwatch` client that compares the cost of using `Complex` to the cost of writing code that directly manipulates two double values, for the task of doing the calculations in `Mandelbrot`. Specifically, create a version of `Mandelbrot` that just does the calculations (remove the code that refers to `Picture`), then create a version of that program that does not use `Complex`, and then compute the ratio of the running times.

-105

-155

**3.2.25** *Quaternions.* In 1843, Sir William Hamilton discovered an extension to complex numbers called quaternions. A quaternion is a vector $a = (a_0, a_1, a_2, a_3)$ with the following operations:

- *Magnitude:* $|a| = \sqrt{a_0^2 + a_1^2 + a_2^2 + a_3^2}$.
- *Conjugate:* the conjugate of $a$ is $(a_0, -a_1, -a_2, -a_3)$.
- *Inverse:* $a^{-1} = (a_0/|a|, -a_1/|a|, -a_2/|a|, -a_3/|a|)$.
- *Sum:* $a + b = (a_0 + b_0, a_1 + b_1, a_2 + b_2, a_3 + b_3)$.
- *Product:* $a * b = (a_0 b_0 - a_1 b_1 - a_2 b_2 - a_3 b_3, a_0 b_1 - a_1 b_0 + a_2 b_3 - a_3 b_2, a_0 b_2 - a_1 b_3 + a_2 b_0 + a_3 b_1, a_0 b_3 + a_1 b_2 - a_2 b_1 + a_3 b_0)$.
- *Quotient:* $a / b = ab^{-1}$.

-205

*Mutating a charge*

Create a data type for quaternions and a test client that exercises all of your code. Quaternions extend the concept of rotation in three dimensions to four dimensions. They are used in computer graphics, control theory, signal processing, and orbital mechanics.

**3.2.26** *Dragon curves.* Write a recursive `Turtle` client `Dragon` that draws dragon curves (see Exercises 1.2.35 and 1.5.9).

% java Dragon 15

*Answer*: These curves, originally discovered by three NASA physicists, were popularized in the 1960s by Martin Gardner and later used by Michael Crichton in the book and movie *Jurassic Park*. This exercise can be solved with remarkably compact code, based on a pair of mutually interacting recursive functions derived directly from the definition in Exercise 1.2.35. One of them, `dragon()`, should draw the curve as you expect; the other, `nogard()`, should draw the curve in *reverse* order. See the booksite for details.

**3.2.27** *Hilbert curves.* A space-filling curve is a continuous curve in the unit square that passes through every point. Write a recursive `Turtle` client that produces these recursive patterns, which approach a space-filling curve that was defined by the mathematician David Hilbert at the end of the 19th century.

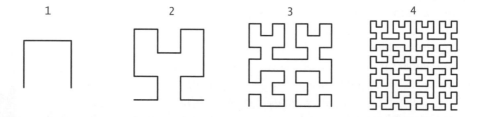

*Partial answer* See the previous exercise. You need a pair of methods: `hilbert()`, which traverses a Hilbert curve, and `treblih()`, which traverses a Hilbert curve *in reverse order*. See the booksite for details.

**3.2.28** *Gosper island.* Write a recursive `Turtle` client that produces these recursive patterns.

**3.2.29** *Data analysis.* Write a data type for use in running experiments where the control variable is an integer in the range $[0, N)$ and the dependent variable is a `double` value. (For example, studying the running time of a program that takes an integer argument would involve such experiments.) Implement the following API.

```
public class Data
```

|  |  |  |
|---|---|---|
| | `Data(int N, int max)` | *create a new data analysis object for the N int values in [0, N)* |
| `double` | `addDataPoint(int i, double x)` | *add a data point (i, x)* |
| `void` | `plot()` | *plot all the data points* |
| `void` | `TukeyPlot()` | *draw a Tukey plot (see Exercise 2.2.18)* |

You can use the static methods in `StdStats` to do the statistical calculations and draw the plots. Use `StdDraw` so clients can use different colors for `plot()` and `TukeyPlot()` (for example, light gray for all the points and black for the Tukey plot). Write a test client that plots the results (percolation probability) of running experiments with `Percolation` as the grid size increases.

**3.2.30** *Elements.* Create a data type `Element` for entries in the *Periodic Table of Elements.* Include data type values for element, atomic number, symbol, and atomic weight and accessor methods for each of these values. Then, create a data type

PeriodicTable that reads values from a file to create an array of Element objects (you can find the file and a description of its format on the booksite) and responds to queries on standard input so that a user can type a molecular equation like H2O and the program responds by printing the molecular weight. Develop APIs and implementations for each data type.

**3.2.31** *Stock prices.* The file DJIA.txt on the booksite contains all closing stock prices in the history of the Dow Jones Industrial Average, in the comma-separated-value format. Create a data type Entry that can hold one entry in the table, with values for date, opening price, daily high, daily low, closing price, and so forth. Then, create a data type Table that reads the file to build an array of Entry objects and supports methods for computing averages over various periods of time. Finally, create interesting Table clients to produce plots of the data. Be creative: this path is well-trodden.

**3.2.32** *Chaos with Newton's method.* The polynomial $f(z) = z^4 - 1$ has four roots: at $1$, $-1$, $i$, and $-i$. We can find the roots using Newton's method in the complex plane: $z_{k+1} = z_k - f(z_k)/f'(z_k)$. Here, $f(z) = z^4 - 1$ and $f'(z) = 4z^3$. The method converges to one of the four roots, depending on the starting point $z_0$. Write a Complex client Newton that takes a command-line argument $N$ and colors pixels in an $N$-by-$N$ Picture white, red, green, or blue by mapping the pixels complex points in a regularly spaced grid in the square of size 2 centered at the origin and coloring each pixel according to which of the four roots the corresponding point converges (black if no convergence after 100 iterations).

`if (g != 255) g = g * 17 % 256;`

**3.2.33** *Equipotential surfaces.* An equipotential surface is the set of all points that have the same electric potential $V$. Given a group of point charges, it is useful to visualize the electric potential by plotting equipotential surfaces (also known as a *contour plot*). Write a program Equipotential that draws a line every $5V$ by computing the potential at each pixel and checking whether the potential at the corresponding point is within 1 pixel of a multiple of $5V$. *Note*: A *very easy* approximate solution to this exercise is obtained from PROGRAM 3.1.7 by scrambling the color values assigned to each pixel, rather than having them be proportional to the grayscale value. For example, the accompanying figure is created by inserting the code above it before creating the `Color`. Explain why it works, and experiment with your own version.

**3.2.34** *Color Mandelbrot plot.* Create a file of 256 integer triples that represent interesting `Color` values, and then use those colors instead of grayscale values to plot each pixel in `Mandelbrot`: Read the values to create an array of 256 `Color` values, then index into that array with the return value of `mand()`. By experimenting with various color choices at various places in the set, you can produce astonishing images. See `mandel.txt` on the booksite for an example.

**3.2.35** *Julia sets.* The *Julia set* for a given complex number $c$ is a set of points related to the Mandelbrot function. Instead of fixing $z$ and varying $c$, we fix $c$ and vary $z$. Those points $z$ for which the modified Mandelbrot function stays bounded are in the *Julia set*; those for which the sequence diverges to infinity are not in the set. All points $z$ of interest lie in the 4-by-4 box centered at the origin. The Julia set for $c$ is connected if and only if $c$ is in the Mandelbrot set! Write a program `Color-Julia` that takes two command line arguments $a$ and $b$, and plots a color version of the Julia set for $c = a + bi$, using the color-table method described in the previous exercise.

**3.2.36** *Biggest winner and biggest loser.* Write a `StockAccount` client that builds an array of `StockAccount` objects, computes the total value of each account, and prints a report for the accounts with the largest value and the account with the smallest value. Assume that the information in the accounts are kept in a single file that contains the information for the accounts, one after the other, in the format given in the text.

# 3.3  Designing Data Types

THE ABILITY TO CREATE DATA TYPES turns every programmer into a language designer.
You do not have to settle for the types of data and associated operations that are
built into the language, because you can
easily create your own types of data and
then write client programs that use them.
Java does not have complex numbers
built in, but you can define `Complex` and
write programs such as `Mandelbrot`. Java
does not have a built-in facility for turtle
graphics, but you can define `Turtle` and
write client programs that take immedi-

ate advantage of this abstraction. Even when Java does have a particular facility, we
can use a data type to tailor it to our needs, as we do when we use our `Std*` libraries
instead the more extensive ones provided by Java for software developers.

Now, the first thing that we strive for when creating a program is an understanding of the types of data that we will need. Developing this understanding is a
*design* activity. In this section, we focus on developing APIs as a critical step in the
development of any program. We need to consider various alternatives, understand
their impact on both client programs and implementations, and refine the design
to strike an appropriate balance between the needs of clients and the possible implementation strategies.

If you take a course in systems programming, you will learn that this design
activity is critical when building large systems, and that Java and similar languages
have powerful high-level mechanisms that support code reuse when writing large
programs. Many of these mechanisms are intended for use by experts building large
systems, but the general approach is worthwhile for every programmer, and some
of these mechanisms are useful when writing small programs.

In this section we discuss *encapsulation*, *immutability*, and *inheritance*, with
particular attention to the use of these mechanisms in data-type design to enable
modular programming, facilitate debugging, and write clear and correct code.

At the end of the section, we discuss Java's mechanisms for use in checking
design assumptions against actual conditions at runtime. Such tools are invaluable
aids in developing reliable software.

**Designing APIs.** In Section 3.1, we wrote client programs that *use* APIs; in Section 3.2, we *implemented* APIs. Now we consider the challenge of *designing* APIs. Treating these topics in this order and with this focus is appropriate because most of the time that you spend programming will be writing client programs.

Often the most important and most challenging steps in building software is designing the APIs. This task takes practice, careful deliberation, and many iterations. However, any time spent designing a good API is certain to be repaid in time saved during debugging or with code reuse.

Articulating an API might seem to be overkill when writing a small program, but you should consider writing every program as though you will need to reuse the code someday—not because you know that you will reuse that code, but because you are quite likely to want to reuse *some* of your code and you cannot know *which* code you will need.

*Standards.* It is easy to understand why writing to an API is so important by considering other domains. From railroad tracks, to threaded nuts and bolts, to fax machines, to radio frequencies, to DVD standards, we know that using a common standard interface enables the broadest usage of a technology. Java itself is another example: your Java programs are clients of the *Java virtual machine*, which is a standard interface that is implemented on a wide variety of hardware and software platforms. By using APIs to separate clients from implementations, we reap the benefits of standard interfaces for every program that we write.

*client*

```
Charge c1 = new Charge(.51, .63, 21.3);

          c1.potentialAt(x, y)
```

*creates objects
and invokes methods*

*API*

```
public class Charge

        Charge(double x0, double y0, double q0)

double potentialAt(double x, double y)      potential at (x, y)
                                                  due to charge

String toString()                                    string
                                              representation
```

*defines signatures
and describes methods*

*implementation*

```
public class Charge
    private final double rx, ry;
    private final double q;

    public Charge(double x0, double y0, double q0)
    {  ...  }

    public double potentialAt(double x, double y)
    {  ...  }

    public String toString()
    {  ...  }
```

*defines instance variables
and implements methods*

*Object-oriented library abstraction*

*Specification problem.* Our APIs are lists of methods, along with brief English-language descriptions of what the methods are supposed to do. Ideally, an API would clearly articulate behavior for all possible inputs, including side effects, and then we would have software to check that implementations meet the specification. Unfortunately, a fundamental result from theoretical computer science, known as the *specification problem*, says that this goal is actually *impossible* to achieve. Briefly, such a specification would have to be written in a formal language like a programming language, and the problem of determining whether two programs perform the same computation is known, mathematically, to be *unsolvable*. (If you are interested in this idea, you can learn much more about the nature of unsolvable problems and their role in our understanding of the nature of computation in a course in theoretical computer science.) Therefore, we resort to informal descriptions with examples, such as those in the text surrounding our APIs.

*Wide interfaces.* A *wide interface* is one that has an excessive number of methods. An important principle to follow in designing an API is to *avoid wide interfaces*. The size of an API naturally tends to grow over time because it is easy to add methods to an existing API, whereas it is difficult to remove methods without breaking existing clients. In certain situations, wide interfaces are justified—for example, in widely used systems libraries such as `String`. Various techniques are helpful in reducing the effective width of an interface. For example, we considered in CHAPTER 2 several libraries that use overloading to provide implementations of basic methods for all types of data. Another approach is to include methods that are orthogonal in functionality. For example, Java's `Math` library includes methods for `sin()`, `cos()`, and `tan()`, but not `sec()`.

*Start with client code.* One of the primary purposes of developing a data type is to simplify client code. Therefore, it makes sense to pay attention to client code form the start when designing an API. Very often, doing so is no problem at all, because a typical reason to develop a data type in the first place is to simplify client code that is becoming cumbersome. When you find yourself with some client code that you are not proud of, one way to proceed is to write a fanciful simplified version of the code that expresses the computation the way you are thinking about it, at some higher level that does not involve the details of the code. If you have done a good job of writing succinct comments to describe your computation, one possible starting point is to think about opportunities to convert the comments into code.

Remember the basic mantra for data types: *whenever you can clearly separate data and associated operations within a program, you should do so.* Whatever the source, it is normally wise to write client code (and develop the API) *before* working on an implementation. Writing two clients is even better. Starting with client code is one way of ensuring that developing an implementation will be worth the effort.

*Avoid dependence on representation.* Usually when developing an API, we have a representation in mind. After all, a data type is a set of values and a set of operations on those values, and it does not make much sense to talk about the operations without knowing the values. But that is different from knowing the representation of the values. One purpose of the data type is to simplify client code by allowing it to avoid details of and dependence on a particular representation. For example, our client programs for Picture and StdAudio work with simple abstract representations of pictures and sound, respectively. The primary value of the APIs for these abstraction is that they allow client code to ignore a substantial amount of detail that is found in the standard representations of those abstractions.

*Pitfalls in API design.* An API may be *too hard to implement*, implying implementations that are difficult or impossible to develop; or *too hard to use*, creating client code that is more complicated than without the API. An API might be too *narrow*, omitting methods that clients need; or *too wide*, including a large number of methods not needed by any client. An API may be *too general*, providing no useful abstractions; or *too specific*, providing abstractions so detailed or so diffuse as to be useless. These considerations are sometimes summarized in yet another motto: *provide to clients the methods they need and no others.*

WHEN YOU FIRST STARTED PROGRAMMING, YOU typed in HelloWorld.java without understanding much about it except the effect that it produced. From that starting point, you learned to program by mimicking the code in the book and eventually developing your own code to solve various problems. You are at a similar point with API design. There are many APIs available in the book, on the booksite, and in online Java documentation that you can study and use, to gain confidence in designing and developing APIs of your own.

**Encapsulation.**  The process of separating clients from implementations by hiding information is known as *encapsulation*. Details of the implementation are kept hidden from clients, and implementations have no way of knowing details of client code, which may even be created in the future.

As you may have surmised, we have been practicing encapsulation in our data type implementations. In SECTION 3.1, we started with the mantra *you do not need to know how a data type is implemented in order to use it*. This statement describes one of the prime benefits of encapsulation. We consider it to be so important that we have not described to you any other way of building a data type. Now, we describe our three primary reasons for doing so in more detail. We use encapsulation:
  • To enable modular programming
  • To facilitate debugging
  • To clarify program code
These reasons are tied together (well-designed modular code is easier to debug and understand than code based entirely on primitive types in long programs).

*Modular programming.*  The programming style that we have been developing since learning functions in CHAPTER 2 has been predicated on the idea of breaking large programs into small modules that can be developed and debugged independently. This approach improves the resiliency of our software by limiting and localizing the effects of making changes, and it promotes code reuse by making it possible to substitute new implementations of a data type to improve performance, accuracy, or memory footprint. The same idea works in many settings. We often reap the benefits of encapsulation when we use system libraries. New versions of the Java system often include new implementations of various data types or static method libraries, but *the APIs do not change*. There is strong and constant motivation to improve data-type implementations because *all* clients can potentially benefit from an improved implementation. The key to success in modular programming is to maintain *independence* among modules. We do so by insisting on the API being the *only* point of dependence between client and implementation. *You do not need to know how a data type is implemented in order to use it*. The flip side of this mantra is that a data-type implementation code can assume that the client knows nothing but the API.

*Example.*  For example, consider Complex (PROGRAM 3.3.1). It has the same name and API as PROGRAM 3.2.6, but uses a different representation for the complex num-

***Program 3.3.1   Complex numbers (alternate)***

```java
public class Complex
{
   private final double r;
   private final double theta;

   public Complex(double re, double im)
   {
      r = Math.sqrt(re*re + im*im);
      theta = Math.atan2(im, re);
   }

   public Complex plus(Complex b)
   {  // Return the sum of this number and b.
      double real = re() + b.re();
      double imag = im() + b.im();
      return new Complex(real, imag);
   }

   public Complex times(Complex b)
   {  // Return the product of this number and b.
      double radius = r * b.r;
      double angle  = theta + b.theta;
      // See Q & A.
   }

   public double abs()
   {  return r;  }

   public double re()  { return r * Math.cos(theta); }
   public double im()  { return r * Math.sin(theta); }

   public String toString()
   {  return re() + " + " + im() + "i";  }

   public static void main(String[] args)
   {
      Complex z0 = new Complex(1.0, 1.0);
      Complex z = z0;
      z = z.times(z).plus(z0);
      z = z.times(z).plus(z0);
      StdOut.println(z);
   }
}
```

| r | *radius* |
|---|---|
| theta | *angle* |

*Polar representation*

*This data type implements the same API as Program 3.2.5. It uses the same instance methods but different instance variables. Since the instance variables are* private, *this program might be used in place of Program 3.2.5 without changing any client code.*

```
% java Complex
-7.0 + 7.0i
```

bers. PROGRAM 3.2.6 uses the *Cartesian* representation, where instance variables x and y represent a complex number $x + iy$. PROGRAM 3.3.1 uses the *polar* representation, where instance variables r and theta represent a complex number in the form $r(\cos\theta + i\sin\theta)$. The polar representation is of interest because certain operations on complex number are easier to perform in the polar representation. Addition and subtraction are easier in the Cartesian representation; multiplication and division are easier in the polar representation. As you will learn in SECTION 4.1, it is often the case that performance differences are dramatic. The idea of encapsulation is that we can substitute one of these programs for the other (for whatever reason) *without changing client code.* The choice between the two implementations depends on the client. Indeed, in principle, the *only* difference to the client should be in different performance properties. This capability is of critical importance for many reasons. One of the most important is that it allows us to improve software constantly: when we develop a better way to implement a data type, all of its clients can benefit. You take advantage of this property every time you install a new version of a software system, including Java itself.

*Polar coordinates*

*Private.*  Java's language support for enforcing encapsulation is the private visibility modifier. When you declare a variable to be private, you are making it impossible for any client (code in another module) to directly access the instance variable (or method) that is the subject of the modifier. Clients can only access the API through the public methods and constructors (the API). Accordingly, you can modify the implementation of private methods (or use different private instance variables) with certain knowledge that no client will be directly affected. Java does not *require* that all instance variables be private, but we insist on this convention in the programs in this book. For example, if the instance variable re and im in Complex (PROGRAM 3.2.6) were public, then a client could write code that directly accesses them. If z refers to a Complex object, z.re and z.im refer to those values. But any client code that does so becomes completely dependent on that implementation, violating a basic precept of encapsulation. A switch to a different implementation, such as the one in PROGRAM 3.3.1, would render that code useless. To protect ourselves against such situations, we always make instance variables private; there is no good reason to make them public. Next, we examine some ramifications of this convention.

*Planning for the future.*  There have been numerous examples of important applications where significant expense can be directly traced to programmers not encapsulating their data types.

- *Zip codes.* In 1963, The United States Postal Service (USPS) began using a five-digit zip code to improve the sorting and delivery of mail. Programmers wrote software that assumed that these codes would remain at five digits forever, and represented them in their programs using a single 32-bit integer. In 1983, the USPS introduced an expanded zip code called ZIP+4, which consists of the original five-digit zip code plus four extra digits.

- *IPv4 vs. IPv6.* The Internet Protocol (IP) is a standard used by electronic devices to exchange data over the internet. Each device is assigned a unique integer or address. IPv4 uses 32-bit addresses and supports about 4.3 billion addresses. Due to explosive growth of the internet, a new version, IPv6, uses 128-bit addresses and supports $2^{128}$ addresses.

- *Vehicle identification numbers.* The 17-character naming scheme for vehicles known as the Vehicle Identification Number (VIN) that was established in 1981 describes the make, model, year, and other attributes of cars, trucks, buses, and other vehicles in the United States. But automakers expect to run out of numbers by 2010. Either the length of the VIN must be increased, or existing VINs must be reused.

In each of these cases, a necessary change to the internal representation means that a large amount of client code that depends on a current standard (because the data type is not encapsulated) will simply not function as intended. The estimated costs for the changes in each of these cases runs to hundreds of millions of dollars! That is a huge cost for failing to encapsulate a single number. These predicaments might seem distant to you, but you can be sure that every individual programmer (that's you) who does not take advantage of the protection available through encapsulation risks losing significant amounts of time and effort fixing broken code when conventions change. Our convention to define *all* of our instance variables with the `private` access modifier provides some protection against such problems. If you adopt this convention when implementing a data type for a zip code, IP address, VIN, or whatever, you can change the representation without affecting clients. The *data-type implementation* knows the data representation, and the *object* holds the data; the *client* holds only a reference to the object and does not know the details.

*Limiting the potential for error.* Encapsulation also helps programmers ensure that their code operates as intended. As an example, we consider yet another horror story: In the 2000 presidential election, Al Gore received *negative* 16,022 votes on an electronic voting machine in Volusia County, Florida. The counter variable was not properly encapsulated in the voting machine software! To understand the problem, consider `Counter` (PROGRAM 3.3.2), which implements a simple counter according to the following API:

```
public class Counter
```
---
|  |  |
|---|---|
| `Counter(String id, int max)` | *create a counter, initialized to* 0 |
| `void increment()` | *increment the counter unless its value is* max |
| `int value()` | *return the value of the counter* |
| `String toString()` | *string representation* |

*API for a counter (see* PROGRAM 3.3.2)

This abstraction is useful in many contexts, including, for example, an electronic voting machine. It encapsulates a single integer and ensures that the only operation that can be performed on the integer is *increment by one*. Therefore, it can never go negative. The goal of data abstraction is to *restrict* the operations on the data. It also *isolates* operations on the data. For example, we could add a new implementation with a logging capability so that `increment()` saves a timestamp for each vote or some other information that can be used for consistency checks. But without the `private` modifier, there could be client code like the following somewhere in the voting machine:

```
Counter c = new Counter("Volusia", VOTERS_IN_VOLUSIA_COUNTY);
c.count = -16022;
```

With `private`, code like this will not compile; without it, Gore's vote count was negative. Using encapsulation is far from a complete solution to the voting security problem, but it is a good start.

*Code clarity.* Precisely specifying a data type is good design also because it leads to client code that can more clearly express its computation. You have seen many examples of such client code in SECTIONS 3.1 and 3.2, and we already mentioned this issue in our discussion of `Histogram` (PROGRAM 3.2.3). Clients of that program are

**Program 3.3.2  Counter**

```java
public class Counter
{
   private final String name;
   private final int maxCount;
   private int count;

   public Counter(String id, int max)
   {  name = id;   maxCount = max;  }

   public void increment()
   {  if (count < maxCount) count++;   }

   public int value()
   {  return count;   }

   public String toString()
   {  return name + ": " + count;   }

   public static void main(String[] args)
   {
     int N = Integer.parseInt(args[0]);
     int T = Integer.parseInt(args[1]);
     Counter[] hits = new Counter[N];
     for (int i = 0; i < N; i++)
        hits[i] = new Counter(i + "", T);

     for (int t = 0; t < T; t++)
        hits[StdRandom.uniform(N)].increment();
     for (int i = 0; i < N; i++)
        StdOut.println(hits[i]);
   }
}
```

| name | counter name |
| maxCount | maximum value |
| count | value |

*This class encapsulates a simple integer counter, assigning it a string name and initializing it to 0 (Java's default initialization), incrementing it each time the client calls increment(), reporting the value when the client calls value(), and creating a string with its name and value in toString().*

```
% java Counter 6 600000
0: 100684
1: 99258
2: 100119
3: 100054
4: 99844
5: 100037
```

more clear than without it because calls on the instance method `addDataPoint()` clearly identify points of interest in the client. One key to good design is to observe that code written with the proper abstractions can be nearly self-documenting. Some aficionados of object-oriented programming might argue that `Histogram` itself would be easier to understand if it were to use `Counter` (see EXERCISE 3.3.5), but that point is perhaps debatable.

WE HAVE STRESSED THE BENEFITS OF encapsulation throughout this book. We summarize them again here, in the context of designing data types. Encapsulation enables modular programming, allowing us to:
   • Independently develop of client and implementation code
   • Substitute improved implementations without affecting clients
   • Support programs not yet written (any client can write to the API)
Encapsulation also isolates data-type operations, which leads to the possibility of:
   • Adding consistency checks and other debugging tools in implementations
   • Clarifying client code
A properly implemented data type (encapsulated) extends the Java language, allowing any client program to make use of it.

**Immutability.**   An *immutable* data type, such as a Java `String`, has the property that the value of an object never changes once constructed. By contrast, a *mutable* data type, such as a Java array, manipulates object values that are intended to change. Of the data types considered in this chapter, `Charge`, `Color`, `Stopwatch`, and `Complex` are all immutable, and `Picture`, `Histogram`, `Turtle`, `StockAccount`, and `Counter` are all mutable. Whether to make a data type immutable is an important design decision and depends on the application at hand.

*Immutable types.*   The purpose of many data types is to encapsulate values that do not change so that they behave in the same way as primitive types. For example, a programmer implementing a `Complex` client might reasonably expect to write the code `z = z0` for two `Complex` variables, in the same way as for `double` or `int` values. But if `Complex` were mutable and the value of `z` were to change *after* the assignment `z = z0`, then the value of `z0` would *also* change (they are both references to the same object)! This unexpected result, known as an *aliasing* bug, comes as a surprise to many newcomers to object-oriented programming. One very important reason to implement immutable types is that we can use immutable objects in assignment statements and as arguments and return values from functions without having to worry about their values changing.

| mutable | immutable |
|---------|-----------|
| Picture | Charge |
| Histogram | Color |
| Turtle | Stopwatch |
| StockAccount | Complex |
| Counter | String |
| Java arrays | primitive types |

*Mutable types.*   For many data types, the very purpose of the abstraction is to encapsulate values as they change. `Turtle` (PROGRAM 3.2.4) is a prime example. Our reason for using `Turtle` is to relieve client programs of the responsibility of tracking the changing values. Similarly, `Picture`, `Histogram`, `StockAccount`, `Counter`, and Java arrays are all types where we expect values to change. When we pass a `Turtle` as an argument to a method, as in `Koch`, we expect the values of the instance variables to change.

*Arrays and strings.*   You have already encountered this distinction as a client programmer, when using Java arrays (mutable) and Java's `String` data type (immutable). When you pass a `String` to a method, you do not need to worry about that method changing the sequence of characters in the `String`, but when you pass an array to a method, the method is free to change the elements of the array. `String` objects are immutable because we generally do *not* want `String` values to change, and Java arrays are mutable because we generally *do* want array values to change. There are also situations where we want to have mutable strings (that is the purpose of Java's `StringBuilder` class) and where we want to have immutable arrays (that is the purpose of the `Vector` class that we consider later in this section).

*Advantages of immutability.* Generally, immutable types are easier to use and harder to misuse because the scope of code that can change their values is far smaller than for mutable types. It is easier to debug code that uses immutable types because it is easier to guarantee that variables in the client code that uses them remain in a consistent state. When using mutable types, you must always be concerned about where and when their values change.

*Cost of immutability.* The downside of immutability is that *a new object must be created for every value.* For example, the expression `z = z.times(z).plus(z0)` involves creating a new object (the return value of `z.times(z)`, then using that object to invoke `plus()`, but never saving a reference to it. A program such as `Mandelbrot` (PROGRAM 3.2.7) might create a large number of such intermediate orphans. However, this expense is normally manageable because Java garbage collectors are typically optimized for such situations. Also, as in the case of `Mandelbrot`, when the point of the calculation is to create a large number of values, we expect to pay the cost of representing them. `Mandelbrot` also creates a large number of (immutable) `Color` objects.

```
Complex z0;
z0 = new Complex(1.0, 1.0);
Complex z = z0;
z = z.times(z).plus(z0);
```

*An intermediate orphan*

*Final.* Java's language support for helping to enforce immutability is the `final` modifier. When you declare a variable to be `final`, you are promising to assign it a value only once, either in an initializer or in the constructor. Code that could modify the value of a `final` variable leads to a compile-time error. In our code, we always use the modifier `final` with instance variables whose values never change. This policy serves as documentation that the value does not change, prevents accidental changes, and makes programs easier to debug. For example, you do not have to include a `final` value in a trace, since you know that its value never changes.

*Reference types.* Unfortunately, `final` guarantees immutability only when instance variables are primitive types, not reference types. If an instance variable of a reference type has the `final` modifier, the value of that instance variable (the reference to an object) will never change—it will always refer to the same object. However, the value of the object itself *can* change. For example, if you have a `final` instance variable that is an array, you cannot change the array (to change its length, say), but you *can* change the individual array elements. Thus, aliasing bugs can arise. For example, this code does *not* implement an immutable type:

```
public class Vector
{
    private final double[] coords;
    public Vector(double[] a)
    {
        coords = a;
    }
    ...
}
```

A client program could create a `Vector` by specifying the entries in an array, and then (bypassing the API) change the elements of the `Vector` after construction:

```
double[] a = { 3.0, 4.0 };
Vector vector = new Vector(a);
a[0] = 17.0;  // Bypasses the public API.
```

The instance variable `coords[]` is `private` and `final`, but `Vector` is mutable because the *client* holds the data, not the *implementation*. To ensure immutability of a data type that includes an instance variable of a mutable type, we need to make a local copy, known as a *defensive copy*. Next, we consider such an implementation.

IMMUTABILITY NEEDS TO BE TAKEN INTO account in any data-type design. Ideally, whether a data type is immutable should be specified in the API, so that clients know that object values will not change. Implementing an immutable type can be a burden in the presence of reference types. For complex types, making the copy is one challenge; ensuring that none of the instance methods change values is another.

**Example: spatial vectors** To illustrate these ideas in the context of a useful mathematical abstraction, we now consider a *vector* data type. Like complex numbers, the basic definition of the vector abstraction is familiar because it has played a central role in applied mathematics for over 100 years. The field of mathematics known as *linear algebra* is concerned with properties of vectors. Linear algebra is a rich and successful theory with numerous applications, and plays an important role in all fields of social and natural science. Full treatment of linear algebra is certainly beyond the scope of this book, but several important applications are based upon elementary and familiar calculations, so we touch upon vectors and linear algebra throughout the book (for example, the random surfer example in SECTION 1.6 is based on linear algebra). Accordingly, it is worthwhile to encapsulate such an abstraction in a data type.

A *spatial vector* is an abstract entity that has a *magnitude* and a *direction*. Spatial vectors provide a natural way to describe properties of the physical world, such as force, velocity, momentum, or acceleration. One standard way to specify a vector is as an arrow from the origin to a point in a Cartesian coordinate system: the direction is the ray from the origin to the point and the magnitude is the length of the arrow (distance from the origin to the point). To specify the vector it suffices to specify the point.

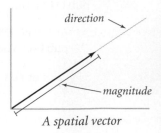

*A spatial vector*

This concept extends to any number of dimensions: an ordered list of $N$ real numbers (the coordinates of an $N$-dimensional point) suffices to specify a vector in $N$-dimensional space. By convention, we use a boldface letter to refer to a vector and numbers or indexed variable names (the same letter in italics) separated by commas within square brackets to denote its value. For example, we might use $\mathbf{x}$ to denote $(x_0, x_1, \ldots, x_{N-1})$ and $\mathbf{y}$ to denote $(y_0, y_1, \ldots, y_{N-1})$.

*API.* The basic operations on vectors are to add two vectors, multiply a vector by a scalar (real number), compute the dot product of two vectors, and compute the magnitude and direction, as follows:

- *Addition*: $\mathbf{x} + \mathbf{y} = (x_0 + y_0, x_1 + y_1, \ldots, x_{N-1} + y_{N-1})$
- *Scalar product*: $t\mathbf{x} = (tx_0, tx_1, \ldots, tx_{N-1})$
- *Dot product*: $\mathbf{x} \cdot \mathbf{y} = x_0 y_0 + x_1 y_1 + \ldots + x_{N-1} y_{N-1}$
- *Magnitude*: $|\mathbf{x}| = (x_0{}^2 + x_1{}^2 + \ldots + x_{N-1}{}^2)^{1/2}$
- *Direction*: $\mathbf{x} / |\mathbf{x}| = (x_0 / |\mathbf{x}|, x_1 / |\mathbf{x}|, \ldots, x_{N-1} / |\mathbf{x}|)$

The result of addition, scalar product, and the direction are vectors, but the magnitude and the dot product are scalar quantities (double values). For example, if $\mathbf{x} = (0, 3, 4, 0)$, and $\mathbf{y} = (0, -3, 1, -4)$, then $\mathbf{x} + \mathbf{y} = (0, 0, 5, -4)$, $3\mathbf{x} = (0, 9, 12, 0)$, $\mathbf{x} \cdot \mathbf{y} = -5$, $|\mathbf{x}| = 5$, and $\mathbf{x} / |\mathbf{x}| = (0, .6, .8, 0)$. The direction vector is a *unit vector*: its magnitude is 1. These definitions lead immediately to an API:

```
public class Vector
```

|  |  |  |
|---|---|---|
|  | Vector(double[] a) | *create a vector with the given Cartesian coordinates* |
| Vector | plus(Vector b) | *sum of this vector and b* |
| Vector | minus(Vector b) | *difference of this vector and b* |
| Vector | times(double t) | *scalar product of this vector and t* |
| double | dot(Vector b) | *dot product of this vector and b* |
| double | magnitude() | *magnitude of this vector* |
| Vector | direction() | *unit vector with same direction as this vector* |
| double | cartesian(int i) | *i th cartesian coordinate of this vector* |
| String | toString() | *string representation* |

*API for a spatial vector (see* PROGRAM 3.3.3*)*

As with Complex, this API does not explicitly specify that this type is immutable, but we know that client programmers (who are likely to be thinking in terms of the mathematical abstraction) will certainly expect that.

*Representation.* As usual, our first choice in developing an implementation is to choose a representation for the data. Using an array to hold the Cartesian coordinates provided in the constructor is a clear choice, but not the only reasonable choice. Indeed, one of the basic tenets of linear algebra is that other sets of $N$ vectors can be used as the basis for a coordinate system: any vector can be expressed as a linear combination of a set of $N$ vectors, satisfying a certain condition known as *linear independence*. This ability to change coordinate systems aligns nicely with encapsulation. Most clients do not need to know about the representation at all and can work with Vector objects and operations. If warranted, the implementation can change the coordinate system without affecting client code.

*Program 3.3.3    Spatial vectors*

```java
public class Vector
{
    private final double[] coords;                    coords[] | Cartesian coordinates

    public Vector(double[] a)
    {  // Make a defensive copy to ensure immutability.
       coords = new double[a.length];
       for (int i = 0; i < a.length; i++)
          coords[i] = a[i];
    }

    public Vector plus(Vector b)
    {  // Sum of this vector and b.
       double[] c = new double[coords.length];
       for (int i = 0; i < coords.length; i++)
          c[i] = coords[i] + b.coords[i];
       return new Vector(c);
    }

    public Vector times(double t)
    {  // Product of this vector and b.
       double[] c = new double[coords.length];
       for (int i = 0; i < coords.length; i++)
          c[i] = t * coords[i];
       return new Vector(c);
    }

    public double dot(Vector b)
    {  // Dot product of this vector and b.
       double sum = 0.0;
       for (int i = 0; i < coords.length; i++)
          sum = sum + (coords[i] * b.coords[i]);
       return sum;
    }

    public double magnitude()
    {  return Math.sqrt(this.dot(this));  }

    public Vector direction()
    {  return this.times(1/this.magnitude());  }

    public double cartesian(int i)
    {  return coords[i];  }
}
```

*This implementation encapsulates the mathematical spatial-vector abstraction. in an immutable Java data type.* Document *(Program 3.3.4) and* Body *(Program 3.4.2) are typical clients.*

*Implementation.* Given the representation, the code that implements all of these operations (`Vector`, in PROGRAM 3.3.3) is straightforward. Two of the methods (`minus()` and `toString()`) are left for exercises, as is the test client. The constructor makes a defensive copy of the client array and none of the methods assign values to the copy, so that `Vector` objects are immutable. The `cartesian()` method is easy to implement in our Cartesian coordinate representation: return the $i$th coordinate in the array. It actually implements a mathematical function that is defined for any `Vector` representation: the geometric projection onto the $i$th Cartesian axis.

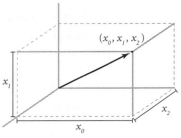

*Projecting a vector (3D)*

*The this reference.* The `magnitude()` and `direction()` methods in `Vector` make use of the name `this`. Java provides the `this` keyword to give us a way to refer within the code of an instance method to the object whose name was used to invoke this method. You can use `this` in code in the same way you use any other name. Some Java programmers *always* use `this` to refer to instance variables. Their scope is the whole class, and this policy is easy to defend because it documents references to instance variables. However, it does result in a surfeit of `this` keywords, so we take the opposite tack and use `this` sparingly in our code.

WHY GO TO THE TROUBLE OF using a `Vector` data type when all of the operations are so easily implemented with arrays? By now the answer to this question should be obvious to you: to enable modular programming, facilitate debugging, and clarify code. The array is a low-level Java mechanism that admits all kinds of operations. By restricting ourselves to just the operations in the `Vector` API (which are the only ones that we need, for many clients), we simplify the process of designing, implementing, and maintaining our programs. Because the type is immutable, we can use it as we use primitive types. For example, when we pass a `Vector` to a method, we are assured its value will not change, but we do not have that assurance with an array. After you have seen several more examples of object-oriented programming, we will discuss some more nuances in support of the assertion that it simplifies design, implementation, and maintenance. In the case of `Vector`, writing programs that use `Vector` and well-defined `Vector` operations is an easy and natural way to take advantage of the extensive amount of mathematical knowledge that has been developed around this abstract concept.

**Inheritance**   Java provides language support for defining relationships among objects, known as *inheritance*. Software developers use these mechanisms widely, so you will study them in detail if you take a course in software engineering. Generally, effective use of such mechanisms is beyond the scope of this book, but we briefly describe them here because there are a few situations where you may encounter them.

*Interfaces.*   Interfaces provide a mechanism for specifying a relationship between otherwise unrelated classes, by specifying a set of common methods that each implementing class must contain. We refer to this arrangement as *interface inheritance* because an implementing class *inherits* methods that are not otherwise in its API through the interface. This arrangement allows us to write client programs that can manipulate objects of varying types, by invoking methods in the interface. As with most new programming concepts, it is a bit confusing at first, but will make sense to you after you have seen a few examples.

*Comparable.*   One interface that you are likely to encounter is Java's `Comparable` interface. The interface associates a *natural order* for values within a data type, using a method named `compareTo()`, as described in the following API:

```
public interface Comparable<Key>
```
---
>         int compareTo(Key b)        *compare this object with b for order*

*API for Java's Comparable interface*

 The `<Key>` notation, which we will introduce in SECTION 4.3, ensures that the two objects being compared have the same type. Assuming a and b are objects of the same type, `a.compareTo(b)` must return:
   • A negative integer if a is *less than* b
   • A positive integer if if a *greater than* b
   • Zero if a is *equal to* b
Additionally, the `compareTo()` method must be consistent: for example, if a is less than b, then b must be greater than a. A class that implements the `Comparable` interface—such as `String`, `Integer`, or `Double`—promises to include a `compareTo()` method according to these rules. As expected, the natural order for strings is alphabetical and for integers is ascending.

To illustrate the utility of having such an interface, we start by considering a sort filter for String objects. The following code takes an integer N from the command-line, reads in N strings from standard input, sorts them, and prints the strings on standard output in alphabetical order.

```
import java.util.Arrays;

public class SortClient
{
    public static void main(String[] args)
    {
        int N = Integer.parseInt(args[0]);
        String[] names = new String[N];
        for (int i = 0; i < N; i++)
            names[i] = StdIn.readString();
        Arrays.sort(names);
        for (int i = 0; i < N; i++)
            StdOut.println(names[i]);
    }
}
```

We will examine sorting in detail in SECTION 4.2, so for the moment, we use a static method Arrays.sort() from Java's java.util library. Now, if we replace the array input with the three lines

```
Integer[] names = new Integer[N];
for (int i = 0; i < N; i++)
    names[i] = StdIn.readInt();
```

SortClient sorts Integer values from standard input. You might speculate that Arrays.sort() has overloaded implementations, one for String and one for Integer. But this is *not* the case because Arrays.sort() must be able to sort an array of *any* type that implements the Comparable interface (even a data type not contemplated when writing the sorting method). To do so, the code in Arrays.sort() declares variables of type Comparable—such variables may store values of type String, Integer, Double, or of *any* type that implements the Comparable interface. When you invoke the compareTo() method of such a variable, Java knows which compareTo() method to call, because it knows the type of the invoking object. This powerful programming mechanism is known as *polymorphism* or *dynamic dispatch*.

To make a class implement the `Comparable` interface, include the phrase `imple-ments Comparable` after the class definition, and then add a `compareTo()` method. For example, modify `Counter` (PROGRAM 3.3.2) as follows:

```
public class Counter implements Comparable<Counter>
{
 ...
   public int compareTo(Counter b)
   {
     if        (count < b.count) return -1;
     else if (count > b.count) return +1;
     else                          return  0;
   }
 ...
}
```

Since you are implementing `compareTo()`, you have the flexibility to specify any sort order whatever. For example, you might create a version of `Counter` to allow clients to sort `Counter` values in *decreasing* order (perhaps for a voting application), by changing the `compareTo()` method as follows:

```
public int compareTo(Counter b)
{
  if        (count < b.count) return +1;
  else if (count > b.count) return -1;
  else                          return  0;
}
```

For another example, if you were to modify `StockAccount` as follows:

```
public class StockAccount implements Comparable<StockAccount>
{
 ...
   public int compareTo(StockAccount b)
   {
      return name.compareTo(b.name);
   }
 ...
}
```

you could then sort an array of `StockAccount` values by account name with `Ar-rays.sort()`. (Note that this `compareTo()` implementation for `StockAccount` uses Java's `compareTo()` method for `String`.) This ability to arrange to write a client to sort any type of data is a persuasive example of interface inheritance.

*Computing with functions.* Often, particularly in scientific computing, we want to compute with *functions*: we want to compute integrals and derivatives, find roots, and so forth. In some programming languages, known as *functional programming languages*, this desire aligns with the underlying design of the language, which uses computing with functions to substantially simplify client code. Unfortunately, *methods are not first-class objects in Java.* As an example, consider the problem of estimating the integral of a positive function (area under the curve) in an interval (*a*, *b*).

*Approximating an integral*

This computation is known as *quadrature* or *numerical integration*. One simple method for estimating the integral is the *rectangle rule*: compute the total area of N equally-spaced rectangles under the curve. To implement this rule, we might try to write the following code to approximate the value of an integral by:

```
public double integrate(double f(double x),
                                    double a, double b, int N)
{
    double delta = (a - b) / N;
    double sum = 0.0;
    for (int i = 0; i < N; i++)
        sum += delta * f(a + delta * (i + 0.5));
}
```

Such a method would enable client code such as this:

```
integrate(Gaussian.phi(), a, b, N)
```

Unfortunately, *this code is not legal in Java.* You cannot pass methods as arguments. We can get around this restriction by defining an interface for functions and using that interface to implement `integrate()`. You can find that solution on the booksite, along with many examples of methods and classes that involve computing with functions in Java, which will be of interest if you plan to take future courses in scientific computing.

*Event-based programming.* Another powerful example of the value of interface inheritance is its use in *event-based programming*. In a familiar setting, consider the problem of extending Draw to respond to user input such as mouse clicks and keystrokes. One way to do so is to define an interface to specify which methods the draw package should call when user input happens. The descriptive term *callback* is sometimes used to describe a call from a method in one class to a method in another class through an interface. You can find on the booksite an example interface DrawListener and information on how to write code to respond to user mouse clicks and keystrokes within Draw.java. You will find it easy to write code that creates a Draw object and includes a method that the Draw method can invoke (*callback* your code) to tell your method the character typed on a user keystroke event or the mouse position on a mouse click. Writing interactive code is fun but challenging because you have to plan for all possible user input actions.

*Subtyping.* Another approach to enabling code reuse is known as *subtyping*. It is a powerful technique that enables a programmer to change the behavior of a class and add functionality without rewriting the entire class from scratch. The idea is to define a new class (*subclass*, or *derived class*) that *inherits* instance variables and instance methods from another class (*superclass*, or *base class*). The subclass contains more methods than the superclass. Subtyping is widely used by systems programmers to build so-called *extensible* libraries. The idea is that one programmer (even you) can add methods to a library built by another programmer (or, perhaps, a team of systems programmers), effectively reusing the code in a potentially huge library. This approach is widely used, particularly in the development of user interfaces, so that the large amount of code required to provide all the facilities that users expect (drop-down menus, cut-and-paste, access to files, and so forth) can be reused. The use of subtyping is controversial among systems programmers (its advantages over interface inheritance are debatable), and we do not use it in this book, because it generally works against encapsulation. Subtyping makes modular programming more difficult for two reasons. First, any change in the superclass affects all sub-classes. The subclass cannot be developed *independently* of the superclass; indeed, it is *completely dependent* on the superclass. This problem is known as the *fragile base class* problem. Second, the subclass code, having access to instance variables, can subvert the intention of the superclass code. For example, the designer of a class such as Vector may have taken great care to make the Vector immutable, but a subclass, with full access to the instance variables, can just change them. However, certain vestiges of the approach are built into Java and therefore unavoidable. Specifically, every class is a subtype of Java's Object class. This structure enables implementation of the "convention" that every class includes an implementations of toString(), equals(), hashCode() (a method that we will encounter later in this section and in CHAPTER 4), and several other methods. Every class inherits these methods from Object through subtyping.

**Application: data mining**   To illustrate some of the concepts discussed in this section in the context of an application, we next consider a software technology that is proving important in addressing the daunting challenges of *data mining*, a term that is widely used to describe the process of searching through the massive amounts of information now accessible to every user on the web (not to mention our own computers). This technology can serve as the basis for dramatic improvements in the quality of web search results, for multimedia information retrieval, for biomedical databases, for plagiarism detection, for research in genomics, for improved scholarship in many fields, for innovation in commercial applications, for learning the plans of evildoers, and for many other purposes. Accordingly, there is intense interest and extensive ongoing research on data mining.

You have direct access to thousands of files on your computer and indirect access to billions of files on the web. As you know, these files are remarkably diverse: there are commercial web pages, music and video, email, program code, and all sorts of other information. For simplicity, we will restrict attention to *text* documents (though the method we will consider applies to pictures, music, and all sorts of other files as well). Even with this restriction, there is remarkable diversity in the types of documents. For reference, you can find these documents on the booksite: Our interest is in finding efficient ways to search through the files using their *content* to characterize documents. One fruitful approach to this problem is to as-

| file name | description | sample text |
|---|---|---|
| Constitution.txt | *legal document* | ... of both Houses shall be determined by ... |
| TomSawyer.txt | *American novel* | ..."Say, Tom, let ME whitewash a little." ... |
| HuckFinn.txt | *American novel* | ...was feeling pretty good after breakfast... |
| Prejudice.txt | *English novel* | ... dared not even mention that gentleman.... |
| Picture.java | *Java code* | ...String suffix = filename.substring(file... |
| DJIA.csv | *financial data* | ...01-Oct-28,239.43,242.46,3500000,240.01 ... |
| Amazon.html | *web page source* | ...<table width="100%" border="0" cellspac... |
| ACTG.txt | *virus genome* | ...GTATGGAGCAGCAGACGCGCTACTTCGAGCGGAGGCATA... |

*Some text documents*

sociate with each document a vector known as a *profile*, which is a function of its content. The basic idea is that the profile should characterize a document, so that documents that are different have profiles that are different and documents that are similar have profiles that are similar. You probably are not surprised to learn that this approach can enable us to distinguish among a novel, a Java program, and a genome, but you might be surprised to learn that content searches can tell the difference between novels written by different authors and can be effective as the basis for many other subtle search criteria.

To start, we need an abstraction for documents. What is a document? What operations do we want to perform on documents? The answers to these questions inform our design and therefore, ultimately, the code that we write. For the purposes of data mining, it is clear that the answer to the first question is that a document is defined by an input stream. The answer to the second question is that we need to be able to compute a number (for example, a `double` value) to measure the similarity between a document and any other document. These considerations lead to the following API.

```
public class Document
```
| | | |
|---|---|---|
| | `Document(String name, int k, int d)` | |
| `double` | `simTo(Document doc)` | *similarity measure between this document and* `doc` |
| `String` | `name()` | *name of this document* |

*API for documents (see* PROGRAM *3.3.4)*

The arguments of the constructor are a file or website name (for use by `In`) and two integers that control the quality of the search. Clients can use `simTo()` to determine the extent of similarity between this `Document` and any other `Document` on a scale of 0 (not similar) to 1 (similar). This simple data type provides a good separation between implementing a similarity measure and implementing clients that use the measure to search among documents.

*Computing profiles* Computing the profile is the first challenge. Our first choice is to use `Vector` to represent a document's profile. But what information should go into computing the profile and how do we compute the value of the `Vector` profile of a `Document` (in the constructor)? Many different approaches have been studied, and researchers are still actively seeking efficient and effective algorithms for this

## Program 3.3.4  Document

```java
public class Document
{
   private final String id;
   private final Vector profile;

   public Document(String name, int k, int d)
   {
      id = name;
      String s = (new In(name)).readAll();
      int N = s.length();
      double[] freq = new double[d];
      for (int i = 0; i < N-k; i++)
      {
         int h = s.substring(i, i+k).hashCode();
         freq[Math.abs(h % d)] += 1;

      }
      profile = (new Vector(freq)).direction();
   }

   public double simTo(Document doc)
   {  return profile.dot(doc.profile);  }

   public String name()
   {  return id;  }

   public static void main(String[] args)
   {
      String name = args[0];
      int k = Integer.parseInt(args[1]);
      int d = Integer.parseInt(args[2]);
      Document doc = new Document(name, k, d);
      StdOut.println(doc.profile);
   }
}
```

| | |
|---|---|
| id | *file name or URL* |
| profile | *unit vector* |

| | |
|---|---|
| name | *document name* |
| k | *length of gram* |
| d | *dimension* |
| s | *entire document* |
| N | *document length* |
| freq[] | *hash frequencies* |
| h | *hash for k-gram* |

---

*This* Vector *client creates a unit vector from a document's k-grams that clients can use to measure its similarity with other documents (see text).*

```
% more genomeA.txt
ATAGATGCATAGCGCATAGC
% java Document genomeA.txt 2 16
[ 0 0 0.51 0.39 0.39 0 0 0 .13 0.39 0 0 0.13 0.13 0.51 0 0 ]
```

task. Our implementation Document (PROGRAM 3.3.4) uses a simple *frequency count* approach. The constructor has two arguments, an integer $k$ and a vector dimension $d$. It scans the document and examines all of the *k-grams* in the document: the substrings of length $k$ starting at each position. In its simplest form, the profile is a vector that gives the relative frequency of occurrence of the $k$-grams in the string: an entry for each possible $k$-gram giving the number of $k$-grams in the content that have that value. For example, suppose that we use $k = 2$ in genomic data, with $d = 16$ (there are 4 possible character values and therefore 16 possible 2-grams). The 2-gram AT occurs 4 times in the string ATAGATGCATAGCGCATAGC, so, for example, the vector entry corresponding to AT would be 4. To build the frequency vector, we need to be able to convert each of the $k$-grams into an integer between 0 and 15 (this integer function of a string is known as a *hash* value). For genomic data, this is an easy exercise (see EXERCISE 3.3.26). Then, we can compute an array to build the frequency vector in one scan through the text, incrementing the array entry corresponding to each $k$-gram encountered. It would seem that we lose information by disregarding the order of the $k$-grams, but the remarkable fact is that the information content of that order is lower than that of their frequency. A Markov model paradigm not dissimilar from the one that we studied for the random surfer in SECTION 1.6 can be used to take order into account— such models are effective, but much more work to implement. Encapsulating the computation in Document gives us the flexibility to experiment with various designs without needing to rewrite Document clients.

|  |  | CTTTCGGTTT GGAACCGAAG CCGCGCGTCT | |  |
|  |  | ATAGATGCAT TGTCTGCTGC AGCGCATAGC AGCATCGTTC | |  |

| 2-gram | hash | count | unit | count | unit |
|--------|------|-------|------|-------|------|
| AA | 0 | 0 | 0 | 2 | .137 |
| AC | 1 | 0 | 0 | 1 | .069 |
| AG | 2 | 4 | .508 | 1 | .069 |
| AT | 3 | 3 | .381 | 2 | .137 |
| CA | 4 | 3 | .381 | 3 | .206 |
| CC | 5 | 0 | 0 | 2 | .137 |
| CG | 6 | 0 | 0 | 4 | .275 |
| CT | 7 | 1 | .127 | 6 | .412 |
| GA | 8 | 3 | .381 | 0 | 0 |
| GC | 9 | 0 | 0 | 5 | .343 |
| GG | 10 | 0 | 0 | 6 | .412 |
| GT | 11 | 1 | .127 | 4 | .275 |
| TA | 12 | 1 | .127 | 2 | .137 |
| TC | 13 | 4 | .508 | 6 | .412 |
| TG | 14 | 0 | 0 | 4 | .275 |
| TT | 15 | 0 | 0 | 2 | .137 |

*Profiling genomic data*

*Hashing.* For ASCII text strings there are 128 different possible char values for each character, so there are $128^k$ possible $k$-grams, and the dimension $d$ would have to be $128^k$ for the simple scheme just described. This number is prohibitively large even for moderately large $k$. For Unicode, with 65,536 characters, even 2-grams lead to huge vector profiles. To ameliorate this problem, we use *hashing*, a fundamental operation related to search algorithms that we consider in SECTION 4.4. Indeed, the problem of converting a string to an integer index is so important that it is built into Java. As just mentioned in our discussion of inheritance, all objects inherit from `Object` a method `hashCode()` that returns an `int` value. Given any string `s`, we compute `Math.abs(s.hashcode() % d)`. This value is an integer between 0 and $d-1$ that we can use as an index into an array to compute frequencies. The profile that we use is the *direction* of the vector defined by frequencies of these values for all $k$-grams in the document (the unit vector with the same direction).

*Comparing profiles.* The second challenge is to compute a similarity measure between two profiles. Again, there are many different ways to compare two vectors. Perhaps the simplest is to compute the Euclidean distance between them. Given vectors **x** and **y**, this distance is defined by:

$$|\mathbf{x} - \mathbf{y}| = ((x_0 - y_0)^2 + (x_1 - y_1)^2 + \ldots + (x_{d-1} - y_{d-1})^2)^{1/2}$$

You are familiar with this formula for $d = 2$ or $d = 3$. With `Vector`, the distance is easy to compute. If x and y are two `Vector` values, then `x.minus(y).magnitude()` is the Euclidean distance between them. If documents are similar, we expect their profiles to be similar and the distance between them to be low. Another widely used similarity measure, known as the *cosine similarity measure*, is even simpler: since our profiles are unit vectors with nonnegative coordinates, their *dot product*

```
% more docs.txt
Consitution.txt
TomSawyer.txt
HuckFinn.txt
Prejudice.txt
Picture.java
DJIA.csv
Amazon.html
ACTG.txt
```

$$\mathbf{x} \cdot \mathbf{y} = x_0 y_0 + x_1 y_1 + \ldots + x_{d-1} y_{d-1}$$

is a number between 0 and 1. Geometrically, this quantity is the cosine of the angle formed by the two vectors (see EXERCISE 3.3.12). The more similar the documents, the closer we expect this measure to be to 1.

*Comparing all pairs.* `CompareAll` (PROGRAM 3.3.5) is a simple and useful `Document` client that provides the information needed to solve the following problem: given a set of documents, find the two that are most similar. Since this specification is a bit subjective, `CompareAll` prints out the cosine similarity measure for all pairs of documents on an input list. For moderate-size $k$ and $d$, the profiles do a remarkably good job of characterizing our sample set of documents. The results say not only that genomic data, financial data, Java code, and web source code are quite different from legal documents and novels, but also that *Tom Sawyer* and *Huckleberry*

*Program 3.3.5   Similarity detection*

```
public class CompareAll
{
  public static void main(String[] args)
  {
    int k = Integer.parseInt(args[0]);
    int d = Integer.parseInt(args[1]);
    int N = StdIn.readInt();
    Document[] a = new Document[N];
    for (int i = 0; i < N; i++)
       a[i] = new Document(StdIn.readString(), k, d);
    StdOut.print("    ");
    for (int j = 0; j < N; j++)
       StdOut.printf("    %.4s", a[j].name());
    StdOut.println();
    for (int i = 0; i < N; i++)
    {
        StdOut.printf("%.4s", a[i].name());
        for (int j = 0; j < N; j++)
           StdOut.printf("%8.2f", a[i].simTo(a[j]));
        StdOut.println();
    }
  }
}
```

| k | length of gram |
|---|---|
| d | dimension |
| N | number of documents |
| a[] | all documents |

*This Document client reads a document list from standard input, computes profiles based on k-gram frequencies for all the documents, and prints a matrix of similarity measures between all pairs of documents. It takes two arguments from the command line: the value of k and the dimension d of the profiles.*

```
% java CompareAll 5 10000 < docs.txt
        Cons    TomS    Huck    Prej    Pict    DJIA    Amaz    ACTG
Cons    1.00    0.66    0.60    0.64    0.17    0.18    0.21    0.11
TomS    0.66    1.00    0.93    0.88    0.10    0.24    0.18    0.14
Huck    0.60    0.93    1.00    0.82    0.07    0.23    0.16    0.12
Prej    0.64    0.88    0.82    1.00    0.10    0.25    0.19    0.15
Pict    0.17    0.10    0.07    0.10    1.00    0.05    0.37    0.03
DJIA    0.18    0.24    0.23    0.25    0.05    1.00    0.16    0.11
Amaz    0.21    0.18    0.16    0.19    0.37    0.16    1.00    0.07
ACTG    0.11    0.14    0.12    0.15    0.03    0.11    0.07    1.00
```

*Finn* are much more similar to each other than to *Pride and Prejudice*. A researcher in comparative literature could use this program to discover relationships between texts; a teacher could also use this program to detect plagiarism in a set of student submissions (indeed, many teachers *do* use such programs on a regular basis); or a biologist could use this program to discover relationships among genomes. You can find many documents on the booksite (or gather your own collection) to test the effectiveness of `CompareAll` for various parameter settings.

*Searching for similar documents.*  Another natural `Document` client is one that uses profiles to search among a large number of documents to identify those that are similar to a given document. For example, web search engines uses clients of this type to present you with pages that are similar to those you have previously visited, online book merchants use clients of this type to recommend books that are similar to ones you have purchased, and social networking websites use clients of this type to identify people whose personal interests are similar to yours. Since In can take web addresses instead of file names, it is feasible to write a program that can surf the web, compute profiles, and return links to pages that have profiles that are similar to the one sought. We leave this client for a challenging exercise.

THIS SOLUTION IS JUST A SKETCH. Many sophisticated algorithms for efficiently computing profiles and comparing them are still being invented and studied by computer scientists. Our purpose here is to introduce you to this fundamental problem domain while at the same time illustrating the power of abstraction in addressing a computational challenge. Vectors are an essential mathematical abstraction, and we can build search solutions by developing *layers of abstraction*: `Vector` is built with the Java array, `Document` is built with `Vector`, and client code uses `Document`. As usual, we have

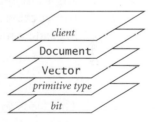

*Layers of abstraction*

spared you from a lengthy account of our many attempts to develop these APIs, but you can see that the data types are designed in response to the needs of the problem, with an eye toward the requirements of implementations. Identifying and implementing appropriate abstractions is the key to effective object-oriented programming. The power of abstraction—in mathematics, physical models, and in computer programs—pervades these examples. As you become fluent in developing data types to address your own computational challenges, your appreciation for this power will surely grow.

**Design-by-contract.**   To conclude, we briefly discuss Java language mechanisms that enable you to verify assumptions about your program *as it is running*.
For example, if you have a data type that represents a particle, you might assert
that its mass is positive and its speed is less than the speed of light. Or if you have a
method to add two vectors of the same length, you might assert that the length of
the resulting vector also has the same length.

*Exceptions.*  An exception is a disruptive event that occurs while a program is running, often to signal an error. The action taken is known as *throwing an exception*.
We have already encountered exceptions thrown by Java system methods in the
course of learning to program: `StackOverflowException`, `DivideByZeroExcep-
tion`, `NullPointerException`, and `ArrayOutOfBoundsException` are typical
examples. You can also create your own exceptions. The simplest kind is a `Run-
timeException` that terminates execution of the program and prints out an error
message.

```
throw new RuntimeException("Error message here.");
```

It is good practice to use exceptions when they can be helpful to the user. For example, in `Vector` (PROGRAM 3.3.3), we should throw an exception in `plus()` if the
two `Vectors` to be added have different dimensions. To do so, we insert the following statement at the beginning of `plus()`:

```
if (coords.length != b.coords.length)
    throw new RuntimeException("Vector dimensions disagree.");
```

This leads to a more informative error message than the `ArrayOutOfBoundsEx-
ception` than the client would otherwise receive.

*Assertions.*  An *assertion* is a boolean expression that you are affirming is `true` at
that point in the program. If the expression is `false`, the program will terminate
and report an error message. Assertions are widely used by programmers to detect
bugs and gain confidence in the correctness of programs. They also serve to document the programmer's intent. For example, in `Counter` (PROGRAM 3.3.2), we might
check that the counter is never negative by adding the following assertion as the last
statement in `increment()`:

```
assert count >= 0;
```

which would identify a negative count. You can also add an optional detail message, such as

```
assert count >= 0 : "Negative count detected in increment()";
```

to help you locate the bug. By default, assertions are disabled, but you can enable them from the command line by using the -enableassertions flag (-ea for short). Assertions are for debugging only: your program should not rely on assertions for normal operation since they may be disabled. When you take a course in systems programming, you will learn to use assertions to ensure that your code *never* terminates in a system error or goes into an infinite loop. One model, known as the *design-by-contract* model of programming, expresses the idea. The designer of a data type expresses a *precondition* (the condition that the client promises to satisfy when calling a method), a *postcondition* (the condition that the implementation promises to achieve when returning from a method), *invariants* (any condition that the implementation promises to satisfy while the method is executing), and *side effects* (any other change in state that the method could cause). During development, these conditions can be tested with assertions. Many programmers use assertions liberally to aid in debugging.

THE LANGUAGE MECHANISMS DISCUSSED THROUGHOUT THIS section illustrate that effective data-type design takes us into deep water in programming-language design. Experts are still debating the best ways to support some of the design ideas that we are discussing. Why does Java not allow functions as arguments? Why does MATLAB not support mutable data types? As mentioned early in CHAPTER 1, it is a slippery slope from complaining about features in a programming language to becoming a programming-language designer. If you do not plan to do so, your best strategy is to use widely available languages. Most systems have extensive libraries that you certainly should use when appropriate, but you often can simplify your client code and protect yourself by building abstractions that can easily transport to other languages. Your main goal is to develop data types so that most of your work is done at a level of abstraction that is appropriate to the problem at hand.

## Q + A

**Q.** What happens if I try to access a `private` instance variable or method from another file?

**A.** You get a compile-time error that says the given instance variable or method has private access in the given class.

**Q.** The instance variables in `Complex` are `private`, but when I am executing the method `times()` for a `Complex` object a, I can access object b's instance variables. Shouldn't they be inaccessible?

**A.** The granularity of private access is at the class level, not the instance level. Declaring an instance variable as private means that it is not directly accessible from any other class. Methods within the `Complex` class can access (read or write) the instance variables of any instance in that class. It might be nice to have a more restrictive access modifier, say, `superprivate`—that would make the granularity at the instance level so that only the invoking object can access its instance variables, but Java does not have such a facility.

**Q** I see the problem with the `times()` method in `Complex`. It needs a constructor that takes polar coordinates as arguments. How can we add such a constructor?

**A.** That is a problem since we already have one constructor that takes two real arguments. A better design would be to have two methods `createRect(x, y)` and `createPolar(r, theta)` in the API that create and return new objects. This design is better because it would provide the *client* with the capability to switch to polar coordinates. This example demonstrates that it is a good idea to think about more than one implementation when developing a data type.

**Q.** Is there a relationship between the `Vector` in this section and the `Vector` class in the Java library?

**A.** No. We use the name because the term *vector* properly belongs to linear algebra and vector calculus.

**Q.** What is a deprecated method?

**A.** A method that is no longer fully supported, but kept in an API to maintain compatibility. For example, Java once included a method `Character.isSpace()`, and programmers wrote programs that relied on using that method's behavior. When the designers of Java later wanted to support additional Unicode whitespace characters, they could not change the behavior of `isSpace()` without breaking client programs. So, instead, they added a new method `Character.isWhiteSpace()` and *deprecated* the old method. As time wears on, this practice certainly complicates APIs.

**Q.** I am interested in the methods that all objects inherit from `Object`. We have been using `toString()` and the use of `hashCode()` in `Document` is interesting, but what about `equals()`? Isn't it important for me to know how about that?

**A.** Well, yes, in principle, but you would be very surprised at how difficult it is to properly implement `equals()`, even for simple objects. For example, the following is an implementation of `equals()` for `Counter`:

```
public boolean equals(Object y)
{
    if (y == this) return true;
    if (y == null) return false;
    if (y.getClass() != this.getClass()) return false;
    Counter b = (Counter) y;
    return (count == b.count);
}
```

## Exercises

**3.3.1**  Represent a point in time by using an `int` to store the number of seconds since January 1, 1970. When will programs that use this representation face a time bomb? How should you proceed when that happens?

**3.3.2**  Create a data type `Location` for dealing with locations on Earth using spherical coordinates (latitude/longitude). Include methods to generate a random location on the surface of the Earth, parse a location "25.344 N, 63.5532 W", and compute the great circle distance between two locations.

**3.3.3**  Create a data type for a three-dimensional particle with position $(r_x, r_y, r_z)$, mass $(m)$, and velocity $(v_x, v_y, v_z)$. Include a method to return its kinetic energy, which equals $1/2\ m\ (v_x^2 + v_y^2 + v_z^2)$. Use `Vector`.

**3.3.4**  If you know your physics, develop an alternate implementation for you data type of the previous exercise based on using the *momentum* $(p_x, p_y, p_z)$ as an instance variable.

**3.3.5**  Develop an implementation of `Histogram` (PROGRAM 3.2.3) that uses `Counter` (PROGRAM 3.3.2).

**3.3.6**  Give an implementation of `minus()` for `Vector` solely in terms of the other `Vector` methods, such as `direction()` and `magnitude()`.

*Answer*:

```
public Vector minus(Vector b)
{
    return this.plus(b.times(-1.0));
}
```

The advantage of such implementations is that they limit the amount of detailed code to check; the disadvantage is that they can be inefficient. In this case, `plus()` and `times()` both create new `Vector` objects, so copying the code for `plus()` and replacing the minus sign with a plus sign is probably a better implementation.

**3.3.7**  Implement the method `toString()` for `Vector`.

**3.3.8** Add the code necessary to make `Vector` implement `Comparable` (using the value of the magnitude to determine the sort order) and write a test client that takes k and N as command-line arguments, reads N *k*-dimensional vectors from standard input, sorts them with `Arrays.sort()`, and prints the sorted result on standard output.

**3.3.10** Implement a data type `Vector2D` for two-dimensional vectors that has the same API as `Vector`, except that the constructor takes two `double` values as arguments. Use two `double` values (instead of an array) for instance variables.

**3.3.11** Implement the `Vector2D` data type of the previous exercise using one `Complex` value as the only instance variable.

**3.3.12** Prove that the dot product of two two-dimensional unit-vectors is the cosine of the angle between them.

**3.3.13** Implement a data type `Vector3D` for three-dimensional vectors that has the same API as `Vector`, except that the constructor takes three `double` values as arguments. Also, add a *cross product* method: the cross product of two vectors is another vector, defined by the equation

$$\mathbf{a} \times \mathbf{b} = \mathbf{c} \, |\mathbf{a}| \, |\mathbf{b}| \, \sin\theta$$

where $\mathbf{c}$ is the unit normal vector perpendicular to both $\mathbf{a}$ and $\mathbf{b}$, and $\theta$ is the angle between $\mathbf{a}$ and $\mathbf{b}$. In Cartesian coordinates, the following equation defines the cross product:

$$(a_0, a_1, a_2) \times (b_0, b_1, b_2) = (a_1 b_2 - a_2 b_1, \, a_2 b_0 - a_0 b_2, \, a_0 b_1 - a_1 b_0)$$

The cross product arises in the definition of torque, angular momentum, and vector operator curl. Also, $|\mathbf{a} \times \mathbf{b}|$ is the area of the parallelogram with sides $\mathbf{a}$ and $\mathbf{b}$.

**3.3.14** Use assertions and exceptions to develop an implementation of `Rational` (see Exercise 3.2.7) that is immune to overflow.

**3.3.15** Add code to `Counter` to throw a `RuntimeException` if the client tries to construct a `Counter` object using a negative value for max.

# Data-type Design Exercises

*This list of exercises is intended to give you experience in developing data types. For each problem, design one or more APIs with API implementations, testing your design decisions by implementing typical client code. Some of the exercises require either knowledge of a particular domain or a search for information about it on the web.*

**3.3.16** *Statistics.* Develop a data type for maintaining statistics of a set of double values. Provide a method to add data points and methods that return the number of points, the mean, the standard deviation, and the variance. Develop two implementations: one whose instance values are the number of points, the sum of the values, and the sum of the squares of the values, and another that keeps an array containing all the points. For simplicity, you may take the maximum number of points in the constructor. Your first implementation is likely to be faster and use substantially less space, but is also likely to be susceptible to roundoff error. See the booksite for a well-engineered alternative.

**3.3.17** *Genome.* Develop a data type to store the genome of an organism. Biologists often abstract the genome to a sequence of nucleotides (A, C, G, or T). The data type should support the methods addCodon(char c) and nucleotideAt(int i), as well as findGene() (see Program 3.1.8). Develop three implementations. First, use one instance variable of type String, implementing addCodon() with string concatenation. Each method call takes time proportional to the size of the current genome. Second, use an array of characters, doubling the size of the array each time it fills up. Third, use a boolean array, using two bits to encode each codon.

**3.3.18** *Time.* Develop a data type for the time of day. Provide client methods that return the current hour, minute, and second, as well as toString() and compareTo() methods. Develop two implementations: one that keeps the time as a single int value (number of seconds since midnight) and another that keeps three int values, one each for seconds, minutes, and hours.

**3.3.19** *Vector fields.* Develop a data type for force vectors in two dimensions. Provide a constructor, a method to add two vectors, and an interesting test client.

**3.3.20** *VIN number.* Develop a data type for VIN numbers that can report back all relevant information.

**3.3.21** *Generating random numbers.* Develop a data type for random numbers. (Convert StdRandom to a data type). Instead of using Math.random(), base your data type on a linear congruential random number generator. This method traces to the earliest days of computing and is also a quintessential example of the value of maintaining state in a computation (implementing a data type). To generate random int values, maintain an int value x (the value of the last "random" number returned). Each time the client asks for a new value, return a*x + b for suitably chosen values of a and b (ignoring overflow). Use arithmetic to convert these values to "random" values of other types of data. As suggested by D. E. Knuth, use the values 3141592621 for a and 2718281829 for b, or check the booksite for other suggestions. Provide a constructor allowing the client to start with an int value known as a seed (the initial value of x). This ability makes it clear that the numbers are not at all random (even though they may have many of the properties of random numbers) but that fact can be used to aid in debugging, since clients can arrange to see the same numbers each time.

**3.3.22** *Encapsulation.* Is the following class immutable?

```
import java.util.Date;
public class Appointment
{
    private Date date;
    private String contact;

    public Appointment(Date date)
    {
        // Code to check for a conflict.
        this.date = date;
        this.contact = contact;
    }
    public Date getDate()
    {   return date;   }
}
```

*Answer:* No. Java's `Date` class is mutable. The method `setDate(seconds)` changes the value of the invoking date to the number of milliseconds since January 1, 1970, 00:00:00 GMT. This has the unfortunate consequence that when a client gets a date with `d = getDate()`, the client program can then invoke `d.setDate()` and change the date in an `Appointment` object type, perhaps creating a conflict. In a data type, we cannot let references to mutable objects escape because the caller can then modify its state. One solution is to create a defensive copy of the `Date` before returning it using `new Date(date.getTime())`; and a defensive copy when storing it via `this.date = new Date(date.getTime())`. Many programmers regard the mutability of `Date` as a Java design flaw. (`GregorianCalendar` is a more modern Java library for storing dates, but it is mutable, too.)

**3.3.23** *Date.* Develop an implementation of Java's `Date` API that is immutable and therefore corrects the defects of the previous exercise.

**3.3.24** *Calendar.* Develop `Appointment` and `Calendar` APIs that can be used to keep track of appointments (by day) in a calendar year. Your goal is to enable clients to schedule appointments that do not conflict and to report current appointments to clients.

**3.3.25** *Vector field.* A vector field associates a vector with every point in a Euclidean space. Write a version of `Potential` (PROGRAM 3.1.7) that takes as input a grid size $N$, computes the `Vector` value of the potential due to the point charges at each point in an $N$-by-$N$ grid of equally spaced points, and draws the unit vector in the direction of the accumulated field at each point. (Modify `Charge` to return a `Vector`.)

**3.3.26** *Genome profiling.* Write a function `hash()` that takes as argument a $k$-gram (string of length $k$) whose characters are all A, C, G, or T and returns an `int` value between 0 and $4^k$ that corresponds to treating the string as base-4 numbers with {A, C, G, T} replaced by {0, 1, 2, 3}, respectively, as suggested by the table in the text. Next, write a function `unhash()` that reverses the transformation. Use your methods to create a class `Genome` that is like `Document`, but is based on exact counting of $k$-grams in genomes. Finally, write a version of `CompareAll` for `Genome` objects and use it to look for similarities among the set of genome files on the booksite.

**3.3.27** *Profiling.* Pick an interesting set of documents from the booksite (or use a collection of your own) and run `CompareAll` with various values of the two parameters, to learn about their effect on the computation.

**3.3.28** *Multimedia search.* Develop profiling strategies for sound and pictures, and use them to discover interesting similarities among songs in the music library and photos in the photo album on your computer.

**3.3.29** *Data mining.* Write a recursive program that surfs the web, starting at a page given as the first command-line argument, looking for pages that are similar to the page given as the second command-line argument, as follows: to process a name, open an input stream, do a `readAll()`, profile it, and print the name if its distance to the target page is greater than the threshold value given as the third command-line argument. Then scan the page for all strings that contain the substring `http://` and (recursively) process pages with those names. *Note*: This program could read a very large number of pages!

# 3.4 Case Study: *N*-body Simulation

SEVERAL OF THE EXAMPLES THAT WE considered in CHAPTERS 1 AND 2 are better expressed as object-oriented programs. For example, BouncingBall (PROGRAM 1.5.6) is naturally implemented as a data type whose values are the position and the velocity of the ball and a client that calls instance methods to move and draw the ball. Such a data type enables, for example, clients that can simulate the motion of several balls at once (see EXERCISE 3.4.1). Similarly, our case study for Percolation in

SECTION 2.4 certainly makes an interesting exercise in object-oriented programming, as does our random surfer case study in SECTION 1.6. We leave the former for an exercise (see EXERCISE 3.4.2) and will revisit the latter in SECTION 4.5. In this section, we consider a new example that exemplifies object-oriented programming.

Our task is to write a program that dynamically simulates the motion of *N* bodies under the influence of mutual gravitational attraction. This problem was first formulated by Newton over 350 years ago, and it is still studied intensely today.

*What is the set of values, and what are the operations on those values?* One reason that this problem is an amusing and compelling example of object-oriented programming is that it presents a direct and natural correspondence between physical objects in the real world and the abstract objects that we use in programming. The shift from solving problems by putting together sequences of statements to be executed to beginning with data type design is a difficult one for many novices. As you gain more experience, you will appreciate the value in this approach to computational problem-solving.

We recall a few basic concepts and equations that you learned in high school physics. Understanding those equations fully is not required to appreciate the code—because of *encapsulation*, these equations are restricted to a few methods, and because of *data abstraction*, most of the code is intuitive and will make sense to you. In a sense, this is the ultimate object-oriented program.

**N-body simulation**   The bouncing ball simulation of Section 1.5 is based on *Newton's first law of motion*: a body in motion remains in motion at the same velocity unless acted on by an outside force. Embellishing that example to include Newton's *second* law of motion (which explains how outside forces affect velocity) leads us to a basic problem that has fascinated scientists for ages. Given a system of $N$ bodies, mutually affected by gravitational forces, the problem is to describe their motion. The same basic model applies to problems ranging in scale from astrophysics to molecular dynamics.

In 1687, Isaac Newton formulated the principles governing the motion of two bodies under the influence of their mutual gravitational attraction, in his famous *Principia*. However, Newton was unable to develop a mathematical description of the motion of *three* bodies. It has since been shown that not only is there no such description in terms of elementary functions, but also that chaotic behavior is possible, depending on initial values. To study such problems, scientists have no recourse but to develop an accurate simulation. In this section, we develop an object-oriented program that implements such a simulation. Scientists are interested in studying such problems at a high degree of accuracy for huge numbers of bodies, so our solution is only an introduction to the subject, but you are likely to be surprised at the ease with which we can develop realistic images depicting the complexity of the motion.

*Body data type.* In `BouncingBall` (Program 1.5.6), we keep the displacement from the origin in the `double` values `rx` and `ry` and the velocity in the `double` values `vx` and `vy`, and displace the ball the amount it moves in one time unit with the statements:

```
rx = rx + vx;
ry = ry + vy;
```

With `Vector` (Program 3.3.3), we can keep the position in the `Vector` value `r` and the velocity in the `Vector` value `v`, and then displace the body the amount it moves in `dt` time units with a single statement:

```
r = r.plus(v.times(dt));
```

In *N*-body simulation, we have several operations of this kind, so our first design decision is to work with `Vector` values instead of individual component values. This decision

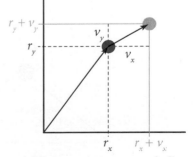

*Adding vectors to move a ball*

leads to code that is clearer, more compact, and more flexible than the alternative of working with individual components. Body (PROGRAM 3.4.1) is a Java class that uses Vector to implement a data type for moving bodies. The values of the data type are Vector values that carry the body's position and velocity, as well as a double value that carries the mass. The data-type operations allow clients to move and to draw the body (and to compute the force vector due to gravitational attraction of another body), as defined by the following API:

```
public class Body
```

|  |  |
|---|---|
| Body(Vector r, Vector v, double mass) | |
| void move(Vector f, double dt) | *apply force* f, *move body for* dt *seconds* |
| void draw() | *draw the ball* |
| Vector forceFrom(Body b) | *force vector between this body and* b |

*API for bodies moving under Newton's laws (see* PROGRAM 3.4.1)

Technically, the body's position (displacement from the origin) is not a vector (it is a point in space, not a direction and a magnitude), but it is convenient to represent it as a Vector because Vector's operations lead to compact code for the transformation that we need to move the body, as just discussed. When we move a Body, we need to change not just its position, but also its velocity.

*Force and motion.* *Newton's second law of motion* says that the force on a body (a vector) is equal to the scalar product of its mass and its acceleration (also a vector): $\mathbf{f} = m\mathbf{a}$. In other words, to compute the acceleration of a body, we compute the

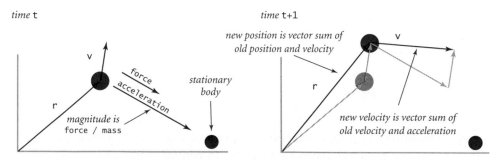

*Motion near a stationary body*

force, then divide by its mass. In Body, the force is a Vector argument f to move(), so that we can first compute the acceleration vector just by dividing by the mass (a scalar value that is kept as a double value in an instance variable) and then compute the change in velocity by adding to it the amount this vector changes over the time interval (in the same way as we used the velocity to change the position). This law immediately translates to the following code for updating the position and velocity of a body due to a given force vector f and amount of time dt:

```
Vector a = f.times(1/mass);
v = v.plus(a.times(dt));
r = r.plus(v.times(dt));
```

This code appears in the move() instance method in Body, to adjust its values to reflect the consequences of that force being applied for that amount of time: the body moves and its velocity changes. This calculation assumes that the acceleration is constant during the time interval.

*Forces among bodies.* The computation of the force imposed by one body on another is encapsulated in the instance method forceFrom() in Body, which takes a Body object as argument and returns a Vector. *Newton's law of universal gravitation* is the basis for the calculation: it says that the magnitude of the gravitational force between two bodies is given by the product of their masses divided by the square of the distance between them (scaled by the gravitational constant G, which is $6.67 \times 10^{-11}$ N m$^2$ / kg$^2$) and that the direction of the force is the line between the two particles. This law translates to the following code for computing a.forceFrom(b):

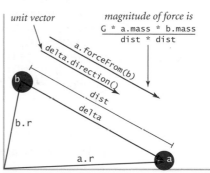

*Force from one body to another*

```
double G = 6.67e-11;
Vector delta = a.r.minus(b.r);
double dist = delta.magnitude();
double F = (G * a.mass * b.mass) / (dist * dist);
return delta.direction().times(F);
```

The *magnitude* of the force vector is the double value F, and the *direction* of the force vector is the same as the direction of the difference vector between the two body's positions. The force vector is the product of magnitude and direction.

*Program 3.4.1    Gravitational body*

```
public class Body
{
    private Vector r;
    private Vector v;
    private final double mass;

    public Body(Vector r0, Vector v0, double m0)
    {   r = r0; v = v0; mass = m0;   }

    public void move(Vector f, double dt)
    {   // Update position and velocity.
        Vector a = f.times(1/mass);
        v = v.plus(a.times(dt));
        r = r.plus(v.times(dt));
    }

    public Vector forceFrom(Body b)
    {   // Compute force on this body from b.
        Body a = this;
        double G = 6.67e-11;
        Vector delta = a.r.minus(b.r);
        double dist = delta.magnitude();
        double F = (G * a.mass * b.mass)
                              / (dist * dist);
        return delta.direction().times(F);
    }

    public void draw()
    {
        StdDraw.setPenRadius(0.025);
        StdDraw.point(r.cartesian(0), r.cartesian(1));
    }
}
```

| | |
|---|---|
| r | *position* |
| v | *velocity* |
| mass | *mass* |

| | |
|---|---|
| f | *force on this body* |
| dt | *time increment* |
| a | *acceleration* |

| | |
|---|---|
| a | *this body* |
| b | *another body* |
| G | *gravitational constant* |
| delta | *vector from* b *to* a |
| dist | *distance from* b *to* a |
| F | *magnitude of force* |

*This data type provides the operations that we need to simulate the motion of physical bodies such as planets or atomic particles. It is a mutable type whose instance variables are the position and velocity of the body, which change in the* move() *method in response to external forces (the body's mass is not mutable). The* forceFrom() *method returns a force vector.*

*Universe data type.* `Universe` (PROGRAM 3.4.2) is a data type that implements the following API:

| public class Universe | |
|---|---|
| `Universe()` | |
| `void increaseTime(double dt)` | *simulate the passing of* `dt` *seconds* |
| `void draw()` | *draw the universe* |

*API for a universe (see PROGRAM 3.4.2)*

Its data-type values define a universe (its size, number of bodies, and an array of bodies) and two data-type operations: `increaseTime()`, which adjusts the positions (and velocities) of all of the bodies, and `draw()`, which draws all of the bodies. The key to the *N*-body simulation is the implementation of `increaseTime()` in `Universe`. The first part of the computation is a double loop that computes the force vector that describes the gravitational force of each body on each other body.

It applies the *principle of superposition*, which says that we can add together the force vectors affecting a body to get a single vector representing all the forces. After it has computed all of the forces, it calls the `move()` operation for each body to apply the computed force for a fixed time quantum.

```
% more 2body.txt
2
5.0e10
0.0e00   4.5e10   1.0e04 0.0e00 1.5e30
0.0e00  -4.5e10  -1.0e04 0.0e00 1.5e30

% more 3body.txt
3
1.25e11
0.0e00   0.0e00 0.05e04 0.0e00 5.97e24
0.0e00   4.5e10   3.0e04 0.0e00 1.989e30
0.0e00  -4.5e10  -3.0e04 0.0e00 1.989e30
```

*File format.* As usual, we use a data-driven design with input taken from standard input. The constructor reads the universe parameters and body descriptions from a file that contains the following information:
- The number of bodies
- The radius of the universe
- The position, velocity, and mass of each body

As usual, for consistency, all measurements are in standard SI units (recall also that the gravitational constant *G* appears in our code). With this defined file format, the code for our `Universe` constructor is straightforward.

*Universe file format examples*

```
public Universe()
{
    N = StdIn.readInt();
    radius = StdIn.readDouble();
    StdDraw.setXscale(-radius, +radius);
    StdDraw.setYscale(-radius, +radius);
    orbs = new Body[N];
    for (int i = 0; i < N; i++)
    {
        double rx = StdIn.readDouble();
        double ry = StdIn.readDouble();
        double[] position = { rx, ry };
        double vx = StdIn.readDouble();
        double vy = StdIn.readDouble();
        double[] velocity = { vx, vy };
        double mass = StdIn.readDouble();
        Vector r = new Vector(position);
        Vector v = new Vector(velocity);
        orbs[i] = new Body(r, v, mass);
    }
}
```

Each Body is described by five double values: the *x* and *y* coordinates of its position, the *x* and *y* components of its initial velocity, and its mass.

TO SUMMARIZE, WE HAVE IN THE test client main() in Universe a data-driven program that simulates the motion of *N* bodies mutually attracted by gravity. The constructor creates an array of *N* Body objects, reading each body's initial position, initial velocity, and mass from standard input. The increaseTime() method calculates the mutual force on the bodies and uses that information to update the acceleration, velocity, and position of each body after a time quantum dt. The main() test client invokes the constructor, then stays in a loop calling increaseTime() and draw() to simulate motion.

You will find on the booksite a variety of files that define "universes" of all sorts, and you are encouraged to run Universe and observe their motion. When you view the motion for even a small number of bodies, you will understand why Newton had trouble deriving the equations that define their paths. The images on the chapter openings for CHAPTERS 2, 3, and 4 of this book show the result of running Universe for the 2-body, 3-body, and 4-body examples in the data files shown here. The 2-body example is a mutually orbiting pair, the 3-body example is a cha-

***Program 3.4.2    N-body simulation***

```
public class Universe
{
   private final double radius;
   private final int N;
   private final Body[] orbs;

   public Universe()
   {  /* See text. */  }

   public void increaseTime(double dt)
   {
      Vector[] f = new Vector[N];
      for (int i = 0; i < N; i++)
         f[i] = new Vector(new double[2]);
      for (int i = 0; i < N; i++)
         for (int j = 0; j < N; j++)
           if (i != j)
              f[i] = f[i].plus(orbs[i].forceFrom(orbs[j]));
      for (int i = 0; i < N; i++)
         orbs[i].move(f[i], dt);
   }

   public void draw()
   {
      for (int i = 0; i < N; i++)
         orbs[i].draw();
   }

   public static void main(String[] args)
   {
      Universe newton = new Universe();
      double dt = Double.parseDouble(args[0]);
      while (true)
      {
         StdDraw.clear();
         newton.increaseTime(dt);
         newton.draw();
         StdDraw.show(10);
      }
   }
}
```

| radius | radius of universe |
|---|---|
| N | number of bodies |
| orbs[] | array of bodies |

% java Universe 20000 < 3body.txt

*880 steps*

*This data-driven program simulates motion in the universe defined by the standard input stream, increasing time at the rate specified on the command line.*

otic situation with a moon jumping between two orbiting planets, and the 4-body example is a relatively simple situation where two pairs of mutually orbiting bodies are slowly rotating. The static images on these pages are made by modifying Universe and Body to draw the bodies in white, and then black on a gray background, as in BouncingBall (PROGRAM 1.5.6): the dynamic images that you get when you run Universe as it stands give a realistic feeling of the bodies orbiting one another, which is difficult to discern in the fixed pictures. When you run Universe on an example with a large number of bodies, you can appreciate why simulation is such an important tool for scientists trying to understand a complex problem. The *N*-body simulation model is remarkably versatile, as you will see if you experiment with some of these files.

*planetary scale*
```
% more 2body.txt
2
5.0e10
0.0e00   4.5e10   1.0e04 0.0e00 1.5e30
0.0e00  -4.5e10  -1.0e04 0.0e00 1.5e30
```

You will certainly be tempted to design your own universe (see EXERCISE 3.4.7). The biggest challenge in creating a data file is appropriately scaling the numbers so that the radius of the universe, time scale, and the mass and velocity of the bodies lead to in-

*subatomic scale*
```
% more 2bodyTiny.txt
2
5.0e-10
0.0e00   4.5e-10   1.0e-16 0.0e00 1.5e-30
0.0e00  -4.5e-10  -1.0e-16 0.0e00 1.5e-30
```

teresting behavior. You can study the motion of planets rotating around a sun or subatomic particles interacting with one another, but you will have no luck studying the interaction of a planet with a subatomic particle. When you work with your own data, you are likely to have some bodies that will fly off to infinity and some others that will be sucked into others, but enjoy!

Our purpose in presenting this example is to illustrate the utility of data types, not present simulation code for production use. There are many issues that scientists have to deal with when using this approach to study natural phenomena. The first is *accuracy*: it is common for inaccuracies in the calculations to accumulate to present dramatic effects in the simulation that would not be observed in nature. For example, our code takes no special action when bodies collide. The second is *efficiency*: the move() method in Universe takes time proportional to $N^2$ and is therefore not usable for huge numbers of bodies. As with genomics, addressing scientific problems related to the *N*-body problem now involves not just knowledge of the original problem domain, but also understanding core issues that computer scientists have been studying since the early days of computation.

For simplicity, we are working with a *two-dimensional* universe, which is realistic only when we are considering bodies in motion on a plane. But an important implication of basing the implementation of `Body` on `Vector` is that a client could use *three-dimensional* vectors to simulate the motion of moving balls in three dimensions (actually, any number of dimensions) without changing the code at all! The `draw()` method projects the position onto the plane defined by the first two dimensions.

The test client in `Universe` is just one possibility: we can use the same basic model in all sorts of other situations (for example, involving different kinds of interactions among the bodies). One such possibility is to observe and measure the current motion of some existing bodies and then run the simulation backwards! That is one method that astrophysicists use to try to understand the origins of the universe. In science, we try to understand the past and to predict the future; with a good simulation, we can do both.

```
% java Universe 25000 < 4body.txt
```

*100 steps*

*500 steps*

*1000 steps*

*3000 steps*

*Simulating a 4-body universe*

**Q.** The `Universe` API is certainly small. Why not just implement that code in a `main()` test client for `Body`?

**A.** Well, our design is an expression of what most people believe about the universe: it was created, and then time moves on. It clarifies the code and allows for maximum flexibility in simulating what goes on in the universe.

**Q.** Why is `forceFrom()` an instance method? Wouldn't it be better for it to be a static method that takes two `Body` objects as arguments?

**A.** Yes, implementing `forceFrom()` as an instance method is one of several possible alternatives, and having a static method that takes two `Body` objects as arguments is certainly a reasonable choice. Some programmers prefer to completely avoid static methods in data-type implementations; another option is to maintain the force acting on each `Body` as an instance variable. Our choice is a compromise between these two.

# *Exercises*

**3.4.1** Write an object-oriented version of `BouncingBall` (PROGRAM 1.5.6). Include a constructor that starts each ball moving a random direction at a random velocity (within reasonable limits) and a test client that takes an integer N from the command line and simulates the motion of N bouncing balls.

**3.4.2** Write an object-oriented version of `Percolation` (PROGRAM 2.4.5). Think carefully about the design before you begin, and be prepared to defend your design decisions.

**3.4.3** What happens in a universe where Newton's second law does not apply? This situation would correspond to `forceTo()` in `Body` always returning the zero vector.

**3.4.4** Create a data type `Universe3D` to model three-dimensional universes. Develop a data file to simulate the motion of the planets in our solar system around the sun.

**3.4.5** Modify `Universe` so that its constructor takes an `In` object and a `Draw` object as arguments. Write a test client that simulates the motion of two different universes (defined by two different files and appearing in two different `Draw` windows). You also need to modify the `draw()` method in `Body`.

**3.4.6** Implement a class `RandomBody` that initializes its instance variables with (carefully chosen) random values instead of using a constructor and a client `RandomUniverse` that takes a single argument *N* from the command line and simulates motion in a random universe with *N* bodies.

## Creative Exercise

**3.4.7**  *New universe.*  Design a new universe with interesting properties and simulate its motion with `Universe`. This exercise is truly an opportunity to be creative!

# Chapter Four

# Algorithms and Data Structures

IN THIS CHAPTER, WE DISCUSS THE fundamental data types that are essential building blocks for a broad variety of applications. This chapter is a guide to using them, whether you choose to use Java library implementations or choose to develop your own variations based on the code given here.

Objects can contain references to other objects, so we can build structures known as *linked structures*, which can be arbitrarily complex. With linked structures and arrays, we can build *data structures* to organize information in such a way that we can efficiently process it with associated *algorithms*. In a data type, we use the set of values to build data structures and the methods that operate on those values to implement algorithms.

The algorithms and data structures that we consider in this chapter introduce a body of knowledge developed over the past 50 years that constitutes the basis for the efficient use of computers for a broad variety of applications. From $N$-body simulation problems in physics to genetic sequencing problems in bioinformatics, the basic methods we describe have become essential in scientific research; from database systems to search engines, these methods are the foundation of commercial computing. As the scope of computing applications continues to expand, so grows the impact of these basic methods.

Algorithms and data structures themselves are valid subjects of scientific study. Accordingly, we begin by describing a scientific approach for analyzing the performance of algorithms, which we use throughout the chapter to study the performance characteristics of our implementations.

# 4.1  Performance

IN THIS SECTION, YOU WILL LEARN to respect a principle that is succinctly expressed in yet another mantra that should live with you whenever you program: *Pay attention to the cost.* If you become an engineer, that will be your job; if you become a biologist or a physicist, the cost will dictate which scientific problems you can address; if you are in business or become an economist, this principle needs no defense; and if you become a software developer, the cost will dictate whether the software that you build will be useful to any of your clients.

To study the cost of running them, we study our programs themselves via the *scientific method*, the commonly accepted body of techniques universally used by scientists to develop knowledge about the natural world. We also apply *mathematical analysis* to derive concise models of the cost.

What features of the natural world are we studying? In most situations, we are interested in one fundamental characteristic: *time*. On each occasion that we run a program, we are performing an experiment involving the natural world, putting a complex system of electronic circuitry through series of state changes involving a huge number of discrete events that we are confident will eventually stabilize to a state with results that we want to interpret. Although developed in the abstract world of Java programming, these events most definitely are happening in the natural world. What will be the elapsed time until we see the result? It makes a great deal of difference to us whether that time is a millisecond, a second, a day, or a week, and therefore we want to learn, through the scientific method, how to properly control the situation, just as when we launch a rocket, build a bridge, or smash an atom.

On the one hand, modern programs and programming environments are complex; on the other hand, they are developed from a simple (but powerful) set of abstractions. It is a small miracle that a program produces the same result each time we run it. To predict the time required, we take advantage of the relative simplicity of the supporting infrastructure that we use to build programs. You may be surprised at the ease with which you can develop cost estimates for many of the programs that you write.

*Scientific method* The following five-step approach briefly summarizes the scientific method.

- *Observe* some feature of the natural world.
- *Hypothesize* a model that is consistent with the observations.
- *Predict* events using the hypothesis.
- *Verify* the predictions by making further observations.
- *Validate* by repeating until the hypothesis and observations agree.

One of the key tenets of the scientific method is that the experiments we design must be reproducible, so that others can convince themselves of the validity of the hypothesis. In addition, the hypotheses we formulate must be *falsifiable*, so that we can know for sure when a hypothesis is wrong (and thus needs revision).

**Observations** Our first challenge is to make quantitative measurements of the running time of our programs. Although measuring the exact running time of our program is difficult, usually we are happy with approximate estimates. There are a

number of tools available to help us obtain such approximations. Perhaps the simplest is a physical stopwatch or the `Stopwatch` (see PROGRAM 3.2.2) data type. We can simply run a program on various inputs, measuring the amount of time to process each input.

Our first qualitative observation about most programs is that there is a *problem size* that characterizes the difficulty of the computational task. Normally, the problem size is either the size of the input or the value of a command-line argument. Intuitively, the running time should increase with the problem size, but the question of *how much* it increases naturally arises every time we develop and run a program.

Another qualitative observation for many programs is that the running time is relatively insensitive

```
% java ThreeSum < 1Kints.txt
```

tick tick tick

0

```
% java ThreeSum < 2Kints.txt
```

tick tick tick tick tick tick
tick tick tick tick tick tick
tick tick tick tick tick tick
tick tick tick tick tick tick

2
391930676 -763182495 371251819
-326747290 802431422 -475684132

*Observing the running time of a program*

to the input itself; it depends primarily on the problem size. If this relationship does not hold, we need to run more experiments to better understand, and perhaps better control, the running time's sensitivity to the input. Since this relationship does often hold, we focus now on the goal of better quantifying the correspondence between problem size and running time.

As a concrete example, we start with `ThreeSum` (PROGRAM 4.1.1), which counts the number of triples in a set of $N$ numbers that sum to 0. This computation may seem contrived to you, but it is deeply related to numerous fundamental computational tasks, particularly those found in computational geometry, so it is a problem worthy of careful study. What is the relationship between the problem size $N$ and running time for `ThreeSum`?

**Hypotheses**     In the early days of computer science, Donald Knuth showed that, despite all of the complicating factors in understanding the running times of our programs, it is possible *in principle* to create accurate models that can help us predict precisely how long a particular program will take. Proper analysis of this sort involves:
   • detailed understanding of the program
   • detailed understanding of the system and the computer
   • advanced tools of mathematical analysis
and so is best left for experts. But every programmer needs to know back-of-the-envelope performance estimates. Fortunately, we can often acquire such knowledge by using a combination of empirical observations and a small set of mathematical tools.

*Doubling hypotheses.*   For a great many programs, we can quickly formulate a hypothesis for the following question: *What is the effect on the running time of doubling the size of the input?* For clarity, we refer to this hypothesis as a *doubling hypothesis.* Perhaps the easiest way to pay attention to the cost is to ask yourself this question about your programs during development and also as you use them in practical applications. Next, we describe how to develop answers via the scientific method.

*Empirical analysis.*   One simple way to develop a doubling hypothesis is to double the size of the input and observe the effect on the running time. For example, `DoublingTest` (PROGRAM 4.1.2) generates a sequence of random input arrays for `ThreeSum`, doubling the array size at each step, and prints the ratio of running times of `ThreeSum.count()` for each input over the previous (which was one-half the size). If you run this program, you will find yourself caught in a prediction-verification cycle: It prints several lines very quickly, but then begins to slow down. Each time it prints a line, you find yourself wondering how long it will be until it

*Program 4.1.1    3-sum problem*

```
public class ThreeSum
{
    public static void printAll(int[] a)
    {   /* See Exercise 4.1.1. */  }

    public static int count(int[] a)
    {   // Count triples that sum to 0.

        int N = a.length;
        int cnt = 0;
        for (int i = 0; i < N; i++)
            for (int j = i+1; j < N; j++)
                for (int k = j+1; k < N; k++)
                    if (a[i] + a[j] + a[k] == 0)
                        cnt++;
        return cnt;
    }

    public static void main(String[] args)
    {   // Count triples that sum to 0 in input.
        int[] a = StdArrayIO.readInt1D();
        int cnt = count(a);
        StdOut.println(cnt);
        if (cnt < 10) printAll(a);
    }
}
```

| N | number of inputs |
|---|---|
| a[] | integer inputs |
| cnt | number of triples that sum to 0 |

The count() *method counts the triples of integers in* a[] *whose sum is 0. The test client invokes* count() *for the integers on standard input and prints the triples if the count is low. The file* 1Kints.txt *contains 1,024 random values from the* int *data type. Such a file is not likely to have such a triple (see Exercise 4.1.28).*

```
more 8ints.txt
8
   30
  -30
  -20
  -10
   40
    0
   10
    5
```

```
% java ThreeSum < 8ints.txt
4
   30 -30    0
   30 -20  -10
  -30 -10   40
  -10    0   10

% java ThreeSum < 1Kints.txt
0
```

prints the next line. Checking the stopwatch as the program runs, it is easy to pre-

*Standard plot*

dict that the elapsed time increases by about a factor of eight to print each line. This prediction is verified by the Stopwatch measurements that the program prints, and leads immediately to the hypothesis that the running time increases by a factor of eight when the input size doubles. We might also plot the running times, either on a standard plot (*left*), which clearly shows that the *rate* of increase of the running time increases with input size, or on a log-log plot. In the case of ThreeSum, the log-log plot (*below*) is a straight line with slope 3, which clearly suggests the hypothesis that the running time satisfies a *power law* of the form $cN^3$ (see EXERCISE 4.1.30).

*Mathematical analysis.* Knuth's basic insight on building a mathematical model to describe the running time of a program is simple: the total running time is determined by two primary factors:

  • The cost of executing each statement
  • The frequency of execution of each statement

The former is a property of the system, and the latter is a property of the algorithm. If we know both for all instructions in the program, we can multiply them together and sum for all instructions in the program to get the running time.

The primary challenge is to determine the frequency of execution of the statements. Some statements are easy to analyze: for example, the statement that sets cnt to 0 in Three-Sum.count() is executed only once. Others require higher-level reasoning: for example, the if statement in ThreeSum.count() is executed precisely $N(N-1)(N-2)/6$ times (that is precisely the number of ways to pick three different numbers from the input array—see EXERCISE 4.1.4).

Frequency analyses of this sort can lead to complicated and lengthy mathematical expressions. To substantially simplify matters in the mathematical analysis, we develop simpler *approximate* expressions in two ways. First, we work with

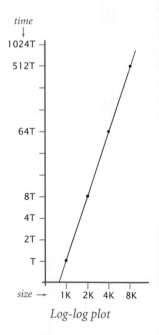

*Log-log plot*

---

***Program 4.1.2   Validating a doubling hypothesis***

```
public class DoublingTest
{
    public static double timeTrial(int N)
    {  // Compute time to solve a random instance of size N.
        int[] a = new int[N];
        for (int i = 0; i < N; i++)
            a[i] = StdRandom.uniform(2000000) - 1000000;
        Stopwatch s = new Stopwatch();
        int cnt = ThreeSum.count(a);
        return s.elapsedTime();
    }

    public static void main(String[] args)
    {  // Print table of doubling ratios.
        double prev = timeTrial(256);
        for (int N = 512; true; N += N)
        {  // Print doubling ratio for problem size N.
            double curr = timeTrial(N);
            StdOut.printf("%7d %4.2f\n", N, curr / prev);
            prev = curr;
        }
    }
}
```

| N | problem size |
|---|---|
| a[] | random integers |
| s | stopwatch |
| curr | time for current size |
| prev | time for previous size |

---

*This program prints a table showing how doubling the problem size affects the running time of* ThreeSum.count() *for problem sizes starting at 256 and doubling for each row of the table. These experiments lead immediately to the hypothesis that the running time increases by a factor of eight when the input size doubles. When you run the program, note carefully that the elapsed time between lines printed increases by a factor of eight for each line, at once verifying the hypothesis.*

```
% java DoublingTest
    512 6.48
   1024 8.30
   2048 7.75
   4096 8.00
   8192 8.05
...
```

```
public class ThreeSum
{
    public static int count(int[] a)
    {
        int N = a.length;
        int cnt = 0;                              ← 1
        for (int i = 0; i < N; i++)
            for (int j = i+1; j < N; j++)         ← N
                for (int k = j+1; k < N; k++)     ~N²/2
                    if (a[i] + a[j] + a[k] == 0)  ~N³/6
                        cnt++;
        return cnt;          depends on input data
    }

    public static void main(String[] args)
    {
        int[] a = StdArrayIO.readInt1D();
        int cnt = count(a);
        StdOut.println(cnt);
    }
}
```

*inner loop*

*Anatomy of a program's statement execution frequencies*

the *leading term* of mathematical expressions by using a mathematical device known as the *tilde notation*. We write $\sim f(N)$ to represent any quantity that, when divided by $f(N)$, approaches 1 as $N$ grows. We also write $g(N) \sim f(N)$ to indicate that $g(N)/f(N)$ approaches 1 as $N$ grows. With this notation, we can ignore complicated parts of an expression that represent small values. For example, the if statement in ThreeSum is executed $\sim N^3/6$ times because $N(N-1)(N-2)/6 = N^3/6 - N^2/2 + N/3$, which certainly, when divided by $N^3/6$, approaches 1 as $N$ grows. This notation is useful when the terms after the leading term are relatively insignificant (for example, when $N = 1000$, this assumption amounts to saying that $-N^2/2 + N/3 \approx -499,667$ is relatively insignificant by comparison with $N^3/6 \approx 166,666,667$, which it is). Second, we focus on the instructions that are executed most frequently, sometimes referred to as the *inner loop* of the program. In this program it is reasonable to assume that the time devoted to the instructions outside the inner loop is relatively insignificant.

The key point in analyzing the running time of a program is this: for a great many programs, the running time satisfies the relationship

$$T(N) \sim cf(N)$$

where $c$ is a constant and $f(N)$ a function known as the *order of growth* of the running time. For typical programs, $f(N)$ is a function such as $\log N$, $N$, $N \log N$, $N^2$, or $N^3$, as you will soon see (customarily, we express order-of-growth functions without any constant coefficient). When $f(N)$ is a power of $N$, as is often the case, this assumption is equivalent to saying that the running time satisfies a power law. In the case of ThreeSum, it is

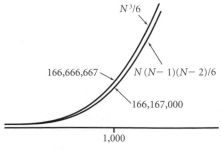

*Leading-term approximation*

a hypothesis already verified by our empirical observations: *the order of growth of the running time of* ThreeSum *is* $N^3$. The value of the constant $c$ depends both on the cost of executing instructions and on details of the frequency analysis, but we normally do not need to work out the value, as you will now see.

The order of growth is a simple but powerful model of running time. For example, knowing the order of growth typically leads immediately to a doubling hypothesis. In the case of ThreeSum, knowing that the order of growth is $N^3$ tells us to expect the running time to increase by a factor of eight when we double the size of the problem because

$$T(2N)/T(N) \rightarrow c(2N)^3/(cN^3) = 8$$

This matches the value resulting from the empirical analysis, thus validating both the model and the experiments. *Study this example carefully, because you can use the same method to better understand the performance of any program that you write.*

Knuth showed that it is possible to develop an accurate mathematical model of the running time of any program, and many experts have devoted much effort to developing such models. But you do not need such a detailed model to understand the performance of your programs: it is typically safe to ignore the cost of the instructions outside the inner loop (because that cost is negligible by comparison to the cost of the instruction in the inner loop) and not necessary to know the value of the constant in the running-time approximation (because it cancels out when you use a doubling hypothesis).

| number of instructions | time per instruction in seconds | frequency | total time |
|:---:|:---:|:---:|:---:|
| 6 | $2 \times 10^{-9}$ | $N^3/6 - N^2/2 + N/3$ | $(2 N^3 - 6 N^2 + 4 N) \times 10^{-9}$ |
| 4 | $3 \times 10^{-9}$ | $N^2/2 - N/2$ | $(6 N^2 + 6 N) \times 10^{-9}$ |
| 4 | $3 \times 10^{-9}$ | $N$ | $(12 N) \times 10^{-9}$ |
| 10 | $1 \times 10^{-9}$ | 1 | $10 \times 10^{-9}$ |
| | | grand total: | $(2 N^3 + 22 N + 10) \times 10^{-9}$ |
| | | tilde notation | $(2 N^3) \times 10^{-9}$ |
| | | order of growth | $N^3$ |

*Analyzing the running time of a program (example)*

These approximations are significant because they relate the abstract world of a Java program to the real world of a computer running it. The approximations are such that characteristics of the particular machine that you are using do not play a significant role in the models—we separate the *algorithm* from the *system*. The order of growth of the running time of `ThreeSum` is $N^3$ does not depend on whether it is implemented in Java, or whether it is running on your laptop, someone else's cellphone, or a supercomputer; it depends primarily on the fact that it examines all the triples. The properties of the computer and the *system* are all summarized in various assumptions about the relationship between program statements and machine instructions, and in the actual running times that we observe as the basis for the doubling hypothesis. The *algorithm* that you are using determines the order of growth. This separation is a powerful concept because it allows us to develop knowledge about the performance of algorithms and then apply that knowledge to any computer. In fact, much of the knowledge about the performance of classic algorithms was developed decades ago, but that knowledge is still relevant to today's computers.

EMPIRICAL AND MATHEMATICAL ANALYSES LIKE THOSE we have described constitute a model (an explanation of what is going on) that might be formalized by listing all of the assumptions mentioned (each instruction takes the same amount of time each time it is executed, running time has the given form, and so forth). Not many programs are worthy of a detailed model, but you need to have an idea of the running time that you might expect for every program that you write. *Pay attention to the cost.* Formulating a doubling hypothesis—through empirical studies, mathematical analysis, or (preferably) both—is a good way to start. This information about performance is extremely useful, and you will soon find yourself formulating and validating hypotheses every time you run a program. Indeed, doing so is a good use of your time while you wait for your program to finish!

**Order of growth classifications**    We use just a few structural primitives (statements, conditionals, loops, and method calls) to build Java programs, so very often the order of growth of our programs is one of just a few functions of the problem size, summarized in the table on the next page. These functions immediately lead to a doubling hypothesis, which we can verify by running the programs. Indeed, you *have* been running programs that exhibit these orders of growth, as you can see in the following brief discussions.

*Constant.* A program whose running time's order of growth is *constant* executes a fixed number of statements to finish its job; consequently its running time does not depend on the problem size. Our first several programs in CHAPTER 1—such as Hel-loWorld (PROGRAM 1.1.1) and LeapYear (PROGRAM 1.2.4)—fall into this classification. They each execute several statements just once. All of Java's operations on primitive types take constant time, as do Java's Math library functions. Note that we do not specify the size of the constant. For example, the constant for Math.tan() is somewhat larger than for Math.abs().

*Logarithmic.* A program whose running time's order of growth is *logarithmic* is barely slower than a constant-time program. The classic example of a program whose running time is logarithmic in the problem size is looking up an entry in an ordered table, which we consider in the next section (see BinarySearch, in PROGRAM 4.2.3). The base of the logarithm is not relevant with respect to the order of growth (since all logarithms with a constant base are related by a constant factor), so we use log $N$ when referring to order of growth. Occasionally, we write more precise formulas using lg $N$ (base 2, or *binary* log) or ln $N$ (base $e$, or *natural* log) because they both arise naturally when studying computer programs. For example, lg $N$, rounded up, is the number of bits in the binary representation of $N$, and ln $N$ arises in the analysis of binary search trees (see SECTION 4.4).

| order of growth | | factor for doubling hypothesis |
|---|---|---|
| description | function | |
| constant | 1 | 1 |
| logarithmic | log $N$ | 1 |
| linear | $N$ | 2 |
| linearithmic | $N \log N$ | 2 |
| quadratic | $N^2$ | 4 |
| cubic | $N^3$ | 8 |
| exponential | $2^N$ | $2^N$ |

*Commonly encountered growth functions*

*Linear.* Programs that spend a constant amount of time processing each piece of input data, or that are based on a single for loop, are quite common. The order of growth of such a program is said to be *linear*—its running time is directly proportional to the problem size. Average (PROGRAM 1.5.3), which computes the average of the numbers on standard input, is prototypical, as is our code to shuffle the entries in an array in SECTION 1.4. Filters such as PlotFilter (PROGRAM 1.5.5) also fall into this classification, as do the various image-processing filters that we considered in SECTION 3.2, which perform a constant number of arithmetic operations per input pixel.

*Linearithmic.* We use the term *linearithmic* to describe programs whose running time for a problem of size $N$ has order of growth $N \log N$. Again, the base of the logarithm is not relevant. For example, CouponCollector (PROGRAM 1.4.2) is linearithmic. The prototypical example is mergesort (see PROGRAM 4.2.6). Several important problems have natural solutions that are quadratic but clever algorithms that are linearithmic. Such algorithms (including mergesort) are critically important in practice because they enable us to address problem sizes far larger than could be addressed with quadratic solutions. In the next section, we consider a general design technique for developing linearithmic algorithms.

*Orders of growth (log-log plot)*

*Quadratic.* A typical program whose running time has order of growth $N^2$ has two nested for loops, used for some calculation involving all pairs of $N$ elements. The force update double loop in NBody (PROGRAM 3.4.2) is a prototype of the programs in this classification, as is the elementary sorting algorithm Insertion (PROGRAM 4.2.4).

*Cubic.* Our example for this section, ThreeSum, is cubic (its running time has order of growth $N^3$) because it has *three* nested for loops, to process all triples of $N$ elements. The running time of matrix multiplication, as implemented in SECTION 1.4 has order of growth $M^3$ to multiply two $M$-by-$M$ matrices, so the basic matrix multiplication algorithm is often considered to be cubic. However, the size of the input (the number of entries in the matrices) is proportional to $N = M^2$, so the algorithm is best classified as $N^{3/2}$, not cubic.

*Exponential.* As discussed in SECTION 2.3, both TowersOfHanoi (PROGRAM 2.3.2) and GrayCode (PROGRAM 2.3.3) have running times proportional to $2^N$ because they process all subsets of $N$ elements. Generally, we use the term "exponential" to refer to algorithms whose order of growth is $b^N$ for any constant $b > 1$, even though different values of $b$ lead to vastly different running times. Exponential algorithms are extremely slow—you will never run one of them for a large problem. They play a critical role in the theory of algorithms because there exists a large class of problems for which it seems that an exponential algorithm is the best possible choice.

THESE CLASSIFICATIONS ARE THE MOST COMMON, but certainly not a complete set. Indeed, the detailed analysis of algorithms can require the full gamut of mathematical tools that have been developed over the centuries. Understanding the running time of programs such as Factor (PROGRAM 1.3.9), PrimeSieve (PROGRAM 1.4.3) and Euclid (PROGRAM 2.3.1), requires fundamental results from number theory. Standard algorithms like BST (PROGRAM 4.4.3) require careful mathematical analysis. Newton (PROGRAM 2.1.1) and Markov (PROGRAM 1.6.3) are prototypes for numerical computation: their running time is dependent on the rate of convergence of a computation to a desired numerical result. Simulations such as Gambler (PROGRAM 1.3.8) and its variants are of interest precisely because detailed mathematical models are not always available.

But a great many of the programs that you will write have straightforward performance characteristics that can be accurately described by one of the orders of growth that we have considered. Accordingly, we can usually work with simple higher-level hypotheses, such as *the order of growth of the running time of mergesort is linearithmic.* For economy, we abbreviate such a statement to just say *mergesort is linearithmic.* Most of our hypotheses about cost are of this form, or of the form *mergesort is faster than insertion sort.* Again, a notable feature of such hypotheses is that they are statements about algorithms, not just about programs.

**Predictions** You can always try to learn the running time of a program by simply running it, but that might be a poor way to proceed when the problem size is large. In that case, it is analogous to trying to learn where a rocket will land by launching it, how destructive a bomb will be by igniting it, or whether a bridge will stand by building it.

Knowing the order of growth of the running time allows us to make decisions about addressing large problems so that we can invest whatever resources we have to deal with the specific problems that we actually need to solve. We typically use the results of verified hypotheses about the order of growth of the running time of programs in one of the following four ways.

*Estimating the feasibility of solving large problems.* To pay attention to the cost, you need to answer this basic question for every program that you write: *Will this program be able to process this input data in a reasonable amount of time?* For example, a cubic algorithm that runs in a couple of seconds for a problem of size $N$ will require a few *weeks* for a problem of size $100N$ because it will be a million $(100^3)$ times slower, and a couple of million seconds is a few weeks. If that is the size of the problem that you need to solve, you have to find a better method. Knowing the order of growth of the running time of an algorithm provides precisely the information that you need to understand limitations on the size of the problems that you can solve. Developing such understanding is the most important reason to study performance. Without it, you are likely have no idea how much time a program will consume; with it, you can make a back-of-the-envelope calculation to estimate costs and proceed accordingly.

| order of growth | predicted running time if problem size is increased by a factor of 100 |
|---|---|
| linear | a few minutes |
| linearithmic | a few minutes |
| quadratic | several hours |
| cubic | a few weeks |
| exponential | forever |

*Effect of increasing problem size for a program that runs for a few seconds*

*Estimating the value of using a faster computer.* To pay attention to the cost, you also may be faced with this basic question, periodically: *How much faster can I solve the problem if I get a faster computer?* Again, knowing the order of growth of the running time provides precisely the information that you need. A famous rule of thumb known as *Moore's Law* implies that you can expect to have a computer with about double the speed and double the memory 18 months from now, or a computer with about 10 times the speed and 10 times the memory in about 5 years. It is natural to think that if you buy a new computer that is 10 times faster and has 10 times more memory than your old one, you can solve a problem 10 times the size, but that is *not* the case for quadratic or cubic algorithms. Whether it is an investment banker running daily financial models or a scientist running a program to analyze experimental data or an engineer running simulations to test a design, it is not unusual for people to regularly run programs that take several hours to complete. Suppose that you are using a program whose running time is cubic, and then buy a new computer that is 10 times faster with 10 times more memory, not just because you need a new computer, but because you face problems that are 10 times larger. The rude awakening is that it will take a several *weeks* to get results, because the larger problems would be a thousand times slower on the old computer and improved by only a factor of 10 on the new computer. This kind of situation is the primary reason that linear and linearithmic algorithms are so valuable because with such an algorithm and a new computer that is 10 times faster with 10 times more memory than an old computer, you can solve a problem that is 10 times larger than could be solved by the old computer in the same amount of time. In other words, you cannot keep pace with Moore's Law if you are using a quadratic or a cubic algorithm.

*Processing multiple instances.* For fast algorithms, we often think in terms of multiple problem instances. For example, consider the effect of Moore's law on a company that provides web services, say, at the rate of a million problems of size $N$ every few seconds. At what rate can problems that are 10 times larger be handled with a computer that is 10 times faster (or with 10 times as many computers)? If the algorithm is linear, the rate stays the same; remarkably, if the algorithm is logarithmic, the rate can be increased by a factor of 10, even though problems are 10 times larger. For example, a company that can handle 10 million requests of size $10N$ per second (using a logarithmic algorithm) is likely to do much better than one competitor that can handle only 1 million requests of size $10N$ per second and another competitor that can handle only 10 million requests of size $N$ per second.

| order of growth | predicted factor of problem size increase if computer speed is increased by a factor of 10 |
|:---:|:---:|
| linear | 10 |
| linearithmic | 10 |
| quadratic | 3-4 |
| cubic | 2-3 |
| exponential | 1 |

*Effect of increasing computer speed on problem size that can be solved in a fixed amount of time*

*Comparing programs.* We are always seeking to improve our programs, and we can often extend or modify our hypotheses to evaluate the effectiveness of various improvements. With the ability to predict performance, we can make design decisions during the development of an implementation that can guide us towards better, more efficient code. As an example, a novice programmer might have written the nested `for` loops in `ThreeSum` as

```
for (int i = 0; i < N; i++)
   for (int j = 0; j < N; j++)
      for (int k = 0; k < N; k++)
         if (i < j && j < k)
            if (a[i] + a[j] + a[k] == 0)
               cnt++;
```

so that frequency of execution of the instructions in the inner loop would be exactly $N^3$ (instead of approximately $N^3/6$). It is easy to formulate and verify the hypothesis that ThreeSum is six times as fast as this variant. Note that improvements like this for code that is *not* in the inner loop will have little or no effect. More generally, given two algorithms that solve the same problem, we want to know which one will solve our problem using fewer computational resources. In many cases, we can determine the order of growth of the running times and develop accurate hypotheses about comparative performance. The order of growth is extremely useful in this process because it allows us to compare one particular algorithm with whole classes of algorithms. For example, once we have a linearithmic algorithm to solve a problem, we become less interested in quadratic or cubic algorithms (even if they are highly optimized) to solve the same problem.


**Caveats**   There are many reasons that you might get inconsistent or misleading results when trying to analyze program performance in detail. All of them have to do with the idea that one or more of the basic assumptions underlying our hypotheses might not be quite correct. We can develop new hypotheses based on new assumptions, but the more details that we need to take into account, the more care is required in the analysis.

*Instruction time.*   The assumption that each instruction always takes the same amount of time is not always correct. For example, most modern computer systems use a technique known as *caching* to organize memory, in which case accessing elements in huge arrays can take much longer if they are not close together in the array. You can observe the effect of caching for ThreeSum by letting DoublingTest run for a while. After seeming to converge to 8, the ratio of running times will jump to a larger value for large arrays because of caching.

*Nondominant inner loop.*   The assumption that the inner loop dominates may not always be correct. The problem size $N$ might not be sufficiently large to make the leading term in the mathematical description of the frequency of execution of instructions in the inner loop so much larger than lower-order terms that we can ignore them. Some programs have a significant amount of code outside the inner loop that needs to be taken into consideration.

*System considerations.* Typically, there are many, many things going on in your computer. Java is one application of many competing for resources, and Java itself has many options and controls that significantly affect performance. Such considerations can interfere with the bedrock principle of the scientific method that experiments should be reproducible, since what is happening at this moment in your computer will never be reproduced again. Whatever else is going on in your system (that is beyond your control) should *in principle* be negligible.

*Too close to call.* Often, when we compare two different programs for the same task, one might be faster in some situations, and slower in others. One or more of the considerations just mentioned could make the difference. Again, there is a natural tendency among some programmers (and some students) to devote an extreme amount of energy running such horseraces to find the "best" implementation, but such work is best left for experts.

*Strong dependence on input values.* One of the first assumptions that we made in order to determine the order of growth of the program's running time of a program was that the running time should be relatively insensitive to the input values. When that is not the case, we may get inconsistent results or be unable to validate our hypotheses. Our running example ThreeSum does not have this problem, but many of the programs that we write certainly do. We will see several examples of such programs in this chapter. Often, a prime design goal is to eliminate the dependence on input values. If we cannot do so, we need to more carefully model the kind of input to be processed in the problems that we need to solve, which may be a significant challenge. For example, if we are writing a program to process a genome, how do we know how it will perform on a different genome? But a good model describing the genomes found in nature is precisely what scientists seek, so estimating the running time of our programs on data found in nature actually amounts to contributing to that model!

*Multiple problem parameters.* We have been focusing on measuring performance as a function of a *single* parameter, generally the value of a command-line argument or the size of the input. However, it is not unusual to have several parameters. For example, the percolation probability estimation method `Estimate.eval()` in Section 2.4 has two parameters: $N$ (the size of the grid) and $T$ (the number of trials). In such cases, we treat the parameters separately, holding one fixed while analyzing the other. In the case of `Estimate.eval()`, the order of growth of the running time is $TN^2$, or linear in $T$ and quadratic in $N$.

Despite all these caveats, understanding the order of growth of the running time of each program is valuable knowledge for any programmer, and the methods that we have described are powerful and broadly applicable. Knuth's insight was that we can carry these methods through to the last detail *in principle* to make detailed, accurate predictions. Typical computer systems are extremely complex and close analysis is best left for experts, but the same methods are effective for developing approximate estimates of the running time of any program. A rocket scientist needs to have some idea of whether a test flight will land in the ocean or in a city; a medical researcher needs to know whether a drug trial will kill or cure all the subjects; and any scientist or engineer using a computer program needs to have some idea of whether it will run for a second or for a year.

**Performance guarantees**    For some programs, we demand that the running time of a program is less than a certain bound, no matter what the input values. To provide such performance *guarantees*, theoreticians take an extremely pessimistic view of the performance of algorithms: what would the running time be in the *worst case*?

For example, such a conservative approach might be appropriate for the software that runs a nuclear reactor or an air traffic control system or the brakes in your car. We want to guarantee that such software completes its job within the bounds that we set because the result could be catastrophic if it does not.

Scientists normally do not contemplate the worst case when studying the natural world: in biology, the worst case might the extinction of the human race; in physics, the worst case might be the end of the universe. But the worst case can be a very real concern in computer systems, where the input may be generated by another (potentially malicious) user, rather than by nature. For example, websites that do not use algorithms with performance guarantees are subject to *denial-of-service* attacks, where hackers flood them with pathological requests that make them run much more slowly than planned.

Performance guarantees are difficult to verify with the scientific method, because we cannot test a hypothesis such as *Mergesort is guaranteed to be linearithmic* without trying all possible input values, which we cannot do because there are far too many of them. We might falsify such a hypothesis by providing inputs for which mergesort is slow, but how can we prove it to be true? We can do this not with experimentation, but with mathematical models. In fact, it is often no more difficult to develop performance guarantees than it is to predict performance. Indeed, it is often the case that the same mathematical model used to prove that a program computes the expected results can also provide the performance guarantees that we need.

Often, randomness provides performance guarantees. For example, it is possible, though extraordinarily unlikely, that `CouponCollector` (PROGRAM 1.4.2) will not terminate, but mathematical analysis provides a way for us to guarantee that its running time is linearithmic. The guarantee is probabilistic, but the chance that it is invalid is less than the chance your computer will be simultaneously struck by lightning and hit by a meteor.

It is the task of the algorithm analyst to discover as much relevant information about an algorithm as possible, and it is the task of the applications programmer to apply that knowledge to develop programs that effectively solve the problems at hand. For example, if you are using a quadratic algorithm to solve a problem but can find an algorithm that is guaranteed to be linearithmic, you certainly are well advised to consider it, because an algorithm that makes the *worst case* linearithmic makes the running time for *every case* linearithmic or better. On the other hand, it is sometimes true that an algorithm that provides worst case performance guarantee is overly complex, adding unnecessary overhead to protect against a situation that you will never encounter. For example, an algorithm that provides a linearithmic guarantee might not be the best one to use, because some other algorithm might solve *your* problem in linear time (your input values might not be the worst case).

Ideally, we want algorithms that lead to clear and compact code that provides both a good guarantee and good performance on input values of interest. Many of the classic algorithms that we consider in this chapter are of importance for a broad variety of applications precisely because they have all of these properties. Using these algorithms as models, you can develop good solutions yourself for typical problems that you face while programming.

**Memory**   As with running time, a program's *memory* usage connects directly to the physical world: a substantial amount of your computer's circuitry enables your program to store values and later retrieve them. The more values you need to have stored at any given instant, the more circuitry you need. To *pay attention to the cost*, you need to be aware of memory usage. You probably are aware of limits on memory usage on your computer (even more so than for time) because you probably have paid extra money to get more memory.

Memory usage is well-defined for Java on your computer (every value will require precisely the same amount of memory each time that you run your program), but Java is implemented on a very wide range of computational devices, and memory consumption is implementation-dependent. For economy, we use the word *typical* to signal values that are particularly subject to machine dependencies. Analyzing memory usage is somewhat different from analyzing time usage, primarily because one of Java's most significant features is its memory allocation system, which is supposed to *relieve* you of having to worry about memory. Certainly, you are well advised to take advantage of this feature when appropriate. Still, it is your responsibility to know, at least approximately, when a program's memory requirements will prevent you from solving a given problem.

| type | bytes |
|---------|-------|
| boolean | 1 |
| byte | 1 |
| char | 2 |
| int | 4 |
| float | 4 |
| long | 8 |
| double | 8 |

*Typical memory requirements for primitive types*

*Primitive types.*   It is easy to estimate memory usage for simple programs like the ones we considered in Chapter 1: Count up the number of variables and weight them by the number of *bytes* according to their type. For example, since the Java int data type is the set of integer values between $-2{,}147{,}483{,}648$ and $2{,}147{,}483{,}647$, a grand total of $2^{32}$ different values, it is reasonable to expect implementations to use 32 bits to represent int values, and similar considerations hold for other primitive types. Typical Java implementations use 8-bit bytes, representing each char value with 2 bytes (16 bits), each int value with 4 bytes (32 bits), each double value with 8 bytes (64 bits), and each boolean value with 1 byte (since computers typically access memory one byte at a time). For example, if you have 1GB of memory on your computer (about 1 billion bytes), you cannot fit more than about 32 million int values or 16 million double values in memory at any one time.

*Objects.*   To determine the memory consumption of an object, we add the amount of memory used by each instance variable to the overhead associated with each object, typically 8 bytes. For example, a `Charge` (PROGRAM 3.2.1) object uses 32 bytes (8 bytes of overhead and 8 bytes for each of its three `double` instance variables). Similarly, a `Complex` object uses 24 bytes. Since many programs create millions of `Color` objects, typical Java implementations pack the information needed for them into 32 bits (three bytes for RGB values and one for transparency). A *reference* to an object typically uses 4 bytes of memory. When a data type contains a reference to an object, we have to account separately for the 4 bytes for the reference and the 8 bytes overhead for each object plus the memory needed for the object's instance variables. In particular, a `Document` (PROGRAM 3.3.4) object uses 16 bytes (8 bytes of overhead and 4 bytes each for the references to the `String` and `Vector` objects) plus the memory needed for the `String` and `Vector` objects themselves (which we consider next).

*String objects.* We account for memory in a `String` object in the same way as for any other object. Java's implementation of a `String` object consumes 24 bytes: a reference to a character array (4 bytes), three `int` values (4 bytes each), and the object overhead (8 bytes). The first `int` value is an offset into the character array; the second is a count (the string length). In terms of the instance variable names in the figure at right, the string that is represented consists of the characters `val[offset]` through `val[offset + count - 1]`. The third `int` value in `String` objects is a *hash code* that saves recomputation in certain circumstances that need not concern us now. In addition to the 24 bytes for the `String` object, we must account for the memory needed for the characters themselves, which are in the array. We account for this space next.

*Typical object memory requirements*

*Arrays.* Arrays in Java are implemented as objects, typically with two instance variables (a pointer to the memory location of the first array element and the length). For *primitive types*, an array of $N$ elements requires 16 bytes of header information plus $N$ times the number of bytes needed to store an element. For example, the `int` array in `Sample` (PROGRAM 1.4.1) uses $4N + 16$ bytes, whereas the `boolean` arrays in `Coupon` (PROGRAM 1.4.2) uses $N + 16$ bytes. Note than a `boolean` array consumes one byte of memory per entry (wasting 7 of the 8 bits)—with some extra work, you could get the job done with $N/8$ bytes (see EXERCISE 4.1.26). An array of *objects* is an array of references to the objects, so we need to add the space for the references to the space required for the objects. For example, the array of `Charge` objects in `Potential` (PROGRAM 3.1.7) uses 16 (array overhead) plus $4N$ (references) plus $32N$ (objects) bytes for a total of $36N + 16$ bytes. This analysis assumes that all of the objects are different: it is possible that multiple array entries could refer to

*Memory requirements for arrays of primitive-type values (left) and objects (right)*

| type | bytes |
|---|---|
| int[] | $4N + 16$ |
| double[] | $8N + 16$ |
| Charge[] | $36N + 16$ |
| int[][] | $4N^2 + 20N + 16$ |
| double[][] | $8N^2 + 20N + 16$ |
| String | $2N + 40$ |

*Typical memory requirements for variable-length data structures*

the same object (aliasing). Normally, we do not need to account for such aliasing in our code, with one significant exception: in conjunction with Java String objects, as discussed next.

*String values and substrings.* A String of length $N$ typically uses 24 bytes (for the String object) plus $2N + 16$ bytes (for the array that contains the characters) for a total of $2N + 40$ bytes. It is typical in string processing to work with substrings, and Java's string representation enables us to do so without having to make copies of the string's characters. When you use the substring() method, you create a new String object (24 bytes) but do not make copies of any characters, so a substring of an existing string takes just 24 bytes. The substring stores an alias to the character array in the original string, and uses the offset and count fields to identify the substring. In other words, a substring takes *constant* extra memory (and forming a substring takes constant time), even when the lengths of the string and the substring are huge. A naive representation that requires copying characters to make substrings would take *linear* time. The ability to create substrings using a constant extra memory (and constant time) is the key to efficiency in many basic string-processing algorithms, as we will see in the next section (PROGRAM 4.2.8). On the other hand, this representation requires that all of the characters in a string be contiguous in *some* array, which implies that the string concatenation method concat() (which is called when the built-in + operator is used) has to copy characters from the two strings into a new array and thus takes time and extra space proportional to the total number of characters in the two strings. Java's StringBuilder class is an alternative that implements string concatenation more efficiently than does String.

```
String genome = "CGCCTGGCGTCTGTAC";
String codon  = genome.substring(6, 3);
```

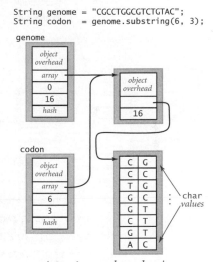

*A* String *and a substring*

*Two-dimensional arrays.* As we saw in SECTION 1.4, a two-dimensional array in Java is an array of arrays. For example, the two-dimensional array in Markov

(PROGRAM 1.6.3) uses 16 bytes (overhead for the array of arrays) plus $4N$ bytes (references to the row arrays) plus $N$ times 16 bytes (overhead from the row arrays) plus $N$ times $N$ times 8 bytes (for the $N$ `double` values in each of the $N$ rows) for a grand total of $8N^2 + 20N + 16 \sim 8N^2$ bytes. If the array entries are objects, then a similar accounting gives $4N^2 + 20N + 16 \sim 4N^2$ bytes for the array of arrays filled with references to objects, to which we need to add the memory for the objects themselves.

THESE BASIC MECHANISMS ARE EFFECTIVE FOR estimating the memory usage of a great many programs, but there are numerous complicating factors that can make the task significantly more difficult. We have already noted the potential effect of aliasing. Moreover, memory consumption is a complicated dynamic process when function calls are involved because the system memory allocation mechanism plays a more important role, with more system dependencies. For example, when your program calls a method, the system allocates the memory needed for the method (for its local variables) from a special area of memory called the *stack*, and when the method returns to the caller, the memory is returned to the stack. For this reason, creating arrays or other large objects in recursive programs is dangerous, since each recursive call implies significant memory usage. When you create an object with new, the system allocates the memory needed for the object from another special area of memory known as the *heap*, and you must remember that every object lives until no references to it remain, at which point a system process known as *garbage collection* reclaims its memory for the heap. Such dynamics can make the task of precisely estimating memory usage of a program challenging.

```
double[][] t = new double[N][N];
```

*Total: $16 + 4N + N \times 16 + N \times 8N = 8N^2 + 20N + 16$*

*Memory requirements for a 2D array*

**Perspective** Good performance is important. An impossibly slow program is almost as useless as an incorrect one, so it is certainly worthwhile to *pay attention to the cost* at the outset, to have some idea of what sorts of problems you might feasibly address. In particular, it is always wise to have some idea of which code constitutes the inner loop of your programs.

Perhaps the most common mistake made in programming is to pay too much attention to performance characteristics. Your first priority is to make your code clear and correct. Modifying a program for the sole purpose of speeding it up is best left for experts. Indeed, doing so is often counterproductive, as it tends to create code that is complicated and difficult to understand. C. A. R. Hoare (the inventor of Quicksort and a leading proponent of writing clear and correct code) once summarized this idea by saying that *"premature optimization is the root of all evil,"* to which Knuth added the qualifier *"(or at least most of it) in programming."* Beyond that, improving the running time is not worthwhile if the available cost benefits are insignificant. For example, improving the running time of a program by a factor of 10 is inconsequential if the running time is only an instant. Even when a program takes a few minutes to run, the total time required to implement and debug an improved algorithm might be substantially more than the time required simply to run a slightly slower one—you may as well let the computer do the work. Worse, you might spend a considerable amount of time and effort implementing ideas that should improve a program but actually do not do so.

Perhaps the second most common mistake made in developing an algorithm is to ignore performance characteristics. Faster algorithms are often more complicated than brute-force solutions, so you might be tempted to accept a slower algorithm to avoid having to deal with more complicated code. However, you can sometimes reap huge savings with just a few lines of good code. Users of a surprising number of computer systems lose substantial time waiting for simple quadratic algorithms to finish solving a problem, even though linear or linearithmic algorithms are available that are only slightly more complicated and could therefore solve the problem in a fraction of the time. When we are dealing with huge problem sizes, we often have no choice but to seek better algorithms.

Improving a program to make it clearer, more efficient, and elegant should be your goal every time that you work on it. If you *pay attention to the cost* all the way through the development of a program, you will reap the benefits every time you use it.

**Q + A**

**Q.** How do I find out how long it takes to add or multiply two `double` values on my computer?

**A.** Run some experiments! The program `TimePrimitives` on the booksite uses `Stopwatch` to test the execution time of various arithmetic operations on primitive types. This technique measures the actual elapsed time as would be observed on a wall clock. If your system is not running many other applications, this can produce accurate results. You can find much more information about refining such experiments on the booksite.

**Q.** How much time do functions such as `Math.sqrt()`, `Math.log()`, and `Math.sin()` take?

**A.** Run some experiments! `Stopwatch` makes it easy to write programs such as `TimePrimitives` to answer questions of this sort for yourself, and you will be able to use your computer much more effectively if you get in the habit of doing so.

**Q.** How much time do string operations take?

**A.** Run some experiments! (Have you gotten the message yet?) The standard implementation is written to allow the methods `length()`, `charAt()`, and `substring()` to run in constant time. Methods such as `toLowerCase()` and `replace()` are linear in the string size. The methods `compareTo()`, and `startsWith()` take time proportional to the number of characters needed to resolve the answer (constant in the best case and linear in the worst case), but `indexOf()` can be slow. String concatenation takes time proportional to the total number of characters in the result.

**Q.** Why does allocating an array of size $N$ take time proportional to $N$?

**A.** In Java, all array elements are automatically initialized to default values (0, `false`, or `null`). In principle, this could be a constant time operation if the system would defer initialization of each element until just before the program accesses that element for the first time, but most Java implementations go through the whole array to initialize each value.

**Q.** How do I find out how much memory is available for my Java programs?

**A.** Since Java will tell you when it runs out of memory, it is not difficult to run some experiments. For example, if you use `PrimeSieve` (PROGRAM 1.4.3) by typing

```
% java PrimeSieve 100000000
```

and get the result

```
50847534
```

but then type

```
% java PrimeSieve 1000000000
```

and get the result

```
Exception in thread "main"
java.lang.OutOfMemoryError: Java heap space
```

then you can figure that you have enough room for an array of 100 million `boolean` values but not for an array of 1 billion `boolean` values. You can increase the amount of memory allotted to Java with command-line flags. The following command executes `PrimeSieve` with the command-line argument 1000000000, requesting a maximum of 1100 megabytes of memory (if available).

```
java -Xmx1100mb PrimeSieve 1000000000
```

**Q.** What does it mean when someone says that the running time of an algorithm is $O(N \log N)$?

**A.** That is an example of a notation known as *big-Oh* notation. We write $f(N)$ is $O(g(N))$ if there exists a constant $c$ such that $f(N) \leq cg(N)$ for all $N$. We also say that the running time of an algorithm is $O(g(N))$ if the running time is $O(g(N))$ for all possible inputs. This notation is widely used by theoretical computer scientists to prove theorems about algorithms, so you are sure to see it if you take a course in algorithms and data structures. It provides a worst-case performance guarantee.

**Q.** So can I use the fact that the running time of an algorithm is $O(N \log N)$ or $O(N^2)$ to predict performance?

**A.** No, because the actual running time might be much less. Perhaps there is some input for which the running time is proportional to the given function, but perhaps the that input is not found among those expected in practice. Mathematically, big-Oh notation is less precise than the tilde notation we use: if $f(N) \sim g(N)$, then $f(N)$ is $O(g(N))$, but not necessarily vice versa. Consequently, big-Oh notation cannot be used to predict performance. For example, knowledge that the running time of one algorithm is $O(N \log N)$ and the running time of another algorithm is $O(N^2)$ does not tell you which will be faster when you run implementations of them. Generally, hypotheses that use big-Oh notation are not useful in the context of the scientific method because they are not falsifiable.

# Exercises

**4.1.1** Implement the method `printAll()` for `ThreeSum`, which prints all of the triples that sum to zero.

**4.1.2** Modify `ThreeSum` to take a command-line argument $x$ and find a triple of numbers on standard input whose sum is closest to $x$.

**4.1.3** Write a program `FourSum` that takes an integer $N$ from standard input, then reads $N$ `long` values from standard input, and counts the number of 4-tuples that sum to zero. Use a quadruple loop. What is the order of growth of the running time of your program? Estimate the largest $N$ that your program can handle in an hour. Then, run your program to validate your hypothesis.

**4.1.4** Prove by induction that the number of distinct pairs of integers between 0 and $N-1$ is $N(N-1)/2$, and then prove by induction that the number of distinct triples of integers between 0 and $N-1$ is $N(N-1)(N-2)/6$.

*Answer for pairs*: The formula is correct for $N = 1$, since there are 0 pairs. For $N > 1$, count all the pairs that do not include $N-1$, which is $N(N-1)/2$ by the inductive hypothesis, and all the pairs that do include $N-1$, which is $N-1$, to get the total

$$(N-1)(N-2)/2 + (N-1) = N(N-1)/2.$$

*Answer for triples*: The formula is correct for $N = 2$. For $N > 2$, count all the triples that do not include $N-1$, which is $(N-1)(N-2)(N-3)/6$ by the inductive hypothesis, and all the triples that do include $N-1$, which is $(N-1)(N-2)/2$, to get the total

$$(N-1)(N-2)(N-3)/6 + (N-1)(N-2)/2 = N(N-1)(N-2)/6.$$

**4.1.5** Show by approximating with integrals that the number of distinct triples of integers between 0 and $N$ is about $N^3/6$.

*Answer*: $\sum_0^N \sum_0^i \sum_0^j 1 \approx \int_0^N \int_0^i \int_0^j dk\,dj\,di = \int_0^N \int_0^i j\,dj\,di = \int_0^N (i^2/2)\,di = N^3/6.$

**4.1.6** What is the value of x after running the following code fragment?

```
int x = 0;
for (int i = 0; i < N; i++)
    for (int j = i + 1; j < N; j++)
        for (int k = j + 1; k < N; k++)
            x++;
```

*Answer*: $N(N-1)(N-2)/6$.

**4.1.7**   Use tilde notation to simplify each of the following formulas, and give the order of growth of each:

    *a.* $N(N-1)(N-2)(N-3)/24$
    *b.* $(N-2)(\lg N - 2)(\lg N + 2)$
    *c.* $N(N+1) - N^2$
    *d.* $N(N+1)/2 + N\lg N$
    *e.* $\ln((N-1)(N-2)(N-3))^2$

**4.1.8**   Determine the order of growth of the running time of the input loop of ThreeSum:

```
int N = Integer.parseInt(args[0]);
int[] a = new int[N];
for (int i = 0; i < N; i++)
    a[i] = StdIn.readInt();
```

*Answer*: Linear. The bottlenecks are the array initialization and the input loop. Depending on your system and the implementation, the readInt() statement might lead to inconsistent timings for small values of $N$. The cost of an input loop like this might dominate in a linearithmic or even a quadratic program with $N$ that is not too large.

**4.1.9**   Determine whether the following code fragment is linear, quadratic, or cubic (as a function of $N$).

```
for (int i = 0; i < N; i++)
    for (int j = 0; j < N; j++)
        if (i == j) c[i][j] = 1.0;
        else        c[i][j] = 0.0;
```

**4.1.10** Suppose the running time of an algorithm on inputs of size one thousand, two thousand, three thousand, and four thousand is 5 seconds, 20 seconds, 45 seconds, and 80 seconds, respectively. Estimate how long it will take to solve a problem of size 5,000. Is the algorithm linear, linearithmic, quadratic, cubic, or exponential?

**4.1.11** Which would you prefer: a quadratic, linearithmic, or linear algorithm?

*Answer*: While it is tempting to make a quick decision based on the order of growth, it is very easy to be misled by doing so. You need to have some idea of the problem size and of the relative value of the leading coefficients of the running time. For example, suppose that the running times are $N^2$ seconds, $100 N \log_2 N$ seconds, and $10000 N$ seconds. The quadratic algorithm will be fastest for $N$ up to about 1000, and the linear algorithm will never be faster than the linearithmic one ($N$ would have to be greater than $2^{100}$, far too large to bother considering).

**4.1.12** Apply the scientific method to develop and validate a hypothesis about order of growth of the running time of the following code fragment, as a function of the input argument n.

```
public static int f(int n)
{
   if (n == 0) return 1;
   return f(n-1) + f(n-1);
}
```

**4.1.13** Apply the scientific method to develop and validate a hypothesis about order of growth of the running time of the collect() method in Coupon (PROGRAM 2.1.3), as a function of the input argument N. *Note*: Doubling is not effective for distinguishing between the linear and linearithmic hypotheses—you might try *squaring* the size of the input.

**4.1.14** Apply the scientific method to develop and validate a hypothesis about order of growth of the running time of Markov (PROGRAM 1.6.3), as a function of the input parameters T and N.

**4.1.15** Apply the scientific method to develop and validate a hypothesis about order of growth of the running time of each of the following two code fragments as a function of N.

```
String s = "";
for (int i = 0; i < N; i++)
   if (StdRandom.bernoulli(0.5)) s += "0";
   else                          s += "1";

StringBuilder sb = new StringBuilder();
for (int i = 0; i < N; i++)
   if (StdRandom.bernoulli(0.5)) sb.append("0");
   else                          sb.append("1");
String s = sb.toString();
```

*Answer*: The first is quadratic; the second is linear.

**4.1.16** Each of the four Java functions below returns a string of length N whose characters are all x. Determine the order of growth of the running time of each function. Recall that concatenating two strings in Java takes time proportional to the sum of their lengths.

```
public static String method1(int N)
{
   if (N == 0) return "";
   String temp = method1(N / 2);
   if (N % 2 == 0) return temp + temp;
   else            return temp + temp + "x";
}

public static String method2(int N)
{
   String s = "";
   for (int i = 0; i < N; i++)
      s = s + "x";
   return s;
}
```

```
public static String method3(int N)
{
    if (N == 0) return "";
    if (N == 1) return "x";
    return method3(N/2) + method3(N - N/2);
}

public static String method4(int N)
{
    char[] temp = new char[N];
    for (int i = 0; i < N; i++)
        temp[i] = 'x';
    return new String(temp);
}
```

**4.1.17** The following code fragment (adapted from a Java programming book) creates a random permutation of the integers from 0 to $N-1$. Determine the order of growth of its running time as a function of $N$. Compare its order of growth with the shuffling code in Section 1.4.

```
int[] a = new int[N];
boolean[] taken = new boolean[N];
int count = 0;
while (count < N)
{
    int r = StdRandom.uniform(N);
    if (!taken[r])
    {
        a[r] = count;
        taken[r] = true;
        count++;
    }
}
```

**4.1.18** What is order of growth of the running time of the following function, which reverses a string s of length N?

```
public static String reverse(String s)
{
    int N = s.length();
    String reverse = "";
    for (int i = 0; i < N; i++)
        reverse = s.charAt(i) + reverse;
    return reverse;
}
```

**4.1.19** What is the order of growth of the running time of the following function, which reverses a string s of length N?

```
public static String reverse(String s)
{
    int N = s.length();
    if (N <= 1) return s;
    String left  = s.substring(0, N/2);
    String right = s.substring(N/2, N);
    return reverse(right) + reverse(left);
}
```

**4.1.20** Give a linear algorithm for reversing a string.

*Answer*:

```
public static String reverse(String s)
{
    int N = s.length();
    char[] a = new char[N];
    for (int i = 0; i < N; i++)
        a[i] = s.charAt(N-i-1);
    return new String(a);
}
```

**4.1.21** Write a program MooresLaw that takes a command-line argument *N* and outputs the increase in processor speed over a decade if microprocessors double every *N* months. How much will processor speed increase over the next decade if speeds double every *N* = 15 months? 24 months?

**4.1.22** Using the model in the text, give the memory requirements for each object of the following data types from CHAPTER 3:
  *a.* Stopwatch
  *b.* Turtle
  *c.* Vector
  *d.* Body
  *e.* Universe

**4.1.23** Estimate, as a function of the grid size $N$, the amount of space used by Visualize (PROGRAM 2.4.3) with the vertical percolation detection (PROGRAM 2.4.2). *Extra credit*: Answer the same question for the case where the recursive percolation detection method in PROGRAM 2.4.5 is used.

**4.1.24** Estimate the size of the biggest two-dimensional array of int values that your computer can hold, and then try to allocate such an array.

**4.1.25** Estimate, as a function of the number of documents $N$ and the dimension $d$, the amount of space used by CompareAll (PROGRAM 3.3.5).

**4.1.26** Write a version of PrimeSieve (PROGRAM 1.4.3) that uses a byte array instead of a boolean array and uses all the bits in each byte, to raise the largest value of N that it can handle by a factor of 8.

**4.1.27** The following table gives running times for various programs for various values of $N$. Fill in the blanks with estimates that you think are reasonable on the basis of the information given.

| program | 1,000 | 10,000 | 100,000 | 1,000,000 |
|---------|-------|--------|---------|-----------|
| A | .001 seconds | .012 seconds | .16 seconds | ? seconds |
| B | 1 minute | 10 minutes | 1.7 hours | ? hours |
| C | 1 second | 1.7 minutes | 2.8 hours | ? days |

Give hypotheses for the order of growth of the running time of each program.

## Creative Exercises

**4.1.28** *ThreeSum analysis.* Calculate the probability that no triple among $N$ random 32-bit integers sums to 0, and give an approximate estimate for $N$ equal to 1000, 2000, and 4000. *Extra credit*: Give an approximate formula for the expected number of such triples (as a function of $N$), and run experiments to validate your estimate.

**4.1.29** *Closest pair.* Design a quadratic algorithm that finds the pair of integers that are closest to each other. (In the next section you will be asked to find a linearithmic algorithm.)

**4.1.30** *Power law.* Show that a log-log plot of the function $cN^b$ has slope $b$ and $x$-intercept $\log c$. What are the slope and $x$-intercept for $4\,N^3\,(\log N)^2$?

**4.1.31** *Sum furthest from zero.* Design an algorithm that finds the pair of integers whose sum is furthest from zero. Can you discover a linear algorithm?

**4.1.32** *The "beck" exploit.* A popular web server supports a function called `no2slash()` whose purpose is to collapse multiple / characters. For example, the string `/d1///d2////d3/test.html` becomes `/d1/d2/d3/test.html`. The original algorithm was to repeatedly search for a / and copy the remainder of the string:

```
void no2slash(char[] name)
{
    for (int x = 0; x < name.length; )
        if (x > 0)
            if ((name[x-1] == '/') && (name[x] == '/'))
                for(int y = x+1; y < name.length; y++)
                    name[y-1] = name[y];
        else x++;
}
```

Unfortunately, the running time of this code is quadratic in the number of / characters in the input. By sending multiple simultaneous requests with large numbers of / characters, a hacker can deluge a server and starve other processes for CPU time, thereby creating a denial-of-service attack. Develop a version of `no2slash()` that runs in linear time and does not allow for the this type of attack.

**4.1.33** *Young tableaux.* Suppose you have in memory an *N*-by-*N* grid of integers a such that a[i][j] < a[i+1][j] and a[i][j] < a[i][j+1] for all i and j, like the table below.

```
 5  23  54  67  89
 6  69  73  74  90
10  71  83  84  91
60  73  84  86  92
99  91  92  93  94
```

Devise an algorithm whose order of growth is linear in *N* to determine whether a given integer *x* is in a given Young tableaux.

*Answer:* Start at the upper-right corner. If the value is *x*, return true. Otherwise, go left if the value is greater than *x* and go down if the value is less than *x*. If you reach bottom left corner, then *x* is not in table. The algorithm is linear because you can go left at most *N* times and down at most *N* times.

**4.1.34** *Subset sum.* Write a program AnySum that takes an integer *N* from standard input, then reads *N* long values from standard input, and counts the number of subsets that sum to 0. Give the order of growth of the running time of your program.

**4.1.35** *String rotation.* Given an array of *N* elements, give a linear time algorithm to rotate the string *k* positions. That is, if the array contains $a_0, a_1, ..., a_{N-1}$, the rotated array is $a_k, a_{k+1}, ..., a_{N-1}, a_0, ..., a_{k-1}$. Use at most a constant amount of extra space (array indices and array values). *Hint:* Reverse three subarrays as in EXERCISE 4.1.20.

**4.1.36** *Finding a duplicated integer.* (*a*) Given an array of *N* integers from 1 to *N* with one value repeated twice and one missing, give an algorithm that finds the missing integer, in linear time and constant extra space. Integer overflow is not allowed. (*b*) Given a read-only array of *N* integers, where each value from 1 to *N*−1 occurs once and one occurs twice, give an algorithm that finds the duplicated value, in linear time and constant extra space. (*c*) Given a read-only array of *N* integers with values between 1 and *N*−1, give an algorithm that finds a duplicated value, in linear time and constant extra space.

**4.1.37** *Factorial.* Design a fast algorithm to compute $N!$ for large values of $N$, using Java's `BigInteger` class. Use your program to compute the longest run of consecutive 9s in 1000000!. Develop and validate a hypothesis for the order of growth of the running time of your algorithm.

**4.1.38** *Maximum sum.* Design a linear algorithm that finds a contiguous subsequence of at most $M$ in a sequence of $N$ `long` integers that has the highest sum among all such subsequences. Implement your algorithm, and confirm that the order of growth of its running time is linear.

**4.1.39** *Pattern matching.* Given an $N$-by-$N$ array of black (1) and white (0) pixels, design a linear algorithm that finds the largest square subarray that consists of entirely black pixels. In the example below there is a 3-by-3 subarray.

```
1 0 1 1 1 0 0 0
0 0 0 1 0 1 0 0
0 0 1 1 1 0 0 0
0 0 1 1 1 0 1 0
0 0 1 1 1 1 1 1
0 1 0 1 1 1 1 0
0 1 0 1 1 0 1 0
0 0 0 1 1 1 1 0
```

Implement your algorithm and confirm that the order of growth of its running time is linear in the number of pixels. *Extra credit*: Design an algorithm to find the largest *rectangular* black subarray.

**4.1.40** *Maximum average.* Write a program that finds a contiguous subarray of at most $M$ elements in an array of $N$ `long` integers that has the highest average value among all such subarrays, by trying all subarrays. Use the scientific method to confirm that the order of growth of the running time of your program is $MN^2$. Next, write a program that solves the problem by first computing `prefix[i] = a[0] + ... + a[i]` for each i, then computing the average in the interval from `a[i]` to `a[j]` with the expression `(prefix[j] - prefix[i]) / (j - i + 1)`. Use the scientific method to confirm that this method reduces the order of growth by a factor of $N$.

**4.1.41** *Sub-exponential function.* Find a function whose order-of-growth is slower than any polynomial function, but faster than any exponential function. *Extra credit*: Find a program whose running time has that order of growth.

# 4.2   Sorting and Searching

THE SORTING PROBLEM IS TO REARRANGE a set of items in ascending order. It is a familiar and critical task in many computational applications: the songs in your music library are in alphabetical order, your email messages are in order of the time received, and so forth. Keeping things in some kind of order is a natural desire. One reason that it is so useful is that it is much easier to *search* for something in a sorted list than an unsorted one. This need is particularly acute in computing, where the list of things to search can be huge and an efficient search can be an important factor in a problem's solution.

Sorting and searching are important for commercial applications (businesses keep customer files in order) and scientific applications (to organize data and computation), and have all manner of applications in fields that may appear to have little to do with keeping things in order, including data compression, computer graphics, computational biology, numerical computing, combinatorial optimization, cryptography, and many others.

We use these fundamental problems to illustrate the idea that *efficient algorithms* are one key to effective solutions for computational problem. Indeed, many different sorting and searching methods have been proposed. Which should we use to address a given task? This question is important because different programs can have vastly differing performance characteristics, enough to make the difference between success in a practical situation and not coming close to doing so, even on the fastest available computer.

In this section, we will consider in detail two classical algorithms for sorting and searching, along with several applications in which their efficiency plays a critical role. With these examples, you will be convinced not just of the utility of these methods, but also of the need to *pay attention to the cost* whenever you address a problem that requires a significant amount of computation.

**Binary search**   The game of "twenty questions" (see PROGRAM 1.5.2) provides an important and useful lesson in the idea of designing and using efficient algorithms for computational problems. The setup is simple: your task is to guess the value of a hidden number that is one of the $N$ integers between 0 and $N-1$. Each time that you make a guess, you are told whether your guess is equal to the hidden number, too high, or too low. As we discussed in SECTION 1.5, an effective strategy is to guess the number in the middle of the interval, then use the answer to halve the interval size. For reasons that will become clear later, we begin by slightly modifying the game to make the questions of the form "is the number less than $m$ ?" with *true* or *false* answers, and assume for the moment that $N$ is a power of two. Now, the basis of an effective method that always gets to the hidden number in a minimal number of questions is to maintain an interval that contains the hidden number and shrinks by half at each step. More precisely, we use a *half-open interval*, which contains the left endpoint but not the right one. We use the notation $[l, h)$ to denote all of the integers greater than or equal to $l$ and less than (but not equal to) $h$. We start with $l = 0$ and $h = N$ and use the following recursive strategy:

| interval | size | Q | A |
|---|---|---|---|
| | 128 | < 64 ? | *false* |
| | 64 | < 96 ? | *true* |
| | 32 | < 80 ? | *true* |
| | 16 | < 72 ? | *false* |
| | 8 | < 76 ? | *false* |
| | 4 | < 78 ? | *true* |
| | 2 | < 77 ? | *false* |
| | 1 | = 77 | |

*Finding a hidden number with binary search*

- *Base case*: If $h - l$ is 1, then the number is $l$.
- *Recursive step*: Otherwise, ask whether the number is less than the number $m = l + (h-l)/2$. If so, look for the number in $[l, m)$; if not, look for the number in $[m, h)$.

This strategy is an example of the general problem-solving method known as *binary search*, which has many applications. TwentyQuestions (PROGRAM 4.2.1) is an implementation.

*Program 4.2.1*    **Binary search (20 questions)**

```
public class TwentyQuestions
{
   public static int search(int lo, int hi)
   { // Find number in [lo, hi)
      if ((hi - lo) == 1) return lo;
      int mid = lo + (hi - lo) / 2;
      StdOut.print("Less than " + mid + "?  ");
      if (StdIn.readBoolean())
           return search(lo, mid);
      else return search(mid, hi);
   }

   public static void main(String[] args)
   { // Play twenty questions.
      int n = Integer.parseInt(args[0]);
      int N = (int) Math.pow(2, n);
      StdOut.print("Think of a number ");
      StdOut.println("between 0 and " + (N-1));
      int v = search(0, N);
      StdOut.println("Your number is " + v);
   }
}
```

| | |
|---|---|
| lo | *smallest possible value* |
| hi - 1 | *largest possible value* |
| mid | *midpoint* |
| n | *number of questions* |
| N | *number of possible values* |

*This code uses binary search to play the same game as Program 1.5.2, but with the roles reversed: you provide the number and the program guesses its value. It takes a command-line argument n, asks you to think of a number between 0 and N−1, where N = 2ⁿ, and always guesses the answer with n questions.*

```
% java TwentyQuestions 7
Think of a number between 0 and 127
Less than 64?  false
Less than 96?  true
Less than 80?  true
Less than 72?  false
Less than 76?  false
Less than 78?  true
Less than 77?  false
Your number is 77
```

*Correctness proof.* First, we have to convince ourselves that the method is *correct*: that it always leads us to the hidden number. We do so by establishing the following facts:
- The interval always contains the hidden number.
- The interval sizes are the powers of two, decreasing from $N$.

The first of these facts is enforced by the code; the second follows by noting that if $(h-l)$ is a power of two, then $(h-l)/2$ is the next smaller power of two and also the size of both halved intervals. These facts are the basis of an induction proof that the method operates as intended. Eventually, the interval size becomes 1, so we are guaranteed to find the number.

*Analysis of running time.* Since $N$ is a power of 2, we write $N = 2^n$, where $n = \lg N$. Now, let $T(N)$ be the number of questions. The recursive strategy immediately implies that $T(N)$ must satisfy the following recurrence relation:

$$T(N) = T(N/2) + 1$$

with $T(1) = 1$. Substituting $2^n$ for $N$, we can telescope the recurrence (apply it to itself) to immediately get a closed-form expression:

$$T(2^n) = T(2^{n-1}) + 1 = T(2^{n-2}) + 2 = \ldots = T(1) + n-1 = n.$$

Substituting back $N$ for $2^n$ (and $\lg N$ for $n$) gives the result

$$T(N) = \lg N$$

We normally use this equation to justify a hypothesis that the running time of a program that uses binary search is logarithmic. *Note*: Binary search and `Twenty-Questions.search()` work even when $N$ is not a power of two—we just assumed that $N$ is a power of two to simplify our proof (see EXERCISE 4.2.14).

*Linear-logarithmic chasm.* The alternative to using binary search is to guess 0, then 1, then 2, then 3, and so forth, until hitting the hidden number. We refer to such an algorithm as a *brute-force* algorithm: it seems to get the job done, but without much regard to the cost (which might prevent it from actually getting the job done for large problems). In this case, the running time of the brute-force algorithm is sensitive to the input value, but could be as much as $N$ and has expected value $N/2$ if the input value is chosen at random. Meanwhile, binary search is guaranteed to use no more than $\lg N$ steps. As you will learn to appreciate, the difference between $N$ and $\lg N$ makes a huge difference in practical applications. *Understanding the enormousness of this difference is a critical step to understanding the importance of algorithm design and analysis.* In the present context, suppose that it takes 1 second to process a guess. With binary search, you can guess the value of any number less than 1 million in 20 seconds; with the brute-force algorithm, it might take 1 million seconds, which is more than 1 week. We will see many examples where such a cost difference is the determining factor in whether or not a practical problem can be feasibly solved.

*Binary representation.* If you look back to PROGRAM 1.3.7, you will immediately recognize that binary search is nearly the same computation as converting a number to binary! Each guess determines one bit of the answer. In our example, the information that the number is between 0 and 127 says that the number of bits in its binary representation is 7, the answer to the first question (is the number less than 64?) tells us the value of the leading bit, the answer to the second question tells us the value of the next bit, and so forth. For example, if the number is 77, the sequence

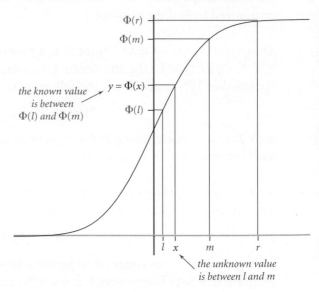

*Binary search (bisection) to invert an increasing function*

of answers no yes yes no no yes no immediately yields 1001101, the binary representation of 77. Thinking in terms of the binary representation is another way to understand the linear-logarithmic chasm: when we have a program whose running time is linear in a parameter $N$, its running time is proportional to the *value* of $N$, whereas a logarithmic running time is just proportional to the *number of digits* in $N$. In a context that is perhaps slightly more familiar to you, think about the following question, which illustrates the same point: would you rather earn $6 or a six-figure salary?

---

### Program 4.2.2    Bisection search (function inversion)

```
public static void PhiInverse(double y)
{  return PhiInverse(y, .00000001, -8, 8)  }

private static double PhiInverse(double y, double delta,
                                double lo, double hi)
{  // Compute x with Phi(x) = y.
   double mid = lo + (hi - lo)/2;
   if (hi - lo < delta) return mid;
   if (Phi(mid) > y)
       return PhiInverse(y, delta, lo, mid);
   else return PhiInverse(y, delta, mid, hi);
}
```

| | |
|---|---|
| y | *argument* |
| delta | *precision* |
| lo | *smallest possible value* |
| mid | *midpoint* |
| hi | *largest possible value* |

---

*This implementation of* PhiInverse() *for our Gaussian library (Program 2.1.2) uses binary search to compute a value x for which* $\Phi(x)$ *is equal to a given value y, within a given precision* delta. *It is a recursive function that halves the interval containing the given value, evaluates the function at the midpoint of the interval, and takes advantage of the fact that* $\Phi$ *is increasing to decide whether the desired point is in the left half or the right half, continuing until the interval size is less than the given precision.*

*Inverting a function.* As an example of the utility of binary search in scientific computing, we revisit a problem that we first encountered in SECTION 2.1: inverting an increasing function. To fix ideas, we refer to the Gaussian cumulative distribution function $\Phi$ when describing the method, but it works for any increasing function. Given a value *y*, our task is to find a value *x* such that $\Phi(x) = y$. In this situation, we use real numbers as the endpoints of our interval, not integers, but we use the same essential method as for guessing a hidden integer: we halve the size of the interval at each step, keeping *x* in the interval, until the interval is sufficiently small that we know the value of *x* to within a desired precision $\delta$. We start with an interval $(l, h)$ known to contain *x* and use the following recursive strategy:

- Compute $m = l + (h - l)/2$.
- *Base case*: If $h - l$ is less than $\delta$, then return *m* as an estimate of *x*.
- *Recursive step*: Otherwise, test whether $\Phi(m) > y$. If so, look for *x* in $(l, m)$; if not, look for *x* in $(m, h)$.

The key to this method is the idea that the function is increasing—for any values $a$ and $b$, knowing that $\Phi(a) < \Phi(b)$ tells us that $a < b$, and vice versa. The recursive step just applies this knowledge: knowing that $y = \Phi(x) < \Phi(m)$ tells us that $x < m$, so that $x$ must be in the interval $(l, m)$, and knowing that $y = \Phi(x) > \Phi(m)$ tells us that $x > m$, so that $x$ must be in the interval $(m, h)$. You can think of the problem as determining which of the $N = (h-l)/\delta$ tiny intervals of size $\delta$ within $(l, h)$ contains $x$, with running time logarithmic in $N$. As with number conversion for integers, we determine one bit of $x$ for each iteration. In this context, binary search is often called *bisection search* because we bisect the interval at each stage.

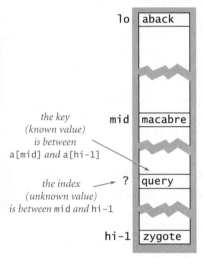

*the key (known value) is between* a[mid] *and* a[hi-1]

*the index (unknown value) is between* mid *and* hi-1

*Binary search in a sorted array (one step)*

*Binary search in a sorted array.* One of the most important uses of binary search is to find a piece of information using a key to guide the search. This usage is ubiquitous in modern computing, to the extent that printed artifacts that depend on the same concepts are well on their way to becoming obsolete. For example, during the last few centuries, people would use a publication known as a *dictionary* to look up the definition of a word, and during much of the last century people would use a publication known as a *phone book* to look up a person's phone number. In both cases, the basic mechanism is the same: entries appear in order, sorted by a key that identifies it (the word in the case of the dictionary, and the person's name in the case of the phone book, sorted in alphabetical order in both cases). You probably use your computer to reference such information, but think about how you would look up a word in a dictionary. A brute-force solution would be to start at the beginning, examine each entry one at a time, and continue until you find the word. No one uses that method: instead, you open the book to some interior page and look for the word on that page. If it is there, you are done; otherwise, you eliminate either the part of the book before the current page or the part of the book after the current page from consideration, and then repeat. We now recognize this method as binary search. Whether or not you look exactly in the middle is immaterial; as long as you eliminate at least a fraction of the entries each time that you look, your search will be logarithmic (see EXERCISE 4.2.15).

---

**Program 4.2.3  *Binary search (sorted array)***

---

```java
public class BinarySearch
{
   public static int search(String key, String[] a)
   {  return search(key, a, 0, a.length);  }

   public static int search(String key,String[] a, int lo, int hi)
   {  // Search for key in a[lo, hi).
      if (hi <= lo) return -1;
      int mid = lo + (hi - lo) / 2;
      int cmp = a[mid].compareTo(key);
      if      (cmp > 0) return search(key, a, lo, mid);
      else if (cmp < 0) return search(key, a, mid+1, hi);
      else              return mid;
   }

   public static void main(String[] args)
   {  // Print keys in StdIn that are not found
      // in the whitelist file args[0].
      In in = new In(args[0]);
      String[] a = in.readAll().split("\\s+");
      while (!StdIn.isEmpty())
      {
         String key = StdIn.readString();
         if (search(key, a) < 0) StdOut.println(key);
      }
   }
}
```

| | |
|---|---|
| key | *string sought* |
| a[] | *sorted list of strings* |
| lo | *smallest possible index* |
| mid | *midpoint* |
| hi - 1 | *largest possible index* |

---

*The* search() *method in this class uses binary search to find the index of a string key in a sorted array (or returns –1 if the string is not in the array). The test client is an exception filter that reads a (sorted) whitelist from the file given on the command line and prints the words from standard input that are not in the whitelist.*

```
more test.txt
bob@office
carl@beach
marvin@spam
bob@office
bob@office
mallory@spam
dave@boat
eve@airport
alice@home
```

```
% more whitelist.txt
alice@home
bob@office
carl@beach
dave@boat

% java BinarySearch whitelist.txt < test.txt
marvin@spam
mallory@spam
eve@airport
```

*Exception filter.* We will consider in SECTION 4.3 the details of implementing the kind of computer program that you use in place of a dictionary or a phone book. PROGRAM 4.2.3 uses binary search to solve the simpler *existence problem*: is a given key in a sorted database of keys, or not? For example, when checking the spelling of a word, you need only know whether your word is in the dictionary and are not interested in the definition. In a computer search, we keep the information in an array, sorted in order of the key (for some applications, the information comes in sorted order; for others, we have to sort it first, using one of the methods discussed later in this section). The binary search in PROGRAM 4.2.3 differs from our other applications in two details. First, the file size $N$ need not be a power of two. Second, it has to allow the possibility that the item sought is not in the array. Coding binary search to account for these details requires some care, as discussed in this section's Q&A and exercises. The test client in PROGRAM 4.2.3 is known as an *exception filter*: it reads in a sorted list of strings from a file (which we refer to as the *whitelist*) and an arbitrary sequence of strings from standard input, and prints those in the sequence that are not in the whitelist. Exception filters have many direct applications. For example, if the whitelist is the words from a dictionary and standard input is a text document, the exception filter will print the misspelled words. Another example arises in web applications: your email application might use an exception filter to reject any mail messages that are not on a whitelist that contains the mail addresses of your friends, or your operating system might have an exception filter that disallows network connections to your computer from any device having an IP address that is not on a preapproved whitelist.

*Weighing an object.* Binary search has been known since antiquity, perhaps partly because of the following application. Suppose that you need to determine the weight of a given object using only a balancing scale. With binary search, you can do so with weights that are powers of two (you need only one weight of each type). Put the object on the left side of the balance and try the weights in decreasing order on the right side. If a weight causes the balance to tilt to the left, remove it; otherwise, leave it. This process is precisely analogous to determining the binary representation of a number by subtracting decreasing powers of two, as in PROGRAM 1.3.7.

twenty questions
(converting to binary)

weighing an object

inverting a function

*Three applications of binary search*

Fast algorithms are an essential element of the modern world, and binary search is a prototypical example that illustrates the impact of fast algorithms. With a few quick calculations, you can convince yourself that problems like finding all the misspelled words in a document or protecting your computer from intruders using an exception filter *require* a fast algorithm like binary search. *Take the time to do so.* You can find the exceptions in a million-entry document to a million-entry whitelist in an instant, whereas that task might take days or weeks using the brute force algorithm. Nowadays, web companies routinely provide services that are based on using binary search *billions* of times in tables with *billions* of entries—without a fast algorithm like binary search, we could not contemplate such services.

Whether it be extensive experimental data or detailed representations of some aspect of the physical world, modern scientists are awash in vast amounts of data. Binary search and fast algorithms like it are essential components of scientific progress. Using a brute-force algorithm is precisely analogous to searching for a word in a dictionary by starting at the first page and turning pages one by one. With a fast algorithm, you can literally search among billions of pieces of information in an instant. Taking the time to identify and use a fast algorithm for search certainly can make the difference between being able to solve a problem easily and spending substantial resources trying to do so (and failing).

**Insertion sort**   Binary search requires that the data be sorted, and sorting has many other direct applications, so we now turn to sorting algorithms. We first consider a brute-force method, then a sophisticated method that we can use for huge data sets.

The brute-force algorithm is known as *insertion sort* and is based on a simple method that people often use to arrange hands of playing cards. Consider the cards one at a time and insert each into its proper place among those already considered (keeping them sorted). The following code mimics this process in a Java method that sorts strings in an array:

```java
public static void sort(String[] a)
{
   int N = a.length;
   for (int i = 1; i < N; i++)
      for (int j = i; j > 0; j--)
         if (a[j-1].compareTo(a[j]) > 0)
            exch(a, j-1, j);
         else break;
}
```

The outer `for` loop sorts the first i entries in the array; the inner `for` loop completes the sort by putting a[i] into its proper position in the array, as in the following example when i is 6:

| i | j | a 0 | 1 | 2 | 3 | 4 | 5 | 6 | 7 |
|---|---|-----|---|---|---|---|---|---|---|
| 6 | 6 | and | had | him | his | was | you | the | but |
| 6 | 5 | and | had | him | his | was | the | you | but |
| 6 | 4 | and | had | him | his | the | was | you | but |
|   |   | and | had | him | his | the | was | you | but |

*Inserting* a[6] *into position by exchanging with larger entries to its left*

Entry a[i] is put in its place among the sorted entries to its left by exchanging it (using the `exch()` method that we first encountered in Section 2.1) with each larger element to its left, moving from right to left, until it reaches its proper position. The black entries in the three bottom rows in this trace are the ones that are compared (and exchanged, on all but the final iteration).

The insertion process just described is executed, first with i equal to 1, then 2, then 3, and so forth, as illustrated in the following trace.

| i | j | 0 | 1 | 2 | 3 | 4 | 5 | 6 | 7 |
|---|---|---|---|---|---|---|---|---|---|
|   |   | was | had | him | and | you | his | the | but |
| 1 | 0 | had | was | him | and | you | his | the | but |
| 2 | 1 | had | him | was | and | you | his | the | but |
| 3 | 0 | and | had | him | was | you | his | the | but |
| 4 | 4 | and | had | him | was | you | his | the | but |
| 5 | 3 | and | had | him | his | was | you | the | but |
| 6 | 4 | and | had | him | his | the | was | you | but |
| 7 | 1 | and | but | had | him | his | the | was | you |
|   |   | and | but | had | him | his | the | was | you |

*Inserting* a[1] *through* a[N-1] *into position (insertion sort)*

This trace displays the contents of the array each time the outer for loop completes, along with the value of j at that time. The highlighted element is the one that was in a[i] at the beginning of the loop, and the other elements printed in black are the other ones that were involved in exchanges and moved to the right one position within the loop. Since the elements a[0] through a[i-1] are in sorted order when the loop completes for each value of i, they are, in particular, in sorted order the final time the loop completes, when the value of i is a.length. This discussion again illustrates the first thing that you need to do when studying or developing a new algorithm: convince yourself that it is correct. Doing so provides the basic understanding that you need in order to study its performance and use it effectively.

*Analysis of running time.* The inner loop of the insertion sort code is within a double for loop, which suggests that the running time is quadratic, but we cannot immediately draw this conclusion, because of the break. For example, in the best case, when the input array is already in sorted order, the inner for loop amounts to nothing more than a comparison (to learn that a[j-1] is less than a[j] for each j from 1 to N-1) and the break, so the total running time is linear. On the other hand, in the reverse-sorted case, the inner loop fully completes without a break, so the frequency of execution of the instructions in the inner loop is $1 + 2 + \ldots + N-1 \sim N^2$ and the running time is quadratic. To understand the performance of insertion sort for *randomly* ordered input, take a careful look at the trace: it is an N-by-N array with one black element corresponding to each exchange. That is, the number of black elements is the frequency of execution of instructions in the inner loop. We expect that each new element to be inserted is equally likely to fall into any position, so that element will move halfway to the left on average. Thus, on the average, we expect only about one-half the elements below the diagonal (about $N^2/4$ in total) to be black,. This leads immediately to the hypothesis that the expected running time of insertion sort for a randomly ordered input array is quadratic.

*Sorting other types of data.*  We want to be able to sort all types of data, not just strings. In a scientific application, we may wish to sort experimental results by numeric values; in a commercial application, we may wish to use monetary amounts, times, or dates; in systems software, we might wish to use IP addresses or account numbers. The idea of sorting in each of these situations is intuitive, but implement-

ing a sort method that works in all of them is a prime example of the need for a functional abstraction mechanism like the one provided by Java. For sorting objects in an array, we need only assume that we can *compare* two elements to see whether the first is bigger than, smaller than, or equal to the second. Java provides the `Comparable` interface for precisely this purpose. Simply put, a class that implements the `Comparable` interface promises to implement a method `compareTo()` for objects of its type so that `a.compareTo(b)` returns a negative integer if a is less than b, a positive integer if a is greater than b, and 0 if a is equal

*Analysis of insertion sort*

to b. The precise meanings of *less than*, *greater than*, and *equal to* are up to the data type, though implementations that do not respect the natural laws of mathematics surrounding these concepts will yield unpredictable results. With this convention, we can implement our sort method so that it sorts arrays of `Comparable` objects, and use `compareTo()` to compare them, as illustrated in `Insertion` (PROGRAM 4.2.4). As discussed in SECTION 3.3, Java's `String` type implements the `Comparable` interface (we have been using its `compareTo()` method), as does the `Date` type and wrappers for primitive numeric types such as `Integer` and `Double`. Thus, we can use `Insertion.sort()` to sort arrays of all of these types of data. It is also easy to implement the interface so that we can sort user-defined types of data, as we saw in SECTION 3.3.

*Program 4.2.4     Insertion sort*

```
public class Insertion
{
   public static void sort(Comparable[] a)
   {  // Sort a[] into increasing order.
      int N = a.length;
      for (int i = 1; i < N; i++)
         // Insert a[i] into position by exchanging
         // it with the larger elements to its left.
         for (int j = i; j > 0; j--)
            if (a[j-1].compareTo(a[j]) > 0)
                 exch(a, j-1, j);
            else break;
   }

   public static void exch(Comparable[] a, int i, int j)
   {  Comparable t = a[j]; a[j] = a[j-1]; a[j-1] = t;  }

   public static void main(String[] args)
   {  // Read strings from standard input, sort them, and print.
      String[] a = StdIn.readAll().split("\\s+");
      sort(a);
      for (int i = 0; i < a.length; i++)
         StdOut.print(a[i] + " ");
      StdOut.println();
   }
}
```

| a[] | array to sort |
|-----|---------------|
| N | number of entries |

*The* sort() *function is an implementation of insertion sort. It sorts arrays of any type of data that implements the* Comparable *interface (has a* compareTo() *method). This method is appropriate for small files or for large files that are nearly in order, but is too slow to use for large files that are out of order.*

```
% more tiny.txt
was had him and you his the but

% java Insertion < tiny.txt
and but had him his the was you

% java Insertion < TomSawyer.txt
tick tick tick tick tick tick tick tick tick tick tick tick tick tick tick tick tick tick tick tick
tick tick tick tick tick tick tick tick tick tick tick tick tick tick tick tick tick tick tick tick
tick tick tick tick tick tick tick tick tick tick tick tick tick tick tick tick tick tick tick tick
tick tick tick tick tick tick tick tick tick tick tick tick tick tick tick tick tick tick tick tick
tick tick tick tick tick tick tick tick tick tick tick tick tick tick tick tick tick tick tick tick
```

*Empirical analysis.* InsertionTest (PROGRAM 4.2.5) tests our hypothesis that insertion sort is quadratic for randomly ordered files by running Insertion.sort() on $N$ random Double values, computing the ratios of running times as $N$ doubles. This ratio converges to 4, which validates the hypothesis that the running time is quadratic, as discussed in the last section. You are encouraged to run Insertion-Test on your own computer. As usual, you might notice the effect of caching or some other system characteristic for some values of $N$, but the quadratic running time should be quite evident, and you will be quickly convinced that insertion sort is too slow to be useful for large inputs.

*Sensitivity to input.* Note that InsertionTest takes a command-line argument T and runs T experiments for each array size, not just one. As we have just observed, one reason for doing so is that *the running time of insertion sort is sensitive to its input values.* This behavior is quite different from (for example) ThreeSum, and means that we have to carefully interpret the results of our analysis. It is not correct to flatly predict that the running time of insertion sort will be quadratic, because your application might involve input for which the running time is linear. When an algorithm's performance is sensitive to input values, you might not be able to make accurate predictions without taking the input values into account.

THERE ARE MANY NATURAL APPLICATIONS FOR which insertion sort *is* quadratic, so we need to consider faster sorting algorithms. As we know from SECTION 4.1, a back-of-the-envelope calculation can tell us that having a faster computer is not much help. A dictionary, a scientific database, or a commercial database can contain billions of entries; how can we sort such a large array?

*Program 4.2.5   Doubling test for insertion sort*

```
public class InsertionTest
{
   public static double timeTrials(int T, int N)
   {  // Sort T random arrays of size N.
      double total = 0.0;
      Double[] a = new Double[N];
      for (int t = 0; t < T; t++)
      {
         for (int i = 0; i < N; i++)
            a[i] = Math.random();
         Stopwatch watch = new Stopwatch();
         Insertion.sort(a);
         total += watch.elapsedTime();
      }
      return total;
   }
   public static void main(String[] args)
   {  // Print doubling ratios for T trials of insertion sort.
      int T = Integer.parseInt(args[0]);
      double prev = timeTrials(T, 512);
      for (int N = 1024; true; N += N)
      {
         double curr =  timeTrials(T, N);
         StdOut.printf("%7d %4.2f\n", N, curr / prev);
         prev = curr;
      }
   }
}
```

| | |
|---|---|
| T | *number of trials* |
| N | *problem size* |
| total | *total elapsed time* |
| watch | *stopwatch* |
| a[] | *array to sort* |
| curr | *total for current size* |
| prev | *total for previous size* |

*The method* timeTrials() *runs* Insertion.sort() *for arrays of random double values. The first argument is the length of the array; the second is the number of trials. Multiple trials produce more accurate results because they dampen system effects and because insertion sort's running time depends on the input.*

```
% java InsertionTest 1
   1024 0.71
   2048 3.00
   4096 5.20
   8192 3.32
  16384 3.91
  32768 3.89
```

```
% java InsertionTest 10
   1024 1.89
   2048 5.00
   4096 3.58
   8192 4.09
  16384 4.83
  32768 3.96
```

**Mergesort**   To develop a faster sorting method, we use recursion (as we did for binary search) and a *divide-and-conquer* approach to algorithm design that every programmer needs to understand. This nomenclature refers to the idea that one way to solve a problem is to *divide* it into independent parts, *conquer* them independently, and then use the solutions for the parts to develop a solution for the full problem. To sort an array with this strategy, we divide it into two halves, sort the two halves independently, and then *merge* the results to sort the full array. This method is known as *mergesort*.

*input*
```
was had him and you his the but
```
*sort left*
```
and had him was you his the but
```
*sort right*
```
and had him was but his the you
```
*merge*
```
and but had him his the was you
```
*Mergesort overview*

We process contiguous subarrays of a given array, using the notation a[lo, hi) to refer to a[lo], a[lo+1], ..., a[hi-1] (adopting the same convention as we used for binary search to denote a half-open interval that excludes a[hi]). To sort a[lo, hi), we use the following recursive strategy:

- *Base case*: If the subarray size is 0 or 1, it is already sorted.
- *Recursive step*: Otherwise, compute mid = lo + (hi - lo)/2, sort (recursively) the two subarrays a[lo, mid) and a[mid, hi), and merge them.

Merge (PROGRAM 4.2.6) is an implementation of this algorithm. The array elements are rearranged by the code that follows the recursive calls, which *merges* the two halves of the array that were sorted by the recursive calls. As usual, the easiest way to understand the merge process is to study a trace of the contents of the array during the merge. The code maintains one index i into the first half, another index j

| i | j | k | aux[k] | 0 | 1 | 2 | 3 | 4 | 5 | 6 | 7 |
|---|---|---|--------|---|---|---|---|---|---|---|---|
|   |   |   |        | and | had | him | was | but | his | the | you |
| 0 | 4 | 0 | and | and | had | him | was | but | his | the | you |
| 1 | 4 | 1 | but | and | had | him | was | but | his | the | you |
| 1 | 5 | 2 | had | and | had | him | was | but | his | the | you |
| 2 | 5 | 3 | him | and | had | him | was | but | his | the | you |
| 3 | 5 | 4 | his | and | had | him | was | but | his | the | you |
| 3 | 6 | 5 | the | and | had | him | was | but | his | the | you |
| 3 | 6 | 6 | was | and | had | him | was | but | his | the | you |
| 4 | 7 | 7 | you | and | had | him | was | but | his | the | you |

*Trace of the merge of the sorted left half with the sorted right half*

*Program 4.2.6   Mergesort*

```
public class Merge
{
    public static void sort(Comparable[] a)
    {  sort(a, 0, a.length);  }
    public static void sort(Comparable[] a, int lo, int hi)
    {  // Sort a[lo, hi).
        int N = hi - lo;
        if (N <= 1) return;
        int mid = lo + N/2;
        sort(a, lo, mid);
        sort(a, mid, hi);
        Comparable[] aux = new Comparable[N];
        int i = lo, j = mid;
        for (int k = 0; k < N; k++)
            if       (i == mid)  aux[k] = a[j++];
            else if (j == hi)    aux[k] = a[i++];
            else if (a[j].compareTo(a[i]) < 0) aux[k] = a[j++];
            else                               aux[k] = a[i++];
        for (int k = 0; k < N; k++)
            a[lo + k] = aux[k];
    }

    public static void main(String[] args)
    {  /* See Program 4.2.4 (and text) */  }
}
```

| a[lo, hi) | subarray to sort |
|---|---|
| N | size of subarray |
| mid | midpoint |
| aux[] | extra array for merge |

*The* sort() *function in this class is a fast method that you can use to sort arrays of any type of data that implements* Comparable. *It is based on a recursive* sort() *that sorts* a[lo, hi) *by sorting its two halves recursively, then merging together the two halves to create the sorted result. The output below and at right is a trace of the sorted subarray for each call to* sort(). *In contrast to* Insertion, *this implementation is suitable for sorting huge arrays.*

```
% java Merge < tiny.txt
  was had him and you his the but
  had was
          and him
  and had him was
                  his you
                      but the
                  but his the you
  and but had him his the was you
```

into the second half, and a third index k into an auxiliary array aux[] that holds the result. The merge implementation is a single loop that sets aux[k] to either a[i] or a[j] (and then increments k and the index for the value that is used). If either i or j has reached the end of its subarray, aux[k] is set from the other; otherwise, it is set to the smaller of a[i] or a[j]. After all of the elements from the two halves have been copied to aux[], the sorted result is copied back to the original array. Take a moment to study the trace just given to convince yourself that this code always properly combines the two sorted subarrays to sort the full array.

The recursive method ensures that the two halves of the array are put into sorted order before the merge. Again, the best way to gain an understanding of this process is to study a trace of the contents of the array each time the recursive sort() method returns. Such a trace for our example is shown next. First a[0] and a[1] are merged to make a sorted subarray in a[0, 2), then a[2] and a[3] are merged to make a sorted subarray in a[2, 4), then these two subarrays of size 2 are merged to make a sorted subarray in a[0, 4), and so forth. If you are convinced that the merge works properly, you need only convince yourself that the code properly divides the array to be convinced that the sort works properly. Note that when the number of elements is not even, the left half will have one fewer element than the right half.

|  | 0 | 1 | 2 | 3 | 4 | 5 | 6 | 7 |
| --- | --- | --- | --- | --- | --- | --- | --- | --- |
|  | was | had | him | and | you | his | the | but |
| sort(a, 0, 8) |  |  |  |  |  |  |  |  |
|   sort(a, 0, 4) |  |  |  |  |  |  |  |  |
|     sort(a, 0, 2) |  |  |  |  |  |  |  |  |
|     return | had | was | him | and | you | his | the | but |
|     sort(a, 2, 4) |  |  |  |  |  |  |  |  |
|     return | had | was | and | him | you | the | the | but |
|   return | and | had | him | was | you | the | the | but |
|   sort(a, 4, 8) |  |  |  |  |  |  |  |  |
|     sort(a, 4, 6) |  |  |  |  |  |  |  |  |
|     return | and | had | him | was | his | you | the | but |
|     sort(a, 6, 8) |  |  |  |  |  |  |  |  |
|     return | and | had | him | was | his | you | but | the |
|   return | and | had | him | was | but | his | the | you |
| return | and | but | had | him | his | the | was | you |

*Trace of recursive mergesort calls*

*Analysis of running time.* The inner loop of mergesort is centered on the auxiliary array. The two `for` loops involve $N$ iterations (and creating the array takes time proportional to $N$), so the frequency of execution of the instructions in the inner loop is proportional to the sum of the subarray sizes for all calls to the recursive function. The value of this quantity emerges when we arrange the calls on levels according to their size. For simplicity, suppose that $N$ is a power of 2, with $N = 2^n$.

$1 \times N/1 = N$
$2 \times N/2 = N$
$4 \times N/4 = N$
$8 \times N/8 = N$

$N/2 \times 2 = N$

Total: $N \lg N$

$\leftarrow \begin{matrix} \lg N \\ levels \end{matrix}$

*Mergesort inner loop count (when N is a power of 2)*

On the first level, we have one call for size $N$; on the second level, we have two calls for size $N/2$; on the third level, we have four calls for size $N/4$; and so forth, down to the last level with $N/2$ calls of size 2. There are precisely $n = \lg N$ levels, giving the grand total $N \lg N$ for the frequency of execution of the instructions in the inner loop of mergesort. This equation justifies a hypothesis that the running time of mergesort is linearithmic. *Note*: When $N$ is not a power of two, the subarrays on each level are not necessarily all the same size, but the number of levels is still logarithmic, so the linearithmic hypothesis is justified for all $N$ (see EXERCISES 4.2.16–17).

You are encouraged to run a doubling test such as PROGRAM 4.2.5 for `Merge.sort()` on your computer. If you do so, you certainly will appreciate that it is much faster for large files than is `Insertion.sort()` and that you can sort huge arrays with relative ease. Validating the hypothesis that the running time is linearithmic is a bit more work, but you certainly can see that mergesort makes it possible for us to address sorting problems that we could not contemplate solving with a brute-force algorithm such as insertion sort.

*Quadratic–linearithmic chasm.* The difference between $N^2$ and $N \lg N$ makes a huge difference in practical applications, just the same as the linear-logarithmic chasm that is overcome by binary search. *Understanding the enormousness of this difference is another critical step to understanding the importance of the design and analysis of algorithms.* For a great many important computational problems, a speedup from quadratic to linearithmic—such as we achieve with mergesort—makes the difference between the ability to solve a problem involving a huge amount of data and not being able to effectively address it at all.

*Divide–and–conquer algorithms.* The same basic approach is effective for many important problems, as you will learn if you take a course on algorithm design. For the moment, you are particularly encouraged to study the exercises at the end of this section, which describe a host of problems for which divide-and-conquer algorithms provide feasible solutions and which could not be addressed without such algorithms.

*Reduction to sorting.* A problem A *reduces* to a problem B if we can use a solution to B to solve A. Designing a new divide-and-conquer algorithm from scratch is sometimes akin to solving a puzzle that requires some experience and ingenuity, so you may not feel confident that you can do so at first. But it is often the case that a simpler approach is effective: given a new problem that lends itself to a quadratic brute-force solution, ask yourself how you would solve it if the data were sorted. It often turns out to be the case that a relatively simple linear pass through the sorted data will do the job. Thus, we get a linearithmic algorithm, with the ingenuity hidden in the mergesort implementation. For example, consider the problem of determining whether the elements in an array are all different. This problem reduces to sorting because we can sort the array, and then pass through the sorted array to check whether any entry is equal to the next—if not, the elements are all different. For another example, an easy way to implement `StdStats.select()` (see SECTION 2.2) is to reduce selection to sorting. We consider next two more complicated examples, and you can find many others in the exercises at the end of this section.

MERGESORT TRACES BACK TO JOHN VON Neumann, an accomplished physicist, who was among the first to recognize the importance of computation in scientific research. Von Neumann made many contributions to computer science, including a basic conception of the computer architecture that has been used since the 1950s. When it came to applications programming, von Neumann recognized that:
   • Sorting is an essential ingredient in many applications.
   • Quadratic algorithms are too slow for practical purposes.
   • A divide-and-conquer approach is effective.
   • Proving programs correct and knowing their cost is important.
Computers are many orders of magnitude faster and have many orders of magnitude more memory, but these basic concepts remain important today. People who use computers effectively and successfully know, as did von Neumann, that brute-force algorithms are often not good enough to do the job.

**Application: frequency counts**    FrequencyCount (Program 4.2.7) reads a sequence of strings from standard input and then prints a table of the distinct values found and the number of times each was found, in decreasing order of the frequencies. This computation is useful in numerous applications: a linguist might be studying patterns of word usage in long texts, a scientist might be looking for frequently occurring events in experimental data, a merchant might be looking for the customers who appear most frequently in a long list of transactions, or a network analyst might be looking for the heaviest users. Each of these applications might involve millions of strings or more, so we need a linearithmic algorithm (or better). FrequencyCount is an example of developing such an algorithm by reduction to sorting. It actually does *two* sorts.

*Computing the frequencies.*    Our first step is to sort the strings on standard input. In this case, we are not so much interested in the fact that the strings are put into sorted order, but in the fact that *sorting brings equal strings together.* If the input is

to be or not to be to

then the result of the sort is

be be not or to to to

with equal strings, such as the two occurrences of be and the three occurrences of to, brought together in the array. Now, with equal strings all together in the array, we can make a single pass through the array to compute all of the frequencies. The Counter data type that we considered in Section 3.3 is the perfect tool for the job. Recall that a Counter has a string instance variable (initialized to the constructor argument), a count instance variable (initialized to 0), and an increment() instance method, which increments the counter by one. We maintain an array of Counter objects and do the following for each string:

• If the string is not equal to the previous one, create a new Counter.
• Increment the most recently created Counter.

At the end, the value of M is the number of different string values, and zipf[i] contains the ith string value and its frequency.

*Sorting the frequencies.*    Next, we sort the Counter objects by frequency. We can do so in client code without any special arrangements because Counter implements the Comparable interface (and therefore has a compareTo() method). We

**Program 4.2.7 Frequency counts**

```java
public class FrequencyCount
{
    public static void main(String[] args)
    { // Print input strings in decreasing order
      // of frequency of occurence.
        String s = StdIn.readAll();
        String[] words = s.split("\\s+");
        Merge.sort(words);
        Counter[] zipf = new Counter[words.length];
        int M = 0;
        for (int i = 0; i < words.length; i++)
        { // Create new counter or increment prev counter.
            if (i == 0 || !words[i].equals(words[i-1]))
                zipf[M++] = new Counter(words[i], words.length);
            zipf[M-1].increment();
        }
        Merge.sort(zipf, 0, M);
        for (int j = M-1; j >= 0; j--)
            StdOut.println(zipf[j]);
    }
}
```

| | |
|---|---|
| s | *input* |
| words[] | *strings in input* |
| zipf[] | *counter array* |
| M | *different strings* |

*This program sorts the words on standard input, uses the sorted list to count the frequency of occurrence of each, and then sorts the frequencies. The test file used below has over 20 million words. The plot compares the $i$th frequency relative to the first (bars) with $1/i$ (blue)..*

```
% java FrequencyCount < Leipzig1M.txt
1160105 the
593492 of
560945 to
472819 a
435866 and
430484 in
205531 for
192296 The
188971 that
172225 is
148915 said
147024 on
141178 was
118429 by
  ...
```

simply sort the array! Note that `FrequencyCount` allocates `zipf[]` to its maximum possible size and sorts a subarray, as opposed to the alternative of making an extra pass through `words[]` to determine the number of distinct entries before allocating `zipf[]`. Leaving its recursive `sort()` function for subarrays `public` (there is not reason not to) allows `MergeSort` to support such applications.

| i | M | a[i] | zipf[i].count() | | | |
|---|---|------|---|---|---|---|
| | | | 0 | 1 | 2 | 3 |
| | 0 | | | | | |
| 0 | 1 | be | 1 | | | |
| 1 | 1 | be | 2 | | | |
| 2 | 2 | not | 2 | 1 | | |
| 3 | 3 | or | 2 | 1 | 1 | |
| 4 | 4 | to | 2 | 1 | 1 | 1 |
| 5 | 4 | to | 2 | 1 | 1 | 2 |
| 6 | 4 | to | 2 | 1 | 1 | 3 |
| | | | 2 | 1 | 1 | 3 |

*Counting the frequencies*

*Zipf's law.* The application highlighted in `Frequency-Count` is elementary linguistic analysis: which words appear most frequently in a text? A phenomenon known as *Zipf's law* says that the frequency of the $i$th most frequent word in a text of $M$ distinct words is proportional to $1/i$, with its constant of proportionality the Harmonic number $H_M$. For example, the second most common word should appear about half as often as the first. This is an empirical hypothesis that holds in a surprising variety of situations ranging from financial data to web usage statistics. The test client run in PROGRAM 4.2.7 validates Zipf's law for a database containing 1 million sentences drawn from popular publications (see the booksite).

| i | | zipf[i] |
|---|---|---------|
| *before* | | |
| 0 | 2 | be |
| 1 | 1 | not |
| 2 | 1 | or |
| 3 | 3 | to |
| *after* | | |
| 0 | 1 | not |
| 1 | 1 | or |
| 2 | 2 | be |
| 3 | 3 | to |

*Sorting the frequencies*

YOU ARE LIKELY TO FIND YOURSELF writing a program sometime in the future for a simple task that could easily be solved by first using a sort. How many distinct values are there? Which value appears most frequently? Are the strings all different? Which is the median element? With a linearithmic sorting algorithm such as mergesort, you can address these problems and many other problems like them, even for huge data sets. `FrequencyCount`, which uses two different sorts, is a prime example. If sorting does not apply directly, some other divide-and-conquer algorithm might apply, or some more sophisticated method might be needed. Without a good algorithm (and an understanding of its performance characteristics), you might find yourself frustrated by the idea that your fast and expensive computer cannot solve a problem that seems to be a simple one. With an ever-increasing set of problems that you know how to solve efficiently, you will find that your computer can be a much more effective tool than you now imagine. To illustrate this idea, we consider next an application to a problem in bioinformatics.

**Application: longest repeated substring**   Another important computational task that reduces to sorting is the problem of finding the *longest repeated substring* in a given string. For example, the longest repeated substring in the string to be or not to be is the string to be. This problem is simple to state and has many important applications, including data compression, cryptography, and computer-assisted music analysis. Think briefly about how you might solve it. Could you find the longest repeated substring in a string that has millions of characters?

Another application is *refactoring code*. Programmers often put together new programs by cutting-and-pasting code from old programs. In a large program built over a long period of time, replacing duplicate code by function calls to a single copy of the code can make the program much easier to understand and maintain. This improvement can easily be accomplished by finding long repeated substrings in the program. Documented success stories of using this approach on large systems have led to its being a standard technique in the repertoire of people who develop large software systems.

Another application is found in computational biology. Are substantial identical substrings to be found in a genome? Again, the basic computational problem underlying this question is to find the longest repeated substring in a string. Scientists are typically interested in more detailed questions (indeed, the nature of the repeated substrings is precisely what scientists seek to understand), but such questions are certainly no easier than the basic question of finding the *longest* repeated substring. Various modifications of our solution to this problem can solve other problems of interest, as addressed in several of the exercises.

With such applications in mind, we now focus on the basic computational problem of finding the longest repeated substring in a given string.

*Longest common prefix.*   As a warm-up, consider the following simple task: given two strings, find their longest common prefix (the longest substring that is a prefix of both strings). For example, the longest common prefix of acctgttaac and accgttaa is acc. The following code for solving this problem is a useful starting point for addressing more complicated tasks:

```
public static String lcp(String s, String t)
{
    int N = Math.min(s.length(), t.length());
    for (int i = 0; i < N; i++)
        if (s.charAt(i) != t.charAt(i))
            return s.substring(0, i);
    return s.substring(0, N);
}
```

This code is trickier than it looks: you should convince yourself that it works properly when the first characters of the two strings are different, when one or both of the strings are of length 0, and the two cases when each of the strings is a prefix of the other.

*Brute-force solution.* Now, how do we find the longest sequence of characters that is repeated in a given string? With lcp(), the following brute-force solution immediately suggests itself:

```
public static String lrs(String s)
{
    String lrs = "";
    for (int i = 0; i < N; i++)
    {
        for (int j = i+1; j < N; j++)
        {
            String x = lcp(s.substring(i, N), s.substring(j, N));
            if (x.length() > lrs.length())
                lrs = x;
        }
    }
    return lrs;
}
```

We compare the substring starting at each string position i with the substring starting at each other starting position j, keeping track of the longest match found. This code is not useful for long strings, because its running time is at least quadratic in the length of the string: by examining the nested for loops, it is easy to see that the number of calls on lcp() is $N-1 + N-2 + ... + 2 + 1 \sim N^2$. Using this code for a genomic sequence with millions of characters would require trillions of lcp() calls, which is infeasible.

*Suffix sort solution.*  The following clever approach, which again takes advantage of sorting in an unexpected way, is an effective way to find the longest repeated subsequence, even in huge strings: we use substring() to make an array of strings that consists of the *suffixes* of s (the substrings starting at each position and going to the end), and then we sort this array. The key to the algorithm is that every substring appears somewhere as a prefix of one of the suffixes in the array. After sorting, the longest repeated substrings will appear in adjacent positions in the array (like the equal keys in FrequencyCount). Thus, we can proceed just as we did for FrequencyCount: make a single pass through the sorted array, keeping track of the longest matching prefixes between adjacent strings. LRS (PROGRAM 4.2.8) is an implementation of this method. This program is significantly more efficient than the brute-force method. Analyzing its performance depends upon an understanding of details of Java's String implementation, which we examine next. The end result is that the running time is linearithmic (unless the length of the repeat is huge), and so we certainly can handle strings with millions of characters.

*String representation.*  The running time of LRS is strongly dependent on the way that Java represents String objects, so we briefly revisit the representation. A value of the String data type is a sequence of characters. Java represents them using an array of characters, plus the offset to the first character and the length. As with arrays, the implementation can return the length in constant time. Also, the string data type is *immutable* (it has no methods to change any string's value), so Java can reuse the array holding the characters. In the present context, the most important consequence of this design is that the substring() method does *not* take time proportional to the length of the result, but instead requires just a few machine instructions: it simply calculates the necessary offset to the first character and length in a straightforward manner.

*input string*
```
 0 1 2 3 4 5 6 7 8 91011121314
 a a c a a g t t t a c a a g c
```

*suffixes*
```
 0  a a c a a g t t t a c a a g c
 1  a c a a g t t t a c a a g c
 2  c a a g t t t a c a a g c
 3  a a g t t t a c a a g c
 4  a g t t t a c a a g c
 5  g t t t a c a a g c
 6  t t t a c a a g c
 7  t t a c a a g c
 8  t a c a a g c
 9  a c a a g c
10  c a a g c
11  a a g c
12  a g c
13  g c
14  c
```

*sorted suffixes*
```
 0  a a c a a g t t t a c a a g c
11  a a g c
 3  a a g t t t a c a a g c
 9  a c a a g c
 1  a c a a g t t t a c a a g c
12  a g c
 4  a g t t t a c a a g c
14  c
10  c a a g c
 2  c a a g t t t a c a a g c
13  g c
 5  g t t t a c a a g c
 8  t a c a a g c
 7  t t a c a a g c
 6  t t t a c a a g c
```

*longest repeated substring*
```
        1           9
 a a c a a g t t t a c a a g c
```

*Computing the LRS by sorting suffixes*

Therefore, the substring operation in Java takes *constant* time and space. Java programmers are well-advised to take advantage of this efficient implementation of substring().

123    288 ← a
      2 ← a.length

288    407 ← a[0]
     311 ← a[1]

311    462
     12

407    459
     9

459   t t t a
460   c a a g
461   c
462   H e l l
463   o ,   W
464   o r l d

*swap references*

311
407

*string objects*

*no other changes*

a[0] = "tttacaagc";    exch(a, 0, 1)
a[1] = "Hello, World";

*Exchanging two strings in an array*

*Sorting strings.* Given an array of strings, we can rearrange them so that they appear in lexicographic order in the array (the order they would appear in a dictionary) with Merge.sort() because String implements the Comparable interface. It is very important to note that this approach is effective for long strings and large objects because of the Java reference representation for objects: *when we exchange two objects, we are exchanging only references, not the whole object.* Now, the cost of *comparing* two strings may be proportional to the length of the strings in the case when their common prefix is very long, but most comparisons in typical string sort applications involve only a few characters. If so, the running time of the string sort is linearithmic.

*Suffix arrays.* From the standpoint of the sort, there is no difference between sorting an array of strings and sorting a suffix array: both refer to an array of references to strings. A suffix array is an array of string objects, each consisting of the standard object overhead, a reference to an array of char values, an offset, a length, (and a hash value). Suffix arrays are characterized by the fact that all of the array references are to the same char array, which holds the string of interest, and that each possible offset and length appears once.

*LRS analysis.* We can now see why the suffix sorting approach to solving the longest repeated substring problem in PROGRAM 4.2.8 is effective, even though the suffixes of a very long string are themselves very long.

## Program 4.2.8   Longest repeated substring

```
public class LRS
{
   public static String lcp(String s, String t)
   {  // See text.  }

   public static String lrs(String s)
   {  // Find the longest repeated substring in s.

      // Create and sort suffix array.
      int N  = s.length();
      String[] suffixes = new String[N];
      for (int i = 0; i < N; i++)
         suffixes[i] = s.substring(i, N);
      Merge.sort(suffixes);

      String lrs = "";
      for (int i = 0; i < N-1; i++)
      {  // LRS is longest common prefix in adjacent strings.
         String x = lcp(suffixes[i], suffixes[i+1]);
         if (x.length() > lrs.length())  lrs = x;
      }
      return lrs;
   }

   public static void main(String[] args)
   {  // Find the longest repeated substring in StdIn.
      String s = StdIn.readAll();
      StdOut.println(lrs(s));
   }
}
```

| | |
|---|---|
| s | input string |
| N | length |
| suffixes[] | suffix array |
| lrs | longest repeated substring |

*To find the longest repeated substring in a string, we form an array of all the string's suffixes, sort the array, and then find the longest common prefix of adjacent strings in the result.*

```
% more example.txt
aacaagtttacaagc
% java LRS < example.txt
acaag
% java LRS < genome.txt
aaactcgacaaacccatttaccccacactttt
```

```
String s = "ATAGATGCATAGCGCATAGCTAGATGTGCTAGCAT"
int N  = s.length();
String[] suffixes = new String[N];
for (int i = 0; i < N; i++)
    suffixes[i] = s.substring(i, N);
```

Total: $16 + 4N + N \times 24 + 16 + 2N = 32 + 30N$

*Memory requirements for a suffix array*

The total length of the suffixes is quadratic, but the actual space used is only linear, because Java represents each substring with a constant amount of extra space. The `substring()` operations all take constant time, most string comparisons involve only a few character comparisons, and all exchanges are fast because they just involve exchanging references. In summary, this discussion supports the hypothesis that the running time of PROGRAM 4.2.8 is linearithmic. We expect the sort to be linearithmic, and then we make a single pass through the string to find the longest common prefix among adjacent substrings.

*Long repeats.* A more precise analysis shows that our suffix sorting approach (and finding the longest repeated substring) is *quadratic* (or worse) in the length of the repeated substring, because each suffix of the repeated substring appears twice as a prefix in the suffix array and requires time proportional to its length for `lcp()` and for comparisons during the sort. Accordingly, computational biologists and computer scientists have developed more sophisticated algorithms to look for repeated substrings whose length is substantially longer than the square root of the string length.

**Lessons** The vast majority of programs that we write involve managing the complexity of addressing a new practical problem by developing a clear and correct solution, breaking the program into modules of manageable size whenever possible, and making use of the basic available resources. From the very start, our approach in this book has been to develop programs along these lines. But as you become involved in ever more complex applications, you will find that a clear and correct solution is not always sufficient, because the cost of computation can be a limiting factor. The examples in this section are a basic illustration of this fact.

*input string*
    a a c a a g t t t a c a a g c

*suffixes of longest repeat (M = 5)*
    a c a a g
      c a a g
        a a g  ← all appear at least
          a g    twice as a prefix of
            g    a suffix string

*sorted suffixes of input*
    a a c a a g t t t a c a a g c
  3 a a g c
    a a g t t t a c a a g c
  5 a c a a g c
    a c a a g t t t a c a a g c
  2 a g c
    a g t t t a c a a g c
    c
  4 c a a g c
    c a a g t t t a c a a g c
  1 g c
    g t t t a c a a g c
  ↑ t a c a a g c
    t t a c a a g c
    t t t a c a a g c

*comparison cost is at least*
$1 + 2 + \ldots + M \sim M^2/2$

*LRS cost is quadratic in repeat length*

*Respect the cost of computation.* If you can quickly solve a small problem with a simple algorithm, fine. But if you need to address a problem that involves a large amount of data or a substantial amount of computation, you need to take into account the cost.

*Reduce to a known problem.* Our use of sorting for frequency counting and for solving the longest repeated substring problem illustrates the utility of understanding fundamental algorithms and using them for problem solving.

*Divide-and-conquer.* It is worthwhile for you to reflect a bit on the power of the divide-and-conquer paradigm, as illustrated by developing a logarithmic search algorithm (binary search) and a linearithmic sorting algorithm (mergesort) that serves as the basis for addressing so many computational problems. Divide-and-conquer is but one approach to developing efficient algorithms.

SINCE THE ADVENT OF COMPUTING, PEOPLE have been developing algorithms such as binary search and mergesort that can efficiently solve practical problems. The field of study known as *design and analysis of algorithms* encompasses the study of design paradigms like divide-and-conquer, techniques to develop hypotheses about algorithms performance, and algorithms for solving fundamental problems like sorting and searching that can be put to use for practical applications of all kinds. Implementations of many of these algorithms are found in Java libraries or other specialized libraries, but understanding these basic tools of computation is like understanding the basic tools of mathematics or science. You can use a matrix-processing package to find the eigenvalues of a matrix, but you still need a course in linear algebra. Now that you *know* that a fast algorithm can make the difference between spinning your wheels and properly addressing a practical problem, you can be on the lookout for situations where algorithm design and analysis can make the difference, and for efficient algorithms like binary search and mergesort that can do the job.

# Q+A

**Q.** Why do we need to go to such lengths to prove a program correct?

**A.** To spare ourselves considerable pain. Binary search is a notable example. For example, you now understand binary search; a classic programming exercise is to write a version that uses a `while` loop instead of recursion. Try solving EXERCISE 4.2.1 without looking back at the code in the book. In a famous experiment, Jon Bentley once asked several professional programmers to do so, and most of their solutions were *not* correct.

**Q.** Are there implementations for sorting and searching in the Java library?

**A.** Yes. The Java library `java.util.Arrays` contains the methods `Arrays.sort()` and `Arrays.binarySearch()` that implement mergesort and binary search for `Comparable` types and a sorting implementation for primitive types based on a version of the *quicksort* algorithm, which is faster than mergesort and also sorts an array in place (without using any extra space).

**Q.** So why not just use them?

**A.** Feel free to do so. As with many topics we have studied, you will be able to use such tools more effectively if you understand the background behind them.

**Q.** Why do I get a `unchecked or unsafe operation` warning when compiling `Insertion` and `Merge`?

**A.** The argument to `sort()` is a `Comparable` array, but nothing, technically, prevents its elements from being of different types. To eliminate the warning, change the signature to:

```
public static <Key extends Comparable<Key>> void sort(Key[] a)
```

We'll learn about the `<Key>` notation in the next section.

# Exercises

**4.2.1**   Develop an implementation of TwentyQuestions that takes the maximum number $N$ as command-line argument. Prove that your implementation is correct.

**4.2.2**   Add code to Insertion to produce the trace given in the text.

**4.2.3**   Add code to Merge to produce the trace given in the text.

**4.2.4**   Give traces of insertion sort and mergesort in the style of the traces in the text, for the input it was the best of times it was.

**4.2.5**   Describe why it is desirable to use immutable keys with binary search.

**4.2.6**   Explain why we use lo + (hi - lo) / 2 to compute the index midway between lo and hi instead of using (lo + hi) / 2.

*Answer*: The latter fails when lo + hi overflows an int.

**4.2.7**   Modify BinarySearch (PROGRAM 4.2.3) so that if the search key is in the array, it returns the smallest index i for which a[i] is equal to key, and otherwise, it returns -i, where i is the smallest index such that a[i] is greater than key.

**4.2.8**   Describe what happens if you apply binary search to an unorderd array. Why shouldn't you check whether the array is sorted before each call to binary search? Could you check that the elements binary search examines are in ascending order?

**4.2.9**   Write a program DeDup that reads strings from standard input and prints them on standard output with all duplicates removed (and in the same order they are found in the input).

**4.2.10**  Find the frequency distribution of words in your favorite book. Does it obey Zipf's law?

**4.2.11**  Find the longest repeated substring in your favorite book.

**4.2.12**  Add code to LRS (PROGRAM 4.2.8) to make it print indices in the original string where the long repeated substring occur.

**4.2.13** Find a pathological input for which LRS (PROGRAM 4.2.8) runs in quadratic time (or worse).

**4.2.14** Show that binary search in a sorted array is logarithmic as long as it eliminates at least a constant fraction of the array at each step.

**4.2.15** Modify BinarySearch (PROGRAM 4.2.3) so that if the search key is not in the array, it returns the largest index i for which a[i] is smaller than key (or -1 if no such index exists).

**4.2.16.** Analyze mergesort mathematically when $N$ is a power of 2, as we did for binary search.

*Answer*: Let $M(N)$ be the frequency of execution of the instructions in the inner loop. Then $M(N)$ must satisfy the following recurrence relation:

$$M(N) = 2M(N/2) + N$$

with $M(1) = 0$. Substituting $2^n$ for $N$ gives

$$M(2^n) = 2M(2^{n-1}) + 2^n$$

which is similar to but more complicated than the recurrence that we considered for binary search. But if we divide both sides by $2^n$, we get

$$M(2^n)/2^n = M(2^{n-1})/2^{n-1} + 1$$

which is *precisely* the recurrence that we had for binary search. That, is $M(2^n)/2^n = T(2^n) = n$. Substituting back $N$ for $2^n$ (and $\lg N$ for $n$) gives the result $M(N) = N\lg N$.

**4.2.17** Analyze mergesort for the case when $N$ not a power of two.

*Partial answer:*  When $N$ is an odd number, one subarray has to have one more entry than the other, so when $N$ is not a power of two, the subarrays on each level are not necessarily all the same size. Still, every element appears in some subarray, and the number of levels is still logarithmic, so the linearithmic hypothesis is justified for all $N$.

## *Creative Exercises*

*The following exercises are intended to give you experience in developing fast solutions to typical problems. Think about using binary search, mergesort, or devising your own divide-and-conquer algorithm. Implement and test your algorithm.*

**4.2.18** *Median.* Add to `StdStats` a method `median()` that computes in linearithmic time the median of a sequence of $N$ integers. *Hint*: Reduce to sorting.

**4.2.19** *Mode.* Add to `StdStats` a method `mode()` that computes in linearithmic time the mode (value that occurs most frequently) of a sequence of $N$ integers. *Hint*: Reduce to sorting.

**4.2.20** *Integer sort.* Write a *linear*-time filter that takes from standard input a sequence of integers that are between 0 and 99 and prints the same set of integers in sorted order on standard output. For example, presented with the input sequence

```
98 2 3 1 0 0 0 3 98 98 2 2 2 0 0 0 2
```

your program should print the output sequence

```
0 0 0 0 0 0 1 2 2 2 2 2 3 3 98 98 98
```

**4.2.21** *Floor and ceiling.* Given a sorted array of `Comparable` items, write methods `floor()` and `ceil()` that returns the index of the largest (or smallest) item not larger (or smaller) than an argument item in logarithmic time.

**4.2.22** *Closest pair.* Given an array of $N$ real numbers, write a static method to find in linearithmic time the pair of integers that are closest in value.

**4.2.23** *Furthest pair.* Given an array of $N$ real numbers, write a static method to find in linear time the pair of integers that are farthest apart in value.

**4.2.24** *Two sum.* Write a static method that takes as argument an array of $N$ `int` values and determines in linearithmic time whether any *two* of them sum to 0.

**4.2.25** *Three sum.* Write a static method that takes as argument an array of $N$ `int` values and determines whether any *three* of them sum to 0. Your program should run in time proportional to $N^2 \log N$. *Extra credit*: Develop a program that solves the problem in quadratic time.

**4.2.26.** *Majority.* An element is a *majority* if it appears more than $N/2$ times. Write a static method that takes an array of $N$ strings as argument and identifies a majority (if it exists) in linear time.

**4.2.27** *Common element.* Write a static method that takes as argument three arrays of strings, determines whether there is any string common to all three arrays, and if so, returns one such string. The running time of your method should be linearithmic in the total number of strings.

**4.2.28** *Prefix-free codes.* In data compression, a set of strings is *prefix-free* if no string is a prefix of another. For example, the set of strings 01, 10, 0010, and 1111 are prefix-free, but the set of strings 01, 10, 0010, 1010 is not prefix-free because 10 is a prefix of 1010. Write a program that reads in a set of strings from standard input and determines whether the set is prefix-free.

**4.2.29** *Longest common substring.* Write a static method that finds the longest common substring of two given strings s and t.

**4.2.30** *Longest repeated, non-overlapping string.* Modify LRS (Program 4.2.8) to find the longest repeated substring that *does not overlap*.

**4.2.31** *Partitioning.* Write a static method that sorts a Comparable array that is known to have at most two different values. *Hint*: Maintain two pointers, one starting at the left end and moving right, the other starting at the right end and moving left. Maintain the invariant that all elements to the left of the left pointer are equal to the smaller of the two values and all elements to the right of the right pointer are equal to the larger of the two values.

**4.2.32** *Dutch national flag.* Write a static method that sorts a Comparable array that is known to have at most three different values. (Edsgar Dijkstra named this the *Dutch-national-flag problem* because the result is three "stripes" of values like the three stripes in the flag.) *Hint*: Reduce to the previous problem, by first partitioning the array into two parts with all elements having the smallest value in the first part and all other elements in the second part, then partition the second part.

**4.2.33** *Quicksort.* Write a recursive program that sorts an array of randomly ordered distinct `Comparable` elements. *Hint*: Use a method like the one described in the previous exercise. First, partition the array into a left part with all elements less than *v*, followed by *v*, followed by a right part with all elements greater than *v*. Then, recursively sort the two parts. *Extra credit*: Modify your method (if necessary) to work properly when the elements are not necessarily distinct.

**4.2.34** *Reverse domain.* Write a program to read in a list of domain names from standard input and print the reverse domain names in sorted order. For example, the reverse domain of `cs.princeton.edu` is `edu.princeton.cs`. This computation is useful for web log analysis. To do so, create a data type `Domain` that implements the `Comparable` interface, using reverse domain name order.

**4.2.35** *Local minimum in an array.* Given an array of *N* real numbers, write a static method to find in logarithmic time a *local minimum* (an index i such that `a[i-1] < a[i] < a[i+1]`).

**4.2.36** *Discrete distribution.* Design a fast algorithm to repeatedly generate numbers from the discrete distribution: Given an array `a[]` of nonnegative real numbers that sum to 1, the goal is to return index i with probability `a[i]`. Form an array `s[]` of cumulated sums such that `s[i]` is the sum of the first i elements of `a[]`. Now, generate a random real number r between 0 and 1, and use binary search to return the index i for which `s[i]` ≤ r < `s[i+1]`.

**4.2.37** *Rhyming words.* Tabulate a list that you can use to find words that rhyme. Use the following approach:
- Read in a dictionary of words into an array of strings.
- Reverse the letters in each word (`confound` becomes `dnuofnoc`, for example).
- Sort the resulting array.
- Reverse the letters in each word back to their original order.

For example, `confound` is adjacent to words such as `astound` and `surround` in the resulting list.

# 4.3    Stacks and Queues

IN THIS SECTION, WE introduce two closely related data types for manipulating arbitrarily large collections of objects: the *stack* and the *queue*. Stacks and queues are special cases of the idea of a *collection*. A collection of objects is characterized by four operations: *create* the collection, *insert* an object, *remove* an object, and test whether the collection *is empty*.

When we insert an object, our intent is clear. But when we remove an object, which one do we choose? Each type of collection is characterized by the rule used for *remove*, and each is amenable to various implementations with differing performance characteristics. You have encountered different ways to answer this question in various real-world situations, perhaps without thinking about it.

For example, the rule used for a queue is to always remove the item that has been in the collection the *most* amount of time. This policy is known as *first-in first-out*, or *FIFO*. People waiting in line to buy a ticket follow this discipline: the line is arranged in the order of arrival, so the one who leaves the line has been there longer than any other person in the line.

A policy with quite different behavior is the rule used for a stack: always remove the item that has been in the collection the *least* amount of time. This policy is known as *last-in first-out*, or *LIFO*. For example, you follow a policy closer to LIFO when you enter and leave the coach cabin in an airplane: people near the front of the cabin board last and exit before those who boarded earlier.

Stacks and queues are broadly useful, so it is important for you to be familiar with their basic properties and the kind of situation where each might be appropriate. They are excellent examples of fundamental data types that we can use to address higher-level programming tasks. They are widely used in systems and applications programming, as we will see in several examples in this section and in SECTION 4.5.

**Pushdown stacks**   A *pushdown stack* (or just a *stack*) is a collection that is based on the last-in-first-out (LIFO) policy.

When you keep your mail in a pile on your desk, you are using a stack. You pile pieces of new mail on the top when they arrive and take each piece of mail from the top when you are ready to read it. People do not process as many papers as they did in the past, but the same organizing principle underlies several of the applications that you use regularly on your computer. For example, many people organize their email as a stack, where messages go on the top when they are received and are taken from the top, with most recently received first (last in, first out). The advantage of this strategy is that we see interesting email as soon as possible; the disadvantage is that some old email might never get read if we never empty the stack.

You have likely encountered another common example of a stack when surfing the web. When you click a hyperlink, your browser displays the new page (and inserts it onto a stack). You can keep clicking on hyperlinks to visit new pages, but you can always revisit the previous page by clicking the back button (remove it from a stack). The last-in-first-out policy offered by a pushdown stack provides just the behavior that you expect.

Such uses of stacks are intuitive, but perhaps not persuasive. In fact, the importance of stacks in computing is fundamental and profound, but we defer further discussions of applications to later in this section. For the moment, our goal is to make sure that you understand how stacks work and how to implement them.

*Operations on a pushdown stack*

Stacks have been used widely since the earliest days of computing. By tradition, we name the stack insert operation *push* and the stack remove operation *pop*, as indicated in the following API:

| public class *StackOfStrings | | |
|---|---|---|
| | *StackOfStrings() | *create an empty stack* |
| boolean | isEmpty() | *is the stack empty?* |
| void | push(String item) | *push a string onto the stack* |
| String | pop() | *pop the stack* |

*API for a pushdown stack for strings*

The asterisk indicates that we will be considering more than one implementation of this API (we consider three in this section: ArrayStackOfStrings, Linked-StackOfStrings, and DoublingStackOfStrings). This API also includes a method to test whether the stack is empty, leaving to the client the responsibility of using isEmpty() to avoid invoking pop() when the stack is empty (an alternative design would be to throw an exception in that case).

This API has an important restriction that is inconvenient in applications: we would like to have stacks that contain other types of data, not just strings. We examine ways to remove this restriction (and the importance of doing so) later in this section.

**Array implementation**    Representing stacks with arrays is a natural idea, but before reading further, it is worthwhile for you to think for a moment about how you would implement a class ArrayStackOfStrings.

The first problem that you might encounter is implementing the constructor ArrayStackOfStrings(). You clearly need an instance variable a[] with an array of strings to hold the stack items, but how big should the array be? One solution is to start with an array of size 0 and make sure that the array size is always equal to the stack size, but that solution necessitates allocating a new array and copying all of the items into it for each push() and pop() operation, which is unnecessarily inefficient and cumbersome. We will temporarily finesse this problem by having the client provide an argument for the constructor that gives the maximum stack size.

Your next problem might stem from the natural decision to keep the items in the array in the order they appear on the stack, with the top element in a[0], the second element in a[1], and so forth. But then each time you push or pop an item, you would have to move all of the other items to reflect the new state of the stack. A simpler and more efficient way to proceed is to keep the items in *reverse* order of their arrival, as illustrated. This policy allows us to add and remove items at the end without moving any of the other items in the stack.

We could hardly hope for a simpler implementation of the stack API than ArrayStackOfStrings (PROGRAM 4.3.1)—all of the methods are one-liners! The instance variables are an array a[] that hold the items in the stack and an integer N that counts the number of items in the stack. To remove an item, we decrement N and then return a[N]; to insert a new item, we set a[N] equal to the new item and then increment N. These operations preserve the following properties:

- The items in the array are in their insertion order.
- The stack is empty when N is 0.
- The top of the stack (if it is nonempty) is at a[N-1].

As usual, thinking in terms of invariants of this sort is the easiest way to verify that an implementation operates as intended. *Be sure that you fully understand this implementation.* Perhaps the best way to do so is to carefully examine a trace of the stack contents for a sequence of push() and pop() operations. The test client in StringStackArray allows for testing with an arbitrary sequence of operations: it does a push() for each string on standard input except the string consisting of a minus sign, for which it does a pop().

| StdIn | StdOut | N | a[] 0 | 1 | 2 | 3 | 4 |
|-------|--------|---|----|----|----|------|----|
|       |        | 0 |    |    |    |      |    |
| to    |        | 1 | to |    |    |      |    |
| be    |        | 2 | to | be |    |      |    |
| or    |        | 3 | to | be | or |      |    |
| not   |        | 4 | to | be | or | not  |    |
| to    |        | 5 | to | be | or | not  | to |
| -     | to     | 4 | to | be | or | not  | to |
| be    |        | 5 | to | be | or | not  | be |
| -     | be     | 4 | to | be | or | not  | be |
| -     | not    | 3 | to | be | or | not  | be |
| that  |        | 4 | to | be | or | that | be |
| -     | that   | 3 | to | be | or | that | be |
| -     | or     | 2 | to | be | or | that | be |
| -     | be     | 1 | to | be | or | that | be |
| is    |        | 2 | to | is | or | not  | to |

*Trace of ArrayStackOfStrings test client*

The primary characteristic of this implementation is that *the push and pop operations take constant time*. The drawback of this implementation is that it requires the client to estimate the maximum size of the stack ahead of time and always uses space proportional to that maximum, which may be unreasonable in some situations. We omit the code in push() to test for a full stack, but later we will examine implementations that address these drawbacks by not allowing the stack to get full (except in an extreme circumstance when there is no memory at all available for use by the Java system).

*Program 4.3.1* **Stack of strings (array)**

```
public class ArrayStackOfStrings
{
    private String[] a;
    private int N = 0;

    public ArrayStackOfStrings(int max)
    {  a = new String[max];  }

    public boolean isEmpty()
    {  return (N == 0);  }

    public void push(String item)
    {  a[N++] = item;  }

    public String pop()
    {  return a[--N];  }

    public static void main(String[] args)
    {  // Create a stack of capacity max
       // and push or pop strings as directed on StdIn.
       int max = Integer.parseInt(args[0]);
       ArrayStackOfStrings s = new ArrayStackOfStrings(max);
       while (!StdIn.isEmpty())
       {
           String item = StdIn.readString();
           if (!item.equals("-"))
               s.push(item);
           else
               StdOut.print(s.pop());
       }
    }
}
```

| a[] | stack values |
| N | number of items |
| N-1 | index of value most recently pushed |

*Stack methods are simple one-liners, as illustrated in this code. The client pushes or pops strings as directed from standard input (a minus sign indicates pop, and any other string indicates push). Code in push() to test whether the stack is full is omitted (see text).*

```
% more tobe.txt
to be or not to - be - - that - - - is

% java ArrayStackOfStrings 5 < tobe.txt
to be not that or be
```

**Linked lists**   For classes such as stacks that implement collections of objects, an important objective is to ensure that *the amount of space used is always proportional to the number of items in the collection*. The use of a fixed-size array to implement stacks in `ArrayStackOfStrings` works against this objective: when you create a huge stack, you are wasting a potentially huge amount of memory at times when the stack is empty or nearly empty. This property makes the array implementation unusable in applications involving large numbers of items moving among large numbers of stacks, which are typical. For example, a transaction system might involve billions of items and thousands of collections of them. We might not be able to afford the memory to allow for the possibility that each of those collections could each hold all of those items. Worse, if all of the items do wind up in one collection, we know that the others would all be empty, so that wasted memory is unnecessary. One of the primary purposes of Java's memory allocation system is to provide the flexibility to handle such situations. Now we consider the use of a fundamental data structure known as a *linked list*, which can provide implementations of collections (and, in particular, stacks) that achieve the objective cited at the beginning of this paragraph.

   A linked list is a recursive data structure defined as follows: *it is either empty (null) or a reference to a node having a reference to a linked list*. The *node* in this definition is an abstract entity that might hold any kind of data, in addition to the node reference that characterizes its role in building linked lists. As with a recursive program, the concept of a recursive data structure can be a bit mindbending at first, but is of great value because of its simplicity.

   With object-oriented programming, implementing linked lists is not difficult. We start with a class for the *node* abstraction:

```
class Node
{
    String item;
    Node next;
}
```

A `Node` has two instance variables: a `String` and a `Node`. The `String` is a place-holder in this example for any data that we might want to structure with a linked list (we can use any set of instance variables); the instance variable of type `Node` characterizes the linked nature of the data structure. To emphasize that we are just using the `Node` class to structure the data, we define no methods. Now, from the recursive definition, we can represent a linked list with a variable of type `Node` simply

by ensuring that its value is either `null` or a reference to a `Node` whose `next` field is
a reference to a linked list.

As with any type of data, we create an object of type `Node` by invoking the
(no-argument) constructor with `new Node()`. The result is a reference to a `Node`
object whose instance variables are both initialized to the value `null`.

For example, to build a linked list that contains the items `to`, `be`, and `or`, we
create a `Node` for each item:

```
Node first  = new Node();
Node second = new Node();
Node third  = new Node();
```

and set the `item` field in each of the nodes
to the desired value:

```
first.item  = "to";
second.item = "be";
third.item  = "or";
```

and set the `next` fields to build the linked
list:

```
first.next  = second;
second.next = third;
```

As a result, `third` is a linked list (it is a reference to a node that contains `null`, which
is the null reference to an empty linked
list), and `second` is a linked list (it is a reference to a node that has a reference to
`third`, which is a linked list), and `first` is
a linked list (it is a reference to a node that
has a reference to `second`, which is a linked
list). The code that we will examine does these assignment statements in a different
order, depicted in the diagram on this page.

```
Node first  = new Node();
first.item  = "to";
```

```
Node second = new Node();
second.item = "be";
first.next  = second;
```

```
Node third  = new Node();
third.item  = "or";
second.next = third;
```

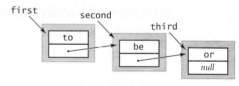

*Linking together a list*

A linked list represents a sequence of items. In the example just considered,
`first` represents the sequence `to  be  or`. We can also use an array to represent a
sequence of items. For example, we could use

```
String[] s = { "to", "be", "or" };
```

to represent the same sequence of strings. The difference is that it is easier to insert items into the sequence and to remove items from the sequence with linked lists. Next, we consider code to accomplish these tasks.

When tracing code that uses linked lists and other linked structures, we use a visual representation where:

- We draw a rectangle to represent each object.
- We put the values of instance variables within the rectangle.
- We use arrows that point to the referenced objects to depict references.

This visual representation captures the essential characteristic of linked lists. For economy, we use the term *links* to refer to node references. For simplicity, when item values are strings (as in our examples), we put the string within the object rectangle rather than the more accurate rendition depicting the string object and the character array that we discussed in SECTION 4.1. (If you work EXERCISE 4.3.12, you will better understand the precise representation of linked lists with string items in Java.) This visual representation allows us to focus on the links.

*save a link to the list*
```
Node oldfirst = first;
```

*create a new node for the beginning*
```
first = new Node();
```

*set the instance variables in the new node*
```
first.item = "not";
first.next = oldfirst;
```

*Inserting a new node at the beginning of a linked list*

Suppose that you want to *insert* a new node into a linked list. The easiest place to do so is at the beginning of the list. For example, to insert the string not at the beginning of a given linked list whose first node is first, we save first in oldfirst, assign to first a new Node, and assign its item field to not and its next field to oldfirst.

Suppose that you want to *remove* the first node from a list. This operation is even easier: simply assign to first the value first.next. Normally, you would

```
first = first.next;
```
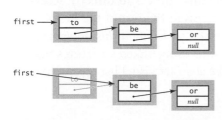

*Removing the first node in a linked list*

retrieve the value of the item (by assigning it to some `String` variable) before doing this assignment, because once you change the value of `first`, you may not have any access to the node to which it was referring. Typically, the node object becomes an orphan, and the memory it occupies is eventually reclaimed by the Java memory management system.

This code for inserting and removing a node from the beginning of a linked list involves just a few assignment statements and thus takes *constant* time (independent of the length of the list). If you hold a reference to a node at an arbitrary position in a list, you can use similar (but more complicated) code to remove the node after it or to insert a node after it, also in constant time. However, we leave those implementations for an exercise (see EXERCISE 4.3.25-26) because inserting and removing at the beginning are the only linked-list operations that we need in order to implement stacks.

*Implementing stacks with linked lists.* `LinkedStackOfStrings` (PROGRAM 4.3.2) uses a linked list to implement a stack of strings, using little more code than the elementary solution that uses arrays.

The implementation is based on a *nested* class `Node` like the one we have been using. Java allows us to define and use other classes within class implementations in this natural way. The class is `private` because clients do not need to know any of the details of the linked lists. One characteristic of a `private` nested class is that its instance variables can be directly accessed from within the enclosing class but nowhere else, so there is no need to declare the `Node` instance variables as `public` or `private`.

`LinkedStackOfStrings` itself has just one instance variable: a reference to the linked list that represents the stack. That single link suffices to directly access the item at the top of the stack and also provides access to the rest of the items in the stack for `push()` and `pop()`. Again, *be sure that you understand this implementation*—it is the prototype for several implementations using linked structures that we will be examining later in this chapter. Using the abstract visual list representation to trace the code is the best way to proceed.

*Linked list traversal.* One of the most common operations we perform on collections is to iterate through the items in the collection. For example, we might wish to implement the `toString()` method that is inherent in every Java API to facilitate debugging our stack code with traces. For `ArrayStackOfStrings`, this implementation is familiar.

**Program 4.3.2 Stack of strings (linked list)**

```
public class LinkedStackOfStrings
{
   private Node first;
   private class Node
   {
      String item;
      Node next;
   }
   public boolean isEmpty()
   {  return (first == null); }
   public void push(String item)
   {  // Add item to top of stack.
      Node oldfirst = first;
      first = new Node();
      first.item = item;
      first.next = oldfirst;
   }
   public String pop()
   {  // Remove item from top of stack.
      String item = first.item;
      first = first.next;
      return item;
   }
   public static void main(String[] args)
   {
      LinkedStackOfStrings s = new LinkedStackOfStrings();
      // See Program 4.3.1 for the test client.
   }
}
```

| first | *first node on list* |
|---|---|

| item | *list item* |
|---|---|
| next | *next node on list* |

*This stack implementation uses a private nested class* Node *as the basis for representing the stack as a linked list of* Node *objects. The instance variable* first *refers to the first (most recently inserted)* Node *on the list. The* next *instance variable in each* Node *refers to the next* Node *(the value of* next *in the final node is* null*). No explicit constructors are needed, because Java initializes the instance variables to* null.

```
% java LinkedStackOfStrings < tobe.txt
to be not that or be
```

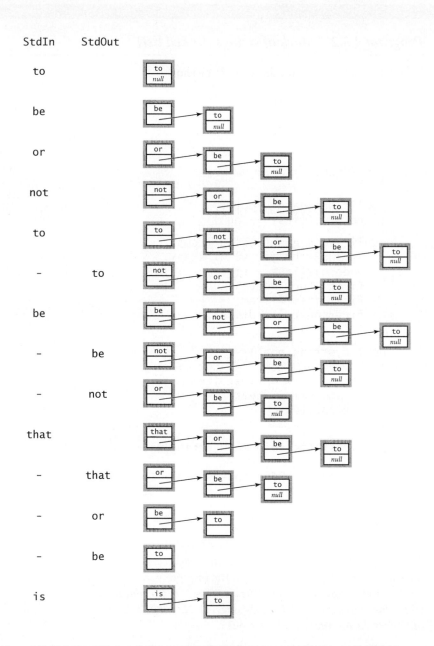

*Trace of* LinkedStackOfStrings *test client*

```
public String toString()
{
    String s = "";
    for (int i = 0; i < N; i++)
        s += a[i] + " ";
    return s;
}
```

As usual, this solution is intended for use only when N is small—it takes quadratic
time because string concatenation takes
linear time. Our focus now is just on the
process of examining every item. There is a
corresponding idiom for visiting the items
in a linked list: We initialize a loop index
variable x that references the first Node of
the linked list. Then, we find the value of
the item associated with x by accessing
x.item, and then update x to refer to the
next Node in the linked list, assigning to it
the value of x.next and repeating this
process until x is null (which indicates
that we have reached the end of the linked
list). This process is known as *traversing*
the list, and is succinctly expressed in this
implementation of    toString() for
LinkedStackOfStrings:

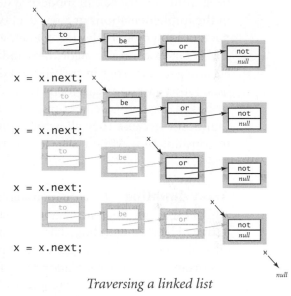

Traversing a linked list

```
public String toString()
{
    String s = "";
    for (Node x = first; x != null; x = x.next)
        s += x.item + " ";
    return s;
}
```

When you program with linked lists, this idiom will become as familiar to you as
the standard idiom for iterating through the items in an array. At the end of this
section, we consider the concept of an *iterator*, which allows us to write client code
to iterate through the objects of a collection without having to program at this level
of detail.

WITH A LINKED-LIST IMPLEMENTATION we can write client programs that use large numbers of stacks without having to worry much about space usage. The same principle applies to collections of data of any sort, so linked lists are widely used in programming. Indeed, typical implementations of the Java memory management system are based on maintaining linked lists corresponding to blocks of memory of various sizes. Before the widespread use of high-level languages like Java, the details of memory management and programming with linked lists was a critical part of any programmer's arsenal. In modern systems, most of these details are encapsulated in the implementations of a few data types like the pushdown stack, including the queue, the symbol table, and the set, which we will consider later in this chapter. If you take a course in algorithms and data structures, you will learn several others and gain expertise in creating and debugging programs that manipulate linked lists. Otherwise, you can focus your attention on understanding the role played by linked lists in implementing these fundamental data types. For stacks, they are significant because they allow us to implement the push() and pop() methods in constant time while using only a small constant factor of extra space (for the links).

**Array doubling**   Next, we consider an alternative approach to accommodating arbitrary growth and shrinkage in a data structure that is an attractive alternative to linked lists. As with linked lists, we introduce it now because the approach is not difficult to understand in the context of a stack implementation and because it is important to know when addressing the challenges of implementing data types that are more complicated than stacks.

   The idea is to modify the array implementation to dynamically adjust the size of the array a[] so that it is both sufficiently large to hold all of the items and not so large as to waste an excessive amount of space. Achieving these goals turns out to be remarkably easy, and we do so in DoublingStackOfStrings (PROGRAM 4.3.3).

   First, in push(), we check whether the array is too small. In particular, we check whether there is room for the new item in the array by checking whether the stack size N is equal to the array size a.length. If there is room, we simply insert the new item with the code a[N++] = item as before; if not, we *double* the size of the array by creating a new array of twice the size, copying the stack items to the new array, and resetting the a[] instance variable to reference the new array.

   Similarly, in pop(), we begin by checking whether the array is too large, and we *halve* its size if that is the case. If you think a bit about the situation, you will see

*Program 4.3.3    Stack of strings (array doubling)*

```java
public class DoublingStackOfStrings
{
   private String[] a = new String[1];
   private int N = 0;

   public boolean isEmpty()
   {  return (N == 0);  }

   private void resize(int max)
   {  // Move stack to a new array of size max.
      String[] temp = new String[max];
      for (int i = 0; i < N; i++)
         temp[i] = a[i];
      a = temp;
   }

   public void push(String item)
   {  // Add item to top of stack.
      if (N == a.length) resize(2*a.length);
      a[N++] = item;
   }

   public String pop()
   {  // Remove item from top of stack.
      String item = a[--N];
      a[N] = null;  // Avoid loitering (see text).
      if (N > 0 && N == a.length/4) resize(a.length/2);
      return item;
   }

   public static void main(String[] args)
   {
      DoublingStackOfStrings s = new DoublingStackOfStrings();
      // See Program 4.3.1 for the test client.
   }
}
```

| a[] | stack items |
| --- | --- |
| N | number of items on stack |

*This implementation achieves the objective of supporting stacks of any size without excessively wasting space by doubling the size of the array when full and halving the size of the array to keep it always at least one-quarter full. On average, all operations are constant-time (see text).*

```
% java DoublingStackOfStrings < tobe.txt
to be not that or be
```

| StdIn | StdOut | N | a.length | a | | | | | | | |
|---|---|---|---|---|---|---|---|---|---|---|---|
| | | | | 0 | 1 | 2 | 3 | 4 | 5 | 6 | 7 |
| | | 0 | 1 | null | | | | | | | |
| to | | 1 | 1 | to | | | | | | | |
| be | | 2 | 2 | to | be | | | | | | |
| or | | 3 | 4 | to | be | or | null | | | | |
| not | | 4 | 4 | to | be | or | not | | | | |
| to | | 5 | 8 | to | be | or | not | to | null | null | null |
| – | to | 4 | 8 | to | be | or | not | null | null | null | null |
| be | | 5 | 8 | to | be | or | not | be | null | null | null |
| – | be | 4 | 8 | to | be | or | not | null | null | null | null |
| – | not | 3 | 8 | to | be | or | null | null | null | null | null |
| that | | 4 | 8 | to | be | or | that | null | null | null | null |
| – | that | 3 | 8 | to | be | or | null | null | null | null | null |
| – | or | 2 | 4 | to | be | null | null | | | | |
| – | be | 1 | 2 | to | null | | | | | | |
| is | | 2 | 2 | to | is | | | | | | |

*Trace of* `DoublingStackOfStrings` *test client*

that the appropriate test is whether the stack size is less than *one-fourth* the array size. Then, after the array is halved, it will be about half full and can accommodate a substantial number of push() and pop() operations before having to change the size of the array again. This characteristic is important: for example, if we were to use to policy of halving the array when the stack size is one-half the array size, then the resulting array would be full, which would mean it would be doubled for a push(), leading to the possibility of an expensive cycle of doubling and halving.

*Amortized analysis.* This doubling and halving strategy is a judicious tradeoff between wasting space (by setting the size of the array to be too big and leaving empty slots) and wasting time (by reorganizing the array after each insertion). The specific strategy in DoublingStackOfStrings guarantees that the stack never overflows and never becomes less than one-quarter full (unless the stack is empty, in which case the array size is 1). If you are mathematically inclined, you might enjoy proving this fact with mathematical induction (see EXERCISE 4.3.20). More important, we can prove that the cost of doubling and halving is always absorbed (to within a constant factor) in the cost of other stack operations. Again, we leave the details to an exercise for the mathematically inclined, but the idea is simple: when push() doubles the size of the array to size *N*, it starts with *N*/2 items in the stack, so the size of the array cannot double again at until the client has made at least *N*/2 additional calls to push() (more if there are some intervening calls to pop()). If we *average* the cost of the push() operation that causes the doubling with the cost of those *N*/2 push() operations, we get a constant. In other words, in Doubling-StackOfStrings, *the total cost of all of the stack operations divided by the number of operations is bounded by a constant.* This statement is not quite as strong as saying that each operation is constant-time, but it has the same implications in many applications (for example, when our primary interest is in total running time). This kind of analysis is known as *amortized analysis*—array doubling is a prototypical example of its value.

*Orphaned items.* Java's garbage collection policy is to reclaim the memory associated with any objects that can no longer be accessed. In the pop() implementation in our initial implementation ArrayStackOfStrings, the reference to the popped item remains in the array. The item is an orphan—we will never use it again within the class, either because the stack will shrink or because it will be overwritten with another reference if the stack grows—but the Java garbage collector has no way to know this. Even when the client is done with the item, the reference in the array may keep it alive. This condition (holding a reference to an item which is no longer needed) is known as *loitering*, which is not the same as a *memory leak* (where even the memory management system has no reference to the item). In this case, loitering is easy to avoid. The implementation of pop() in DoublingStackOfStrings sets the array entry corresponding to the popped item to null, thus overwriting the unused reference and making it possible for the system to reclaim the memory associated with the popped item when the client is finished with it.

WITH AN ARRAY-DOUBLING IMPLEMENTATION (as with a linked-list implementation), we can write client programs that use large numbers of stacks without having to worry much about space usage. Again, the same principle applies to collections of data of any sort. For some data types that are more complicated than stacks, array doubling is preferred over linked lists because the ability to access any item in the array in constant time (through indexing) is critical for implementing certain operations (see, for example, RandomQueue in EXERCISE 4.3.36). Again as with linked lists, it is best to keep array-doubling code local to the implementation of fundamental data types and not worry about using it in client code.

**Parameterized data types**   We have developed stack implementations that allow us to build stacks of one particular type (`String`). But when developing client programs, we need implementations for collections of other types of data, not necessarily `String` objects. A commercial transaction processing system might need to maintain collections of customers, accounts, merchants, and transactions; a university course scheduling system might need to maintain collections of classes, students, and rooms; a portable music player might need to maintain collections of songs, artists, and albums; a scientific program might need to maintain collections of `double` or `int` values. In any program that you write, you should not be surprised to find yourself maintaining collections for any type of data that you might create. How would you do so? After considering two simple approaches (and their shortcomings) that use the Java language constructs we have discussed so far, we introduce a more advanced construct that can help us properly address this problem.

*Create a new collection data type for each item data type.*   We could create classes `StackOfInts`, `StackOfCustomers`, `StackOfStudents`, and so forth to supplement `StackOfStrings`. This approach requires that we duplicate the code for each type of data, which violates a basic precept of software engineering that we should reuse (not copy) code whenever possible. You need a different class for every type of data that you want to put on a stack, so maintaining your code becomes a nightmare: whenever you want or need to make a change, you have to do so in each version of the code. Still, this approach is widely used because many programming languages (including early versions of Java) do not provide any better way to solve the problem. Breaking this barrier is the sign of a sophisticated programmer and programming environment. Can we implement stacks of `String` objects, stacks of integers, and stacks of data of any type whatsoever with just one class?

*Use collections of Objects.*   We could develop a stack whose elements are all of type `Object`. Using inheritance, we can legally push an object of any type (if we want to push an object of type `Apple`, we can do so because `Apple` is a subclass of `Object`, as are all other classes). When we pop the stack, we must cast it back to the appropriate type (everything on the stack is an `Object`, but our code is processing objects of type `Apple`). In summary, if we create a class `StackOfObjects` by changing `String` to `Object` everywhere in one of our `*StackOfStrings` implementations, we can write code like

```
StackOfObjects stack = new StackOfObjects();
Apple a = new Apple();
stack.push(a);
...
a = (Apple) (stack.pop());
```

thus achieving our goal of having a single class that creates and manipulates stacks of objects of any type. However, this approach is undesirable because it exposes clients to subtle bugs in client programs that cannot be detected until runtime. For example, there is nothing to stop a programmer from putting different types of objects on the same stack, as in the following example:

```
ObjectStack stack = new ObjectStack();
Apple  a = new Apple();
Orange b = new Orange();
stack.push(a);
stack.push(b);
a = (Apple)  (stack.pop()); // Throws a ClassCastException.
b = (Orange) (stack.pop());
```

Using type casting in this way amounts to *assuming* that clients will cast objects popped from the stack to the proper type, avoiding the protection provided by Java's type system. One reason that programmers use the type system is to protect against errors that arise from such implicit assumptions. The code cannot be type-checked at compile time: there might be an incorrect cast that occurs in a complex piece of code that could escape detection until some particular runtime circumstance arises. We seek to avoid such errors because they can appear long after an implementation is delivered to a client, who would have no way to fix them.

*Java generics.*  A specific mechanism in Java known as *generic types* solves precisely the problem that we are facing. With generics, we can build collections of objects of a type to be specified by client code. The primary benefit of doing so is to discover type mismatch errors at compile time (when the software is being developed) instead of at runtime (when the software is being used by a client, perhaps long after development). Conceptually, generics are a bit confusing at first (their impact on the programming language is sufficiently deep that they were not included in early versions of Java), but our use of them in the present context involves just a small bit of extra Java syntax and is easy to understand. We name the generic class `Stack` and choose the generic name `Item` for the type of the objects in the stack (you

*Program 4.3.4    Generic stack*

```java
public class Stack<Item>
{
   private Node first;
   private class Node
   {
      Item item;
      Node next;
   }
   public boolean isEmpty()
   {  return (first == null); }
   public void push(Item item)
   {  // Add item to top of stack.
      Node oldfirst = first;
      first = new Node();
      first.item = item;
      first.next = oldfirst;
   }
   public Item pop()
   {  // Remove item from top of stack.
      Item item = first.item;
      first = first.next;
      return item;
   }
   public static void main(String[] args)
   {
      Stack<String> s = new Stack<String>();
      // See Program 4.3.1 for the test client.
   }
}
```

| first | *first node on list* |

| item | *list item* |
| next | *next node on list* |

*This code is almost identical to Program 4.3.2, but is worth repeating because it demonstrates how easy it is to use generics to allow clients to make collections of any type of data. The keyword* Item *in this code is a type parameter, a placeholder for an actual type name provided by clients.*

```
% java Stack < tobe.txt
to be not that or be
```

can use any name). The code of `Stack` (PROGRAM 4.3.4) is identical to the code of `LinkedStackOfStrings` (we drop the `Linked` modifier because we have a good implementation for clients who do not care about the representation), except that we replace every occurrence of `String` with `Item` and declare the class with the following first line of code:

```
public class Stack<Item>
```

The name `Item` is a *type parameter*, a symbolic placeholder for some actual type to be used by the client. You can read `Stack<Item>` as *stack of items*, which is precisely what we want. When implementing `Stack`, we do not know the actual type of `Item`, but a client can use our stack for any type of data, including one defined long after we develop our implementation. The client code provides an actual type when the stack is created:

```
Stack<Apple> stack = new Stack<Apple>();
Apple a = new Apple();
...
stack.push(a);
```

If you try to push an object of the wrong type on the stack, like this:

```
Stack<Apple> stack = new Stack<Apple>();
Apple   a = new Apple();
Orange b = new Orange();
stack.push(a);
stack.push(b);        // Compile-time error.
```

you will get a compile-time error:

```
push(Apple) in Stack<Apple> cannot be applied to (Orange)
```

Furthermore, in our `Stack` implementation, Java can use the type parameter `Item` to check for type mismatch errors—even though no actual type is yet known, variables of type `Item` must be assigned values of type `Item`, and so forth.

*Auto-boxing.* One slight difficulty with generic code like PROGRAM 4.3.4 is that the type parameter stands for a *reference type*. How can we use the code for primitive types such as `int` and `double`? The Java language feature known as *auto-boxing* and *auto-unboxing* enables us to reuse generic code with primitive types as well. Java supplies built-in object types known as *wrapper types*, one for each of the primitive types: Boolean, Byte, Character, Double, Float, Integer, Long, and Short correspond to boolean, byte char, double, float, int, long, and short, respectively. These classes consist primarily of static methods such as Integer.parseInt() and Integer.toBinaryString(), and they also include non-static methods such as compareTo() and equals(). Java automatically converts between these reference types and the corresponding primitive types—in assignments, method arguments, and arithmetic/logic expressions—so that we can write code like the following:

```
Stack<Integer> stack = new Stack<Integer>();
stack.push(17);        // Auto-boxing    (int -> Integer).
int a = stack.pop(); // Auto-unboxing (Integer -> int).
```

In this example, Java automatically casts (auto-boxes) the primitive value 17 to be of type Integer when we pass it to the push() method. The pop() method returns an Integer, which Java casts (auto-unboxes) to an int before assigning it to the variable a. This feature is convenient for writing code, but involves a significant amount of processing behind the scenes that can affect performance. In some performance-critical applications, a class like StackOfInts might be necessary, after all.

GENERICS PROVIDE THE SOLUTION THAT WE seek: they enable code reuse and at the same time provide type safety. Studying Stack carefully and being sure that you understand each line of code will pay dividends in the future, as the ability to parameterize data types is an important high-level programming technique that is well-supported in Java. You do not have to be an expert to take advantage of this powerful feature.

**Stack applications**   Pushdown stacks play an essential role in computation. If you study operating systems, programming languages, and other advanced topics in computer science, you will learn that not only are stacks used explicitly in many applications, but they also still serve as the basis for executing programs written in high-level languages such as Java.

*Arithmetic expressions.*   Some of the first programs that we considered in CHAPTER 1 involved computing the value of arithmetic expressions like this one:

```
( 1 + ( ( 2 + 3 ) * ( 4 * 5 ) ) )
```

If you multiply 4 by 5, add 3 to 2, multiply the result, and then add 1, you get the value 101. But how does the Java system do this calculation? Without going into the details of how the Java system is built, we can address the essential ideas just by writing a Java program that can take a string as input (the expression) and produce the number represented by the expression as output. For simplicity, we begin with the following explicit recursive definition: an *arithmetic expression* is either: a number or a left parenthesis followed by an arithmetic expression followed by an operator followed by another arithmetic expression followed by a right parenthesis. For simplicity, this definition is for *fully parenthesized* arithmetic expressions, which specifies precisely which operators apply to which operands—you are a bit more familiar with expressions like 1 + 2 * 3, in which we use precedence rules instead of parentheses. The same basic mechanisms that we consider can handle precedence rules, but we avoid that complication. For specificity, we support the familiar binary operators *, +, -, and /, as well as a square-root operator sqrt that takes only one argument. We could easily allow more operators and more kinds of operators to embrace a large class of familiar mathematical expressions, involving trigonometric, exponential, and logarithmic functions and whatever other operators we might wish to include. Our focus is on understanding how to interpret the string of parentheses, operators, and numbers to enable performing in the proper order the low-level arithmetic operations that are available on any computer.

*Arithmetic expression evaluation.*  Precisely how can we convert an arithmetic expression—a string of characters—to the value that it represents? A remarkably simple algorithm that was developed by Edsgar Dijkstra in the 1960s uses two push-down stacks (one for operands and one for operators) to do this job. An expression consists of parentheses, operators, and operands (numbers). Proceeding from left to right and taking these entities one at a time, we manipulate the stacks according to four possible cases, as follows:
   • Push *operands* onto the operand stack.
   • Push *operators* onto the operator stack.
   • Ignore *left* parentheses.
   • On encountering a *right* parenthesis, pop an operator, pop the requisite number of operands, and push onto the operand stack the result of applying that operator to those operands.
After the final right parenthesis has been processed, there is one value on the stack, which is the value of the expression. This method may seem mysterious at first, but

*Program 4.3.5    Expression evaluation*

```
public class Evaluate
{
   public static void main(String[] args)
   {
      Stack<String> ops  = new Stack<String>();
      Stack<Double> vals = new Stack<Double>();
      while (!StdIn.isEmpty())
      { // Read token, push if operator.
         String s = StdIn.readString();
         if      (s.equals("("))                    ;
         else if (s.equals("+"))    ops.push(s);
         else if (s.equals("-"))    ops.push(s);
         else if (s.equals("*"))    ops.push(s);
         else if (s.equals("/"))    ops.push(s);
         else if (s.equals("sqrt")) ops.push(s);
         else if (s.equals(")"))
         { // Pop, evaluate, and push result if token is ")".
            String op = ops.pop();
            double v = vals.pop();
            if      (op.equals("+"))    v = vals.pop() + v;
            else if (op.equals("-"))    v = vals.pop() - v;
            else if (op.equals("*"))    v = vals.pop() * v;
            else if (op.equals("/"))    v = vals.pop() / v;
            else if (op.equals("sqrt")) v = Math.sqrt(v);
            vals.push(v);
         } // Token not operator or paren: push double value.
         else vals.push(Double.parseDouble(s));
      }
      StdOut.println(vals.pop());
   }
}
```

| ops  | operator stack |
|------|----------------|
| vals | operand stack  |
| s    | current token  |
| v    | current value  |

This Stack *client uses two stacks to evaluate arithmetic expressions, illustrating an essential computational process: interpreting a string as a program and executing that program to compute the desired result. Executing a Java program is nothing other than a more complicated version of this same process.*

```
% java Evaluate
( 1 + ( ( 2 + 3 ) * ( 4 * 5 ) ) )
101.0
```

```
% java Evaluate
( ( 1 + sqrt ( 5.0 ) ) / 2.0 )
1.618033988749895
```

it is easy to convince yourself that it computes the proper value: any time the algorithm encounters a subexpression consisting of two operands separated by an operator, all surrounded by parentheses, it leaves the result of performing that operation on those operands on the operand stack. The result is the same as if that value had appeared in the input instead of the subexpression, so we can think of replacing the subexpression by the value to get an expression that would yield the same result. We can apply this argument again and again until we get a single value. For example, the algorithm computes the same value of all of these expressions:

```
( 1 + ( ( 2 + 3 ) * ( 4 * 5 ) ) )
( 1 + ( 5 * ( 4 * 5 ) ) )
( 1 + ( 5 * 20 ) )
( 1 + 100 )
101
```

`Evaluate` (PROGRAM 4.3.5) is an implementation of this method. This code is a simple example of an *interpreter*: a program that interprets the computation specified by a given string and performs the computation to arrive at the result. A *compiler* is a program that converts the string into code on a lower-level machine that can do the job. This conversion is a more complicated process than the step-by-step conversion used by an interpreter, but it is based on the same underlying mechanism. Initially, Java was based on using an interpreter. Now, however, the Java system includes a compiler that converts arithmetic expressions (and, more generally, Java programs) into code for the *Java virtual machine*, an imaginary machine that is easy to simulate on an actual computer.

*Trace of expression evaluation (Program 4.3.5)*

*Stack-based programming languages.* Remarkably, Dijkstra's 2-stack algorithm also computes the same value as in our example for this expression:

> ( 1 ( ( 2 3 + ) ( 4 5 * ) * ) + )

In other words, we can put each operator *after* its two operands instead of *between* them. In such an expression, each right parenthesis immediately follows an operator so we can ignore *both* kinds of parentheses, writing the expressions as:

> 1 2 3 + 4 5 * * +

This notation is known as *reverse Polish notation,* or *postfix.* To evaluate a postfix expression, we use one stack (see EXERCISE 4.3.15). Proceeding from left to right, taking these entities one at a time, we manipulate the stacks according to just two possible cases, as follows:

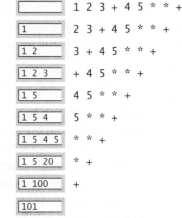

- Push operands onto the operand stack.
- On encountering an operator, pop the requisite number of operands and push onto the operand stack the result of applying the operator to those operands.

Again, this process leaves one value on the stack, which is the value of the expression. This representation is so simple that some programming languages, such as Forth (a scientific programming language) and POSTSCRIPT (a page description language that is used on most printers) use explicit stacks. For example, the string 1 2 3 + 4 5 * * + is a legal program in both FORTH and POSTSCRIPT that leaves the value 101 on the execution stack. Aficionados

*Trace of postfix evaluation*

of these and similar stack-based programming languages prefer them because they are simpler for many types of computation. Indeed, the Java virtual machine itself is stack-based.

*Function-call abstraction.* Most programs use stacks implicitly because they support a natural way to implement function calls, as follows: at any point during the execution of a method, define its *state* to be the values of all of its variables *and* a pointer to the next instruction to be executed. One of the fundamental characteristics of computing environments is that every computation is fully determined by its state (and the value of its inputs). In particular, the system can suspend a com-

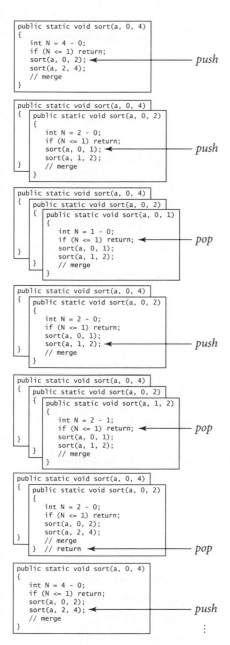

```
public static void sort(a, 0, 4)
{
    int N = 4 - 0;
    if (N <= 1) return;
    sort(a, 0, 2);  ◄────────────  push
    sort(a, 2, 4);
    // merge
}
```

```
public static void sort(a, 0, 4)
{   public static void sort(a, 0, 2)
    {
        int N = 2 - 0;
        if (N <= 1) return;
        sort(a, 0, 1);  ◄────────  push
        sort(a, 1, 2);
    }   // merge
}       }
```

```
public static void sort(a, 0, 4)
{   public static void sort(a, 0, 2)
    {   public static void sort(a, 0, 1)
        {
            int N = 1 - 0;
            if (N <= 1) return;  ◄──── pop
            sort(a, 0, 1);
        }   sort(a, 1, 2);
    }       // merge
}           }
```

```
public static void sort(a, 0, 4)
{   public static void sort(a, 0, 2)
    {
        int N = 2 - 0;
        if (N <= 1) return;
        sort(a, 0, 1);
    }   sort(a, 1, 2);  ◄────────  push
}       // merge
        }
```

```
public static void sort(a, 0, 4)
{   public static void sort(a, 0, 2)
    {   public static void sort(a, 1, 2)
        {
            int N = 2 - 1;
            if (N <= 1) return;  ◄──── pop
        }   sort(a, 0, 1);
    }       sort(a, 1, 2);
}           // merge
            }
```

```
public static void sort(a, 0, 4)
{   public static void sort(a, 0, 2)
    {
        int N = 2 - 0;
        if (N <= 1) return;
        sort(a, 0, 2);
    }   sort(a, 2, 4);
        // merge
}   } // return  ◄────────────  pop
```

```
public static void sort(a, 0, 4)
{
    int N = 4 - 0;
    if (N <= 1) return;
    sort(a, 0, 2);
    sort(a, 2, 4);  ◄────────────  push
    // merge
}                               ⋮
```

*Using a stack to support function calls*

putation by saving away its state, then restart it by restoring the state. If you take a course about operating systems, you will learn the details of this process, because it is critical to much of the behavior of computers that we take for granted (for example, switching from one application to another is simply a matter of saving and restoring state). Now, the natural way to implement the function-call abstraction, which is used by virtually all modern programming environments, is to use a stack. To *call* a function, *push* the state on a stack. To *return* from a function call, *pop* the state from the stack to restore all variables to their values before the function call, substitute the function return value (if there is one) in the expression containing the function call (if there is one), and resume execution at the next instruction to be executed (whose location was saved as part of the state of the computation). This mechanism works whenever functions call one another, even recursively. Indeed, if you think about the process carefully, you will see that it is essentially the *same* process that we just examined in detail for expression evaluation. A program is a sophisticated expression.

THE PUSHDOWN STACK IS A FUNDAMENTAL computational abstraction. Stacks have been used for expression evaluation, implementing the function-call abstraction, and other basic tasks since the earliest days of computing. We will examine another (tree traversal) in SECTION 4.4. Stacks are used explicitly and extensively in many areas of computer science, including algorithm design, operating systems, compilers, and numerous other computational applications.

**FIFO queues**   A *FIFO queue* (or just a *queue*) is a collection that is based on the first-in-first-out (FIFO) policy.

The policy of doing tasks in the same order that they arrive is one that we encounter frequently in everyday life, from people waiting in line at a theater, to cars waiting in line at a toll booth, to tasks waiting to be serviced by an application on your computer.

One bedrock principle of any service policy is the perception of fairness. The first idea that comes to mind when most people think about fairness is that whomever has been waiting the longest should be served first. That is precisely the FIFO discipline, so queues play a central role in numerous applications. Queues are a natural model for so many everyday phenomena, and their properties were studied in detail even before the advent of computers.

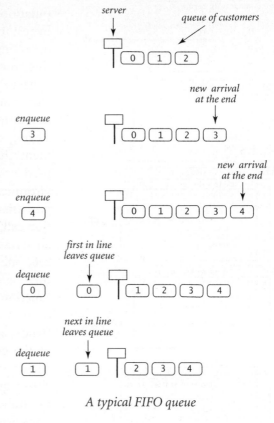

*A typical FIFO queue*

As usual, we begin by articulating an API. Again by tradition, we name the queue insert operation *enqueue* and the remove operation *dequeue*, as indicated in the following API:

```
public class Queue<Item>
```
|            |                      |                       |
|-----------:|----------------------|-----------------------|
|            | Queue<Item>()        | *create an empty queue* |
| boolean    | isEmpty()            | *is the queue empty?* |
| void       | enqueue(Item item)   | *enqueue an item*     |
| Item       | dequeue()            | *dequeue an item*     |
| int        | length()             | *queue length*        |

*API for a generic FIFO queue*

As specified in this API, we will use generics in our implementations, so that we can write client programs that safely build and use queues of any reference type. We include a `length()` method, even though we did not have such a method for stacks because queue clients often do need to be aware of the number of items in the queue, whereas most stack clients do not (see PROGRAM 4.3.8 and EXERCISE 4.3.9).

Applying our knowledge from stacks, we can use linked lists or array doubling to develop implementations where the operations take constant time and the memory associated with the queue grows and shrinks with the number of elements in the queue. As with stacks, each of these implementations represents a classic programming exercise. You may wish to think about how you might achieve these goals in an implementation before reading further.

*Linked-list implementation.* To implement a queue with a linked list, we keep the items in order of their arrival (the reverse of the order that we used in `Stack`). The implementation of `dequeue()` is the same as the `pop()` implementation in `Stack` (save the item in the first list node, remove the first list node from the queue, and return the saved item). Implementing `enqueue()`, however, is a bit more challenging: how do we add a node to the *end* of a linked list? To do so, we need a link to the last node in the list, because that node's link has to be changed to reference a new node containing the item to be inserted. In `Stack`, the only instance variable is a reference to the *first* node in the list; with only that information, our only recourse is to traverse all the nodes in the list to get to the end. That solution is unattractive when lists might be lengthy. A reasonable alternative is to maintain a second instance variable that always references the *last* node in the list. Adding an extra instance variable that needs to be

*save a link to the last node*
```
Node oldlast = last;
```

*create a new node for the end*
```
Node last = new Node();
last.item = "not";
```

*link the new node to the end of the list*
```
oldlast.next = last;
```

*Inserting a new node at the end of a linked list*

*Program 4.3.6  Generic FIFO queue (linked list)*

```java
public class Queue<Item>
{
   private Node first;
   private Node last;

   private class Node
   {
      Item item;
      Node next;
   }

   public boolean isEmpty()
   {  return (first == null);  }

   public void enqueue(Item item)
   {  // Add item to the end of the list.
      Node oldlast = last;
      last = new Node();
      last.item = item;
      last.next = null;
      if (isEmpty()) first = last;
      else           oldlast.next = last;
   }

   public Item dequeue()
   {  // Remove item from the beginning of the list.
      Item item = first.item;
      first = first.next;
      if (isEmpty()) last = null;
      return item;
   }

   public static void main(String[] args)
   {  // Test client is similar to Program 4.3.2.
      Queue<String> q = new Queue<String>();
   }

}
```

| first | *first node on list* |
|---|---|
| last | *last node on list* |

| item | *list item* |
|---|---|
| next | *next node on list* |

*This implementation is very similar to our linked-list stack implementation (Program 4.3.2):
dequeue() is almost the same as pop(), but enqueue() links the new item onto the end of the
list, not the beginning as in push(). To do so, it maintains an instance variable that references
the last node on the list. The length() method is left for an exercise (see Exercise 4.3.11).*

```
% java Queue < tobe.txt
to be or not to be
```

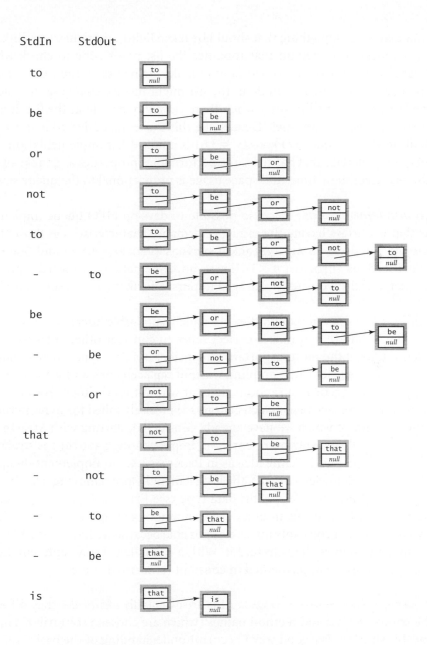

*Trace of* Queue *test client (see Program 4.3.6)*

maintained is not something that should be taken lightly, particularly in linked-list code, because every method that modifies the list needs code to check whether that variable needs to be modified (and to make the necessary modifications). For example, removing the first node in the list might involve changing the reference to the last node in the list, since when there is only one node in the list, it is both the first one and the last one! (Details like this make linked-list code notoriously difficult to debug.) `Queue` (PROGRAM 4.3.6) is a linked-list implementation of our FIFO queue interface that has the same performance properties as `Stack`: all of the methods are constant-time, and space usage is proportional to the queue size.

*Array implementations.* It is also possible to develop FIFO queue implementations that use arrays having the same performance characteristics as those that we developed for stacks in `ArrayStackOfStrings` (PROGRAM 4.3.1) and `Doubling-StackOfStrings` (PROGRAM 4.3.3). These implementations are worthy programming exercises that you are encouraged to pursue further (see EXERCISE 4.3.18).

*Random queues.* Even though they are widely applicable, there is nothing sacred about FIFO and LIFO. It makes perfect sense to consider other rules for removing items. One of the most important to consider is a data type where `dequeue()` removes a *random* element (sampling without replacement), and we have a method `sample()` that returns a random element without removing it from the queue (sampling with replacement). Such actions are precisely called for in numerous applications, some of which we have already considered, starting with `Sample` (PROGRAM 1.4.1). With an array representation, implementing `sample()` is straightforward, and we can use the same idea as in PROGRAM 1.4.1 to implement `dequeue()` (exchange a random element with the last element before removing it). We use the name `RandomQueue` to refer to this data type (see EXERCISE 4.3.36). Note that this solution depends on using an array representation; getting to a random element from a linked list in constant time is not possible because we have to start from the beginning and traverse links to find it. With a (doubling) array representation, all of the operations are implemented in constant (amortized) time.

THE QUEUE, RANDOM QUEUE, AND STACK APIs are essentially *identical*—they differ only in the choice of class and method names (which are chosen arbitrarily). Thinking about this situation is a good way to cement understanding of the basic issues surrounding data types that we introduced in SECTION 3.3. The true differences among these data types are in the semantics of the *remove* operation—which item is to be removed? The differences between stacks and queues are in the English-language descriptions of what they do. These differences are akin to the differences between `Math.sin(x)` and `Math.log(y)`, but we might want to articulate them with a formal description of stacks and queues (in the same way as we have mathematical descriptions of the sine and logarithm functions). But precisely describing what we mean by first-in-first-out or last-in-first-out or random-out is not so simple. For starters, what language would you use for such a description? English? Java? Mathematical logic? The problem of describing how a program behaves is known as the *specification problem*, and it leads immediately to deep issues in computer science. One reason for our emphasis on clear and concise code is that the code itself can serve as the specification for simple data types such as stacks and queues.

**Queue applications**   In the past century, FIFO queues proved to be accurate and useful models in a broad variety of applications, ranging from manufacturing processes to telephone networks to traffic simulations. A field of mathematics known as *queuing theory* has been used with great success to help understand and control complex systems of all kinds. FIFO queues also play an important role in computing. You often encounter queues when you use your computer: a queue might hold songs on a playlist, documents to be printed, or events in a game.

Perhaps the ultimate queue application is the internet itself, which is based on huge numbers of messages moving through huge numbers of queues that have all sorts of different properties and are interconnected in all sorts of complicated ways. Understanding and controlling such a complex system involves solid implementations of the queue abstraction, application of mathematical results of queueing theory, and simulation studies involving both. We consider next a classic example to give a flavor of this process.

*M/D/1 queue.*   One of the simplest queueing models is known as an *M/D/1* queue. The *M* indicates that arrivals obey a *Markov* process (in this context, a *Poisson process* where arrivals obey a specific probability distribution that has been shown to accurately model many real-world situations), the *D* indicates that departures are deterministic (happen at a fixed rate), and the 1 indicates that there is one server. It is an appropriate model for a situation like a single line of cars entering a toll booth: they arrive at randomly spaced intervals, but leave at fixed intervals. An *M/D/1* queue is parameterized by its *arrival rate* $\lambda$ (for example, the number of cars per minute arriving at the toll booth) and its *departure rate* $\mu$ (for example, the number of cars per minute that can pass through the toll booth) and is characterized by three properties:

- There is one server (a FIFO queue).
- Arrivals are described by a Poisson process with rate $\lambda$, where the arrivals come from an *exponential distribution* (see EXERCISE 2.2.14).
- Departures happen at a fixed rate of $\mu$ when the queue is nonempty.

Note that the queue will grow without bound unless $\mu > \lambda$. Otherwise, customers enter and leave the queue in an interesting dynamic process. Also note that the time between arrivals is $1/\lambda$ minutes, on the average, and the time between departures, when the queue is nonempty, is $1/\mu$ minutes.

*Analysis.* In practical applications, people are interested in the effect of the values of the parameters on various properties of the queue. If you are a customer, you may want to know the expected amount of time you will have to wait in the queue; if you are designing the system, you might want to know how many customers are likely to be in the queue, or something more complicated, such as the likelihood that the queue size will exceed a given maximum size. For simple models, probability theory yields formulas expressing these quantities as functions of $\lambda$ and $\mu$. For M/D/1 queues, it is known that:

- The average number of customers in the system $L$ is $\lambda^2 / (2\,\mu\,(\mu - \lambda)) + \lambda/\mu$.
- The average wait time $W$ is $\lambda / (2\,\mu\,(\mu - \lambda)) + 1/\mu$.

For example, if the cars arrive at an average rate of 10 per minute and the service rate is 15 per minute, then the average number of cars in the system will be 4/3 and the average wait time will be 2/15 minutes or 8 seconds. These formulas confirm that the wait time (and queue length) grow without bound as $\lambda$ approaches $\mu$. They also obey a general rule known as *Little's law*: the average number of customers in the system is $\lambda$ times the average wait time ($L = \lambda W$) for many types of queues.

| | arrival | departure | wait |
|---|---|---|---|
| 0 | 0 | 5 | 5 |
| 1 | 2 | 10 | 8 |
| 2 | 7 | 15 | 8 |
| 3 | 17 | 23 | 6 |
| 4 | 19 | 28 | 9 |
| 5 | 21 | 30 | 9 |

*An M/D/1 queue*

### Program 4.3.7  M/D/1 queue simulation

```java
public class MD1Queue
{
   public static void main(String[] args)
   {
      double lambda = Double.parseDouble(args[0]);
      double mu     = Double.parseDouble(args[1]);
      Histogram hist = new Histogram(60 + 1);
      Queue<Double> queue = new Queue<Double>();
      double nextArrival = StdRandom.exp(lambda);
      double nextService = nextArrival + 1/mu;
      while (true)
      {
         while (nextArrival < nextService)
         {  // Simulate an arrival.
            queue.enqueue(nextArrival);
            nextArrival += StdRandom.exp(lambda);
         }  // Arrivals done; simulate a service.
         double wait = nextService - queue.dequeue();
         StdDraw.clear();
         hist.addDataPoint(Math.min(60,  (int) (wait)));
         hist.draw();
         StdDraw.show(20);
         if (queue.isEmpty())
            nextService = nextArrival + 1/mu;
         else
            nextService = nextService + 1/mu;
      }
   }
}
```

| | |
|---|---|
| lambda | *arrival rate* |
| mu | *service rate* |
| hist | *histogram* |
| queue | *M/D/1 queue* |
| wait | *time on queue* |

*This simulation of an M/D/1 queue keeps track of time with two variables* nextArrival *and* nextService *and a single* Queue *of* double *values to calculate wait times. The value of each item on the queue is the (simulated) time it entered the queue. The waiting times are plotted using* Histogram *(Program 3.2.3).*

% java MD1Queue .167 .25

% java MD1Queue .167 .22

*Simulation.* MD1Queue (PROGRAM 4.3.7) is a Queue client that you can use to validate these sorts of mathematical results. It is a simple example of an *event-based simulation*: we generate *events* that take place at particular times and adjust our data structures accordingly for the events, simulating what happens at the time they occur. In an *M/D/*1 queue, there are two kinds of events: we either have a customer *arrival* or a customer *service*, so we maintain two variables:

- nextService is the time of the next service.
- nextArrival is the time of the next arrival.

To simulate an arrival event, we enqueue a double value (nextArrival, the time of arrival); to simulate a service, we dequeue a value, compute the wait time (nextService, which is the time of service, minus the value that came off the queue, which is the time of arrival) and add the wait time data point to the histogram (see PROGRAM 3.2.3). The shape that results after a large number of trials is characteristic of the M/D/1 queueing system. From a practical point of view, one of the most important characteristics of the process, which you can discover for yourself by running MD1-Queue for various values of $\lambda$ and $\mu$, is that average wait time (and queue length) can increase dramatically when the service rate approaches the arrival rate. When the service rate is high, the histogram has a visible tail where the frequency of customers having a given wait time decreases to being negligible as the wait time increases. But when the service rate is close to the arrival rate, the tail of the histogram stretches to the point that most values are in the tail, so the frequency of customers having at least the highest wait time displayed dominates.

AS IN MANY OTHER APPLICATIONS THAT we have studied, the use of simulation to validate a well-understood mathematical model is a starting point for studying more complex situations. In practical applications of queues, we may have multiple queues, multiple servers, multi-stage servers, limits on queue size, and many other restrictions. Moreover, the distributions of arrival and service times may not be possible to characterize mathematically. In such situations, we may have no recourse but to use simulations. It is quite common for a system designer to build a computational model of a queuing system (such as MD1Queue) and to use it to adjust design parameters (such as the service rate) to properly respond to the outside environment (such as the arrival rate).

**Iterable collections** As mentioned earlier in this section, one of the fundamental operations on arrays and linked lists is the for loop idiom that we use to process each entry. This common programming paradigm need not be limited to low-level data structures such as arrays and linked lists. For any collection, the ability to process all of its items (perhaps in some specified order) is a valuable capability. The client's requirement is just to process each of the items in some way, or to *iterate* through the items in the collection. This paradigm is so important that it has achieved first-class status in Java and many other modern languages (the programming language itself has specific mechanisms to support it, not just the libraries). With it, we can write clear and compact code that is free from dependence on the details of a collection's implementation.

To introduce the concept, we start with a snippet of client code that prints all of the items in a collection of strings, one per line:

```
Stack<String> collection = new Stack<String>();
...
for (String s : collection)
   StdOut.println(s);
...
```

This construct is known as the *foreach* statement: you can read the for statement as *for each string s in the collection, print s*. This client code does not need to know anything about the representation or the implementation of the collection; it just wants to process each of the items in the collection. The same for loop would work with a Queue of strings or any other *iterable* collection.

We could hardly imagine code that is more clear and compact. However, implementing a collection that supports it requires some extra work, which we now consider in detail. First, the foreach construct is shorthand for a while construct (just like the for statement itself). For example, the foreach statement above is exactly equivalent to the following while construct:

```
Iterator<String> i = collection.iterator();
while (i.hasNext())
{
   String s = i.next();
   StdOut.println(s);
}
```

This code exposes the three necessary elements that we need to implement in any iterable collection:

- The collection must implement an `iterator()` method that returns an `Iterator` object.
- The `Iterator` class must include two methods: `hasNext()` (which returns a `boolean` value) and `next()` (which returns an item from the collection).

In Java, we use the `interface` mechanism to express the idea that a class implements a specific method (see SECTION 3.3). For iterable collections, the necessary interfaces are already defined for us in Java.

To make a class iterable, the first step is to add the phrase `implements Iterable<Item>` to its declaration, matching the interface

```
public interface Iterable<Item>
{
    Iterator<Item> iterator();
}
```

(which is in `java.lang.Iterable`), and to add a method to the class that returns an `Iterator<Item>`. Iterators are generic; we can either use them in a generic class or just use them to provide clients with the ability to iterate through a specific type of objects.

What is an iterator? An object from a class that implements the methods `hasNext()` and `next()`, as defined in the following interface (which is in `java.util.Iterator`):

```
public interface Iterator<Item>
{
    boolean hasNext();
    Item next();
    void remove();
}
```

Although the interface requires a `remove()` method, we always use an empty method for `remove()` in this book, because interleaving iteration with operations that modify the data structure is best avoided.

As illustrated in the following two examples, implementing an iterator class is often straightforward for array and linked-list representations of collections.

*Implementing an iterator for a class that uses an internal array.* As a first example, we will consider all of the steps needed to make `ArrayStackOfStrings` (PROGRAM 4.3.1) iterable. First, change the class declaration to:

```
public class ArrayStackOfStrings implements Iterable<String>
```

In other words, we are promising to provide an `iterator()` method so that a client can use a foreach statement to iterate through the strings in the stack. The `iterator()` method itself is simple:

```
public Iterator<String> iterator()
{   return new ArrayIterator();   }
```

It just returns an object from a private nested class that implements the `Iterator` interface (which provides `hasNext()`, `next()`, and `remove()` methods):

```
private class ArrayIterator implements Iterator<String>
{
    private int i = N-1;
    public boolean hasNext()
    {   return i >= 0;   }
    public Item next()
    {   return a[i--];   }
    public void remove()
    { }
}
```

Note that the nested class can access the instance variables of the enclosing class, in this case `a[]` and `N` (this ability is the main reason we use nested classes for iterators). One crucial detail remains: we have to include

```
import java.util.Iterator;
```

at the beginning of the program because (for historical reasons) `Iterator` is not part of the standard library (even though `Iterable` *is* part of the standard library). Now a client using the foreach statement for this class will get behavior equivalent to the common `for` loop for arrays, but does not need to be aware of the array representation (an implementation detail). This arrangement is of critical importance for implementations of fundamental data types like those included in Java libraries. For example, it frees us to switch to a totally different representation *without having to change any client code*. More important, taking the client's point of view, it allows clients to use iteration *without having to know any details of the class implementation.*

*Implementing an iterator for a class that uses a linked list.* The same specific steps (with different code) are effective to make `Queue` (Program 4.3.6) iterable, even though it is generic. First, we change the class declaration to:

```
public class Queue<Item> implements Iterable<Item>
```

In other words, we are promising to provide an `iterator()` method so that a client can use a foreach statement to iterate through the items in the stack, whatever their type. Again, the `iterator()` method itself is simple:

```
public Iterator<Item> iterator()
{   return new ListIterator();   }
```

As before, we have a private nested class that implements the `Iterator` interface:

```
private class ListIterator implements Iterator<Item>
{
    Node current = first;
    public boolean hasNext()
    {   return current != null; }
    public Item next()
    {
        Item item = current.item;
        current = current.next;
        return item;
    }
    public void remove()
    { }
}
```

Again, a client can build a queue of objects of any type and then iterate through the objects without any awareness of the linked-list representation:

```
Queue<String> queue = new Queue<String>();
...
for (String s : queue)
    StdOut.println(s);
```

This client code is a clearer expression of the computation and therefore easier to write and maintain than code based on the low-level representation.

Our stack iterator goes through the items in LIFO order and our queue iterator goes through them in FIFO order, even though there is no requirement to do so: we could return the items in any order whatsoever. However, when developing iterators, it is wise to follow a simple rule: if a data type specification implies a natural iteration order, *use it*.

Iterator implementations may seem a bit complicated to you at first, but they are worth the effort. You will not find yourself implementing them very often, but when you do, you will enjoy the benefits of clear and correct client code and code reuse. Moreover, as with any programming construct, once you begin to enjoy these benefits, you will find yourself taking advantage of them often.

Making a class iterable certainly changes its API, but to avoid overly complicated API tables, we simply use the adjective *iterable* to indicate that we have included the appropriate code to a class, as described in this section, and to indicate that you can

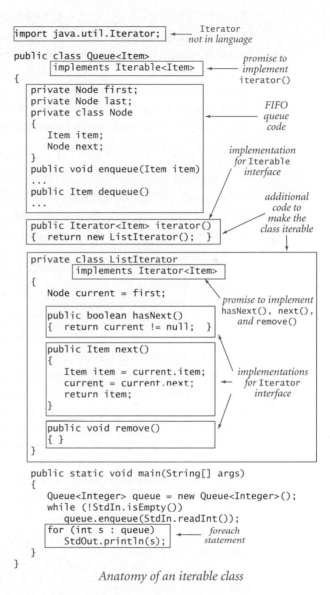

*Anatomy of an iterable class*

use the foreach statement in client code. From this point forward we will use in client programs the iterable (and generic) `Stack`, `Queue`, and `RandomQueue` data types described here.

**Resource allocation**   Next, we examine an application that illustrates the language features that we have been considering. A *resource-sharing* system involves a large number of loosely cooperating *servers* who want to share resources. Each server agrees to maintain a queue of items for sharing, and a central authority distributes the items to the servers (and informs users where they may be found). For example, the items might be songs, photos, or videos to be shared by a large number of users. To fix ideas, we will think in terms of millions of items and thousands of servers.

We will consider the kind of program that the central authority might use to distribute the items, ignoring the dynamics of deleting items from the systems, adding and deleting servers, and so forth.

If we use a *round-robin* policy, cycling through the servers to make the assignments, we get a balanced allocation, but it is rarely possible for a distributor to have such complete control over the situation: for example, there might be a large number of independent distributors, so none of them could have up-to-date information about the servers. Accordingly, such systems often use a *random* policy, where the assignments are based on random choice. An even better policy is to choose a random *sample* of servers and assign a new item to the one that has smallest number of items. For small queues, differences among these policies is immaterial, but in a system with millions of items on thousands of servers, the differences can be quite significant, since each server has a fixed amount of resources to devote to this process. Indeed, similar systems are used in internet hardware, where some queues might be implemented in special-purpose hardware, so queue length translates directly to extra equipment cost. But how big a sample should we take?

LoadBalance (PROGRAM 4.3.8) is a simulation of the sampling policy, which we can use to study this question. This program makes good use of the high-level constructs (generics and iterators) that we have been considering to provide an easily understood program that we can use for experimentation. We maintain a random queue of queues of strings and build the computation around an inner loop where we put each new request on the smallest of a sample of queues, using the sample() method from RandomQueue to randomly sample queues. The surprising end result is that samples of size *two* lead to near-perfect balancing, so there is no point in taking larger samples.

*Program 4.3.8    Load balancing simulation*

```java
public class LoadBalance
{
   public static void main(String[] args)
   { // Assign N items to M servers, using
     // shortest-in-a-sample (of size S) policy.
     int M = Integer.parseInt(args[0]);
     int N = Integer.parseInt(args[1]);
     int S = Integer.parseInt(args[2]);

     // Create server queues.
     RandomQueue<Queue<Integer>> servers;
     servers = new RandomQueue<Queue<Integer>>();
     for (int i = 0; i < M; i++)
        servers.enqueue(new Queue<Integer>());

     for (int j = 0; j < N; j++)
     {  // Assign an item to a server.
        Queue<Integer> min = servers.sample();
        for (int k = 1; k < S; k++)
        {  // Pick a random server, update if new min.
           Queue<Integer> q = servers.sample();
           if (q.length() < min.length()) min = q;
        }  // min is the shortest server queue.
        min.enqueue(j);
     }

     int i = 0;
     double[] lengths = new double[M];
     for (Queue<Integer> q: servers)
        lengths[i++] = q.length();
     StdDraw.setYscale(0, 2.0*N/M);
     StdStats.plotBars(lengths);
   }
}
```

| | |
|---|---|
| M | *number of servers* |
| N | *number of items* |
| S | *sample size* |
| servers | *queues* |
| min | *shortest in sample* |
| max | *current value* |

*This generic* Queue *client simulates the process of assigning N items to a set of M servers. Requests are put on the shortest of a sample of S queues chosen at random.*

% java LoadBalance 50 500 1

% java LoadBalance 50 500 2

WE HAVE CONSIDERED IN DETAIL the issues surrounding the space and time usage of basic implementations of the stack and queue APIs not just because these data types are important and useful, but also because you are likely to encounter the very same issues in the context of your own data type implementations.

Should you use a pushdown stack, a FIFO queue, or a random queue when developing a client that maintains collections of data? The answer to this question depends on a high-level analysis of the client to determine which of the LIFO, FIFO, or random disciplines is appropriate.

Should you use an array, a linked list, or a doubling array to structure your data? The answer to this question depends on low-level analysis of performance characteristics. With an *array*, the advantage is that you can access any element in constant time and the disadvantage that you need to know the maximum size in advance. A *linked list* has the advantage that you do not need to know the maximum size in advance and the disadvantage that you cannot access an arbitrary element in constant time. A *doubling array* combines the advantages of arrays and linked lists (you can access any element in constant time but do not need to know the maximum size in advance) but has the (slight) disadvantage that the constant running time is on an amortized basis. Each is appropriate in various different situations; you are likely to encounter all three in most programming environments. For example, the Java class `java.util.ArrayList` uses a doubling array, and the Java class `java.util.LinkedList` uses a linked list.

The powerful high-level constructs and new language features that we have considered in this section (generics and iterators) are not to be taken for granted. They are sophisticated language features that did not come into widespread use in mainstream languages until the turn of the century, and they still are used mostly by professional programmers. But their use is skyrockcting because they are well-supported in Java and C++, because new languages such as PYTHON and RUBY embrace them, and because many people are learning to appreciate the value of using them in client code. By now, you know that learning to use a new language feature is not so different from learning to ride a bicycle or implement `HelloWorld`: it seems completely mysterious until you have done it for the first time, but quickly becomes second nature. Learning to use generics and iterators will be well worth your time.

## Q+A

**Q.** When do I use new with Node?

**A.** Just as with any other class, you should only use new when you want to create a new Node object (a new element in the linked list). You should not use new to create a new reference to an existing Node object. For example, the code

```
Node oldfirst = new Node();
oldfirst = first;
```

creates a new Node object, then immediately loses track of the only reference to it. This code does not result in an error, but it is a bit untidy to create orphans for no reason.

**Q.** Why declare Node as a nested class? Why private?

**A.** By declaring the nested class Node to be private, we restrict access to methods within the enclosing class. *Note for experts*: A nested class that is not static is known as an *inner* class, so technically our Node classes are inner classes, though the ones that are not generic could be static.

**Q.** When I type javac LinkedStackOfStrings.java to run Program 4.3.2 and similar programs, I find a file LinkedStackOfStrings$Node.class in addition to LinkedStackOfStrings.class. What is the purpose of that file?

**A.** That file is for the nested class Node. Java's naming convention is to use $ to separate the name of the outer class from the nested class.

**Q.** Should a client be allowed to insert null items onto a stack or queue?

**A.** This question arises frequently when implementing collections in Java. Our implementation (and Java's stack and queue libraries) do permit the insertion of null values.

**Q.** Are there Java libraries for stacks and queues?

**A.** Yes and no. Java has a built-in library called `java.util.Stack`, but you should avoid using it when you want a stack. It has several additional operations that are not normally associated with a stack, e.g., getting the `i`th element. It also allows adding an element to the bottom of the stack (instead of the top), so it can implement a queue! Although having such extra operations may appear to be a bonus, it is actually a curse. We use data types not because they provide every available operation, but rather because they allow us to precisely specify the operations we need. The prime benefit of doing so is that the system can prevent us from performing operations that we do not actually want. The `java.util.Stack` API is an example of a *wide interface*, which we generally strive to avoid.

**Q.** I want to use an array representation for a generic stack, but code like the following will not compile. What is the problem?

```
private Item[] a = new Item[max];
```

**A.** Good try. Unfortunately, creating arrays of generics is not allowed in Java 1.5. Experts still are vigorously debating this decision. As usual, complaining too loudly about a language feature puts you on the slippery slope toward becoming a language designer. There is a way out, using a cast. You can write:

```
private Item[] a = (Item[]) new Object[max];
```

**Q.** Can I use a foreach loop with arrays?

**A.** Yes (even though arrays do not implement the `Iterator` interface). The following one-liner prints out the command-line arguments:

```
public static void main(String[] args)
{  for (String s : args) StdOut.println(s);  }
```

**Q.** Why not have a single `Collection` data type that implements methods to add items, remove the most recently inserted, remove the least recently inserted, remove random, iterate, return the number of items in the collection, and whatever other operations we might desire? Then we could get them all implemented in a single class that could be used by many clients.

**A.** This is an example of a *wide interface*, which, as we pointed out in Section 3.3, are to be avoided. One reason to avoid wide interfaces is that it is difficult to construct implementations that are efficient for *all* operations. A more important reason is that narrow interfaces enforce a certain discipline on your programs, which makes client code much easier to understand. If one client uses `Stack<String>` and another uses `Queue<Customer>`, we have a good idea that the LIFO discipline is important to the first and the FIFO discipline is important to the second. Another approach is to use inheritance to try to encapsulate operations that are common to all collections. However, such implementations are for experts, whereas any programmer can learn to build generic implementations such as `Stack` and `Queue`.

## *Exercises*

**4.3.1**  Add a method `isFull()` to `ArrayStackOfStrings` (PROGRAM 4.3.1)

**4.3.2**  Give the output printed by `java ArrayStackOfStrings 5` for the input:

    it was - the best - of times - - - it was - the - -

**4.3.3**  Suppose that a client performs an intermixed sequence of (stack) *push* and *pop* operations. The push operations put the integers 0 through 9 in order on to the stack; the pop operations print out the return value. Which of the following sequence(s) could *not* occur?

    *a.* 4 3 2 1 0 9 8 7 6 5
    *b.* 4 6 8 7 5 3 2 9 0 1
    *c.* 2 5 6 7 4 8 9 3 1 0
    *d.* 4 3 2 1 0 5 6 7 8 9
    *e.* 1 2 3 4 5 6 9 8 7 0
    *f.* 0 4 6 5 3 8 1 7 2 9
    *g.* 1 4 7 9 8 6 5 3 0 2
    *h.* 2 1 4 3 6 5 8 7 9 0

**4.3.4**  Write a stack client `Reverse` that reads in strings from standard input and prints them in reverse order.

**4.3.5**  Assume that standard input has some unknown number $N$ of `double` values. Write a method that reads all the values and returns an array of length $N$ containing them, in the order they appear on standard input.

**4.3.6**  Write a stack client `Parentheses` that reads in a text stream from standard input and uses a stack to determine whether its parentheses are properly balanced. For example, your program should print `true` for `[()]{}{[()()]()}` and `false` for `[(])`. *Hint*: Use a stack.

**4.3.7**  What does the following code fragment print when N is 50? Give a high-level description of what the code fragment in the previous exercise does when presented with a positive integer N.

```
Stack<Integer> stack = new Stack<Integer>();
while (N > 0)
{
   stack.push(N % 2);
   N = N / 2;
}
while (!stack.isEmpty())
   StdOut.print(stack.pop());
StdOut.println();
```

*Answer*: Prints the binary representation of N (110010 when N is 50).

**4.3.8** What does the following code fragment do to the queue q?

```
Stack<String> stack = new Stack<String>();
while (!q.isEmpty())
   stack.push(q.dequeue());
while (!stack.isEmpty())
   q.enqueue(stack.pop());
```

**4.3.9** Add a method peek() to Stack (PROGRAM 4.3.4) that returns the most recently inserted element on the stack (without popping it).

**4.3.10** Give the contents and size of the array for DoublingStackOfStrings with the input:

```
it was - the best - of times - - - it was - the - -
```

**4.3.11** Add a method length() to Queue (PROGRAM 4.3.6) that returns the number of elements on the queue. *Hint*: Make sure that your method takes constant time by maintaining an instance variable N that you initialize to 0, increment in enqueue(), decrement in dequeue(), and return in length().

**4.3.12** Draw a memory usage diagram in the style of the diagrams in SECTION 4.1 for the three-node example used to introduce linked lists in this section.

**4.3.13** Write a program that takes from standard input an expression without left parentheses and prints the equivalent infix expression with the parentheses inserted. For example, given the input:

```
1 + 2 ) * 3 - 4 ) * 5 - 6 ) ) )
```

your program should print

```
( ( 1 + 2 ) * ( ( 3 - 4 ) * ( 5 - 6 ) )
```

**4.3.14** Write a filter `InfixToPostfix` that converts an arithmetic expression from infix to prefix.

**4.3.15** Write a program `EvaluatePostfix` that takes a postfix expression from standard input, evaluates it, and prints the value. (Piping the output of your program from the previous exercise to this program gives equivalent behavior to `Evaluate`, in PROGRAM 4.3.5).

**4.3.16** Suppose that a client performs an intermixed sequence of (queue) *enqueue* and *dequeue* operations. The enqueue operations put the integers 0 through 9 in order on to the queue; the dequeue operations print out the return value. Which of the following sequence(s) could *not* occur?

*a.* 0 1 2 3 4 5 6 7 8 9

*b.* 4 6 8 7 5 3 2 9 0 1

*c.* 2 5 6 7 4 8 9 3 1 0

*d.* 4 3 2 1 0 5 6 7 8 9

**4.3.17** Write an iterable `Stack` *client* that has a static method `copy()` that takes a stack of strings as argument and returns a copy of the stack. *Note*: This ability is a prime example of the value of having an iterator, because it allows development of such functionality without changing the basic API. See EXERCISE 4.3.47 for a better interface.

**4.3.18** Develop a class DoublingQueueOfStrings that implements the queue abstraction with a fixed-size array, and then extend your implementation to use array doubling to remove the size restriction.

**4.3.19** Write a Queue client that takes a command-line argument k prints the kth from the last string found on standard input.

**4.3.20** (For the mathematically inclined.) Prove that the array in DoublingStackOfStrings is never less than one-quarter full. Then prove that, for any DoublingStackOfStrings client, the total cost of all of the stack operations divided by the number of operations is a constant.

**4.3.21** Modify MD1Queue to make a program MM1Queue that simulates a queue for which both arrival and service are Poisson processes. Verify Little's law for this model.

**4.3.22** Develop a class StackOfInts that uses a linked-list representation (but no generics). Write a client that compares the performance of your implementation with Stack<Integer> to determine the performance penalty from autoboxing on your system.

## Linked List Exercises

*This list of exercises is intended to give you experience in working with linked lists. The easiest way to work them is to make drawings using the visual representation described in the text.*

**4.3.23** Write a method `delete()` that takes an `int` argument k and deletes the kth element in a linked list, if it exists.

**4.3.24** Write a method `find()` that takes a linked list and a string key as arguments and returns `true` if some node in the list has key as its item field, `false` otherwise.

**4.3.25** Suppose x is a linked-list node. What is the effect of the following code fragment?

```
x.next = x.next.next;
```

*Answer*: Deletes from the list the node immediately following x.

**4.3.26** Suppose that x is a linked list node. What does the following code fragment do?

```
t.next = x.next;
x.next = t;
```

*Answer*: Inserts node t immediately after node x.

**4.3.27** Why does the following code fragment not do the same thing as in the previous question?

```
x.next = t;
t.next = x.next;
```

*Answer*: When it comes time to update `t.next`, `x.next` is no longer the original node following x, but is instead t itself!

**4.3.28** Write a method `removeAfter()` that takes a linked-list `Node` as argument and removes the node following the given one (and does nothing if the argument or the next field in the argument node is null).

**4.3.29** Write a method `insertAfter()` that takes two linked-list `Node` arguments and inserts the second after the first on its list (and does nothing if either argument is null).

**4.3.30** Write a method `remove()` that takes a linked list and a string `key` as arguments and removes all of the nodes in the list that have `key` as its item field.

**4.3.31** Write a method `max()` that takes a reference to the first node in a linked list as argument and returns the value of the maximum key in the list. Assume that all keys are positive integers, and return 0 if the list is empty.

**4.3.32** Develop a recursive solution to the previous question.

**4.3.33** Write a recursive method to print the elements of a linked list in reverse order. Do not modify any of the links. *Easy*: Use quadratic time, constant extra space. *Also easy*: Use linear time, linear extra space. *Not so easy*: Develop a divide-and-conquer algorithm that uses linearithmic time and logarithmic extra space.

**4.3.34** Write a recursive method to randomly shuffle the elements of a linked list by modifying the links. *Easy*: Use quadratic time, constant extra space. *Not so easy*:: Develop a divide-and-conquer algorithm that uses linearithmic time and logarithmic extra space.

## *Creative Exercises*

**4.3.35** *Deque.* A double-ended queue or *deque* (pronounced deck) is a combination of a stack and and a queue. It stores a collection of items and supports the following API:

public class Deque<Item>
_____

|  |  |  |
|---|---|---|
|  | Deque() | *create an empty deque* |
| boolean | isEmpty() | *is the deque empty?* |
| void | enqueue(Item item) | *add an item to the end* |
| void | push(Item item) | *add an item to the beginning* |
| Item | pop() | *remove an item from the beginning* |
| Item | dequeue() | *remove an item from the end* |

*API for a generic double-ended queue*

Write a class Deque that uses a linked list to implement this API.

**4.3.36** *Random queue.* A *random queue* stores a collection of items and supports the following API:

public class RandomQueue<Item>
_____

|  |  |  |
|---|---|---|
|  | RandomQueue() | *create an empty random queue* |
| boolean | isEmpty() | *is the queue empty?* |
| void | enqueue(Item item) | *add an item* |
| Item | dequeue() | *remove and return a random item (sample without replacement)* |
| Item | sample() | *return a random item, but do not remove (sample with replacement)* |

*API for a generic random queue*

Write a class RandomQueue that implements this API. *Hint*: Use an array representation (with doubling). To remove an item, swap one at a random position (indexed 0 through N-1) with the one at the last position (index N-1). Then delete and return the last object, as in `DoublingStack`. Write a client that prints a deck of cards in random order using `RandomQueue<Card>`.

**4.3.37** *Random iterator.* Write an iterator for `RandomQueue<Item>` from the previous exercise that returns the items in random order. *Note*: This exercise is more difficult than it looks.

**4.3.38** *Josephus problem.* In the Josephus problem from antiquity, $N$ people are in dire straits and agree to the following strategy to reduce the population. They arrange themselves in a circle (at positions numbered from 0 to $N-1$) and proceed around the circle, eliminating every $M$th person until only one person is left. Legend has it that Josephus figured out where to sit to avoid being eliminated. Write a `Queue` client `Josephus` that takes $N$ and $M$ from the command line and prints out the order in which people are eliminated (and thus would show Josephus where to sit in the circle).

```
% java Josephus 7 2
1 3 5 0 4 2 6
```

**4.3.39** *Delete ith element.* Implement a class that supports the following API:

```
public class GeneralizedQueue<Item>
```

|        | GeneralizedQueue()   | *create an empty queue*                                      |
|-------:|----------------------|-------------------------------------------------------------|
| boolean | isEmpty()           | *is the queue empty?*                                        |
|   void | insert(Item item)    | *add an item*                                                |
|   Item | delete(int i)        | *delete and return the $i$th least recently inserted item*  |

*API for a generic generalized queue*

First, develop an implementation that uses an array implementation, and then develop one that uses a linked-list implementation. (See Exercise 4.4.48 for a more efficient implementation that uses a BST.)

**4.3.40** *Ring buffer.* A ring buffer, or circular queue, is a FIFO data structure of a fixed size $N$. It is useful for transferring data between asynchronous processes or for storing log files. When the buffer is empty, the consumer waits until data is deposited; when the buffer is full, the producer waits to deposit data. Develop an API for a ring buffer and an implementation that uses an array representation (with circular wrap-around).

**4.3.41** *Merging two sorted queues.* Given two queues with strings in ascending order, move all of the strings to a third queue so that the third queue ends up with the strings in ascending order.

**4.3.42** *Nonrecursive mergesort.* Given $N$ strings, create $N$ queues, each containing one of the strings. Create a queue of the $N$ queues. Then, repeatedly apply the sorted merging operation to the first two queues and reinsert the merged queue at the end. Repeat until the queue of queues contains only one queue.

**4.3.43** *Queue with two stacks.* Show how to implement a queue using two stacks. *Hint*: If you push elements onto a stack and then pop them all, they appear in reverse order. Repeating the process puts them back in FIFO order.

**4.3.44** *Move-to-front.* Read in a sequence of characters from standard input and maintain the characters in a linked list with no duplicates. When you read in a previously unseen character, insert it at the front of the list. When you read in a duplicate character, delete it from the list and reinsert it at the beginning. Name your program MoveToFront: it implements the well-know *move-to-front* strategy, which is useful for caching, data compression, and many other applications where items that have been recently accessed are more likely to be reaccessed.

**4.3.45** *Topological sort.* You have to sequence the order of N jobs that are numbered from 0 to N-1 on a server. Some of the jobs must complete before others can begin. Write a program TopologicalSorter that takes N as a command-line argument and a sequence on standard input of ordered pairs of jobs i j, and then prints a sequence of integers such that for each pair i j in the input, job i appears before job j. Use the following algorithm: First, from the input, build, for each job, (*i*) a queue of the jobs that must follow it and (*ii*) its *indegree* (the number of jobs that must come before it). Then, build a queue of all nodes whose indegree is 0 and repeatedly delete some job with zero indegree, maintaining all the data structures. This process has many applications: for example, you can use it to model course prerequisites for your major so that you can find a sequence of courses to take in order to graduate.

**4.3.46** *Text editor buffer.* Develop a data type for a buffer in a text editor that implements the following API:

```
public class Buffer
```
---
|        | Buffer()        | *create an empty buffer* |
|-------:|-----------------|--------------------------|
|   void | insert(char c)  | *insert c at the cursor position* |
|   char | delete()        | *delete and return the character at the cursor* |
|   void | left(int k)     | *move the cursor k positions to the left* |
|   void | right(int k)    | *move the cursor k positions to the right* |
|    int | size()          | *number of characters in the buffer* |

*API for a text buffer*

*Hint*: Use two stacks.

**4.3.47** *Copy a stack.* Create a new constructor for the linked list implementation of Stack so that

```
Stack<Item> t = new Stack<Item>(s);
```

makes t a reference to a new and independent copy of the stack s. You should be able to push and pop from either s or t without influencing the other.

**4.3.48** *Copy a queue.* Create a new constructor so that

```
Queue<Item> r = new Queue<Item>(q);
```

makes r a reference to a new and independent copy of the queue q. *Hint*: Delete all of the elements from q and add these elements to both q and r.

**4.3.49** *Reverse a linked list.* Write a function that takes the first Node in a linked list as argument and reverses the list, returning the first Node in the result.

*Iterative solution*: To accomplish this task, we maintain references to three consecutive nodes in the linked list, reverse, first, and second. At each iteration, we extract the node first from the original linked list and insert it at the beginning of the reversed list. We maintain the invariant that first is the first node of what's left of the original list, second is the second node of what's left of the original list, and reverse is the first node of the resulting reversed list.

```
public Node reverse(Node list)
{
   Node first   = list;
   Node reverse = null;
   while (first != null) {
       Node second = first.next;
       first.next  = reverse;
       reverse     = first;
       first       = second;
   }

   return reverse;
}
```

When writing code involving linked lists, we must always be careful to properly handle the exceptional cases (when the linked list is empty, when the list has only one or two nodes) and the boundary cases (dealing with the first or last items). This is usually much trickier than handling the normal cases.

*Recursive solution*: Assuming the linked list has $N$ elements, we recursively reverse the last $N-1$ elements, and then carefully append the first element to the end.

```
public Node reverse(Node first)
{
    Node second = first.next;
    Node rest = reverse(second);
    second.next = first;
    first.next  = null;
    return rest;
}
```

**4.3.50** *Queue simulations.* Study what happens when you modify MD1Queue to use a stack instead of a queue. Does Little's law hold? Answer the same question for a random queue. Plot histograms and compare the standard deviations of the waiting times.

**4.3.51** *More queue simulations.* Instrument LoadBalance to print the average queue length and the maximum queue length instead of plotting the histogram, and use it to run simulations for 1 million items on 100,000 queues. Print the average value of the maximum queue length for 100 trials each with sample sizes 1, 2, 3, and 4. Do your experiments validate the conclusion drawn in the text about using a sample of size 2?

**4.3.52** *Listing files.* A folder is a list of files and folders. Write a program that takes the name of a folder as a command-line argument and prints out all of the files contained in that folder, with the contents of each folder recursively listed (indented) under that folder's name. *Hint*: Use a queue, and see java.io.File.

# 4.4    Symbol Tables

A SYMBOL TABLE IS A DATA type that we use to associate *values* with *keys*. Clients can store (*put*) an entry into the symbol table by specifying a key-value pair and then can retrieve (*get*) the value correspond-ing to a particular key from the symbol table. For example, a university might associate information such as a student's name, home address, and grades (the value) with that student's social security number (the key), so that each student's record can be accessed by specifying a So-

cial Security number. The same approach might be appropriate for a scientist who needs to organize data, a business that needs to keep track of customer transac-tions, an internet search engine that has to associate keywords with web pages, or in countless other ways.

Because of their fundamental importance, symbol tables have been heavily used and studied since the early days of computing. The development of imple-mentations that guarantee good performance continues to be an active area of re-search interest. Several other operations on symbol tables beyond the characteristic *put* and *get* operations naturally arise, and guaranteeing good performance for a given set of operations can be quite challenging.

In this chapter we consider a basic API for the symbol-table data type and a classic implementation of that API. Our API adds to the *put* and *get* operations the abilities to test whether any value has been associated with a given key (*contains*) and to *iterate* through the keys in the table in order.

The implementation that we consider is based on a data structure known as the *binary search tree (BST)*. It is a remarkably simple solution that performs well in many practical situations and also serves as the basis for the industrial-strength symbol-table implementations that are found in modern programming environ-ments. The BST code that we consider for symbol tables is only slightly more com-plicated than the linked-list code that we considered for stacks and queues, but it will introduce you to a new dimension in structuring data that has far-reaching impact.

**API**   A *symbol table* is a collection of key-value pairs. We use a generic type `Key` for keys and a generic type `Value` for values—every symbol-table entry associates a `Value` with a `Key`. In most applications, the keys have some natural ordering, so (as we did with sorting) we require the key type `Key` to implement Java's `Comparable` interface. These assumptions lead to the following basic API:

---

`public class *ST<Key extends Comparable<Key>, Value>`

---

| | | |
|---|---|---|
| | `*ST()` | *create a symbol table* |
| `void` | `put(Key key, Value v)` | *put* key-value *pair into the table* |
| `Value` | `get(Key key)` | *return value paired with* key, `null` *if* key *not in table* |
| `boolean` | `contains(Key key)` | *is there a value paired with* key? |

*Note*: *Implementations should also implement the* `Iterable<Key>` *interface to enable clients to access keys in sorted order with foreach loops.*

*API for a generic symbol table*

As usual, the asterisk is a placeholder to indicate that multiple implementations might be considered. In this section, we provide one basic implementation BST (we describe some elementary implementations briefly in the text and some other implementations in the exercises). This API reflects several design decisions, which we now enumerate.

*Comparable keys.*   As you will see, we take advantage of key ordering to develop efficient implementations of *put* and *get*. An even more basic symbol-table API, suitable for some applications, might omit `extends Comparable`. Since keys in most applications are numbers or strings, this requirement is generally not restrictive.

*Immutable keys.*   We assume the keys do not change their value while in the symbol table. The simplest and most commonly used types of keys, `String` and built-in wrapper types such as `Integer` and `Double`, are immutable.

*Replace-the-old-value policy.*   If a key-value pair is inserted into the symbol table that already associates another value with the given key, we adopt the convention that the new value replaces the old one (just as with an array assignment statement). The `contains()` method gives the client the flexibility to avoid doing so, if desired.

*Not found.* The method `get()` returns `null` if no entry with the given key has previously been *put* into the table. This choice has two implications, discussed next.

*Null keys and values.* Clients are not permitted to use `null` as a key or value. This convention enables us to implement `contains()` as follows:

```
public boolean contains(Key key)
{   return get(key) != null;   }
```

*Remove.* We do not include a method for removing keys from the symbol table. Many applications do require such a method, but we leave implementations as an exercise (see EXERCISE 4.4.13) or for a more advanced course in data structures in algorithms.

*Iterable.* As indicated in the note in the API, we assume that the data type implements the `Iterable` interface to provide an appropriate iterator that allows clients to visit the contents of the table. Since keys are `Comparable`, the natural order of iteration is in order of the keys. Accordingly, we will implement `Iterable<Key>` and clients can use *get* to get values associated with keys if desired.

*Variations.* Computer scientists have identified numerous other useful operations on symbol tables, and APIs based on various subsets of them have been widely studied. We consider several of these operations at the end of this section.

Symbol tables are among the most widely studied data structures in computer science, so the impact of these and many alternative design decisions has been carefully studied, as you will learn if you take later courses in computer science. In this chapter, our approach is to introduce you to the most important properties of symbol tables by considering two prototypical client programs, developing an efficient implementation, and studying the performance characteristics of that implementation, to show you that it can meet the needs of typical clients, even when the tables are huge.

**Symbol table clients**    Once you gain some experience with the idea, you will find that symbol tables are broadly useful. To convince you of this fact, we start with two prototypical examples, each of which arises in a large number of important and familiar practical applications.

*Dictionary lookup.*  The most basic kind of symbol-table client builds a symbol table with successive *put* operations in order to support *get* requests. We maintain a collection of data so that we can quickly access the data we need. Most applications also take advantage of the idea that a symbol table is a *dynamic* dictionary, where it is easy to look up information *and* to update the information in the table. The following list of familiar examples illustrates the utility of this approach.

- *Phone book.* When keys are people's names and values are their phone numbers, a symbol table models a phone book. A very significant difference from a printed phone book is that we can add new names or change existing phone numbers. We could also use the phone number as the key and the name as the value. If you have never done so, try typing your phone number (with area code) into the search field in your browser.

- *Dictionary.* Associating a word with its definition is a familiar concept that gives us the name "dictionary." For centuries people kept printed dictionaries in their homes and offices in order to check the definitions and spellings (values) of words (keys). Now, because of good symbol-table implementations, people expect built-in spell checkers and immediate access to word definitions on their computers.

- *Account information.* People who own stock now regularly check the current price on the web. Several services on the web associate a ticker symbol (key) with the current price (value), usually along with a great deal of other information. Commercial applications of this sort abound, including financial institutions associating account information with a name or account number or educational institutions associating grades with a student name or identification number.

- *Genomics.* Symbols play a central role in modern genomics, as we have already seen (see PROGRAM 3.1.8). The simplest example is the use of the letters A, C, T, and G to represent the nucleotides found in the DNA of living organisms. The next simplest is the correspondence between codons (nucleotide triplets) and amino acids (TTA corresponds to leucine, TCT to cycstine, and so forth), then the correspondence between sequences of amino acids and proteins, and so forth. Researchers in genomics routinely use various types of symbol tables to organize this knowledge.

- *Experimental data.* From astrophysics to zoology, modern scientists are awash in experimental data, and organizing and efficiently accessing this data is vital to understanding what it means. Symbol tables are a critical starting point, and advanced data structures and algorithms that are based on symbol tables are now an important part of scientific research.
- *Programming languages.* One of the earliest uses of symbol tables was to organize information for programming. At first, programs were simply sequences of numbers, but programmers very quickly found that using symbolic names for operations and memory locations (variable names) was far more convenient. Associating the names with the numbers requires a symbol table. As the size of programs grew, the cost of the symbol-table operations became a bottleneck in program development time, which led to the development of data structures and algorithms like the one we consider in this section.

|  | key | value |
|---|---|---|
| *phone book* | name | phone number |
| *dictionary* | word | definition |
| *account* | account number | balance |
| *genomics* | codon | amino acid |
| *data* | data/time | results |
| *Java compiler* | variable name | memory location |
| *file share* | song name | machine |
| *internet DNS* | website | IP address |

*Typical dictionary applications*

- *Files.* We use symbol tables regularly to organize data on computer systems. Perhaps the most prominent example is the *file system*, where we associate a file name (key) with the location of its contents (value). Your music player uses the same system to associate song titles (keys) with the location of the music itself (value).
- *Internet DNS.* The domain name system (DNS) that is the basis for organizing information on the internet associates URLs (keys) that humans understand (such as `www.princeton.edu` or `www.wikipedia.org`) with IP addresses (values) that computer network routers understand (such as `208.216.181.15` or `207.142.131.206`). This system is the next-generation "phone book." Thus, humans can use names that are easy to remember and machines can efficiently process the numbers. The number of symbol-table lookups done each second for this purpose on internet routers around the

world is huge, so performance is of obvious importance. Millions of new computers and other devices are put onto the internet each year, so these symbol tables on internet routers need to be dynamic.

Despite its scope, this list is still just a representative sample, intended to give you a flavor of the scope of applicability of the symbol-table abstraction. Whenever you specify something by name, there is a symbol table at work. Your computer's file system or the web might do the work for you, but there is still a symbol table there somewhere.

For example, to build a table associating codons with amino acid names, we can write code like this:

```
ST<String, String> amino;
amino = new ST<String, String>();
amino.put("TTA", "leucine");
...
```

The idea of associating information with a key is so fundamental that many high-level languages have a built-in support for *associative arrays*, where you can use standard array syntax but with keys inside the brackets instead of an integer index. In such a language, you could write `amino["TTA"] = "leucine"` instead of `amino.put("TTA", "leucine")`. Although Java does not (yet) support such syntax, thinking in terms of associative arrays is a good way to understand the basic purpose of symbol tables.

Lookup (PROGRAM 4.4.1) builds a set of key-value pairs from a file of comma-separated values (see SECTION 3.1) as specified on the command line and then prints out values corresponding to keys read from standard input. The command-line arguments are the file name and two integers, one specifying the field to serve as the key and the other specifying the field to

```
% more amino.csv
TTT,Phe,F,Phenylalanine
TTC,Phe,F,Phenylalanine
TTA,Leu,L,Leucine
TTG,Leu,L,Leucine
TCT,Ser,S,Serine
TCC,Ser,S,Serine
TCA,Ser,S,Serine
TCG,Ser,S,Serine
TAT,Tyr,Y,Tyrosine
TAC,Tyr,Y,Tyrosine
TAA,Stop,Stop,Stop
...
GCA,Ala,A,Alanine
GCG,Ala,A,Alanine
GAT,Asp,D,Aspartic Acid
GAC,Asp,D,Aspartic Acid
GAA,Gly,G,Glutamic Acid
GAG,Gly,G,Glutamic Acid
GGT,Gly,G,Glycine
GGC,Gly,G,Glycine
GGA,Gly,G,Glycine
GGG,Gly,G,Glycine

% more DJIA.csv
...
20-Oct-87,1738.74,608099968,1841.01
19-Oct-87,2164.16,604300032,1738.74
16-Oct-87,2355.09,338500000,2246.73
15-Oct-87,2412.70,263200000,2355.09
...
30-Oct-29,230.98,10730000,258.47
29-Oct-29,252.38,16410000,230.07
28-Oct-29,295.18,9210000,260.64
25-Oct-29,299.47,5920000,301.22
...

% more ip.csv
...
www.ebay.com,66.135.192.87
www.princeton.edu,128.112.128.15
www.cs.princeton.edu,128.112.136.35
www.harvard.edu,128.103.60.24
www.yale.edu,130.132.51.8
www.cnn.com,64.236.16.20
www.google.com,216.239.41.99
www.nytimes.com,199.239.136.200
www.apple.com,17.112.152.32
www.slashdot.org,66.35.250.151
www.espn.com,199.181.135.201
www.weather.com,63.111.66.11
www.yahoo.com,216.109.118.65
...
```

*Typical comma-separated-value (CSV) files*

*Program 4.4.1    Dictionary lookup*

```java
public class Lookup
{
   public static void main(String[] args)
   { // Build dictionary, provide values for keys in StdIn.
      In in = new In(args[0]);
      int keyField = Integer.parseInt(args[1]);
      int valField = Integer.parseInt(args[2]);

      String[] database = in.readAll().split("\n");
      StdRandom.shuffle(database);

      BST<String, String> st = new BST<String, String>();
      for (int i = 0; i < database.length; i++)
      { // Extract key, value from one line and add to ST.
         String[] tokens = database[i].split(",");
         String key = tokens[keyField];
         String val = tokens[valField];
         st.put(key, val);
      }

      while (!StdIn.isEmpty())
      { // Read key and provide value.
         String s = StdIn.readString();
         if (st.contains(s))
              StdOut.println(st.get(s));
         else StdOut.println("Not found");
      }
   }
}
```

| | |
|---|---|
| in | *input stream (.csv)* |
| keyField | *key position* |
| valField | *value position* |
| database[] | *lines in input* |
| st | *symbol table (BST)* |
| tokens | *values on a line* |
| key | *key* |
| val | *value* |
| s | *query* |

*This data-driven symbol table client reads key-value pairs from a comma-separated file, then prints out values corresponding to keys on standard input. Both keys and values are strings.*

```
% java Lookup amino.csv 0 3
TTA
Leucine
ABC
Not found
TCT
Serine

% java Lookup amino.csv 3 0
Glycine
GGG
```

```
% java Lookup ip.csv 0 1
www.google.com
216.239.41.99

% java Lookup ip.csv 1 0
216.239.41.99
www.google.com

% java Lookup DJIA.csv 0 1
29-Oct-29
252.38
```

serve as the value. Examples of similar but slightly more sophisticated test clients are described in the exercises. For instance, we could make the dictionary dynamic by also allowing standard-input commands to change the value associated with a key (see EXERCISE 4.4.1).

Your first step in understanding symbol tables is to download Lookup.java and BST.java (the symbol-table implementation that we consider next) from the booksite to do some symbol-table searches. You can find numerous comma-separated-value (.csv) files that are related to various applications that we have described, including amino.csv (codon-to-amino-acid encodings), DJIA.csv (opening price, volume, and closing price of the stock market average, for every day in its history), and ip.csv (a selection of entries from the DNS database). When choosing which field to use as the key, remember that *each key must uniquely determine a value*. If there are multiple *put* operations to associate values with a key, the table will remember only the most recent one (think about associative arrays). We will consider next the case where we want to associate multiple values with a key.

Later in this chapter, we will see that the cost of the *put* operations and the *get* requests in Lookup is logarithmic in the size of the table. This fact implies that you may experience a small delay getting the answer to your first request (for all the *put* operations to build the table), but you get immediate response for all the others.

*Indexing.* Index (PROGRAM 4.4.2) is a prototypical example of a symbol-table client that uses an intermixed sequence of calls to get() and put(): it reads in a list of strings from standard input and prints a sorted table of all the different strings along with a list of integers specifying the positions where each string appeared in the input. We have a large amount of data and want to know where certain strings of interest occur. In this case, we seem to be associating multiple values with each key, but we actually associating just one: a queue. Again, this approach is familiar:

- *Book index.* Every textbook has an index where you look up a word and get the page numbers containing that word. While no reader wants to see every word in the book in an index, a program like Index can provide a starting point for creating a good index.
- *Programming languages.* In a large program that uses a large number of symbols, it is useful to know where each name is used. A program like Index can be a valuable tool to help programmers keep track of where symbols are used in their programs. Historically, an explicit printed symbol table was one of the most important tools used by programmers to manage large

programs. In modern systems, symbol tables are the basis of software tools that programmers use to manage names of modules in systems.

- *Genomics.* In a typical (if oversimplified) scenario in genomics research, a scientist wants to know the positions of a given genetic sequence in an existing genome or set of genomes. Existence or proximity of certain sequences may be of scientific significance. The starting point for such research is an index like the one produced by Index, modified to take into account the fact that genomes are not separated into words.
- *Web search.* When you type a keyword and get a list of websites containing that keyword, you are using an index created by your web search engine. There is one value (the list of pages) associated with each key (the query), although the reality is a bit more dynamic and complicated because we often specify multiple keys and the pages are spread through the web, not kept in a table on a single computer.
- *Account information.* One way for a company that maintains customer accounts to keep track of a day's transactions is to keep an index of the list of the transactions. The key is the account number; the value is the list of occurrences of that account number in the transaction list.

| | key | value |
|---|---|---|
| *book* | term | page numbers |
| *genomics* | DNA substring | locations |
| *web search* | keyword | websites |
| *business* | customer name | transactions |

*Typical indexing applications*

Index (PROGRAM 4.4.2) takes three command-line arguments: a file name and two integers. The first integer is the minimum string length to include in the symbol table, and the second is the minimum number of occurrences (among the words that appear in the text) to include in the printed index. Again, several similar clients for various useful tasks are discussed in the exercises. For example, one common scenario is to build multiple indices on the same data, using different keys. In our account example, one index might use customer account numbers for keys and another might use vendor account numbers.

As with Lookup, you are certainly encouraged to download Index from the booksite and run it on various input files to gain further appreciation for the utility of symbol tables. If you do so, you will find that it can build large indices for huge files with little delay, because each *put* operation and *get* request is taken care of immediately. Providing this immediate response for huge dynamic tables is one of the classic contributions of algorithmic technology.

## Program 4.4.2    *Indexing*

```
public class Index
{
   public static void main(String[] args)
   {
      int minlen = Integer.parseInt(args[0]);
      int minocc = Integer.parseInt(args[1]);

      String[] words = StdIn.readAll().split("\\s+");

      BST<String, Queue<Integer>> st;
      st = new BST<String, Queue<Integer>>();

      for (int i = 0; i < words.length; i++)
      {  // Add word position to data structure.
         String s = words[i];
         if (s.length() < minlen) continue;
         if (!st.contains(s))
            st.put(s, new Queue<Integer>());
         Queue<Integer> q = st.get(s);
         q.enqueue(i);
      }

      for (String s : st)
      {  // Print words whose occurrence count exceeds threshold.
         Queue<Integer> q = st.get(s);
         if (q.length() >= minocc)
            StdOut.println(s + ": " + q);
      }
   }
}
```

| minlen | minimum length |
|---|---|
| minocc | occurence threshold |
| words[] | words in StdIn |
| st | symbol table |
| s | current word |
| q | queue of positions for current word |

*This symbol table client indexes a text file by word position. Keys are words, and values are queues of positions where the word occurs in the file.*

```
% java Index 9 30 < TaleOfTwoCities.txt
confidence: 2794 23064 25031 34249 47907 48268 48577 ...
courtyard: 11885 12062 17303 17451 32404 32522 38663 ...
evremonde: 86211 90791 90798 90802 90814 90822 90856 ...
expression: 3777 5575 6574 7116 7195 8509 8928 15015 ...
gentleman: 2521 5290 5337 5698 6235 6301 6326 6338 ...
influence: 27809 36881 43141 43150 48308 54049 54067 ...
monseigneur: 85 90 36587 36590 36611 36636 36643 ...
prisoners: 1012 20729 20770 21240 22123 22209 22590 ...
something: 3406 3765 9283 13234 13239 15245 20257 ...
sometimes: 4514 4530 4548 6082 20731 33883 34239 ...
vengeance: 56041 63943 67705 79351 79941 79945 80225 ...
```

**Symbol table implementations**   All of these examples are certainly persuasive evidence of the importance of symbol tables. Symbol-table implementations have been heavily studied, many different algorithms and data structures have been invented for this purpose, and modern programming environments (including Java) have several different symbol-table implementations. You are going to learn a remarkably simple one that serves as the basis for many others. As usual, knowing how a basic implementation works will help you appreciate, choose among, and more effectively use the advanced ones, or help implement your own version for some specialized situation that you might encounter.

*put CAT into the array*

*larger keys all have to move*

*Put into a sorted array takes linear time*

One reason for the proliferation of algorithms and implementations is that the needs of symbol-table clients can vary widely. On the one hand, when the symbol table or the number of operations to be performed is small, any implementation will do. On the other hand, symbol tables for some applications are so huge that they are organized as databases that reside on external storage or the web. In this section, we focus on the huge class of clients like `Index` and `Lookup` whose needs fall between these extremes, where we need to be able to use *put* operations to build and maintain large tables dynamically while also responding immediately to a large number of *get* requests.

We already considered the idea of a dictionary when we considered binary search in Section 4.2. It is not difficult to build a symbol-table implementation that is based on binary search (see Exercise 4.4.5) but such an implementation is not feasible for use with a client like `Index`, because it depends on maintaining an array sorted in order of the keys. Each time a new key is added, larger keys have to be shifted one position higher in the array, which implies that the total time required to build the table is quadratic in the size of the table. Alternatively, we might consider basing an implementation on an unordered linked list. But such an implementation is also not feasible for use with a client like `Lookup` or `Index`, because the only way to search for a key in a list is to traverse its links, so the total time required for searches is the product of the number of searches and the size of

*Get in a linked list takes linear time*

the table, which again is prohibitive. Implementing *put* is also slow because we have to search first to avoid putting duplicate keys in the symbol table. Even keeping the list in sorted order does not help much—for example, traversing all the links is still required to add a new node to the end of the list.

To implement a symbol-table that is feasible for use with clients such as Look-up and Index, we need the flexibility of linked lists and the efficiency of binary search. Next, we consider a data structure that provides this combination.

**Binary search trees**    The *binary tree* is a mathematical abstraction that plays a central role in the efficient organization of information. Like arrays and linked lists, a binary tree is a data type that stores a collection of data. Binary trees play an important role in computer programming because they strike an efficient balance between flexibility and ease of implementation.

For symbol-table implementations, we use a special type of binary tree to organize the data and to provide a basis for efficient implementations of the symbol-table *put* operations and *get* requests. A *binary search tree (BST)* associates comparable keys with values, in a structure defined recursively. A BST is one of the following:

- Empty (null)
- A node having a key-value pair and two references to BSTs, a *left* BST with smaller keys and a *right* BST with larger keys

The key type must implement Comparable, but the type of the value is not specified, so a BST node can hold any kind of data in addition to the (characteristic) references to BSTs. As with our linked-list definition in SECTION 4.3, the idea of a recursive data structure can be a bit mind bending, but all we are doing is adding a second link (and imposing an ordering restriction) to our linked-list definition.

To implement BSTs, we start with a class for the *node* abstraction, which has references to a key, a value, and left and right BST:

```
class Node
{
    Key key;
    Value val;
    Node left, right;
}
```

This definition is like our definition of nodes for linked lists, except that it has *two* links, not just one. From the recursive definition of BSTs, we can represent a BST with a variable of type Node by ensuring that its value is either null or a reference to a Node whose left and right fields are references to BSTs, and by ensuring that the ordering condition is satisfied (keys in the left BST are smaller than key and keys in the right BST are larger than key). To (slightly) simplify the code, we add a constructor to Node that initializes key and val:

*Binary search tree*

```
Node(Key key, Value val)
{
    this.key = key;
    this.val = val;
}
```

The result of new Node(key, val) is a reference to a Node object (which we can assign to any variable of type Node) whose key and val instance variables are set to the given values and whose left and right instance variables are both initialized to null.

As with linked lists, when tracing code that uses BSTs, we can use a visual representation of the changes:

• We draw a rectangle to represent each object.
• We put the values of instance variables within the rectangle.
• We depict references as arrows that point to the referenced object.

Most often, we use an even simpler abstract representation where we draw rectangles containing keys to represent nodes (suppressing the values) and connect the nodes with arrows that represent links. This abstract representation allows us to focus on the structure.

For example, suppose that `Key` is `String` and `Value` is `Integer`. To build a one-node BST that associates the key `it` with the value 0, we just create a `Node`:

        Node first = new Node("it", 0);

Since the left and right links are both null, both refer to BSTs, so this node is a BST. To add a node that associates the key `was` with the value 1, we create another `Node`:

        Node second = new Node("was", 1);

(which itself is a BST) and link to it from the right field of the first `Node`

        first.right = second;

The second node has to go to the right of the first because `was` comes after `it` in `Comparable` order (or we could have chosen to set `second.left` to `first`). Now we can add a third node that associates the key `the` with the value 2 with the code:

        Node third = new Node("the", 2);
        second.left = third;

and a fourth node that associates the key `best` with the value 3 with the code

        Node fourth = new Node("best", 3);
        first.left = fourth;

Note that each of our links—`first`, `second`, `third`, and `fourth`—are, by definition, BSTs (they each are either null or refer to BSTs, and the ordering condition is satisfied at each node).

We often use tree-based terminology when discussing BSTs. We refer to the node at the top as the *root* of the tree, the node referenced by its left link as the *left subtree*, and the node referenced by its right link as the *right subtree*. Traditionally, computer scientists draw trees upside down, with the root at the top. Nodes whose links are both null are called *leaf* nodes. In

*Linking together a BST*

general, a tree may have multiple links per node, the order of the links may not be significant, and no keys or values in the nodes. General trees have many applications in science, mathematics, and computational applications, so you are certain to encounter the model on many occasions.

In the present context, we take care to ensure that we always link together nodes such that *every* Node that we create is the root of a BST (has a key, a value, a link to a left BST with smaller values, and a link to a right BST with a larger value). From the standpoint of the BST data structure, the value is immaterial, so we often ignore it, but we include it in the definition because it plays such a central role in the symbol-table concept. We also intentionally confuse our nomenclature, using ST to signify both "symbol table" and "search tree" because search trees play such a central role in symbol-table implementations.

A BST represents an *ordered* sequence of items. In the example just considered, first represents the sequence best it the was. We can also use an array to represent a sequence of items. For example, we could use:

```
String[] a = { "best", "it", "the", "was" };
```

to represent the same ordered sequence of strings. Given a set of distinct keys, there is only one way to represent them in an ordered array, but there are many ways to represent it in a BST (see Exercise 4.4.7). This flexibility allows us to develop efficient symbol-table implementations. For instance, in our example we were able to insert each new item by creating a new node and changing just one link. As it turns out, it is always possible to do so. Equally important, we can easily find a given key in the tree and find the place where we need to add a link to a new node with a given key. Next, we consider symbol-table code that accomplishes these tasks.

Suppose that you want to *search* for a node with a given key in a BST (or to *get* a value with a given key in a symbol table). There are two possible outcomes: the search might be *successful* (we find the key in the BST; in a symbol-table implementation, we return the associated value)

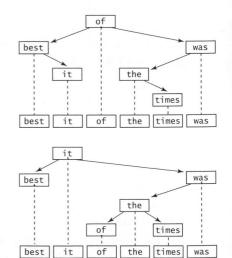

*Two BSTs representing the same sequence*

or it might be *unsuccessful* (there is no key in the BST with the given key; in a symbol-table implementation, we return null).

A recursive searching algorithm is immediate: Given a BST (a reference to a Node), first check whether the tree is empty (the reference is null). If so, then terminate the search as unsuccessful (in a symbol-table implementation, return null). If the tree is nonempty, check whether the key in the node is equal to the search key. If so, then terminate the search as successful (in a symbol-table implementation, return the value associated with the key). If not, compare the search key with the key in the node. If it is smaller, search (recursively) in the left subtree; if it is greater, search (recursively) in the right subtree.

Thinking recursively, it is not difficult to become convinced that this method behaves as intended, based upon the invariant that the key is in the BST if and only if it is in the current subtree. The key property of the recursive method is that we always have just one node to examine in order to decide what to do next. Moreover, we typically examine only a small number of the nodes in the tree: whenever we go to one of the subtrees at a node, we never will examine any of the nodes in the other subtree.

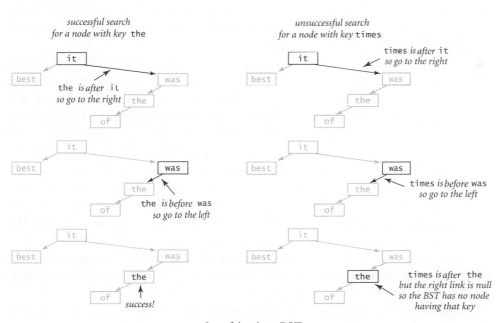

*Searching in a BST*

Suppose that you want to *insert* a new node into a BST (in a symbol-table implementation, *put* a new key-value pair into the data structure). The logic is similar to searching for a key, but the implementation is trickier. The key to understanding it is to realize that only one link must be changed to point to the new node, and that link is precisely the link that would be found to be null in an unsuccessful search for the key in that node.

If the BST is empty, we create and return a new Node containing the key-value pair; if the search key is less than the key at the root, we set the left link to the result of inserting the key-value pair into the left subtree; if the search key is greater, we set the right link to the result of inserting the key-value pair into the right subtree; otherwise, if the search key is equal, we overwrite the existing value with the new value. Resetting the link after the recursive call in this way is usually unnecessary, because the link changes only if the subtree is empty, but it is as easy to set the link as it is to test to avoid setting it.

BST (PROGRAM 4.4.3) is a symbol-table implementation based on these two recursive algorithms. If you compare this code with our binary search implementation BinarySearch (PROGRAM 4.2.3) and our stack and queue implementations Stack (PROGRAM 4.3.4) and Queue (PROGRAM 4.3.6), you will appreciate the elegance and simplicity of this code. *Take the time to think recursively and convince yourself that this code behaves as intended.* Perhaps the simplest way to do so is to trace the construction of an initially empty BST from a sample set of keys. Your ability to do so is a sure test of your understanding of this fundamental data structure.

*insert* times

*Inserting a new node into a BST*

Moreover, the put() and get() methods in BST are remarkably efficient: typically, each accesses a small number of the nodes in the BST (those on the path

***Program 4.4.3   BST symbol table***

```
public class BST<Key extends Comparable<Key>, Value>
{
   private Node root;
   private class Node
   {
      Key key;
      Value val;
      Node left, right;
      Node(Key key, Value val)
      {  this.key = key; this.val = val;  }
   }
   public Value get(Key key)
   {  return get(root, key);  }
   private Value get(Node x, Key key)
   {
      if (x == null) return null;
      int cmp = key.compareTo(x.key);
      if      (cmp < 0) return get(x.left,  key);
      else if (cmp > 0) return get(x.right, key);
      else              return x.val;
   }
   public boolean contains(Key key)
   {  return (get(key) != null);  }
   public void put(Key key, Value val)
   {  root = put(root, key, val);  }
   private Node put(Node x, Key key, Value val)
   {
      if (x == null) return new Node(key, val);
      int cmp = key.compareTo(x.key);
      if      (cmp < 0) x.left  = put(x.left,  key, val);
      else if (cmp > 0) x.right = put(x.right, key, val);
      else              x.val = val;
      return x;
   }
}
```

| root | *BST root* |
|------|-----------|

| key | *key* |
|-----|-------|
| val | *value* |
| left | *left subtree* |
| right | *right subtree* |

*This implementation of the symbol-table data type is centered on the recursive BST data structure and recursive methods for traversing it.*

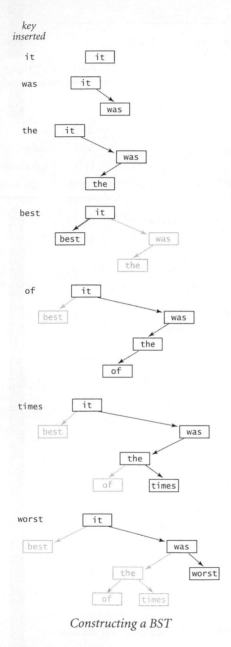

*key
inserted*

it

was

the

best

of

times

worst

*Constructing a BST*

from the root to the node sought or to the null link that is replaced by a link to the new node). Next, we show that *put* operations and *get* requests take logarithmic time (under certain assumptions). Also, put() only creates one new Node and adds one new link. If you make a drawing of a BST built by inserting some keys into an initially empty tree, you certainly will be convinced of this fact—you can just draw each new node somewhere at the bottom of the tree.

**Performance characteristics of BSTs**  The running times of BST algorithms are ultimately dependent on the shape of the trees, and the shape of the trees is dependent on the order in which the keys are inserted. Understanding this dependence is a critical factor in being able to use BSTs effectively in practical situations.

*Best case.* In the best case, the tree is perfectly balanced (each Node has exactly two non-null children), with lg $N$ nodes between the root and each leaf node. In such a tree, it is easy to see that the cost of an unsuccessful search is logarithmic, because that cost satisfies the same recurrence relation as the cost of binary search (see SECTION 4.2) so that the cost of every *put* operation and *get* request is proportional to lg $N$ or less. You would have to be quite lucky to get a perfectly balanced tree like this by inserting keys one by one in practice, but it is worthwhile to know the best possible performance characteristics.

*Average case.* If we insert random keys, we might expect the search times to be logarithmic as well, because the first element becomes the root of the tree and should divide the keys roughly in half. Applying the same argument to the subtrees, we expect to get about the same result as for the best case. This intuition is in-

*Best case (perfectly balanced) BSTs*

deed validated by careful analysis: a classic mathematical derivation shows that the time required for *put* and *get* in a tree constructed from randomly ordered keys is logarithmic (see the booksite for references). More precisely, *the expected number of key comparisons is ~2 ln N for a random put or get in a key built from N randomly ordered keys.* In a practical application such as Lookup, when we can explicitly randomize the order of the keys, this result suffices to (probabilistically) guarantee logarithmic performance. Indeed, since 2 ln $N$ is about 1.39 lg $N$, the *average* case is only about 39% higher than the *best* case. In an application like Index, where we have no control of the order of insertion, there is no guarantee, but typical data gives logarithmic performance (see EXERCISE 4.4.17). As with binary search, this fact is very significant because of the enormousness of the logarithmic-linear chasm: with a BST-based symbol table implementation, we can perform millions of operations per second (or more), even in a huge table.

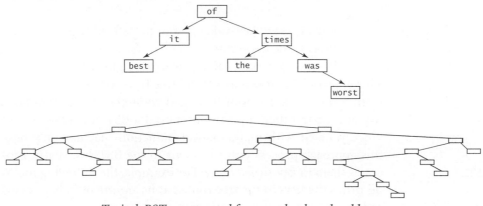

*Typical BSTs constructed from randomly ordered keys*

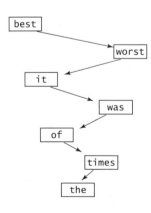

*Worst-case BSTs*

*Worst case.* In the worst case, each node has exactly one null link, so the BST is like a linked list with an extra wasted link, where *put* operations and *get* requests take linear time. Unfortunately, this worst case is not rare in practice—it arises, for example, when we insert the keys in order.

Thus, good performance of the basic BST implementation is dependent on the keys being sufficiently similar to random keys that the tree is not likely to contain many long paths. If you are not sure that assumption is justified, *do not use a simple BST*. Your only clue that something is amiss will be slow response time as the problem size increases. (*Note*: It is not unusual to encounter software of this sort!) Remarkably, there are BST variants that eliminate this worst case and guarantee logarithmic performance per operation, by making all trees nearly perfectly balanced. One popular variant is known as a *red-black tree*. The Java library `java. util.TreeMap` implements a symbol table using this approach.

**Traversing a BST**   Perhaps the most basic tree-processing function is known as *tree traversal*: given a (reference to) a tree, we want to systematically process every key-value pair in the tree. For linked lists, we accomplish this task by following the single link to move from one node to the next. For trees, however, we have decisions to make, because there are generally *two* links to follow. Recursion comes immediately to the rescue. To process every key in a BST:

•        Process every key-value pair in the left subtree.
•        Process the key-value pair at the root.
•        Process every key-value pair in the right subtree.

This approach is known as *inorder* tree traversal, to distinguish it from *preorder* (do the root first) and *postorder* (do the root last), which arise in other applications. Given a BST, it is easy to convince yourself with mathematical induction that not only does this approach process every key pair in the BST, but that it processes them in *key-sorted order*. For example, the following method prints the keys in the tree rooted at its argument in key-sorted order:

```
private static void traverse(Node x)
{
   if (x == null) return;
   traverse(x.left);
   StdOut.println(x.key);
   traverse(x.right);
}
```

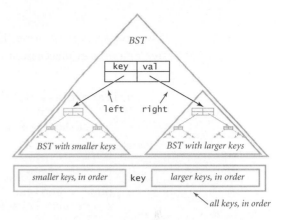

This remarkably simple method is worthy of careful study. It can be used as a basis for a `toString()` implementation for BSTs (see EXERCISE 4.4.11) and also a starting point for developing the iterator that we need to provide clients the ability to use a foreach loop to process the entries in key-sorted order.

*Recursive inorder traversal of a binary search tree*

*Implementing an iterable symbol table.* A close look at the recursive `traverse()` method just considered leads to a way to make our BST data type `Iterable`. For simplicity, we just process the keys because we can *get* the values when we need them. Our goal is to enable client code like the following:

```
BST<String, Double> st = new BST<String, Double>();
...
for (String key: st)
   StdOut.println(key + " " + st.get(key));
...
```

Index (PROGRAM 4.4.2) is another example of such client code.

As usual, we first promise to provide an `iterator()` method by adding the phrase `implements Iterable<Key>` to the class declaration. This addition is a commitment to provide an `iterator()` method for iterating through the keys in the table, in key-sorted order. As usual, the `iterator()` method itself is simple:

```
public Iterator<Key> iterator()
{  return new BSTIterator();  }
```

We need a `private` nested class that implements the `Iterator` interface, but implementing such a class is a bit of a challenge. We cannot directly use recursive traversal, because we need to be able to pause and restart the process. To this end, we maintain an explicit `Stack` that contains the sequence of nodes from the root down to the current node. The system call stack during the execution of the recursive `traverse()` has essentially this same information.

```
private class BSTIterator implements Iterator<Key>
{
    Stack<Node> stack = new Stack<Node>();

    BSTIterator()
    // see below

    public boolean hasNext()
    {   return !stack.isEmpty();   }

    public Key next()
    // see below

    public void remove()
    { }
}
```

To complete this implementation, we need a `BSTIterator()` constructor that initializes the stack and a `next()` method that returns the next key. The recursive `traverse()` method calls itself for the left link of each node until reaching a null link (at the node with the smallest key in the BST). Therefore, to prepare for processing the smallest key, we need to initialize the stack to contain the nodes in the BST reached by following left links from the root. To do so, we use a helper method:

```
private void pushLeft(Node x)
{
    while (x != null)
    {
        stack.push(x);
        x = x.left;
    }
}

BSTIterator()
{   pushLeft(root);   }
```

In particular, the node with the smallest key in the BST is on the top of the stack after this initialization. Now, to process a key, we pop the top node from the stack and process its right subtree using the same method:

```
public Key next()
{
   Node x = stack.pop();
   pushLeft(x.right);
   return x.key;
}
```

Convincing yourself that these methods allow clients like `Index` to iterate through the keys of a BST in key order by tracing their operation on some sample trees will teach you a great deal about BSTs, stacks, and recursion.

**Extended symbol table operations**    The flexibility of BSTs enables the implementation of many useful additional operations beyond those dictated by the symbol table API. We leave implementations of these operations for exercises and leave further study of their performance characteristics and applications for a course in algorithms and data structures.

*Minimum and maximum.* To find the smallest key in a BST, follow left links from the root until reaching `null`. The last key encountered is the smallest in the BST. The same procedure following right links lead to the largest key.

*Size.* To keep track of the number of nodes in a BST, keep an extra instance variable N in BST that counts the number of nodes in the tree. Initialize it to 0 and increment it whenever creating a new `Node`. Alternatively, keep an extra instance variable N in `Node` that counts the number of nodes in the subtree rooted at that node. Initialize it to 1 and increment it for each node on the search path when inserting a new `Node`, taking care to handle properly the duplicate-key case, when no new `Node` is added (see Exercise 4.4.20).

*Remove.* Many applications demand the ability to remove a key-value pair with a given key. You can find explicit code for removing a node from a BST on the booksite or in a book on algorithms and data structures. An easy, lazy way to implement `remove()` relies on the fact that our symbol table API disallows `null` values:

```
public void remove(Key key)
{
   if (contains(key))
      put(key, null);
}
```

This approach necessitates periodically cleaning out nodes in the BST with `null` values, because performance will degrade unless the size of the data structure stays proportional to the number of key-value pairs in the table.

*Range search.* With a recursive method like `traverse()`, we can count the number of keys that fall between two given values or return an iterator for keys falling between two given values. For example, a financial institution might build a symbol-table whose keys are account balances to be able to process accounts whose balances are above certain limits.

*Order statistics.* If we maintain an instance variable in each node having the size of the subtree rooted at each node, we can implement a recursive method that returns the $k$th largest key in the BST in logarithmic time.

This list is representative; numerous other important operations have been invented for BSTs that are broadly useful in applications.

HENCEFORTH, WE WILL USE THE REFERENCE implementation ST that implements our basic interface using the symbol-table implementation in `java.util.TreeMap`, which is based on advanced type of BST known as the *red-black tree*. Red-black trees, which you are likely to encounter if you take an advanced course in data structures and algorithms, are of interest because they support a logarithmic-time guarantee for `get()`, `put()`, and many of the other operations just described.

**Set data type**    As a final example, we consider a data type that is simpler than a symbol table, still broadly useful, and easy to implement with BSTs. A *set* is a collection of distinct keys, like a symbol table with no values. We could use ST and ignore the values, but client code that uses the following API is simpler and clearer:

| public class SET<Key extends Comparable<Key>> | | |
|---|---|---|
| | SET() | *create a set* |
| boolean | isEmpty() | *is the set empty?* |
| void | add(Key key) | *add key to the set* |
| boolean | contains(Key key) | *is key in the set?* |

*Note: Implementations should also implement the `Iterable<Key>` interface to enable clients to access keys in sorted order with foreach loops*

*API for a generic set*

---

### Program 4.4.4 Dedup filter

```
public class DeDup
{
   public static void main(String[] args)
   { // Filter out duplicate strings.
      SET<String> distinct = new SET<String>();
      while (!StdIn.isEmpty())
      { // Read a string, ignore if duplicate.
         String key = StdIn.readString();
         if (!distinct.contains(key))
         { // Save and print new string.
            distinct.add(key);
            StdOut.print(key);
         }
         StdOut.println();
      }
   }
}
```

| distinct | set of distinct string values in StdIn |
| key | current string |

*This* SET *client is a filter that removes duplicate strings in the input stream, using a* SET *containing the distinct strings encountered so far.*

```
% java DeDup < TaleOfTwoCities.txt
it was the best of times worst age wisdom foolishness...
```

As with symbol tables, there is no intrinsic reason that the key type should implement the Comparable interface. However, processing Comparable items is typical, and we can take advantage of item comparison to develop efficient implementations, so we include Comparable in the interface. Implementing SET by deleting references to val in our BST code is a straightforward exercise (see EXERCISE 4.4.15).

DeDup (PROGRAM 4.4.4) is a SET client that reads a sequence of strings from standard input and prints out the first occurrence of each string (thereby removing duplicates). You can find many other examples of SET clients in the exercises at the end of this section. In the next section, you will see the importance of identifying such a fundamental abstraction, illustrated in the context of a case study.

**Perspective**   The use of binary search trees to implement symbol tables and sets is a sterling example of exploiting the tree abstraction, which is ubiquitous and familiar. Trees lie at the basis of many scientific topics, and are widely used in computer science. We are accustomed to many tree structures in everyday life, including family trees, sports tournaments, the organization chart of a company, and parse trees in grammar. Trees also arise in numerous computational applications, including function call trees, parse trees for programming languages, and file systems. Many important applications are rooted in science and engineering, including phylogenetic trees in computational biology, multidimensional trees in computer graphics, minimax game trees in economics, and quad trees in molecular dynamics simulations. Other, more complicated, linked structures can be exploited as well, as you will see in Section 4.5.

Symbol table implementations are a prime topic of further study in algorithms and data structures. Examples include balanced BSTs, hashing, and tries. Implementations of many of these algorithms and data structures are found in Java and most other computational environments. Different APIs and different assumptions about keys call for different implementations. Researchers in algorithms and data structures still study symbol-table implementations of all sorts.

People use dictionaries, indexes, and other kinds of symbol tables every day. Within a short amount of time, applications based on symbol tables will completely replace phone books, encyclopedias, and all sorts of physical artifacts that served us well in the last millennium. Without symbol-table implementations based on data structures such as BSTs, such applications would not be feasible; with them, we have the feeling that anything that we need is instantly accessible online.

**Q + A**

**Q.** Why use immutable symbol table keys?

**A.** If we changed a key while it was in the BST, it would invalidate the ordering restriction.

**Q.** Why not use the Java library methods for symbol tables?

**A.** Now that you understand how a symbol table works, you are certainly welcome to use the industrial-strength versions `java.util.TreeMap` and `java.util.HashMap`. They follow the same basic API as BST, but they allow null keys and use the names `containsKey()` and `keySet()` instead of `contains()` and `iterator()`, respectively. They also contain additional methods such as `remove()`, but they do not provide any efficient way to add some of the additional methods that we mentioned, such as order statistics. You can also use `java.util.TreeSet` and `java.util.HashSet`, which implement an API like our SET.

## *Exercises*

**4.4.1**   Modify Lookup to to make a program LookupAndPut that allows *put* operations to be specified on standard input. Use the convention that a plus sign indicates that the next two strings typed are the key-value pair to be inserted.

**4.4.2**   Modify Lookup to make a program LookupMultiple that handles multiple values having the same key by putting the values on a queue, as in Index, and then printing them all out on a *get* request, as follows:

```
% java LookupMultiple amino.csv 3 0
Leucine
TTA TTG CTT CTC CTA CTG
```

**4.4.3**   Modify Index to make a program IndexByKeyword that takes a file name from the command line and makes an index from standard input using only the keywords in that file. *Note*: Using the same file for indexing and keywords should give the same result as Index.

**4.4.4**   Modify Index to make a program IndexLines that considers only consecutive sequences of letters as keys (no punctuation or numbers) and uses line numbers instead of word position as the value. This functionality is useful for programs, as follows:

```
% java IndexLines 6 0 < Index.java
continue 12
enqueue 15
Integer 4 5 7 8 14
parseInt 4 5
println 22
```

**4.4.5**   Develop an implementation BinarySearchST of the symbol-table API that maintains parallel arrays of keys and values, keeping them in key-sorted order. Use binary search for *get*, and move larger elements to the right one position for *put* (use array doubling to keep the array size proportional to the number of key-value pairs in the table). Test your implementation with Index, and validate the hypothesis that using such an implementation for Index takes time proportional to the product of the number of strings and the number of distinct strings in the input.

**4.4.6** Develop an implementation `LinkedListST` of the symbol-table API that maintains a linked list of nodes containing keys and values, keeping them in arbitrary order. Test your implementation with `Index`, and validate the hypothesis that using such an implementation for `Index` takes time proportional to the product of the number of strings and the number of distinct strings in the input.

**4.4.7** Draw all the different BSTs that can represent the key sequence `best of it the time was`.

**4.4.8** Draw the BST that results when you insert items with keys

> E A S Y Q U E S T I O N

in that order into an initially empty tree.

**4.4.9** Suppose we have integer keys between 1 and 1000 in a BST and search for 363. Which of the following *cannot* be the sequence of keys examined?

> *a.* 2 252 401 398 330 363
> *b.* 399 387 219 266 382 381 278 363
> *c.* 3 923 220 911 244 898 258 362 363
> *d.* 4 924 278 347 621 299 392 358 363
> *e.* 5 925 202 910 245 363

**4.4.10** Suppose that the following 31 keys appear (in some order) in a BST of height 5:

> 10 15 18 21 23 24 30 30 38 41 42 45 50 55 59
> 60 61 63 71 77 78 83 84 85 86 88 91 92 93 94 98

Draw the top three nodes of the tree (the root and its two children).

**4.4.11** Implement `toString()` for BST, using a recursive helper method like `traverse()`. As usual, you can accept quadratic performance because of the cost of string concatenation. *Extra credit*: Write a linear-time `toString()` method for BST that uses `StringBuilder`.

**4.4.12** True or false: Given a BST, let *x* be a leaf node, and let *p* be its parent. Then either (i) the key of *p* is the smallest key in the BST larger than the key of *x* or (ii) the key of *p* is the largest key in the BST smaller than the key of *x*.

**4.4.13** Modify BST to add a method `remove()` that takes a `key` argument and removes that `key` (and the corresponding value) from the symbol table, if it exists. Implement it by setting the value associated with the given `key` to `null`.

**4.4.14** Modify the symbol-table API to handle values with duplicate keys by having `get()` return an *iterator* for the values having a given key. Implement BST and `Index` as dictated by this API. Discuss the pros and cons of this approach versus the one given in the text.

**4.4.15** Modify BST to implement the SET API given at the end of this section.

**4.4.16** A *concordance* is an alphabetical list of the words in a text that gives all word positions where each word appears. Thus, `java Index 0 0` produces a concordance. In a famous incident, one group of researchers tried to establish credibility while keeping details of the Dead Sea Scrolls secret from others by making public a concordance. Write a program `InvertConcordance` that takes a command-line argument N, reads a concordance from standard input, and prints the first N words of the corresponding text on standard output.

**4.4.17** Run experiments to validate the claims in the text that the *put* operations and *get* requests for `Lookup` and `Index` are logarithmic in the size of the table when using BST. Develop test clients that generate random keys and also run tests for various data sets, either from the booksite or of your own choosing.

**4.4.18** Modify BST to add a method `size()` that returns the number of elements in the table. Use the approach of storing within each `Node` the number of nodes in the subtree rooted there.

**4.4.19** Modify BST to add a method `rangeCount()` that takes two `Key` arguments and returns the number of keys in a BST between the two given keys. Your method should take time proportional to the height of the tree. *Hint*: First work the previous exercise.

**4.4.20** Modify BST to add methods min() and max() that return the smallest (or largest) key in the table (or null if no such key exists).

**4.4.21** Modify BST to implement a symbol-table API where keys are arbitrary objects. Use hashCode() to convert keys to integers and use integer keys in the BST. *Note*: This exercise is trickier than it might seem, because of the possibility that hashCode() can return the same integer for two different objects.

**4.4.22** Modify your SET implementation from EXERCISE 4.4.15 to add methods floor() and ceil() that take as argument a Key and return the largest (smallest) element in the set that is no larger (no smaller) than the given Key.

**4.4.23** Write an ST client that creates a symbol table mapping letter grades to numerical scores, as in the table below, and then reads from standard input a list of letter grades and computes their average (GPA).

| A+ | A | A- | B+ | B | B- | C+ | C | C- | D | F |
|------|------|------|------|------|------|------|------|------|------|------|
| 4.33 | 4.00 | 3.67 | 3.33 | 3.00 | 2.67 | 2.33 | 2.00 | 1.67 | 1.00 | 0.00 |

# Binary Tree Exercises

*This list of exercises is intended to give you experience in working with binary trees that are not necessarily BSTs. They all assume a* Node *class with three instance variables: a positive* double *value and two* Node *references. As with linked lists, you will find it helpful to make drawings using the visual representation shown in the text.*

**4.4.24** Implement the following methods that each take as argument a Node that is the root of a binary tree.

| | |
|---|---|
| int size() | *number of nodes in the tree* |
| int leaves() | *number of nodes whose links are both* null |
| double total() | *sum of the key values in all nodes* |

Your methods should all run in linear time.

**4.4.25** Implement a linear-time method height() that returns the maximum number of nodes on any path from the root to a leaf node (the height of the null tree is 0; the height of a one-node tree is 1).

**4.4.26** A binary tree is *heap-ordered* if the key at the root is larger than the keys in all of its descendants. Implement a linear-time method heapOrdered() that returns true if the tree is heap-ordered, and false otherwise.

**4.4.27** A binary tree is *balanced* if both its subtrees are balanced and the height of its two subtrees differ by at most 1. Implement a linear-time method balanced() that returns true if the tree is balanced, and false otherwise.

**4.4.28** Two binary trees are *isomorphic* if only their key values differ (they have the same shape). Implement a linear-time static method isomorphic() that takes two tree references as arguments and returns true if they refer to isomorphic trees, and false otherwise. Then, implement a linear-time static method eq() that takes two tree references as arguments and returns true if they refer to identical trees (isomorphic with the same key values), and false otherwise.

**4.4.29** Implement a linear-time method isBST() that returns true if the tree is a BST, and false otherwise.

*Solution*: This task is a bit more difficult than it might seem. Use an overloaded recursive method `isBST()` that takes two additional arguments `min` and `max` and returns `true` if the tree is a BST and all its values are between `min` and `max`.

```
public static boolean isBST()
{   return isBST(root, 0, Double.POSITIVE_INFINITY);   }

private boolean isBST(Node x, int min, int max)
{
    if (x == null) return true;
    if (x.val <= min || x.val >= max)  return false;
    if (!isBST(x.left, min, x.val))    return false;
    if (!isBST(x.right, x.val, max))   return false;
}
```

**4.4.30** Write a method `levelOrder()` that prints BST keys in *level order*: first print the root, then the nodes one level below the root, left to right, then the nodes two levels below the root (left to right), and so forth. *Hint*: Use a `Queue<Node>`.

**4.4.31** Compute the value returned by `mystery()` on some sample binary trees and then formulate a hypothesis about its behavior and prove it.

```
public int mystery(Node x)
{
    if (x == null) return 0;
    return mystery(x.left) + mystery(x.right);
}
```

*Answer*: Returns 0 for any binary tree.

## Creative Exercises

**4.4.32** *Spell checking.* Write a SET client `SpellChecker` that takes as command-line argument the name of a file containing a dictionary of words, and then reads strings from standard input and prints out any string that is not in the dictionary. You can find a dictionary file on the booksite. *Extra credit*: Augment your program to handle common suffixes such as -ing or -ed.

**4.4.33** *Spell correction.* Write an ST client `SpellCorrector` that serves as a filter that replaces commonly misspelled words on standard input with a suggested replacement, printing the result to standard output. Take as command-line argument a file that contains common misspellings and corrections. You can find an example on the booksite.

**4.4.34** *Web filter.* Write a SET client `WebBlocker` that takes as command-line argument the name of a file containing a list of objectionable websites, and then reads strings from standard input and prints out only those websites not on the list.

**4.4.35** *Set operations.* Add methods `union()` and `intersection()` to SET that each take two sets as arguments and return the union and intersection, respectively, of those two sets.

**4.4.36** *Frequency symbol table.* Develop a data type `FrequencyTable` that supports the following operations: `click()` and `count()`, both of which take `String` arguments. The data-type value is an integer that keeps track of the number of times the `click()` operation has been called with the given `String` as argument. The `click()` operation increments the count by one, and the `count()` operation returns the value, possibly 0. Clients of this data type might include a web traffic analyzer, a music player that counts the number of times each song has been played, phone software for counting calls, and so forth.

**4.4.37** *1D range searching.* Develop a data type that supports the following operations: insert a date, search for a date, and count the number of dates in the data structure that lie in a particular interval. Use Java's `java.util.Date` data type.

**4.4.38** *Non-overlapping interval search.* Given a list of non-overlapping intervals of integers, write a function that takes an integer argument and determines in which, if any, interval that value lies. For example, if the intervals are 1643–2033,

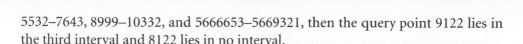

5532–7643, 8999–10332, and 5666653–5669321, then the query point 9122 lies in the third interval and 8122 lies in no interval.

**4.4.39**  *IP lookup by country.* Write a BST client that uses the data file `ip-to-country.csv` found on the booksite to determine from which country a given IP address is coming . The data file has five fields: beginning of IP address range, ending of IP address range, two-character country code, three character country code, and country name. The IP addresses are non-overlapping. Such a database tool can be used for credit card fraud detection, spam filtering, auto-selection of language on a website, and web server log analysis.

**4.4.40**  *Inverted index of web.* Given a list of web pages, create a symbol table of words contained in the web pages. Associate with each word a list of web pages in which that word appears. Write a program that reads in a list of web pages, creates the symbol table, and support single word queries by returning the list of web pages in which that query word appears.

**4.4.41**  *Inverted index of web.* Extend the previous exercise so that it supports multi-word queries. In this case, output the list of web pages that contain at least one occurrence of each of the query words.

**4.4.42**  *Multiple word search.* Write a program that takes k words from the command line, reads in a sequence of words from standard input, and identifies the smallest interval of text that contains all of the k words (not necessarily in the same order). You do not need to consider partial words.

*Hint*: For each index $i$, find the smallest interval $[i, j]$ that contains the $k$ query words. Keep a count of the number of times each of the $k$ query words appear. Given $[i, j]$, compute $[i+1, j']$ by decrementing the counter for word $i$. Then, gradually increase $j$ until the interval contains at least one copy of each of the $k$ words (or, equivalently, word $i$).

**4.4.43**  *Repetition draw in chess.* In the game of chess, if a board position is repeated three times with the same side to move, the side to move can declare a draw. Describe how you could test this condition using a computer program.

**4.4.44** *Registrar scheduling.* The Registrar at a prominent northeastern university recently scheduled an instructor to teach two different classes at the same exact time. Help the Registrar prevent future mistakes by describing a method to check for such conflicts. For simplicity, assume all classes run for 50 minutes and start at 9, 10, 11, 1, 2, or 3.

**4.4.45** *Entropy.* We define the relative entropy of a text corpus with $N$ words, $k$ of which are distinct as

$$E = 1 / (N \lg N) \, (p_0 \lg(k/p_0) + p_1 \lg(k/p_1) + \ldots + p_{k-1} \lg(k/p_{k-1}))$$

where $p_i$ is the fraction of times that word $i$ appears. Write a program that reads in a text corpus and prints out the relative entropy. Convert all letters to lowercase and treat punctuation marks as whitespace.

**4.4.46** *Order statistics.* Add to BST a method `select()` that takes an integer argument $k$ and returns the $k$th largest key in the BST. Maintain subtree sizes in each node (see Exercise 4.4.18). The running time should be proportional to the height of the tree.

**4.4.47** *Rank query.* Add to BST a method `rank()` that takes a key as argument and returns the integer i such that key is the ith largest element in the BST. Maintain subtree sizes in each node (see Exercise 4.4.18). The running time should be proportional to the height of the tree.

**4.4.48** *Delete ith element.* Implement a class that supports the following API:

```
public class GeneralizedQueue<Item>
```

|        | GeneralizedQueue()   | *create an empty queue*                                  |
|--------|----------------------|---------------------------------------------------------|
| boolean | isEmpty()           | *is the queue empty?*                                    |
| void   | insert(Item item)    | *insert an item*                                         |
| Item   | delete(int i)        | *delete and return the ith least recently inserted item* |

*API for a generic generalized queue*

Use a BST that associates the *k*th element inserted with the key *k* and maintains in each node the total number of nodes in the subtree rooted at that node. To find the *i*th least recently added item, search for the *i*th smallest element in the BST.

**4.4.49** *Sparse vectors.* An *N*-dimensional vector is *sparse* if its number of nonzero values is small. Your goal is to represent a vector with space proportional to its number of nonzeros, and to be able to add two sparse vectors in time proportional to the total number of nonzeros. Implement a class that supports the following API:

```
public class SparseVector
```
---

|            | SparseVector()             | *create a vector*       |
|-----------:|----------------------------|-------------------------|
| void       | put(int i, double v)       | *set $a_i$ to v*        |
| double     | get(int i)                 | *return $a_i$*          |
| double     | dot(SparseVector b)        | *vector dot product*    |
| SparseVector | plus(SparseVector b)     | *vector addition*       |

*API for a sparse vector of* double *values*

**4.4.50** *Sparse matrices.* An *N*-by-*N* matrix is *sparse* if its number of nonzeros is proportional to *N* (or less). Your goal is to represent a matrix with space proportional to *N*, and to be able to add and multiply two sparse matrices in time proportional to the total number of nonzeros (perhaps with an extra log *N* factor). Implement a class that supports the following API:

```
public class SparseMatrix
```
---

|              | SparseMatrix()               | *create a matrix*    |
|-------------:|------------------------------|----------------------|
| void         | put(int i, int j, double v)  | *set $a_{ij}$ to v*  |
| double       | get(int i, int j)            | *return $a_{ij}$*    |
| SparseMatrix | plus(SparseMatrix b)         | *matrix addition*    |
| SparseMatrix | times(SparseMatrix b)        | *matrix product*     |

*API for a sparse matrix of* double *values*

**4.4.51** *Queue with no duplicates.* Create a data type that is a queue, except that an element may only appear on the queue at most once at any given time. Ignore requests to insert an item if it is already on the queue.

**4.4.52** *Mutable string.* Create a data type that supports the following API on a string. Use a BST to implement all operations in logarithmic time.

```
public class MutableString
```
---
|  |  |
|---|---|
| MutableString() | *create an empty string* |
| void get(int i) | *return the i th character in the string* |
| void insert(int i, char c) | *insert c and make it the i th character* |
| char delete(int i) | *delete and return the i th character* |
| int length() | *return the length of the string* |

*API for a mutable string*

**4.4.53** *Assignment statements.* Write a program to parse and evaluate programs consisting of assignment and print statements with fully parenthesized arithmetic expressions (see PROGRAM 4.3.5). For example, given the input

```
A = 5
B = 10
C = A + B
D = C * C
print(D)
```

your program should print the value 225. Assume that all variables and values are of type `double`. Use a symbol table to keep track of variable names.

**4.4.54** *Random element.* Add to your SET implementation from EXERCISE 4.4.15 a method `random()` that returns a random key. The running time should be proportional to the length of the path from the root to the node returned. *Hint:* Add to Node an `int` instance variable `size` to contain the size of the subtree rooted at each node and update the rest of the code to maintain `size`.

**4.4.55** *Dynamic discrete distribution.* Create a data type that supports the following two operations: add() and random(). The add() method should insert a new item into the data structure if it has not been seen before; otherwise, it should increase its frequency count by one. The random() method should return an element at random, where the probabilities are weighted by the frequency of each element. Use space proportional to the number of items.

**4.4.56** *Random phone numbers.* Write a program that takes a command-line argument $N$ and prints $N$ random phone numbers of the form (xxx) xxx-xxxx. Use a SET to avoid choosing the same number more than once. Use only legal area codes (you can find a file of such codes on the booksite).

**4.4.57** *Codon usage table.* Write a program that uses a symbol table to print out summary statistics for each codon in a genome taken from standard input (frequency per thousand), like the following:

```
UUU 13.2   UCU 19.6   UAU 16.5   UGU 12.4
UUC 23.5   UCC 10.6   UAC 14.7   UGC  8.0
UUA  5.8   UCA 16.1   UAA  0.7   UGA  0.3
UUG 17.6   UCG 11.8   UAG  0.2   UGG  9.5
CUU 21.2   CCU 10.4   CAU 13.3   CGU 10.5
CUC 13.5   CCC  4.9   CAC  8.2   CGC  4.2
CUA  6.5   CCA 41.0   CAA 24.9   CGA 10.7
CUG 10.7   CCG 10.1   CAG 11.4   CGG  3.7
AUU 27.1   ACU 25.6   AAU 27.2   AGU 11.9
AUC 23.3   ACC 13.3   AAC 21.0   AGC  6.8
AUA  5.9   ACA 17.1   AAA 32.7   AGA 14.2
AUG 22.3   ACG  9.2   AAG 23.9   AGG  2.8
GUU 25.7   GCU 24.2   GAU 49.4   GGU 11.8
GUC 15.3   GCC 12.6   GAC 22.1   GGC  7.0
GUA  8.7   GCA 16.8   GAA 39.8   GGA 47.2
```

**4.4.58** *Unique substrings of length L.* Write a program that reads in text from standard input and calculates the number of unique substrings of length L that it contains. For example, if the input is cgcgggcgcg, then there are five unique substrings of length 3: cgc, cgg, gcg, ggc, and ggg. This calculation is useful in data compression. *Hint*: Use the string method substring(i, i + L) to extract the ith substring and insert into a symbol table. Test your program on a large genome from the booksite and on the first 10 million digits of $\pi$.

**4.4.59** *Password checker.* Write a program that reads in a string from the command line and a dictionary of words from standard input, and checks whether it is a "good" password. Here, assume "good" means that it (*i*) is at least eight characters long, (*ii*) is not a word in the dictionary, (*iii*) is not a word in the dictionary followed by a digit 0-9 (e.g., hello5), (*iv*) is not two words separated by a digit (e.g., hello2world), and (*v*) none of (*ii*) through (*iv*) hold for reverses of words in the dictionary.

# 4.5   Case Study: Small World

THE MATHEMATICAL MODEL THAT WE USE for studying the nature of pairwise connections among entities is known as the *graph*. Graphs are important for studying the natural world and for helping us to better understand and refine the networks that we create. From models of the nervous system in neurobiology, to the study of the spread of infectious diseases in medical science, to the development of the telephone system, graphs have played a critical role in science and engineering over the past century, including the development of the internet itself.

Some graphs exhibit a specific property known as the *small-world phenomenon*. You may be familiar with this property, which is sometimes known as *six degrees of separation*. It is the basic idea that, even though each of us has relatively few acquaintances, there is a relatively short chain of acquaintances (the six degrees of separation) separating us from one another. This hypothesis was validated experimentally by Stanley Milgram in the 1960s and modelled mathematically by Duncan Watts and Stephen Strogatz in the 1990s. In recent years, the principle has proven important in a remarkable variety of applications. Scientists are interested in small-world graphs because they model natural phenomena, and engineers are interested in building networks that take advantage of the natural properties of small-world graphs.

In this section, we address basic computational questions surrounding the study of small-world graphs. Indeed, the simple question

*Does a given graph exhibit the small-world phenomenon?*

can present a significant computational burden. To address this question, we will consider a graph-processing data type and several useful graph-processing clients. In particular, we will examine a client for computing *shortest paths*, a computation which has a vast number of important applications in its own right.

A persistent theme of this section is that the algorithms and data structures that we have been studying play a central role in graph processing. Indeed, you will see that several of the fundamental data types introduced earlier in this chapter help us to develop elegant and efficient code for studying the properties of graphs.

**Graphs** To nip in the bud any terminological confusion, we start right away with some definitions. A *graph* is comprised of a set of *vertices* and a set of *edges*. Each edge represents a connection between two vertices. Two vertices are *neighbors* if they are connected by an edge, and the *degree* of a vertex is its number of neighbors. Note that there is no relationship between a graph and the idea of a function graph (a plot of a function values) or the idea of graphics (drawings). We often visualize graphs by drawing labelled geometric shapes (vertices) connected by lines (edges), but it is always important to remember that it is the connections that are essential, not the way we depict them.

The following list suggests the diverse range of systems where graphs are appropriate starting points for understanding structure.

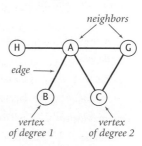

*Graph terminology*

*Human biology.* Arteries and veins connect organs, synapses connect neurons, and joints connect bones, so an understanding of the human biology depends on understanding appropriate graph models. Perhaps the largest and most important such modelling challenge in this arena is the human brain. How do local connections among neurons translate to consciousness, memory, and intelligence?

*Social networks.* People have relationships with other people. From the study of infectious diseases to the study of political trends, graph models of these relation-

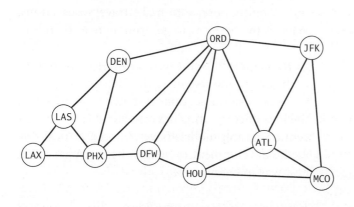

*Graph model of a transportation system*

| vertices | edges |
|---|---|
| JFK | JFK MCO |
| MCO | ORD DEN |
| ATL | ORD HOU |
| ORD | DFW PHX |
| HOU | JFK ATL |
| DFW | ORD DFW |
| PHX | ORD PHX |
| DEN | ATL HOU |
| LAX | DEN PHX |
| LAS | PHX LAX |
|  | JFK ORD |
|  | DEN LAS |
|  | DFW HOU |
|  | ORD ATL |
|  | LAS LAX |
|  | ATL MCO |
|  | HOU MCO |
|  | LAS PHX |

| system | vertex | edge |
| --- | --- | --- |
| *natural phenomena* | | |
| circulatory | organ | blood vessel |
| skeletal | joint | bone |
| nervous | neuron | synapse |
| social | person | relationship |
| epidemiological | person | infection |
| chemical | molecule | bond |
| N-body | particle | force |
| genetic | gene | mutation |
| biochemical | protein | interaction |
| *engineered systems* | | |
| transportation | airport | route |
| | intersection | road |
| communication | telephone | wire |
| | computer | cable |
| | web page | link |
| distribution | power station | power line |
| | home | |
| | reservoir | pipe |
| | home | |
| | warehouse | truck route |
| | retail outlet | |
| mechanical | joint | beam |
| software | module | call |
| financial | account | transaction |

*Typical graph models*

ships are critical to our understanding of their implications. Hoes does information propagate in online networks?

*Physical systems.* Atoms connect to form molecules, molecules connect to form a material or a crystal, and particles are connected by mutual forces such as gravity or magnetism. Graph models are appropriate for studying the percolation problem that we considered in SECTION 2.4, the interacting charges that we considered in SECTION 3.1, and the N-body problem that we considered in SECTION 3.4. How do local interactions propagate through such systems as they evolve?

*Transportation systems.* Train tracks connect stations, roads connect intersections, and airline routes connect airports, so all of these systems naturally admit a simple graph model. No doubt you have used applications that are based on such models when getting directions from an interactive mapping program or a GPS device, or using an online service to make travel reservations. What is the best way to get from here to there?

*Communications systems.* From electric circuits, to the telephone system, to the internet, to wireless services, communications systems are all based on the idea of connecting devices. For at least the past century, graph models have played a critical role in the development of such systems. What is the best way to connect the devices?

*Resource distribution.* Power lines connect power stations and home electrical systems, pipes connect reservoirs and home plumbing, and truck

| vertices | edges | |
|----------|-------|---------|
| aaa.edu | aaa.edu | www.com |
| www.com | www.com | fff.org |
| mmm.net | www.com | mmm.net |
| fff.org | www.com | ttt.gov |
| ttt.gov | www.com | fff.org |
| | www.com | mmm.net |
| | mmm.net | fff.org |
| | fff.org | aaa.edu |
| | ttt.gov | aaa.edu |
| | ttt.gov | mmm.net |

*Graph model of the web*

routes connect warehouses and retail outlets. The study of effective and reliable means of distributing resources depends on accurate graph models. Where are the bottlenecks in a distribution system?

*Mechanical systems.* Trusses or steel beams connect joints in a bridge or a building. Graph models help us to design these systems and to understand their properties. What forces must a joint or a beam withstand?

*Software systems.* Methods in one program module invoke methods in other modules. As we have seen throughout this book, understanding relationships of this sort is a key to success in software design. Which modules will be affected by a change in an API?

*Financial systems.* Transactions connect accounts, and accounts connect customers to financial institutions. These are but a few of the graph models that people use to study complex financial transactions, and to profit from better understanding them. Which transactions are routine and which are indicative of a significant event that might translate to profits?

SOME OF THESE ARE MODELS OF natural phenomena, where our goal is to gain a better understanding of the natural world by developing simple models and then using them to formulate hypotheses that we can test. Other graph models are of networks that we engineer, where our goal is to build a better network or to better maintain a network by understanding its basic characteristics.

Graphs are useful models whether they are small or massive. A graph having just dozens of vertices and edges (for example, one modeling a chemical compound, where vertices are molecules and edges are bonds) is already a complicated combinatorial object because there are a huge number of possible graphs, so understanding the structures of the particular ones at hand is important. A graph having billions or trillions of vertices and edges (for example, a government database containing all phone calls or a graph model of the human nervous system) is vastly more complex, and presents significant computational challenges.

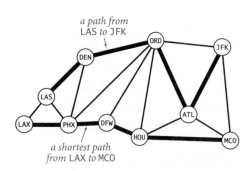

*a path from LAS to* JFK

*a shortest path from* LAX *to* MCO

*Paths in a graph*

Processing graphs typically involves building a graph from information in a database and then answering questions about the graph. Beyond the application-specific questions in the examples just cited, we often need to ask basic questions about graphs. How many vertices and edges does the graph have? What are the neighbors of a given vertex? Some questions depend on an understanding of the structure of a graph. For example, a *path* in a graph is a sequence of vertices connected by edges. Is there a path connecting two given vertices? What is the shortest such path? What is the maximum length of a shortest path in the graph (the graph's *diameter*)?

We have already seen in this book several examples of questions from scientific applications that are much more complicated than these. What is the probability that a random surfer will land on each vertex? What is the probability that a system represented by a certain graph percolates?

As you encounter complex systems in later courses, you are certain to encounter graphs in many different contexts. You may also study their properties in detail in later courses in mathematics, operations research, or computer science. Some graph-processing problems present insurmountable computational challenges; others can be solved with relative ease with data-type implementations of the sort we have been considering.

**Graph data type**   Graph-processing algorithms generally first build an internal representation of a graph by adding edges, then process it by iterating through the vertices and through the edges that are adjacent to a vertex. The following API supports such processing:

```
public class Graph
```

| | | |
|---|---|---|
| | Graph() | *create an empty graph* |
| | Graph(In in, String delim) | *read graph from input stream* |
| void | addEdge(String v, String w) | *add edge* v-w |
| int | V() | *number of vertices* |
| int | E() | *number of edges* |
| Iterable<String> | vertices() | *vertices in the graph* |
| Iterable<String> | adjacentTo(String v) | *neighbors of* v |
| int | degree(String v) | *number of neighbors of* v |
| boolean | hasVertex(String v) | *is* v *a vertex in the graph?* |
| boolean | hasEdge(String v, String w) | *is* v-w *an edge in the graph?* |

*API for a graph with* String *vertices*

As usual, this API reflects several design choices, each made from among various alternatives, some of which we now briefly discuss.

*Undirected graph.*   Edges are *undirected*: an edge that connects v to w is the same as one that connects w to v. Our interest is in the connection, not the direction. Directed edges (for example, one-way streets in road maps) require a slightly different data type (see EXERCISE 4.5.35).

*String vertex type.*   We might use a generic vertex type, to allow clients to build graphs with objects of any type. We leave this sort of implementation for an exercise, however, because the resulting code becomes a bit unwieldy (see EXERCISE 4.5.9). The String vertex type suffices for the applications that we consider here.

*Implicit vertex creation.*   When a String is used as an argument to addEdge(), we assume that it is a vertex name. If no edge using that String has yet been added, our implementation creates a vertex with that name. The alternative design of having an `addVertex()` method requires more client code (to create the vertices) and more cumbersome implementation code (to check that edges connect vertices that have previously been created).

*Self-loops and parallel edges.* Although the API does not explicitly address the issue, we assume that implementations *do* allow self-loops (edges connecting a vertex to itself) but *do not* allow parallel edges (two copies of the same edge). Checking for self-loops and parallel edges is easy; our choice is to omit both checks.

*Client query methods.* We also include the methods `V()` and `E()` in our API to provide to the client the number of vertices and edges in the graph. Such methods should provide the requisite information in constant time. Similarly, the methods `degree()`, `hasVertex()`, and `hasEdge()` are useful in client code. We leave as exercises the implementation of these methods, but assume them to be in our `Graph` API.

NONE OF THESE DESIGN DECISIONS ARE sacrosanct; they are simply the choices that we have made for the code in this book. Some other choices might be appropriate in various situations, and some decisions are still left to implementations. It is wise to carefully consider the choices that you make for design decisions like this *and to be prepared to defend them.*

`Graph` (PROGRAM 4.5.1) implements this API. Its internal representation is a *symbol table of sets*: the keys are vertices and the values are the sets of neighbors—the vertices adjacent to the key. This representation uses the two data types `ST` and `SET` that we introduced in SECTION 4.4. It has three important properties:

- Clients can efficiently iterate through the graph vertices.
- Clients can efficiently iterate through a vertex's neighbors.
- Space usage is proportional to the number of edges.

These properties follow immediately from basic properties of `ST` and `SET`. As you will see, the two iterators are at the heart of graph processing.

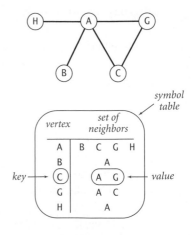

*Symbol-table-of-sets graph representation*

**Program 4.5.1 Graph data type**

```java
public class Graph
{
    private ST<String, SET<String>> st;

    public Graph()
    {  st = new ST<String, SET<String>>();  }

    public void addEdge(String v, String w)
    {  // Put v in w's SET and w in v's SET.
        if (!st.contains(v)) st.put(v, new SET<String>());
        if (!st.contains(w)) st.put(w, new SET<String>());
        st.get(v).add(w);
        st.get(w).add(v);
    }

    public Iterable<String> adjacentTo(String v)
    {  return st.get(v);  }

    public Iterable<String> vertices()
    {  return st;  }

    // See exercise 4.5.1-4 for V(), E(), degree(),
    // hasVertex(), and hasEdge().

    public static void main(String[] args)
    {  // Read edges, print Graph (sets of neighbors).
        Graph G = new Graph();
        while (!StdIn.isEmpty())
            G.addEdge(StdIn.readString(), StdIn.readString());
        StdOut.print(G);
    }
}
```

| st | symbol table of vertex neighbor sets |
|---|---|

| adjacentTo() | neighbor iterator |
|---|---|
| vertices() | vertex iterator |

This implementation uses ST and SET (see Section 4.4) to implement the graph data type. Clients build graphs by adding edges and process them by iterating the vertex set and the set of vertices adjacent to a given vertex. See the text for toString() and a matching constructor that reads a graph from an input stream.

```
% more tiny.txt
A B
A C
C A
C G
A G
H A
```

```
% java Graph < tiny.txt
A B C G H
B A
C A G
G A C
H A
```

As a simple example of client code, consider the problem of printing a Graph. A natural way to proceed is to print a list of the vertices, along with a list of immediate neighbors of each vertex. We use this approach to implement toString() in Graph, as follows:

```
public String toString()
{
   String s = "";
   for (String v : vertices())
   {
      s += v + " ";
      for (String w : adjacentTo(v))
         s += w + " ";
      s += "\n";
   }
   return s;
}
```

This code prints two representations of each edge, once when discovering that w is a neighbor of v and once when discovering that v is a neighbor of w. Many graph algorithms are based on this basic paradigm of processing each edge in the graph in this way, and it is important to remember that they process each edge twice. As usual, this implementation is intended for use only for small graphs, as the running time is quadratic in the string length because string concatenation is linear-time.

The output format just considered defines a reasonable file format: each line is a vertex name followed by the names of neighbors of that vertex. Accordingly, our basic graph API includes a constructor for building a graph from an input stream in this format (list of vertices with neighbors). For flexibility, we allow for the use of other delimiters besides spaces for vertex names (so that, for example, vertex names may contain spaces), as in the following implementation:

```
public Graph(In in, String delimiter)
{
   st = new ST<String, SET<String>>();
   while (!in.isEmpty())
   {
      String line = in.readLine();
      String[] names = line.split(delimiter);
      for (int i = 1; i < names.length; i++)
         addEdge(names[0], names[i]);
   }
}
```

Adding this constructor and `toString()` to `Graph` provides a complete data type suitable for a broad variety of applications, as we will now see. Note that this same constructor (with a space delimiter) works properly when the input is a list of edges, one per line, as in the test client for PROGRAM 4.5.1.

**Graph client example**   As a first graph-processing client, we consider an example of social relationships, one that is certainly familiar to you and for which extensive data is readily available.

On the booksite you can find the file `movies.txt` (and many similar files), which contains a list of movies and the performers who appeared in them. Each line gives the name of a movie followed by the cast (a list of the names of the performers who appeared in that movie). Since names have spaces and commas in them, the / character is used as a delimiter. (Now you can see why our file input `Graph` constructor takes the delimiter as an argument.)

If you study `movies.txt`, you will notice a number of characteristics that, though minor, need attention when working with the database:

- Movies always have the year in parentheses after the title.
- Special characters are present.
- Multiple performers with the same name are differentiated by Roman numerals within parentheses.
- Cast lists are not in alphabetical order.

Depending on your terminal and operating system settings, special characters may be replaced by blanks or question marks. These types of anomalies are common in working with large amounts of real-world data. We can either choose to live with them or write filters to minimize any annoyances.

```
% more movies.txt
...
Tin Men (1987)/DeBoy, David/Blumenfeld, Alan/... /Geppi, Cindy/Hershey, Barbara
Tirez sur le pianiste (1960)/Heymann, Claude/.../Berger, Nicole (I)
Titanic (1997)/Mazin, Stan/...DiCaprio, Leonardo/.../Winslet, Kate/...
Titus (1999)/Weisskopf, Hermann/Rhys, Matthew/.../McEwan, Geraldine
To Be or Not to Be (1942)/Verebes, Ernö (I)/.../Lombard, Carole (I)
To Be or Not to Be (1983)/.../Brooks, Mel (I)/.../Bancroft, Anne/...
To Catch a Thief (1955)/París, Manuel/.../Grant, Cary/.../Kelly, Grace/...
To Die For (1995)/Smith, Kurtwood/.../Kidman, Nicole/.../ Tucci, Maria
...
```

*Movie database example*

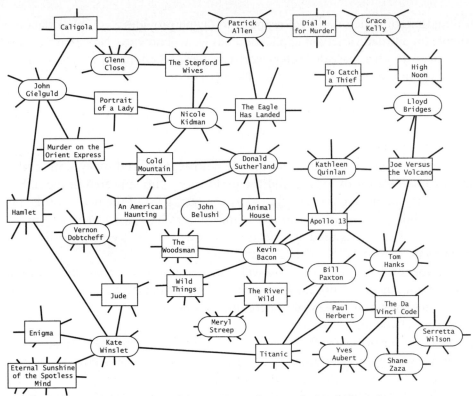

*A tiny portion of the movie-performer relationship graph*

Using Graph, we can write a simple and convenient client for extracting information from movies.txt. We begin by building a Graph to better structure the information. What should the vertices and edges model? Should the vertices be movies with edges connecting two movies if a performer has appeared in both? Should the vertices be performers with edges connecting two performers if both have appeared in the same movie? These choices are both plausible, but which should we use? This decision affects both client and implementation code. Another way to proceed (which we choose because it leads to simple implementation code) is to have vertices for *both* the movies and the performers, with an edge connecting each movie to each performer in that movie. As you will see, programs that process this graph can answer a great variety of interesting questions. The Graph client IndexGraph (PROGRAM 4.5.2) is a first example that takes a query, such as the name of a movie, and prints the list of performers that appear in that movie.

## Program 4.5.2 *Using a graph to invert an index*

```
public class IndexGraph
{
   public static void main(String[] args)
   {  // Build a graph and process queries.
      In in = new In(args[0]);
      String delimiter = args[1];
      Graph G = new Graph(in, delimiter);
      while (!StdIn.isEmpty())
      {  // Read a vertex and print its neighbors.
         String v = StdIn.readLine();
         for (String w : G.adjacentTo(v))
            StdOut.println("  " + w);
      }
   }
}
```

| | |
|---|---|
| in | *input stream* |
| delimiter | *input delimiter* |
| G | *graph* |
| v | *query* |
| w | *neighbor of* v |

*This* Graph *client builds a graph, then accepts vertex names from standard input and prints its neighbors. When the file is an index, it creates a bipartite graph and amounts to an interactive inverted index.*

```
% java IndexGraph tiny.txt " "
C
  A
  G
A
  B
  C
  G
  H
```

```
% java IndexGraph movies.txt "/"
Da Vinci Code, The (2006)
  Aubert, Yves
  ...
  Herbert, Paul
  ...
  Wilson, Serretta
  Zaza, Shane
Bacon, Kevin
  Animal House (1978)
  Apollo 13 (1995)
  ...
  Wild Things (1998)
  River Wild, The (1994)
  Woodsman, The (2004)
```

Typing a movie name and getting its cast is not much more than regurgitating the corresponding line in `movies.txt` (though the `IndexGraph` test client does print the cast list sorted by last name, as that is the default iteration order provided by `SET`). A more interesting feature of `IndexGraph` is that you can type the name of a *performer* and get the list of *movies* in which that performer has appeared. Why does this work? Even though the database seems to connect movies to performers and not the other way around, the edges in the graph are *connections* that also connect performers to movies.

A graph in which connections all connect one kind of vertex to another kind of vertex is known as a *bipartite* graph. As this example illustrates, bipartite graphs have many natural properties that we can often exploit in interesting ways.

As we saw at the beginning of SECTION 4.4, the indexing paradigm is general and very familiar. It is worth reflecting on the fact that building a bipartite graph provides a simple way to automatically invert *any* index! The `movies.txt` database is indexed by movie, but we can query it by performer. You could use `IndexGraph` in precisely the same way to print the index words appearing on a given page or the codons corresponding to a given amino acid, or to invert any of the other indices discussed at the beginning of SECTION 4.2. Since `IndexGraph` takes the delimiter as a command-line argument, you can use it to create an interactive inverted index for a `.csv` file or a test file with space delimiters.

```
% more amino.csv
TTT,Phe,F,Phenylalanine
TTC,Phe,F,Phenylalanine
TTA,Leu,L,Leucine
TTG,Leu,L,Leucine
TCT,Ser,S,Serine
TCC,Ser,S,Serine
TCA,Ser,S,Serine
TCG,Ser,S,Serine
TAT,Tyr,Y,Tyrosine
...
GGA,Gly,G,Glycine
GGG,Gly,G,Glycine

% java IndexGraph amino.csv ","
TTA
   Lue
   L
   Leucine
Serine
   TCT
   TCC
   TCA
   TCG
```

This inverted-index functionality is a direct benefit of the graph *data structure*. Next, we examine some of the added benefits to be derived from *algorithms* that process the data structure.

*Inverting an index*

**Shortest paths in graphs**   Given two vertices in a graph, a *path* is a sequence of edges connecting them. A *shortest path* is one with minimal length over all such paths (there typically are multiple shortest paths). Finding a shortest path connecting two vertices in a graph is a fundamental problem in computer science. Shortest paths have been famously and successfully applied to solve large-scale problems in a broad variety of applications, from routing the internet to financial arbitrage transactions to studying the dynamics of neurons in the brain.

As an example, imagine that you are a customer of an imaginary no-frills airline that serves a limited number of cities with a limited number of routes. Assume that best way to get from one place to another is to minimize your number of flight segments, because delays in transferring from one flight to another are likely to be lengthy (or perhaps the best thing to do is to consider paying more for a direct flight on another airline!). A shortest-path algorithm is just what you need to plan a trip. Such an application appeals to intuition in understanding the basic problem and our approach to solving it. After covering these topics in the context of this example, we will consider an application where the graph model is more abstract.

Depending upon the application, clients have various needs with regard to shortest paths. Do we want the shortest path connecting two given vertices? Just the length of such a path? Will we have a large number of such queries? Is one particular vertex of interest? In huge graphs or for huge numbers of queries, we have to pay particular attention to such questions because the cost of computing paths might prove to be prohibitive. We start with the following API:

```
public class PathFinder
```
---

| | | |
|---|---|---|
| | PathFinder(Graph G, String s) | *constructor* |
| int | distanceTo(String v) | *length of shortest path from* s *to* v *in* G |
| Iterable<String> | pathTo(String v) | *shortest path from* s *to* v *in* G |

*API for single-source shortest paths in a* Graph

Clients can construct a PathFinder for a given graph and a given vertex, and then use the PathFinder either to find the length of the shortest path or to iterate through the vertices on the shortest path to any other vertex in the graph. An implementation of these methods is known as a *single-source shortest-path algorithm*. A classic algorithm known as *breadth-first search* provides a direct and elegant solution.

*Single-source client.* Suppose that you have available to you the graph of vertices and connections for your no-frills airline's route map. Then, using your home city as a source, you can write a client that prints your route any time you want to go on a trip. PROGRAM 4.5.3 is a client for `PathFinder` that provides this functionality for any graph. This sort of client is particularly useful in applications where we anticipate numerous queries from the same source. In this situation, the cost of building a `PathFinder` is amortized over the cost of all the queries. You are encouraged to explore the properties of shortest paths by running `PathFinder` on our sample input `routes.txt` or any input model that you choose. The exercises at the end of this section describe several models that you might consider.

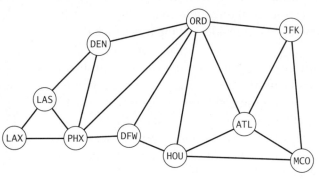

| source | destination | distance | shortest paths |
|--------|-------------|----------|----------------|
| JFK | LAX | 3 | JFK-ORD-PHX-LAX |
| LAS | MCO | 4 | LAS-PHX-DFW-HOU-MCO *and four others* |
| HOU | JFK | 2 | HOU-ATL-JFK *and two others* |

*Examples of shortest paths in a graph*

*Degrees of separation.* One of the classic applications of shortest-paths algorithms is to find the *degrees of separation* of individuals in social networks. To fix ideas, we discuss this application in terms of a recently popularized pastime known as the *Kevin Bacon game*, which uses the movie-performer graph that we just considered. Kevin Bacon is a prolific actor who has appeared in many movies. We assign every performer who has appeared in a movie a *Kevin Bacon number*: Bacon himself is 0, any performer who has been in the same cast as Bacon has a Kevin Bacon number of 1, any other performer (except Bacon) who has been in the same cast as a performer whose number is 1 has a Kevin Bacon number of 2, and so forth. For example, Meryl Streep has a Kevin Bacon number of 1 because she appeared in *The River Wild* with Kevin Bacon. Nicole Kidman's number is 2: although she did not appear in any movie with Kevin Bacon, she was in *Cold Mountain* with Donald Sutherland, and Sutherland appeared in *Animal House* with Kevin Bacon. Given the name of a performer, the simplest version of the game is to find some alternating sequence of movies and performers that lead back to Kevin Bacon. For example, a movie

**Program 4.5.3    *Shortest-paths client***

```
public class PathFinder
{
    // See Program 4.5.5 for implementation.

    public static void main(String[] args)
    { // Read a graph and process queries
      // for shortest paths from s.
        In in = new In(args[0]);
        String delimiter = args[1];
        Graph G = new Graph(in, delimiter);
        String s = args[2];
        PathFinder pf = new PathFinder(G, s);
        while (!StdIn.isEmpty())
        { // Print distance and shortest path from s to input t.
            String t = StdIn.readLine();
            int d = pf.distanceTo(t);
            for (String v : pf.pathTo(t))
                StdOut.println("    " + v);
            StdOut.println("distance " + d);
        }
    }
}
```

| | |
|---|---|
| in | *input stream* |
| delimiter | *input delimiter* |
| G | *graph* |
| s | *source* |
| pf | PathFinder *from s* |
| t | *destination query* |
| v | *vertex on path* |

*This* PathFinder *test client takes a file name, a delimiter, and a source vertex as command-line arguments. It builds a graph from the file, assuming that each line of the file specifies a vertex and a list of vertices connected to that vertex, separated by the delimiter. When you type a destination on standard input, you get the shortest path from the source to that destination.*

```
% more routes.txt
JFK MCO
ORD DEN
ORD HOU
DFW PHX
JFK ATL
ORD DFW
ORD PHX
ATL HOU
DEN PHX
PHX LAX
JFK ORD
DEN LAS
DFW HOU
ORD ATL
LAS LAX
ATL MCO
HOU MCO
LAS PHX
```

```
% java PathFinder routes.txt " " JFK
LAX
    JFK
    ORD
    PHX
    LAX
distance 3
MCO
    JFK
    MCO
distance 1
DFW
    JFK
    ORD
    DFW
distance 2
```

buff might know that Tom Hanks was in *Joe Versus the Volcano* with Lloyd Bridges, who was in *High Noon* with Grace Kelly, who was in *Dial M for Murder* with Patrick Allen, who was in *The Eagle Has Landed* with Donald Sutherland, who we know was in *Animal House* with Kevin Bacon. But this knowledge does not suffice to establish Tom Hanks's Bacon number (it is actually 1 because he was in *Apollo 13* with Kevin Bacon). You can see that the Kevin Bacon number has to be defined by counting the movies in the *shortest* such sequence, so it is hard to be sure whether someone wins the game without using a computer. Remarkably, the PathFinder test client in PROGRAM 4.5.3 is just the program you need to find a shortest path that establishes the Kevin Bacon number of any performer in movies.txt—the number is precisely half the distance. You might enjoy using this program, or extending it to answer some enter-

```
% java PathFinder movies.txt "/" "Bacon, Kevin"
Kidman, Nicole
    Bacon, Kevin
    Animal House (1978)
    Sutherland, Donald (I)
    Cold Mountain (2003)
    Kidman, Nicole
distance 4
Hanks, Tom
    Bacon, Kevin
    Apollo 13 (1995)
    Hanks, Tom
distance 2
```

*Degrees of separation from Kevin Bacon*

taining questions about the movie business or in one of many other domains. For example, mathematicians play this same game with the graph defined by paper co-authorship and their connection to Paul Erdös, a prolific 20th-century mathematician. Similarly, everyone in New Jersey seems to have a Bruce Springsteen number of 2, because everyone in the state seems to know someone who claims to know Bruce.

*Other clients.* PathFinder is a versatile data type that can be put to many practical uses. For example, it is easy to develop a client that handles pairwise source-destination requests on standard input, by building a PathFinder for each vertex (see EXERCISE 4.5.17). Travel services use precisely this approach to handle requests at a very high service rate. Since this client builds a PathFinder for each vertex (each of which might consume space proportional to the number of vertices), space usage might be a limiting factor in using it for huge graphs. For an even more performance-critical application that is conceptually the same, consider an internet router that has a graph of connections among machines available and must decide the best next stop for packets heading to a given destination. To do so, it can build a `PathFinder` with itself as the source, then send a packet heading to destination w to `pf.pathTo(w).next()`, the next stop on the shortest path to w. Or a central authority might build a `PathFinder` for each of several dependent routers and use them to issue routing instructions. The ability to handle such requests at a high service rate is one of the prime responsibilities of internet routers, and shortest-paths algorithms are a critical part of the process.

*Shortest-path distances.* We define the *distance* between two vertices to be the length of the shortest path between them. The first step in understanding breadth-first search is to consider the problem of computing distances between the source and each vertex (the implementation of `distanceTo()` in `PathFinder`). Our ap-

| v | queue contents | ATL | DEN | DFW | HOU | JFK | LAS | LAX | MCO | ORD |
|---|---|---|---|---|---|---|---|---|---|---|
| *initialize for distance 0* | JFK | | | | | 0 | | | | |
| *distance 1* | | | | | | | | | | |
| JFK | | | | | | 0 | | | | |
| JFK | ATL | 1 | | | | 0 | | | | |
| JFK | ATL MCO | 1 | | | | 0 | | | 1 | |
| JFK | ATL MCO ORD | 1 | | | | 0 | | | 1 | 1 |
| *distance 2* | | | | | | | | | | |
| ATL | MCO ORD | 1 | | | | 0 | | | 1 | 1 |
| ATL | MCO ORD HOU | 1 | | | 2 | 0 | | | 1 | 1 |
| MCO | ORD HOU | 1 | | | 2 | 0 | | | 1 | 1 |
| ORD | HOU | 1 | | | 2 | 0 | | | 1 | 1 |
| ORD | HOU DEN | 1 | 2 | | 2 | 0 | | | 1 | 1 |
| ORD | HOU DEN DFW | 1 | 2 | 2 | 2 | 0 | | | 1 | 1 |
| ORD | HOU DEN DFW PHX | 1 | 2 | 2 | 2 | 0 | | | 1 | 1 |
| *distance 3* | | | | | | | | | | |
| HOU | DEN DFW PHX | 1 | 2 | 2 | 2 | 0 | | | 1 | 1 |
| DEN | DFW PHX | 1 | 2 | 2 | 2 | 0 | | | 1 | 1 |
| DEN | DFW PHX LAS | 1 | 2 | 2 | 2 | 0 | 3 | | 1 | 1 |
| DFW | PHX LAS | 1 | 2 | 2 | 2 | 0 | 3 | | 1 | 1 |
| PHX | LAS | 1 | 2 | 2 | 2 | 0 | 3 | | 1 | 1 |
| PHX | LAS LAX | 1 | 2 | 2 | 2 | 0 | 3 | 3 | 1 | 1 |
| *check for distance 4* | | | | | | | | | | |
| LAS | LAX | 1 | 2 | 2 | 2 | 0 | 3 | 3 | 1 | 1 |
| LAX | | 1 | 2 | 2 | 2 | 0 | 3 | 3 | 1 | 1 |

*Using breadth-first search to compute shortest path distances in a graph* proach is to compute and save away all the distances in the constructor, and then just return the requested value when a client invokes `distanceTo()`. To associate an integer distance with each vertex name, we use a symbol table:

```
ST<String, Integer> dist = new ST<String, Integer>();
```

The purpose of this symbol table is to associate with each vertex an integer: the length of the shortest path (the distance) from that vertex to s. We begin by giving s the distance 0 with `dist.put(s, 0)`, and we assign to s's neighbors the distance 1 with the following code:

```
for (String v : G.adjacentTo(s))
    dist.put(v, 1)
```

But then what do we do? If we blindly set the distances to all the neighbors of each of those neighbors to 2, then not only would we face the prospect of unnecessarily setting many values twice (neighbors may have many common neighbors), but also we would set s's distance to 2 (it is a neighbor of each of its neighbors), and we clearly do not want that outcome. The solution to these difficulties is simple:
  • Consider the vertices in order of their distance from s.
  • Ignore vertices whose distance to s is already known.
To organize the computation, we use a FIFO queue. Starting with s on the queue, we perform the following operations until the queue is empty:
  • Dequeue a vertex v.
  • Assign all of v's unknown neighbors a distance 1 greater than v's distance.
  • Enqueue all of the unknown neighbors.

This method dequeues the vertices in nondecreasing order of their distance from the source s. Following a trace of this method on a sample graph will help to persuade you that it is correct. Showing that this method labels each vertex v with its distance to s is an exercise in mathematical induction (see EXERCISE 4.5.12).

*Shortest paths tree.* We need not only distances from the source, but also paths. To implement `pathTo()`, we use a subgraph known as the *shortest-paths tree*, defined as follows:
  • Put the source at the root of the tree.
  • Put vertex v's neighbors in the tree if they are added to the queue, with an edge connecting each to v.

Since we enqueue each vertex only once, this structure is a proper tree: it consists of a root (the source) connected to one subtree for each neighbor of the source. Studying such a tree, you can see immediately that the distance from each vertex to the root in the tree is the same as the shortest path distance to the source in the graph. More importantly, each path in the tree is a shortest path in the graph. This observation is important because it gives us an easy way to provide clients with the shortest paths themselves (implement `pathTo()` in `PathFinder`). First, we maintain a symbol table associating each vertex with the vertex one step nearer to the source on the shortest path:

*graph*

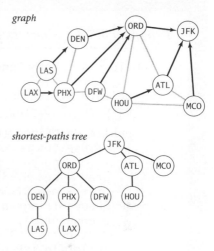

```
ST<String, String> prev;
prev = new ST<String, String>();
```

*parent-link representation*

| ATL | DEN | DFW | HOU | JFK | LAS | LAX | MCO | ORD | PH |
|-----|-----|-----|-----|-----|-----|-----|-----|-----|-----|
| JFK | ORF | ORD | ATL |     |     | DEN | PHX | JFK | JFK | OR |

*Shortest-paths tree*

To each vertex w, we want to associate the previous stop on the shortest path from the source to w. Augmenting the shortest-distances method to also compute this information is easy: when we enqueue w because we first discover it as a neighbor of v, we do so precisely becauset v is the previous stop on the shortest path from the source to w, so we can call `prev.put(w, v)`. The prev data structure is nothing more than a representation of the shortest path tree: it provides a link from each node to its parent in the tree. Then, to respond to a client request for the path from the source to w (a call to `pathTo(w)` in `PathFinder`), we follow these links *up* the tree from w, which traverses the path in reverse order, so we push each vertex encountered onto a stack and then return that stack (an `It-erable`) to the client. At the top of the stack is s; at the bottom of the stack is v; and the

*shortest-paths tree (parent-link representation)*

*stack contents*

*Recovering a path from the tree with a stack*

*Program 4.5.4    Shortest-paths implementation*

```
public class PathFinder
{
    private ST<String, String>  prev;
    private ST<String, Integer> dist;

    public PathFinder(Graph G, String s)
    { // Use BFS to compute distances and previous node
      // on shortest path from s to each vertex.
        prev = new ST<String, String>();
        dist = new ST<String, Integer>();
        Queue<String> q = new Queue<String>();
        q.enqueue(s);
        dist.put(s, 0);
        while (!q.isEmpty())
        { // Process next vertex on queue.
            String v = q.dequeue();
            for (String w : G.adjacentTo(v))
            { // Check whether distance is already known.
                if (!dist.contains(w))
                { // Add to queue and save shortest-path information.
                    q.enqueue(w);
                    dist.put(w, 1 + dist.get(v));
                    prev.put(w, v);
                }
            }
        }
    }

    public int distanceTo(String v)
    {  return dist.get(v);  }

    public Iterable<String> pathTo(String v)
    { // Return iterable object having shortest path from s to v.
        Stack<String> path = new Stack<String>();
        while (dist.contains(v))
        { // Push current vertex; move to previous vertex on path.
            path.push(v);
            v = prev.get(v);
        }
        return path;
    }
}
```

| prev | *previous vertex on shortest path from* s |
|------|-------------------------------------------|
| dist | *distance to* s |

| G | *graph* |
|---|---------|
| s | *source* |
| q | *queue of vertices* |
| v | *current vertex* |
| w | *neighbors of* v |

| PathFinder() | *constructor for* s *in* G |
|--------------|----------------------------|
| distanceTo() | *distance from* s *to* v |
| pathTo() | *path from* s *to* v |

*This class allows clients to find (shortest) paths connecting a specified vertex to other vertices in a graph. See Program 4.5.3 and Exercise 4.5.17 for sample clients.*

vertices on the path from s to v are in between, so the client gets the path from s to v when using the return value from `pathTo()` in a foreach statement.

*Breadth-first search.* `PathFinder` (PROGRAM 4.5.4) is an implementation of the single-source shortest paths API that is based on the ideas just discussed. It maintains two symbol tables, one for the distance from each vertex to the source and the other for the previous stop on the shortest path from the source to each vertex. The constructor uses a queue to keep track of vertices that have been encountered (neighbors of vertices to which the shortest path has been found but whose neighbors have not yet been examined). The process is referred to as breadth-first search (BFS) because it searches broadly in the graph. By contrast, another important graph-search method known as depth-first search is based on a recursive method like the one we used for percolation in PROGRAM 2.4.5 and searches deeply into the graph. Depth-first search tends to find long paths; breadth-first search is guaranteed to find shortest paths.

*Performance.* The cost of graph-processing algorithms typically depends on two graph parameters: the number of vertices $V$ and the number of edges $E$. As implemented in `PathFinder`, *the time required by breadth-first search is linearithmic in the size of the input*, proportional to $E \log V$. To convince yourself of this fact, first observe that the outer (`while`) loop iterates at most $V$ times, once for each vertex, because we are careful to ensure that each vertex is enqueued at most once. Then observe that the inner (`for`) loop iterates a total of at most $2E$ times over all iterations, because we are careful to ensure that each edge is examined at most twice, once for each of the two vertices it connects. Each iteration of the loop requires at least one `contains()` operation and perhaps two `put()` operations, on symbol tables of size at most $V$. This linearithmic-time performance depends upon using a symbol-table implementation like BST (PROGRAM 4.4.3) that has a linear-time iterator and logarithmic-time search.

*Adjacency matrix representation.* Without proper data structures, fast performance for graph-processing algorithms is sometimes not easy to achieve, and so should not be taken for granted. For example, another graph representation that is often used, known as the *adjacency matrix representation*, uses a symbol table to map vertex names to integers between 0 and $V-1$, then maintains a $V$-by-$V$ boolean array with `true` in the entry in row i and column j (and the entry in row j and column i) if there is an edge connecting the vertex corresponding to i with the vertex corresponding to j, and `false` if there is no such edge. We have already used similar representations in this book, when studying the random surfer model for ranking web pages in SECTION 1.6. The adjacency matrix representation is simple, but infeasible for use with huge graphs—a graph with a million vertices would require an adjacency matrix with a *trillion* entries. Understanding this distinction for graph-processing problems makes the difference between solving a problem that arises in a practical situation and not being able to address it at all.

BREADTH-FIRST SEARCH IS A FUNDAMENTAL ALGORITHM that you could use to find your way around an airline route map or a big city subway (see EXERCISE 4.5.34) or in numerous similar situations. As indicated by our degrees-of-separation example, it also is used for countless other applications, from crawling the web or routing packets on the internet to studying infectious disease, models of the brain, or relationships among genomic sequences. Many of these algorithms involve huge graphs, so an efficient algorithm is absolutely necessary.

An important generalization of the shortest-paths model is to associate a weight (which may represent distance or time) with each edge and seek to find a path that minimizes the sum of the edge weights. If you take later courses in algorithms or in operations research, you will learn a generalization of breadth-first search known as *Dijkstra's algorithm* that solves that problem in linearithmic time. When you get directions from a GPS device or a map application on the web, Dikstra's algorithm is the basis for solving the associated shortest-path problems. These important and omnipresent applications are just the tip of an iceberg, because graph models are much more general than maps.

**Small-world graphs**   Scientists have identified a particularly interesting class of graphs that arise in numerous applications in the natural and social sciences. Small-world graphs are characterized by the following three properties:
- They are *sparse.*
- They exhibit *local clustering* of edges around vertices.
- They have a *short average distance between vertices.*

We refer to graphs having these three properties collectively as exhibiting the *small-world phenomenon.* The term *small world* refers to the idea that the preponderance of vertices have both local clustering and short paths to other vertices. The modifier *phenomenon* refers to the somewhat unexpected fact that *all* distances are short in so many sparse graphs with local clustering that arise in practice. Beyond the social-relationships applications just considered, small-world graphs have been used to study the marketing or products or ideas, the formation and spread of fame and fads, the analysis of the internet, the construction of secure peer-to-peer networks, the development of routing algorithms, and wireless networks, the design of electrical power grids, modeling information processing in the human brain, the study of phase transitions in oscillators, the spread of infectious viruses (in both living organisms and computers), and many other applications too numerous to list. Starting with the seminal work of Watts and Strogatz in the 1990s, an intensive amount of research has gone into quantifying the small-world phenomenon.

A key question in such research is the following: *Given a graph, how can we tell whether it is a small-world graph or not?* To answer this question, we begin by imposing the conditions that the graph is not small (say, 1,000 vertices or more) and that it is connected (there exists *some* path connecting each pair of vertices). Then, we need to settle on specific thresholds for each of the small-world properties:

- By *sparse*, we mean the average vertex degree is less than $10 \lg V$.
- By *locally clustered*, we mean that a certain quantity known as the *cluster coefficient* should be greater than 10%.
- By *short average distance*, we mean the average distance between two vertices is less than $10 \lg V$.

*Average vertex degree*

| vertex | degree |
|--------|--------|
| A | 4 |
| B | 1 |
| C | 2 |
| G | 2 |
| H | 1 |
| total | 10 |

average degree $= 10/5 = 2$

*Average path length*

| vertex pair | shortest path | length |
|-------------|---------------|--------|
| A B | A–B | 1 |
| A C | A–C | 1 |
| A G | A–G | 1 |
| A H | A–H | 1 |
| B C | B–A–C | 2 |
| B G | B–A–G | 2 |
| B H | B–A–H | 2 |
| C G | C–G | 1 |
| C H | C–A–H | 2 |
| G H | G–A–H | 2 |
| | total | 15 |

$\dfrac{total\ length}{number\ of\ pairs} = 15/10 = 1.5$

*Cluster coefficient*

| vertex | degree | edges in neighborhood possible | actual |
|--------|--------|----------|--------|
| A | 4 | 10 | 5 |
| B | 1 | 1 | 1 |
| C | 2 | 3 | 3 |
| G | 2 | 3 | 3 |
| H | 1 | 1 | 1 |
| totals | | 18 | 13 |

$\dfrac{total\ possible}{total\ actual} = 13/18 \approx .72$

*Calculating small-world graph characteristics*

The definition of *cluster coefficient* is a bit more complicated than vertex distance. We use a version of a definition suggested by Watts and Strogatz that is not difficult to compute. If a vertex has $t$ neighbors, the total number of possible edges that connect those neighbors (including the vertex itself) is $t(t+1)/2$. We define the cluster coefficient as the percentage of those edges that are in the graph, using the totals over all the vertices. Thus, if that percentage is greater than 10%, we say that most edges are locally clustered around the vertices.

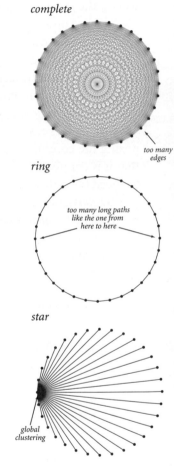

*complete*

*too many edges*

*ring*

*too many long paths like the one from here to here*

*star*

*global clustering*

*Three graph models*

To better familiarize you with these definitions, we next define some simple graph models, and consider whether they describe small-world graphs by checking whether they exhibit the three requisite properties.

**Complete graphs.** A *complete* graph with $V$ vertices has $V(V-1)/2$ edges, one connecting each pair of vertices. Complete graphs are *not* small-world graphs. They have short distances (the distance between all pairs of nodes is 1) and exhibit local clustering (cluster coefficient is 1), but they are *not* sparse (the average vertex degree is $V-1$, which is much greater than 10 lg $V$ for large $V$).

**Ring graphs.** Suppose that the vertices are the integers 0 to $V-1$. In a ring graph, edges connect vertex $i$ to vertex $i+1$ and $V-1$ to 0. Ring graphs are also *not* small-world graphs. They are sparse (average vertex degree 2) and exhibit local clustering (cluster coefficient .33), but they do not have short distances (the average distance between nodes is linear—see EXERCISE 4.5.22).

**Star graphs.** In a star graph, edges connect one vertex to each of the others, but there are no other edges. Star graphs are also *not* small-world graphs. They are sparse (average vertex degree 2) and have short distances (average distance between nodes is slightly less than 2), but they do *not* exhibit local clustering, because the cluster coefficient is about $4/N$ (see EXERCISE 4.5.22).

These examples illustrate that developing a graph model that satisfies all three constraints simultaneously is a puzzling challenge. Take a moment to try to design a graph model that you think might do so. After you have thought about this problem, you will realize that you are likely to need a program to help with calculations. Also, you may agree that it is quite surprising that they are found so often in practice. Indeed, you might be wondering if *any* graph is a small-world graph!

Choosing 10% for the local clustering threshold instead of some other fixed percentage is somewhat arbitrary, as is the choice of 10 lg $V$ for the sparsity and short path length thresholds, but we often do not come close to these borderline values. For example, consider the graph defined by pages on the web connected by links. Analysts have estimated that the average distance between two pages on the web is less than lg $V$. If there are billions of pages, this estimate says that the number of clicks to get from one document to another is about 30 (and each time the web grows by a factor of 1,000, only about 10 more clicks will be needed). These real-world path lengths are very short, much lower than our 10 lg $V$ estimate, which would be over 300 for billions of vertices (but still much, much less than $V$).

Having settled on the definitions, testing whether a graph is a small-world graph can still be a significant computational burden. As you probably have suspected, the graph-processing data types that we

| model | sparse? | short paths? | locally clustered? |
|-------|---------|--------------|--------------------|
| complete | ○ | ● | ● |
| ring | ● | ○ | ● |
| star | ● | ● | ○ |

*Small-world properties of graph models*

have been considering provide precisely the tools that we need. The `Graph` and `PathFinder` client `SmallWorld` (PROGRAM 4.5.5) implements these tests. Without the efficient data structures and algorithms that we have been considering, the cost of this computation would be prohibitive. Even so, for huge graphs, we need to resort to sampling to get estimates of some of the quantities.

*A classic small-world graph.* Our movie-performer graph is not a small-world graph, because it is bipartite and therefore has a very low cluster coefficient. However, the simpler *performer relationship* graph defined by connecting two performers by an edge if they appeared in the same movie is a classic example of a small-world graph. Since a performer relationship graph has many more edges than the corresponding movie-performer graph, we will work for the moment with the smaller graph represented by the file `moviesG.txt` (G-rated movies). Performer graphs are easy to construct from files in the format represented by `movies*.txt`.

Each line represents a movie and gives a set of actors who are connected because of that movie (each slash-delimited string after the first is an actor's name); we build a *complete subgraph* connecting all pairs of actors in that movie by adding a graph edge connecting each pair. Doing so for each movie in the database gives a graph that connects the performers, as desired.

Note that the movie names are not relevant in the performer relationship graph—only in the performer relationships implied by the movie. One alternative might be to use a `Graph` implementation that assigns names to edges, not just vertices, but our movie-performer graph is a much better solution if the edge names are also of interest.

Now, for `moviesG.txt`, our `Small-World` client tells us that the resulting graph has 20,734 vertices and 1,784,567 edges (so the average vertex degree is 139.0, just less than 10 lg $V$ = 143.4), which means it is sparse; its average path length is 7.3 (much less than 143.4), so it has short paths; and its cluster coefficient is .92, so it has local clustering. We have found a small-world graph! These calculations validate the hypothesis that social relationship graphs of this sort exhibit the small-world phenomenon. You are encouraged to find other real-world graphs and to test them with `Small-World`. You will find many suggestions in the exercises at the end of this section.

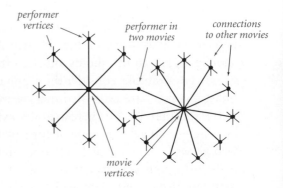

*movie-performer relationship graph*

*Two ways to represent the movie database*

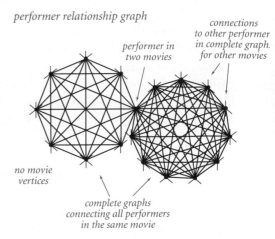

*performer relationship graph*

One approach to understanding something like the small-world phenomenon is to develop a mathematical model that we can use to test hypotheses and to make predictions. We conclude by returning to the problem of developing a graph model that can help us to better under-

---

### Program 4.5.5  Small-world test

```java
public class SmallWorld
{
   public static double avgDegree(Graph G)
   {  return 2*G.E() / G.V();  }

   public static double avgDistance(Graph G)
   {  // Compute average vertex distance.
      int total = 0;
      for (String v : G.vertices())
      {  // Add to total distances from v.
         PathFinder pf = new PathFinder(G, v);
         for (String w : G.vertices())
            total += pf.distanceTo(w);
      }
      return (double) total / (G.V() * (G.V() - 1));
   }

   public static double clusterCoeff(Graph G)
   {  // Compute cluster coefficient.
      int possible = 0;
      int edges = 2*G.E();
      for (String v : G.vertices())
      {  // Cumulate local edge totals.
         for (String u : G.adjacentTo(v))
            for (String w : G.adjacentTo(v))
               if (G.hasEdge(u, w)) edges++;
         int t = G.degree(v);
         possible += (t + 1)*t;
      }
      return (double) edges / possible;
   }

   public static void main(String[] args)
   {  /* See Exercise 4.5.19. */  }
```

| G | graph |
|---|---|
| total | cumulative sum of distances between vertices |
| v | vertex iterator variable |
| w | neighbors of v |

| G | graph |
|---|---|
| possible | cumulative sum of possible local edges |
| edges | cumulative sum of actual local edges |
| v | vertex iterator variable |
| u, w | neighbors of v |

*This client reads a graph from standard input and computes the values of various graph parameters to test whether the graph exhibits the small-world phenomenon.*

```
% java MoviesToPerformers "/" < moviesG.txt | java SmallWorld
20734 vertices
average degree 139.0
average distance 7.3
cluster coefficient .92
```

```
public class MoviesToPerformers
{
   public static void main(String[] args)
   {
      String delimiter = args[0];
      while (!StdIn.isEmpty())
      {
         String line = StdIn.readLine();
         String[] names = line.split(delimiter);
         for (int i = 1; i < names.length; i++)
            for (int j = i+1; j < names.length; j++)
               StdOut.println(names[i] + delim + names[j]);
      }
   }
}

% java MoviesToPerformers "/" < moviesG.txt > performersG.txt
% more performersG.txt
...
DeBoy, David/Blumenfeld, Alan
...
DeBoy, David/Geppi, Cindy
DeBoy, David/Hershey, Barbara
...
Blumenfeld, Alan/Geppi, Cindy
Blumenfeld, Alan/Hershey, Barbara
...
```

*Converting the movie-performer graph to a performer-performer graph*

stand the small-world phenomenon. The trick to developing such a model is to introduce random edges.

*Random graphs.* One well-studied graph model is the *random graph*. The simplest way to generate a *random sparse graph* is to add edges connecting random vertices, each chosen from $V$ possibilities, until $E$ different edges have been generated. Sparse random graphs with a sufficient number of edges are known to have short distances but are *not* small-world graphs, because they do not exhibit local clustering—see EXERCISE 4.5.41.

*Ring graphs with random shortcuts.* One of the most surprising facts to emerge from the work of Watts and Strogatz is that adding a relatively small number of random edges to a graph with local clustering produces small-world graphs. To gain some insight on why this is the case, consider a ring graph, where the distances between vertices on opposite sides is ~$V/2$. Adding ~$V/2$ edges around the ring connecting vertex $i$ to vertex $i+2$ (mod $V$) cuts the length of these longest shortest paths to ~$V/4$, but adding just *one* shortcut across the graph accomplishes about the same effect. Adding $V/2$ random shortcuts just increases the average number of neighbors by 1 and does not significantly affect the local clustering, but it is extremely likely to yield a short average path length. Adding random shortcuts to a ring graph does the trick: adding a random edge from each vertex adds only 1 to the average vertex degree and does not lower the cluster coefficient much below 1, but it *does* significantly lower the average distance between vertices, making them logarithmic.

*random*

*ring with random shortcuts*

*Two additional graph models*

Generators that create graphs drawn from such models are simple to develop, and we can use `SmallWorld` to determine whether the graphs exhibit the small-world phenomenon. We also can check the analytic results that we derived for simple graphs such as `tiny.txt`, complete graphs, and ring graphs. As with most scientific research, new questions arise as quickly as we answer old ones. How many random shortcuts do we need to add to get a short average path length? What is the average path length and the cluster coefficient in a random graph? What other graph models might be appropriate for study? How many samples do we need to accurately estimate the cluster coefficient or the average path length in a huge graph? You can find in the exercises many suggestions for addressing such questions and for further investigations of the small-world phenomenon. With the basic tools and the approach to programming developed in this book, you are well equipped to address this and many other scientific questions.

| model | average degree | average path length | cluster coefficient |
|---|---|---|---|
| *complete* | 999 ○ | 1 ● | 1.0 ● |
| *ring* | 2 ● | 250 ○ | .66 ● |
| *star* | 2 ● | 2 ● | .004 ○ |
| *3V random edges* | 3 ● | 3 ● | .02 ○ |
| *ring with V random shortcuts* | 3 ● | 3 ● | .62 ● |

*Small-world parameters*
*for various 1,000-vertex graphs*

**Lessons**    This case study illustrates the importance of algorithms and data structures in scientific research. It also reinforces several of the lessons that we have learned throughout this book, which are worth repeating.

*Carefully design your data type.*    One of our most persistent messages throughout this book is that effective programming is based on a precise understanding of the possible set of data-type values and the operations on them. Using a modern object-oriented programming languages such as Java provides a path to this understanding because we design, build, and use our own data types. Our Graph data type is a fundamental one, the product of many iterations and experience with the design choices that we have discussed. The clarity and simplicity of our client code is testimony to the value of taking seriously the design and implementation of basic data types in any program.

*Develop code incrementally.*    As with all of our other case studies, we build software one module at a time, testing and learning about each module before moving to the next.

*Solve problems that you understand before addressing the unknown.*    Our shortest-paths example involving air routes between a few cities is a simple one that is easy to understand. It is just complicated enough to hold our interest while debugging and following through a trace, but not so complicated as to make these tasks unnecessarily laborious.

*Keep testing and check results.*    When working with complex programs that process huge amounts of data, you cannot be too careful in checking your results. Use common sense to evaluate every bit of output that your program produces. Novice programmers have an optimistic mindset ("if the program produces an answer, it must be correct"); experienced programmers know that a pessimistic mindset ("there must be something wrong with this result") is far better.

*Use real-world data.*    The movies.txt file from the *Internet Movie Database* is just one example of the data files that are now omnipresent on the web. In past years, such data was often cloaked behind private or parochial formats, but most people are now realizing that simple text formats are much preferred. The various methods in Java's String data type make it easy to work with real data, which is the best way to formulate hypotheses about real-world phenomena. Start working with small files in the real-world format, so that you can test and learn about performance before attacking huge files.

*Reuse software.* Another of our most persistent messages is that effective programming is based on an understanding of the fundamental data types available for our use, so that we do not have to rewrite code for basic functions. Our use of ST and SET in Graph is a prime example—most programmers still use lower-level representations and implementations that use linked lists or arrays for graphs, which means, inevitably, that they are rewriting code for simple operations such as maintaining and traversing linked lists. Our shortest-paths class PathFinder uses Graph, ST, SET, Stack, and Queue, an all-star lineup of fundamental data structures.

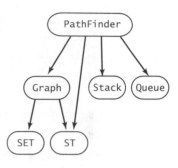

*Code reuse for* Pathfinder

*Maintain flexibility.* Reusing software often means using Java library classes. These classes are generally very wide interfaces (many methods), so it is always wise to define and implement your own APIs with narrow interfaces between clients and implementations, even if your implementations are all calls on Java library methods. This approach provides the flexibility that you need to switch to more effective implementations when warranted and avoids dependence on changes to parts of the library that you do not use. For example, using ST in our Graph implementations gives us the flexibility to use Java's java.util.TreeMap or our BST symbol-table implementation without having to change Graph at all.

*Performance matters.* Without good algorithms and data structures, many of the problems that we have addressed in this chapter would go unsolved, because naïve methods require an impossible amount of time or space. Maintaining an awareness of the approximate resource needs of our programs is essential.

THIS CASE STUDY IS AN APPROPRIATE place to end the book because the programs that we have considered are a starting point, not a complete study. This book is a starting point, too, for your further study in science, mathematics, or engineering. The approach to programming and the tools that you have learned here should prepare you well for addressing any computational problem whatsoever.

# Q + A

**Q.** How many different graphs are there with $V$ given vertices?

**A.** With no self-loops or parallel edges, there are $V(V-1)/2$ possible edges, each of which can be present or not present, so the grand total is $2^{V(V-1)/2}$. The number grows to be huge quite quickly, as shown in the following table:

| $V$ | 1 | 2 | 3 | 4 | 5 | 6 | 7 | 8 | 9 |
|---|---|---|---|---|---|---|---|---|---|
| $2^{V(V-1)/2}$ | 1 | 2 | 8 | 64 | 1024 | 32768 | 2097152 | 268435456 | 68719476736 |

These huge numbers provide some insight into the complexities of social relationships. For example, if you just consider the next nine people that you see on the street, there are over 68 *trillion* mutual-acquaintance possibilities!

**Q.** Can a graph have a vertex that is not connected to any other vertex by an edge?

**A.** Good question. Such vertices are known as *isolated vertices*. Our implementation disallows them. Another implementation might choose to allow isolated vertices by including an explicit `addVertex()` method for the *add a vertex* operation.

**Q.** Why not just use a linked-list representation for the neighbors of each vertex?

**A.** You can do so, but you are likely to wind up re-implementing basic linked-list code as you discover that you need the size, an iterator, and so forth.

**Q.** Why do the `V()` and `E()` query methods need to have constant-time implementations?

**A.** It might seem that most clients would call such methods only once, but an extremely common idiom is to use code like

```
for (int i = 0; i < G.E(); i++) {  ...  }
```

which would take quadratic time if you were to use a lazy algorithm that counts the edges instead of maintaining an instance variable with the number of edges. See EXERCISE 4.5.1.

**Q.** Why are `Graph` and `PathFinder` in separate classes? Wouldn't it make more sense to include the `PathFinder` methods in the `Graph` API?

**A.** Finding shortest paths is just one of many graph-processing algorithms. It would be poor software design to include all of them in a single interface. Please reread the discussion of wide interfaces in SECTION 3.3.

# Exercises

**4.5.1**   Add to Graph the implementations of V() and E() that return the number of vertices and edges in the graph, respectively. Make sure that your implementations are constant-time. *Hint*: For V(), you may assume that the size() method in ST is constant-time; for E(), maintain an instance variable that holds the value.

**4.5.2**   Add a method degree() to Graph that takes a String as input and returns the degree of the named vertex. Use this method to find the performer in movies.txt who has appeared in the most movies.

*Answer*:

```
public int degree(String v)
{
    if (st.contains(v)) return st.get(v).size();
    else                return 0;
}
```

**4.5.3**   Add to Graph a method hasVertex() that takes a String argument and returns true if it names a vertex in the graph, and false otherwise.

**4.5.4**   Add to Graph a method hasEdge() that takes two String arguments and returns true if they specify an edge in the graph, and false otherwise.

**4.5.5**   Create a copy constructor for Graph that takes as argument a graph G, then creates and initializes a new, independent copy of the graph. Any future changes to G should not affect the newly created graph.

**4.5.6**   Write a version of Graph that supports explicit vertex creation and allows self-loops, parallel edges, and isolated vertices. *Hint*: Use a Queue for the adjacency lists instead of a SET.

**4.5.7**   Add to Graph a method remove() that takes two String arguments and deletes the specified edge from the graph, if present.

**4.5.8**   Add to Graph a method subgraph() that takes a SET<String> as argument and returns the induced subgraph (the graph comprised of those vertices and all edges from the original graph that connect any two of them).

**4.5.9** Write a version of `Graph` that supports generic vertex types (easy). Then, write a version of `PathFinder` that uses your implementation to support finding shortest paths using generic vertex types (more difficult).

**4.5.10** Create a version of `Graph` from the previous exercise to support bipartite graphs (graphs whose edges all connect a vertex of one generic type to a vertex of another generic type).

**4.5.11** *True or false*: At some point during breadth-first search the queue can contain two vertices, one whose distance from the source is 7 and one whose distance is 9.

*Answer*: False. The queue can contain vertices of at most two distinct distances $d$ and $d+1$. Breadth first search examines the vertices in increasing order of distance from the source. When examining a vertex at distance $d$, only vertices of distance $d+1$ can be enqueued.

**4.5.12** Prove by induction on the set of vertices visited that `PathFinder` finds the shortest path distances from the source to each vertex.

**4.5.13** Suppose you use a stack instead of a queue for breadth-first search in `Path-Finder`. Does it still find a path? Does it still correctly compute shortest paths? In each case, prove that it does or give a counterexample.

**4.5.14** What would be the effect of using a queue instead of a stack when forming the shortest path in `pathTo()`?

**4.5.15** Add a method `isReachable(v)` to `PathFinder` that returns `true` if there exists *some* path from the source to v, and `false` otherwise.

**4.5.16** Write a `Graph` client that uses the constructor given in the text to read a `Graph` from a file, then prints the edges in the graph, one per line.

**4.5.17** Implement a `PathFinder` client `AllShortestPaths` that builds a `Path-Finder` for each vertex, with a test client that takes from standard input two-vertex queries and prints the shortest path connecting them.

*Answer*:

```
public class AllShortestPaths
{
    public static void main(String[] args)
    {
        In in = new In(args[0]);
        Graph G = new Graph(in, " ");
        ST<String, PathFinder> allpaths;
        allpaths = new ST<String, PathFinder>();
        for (String s : G.vertices())
            allpaths.put(s, new PathFinder(G, s));

        while (!StdIn.isEmpty())
        {
            String s = StdIn.readString();
            String t = StdIn.readString();
            for (String v : allpaths.get(s).pathTo(t))
                StdOut.print(" " + v);
        }
    }
}
```

Modify this code to use a delimiter, so that you can type the two-string queries on one line (separated by the delimiter) and get as output a shortest chain between them. *Note*: For movies.txt, the query strings may both be performers, both be movies, or be a performer and a movie.

**4.5.18** Write a program that plots average distance versus the number of random edges as random shortcuts are added to a ring graph.

**4.5.19** Implement a test client main() for SmallWorld (PROGRAM 4.5.5) that produces the output given in the sample runs. Your program should take a delimiter as command-line argument and read the graph from StdIn in our standard edge-list format. You program should be a Graph and PathFinder client that builds the graph; computes the number of vertices, average degree, average path length, and cluster coefficient for the graph; and indicates whether the values are too large or too small for the graph to exhibit the small-world phenomenon.

*Partial answer*:

```java
public static void main(String[] args)
{
    In stdin = new In();
    String delim = args[0];
    Graph G = new Graph(stdin, delim);

    StdOut.printf("%d vertices", G.V());
    if (G.V() < 1000)
    {   StdOut.print(" (too small) ");
    StdOut.println();

    double val = avgDegree(G);
    StdOut.printf("average degree %7.3f", val);
    if (val > 10.0 * Math.log(G.V()) / Math.log(2))
    {   StdOut.print(" (too big) ");
    StdOut.println();
    ...
}
```

**4.5.20** Add to `SmallWorld` a method `isSmallWorld()` that takes a graph as argument and returns `true` if the graph exhibits the small-world phenomenon (as defined by the specific thresholds given in the text) and `false` otherwise.

**4.5.21** Add to `SmallWorld` a method `clusterCoefficient()` that takes a graph and an integer k as arguments and computes a cluster coefficient for the graph based on total edges present and total edges possible among the set of vertices within distance k of each vertex. Your program should produce results identical to the method in `SmallWorld` when k is 1.)

**4.5.22** Compute the average distance between two vertices in a ring graph with $N$ vertices, and compute the cluster coefficient of a star graph with $N$ vertices.

*3-circle graph*

**4.5.23** In a *k-circle graph* (for any given constant $k$), edges connect vertex $i$ to vertex $i+j$ (mod $V$) for all postive $j$ less than $k$. Write a `SmallWorld` and `Graph` client that generates $k$-circle graphs and tests whether they exhibit the small-world phenomenon (first do EXERCISE 4.5.20).

**4.5.24** In a *grid graph*, vertices are arranged in an *N*-by-*N* grid, with edges connecting each vertex to its neighbors above, below, to the left, and to the right in the grid. Write a `SmallWorld` and `Graph` client that generates grid graphs and tests whether they exhibit the small-world phenomenon (first do Exercise 4.5.20).

**4.5.25** Extend your solutions of the previous two exercises to also take a command-line argument `M` and to add `M` random edges to the graph. Experiment with your programs for 1,024-vertex graphs to find small-world graphs with as few edges as possible.

*Grid graph*

## *Creative Exercises*

**4.5.26** *Large Bacon numbers.* Find the performers in movies.txt with the largest, but finite, Kevin Bacon number.

**4.5.27** *Histogram.* Write a program BaconHistogram that prints a histogram of Kevin Bacon numbers, indicating how many performers from movies.txt have a Bacon number of 0, 1, 2, 3, ... . Include a category for those who have an infinite number (not connected at all to Kevin Bacon).

**4.5.28** *Performer graph.* As mentioned in the text, an alternate way to compute Kevin Bacon numbers is to build a graph where there is a vertex for each performer (but not for each movie), and where two performers are connected by an edge if they appear in a movie together. Calculate Kevin Bacon numbers by running breadth-first searches on the performer graph. Compare the running time with the running time on movies.txt. Explain why this approach is so much slower. Also explain what you would need to do to include the movies along the path, as happens automatically with our implementation.

**4.5.29** *Connected components.* A *connected component* in an undirected graph is a maximal set of vertices that are mutually reachable. Write a Graph client CCFinder that computes the connected components of a graph. Include a constructor that takes a Graph as an argument and computes all of the connected components using breadth-first search. Include a method areConnected(v, w) that returns true if v and w are in the same connected component and false otherwise. Also add a method components() that returns the number of connected components.

**4.5.30** *Flood fill / image processing.* An image is a two-dimensional array of Color values (see SECTION 3.1) that represent pixels. A *blob* is a collection of neighboring pixels of the same color. Write a Graph client whose constructor builds a grid graph (see EXERCISE 4.5.24) from a given image and supports the *flood fill* operation. Given pixel coordinates i and j and a color c, change the color of that pixel and all the pixels in the same blob to c.

**4.5.31** *Word ladders.* Write a program WordLadder that takes two 5-letter strings from the command line, and reads in a list of 5-letter words from standard input, and prints out a shortest word ladder using the words on standard input connecting the two strings (if it exists). Two words can be connected in a word ladder chain if they differ in exactly one letter. As an example, the following word ladder connects green and brown:

green greet great groat groan grown brown

Write a simple filter to get the 5-letter words from a system dictionary for standard input or download a list from the booksite. (This game, originally known as *doublet*, was invented by Lewis Carroll.)

**4.5.32** *All paths.* Write a Graph client AllPaths whose constructor takes a Graph as argument and supports operations to count or print out all simple paths between two given vertices s and t in the graph. A simple path does not revisit any vertex more than once. In two-dimensional grids, such paths are referred to as self-avoiding walks (see Section 1.4). It is a fundamental problem in statistical physics and theoretical chemistry, e.g., to model the spatial arrangement of linear polymer molecules in a solution. *Warning*: There might be exponentially many paths.

**4.5.33** *Percolation.* Develop a graph model for percolation, and write a Graph client that performs the same computation as Percolation (Program 2.4.5).

**4.5.34** *Subway graphs.* In the Tokyo subway system, routes are labeled by letters and stops by numbers, such as G-8 or A-3. Stations allowing transfers are sets of stops. Find a Tokyo subway map on the web, develop a simple database format, and write a Graph client that reads a file and can answer shortest-path queries for the Tokyo subway system. If you prefer, do the Paris subway system, where routes are sequences of names and transfers are possible when two routes have the same name.

**4.5.35** *Directed graphs.* Implement a Digraph data type that represents *directed* graphs, where the direction of edges is significant: addEdge(v, w) means to add an edge from v to w but *not* from w to v. Replace adjacentTo() with two methods, one to give the set of vertices having edges directed to them *from* the argument vertex, the other to give the set of vertices having edges directed from them *to* the argument vertex. Explain how PathFinder would need to be modified to find shortest paths in directed graphs.

**4.5.36** *Random surfer.* Modify your `Digraph` class of the previous exercise to make a `MultiDigraph` class that allows parallel edges. For a test client, run a random surfer simulation that matches `RandomSurfer` (Program 1.6.2).

**4.5.37** *Transitive closure.* Write a `Digraph` client `TransitiveClosure` whose constructor takes a `Digraph` as an argument and whose method `isReachable(v, w)` returns `true` if w is reachable from v along a directed path in the digraph and `false` otherwise. *Hint*: Run breadth-first search from each vertex, as in `AllShortestPaths` (Exercise 4.5.17).

**4.5.38** *Cover time.* A *random walk* in a connected undirected graph moves from a vertex to one of its neighbors, each chosen with equal probability. (This process is the random surfer analog for undirected graphs.) Write programs to run experiments so that support the development of hypotheses on the number of steps used to visit every vertex in the graph. What is the cover time for a complete graph with $V$ vertices? A ring graph? Can you find a family of graphs where the cover time grows proportionally to $V^3$ or $2^V$?

**4.5.39** *Center of the Hollywood universe.* We can measure how good a center Kevin Bacon is by computing each performer's *Hollywood number* or average path length. The Hollywood number of Kevin Bacon is the average Bacon number of all the performers (in its connected component). The Hollywood number of another performer is computed the same way, making that performer the source instead of Kevin Bacon. Compute Kevin Bacon's Hollywood number and find a performer with a better Hollywood number than Kevin Bacon. Find the performers (in the same connected component as Kevin Bacon) with the best and worst Hollywood numbers.

**4.5.40** *Diameter.* The *eccentricity* of a vertex is the greatest distance between it and any other vertex. The *diameter* of a graph is the greatest distance between any two vertices (the maximum eccentricity of any vertex). Write a `Graph` client `Diameter` that can compute the eccentricity of a vertex and the diameter of a graph. Use it to find the diameter of the graph represented by `movies.txt`.

**4.5.41** *Erdös-Renyi graph model.* In the classical random graph model, we build a random graph on $V$ vertices by including each possible edge with probability $p$. Write a Graph client to verify the following properties:
- *Connectivity thresholds*: If $p < 1/V$ and $V$ is large, then most of connected components are small, with the largest logarithmic in size. If $p > 1/V$, then there is almost surely a giant component containing almost all vertices. If $p < \ln V / V$, the graph is disconnected with high probability; if $p > \ln V / V$, the graph is connected with high probability.
- *Distribution of degrees*: The distribution of degrees follows a binomial distribution, centered on the average, so most vertices have similar degrees. The probability that a vertex is connected to $k$ other vertices decreases exponentially in $k$.
- *No hubs*: The maximum vertex degree when $p$ is a constant is at most logarithmic in $V$.
- *Little local clustering*: The cluster coefficient is close to 0 if the graph is sparse and connected. Random graphs are not small-world graphs.
- *Small diameter*: If $p > \ln V / V$, the diameter is logarithmic.

**4.5.42** *Power law of web links.* The indegrees and outdegrees of pages in the web obey a power law that can be modeled by a *preferred attachment* process. Suppose that each web page has exactly one outgoing link. Each page is created one at a time, starting with a single page that points to itself. With probability $p < 1$, it links to one of the existing pages, chosen uniformly at random. With probability $1-p$, it links to an existing page with probability proportional to the number of incoming links of that page. This rule reflects the common tendency for new web pages to point to popular pages. Write a program to simulate this process and plot a histogram of the number of incoming links.

*Partial answer*: The fraction of pages with indegree $k$ is proportional to $k^{(-1/(1-p))}$.

**4.5.43** *Watts-Strogatz graph model.* (See EXERCISE 4.5.25.) Watts and Strogatz proposed a hybrid model that contains typical links of vertices near each other (people know their geographic neighbors), plus some random long-range connection links. Plot the effect of adding random edges to an $N$-by-$N$ grid graph on the average path length and on the cluster coefficient, for $N = 100$. Do the same for $k$-circle graphs, for various values of $k$ up to $10 \log V$, for $V = 10,000$

**4.5.44** *Kleinberg graph model.*   There is no way for participants in the Watts-Strogatz model to find short paths in a decentralized network. But Milgram's experiment also had a striking algorithmic component—individuals can find short paths! Jon Kleinberg proposed making the distribution of shortcuts obey a power law, with probability proportional to the $d$th power of the distance (in $d$ dimensions). Each vertex has *one* long-range neighbor. Write a program to generate graphs according to this model, with a test client that uses `SmallWorld` to test whether they exhibit the small-world phenomenon. Plot histograms to show that the graphs are uniform over all distance scales (same number of links at distances 1–10 as 10–100 or 100–1000. Write a program to compute the average lengths of paths obtained by taking the edge that brings the path as close to target as possible in terms of lattice distance, and test the hypothesis that this average is proportional to $(\log V)^2$.

# *Context*

I N THIS CLOSING SECTION, WE PLACE your newly-acquired knowledge of programming in a broader context by briefly describing some of the basic elements of the world of computation that you are likely to encounter. It is our hope that this information will whet your appetite to use your knowledge of programming as a platform for learning more about the role of computation in the world around you.

You now know how to program. Just as learning to drive an SUV is not difficult when you know how to drive a car, learning to program in a different language will not be difficult for you. Many scientists regularly use several different languages, for various different purposes. The primitive data types, conditionals, loops, and functional abstraction of CHAPTERS 1 AND 2 (that served programmers well for the first couple of decades of computing) and the object-oriented programming approach of CHAPTER 3 (that is used by modern programmers) are basic models found in many programming languages. Your skill in using them and the fundamental data types of CHAPTER 4 will prepare you to cope with libraries, program development environments, and specialized applications of all sorts. You are also well-positioned to appreciate the power of abstraction in designing complex systems and understanding how they work.

The study of *computer science* is much more than learning to program. Now that you are familiar with programming and conversant with computing, you are well-prepared to learn about some of the outstanding intellectual achievements of the past century, some of the most important unsolved problems of our time, and their role in the evolution of the computational infrastructure that surrounds us. Perhaps even more significant, as we have hinted throughout the book, is that computation is playing an ever increasing role in our understanding of nature, from genomics to molecular dynamics to astrophysics. Further study of the basic precepts of computer science is certain to pay dividends for you.

*Java libraries.* The Java system provides extensive resources for your use. We have made extensive use of some Java libraries, such as `Math` and `String`, but have ignored most of them. One of Java's unique features is that a great deal of information about the libraries is readily available online. If you have not yet browsed through the Java libraries, now is the time to do so. You will find that most of this code is for use by professional developers, but there are a number of libraries that you are likely to find to be interesting. Perhaps the most important thing for you to keep in mind when studying libraries is that you do *need* to use them, but you *can* use them. When you find an API that seems to meet your needs, take advantage of it, by all means.

*Programming environments.* You will certainly find yourself using other programming environments besides Java in the future. Many programmers, even experienced professionals, are caught between the past, because of huge amounts of legacy code in old languages such as C, C++, and FORTRAN, and the future, because of the availability of modern tools like Ruby, Python, and JavaScript. Perhaps the most important thing for you to keep in mind when using a programming language is that you do not *need* to use it. If some other language might better meet your needs, take advantage of it, by all means. People who insist on staying within a single programming environment, for whatever reason, are missing opportunities.

*Scientific computing.* In particular, computing with numbers can be very tricky, because of accuracy and precision, so the use of libraries of mathematical functions is certainly justified. Many scientists use FORTRAN, an old scientific language; many others use MATLAB, a language that was developed specifically for computing with matrices. The combination of good libraries and built-in matrix operations makes MATLAB an attractive choice for many problems. However, since MATLAB lacks support for mutable types and other modern facilities, Java is a better choice for many other problems. *You* can use both! The same mathematical libraries used by MATLAB and FORTRAN programmers are accessible from Java (and by modern scripting languages).

*Computer systems.* Properties of specific computer systems once completely determined the nature and extent of problems that could be solved, but now they hardly intrude. You can still count on having a faster machine with much more memory next year at this time. Strive to keep your code machine-independent, so that you can easily make the switch. More importantly, the web is playing an increasingly critical role in commercial and scientific computing, as you have seen in many examples in this book. You can write programs that process data that is maintained elsewhere, programs that interact with programs executing elsewhere, and take advantage of many other properties of the extensive and evolving computational infrastructure. Do not hesitate to do so. People who invest significant effort in writing programs for specific machines, even high-powered supercomputers, are missing opportunities.

*Theoretical computer science.* By contrast, fundamental limits on computation have been apparent from the start and continue to play an important role in determining the kinds of problems that we can address. You might be surprised to learn that there are some problems that no computer program can solve and many other problems, which arise commonly in practice, that are thought to be too difficult to solve on any conceivable computer. Everyone who depends on computation for problem solving, creative work, or research needs to respect these facts.

YOU HAVE CERTAINLY COME A LONG way since you tentatively created, compiled, and ran `HelloWorld`, but you certainly still have a great deal to learn. Keep programming, and keep learning about programming environments, scientific computing, computer systems, and theoretical computer science, and you will open opportunities for yourself that people who do not program cannot even conceive.

# Index

# M

Magritte, René 353
`main()` method 6, 199
  command-line arguments 199
  in each class 221
Mandelbrot, Benoît 394
Mandelbrot set 394–397
Markov, Andrey 168
Markov chain 168
  mixing a 171
  squaring a 171
Markov process 581
Mathematical analysis 476
Mathematical function
  closed form 194
  implementing 193
  no closed form 194
Mathematical induction
  See *Induction*
`Math` library 29, 716
Matlab 3
  matrix operations 696
  mutable types 447
  pass by value 208
Matrix 102
  addition 105
  Hadamard 117, 308
  library 249
  multiplication 105–106, 171
  sparse 645
  transpose 114
McCarthy's 91 function 285
M/D/1 queue 581
Mean 154, 236
Memoization 275
Memory address. See *Pointer*
Memory allocation 356–358
  heap 494
  of a linked list 555, 562

of an array 90
  stack 494
Memory leak 357, 565
Memory representation
  aliased variables 353
  array of objects 355
  object 321
  orphaned object 356
  substring 537
  two-dimensional array 103
Memory usage 490–494
  arrays 492
  objects 490–491
  primitive types 490
  strings 491
  substrings 493
  two-dimensional arrays 493
Mergesort 527–530
  nonrecursive 604
Method 6
  static 184–217
  instance 373
Midpoint displacement method
    270–272
Milgram, Stanley 650
M/M/1 queue 599
Modular programming 183,
    218–219, 243–245, 420
Module 183, 220
Monochrome luminance
  See *Luminance*
Monte Carlo simulation 286
  See also *Simulation*
Moore's law 484–485
`more` command 135
Multidimensional array 107
Mutability
  defined 427–429
  of arrays 427–429

# N

NaN (not a number) 185
Natural ordering 434
N-body simulation 456–469
Nested class 558, 593
Nesting 58
`new` operator
  with arrays 87
  with objects 319
Newline character 19
Newton, Isaac 61, 84, 457
Newton's method 61, 186
N log N running time
  See *Linearithmic running time*
`Node` data type
  in a binary tree 620–621
  in a linked list 555
Normal distribution
  See *Gaussian distribution*
`null` literal
  array elements 87
  as a default value 403
  defined 403
  with linked lists 556
  with binary trees 619
Null pointer exception 403
Number conversion 63, 80

# O

Object 315
  create an 319
  identity 354
  memory representation 321
  orphaned 356
  type conversion 322
`Object` class 438
Object-oriented programming
    315–469

Tree
 See also *Binary search tree*
 See also *Binary tree*
 function call 261
 H-tree 268
true literal 25
Truth table 25
Turing, Alan 399
Turing machine 151
Turtle graphics 382–389
Twenty questions 128–129, 512
Two-dimensional array
  102–110
 column-major order 105
 initialization 102
 input and output 229
 memory representation 103
 memory usage 493
 ragged 106
 row-major order 105
Type. See *Data type*
Type conversion
 auto-boxing 569
 auto-unboxing 569
 objects 322
 primitive type to String 18
 promotion 32
 String to primitive type 30
Type parameter 569

U

Uniform distribution 43, 226
Uninitialized variable
 primitive type 35, 90
 reference type 322
Unix operating system 123, 134
Unreachable code 207

V

Variable
 argument 374
 defined 15
 global 245, 405
 instance 372, 374
 local 374
 scope of 56, 374
 static 245, 405
 visibility of 372
Variance 236
Vector 88
 dot product 88, 200
 sparse 645
 spatial 430–433
 Vector API 431, 721
Vector image 329
Visibility modifier 372
void literal 10, 30, 207
von Neumann, John 531

W

Watts, Duncan 650
Weighing an object 518
while loop 49–54
Whitespace 10, 126, 339
Wide interface 418, 595, 683
Worst-case 488–489
Wrapper type 569

X

Xor function 39

Z

Zero-based indexing 89, 112
Zipf's law 534

# Index of Programs

## Object-Oriented Programming

## Algorithms and Data Structures

# APIs

## public class System.out/StdOut/Out

|  |  |  |
|---|---|---|
|  | Out(String name) | *create output stream from* name |
| void | print(String s) | *print* s |
| void | println(String s) | *print* s, *followed by newline* |
| void | println() | *print a new line* |
| void | printf(String f, ... ) | *formatted print* |

*Note: Methods are static and constructor does not apply for* System.out/StdOut.

## public class Math

|  |  |  |
|---|---|---|
| double | abs(double a) | *absolute value of a* |
| double | max(double a, double b) | *maximum of a and b* |
| double | min(double a, double b) | *minimum of a and b* |

*Note 1:* abs(), max(), *and* min() *are defined also for* int, long, *and* float.

|  |  |  |
|---|---|---|
| double | sin(double theta) | *sine function* |
| double | cos(double theta) | *cosine function* |
| double | tan(double theta) | *tangent function* |

*Note 2: Angles are expressed in radians. Use* toDegrees() *and* toRadians() *to convert.*
*Note 3: Use* asin(), acos(), *and* atan() *for inverse functions.*

|  |  |  |
|---|---|---|
| double | exp(double a) | *exponential ($e^a$)* |
| double | log(double a) | *natural log ($\log_e a$, or $\ln a$)* |
| double | pow(double a, double b) | *raise a to the bth power ($a^b$)* |
| long | round(double a) | *round to the nearest integer* |
| double | random() | *random number in $[0, 1)$* |
| double | sqrt(double a) | *square root of a* |
| double | E | *value of e (constant)* |
| double | PI | *value of $\pi$ (constant)* |

## public class StdIn/In

|  |  |  |
|---:|:---|:---|
|  | `In(String name)` | *create input stream from* `name` |
| `boolean` | `isEmpty()` | `true` *if no more values, else* `false` |
| `int` | `readInt()` | *read a value of type* `int` |
| `double` | `readDouble()` | *read a value of type* `double` |
| `long` | `readLong()` | *read a value of type long* |
| `boolean` | `readBoolean()` | *read a value of type* `boolean` |
| `char` | `readChar()` | *read a value of type* `char` |
| `String` | `readString()` | *read a value of type* `String` |
| `String` | `readLine()` | *read the rest of the line* |
| `String` | `readAll()` | *read the rest of the text* |

*Note*: *Methods are static and constructor does not apply for* `StdIn`.

## public class String

|  |  |  |
|---:|:---|:---|
|  | `String(String s)` | *create a string with the same value as* `s` |
| `int` | `length()` | *string length* |
| `char` | `charAt(int i)` | `i`*th character* |
| `String` | `substring(int i, int j)` | `i`*th through* `(j-1)`*st characters* |
| `boolean` | `contains(String sub)` | *does string contain* `sub` *as a substring?* |
| `boolean` | `startsWith(String pre)` | *does string start with* `pre`*?* |
| `boolean` | `endsWith(String post)` | *does string end with* `post`*?* |
| `int` | `indexOf(String p)` | *index of first occurrence of* `p` |
| `int` | `indexOf(String p, int i)` | *index of first occurrence of* `p` *after* `i` |
| `String` | `concat(String t)` | *this string with* `t` *appended* |
| `int` | `compareTo(String t)` | *string comparison* |
| `String` | `replaceAll(String a, String b)` | *result of changing* `a`s *to* `b`s |
| `String[]` | `split(String delim)` | *strings between occurrences of* `delim` |
| `boolean` | `equals(String t)` | *is this string's value the same as* `t`*'s?* |

## public class StdDraw/Draw

|  |  |  |
|---|---|---|
|  | Draw() | *create a new* Draw *object* |
| void | line(double x0, double y0, double x1, double y1) | |
| void | point(double x, double y) | |
| void | text(double x, double y, String s) | |
| void | circle(double x, double y, double r) | |
| void | filledCircle(double x, double y, double r) | |
| void | square(double x, double y, double r) | |
| void | filledSquare(double x, double y, double r) | |
| void | polygon(double[] x, double[] y) | |
| void | filledPolygon(double[] x, double[] y) | |
| void | setXscale(double x0, double x1) | *reset x range to* $(x_0, x_1)$ |
| void | setYscale(double y0, double y1) | *reset y range to* $(y_0, y_1)$ |
| void | setPenRadius(double r) | *set pen radius to* r |
| void | setPenColor(Color c) | *set pen color to* c |
| void | setFont(Font f) | *set text font to* f |
| void | setCanvasSize(int w, int h) | *set canvas to* w-by-h *window* |
| void | clear(Color c) | *clear the canvas; color it* c |
| void | show(int dt) | *show all; pause* dt *milliseconds* |
| void | save(String filename) | *save to a* .jpg *or* .png *file* |

*Note*: *Methods are static and constructor does not apply for* StdDraw.

## public class StdAudio

|  |  |  |
|---|---|---|
| void | play(String file) | *play the given .wav file* |
| void | play(double[] a) | *play the given sound wave* |
| void | play(double x) | *play sample for 1/44100 second* |
| void | save(String file, double[] a) | *save to a .wav file* |
| double[] | read(String file) | *read from a .wav file* |

## public class StdRandom

| | | |
|---:|---|---|
| int | uniform(int N) | *integer between* 0 *and* N-1 |
| double | uniform(double lo, double hi) | *real between* lo *and* hi |
| boolean | bernoulli(double p) | *true with probability* p |
| double | gaussian() | *normal, mean* 0, *standard deviation* 1 |
| double | gaussian(double m, double s) | *normal, mean* m, *standard deviation* s |
| int | discrete(double[] a) | i *with probability* a[i] |
| void | shuffle(double[] a) | *randomly shuffle the array* a[] |

## public class StdArrayIO

| | | |
|---:|---|---|
| double[] | readDouble1D() | *read a one-dimensional array of* double *values* |
| double[][] | readDouble2D() | *read a two-dimensional array of* double *values* |
| void | print(double[] a) | *print a one-dimensional array of* double *values* |
| void | print(double[][] a) | *print a two-dimensional array of* double *values* |

*Note 1.* 1D *format is an integer N followed by N values.*

*Note 2.* 2D *format is two integers M and N followed by M×N values in row-major order.*

*Note 3. Methods for* int *and* boolean *are also included.*

## public class StdStats

| | | |
|---:|---|---|
| double | max(double[] a) | *largest value* |
| double | min(double[] a) | *smallest value* |
| double | mean(double[] a) | *average* |
| double | var(double[] a) | *sample variance* |
| double | stddev(double[] a) | *sample standard deviation* |
| double | median(double[] a) | *median* |
| void | plotPoints(double[] a) | *plot points at* (i, a[i]) |
| void | plotLines(double[] a) | *plot lines connecting* (i, a[i]) |
| void | plotBars(double[] a) | *plot bars to points at* (i, a[i]) |

*Note: overloaded implementations are included for all numeric types* `public class Picture`

---

|                |                                  |                                                    |
|---------------:|----------------------------------|----------------------------------------------------|
|                | `Picture(String name)`           | *create a picture from a file*                     |
|                | `Picture(int w, int h)`          | *create a blank w-by-h picture*                    |
|          `int` | `width()`                        | *return the width of the picture*                  |
|          `int` | `height()`                       | *return the height of the picture*                 |
|        `Color` | `get(int i, int j)`              | *return the color of pixel (i, j)*                 |
|         `void` | `set(int i, int j, Color c)`     | *set the color of pixel (i, j) to* c               |
|         `void` | `show()`                         | *display the image in a window*                    |
|         `void` | `save(String name)`              | *save the image to a file*                         |

`public class Stopwatch`

---

|                |                     |                                                        |
|---------------:|---------------------|--------------------------------------------------------|
|                | `Stopwatch()`       | *create a new stopwatch and start it running*          |
|       `double` | `elapsedTime()`     | *return the elapsed time since creation, in seconds*   |

`public class Histogram`

---

|                |                      |                                                               |
|---------------:|----------------------|---------------------------------------------------------------|
|                | `Histogram(int N)`   | *create a dynamic histogram for the N integer values in [0, N)* |
|       `double` | `addDataPoint(int i)`| *add an occurrence of the value i*                            |

`public class Turtle`

---

|                |                                          |                                                                                  |
|---------------:|------------------------------------------|----------------------------------------------------------------------------------|
|                | `Turtle(double x0, double y0, double a0)`| *create a new turtle at $(x_0, y_0)$ facing $a_0$ degrees counterclockwise from x-axis* |
|         `void` | `turnLeft(double delta)`                 | *rotate* `delta` *degrees counterclockwise*                                       |
|         `void` | `goForward(double step)`                 | *move distance* `step`*, drawing a line*                                          |

## public class Counter

|          | Counter(String id, int max) | *create a counter, initialized to 0* |
|---------:|-----------------------------|--------------------------------------|
| void | increment() | *increment counter unless its value is max* |
| int | value() | *return the value of the counter* |
| String | toString() | *string representation* |

## public class Complex

|          | Complex(double real, double imag) | |
|---------:|-----------------------------------|---|
| Complex | plus(Complex b) | *sum of this number and b* |
| Complex | times(Complex b) | *product of this number and b* |
| double | abs() | *magnitude* |
| double | re() | *real part* |
| double | im() | *imaginary part* |
| String | toString() | *string representation* |

## public class Vector

|          | Vector(double[] a) | *create a vector with the given Cartesian coordinates* |
|---------:|--------------------|--------------------------------------------------------|
| Vector | plus(Vector b) | *sum of this vector and b* |
| Vector | minus(Vector b) | *difference of this vector and b* |
| Vector | times(double t) | *scalar product of this vector and t* |
| double | dot(Vector b) | *dot product of this vector and b* |
| double | magnitude() | *magnitude of this vector* |
| Vector | direction() | *unit vector with same direction as this vector* |
| double | cartesian(int i) | *ith cartesian coordinate of this vector* |
| String | toString() | *string representation* |

## public class Stack<Item>

|  | Stack<Item> | *create an empty stack* |
|---|---|---|
| boolean | isEmpty() | *is the stack empty?* |
| void | push(Item item) | *push an item onto the stack* |
| Item | pop() | *pop the stack* |

## public class Queue<Item>

|  | Queue<Item>() | *create an empty queue* |
|---|---|---|
| boolean | isEmpty() | *is the queue empty?* |
| void | enqueue(Item item) | *enqueue an item* |
| Item | dequeue() | *dequeue an item* |
| int | length() | *queue length* |

## public class ST<Key extends Comparable<Key>, Value>

|  | ST() | *create a symbol table* |
|---|---|---|
| void | put(Key key, Value v) | *put key-value pair into the table* |
| Value | get(Key key) | *return value paired with key, null if key not in table* |
| boolean | contains(Key key) | *is there a value paired with key?* |

## public class SET<Key extends Comparable<Key>>

|  | SET() | *create a set* |
|---|---|---|
| boolean | isEmpty() | *is the set empty?* |
| void | add(Key key) | *add key to the set* |
| boolean | contains(Key key) | *is key in the set?* |

## public class Graph

| | | |
|---:|---|---|
| | Graph() | *create an empty graph* |
| | Graph(In in, String delim) | *read graph from input stream* |
| void | addEdge(String v, String w) | *add edge* v-w |
| int | V() | *number of vertices* |
| int | E() | *number of edges* |
| Iterable&lt;String&gt; | vertices() | *vertices in the graph* |
| Iterable&lt;String&gt; | adjacentTo(String v) | *neighbors of* v |
| int | degree(String v) | *number of neighbors of* v |
| boolean | hasVertex(String v) | *is* v *a vertex in the graph?* |
| boolean | hasEdge(String v, String w) | *is* v-w *an edge in the graph?* |

## public class PathFinder

| | | |
|---:|---|---|
| | PathFinder(Graph G, String s) | *create an object that finds paths in* G *from* s |
| int | distanceTo(String v) | *length of shortest path from* s *to* v *in* G |
| Iterable&lt;String&gt; | pathTo(String v) | *shortest path from* s *to* v *in* G |